Emergency Radiology of the Acutely Ill or Injured Child

SECOND EDITION

Emergency Radiology of the Acutely Ill or Injured Child

SECOND EDITION

Leonard E. Swischuk, M.D.

Professor of Radiology and Pediatrics
Director, Division of Pediatric Radiology
Child Health Center
The University of Texas Medical Branch
Galveston, Texas

WILLIAMS & WILKINS
Baltimore • Hong Kong • London • Sydney

Senior Editor: George Stamathis
Associate Editor: Carol Eckhart
Copy Editor: William Vinck
Design: JoAnne Janowiak
Illustration Planning: Reginald R. Stanley
Production: Anne G. Seitz

Made in the United States of America

First Edition, 1979

Main entry under title:

Library of Congress Cataloging in Publication Data

Swischuk, Leonard, E., 1937–
    Emergency radiology of the acutely ill or injured child.

    Includes bibliographies and index.
    1. Pediatric   radiography.   2. Pediatric   emergencies.   I. Title.   [DNLM:
1. Emergency Service, Hospital. 2. Radiography—in infancy & childhood. WN 240
S978e] RJ51.R3S9 1985   618.92′007′572   85-9294 ISBN 0-683-08049-0

Composed and printed at the
Waverly Press, Inc.   88 89 90 91   10 9 8 7 6 5 4 3

To Janie
My Wife and Very Best Friend
and
Our Children
Tim, Jim, Mike, and Peter

Preface to the Second Edition

My aims in this second edition are to retain most of what made the first edition successful and to add, wherever necessary, data pertaining to the newer diagnostic modalities. In addition, certain areas have been refined, some new illustrations added, others replaced by better ones, and all of the references have been updated.

It has been my pleasure, once again, to work with Williams and Wilkins in producing this textbook, and once again, I am indebted to Carmen Floeck, my secretary, and Milan Autengruber our department photographer. Both of these individuals work so closely with me, and so diligently, that without them it would be much more difficult, if not quite possible, to produce my manuscripts in time, and of the quality required for rapid publication.

Finally, and most important I must thank my partner Dr. C. Keith Hayden, Jr. We are a team, and I am forever indebted to him for always working so closely with me, and yet growing in his own right.

Preface to the First Edition

I have always enjoyed the challenge of emergency medicine, for the diseases encountered are varied, and the diagnosis usually must be accomplished promptly. While many of these diagnoses can be established with the history and physical examination, in other instances they are made with the aid of roentgenograms. It is this aspect of emergency medicine to which this book is devoted, and I have attempted to present material and concepts which, over the years, have proven useful to me. In this regard, my aim was to outline general approaches to diagnostic problems, helpful rules of thumb, and specific diagnostic signs. Every so often, I felt it appropriate to delve more deeply into the pathophysiologic-roentgenographic correlations of certain diseases, but overall the main theme remained: how to approach a problem and then how to utilize the roentgenogram so as to have it yield the desired data.

The subject material in this book truly is "bread and butter" radiology, and I have tried to be as practical and clinical as possible. Most of the acute conditions commonly seen in the emergency room, outpatient clinic, or office practice have been covered, and in this regard, the main emphasis is on the evaluation of the initial films obtained. These films, of course, most often are plain films, and truly this is where the radiologist

can excel. The radiologist must remain the expert on the plain film for in spite of all of the new modalities and augmented diagnostic procedures available, the plain film remains the mainstay of the roentgenographic examination. As far as interpreting the roentgenogram, not only must one know all of the abnormal configurations encountered, but one also must be familiar with all of the normal variations which mimic pathology. In the pediatric age group, this is an especially significant problem in the skull, spine, and extremities. Because of this, I have included considerable material on normal variations causing problems, and as much as possible have placed this material next to the pathology which it mimics.

So many individuals have been of assistance to me during the time it took to write this book that it would be impossible to thank them all personally. There are many who have worked with me, many who have offered their material for inclusion, many who have offered constructive criticism and advice, and many who have offered simple encouragement. I thank all of them, and to those who allowed me to use some of their material in this book, I offer special thanks and hope that I have assigned appropriate credit in every instance. I must also thank the various residents who have passed through the Department of Radiology here in Galveston, for all of them have been most helpful in the accumulation of the material on a day-to-day basis. I hope that if they recognize a case they will take some satisfaction in seeing it being used to make a teaching point.

Two individuals, however, stand out so much that it is difficult for me to thank them enough. The first is my former secretary. Jonell Hoffman, and the second, our photographer, Milan Autengruber. Extra effort on their part became a routine daily task, and for this I am deeply indebted to both of them. I would also like to express my appreciation to Lester Murray, Mr. Autengruber's assistant; my former secretary, Cynthia Caldwell, who typed some of the early manuscript; and Donna Lofton in our Department of Medical Illustrations for her assistance with the various drawings in this book. In addition, I must thank the radiology technicians who currently work for me and those who have worked for me in the past. There are too many of them to list individually, but all of them are exceptionally devoted, and needless to say, if they had not produced the roentgenograms I use, I would have nothing to illustrate with. My sincerest thanks to all of them.

I also would like to thank Dr. Robert N. Cooley, our former Chairman; and Dr. Melvyn H. Schreiber, our current Chairman, for their constant support for my various projects; and Dr. C. Keith Hayden, my very capable and helpful associate for his daily physical and moral support. He has been of great assistance to me, and I express my sincerest appreciation to him.

Finally, I would like to express my gratitude to The Williams & Wilkins Company for their unfailing confidence and cooperation. More specifically, however, I am indebted to their astute Chief Radiology Editor, Ruby Richardson, for her perception of the tempo of medical publishing, and her overall flexibility and foresight have once again made it exceptionally easy and rewarding to compile a manuscript. She is a most dynamic and devoted individual whom I am fortunate to know and very pleased to call my friend.

Leonard E. Swischuk, M.D.

Contents

CHAPTER 1
The Chest

LOWER RESPIRATORY TRACT INFECTION (PNEUMONIA, BRONCHITIS, AND BRONCHIOLITIS)

Most childhood lower respiratory tract infections are of viral etiology, i.e., respiratory syncytial virus, parainfluenza and influenza viruses, adenovirus, and the virus-like agent, *Mycoplasma pneumoniae* (2, 3, 6, 10–15). Many of these infections show distinct seasonal variation, and most usually come in epidemics (2, 3, 6, 14). Because of this, it is of some value to be aware of the "local virus going around the community." Knowledge of this type can aid in evaluating subsequent patients.

Bacterial lower respiratory tract infections show less seasonal variation and certainly are not prone to produce epidemics. Generally, they result in parenchymal alveolar pneumonias, and this is distinctly different from viral lower respiratory tract infections. With viral lower respiratory tract infections, the predominant manifestation usually is bronchitis or bronchiolitis. This also is true of pertussis and chlamydia infections, while mycoplasma infections can behave either as viral or bacterial infections.

Bacterial infections most often are caused by the following organisms: *Diplococcus (Streptococcus) pneumoniae, Staphylococcus aureus, Haemophilus influenzae,* and hemolytic streptococcus. *D. pneumoniae* (typical lobar pneumonia) infections are generally more common in older children while *H. influenzae* infections tend to occur more commonly in infants and young children, i.e., between the ages of 2 months and 3 years. *S. aureus* infections also are a little more common in infants and young children, but not to the same extent as *H. influenzae* infections. These age group categorizations, of course, are mere generalizations and are not intended to be used with too much specificity or rigidity.

In addition to these features, there has been considerable recent attention to the problem of persistent airway hyperactivity after viral infection. This is especially prone to occur with respiratory syncytial virus producing bronchiolitis in infants (1, 4, 5, 6–9, 16). Most of these studies seem to suggest that hyperactivity results from the initial infection, but there is some question as to whether these individuals have hyperactive airways to begin with, and then overrespond to a viral infection.

REFERENCES

1. Cloutier, M., and Loughlin, G.M., Chronic cough in children, manifestation of airway hyperreactivity. Pediatrics 67: 6–12, 1981.
2. Glezen, W.P., Loda, F.A., Clyde, W.A., Jr., Senior, R.J., Shaeffer, C.I., Conley, W.G., and Denny, F.W.: Epidemiologic patterns of acute lower respiratory disease of children in a pediatric group practice. J. Pediatr. 78: 397–406, 1971.
3. Glezen, W.B., and Denny, F.W.: Epidemiology of acute lower respiratory disease in children. N. Engl. J. Med. 288: 498–505, 1973.
4. Gurwitz, D., Mindorff, C., and Levison, H.: Increased incidence of bronchial reactivity in children with a history of bronchiolitis. J. Pediatr. 98: 551–555, 1981.
5. Hall, C.B., Hall, W.J., and Speers, D.M.: Clinical and physiological manifestations of bronchiolitis and pneumonia. Am. J. Dis. Child. 133: 798–802.
6. Henderson, F.W., Clyde, W.A., Jr., Collier, A.M., Denny,

F.W., Senior, R.J., Shaeffer, C.I., Conley, W.G., III, Christian, R.M., and Hill, C.: The etiologic and epidemiologic spectrum of bronchiolitis in pediatric practice. J. Pediatr. 95: 183–190, 1979.

7. Horn, M.E.C., Reed, S.E., and Taylor, P.: Role of viruses and bacteria in acute wheezy bronchitis in childhood: a study of sputum. Arch. Dis. Child. 54: 587–592, 1979.

8. Hyde, J.S., and Saed, A.M.: Acute bronchiolitis and the asthmatic child. J. Asthma Res. 4: 137–154, 1966.

9. Kattan, M., Keens, T.G., Lapierre, J.-G., Levison, H., Bryan, A.C., and Reilly, B.J.: Pulmonary function abnormalities in symptom-free children after bronchiolitis. Pediatrics 59: 683–688, 1977.

10. Maletzky, A.J., Cooney, M.K., Luce, R., Kenny, G.E., and Grayston, J.T.: Epidemiology of viral and mycoplasmal agents associated with childhood lower respiratory illness in a civilian population. J. Pediatr. 78: 407–414, 1971.

11. McConnochie, K.M.: Bronchiolitis. Am. J. Dis. Child. 137: 11–13, 1983.

12. Mok, J.Y.Q., Waugh, P.R., and Simpson, H.: *Mycoplasma pneumoniae* infection. Arch. Dis. Child. 54: 506–511, 1979.

13. Mufson, M.A., Krause, H.E., Mocega, H.E., and Dawson, F.W.: Viruses, *Mycoplasma pneumoniae* and bacteria associated with lower respiratory tract disease among infants. Am. J. Epidemiol. 91: 192–202, 1970.

14. Rooney, J.C., Williams, H.E.: Relationship between proved viral bronchiolitis and subsequent wheezing. J. Pediatr. 79: 744–747, 1971.

15. Smith, C.B., and Overall, J.C., Jr.: Clinical and epidemiologic clues to the diagnosis of respiratory infections. Radiol. Clin. North Am. 11: 261–278, 1973.

16. Stokes, G.M., Milner, A.D., Hodges, I.G.C., and Groggins, R.C.: Lung function abnormalities after acute bronchiolitis. J. Pediatr. 98: 871–874, 1981.

BASIC ROENTGENOGRAPHIC PATTERNS OF LOWER RESPIRATORY TRACT INFECTION

The Viral Spectrum. Any viral infection of the lower respiratory tract can produce roentgenographic patterns ranging from the infiltrate-free lungs seen with many cases of bronchiolitis, through parahilar peribronchial infiltrates with or without atelectasis, reticulonodular infiltrates, or hazy lungs (Figs. 1.1 and 1.2). Overall, however, the most common pattern is that of parahilar peribronchial infiltration, attesting to the fact that these infections basically are interstitial, and tracheobronchial infections, rather than alveolar pneumonias (2, 4, 13).

Roentgenographically, so-called "parahilar peribronchial" infiltration results in prominent and "dirty" parahilar regions (Fig. 1.3). At the onset, however, it must be indicated that interpretation of this pattern is quite subjective and will vary from viewer to viewer. Generally speaking, the prominent hilar regions are due in part to inflammation of the bronchial walls and peribronchial tissues (2) and in part to associated adenopathy. However, lymphadenopathy is quite variable, and while some children can present with well circumscribed and enlarged lymph nodes, others show no adenopathy at all, or nothing more than a generalized increase in density of the parahilar areas (Fig. 1.4). In some of these latter cases, the findings are best appreciated on the lateral chest roentgenogram, for on this view both hilar regions are superimposed, and their combined increase in density is easier to appreciate (Fig. 1.3B).

Air trapping also is a common feature of this type of viral lower respiratory tract infection, and indeed it is a feature of all types

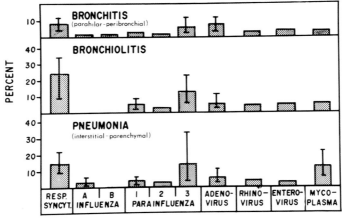

Figure 1.1. *Types of lower respiratory tract infection with various viruses—epidemiologic aspects.* Note that any given virus can produce frank pneumonia, bronchiolitis, or bronchitis (parahilar peribronchial infiltrate). (Modified from Smith, C.B., and Overall, J.C., Jr.: Clinical and epidemiologic clues to the diagnosis of respiratory infections. Radiol. Clin. North Am. 11: 261–278, 1973. Reprinted with permission.)

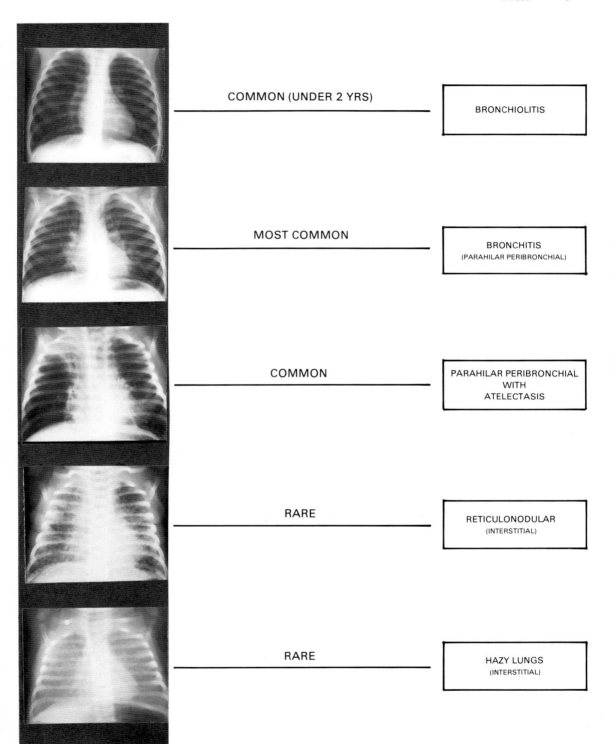

Figure 1.2. *Viral lower respiratory tract infection; basic roentgenographic patterns.* Any virus can produce a number of roentgenographic patterns. The spectrum ranges from relatively infiltrate-free bronchiolitis to parahilar peribronchial infiltrates, with or without atelectasis. Atelectasis may be segmental or lobar. Less commonly diffuse reticulonodular interstitial infiltrates occur, and equally rarely one may see diffusely hazy lungs due to interstitial disease. Parahilar peribronchial infiltrate is the most common, and overlap of one pattern with another also is common.

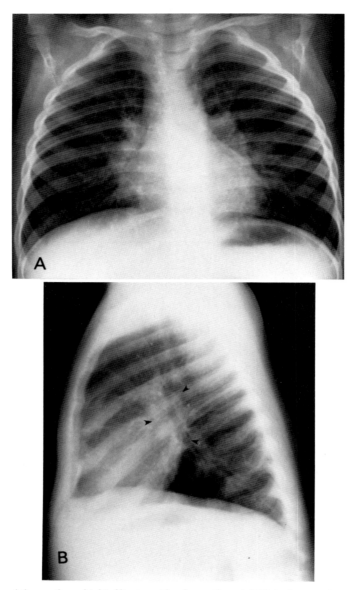

Figure 1.3. *Viral parahilar peribronchial infiltrates with adenopathy.*   (*A*) Note the prominent hilar regions due in part to hilar adenopathy and in part to peribronchial inflammation. The peripheral lung fields are relatively clear. (*B*) Lateral view demonstrates the characteristic increase in density and prominence of the superimposed hilar regions (*arrows*).

of viral lower respiratory tract infection. The inflammatory thickening and edema of the bronchial and peribronchial tissues predisposes to more than normal narrowing of the airways during expiration and thus air trapping occurs. In addition, reactive bronchospasm occurs, and as will be seen later, such air trapping often is most pronounced in cases of bronchiolitis. It also is a greater problem in asthmatics and infants with hyperreactive airway disease.

Clinically infants and children with parahilar peribronchial infiltrates commonly present with a cough, tachypnea, and a generally "miserable" clinical picture. They look sick and feel sick, and in addition, upper airway infection is commonly associated. Consequently, many also have croup,

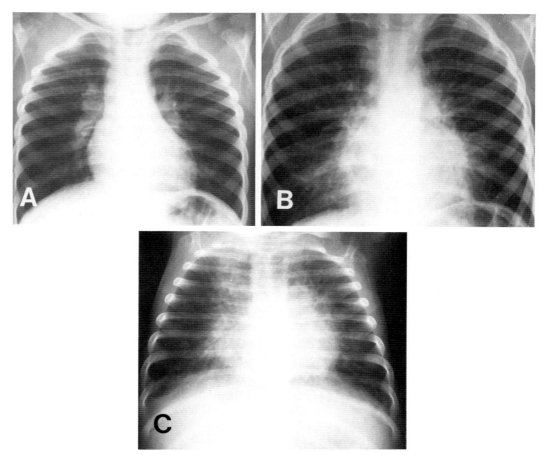

Figure 1.4. *Parahilar peribronchial infiltrates and hilar adenopathy—variable appearance.* (*A*) Note the prominent hilar regions with enlarged, readily recognizable, hilar lymph nodes. Parahilar peribronchial infiltration is minimal. (*B*) Another patient with less prominent hilar adenopathy but more extensive parahilar peribronchial infiltrates. (*C*) In this patient note lack of hilar adenopathy but extensive parahilar peribronchial infiltration leading to haziness of the cardiac edges or the so-called "shaggy heart" appearance.

or at least a croupy cough, sinus congestion, and coryza. Overall, however, most of these children do not require hospitalization, especially if they are older. Actually, what it amounts to is that they have an old-fashioned "chest cold" with a low grade fever. In these patients, oral temperature seldom exceeds 102°F. An exception might be made for infants under 2 years of age, but even then, when corrections are made for rectal temperature readings, fevers still generally are 102°F or less. On the other hand in the early viremic stage of these infections, fevers may be higher, but chest symptoms usually still are minimal or absent and the chest x-ray normal. However by the time respiratory symptoms develop to the point of such con-

cern that a roentgenogram is obtained, fevers drop and infiltrates appear.

On auscultation the lungs frequently are "very noisy and juicy" and while many of these noises are transmitted, upper airway sounds, true rales, rhonchi, and even wheezes can be heard. However, these sounds are variable from moment to moment, and generally correlate poorly with any attempts to match them, lobe for lobe, with the roentgenographic findings. The reason for this is that most of the sounds result from numerous, incomplete, fleeting obstructions of the airways caused by mucous plugs and bronchospasm.

When parenchymal involvement in viral lower respiratory tract occurs, it is interstitial and not alveolar. Indeed, true alveolar consolidations probably do not exist, and what is assumed to be a parenchymal consolidation is an area of atelectasis. This occurs quite frequently, for atelectasis, both lobar and segmental, abounds in viral lower respiratory tract infection.

In terms of interstitial involvement, the most common pattern is that of streaky or reticular infiltrates, radiating outward from the hilar regions. The pattern is merely the extension of the more common parahilar peribronchial pattern and such extension of the reticulations into the lung periphery can be impressive (Fig. 1.4). Overall, both this and the parahilar peribronchial configuration lead to the typical "shaggy" heart. This appearance first was described with pertussis pneumonia, but is much more common with viral or *M. pneumoniae* infections. With pertussis infection, the reason the "shaggy" heart is seen is that the infection, just as with viruses, is a bronchitis, and not a peripheral alveolar infection (13). It is only later that superimposed bacterial infection may lead to consolidation, but in the early stages parahilar peribronchial infiltrates predominate (Fig. 1.5). Similar findings usually also occur in chlamydia infections in infants and, in terms of pertussis infection, it should be noted that not all cases need show the "shaggy" heart, nor any infiltrate at all.

In still other cases of viral lower respiratory tract infection, a diffuse haziness of the lungs is seen and, in some cases, this pattern involves both lungs in their entirety, while in others, the findings tend to be more pronounced in the lung bases (Fig. 1.6). In either case, the pattern is interstitial, and must be differentiated from a similar one occurring with pulmonary edema. Less commonly, patients with viral lower respiratory infection present with miliary or reticulonodular infiltrates scattered throughout the lungs (Fig. 1.7) and the findings then must be differentiated from those of miliary tuberculosis.

True, alveolar infiltrates, with viral lower respiratory tract infection are uncommon, and as has been alluded to earlier, of questionable existence. Even with more aggressive viral infections, such as those caused by adenovirus, the apparent lobar consolidations and patches of fluffy alveolar infiltrate represent areas of atelectasis (3, 8, 9, 12, 15). Indeed, atelectasis probably is responsible for most, if not all, "apparent" alveolar infiltrates seen in children with viral lower respiratory tract infections. Roentgenographically, however, often it is difficult to be absolutely certain that one is dealing with a viral infection only (22), for even though extensive interstitial disease always is present, the "apparent superimposed consolidation" remains worrisome (Fig. 1.8).

The problem of atelectasis mimicking consolidation in viral lower respiratory tract infection is discussed in more detail at the end of this section, but for the time being, it should be realized that such patients may not be as ill as the roentgenographic findings would suggest. In other words, the multiple areas of segmental atelectasis do not inter-

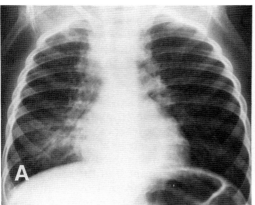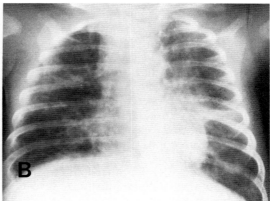

Figure 1.5. *Parahilar peribronchial infiltrates; nonviral.* (*A*) Note typical parahilar peribronchial infiltrates in pertussis infection. (*B*) Chlamydia infection producing similar parahilar peribronchial infiltrates. Also note an area of segmental atelectasis in the left mid-lung field.

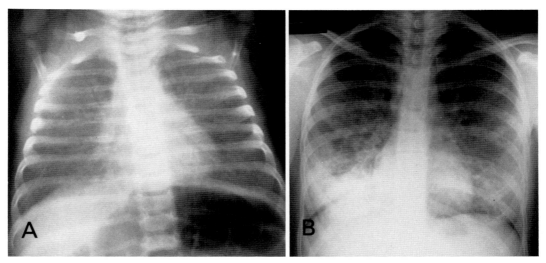

Figure 1.6. *Hazy lungs—viral pneumonitis.* (*A*) Note diffuse haziness throughout both lungs. This is not a common pattern, but nonetheless one which can be seen with viral interstitial pneumonitis. (*B*) Similar findings localized to the bases in a patient with desquamative interstitial pneumonia.

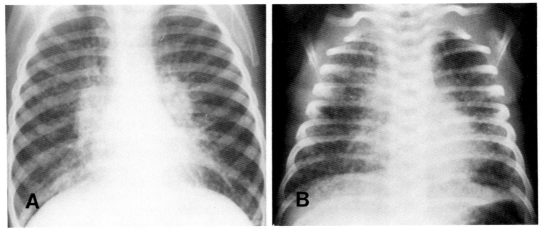

Figure 1.7. *Viral infection; reticulonodular infiltrates.* (*A*) Note parahilar peribronchial infiltrates with some early peripheral reticularity. (*B*) Another patient with more extensive reticulonodular infiltrates. This infant was acutely ill with viral disease.

fere that much with ventilation, and certainly do not make the patient toxic or febrile. This is most important to appreciate, for it will explain those instances where there is gross discrepancy between the patient's clinical condition and roentgenograms. Simply stated, while the roentgenogram "sees" atelectasis, the stethoscope cannot "hear" atelectasis, and consequently, roentgenographic-auscultative correlation is poor. Indeed, ***what one sees is not what one hears and vice versa.***

At the other end of the spectrum of viral lower respiratory tract infection is the young infant with bronchiolitis. Bronchiolitis is a distinct clinicoroentgenographic entity which is frequently, but not exclusively, caused by respiratory syncytial virus (1, 5, 7, 10, 17, 20, 21, 23). Its incidence peaks at around 6 months, but it is common up to 2 years of age or so. In this regard, it may be that, since these young infants are still relatively immature immunologically, they are less able to deal with the viral infection (17).

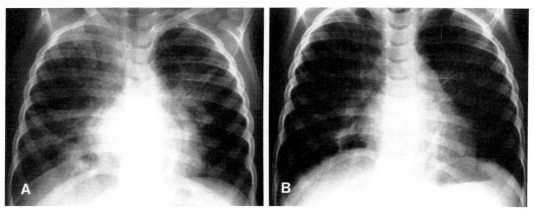

Figure 1.8. *Viral atelectatic (pseudoconsolidation) parenchymal infiltrates.* (*A*) There is a basic pattern of bilateral parahilar, peribronchial infiltration in this patient. However, ill-defined parenchymal infiltrates are suggested in the right upper, middle, and left upper lobes. (*B*) Four days later marked improvement has occurred. Only parahilar peribronchial infiltrates and a few wedge-like streaks of atelectasis remain. No bacterial infection would clear this quickly. Adenoviral infection was strongly suspected in this infant. White blood count showed a pronounced lymphocytosis.

Parahilar peribronchial infiltrates and patches of atelectasis may be seen in these infants, but most show a surprisingly clear chest (Fig. 1.9). This has been noted by others (11), and certainly is our experience.

Pronounced overaeration due to air trapping always is present in bronchiolitis and, to be sure, is the hallmark of this disease. It leads to severe respiratory distress and clinically these infants show marked dyspnea, tachypnea, air hunger, paroxysmal coughing, and cyanosis. Fine rales may be heard at the end of inspiration and in early expiration, and in some infants expiratory wheezes are present. However, unlike the wheezes in asthma, they do not dissipate significantly when epinephrine is administered. Bronchiolar inflammation and expiratory constriction play havoc with the already normally narrow bronchioles in these young infants, and peripheral air trapping becomes pronounced. Simply speaking, the chests in these infants are "frozen" in deep inspiration, and they do not move air.

In passing, it should be noted that there often is some confusion between bronchiolitis and asthma (6, 16). Most physicians have had the experience where some infants with bronchiolitis eventually turn out to have true asthma, but generally speaking the diagnosis of asthma is not made with confidence under the age of 2 years. On the other hand, overlap must occur and the possibility

of underlying asthma should be borne in mind when one is presented with an infant who has repeated bouts of bronchiolitis. Similarly, repeated bouts of bronchiolitis should raise the possibility of underlying cystic fibrosis, for it is not unusual for infants with this disease to first present with what appear to be repeated, or especially severe and refractory, bouts of bronchiolitis. Finally, it should be noted that the roentgenographic picture of bronchiolitis also can be mimicked by centrally obstructing lesions such as vascular rings and mediastinal masses and cysts, and by dehydration and acidosis. In the latter infants, acidosis leads to an increase in respiratory rate and diaphragmatic excursion (to blow off excess CO_2), and the low blood volume of dehydration leads to a diminution in caliber of the pulmonary blood vessels. Together these findings result in lungs which appear overaerated and underperfused (Fig. 1.137), a picture virtually indistinguishable from that seen with bronchiolitis. Clinical correlation, however, usually quickly deciphers the situation and correctly identifies the problem.

Before proceeding to a discussion of the very common problem of focal aeration disturbances associated with viral lower respiratory tract infection, it should be emphasized that the preceding categorizations of the roentgenographic patterns of viral lower respiratory tract infection are intended as

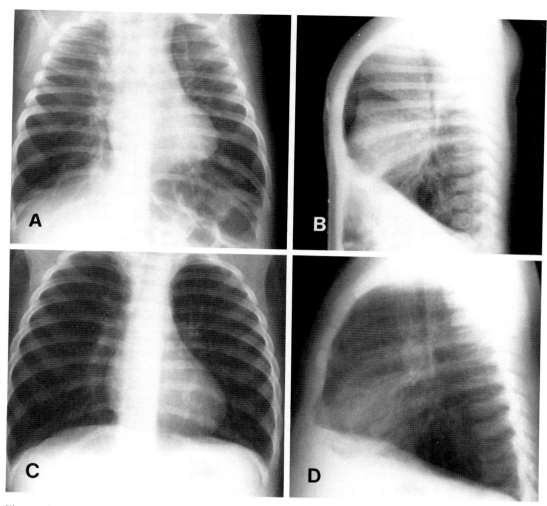

Figure 1.9. *Bronchiolitis with parahilar peribronchial infiltrates.* (*A*) Note marked overaeration of both lungs and some parahilar peribronchial infiltration. (*B*) Lateral view showing marked depression and flattening of the diaphragmatic leaflets secondary to overaeration. In the upper retrosternal area note how the marked degree of overaeration has caused the thymus gland to separate from the heart. (*C*) Note that even though there is considerable overaeration, there is a complete absence of peripheral infiltrates, and minimal, if any, parahilar infiltration. (*D*) Lateral view shows marked overaeration with a characteristically bell-shaped chest and markedly depressed and flattened diaphragmatic leaflets.

initial anchor points only. One should not be too rigid in their application, for overlap of one pattern with another is common. In addition, viral lower respiratory tract infections are prone to produce lingering roentgenographic abnormalities in the face of an improving, or completely improved, clinical picture. This, of course, is one more time for clinical-roentgenographic correlation, and indeed, all of the roentgenographic patterns discussed in this section should be correlated with the clinical picture, for only

then will they benefit the patient and physician most. If all of the clinical and laboratory parameters suggest good health, reassess the roentgenographic findings; do not discard them, just reassess them. Roentgenograms are for interpretation—patients are for treating.

As has just been alluded to, *temporary aeration disturbances such as segmental atelectasis and focal obstructive emphysema are extremely common with viral lower respiratory tract infections* (19). They result from bronchial obstruction secondary to mucosal inflammation, endobronchial secretions, and mucous plugs, and the resulting roentgenographic pictures can be most misleading. Areas of segmental atelectasis, in particular, have a propensity to mimic pneumonia and distract one's attention from the real problem. This can hardly be avoided for it is truly difficult to be sure that atelectasis only is the problem, and actually lobar consolidation usually will be favored (Fig. 1.10). Because of this, antibiotics will be administered, and, of course, this is not without cause. However, at the same time it should be realized that when these suspicious infiltrates clear in just a day or two, it is not because of unusually rapid clearing of the presumed pneumonia, but rather, because of the dislodging of atelectasis producing mucous plugs (Fig. 1.10). Once this phenomenon is appreciated, it becomes easier to understand why some children with viral lower respiratory tract infections seem to show most abnormal and disturbing roentgenographic findings in the face of surprisingly mild symptoms. The reason for this is that they do not really have pneumonia as the roentgenograms might suggest. Their basic problem still is one of bronchitis with parahilar peribronchial infiltrates; it just

happens that the multiple areas of segmental atelectasis confuse the issue by mimicking alveolar consolidation (Fig. 1.10). Such atelectasis is common in children (22), and occurs because of insufficiency of the collateral air-drift phenomenon occurring through the ducts of Lambert and the pores of Kohn (4). In children this mechanism is not as well developed as in adults and so areas of atelectasis tend to persist. In terms of segmental atelectasis, usually it tends to remain somewhat central in its distribution (Fig. 1.10*A*), and this finding is most helpful in distinguishing these infiltrates, from the more peripheral, and diffuse, infiltrates seen with bacterial, alveolar infection (see Fig. 1.20*B*).

When a major bronchus is plugged by mucus, and the entire lobe collapses, the findings often are easier to assess (Fig. 1.11). On the other hand, even in some of these cases, the findings may be puzzling (Fig. 1.12). Of course, in any of these cases, if volume loss is marked, and clearly apparent, atelectasis should be one's first diagnosis. Volume loss is not a prominent feature of acute consolidating pneumonia, for it is only when the pneumonia is healing and contracting (10 days or so later) that significant volume loss occurs. In the acute stages, vol-

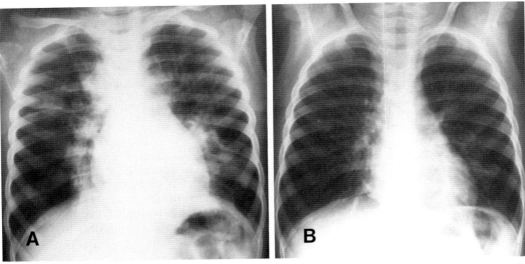

Figure 1.10. *Parahilar peribronchial infiltrates with central segmental atelectasis.* (*A*) Note extensive parahilar peribronchial infiltrates and central predominance of patchy densities. Such densities often are misinterpreted for alveolar pneumonia but in fact are due to segmental atelectasis. However, only with considerable experience would one be able to confidently suggest that viral disease only is the problem. (*B*) Twenty-four hours later, however, note how much clearing has occurred. This could happen only with atelectasis. Parahilar peribronchial infiltration remains and a few wedge-like and linear streaks of atelectasis persist.

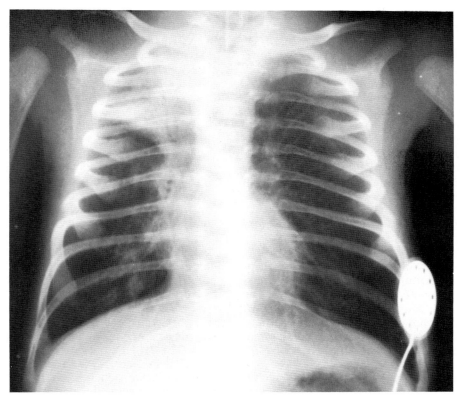

Figure 1.11. *Atelectasis with viral lower respiratory tract infection.* This infant with bronchiolitis has widespread air trapping and a moderate degree of parahilar peribronchial infiltration. However, also note clear-cut atelectasis of the right upper lobe. The minor fissure is markedly elevated and there is ipsilateral shift of the mediastinum.

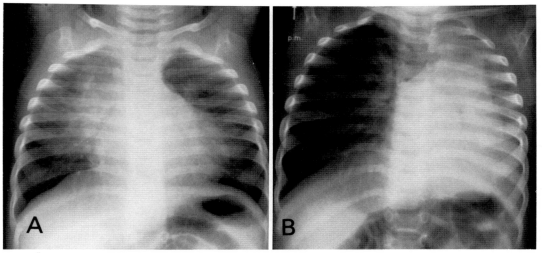

Figure 1.12. *Massive atelectasis, shifting from side to side with viral lower respiratory tract infection.* (*A*) Note parahilar peribronchial infiltrates and what would appear to be a large infiltrate in the right upper lobe. (*B*) The next day note that the entire right lung is clear and that the apparent infiltrate in the right upper lobe has disappeared. However, the left lung has now collapsed. Such rapid clearing of the right lung is too fast for pneumonia; it represents clearing atelectasis after dislodging of a mucous plug. On this inspiratory film the right lung also shows so-called compensatory overaeration; in other words it is larger than it should be because the patient is compensating for the nonventilating left lung.

ume loss usually is minimal (see Fig. 1.14), and for this reason, it is most important to appreciate the degree of volume loss in an involved lobe (22). *If volume loss is significant, atelectasis should be favored, while if it is minimal, consolidation is more likely.*

Obstructive emphysema, rather than atelectasis, due to mucous plugging is a less common feature of viral lower respiratory tract infection, but does occur (Fig. 1.13). In these cases, it is not uncommon to misinterpret the problem as being due to multiple sites of juxtalobar atelectasis, rather than unilobar emphysema. Pleural effusions, usually of small volume, occasionally can be encountered with viral lower respiratory tract infections (13), but generally speaking are uncommon.

Lobar Consolidation. Lobar consolidations most commonly are the result of pneumococcal or *H. influenzae* infections; the latter being more common in infants. *M. pneumoniae* and *S. aureus* are less common causes, and consolidations secondary to *Klebsiella*, *Pseudomonas*, and other such infections generally are rare. *M. pneumoniae* consolidations tend to occur in older children. Viral consolidations probably are nonexistent, and fungal consolidations may be encountered in endemic areas.

Clinically, patients with bacterial lobar consolidations present with abrupt onset of fever (usually 103°F orally or over), lassitude, malaise, and a cough. However, there is a smaller group of patients who first acquire a viral illness, and then a week or so later, develop a superimposed bacterial infection. When they do, symptoms characteristic of bacterial infection become apparent, and the toxic, febrile, clinical picture is quite suggestive of the diagnosis. Auscultatory-roentgenographic correlation with bacterial consolidation, as opposed to viral bronchitis, is good, and roentgenograms usually confirm the location of the clinically suspected pneumonia. Its appearance can range from a small peripheral infiltrate to a completely consolidated lobe and its size depends on the age of the pneumonia (Fig. 1.14). Occasionally, in the early stages these infiltrates may be more nodular (see Fig. 1.20) than homogeneous, but overall the homogeneous pattern prevails.

In most cases consolidations begin peripherally (Fig. 1.14A), but one does not always appreciate this fact, for the apparent location of the infiltrate depends on the view obtained. Nonetheless, this peripheral origin is important to appreciate when it comes to differentiating early consolidation from at-

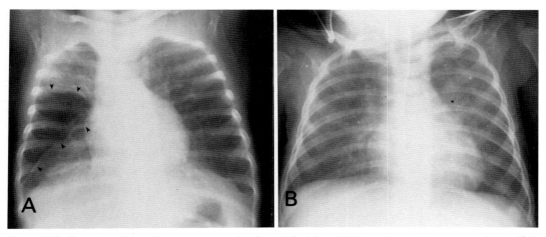

Figure 1.13. *Transient obstructive emphysema of right middle lobe.* (*A*) Note the emphysematous right middle lobe (*arrows*) and the partially collapsed right upper and right lower lobes in this patient with viral lower respiratory tract infection. The *upper arrows* delineate the minor fissure while the *lower arrows* delineate the major fissure. (*B*) A few days later with clearing of the infection the right middle lobe emphysema disappears. On the first film (*A*) the clue to the proper diagnosis lies in the fact that the entire chest is overaerated. In cases of congenital lobar emphysema, there is no reason for the entire chest to be overaerated, only the involved lobe. In this infant the basic problem was bronchiolitis and because of this the whole chest was overaerated; obstructive emphysema due to mucous plugging of the right middle lobe bronchus was an added problem.

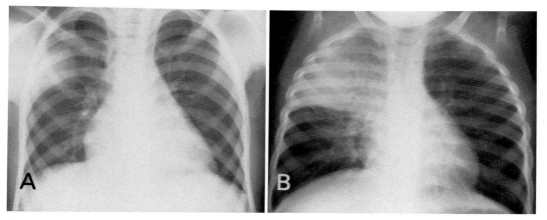

Figure 1.14. *Lobar consolidation.*   (*A*) Early, peripheral consolidation in right upper lobe. Note that the remainder of the right lung, and the entire left lung remain clear. There are no parahilar peribronchial infiltrates. (*B*) Complete consolidation of the right upper lobe with characteristic air bronchogram. The minor fissure is only slightly elevated, attesting to minimal volume loss. There is another early, incomplete consolidation developing in the right middle lobe, but the entire left lung is perfectly clear. Both patients had pneumococcal pneumonia.

electasis. With atelectasis it would be most unusual for a peripheral density to occur without a central counterpart. In other words, usually there is no clear space between the area of increased density due to atelectasis, and the mediastinum (compare Fig. 1.11 and Fig. 1.14*B*).

Interpretation of roentgenograms showing classic lobar consolidation, restricted to one lobe, is relatively straightforward. Usually, with a fresh pneumonia, there is little in the way of volume loss (Fig. 1.14*B*), a point quite different from atelectasis, where volume loss is the key feature. It is only with old, resolving consolidating pneumonias that volume loss may become marked. In addition, of course, an air bronchogram also usually is visualized with consolidation (Fig. 1.14*B*), but is not always clearly visible. This is especially true when the consolidation is incomplete (Fig. 1.15, *A* and *B*). In still other instances, more than one lobe may be involved (Fig. 1.15, *C* and *D*), but unilobar involvement is most common. Consolidating pneumonias also may appear as a pulmonary nodule or mediastinal mass and this aspect of consolidating pneumonias is discussed in detail later (see Fig. 1.22).

Finally, one or two pitfalls in the interpretation of roentgenograms in patients suspected of having consolidating pneumonia should be borne in mind. The most important of these deals with the patient who obtains the chest roentgenogram early in the course of the disease. In such cases, because of the usual delay period of up to 12 hours from the onset of symptoms to the appearance of a roentgenographically demonstrable infiltrate, the roentgenogram can be normal. Clinically, however, fever, cough, and decreased air entry into the involved lobe are usually clearly apparent, but because the roentgenogram appears so normal one may be taken aback by the situation. At the other end of the spectrum, it is equally important to note that it is not uncommon for auscultation to fail to detect a well developed lobar pneumonia which turns out to be startlingly present roentgenographically. These cases represent instances of advanced consolidation and most likely breath sounds from the adjacent normal lung are so well transmitted through the consolidated lobe that it sounds normal on cursory auscultation.

With the approach just outlined, and with practice, one usually can determine whether an infection is of viral or bacterial origin from the roentgenograms alone (22). Basically one is dealing with the categories of pulmonary infiltrate outlined in Table 1.1 and problems in interpretation usually do not arise unless parahilar peribronchial infiltrates are associated with peripheral alveolar infiltrates. The problem, then, is to decide whether these infiltrates are due to atelectasis or consolidation, and no matter how experienced one becomes, certain cases will remain truly indeterminate (22). However, if

Table 1.1. *Infiltrate Patterns and Etiologic Agents*[a]

Roentgenographic Pattern	V	B	M	V/2nd B
A. Lobar				
Consolidation	−	+	+	−
Fluffy-nodular	−	+	+	−
Interstitial-reticulonodular	?	−	+	−
B. Widespread Bilateral				
PHPB only	+	−	+	−
PHPB with atelectasis	+	−	+	−
PHPB with consolidation	−	−	−	+
Fluffy patchy central	+	−	+	−
Fluffy patchy peripheral	−	+	?	−
Reticulonodular	+	−	+	−
Hazy lungs	+	−	−	−

[a] V = viral, B = bacterial, M = *Mycoplasma pneumoniae*, V/2nd B = viral with secondary bacterial, and PHPB = parahilar peribronchial infiltration.

either atelectasis or consolidation is strongly suggested, one can favor a viral or bacterial etiology (Figs. 1.16 and 1.17). Otherwise the indeterminate designation will persist, and final diagnosis will rest with clinical correlation.

In terms of such correlation, viral infections usually come to roentgenographic examination 2 or 3 days after onset of the illness, have lower presenting fevers (102°F or lower orally) and usually do not produce particularly ill patients. An exception occurs with bronchiolitis in infancy where the infant is quite ill, but still more from profound air trapping than toxicity. On the other hand, it should be noted that infants with viral infection tend to appear a little more

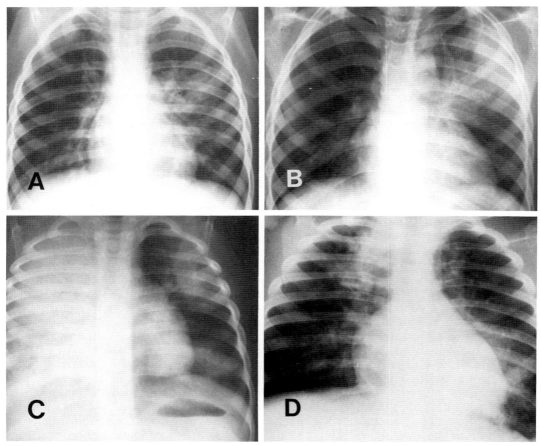

Figure 1.15. *Less typical lobar consolidations.* (*A*) Note ill-defined hazy parenchymal infiltrate in the left mid-lung. This infiltrate was of streptococcal origin. (*B*) Another patient with a more typical appearing consolidation peripherally, but a somewhat streaky appearance medially. (*C*) Multilobar consolidation. Note that the right lung is totally consolidated. This is rather rare with consolidating pneumonias but can occur. On the left, two other consolidations are developing. (*D*) Another patient with multilobar consolidation. First note increased density behind the left side of the heart due to a left lower lobe consolidation. The fluffy, indistinct edge, projected just past the left cardiac border is common with developing consolidations. The second consolidation is developing in the right upper lobe. Note that none of these consolidations are associated with volume loss.

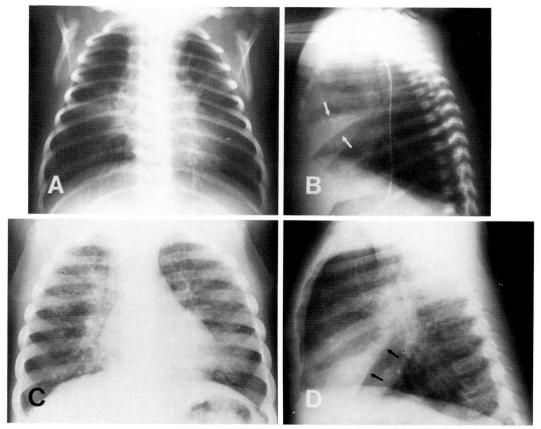

Figure 1.16. *Viral parahilar peribronchial infiltrates with confusing alveolar infiltrates.* (*A*) Young infant with widespread overaeration, parahilar peribronchial infiltrates, and patchy infiltrates along both sides of the cardiac silhouette. (*B*) Lateral view clearly shows that the changes are due to right middle lobe and lingular, atelectasis (*arrows*), and thus, viral disease is favored. This patient had bronchiolitis. (*C*) Another infant with widespread parahilar peribronchial infiltrates and a questionable area of consolidation in the lingula. (*D*) Once again, however, the lateral view suggests atelectasis as the major fissure is displaced forward (*arrows*). Both of these patients had viral disease.

ill than older children with the same infection. However, if white blood cell counts are obtained, there will be a definite lymphocytosis with viral infections. Bacterial infections produce an increase in neutrophils, a concomitant left shift, and an increase in bands. This occurs whether the bacterial infection is primary or secondarily imposed on a viral problem.

Other features of bacterial infections include abrupt onset of symptoms (under 24–36 hours) and higher fevers (103°F or over orally). This same, abrupt onset, in change of symptomatology usually also occurs in those patients who develop a bacterial infection on top of a previously existing viral infection. The reverse, that is, having a bacterial infection first, and then a viral infec-

tion, is not commonplace. Finally, it should be recalled that *M. pneumoniae* infections can mimic viral infections, both clinically and roentgenographically.

Miscellaneous Patterns of Pneumonia. Other patterns of pulmonary infiltration seen with pneumonia include diffuse, hazy lungs, miliary and reticulonodular infiltrates, patchy parenchymal infiltrates, and so-called round or mass-like pneumonias. Always bacterial, these latter pneumonias are discussed in more detail in the next section.

As far as diffusely hazy lungs are concerned, as noted earlier, most often they are seen with viral, interstitial pneumonitis (see Fig. 1.6). Similar infiltrates also can be seen with *Pneumocystis carinii* pneumonia, or

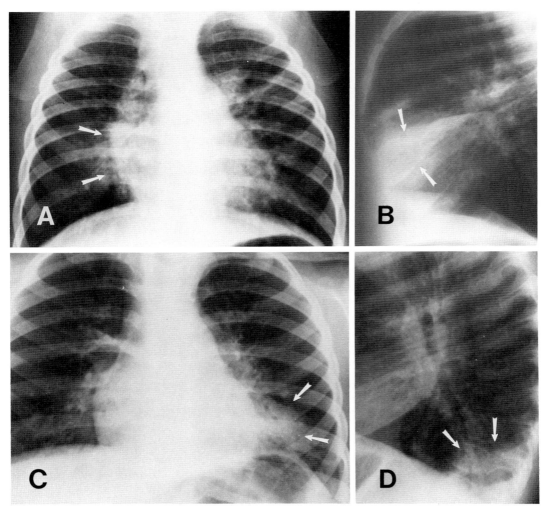

Figure 1.17. *Viral parahilar peribronchial infiltrates with confusing alveolar infiltrates.* (*A*) Note extensive parahilar peribronchial infiltrates and central densities due to segmental atelectasis. The one along the right cardiac border (*arrows*) is suspicious. Consolidation vs. atelectasis? (*B*) Lateral view clearly shows the density to be due to atelectasis of the right middle lobe (arrows). (*C*) Another patient with parahilar peribronchial infiltrates, a streak of segmental atelectasis in the right upper lobe, and a suspicious density along the left cardiac border (*arrows*). Consolidation or atelectasis? (*D*) Lateral view confirms the streak of atelectasis in the right upper lobe, but the density in the left lower lobe is very peripheral (*arrows*). The peripheral location favors consolidation. This patient had viral disease with secondary bacterial infection.

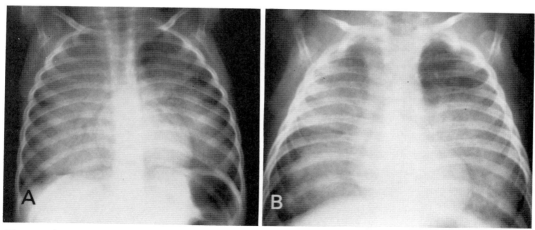

Figure 1.18. *Dense, hazy infiltrates of the lungs.* (*A*) Note diffuse, dense, haziness of both lung fields in this infant with biopsy-proven nonspecific interstitial pneumonia of viral origin. Some early fibrosis also was present. (*B*) Another infant with a dense pattern of diffuse, hazy infiltrates in both lungs secondary to lipoid aspiration. (From Swischuk, L.E.: *Radiology of the Newborn and Young Infant,* Williams & Wilkins, Baltimore, 1980).

lipoid pneumonitis (Fig. 1.18) and on a chronic basis with pulmonary hemosiderosis, pulmonary fibrosis, and pulmonary alveolar proteinosis. When hazy infiltrates are limited to the lung bases, most often the problem is viral pneumonitis (see Fig. 1.6*B*) and very often it is due to desquamative interstitial pneumonia (DIP). However, edema, secondary to the vasculitis seen with the collagen vascular diseases, also produces hazy lung bases, and indeed, edema due to any cause can produce this pattern.

Widespread, small, miliary nodules most often are seen with miliary tuberculosis (Fig. 1.19*A*). On occasion, however, a viral or mycoplasma pneumonitis can produce a similar picture. These nodules, however, are usually a little larger and irregular and the overall pattern may be more reticulonodular (Fig. 1.19*C*). In adults, and in immunosuppressed children, chickenpox pneumonia also is known to produce such a pattern.

Patchy, or fluffy parenchymal infiltrates, limited to one lobe usually represent bacterial or *M. pneumoniae* infection. The former, however, is more common, and the pattern does not exist with viral infections. As far as bacterial infections are concerned, the problem most often is staphylococcal or streptococcal infection (Fig. 1.20*A*) and staphylococcal infection is greatly favored when these infiltrates are diffuse and involve both lungs (Fig. 1.20*B*). One is not likely to see such a pattern with *D. pneumoniae* infection, but it is possible to see it with *H. influenzae* infections. Allergic pneumonitis

from any number of causes, and the bleeding of idiopathic hemosiderosis also can produce diffuse, patchy or fluffy infiltrates. Occasionally, one also can see the same problem with fungal infections.

Viral infections also commonly produce multiple patchy infiltrates throughout the lungs, but in these cases the infiltrates are due to multiple areas of segmental, and subsegmental atelectasis, and not alveolar infection. The problem has been discussed in detail in previous sections, but it is important to recall that the infiltrates in these cases are clustered toward the central lung zones (see Fig. 1.10). With true, inflammatory, alveolar infiltrates, peripheral distribution is more the case (Fig. 1.20*B*).

Reticular, reticulonodular, or streaky infiltrates limited to one lobe, in our experience, are not of bacterial origin (Fig. 1.21). Rather, they almost always are due to *M. pneumoniae* infections (22), and occasionally, may be accompanied by early lobar atelectasis (Fig. 1.21). Viral infections conceivably also could produce such a pattern, but we do not feel that such an occurrence is very common. Indeed, we question as to whether it exists at all, for viral infections usually involve the tracheobronchial tree diffusely. The clinical picture in patients with lobar, reticulonodular, or reticular infiltrates due to *M. pneumoniae* infection usually is one of a low grade fever and cough lasting for 2 or 3 weeks prior to roentgenogram examination.

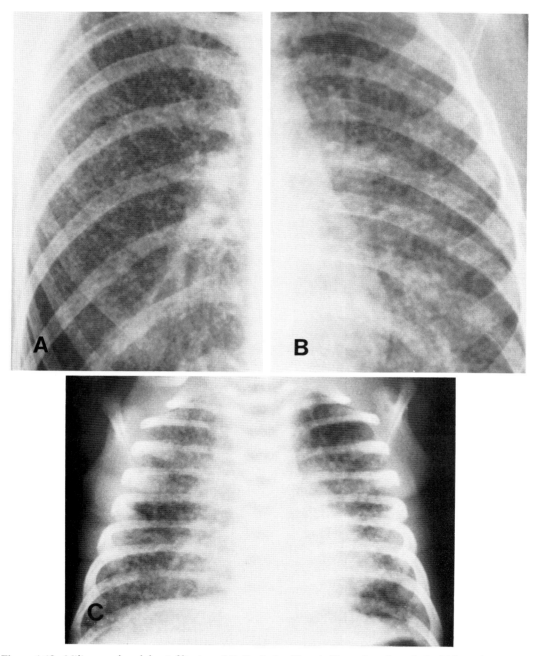

Figure 1.19. *Miliary and nodular infiltrates.* (*A*) Typical miliary infiltrate in tuberculosis. This patient was 10 years old. Occasionally viral infections can produce a similar picture, but the individual nodules are usually a little larger and more ragged. (*B*) Larger nodules in an infant with widespread tuberculosis. (*C*) Reticulonodular infiltrate in viral pneumonitis. (Same patient as in Fig. 1.7*B*).

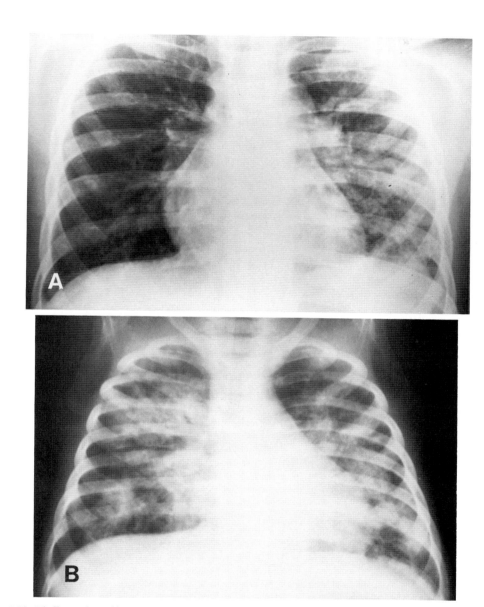

Figure 1.20. *Fluffy patchy infiltrates.* (*A*) Fluffy or patchy infiltrate in left lung due to streptococcal pneumonia. Most often such infiltrates are bacterial in origin. (*B*) Widespread patchy parenchymal infiltrates, somewhat fluffy, in widespread *Staphylococcus aureus* pneumonia. Note that the infiltrates appear "soft" and extend into the periphery of the lungs. They should be differentiated from the patchy infiltrates of diffuse, segmental atelectasis which tend to cluster toward the center of the lungs (see Fig. 1.10).

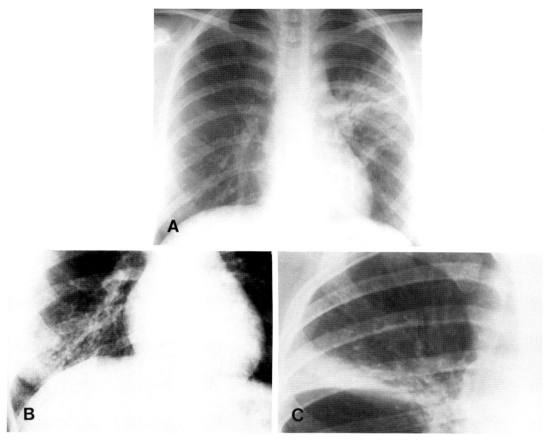

Figure 1.21. *Reticulonodular and streaky infiltrates in one lobe.* (*A*) Note streaky, reticular infiltrate in the left upper lobe. (*B*) Reticulonodular infiltrate in the right lower lobe. (*C*) Reticulonodular infiltrate in the right upper lobe, associated with early atelectasis. All of these patients had *Mycoplasma pneumoniae* infection.

REFERENCES

1. Chanock, R.M., Kim, H.W., Vargosko, A.J., Deleva, A., Johnson, K.M., Cumming, C., and Parrot, R.H.: Respiratory syncitial virus; I. Virus recovery and other observations during the 1960 outbreak of bronchiolitis, pneumonia and minor respiratory diseases in children. J.A.M.A. 176: 647–653, 1961.
2. Conte, P., Heitzman, E.R., and Markarian, B.: Viral pneumonia, roentgen pathological correlations. Radiology 95: 267–272, 1970.
3. Gold, R., Wilt, J.C., Adhikari, P.K., and MacPherson, R.I.: Adenoviral pneumonia and its complications in infancy and childhood. J. Can. Assoc. Radiol. 20: 4, 1969.
4. Griscom, N.T., Wohl, M.E.B., and Kirkpatrick, J.A., Jr.: Lower respiratory infections: how infants differ from adults. Radiol. Clin. North Am. 16: 367–387, 1978.
5. Heycock, J.B., and Noble, T.C.: 1230 cases of acute bronchiolitis in infancy. Br. Med. J. 2: 879, 1962.
6. Hyde, J.S., and Saed, A.M.: Acute bronchiolitis and the asthmatic child. J. Asthma Res. 4: 137–154, 1966.
7. Jacobs, J.A., Peacock, Corner, B.D., Caul, E.O., and Clarke, S.K.R.: Respiratory syncytial and other viruses associated with respiratory disease in infants. Lancet 1: 871–876, 1971.
8. James, A.G., Lang, W.R., Liang, A.Y., Mackay, R.J., Morris, M.C., Newman, J.N., Osborne, D.R., and White, P.R.: Adenovirus type 21 bronchopneumonia in infants and young children. J. Pediatr. 95: 530–533, 1979.
9. Kim, K.S., and Gohd, R.S.: Fatal pneumonia caused by adenovirus type 35. Am. J. Dis. Child. 135: 473–475, 1981.
10. Kirkpatrick, J.A., and Wagner, M.L.: Roentgen manifestations of bronchiolitic inflammatory disease. Pediatr. Clin. North Am. 10: 633–642, 1963.
11. Koch, D.A.: Roentgenologic considerations of capillary bronchiolitis. A.J.R. 82: 433–436, 1959.
12. Lanning, P., Simila, S., and Linna, O.: Late pulmonary sequelae after type 7 adenovirus pneumonia. Ann. Radiol. 23: 132–136, 1980.
13. Murphy, S., and Florman, A.L.: Lung defenses against infection: a clinical correlation. Pediatrics 72: 1, 1983.
14. Osborne, D.: Radiologic appearance of viral disease of the lower respiratory tract in infants and children. A.J.R. 13: 29–33, 1978.
15. Osborne, D., and White, P.: Radiology of epidemic adenovirus 21 infection of the lower respiratory tract in infants and young children. A.J.R. 133: 397–400, 1979.
16. Rice, R.P., and Loda, F.: A roentgenographic analysis of respiratory syncytial virus pneumonia in infants. Radiology 87: 1021–1027, 1966.
17. Ross, C.A.C., Pinkerton, I.W., and Assaad, F.A.: Pathogenesis of respiratory syncytial virus diseases in infancy. Arch. Dis. Child. 46: 702–704, 1971.
18. Scanlon, G.A., and Unger, J.D.: The radiology of bacterial

and viral pneumonias. Radiol. Clin. North Am. 11: 317–338, 1973.

19. Shopfner, C.E.: Aeration disturbances secondary to pulmonary infection. A.J.R. 120: 261–273, 1974.

20. Simpson, W., Hacking, P.M., Court, S.D.M., and Gardner, P.S.: The radiological findings in respiratory syncytial virus infection in children; I. Definitions and interobserver variation in the assessment of abnormalities on the chest x-ray. Pediatr. Radiol. 2: 97–100, 1974.

21. Simpson, W., Hacking, P.M., Court, S.D.M., and Gardner, P.S.: The radiological findings in respiratory syncytial virus infection in children; II. The correlation of radiological categories with clinical and virological findings. Pediatr. Radiol. 2: 155–160, 1974.

22. Swischuk, L.E., and Hayden, C.K.: Lower respiratory tract infection in children: viral or bacterial—can you tell the difference? (in preparation)

23. Wright, F.H., and Beem, N.O.: Diagnosis and treatment: management of acute viral bronchiolitis in infancy. Pediatrics 35: 334–337, 1965.

Round Pneumonias (1–3). If you have never seen a round pneumonia you will never guess that that is what it is. Most often these so-called round, spherical, or oval pneumonias represent pneumococcal infections in an early consolidative phase. Some of them appear so round that they defy distinction from a pulmonary nodule or oval mass (Fig. 1.22). In other instances, a mediastinal mass might be suggested (Fig. 1.23), but the fact that one sees these pneumonias in such a configuration is purely fortuitous. If one could examine these patients a few hours later, a more typical picture of consolidation would be present (Fig. 1.24).

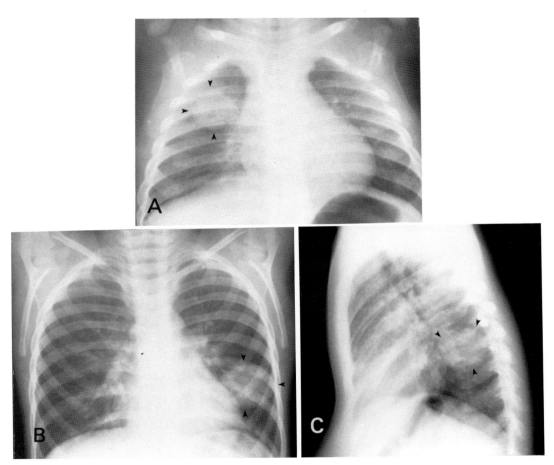

Figure 1.22. *Round or oval pneumonias—pseudopulmonary nodules or masses.* (*A*) Note the perfectly round pneumonia in the right upper lobe. This configuration could easily be mistaken for a pulmonary nodule. Clinical correlation is most important. (*B*) Perfectly oval configuration of lobar pneumonia in left lower lobe. The configuration defies distinction from a pulmonary mass. (*C*) Lateral view confirms the left lower lobe location of this pneumonia (*arrows*). This patient had pneumococcal pneumonia.

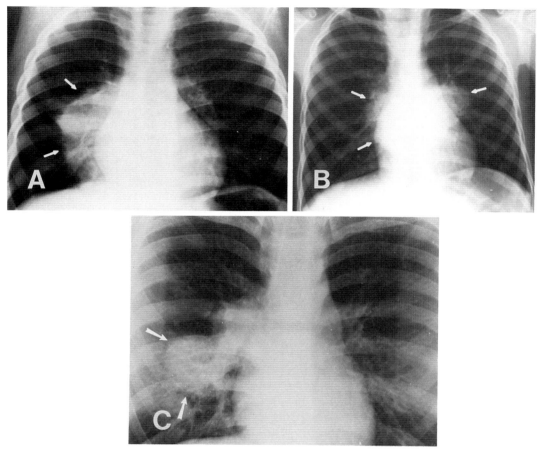

Figure 1.23. *Mass-like pneumonias.*   (*A*) Note mass-like configuration of this right lower lobe pneumonia (*arrows*). (*B*) Another patient with bilateral superior segment pneumonias mimicking a paraspinal mass (*arrows*). (*C*) Round pneumonia (*arrows*) with associated adenopathy on the right. All of these patients responded briskly to antibiotics.

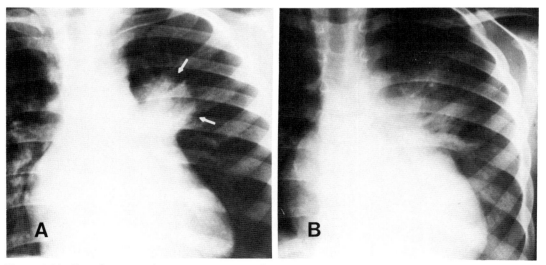

Figure 1.24. *Round pneumonia progressing to regular pneumonia.* (*A*) Note round pneumonia mimicking adenopathy on the left (*arrows*). (*B*) Next day a more typical consolidation has evolved.

The clue to proper diagnosis of these cases, of course, is clinical. These children almost always come to the attention of a physician because of an abrupt onset of fever, cough, and malaise. Usually they have a fever of between 103 and 105°F and auscultative findings which suggest a pneumonia. Under these circumstances do not think of tumor or a pulmonary nodule, think of a consolidating lobar pneumonia, usually pneumococcal in origin.

REFERENCES

1. Greenfield, H., and Gyepes, M.T.: Oval-shaped consolidations simulating new growth of the lung. A.J.R. 91: 125–131, 1964.
2. Rose, R. W., and Ward, B. H.: Spherical pneumonias in children simulating pulmonary and mediastinal masses. Radiology 106: 179–182, 1973.
3. Talner, L.B.: Pulmonary pseudotumors in childhood. A.J.R. 100: 208–213, 1967.

LOOKING FOR THE PNEUMONIA

Know Your Normal Chest First. It is most important that one be thoroughly familiar with the normal chest before one attempts to identify pneumonias, and in this regard it is a matter of studying the normal shape and densities of the various structures visualized (Fig. 1.25). For example, both hilar regions should be of relatively equal density, and the cardiac silhouette to either side of the spine should be of about the same density. Indeed, analysis of the chest roentgenogram is a matter of comparing one side with the other, not only in terms of anatomic boundaries, but also in terms of comparative densities. To be sure, it is the latter comparison which often turns out to be the more useful in detecting early or hidden infiltrates.

One also should note that the margins of the heart and diaphragmatic leaflets, as they lie in juxtaposition to normally aerated lung, are crisp and distinct. This observation is useful when it comes to utilizing and understanding Felson's silhouette sign. This sign is discussed in detail in the next section, but as a preliminary consideration it should be noted that if any of the cardiac or diaphragmatic edges become hazy or fuzzy one should suspect an adjacent abnormality such as pulmonary infiltration or atelectasis.

On lateral view an important normal finding is that the space behind the heart is characteristically radiolucent (Fig. 1.25B); it represents the superimposed, normally aer-

ated, lower lobes. Above this area the soft tissues of the upper chest wall, axillae, and shoulder cause the lung fields to become progressively more opaque. Characteristically, then, the posterior half of the chest should become more radiolucent as one passes from top to bottom and, if it does not (i.e., the lower retrocardiac space is of equal or greater density than the superior retrocardiac space), one should suspect a pneumonia in one or other of the lower lobes (compare Fig. 1.25B with Fig. 1.32B). However one pitfall must be avoided and that is not to interpret normal pulmonary vascular markings in this area as being representative of an infiltrate (Fig. 1.25C). The characteristic angle and linear configuration of the pulmonary vessels are the clues to proper diagnosis. The upper retrosternal space also should be radiolucent, except in young infants where the normal thymus gland causes the radiolucency to be replaced by radiodensity or whiteness. If this should occur in older children look for an anterior segment, upper lobe pneumonia, or by the same token, a superior mediastinal mass.

The right diaphragmatic leaflet normally is a little higher than the left, and because of this, it is often projected at a higher level on lateral view. Occasionally the leaflets are superimposed but most often they appear as separate structures. The right diaphragmatic leaflet also can be identified by the fact that it is usually seen in its entirety (Fig. 1.26). In other words, it can be seen as a distinct structure right up to its insertion onto the anterior chest wall. The left leaflet, on the other hand, usually is seen only as far as the posterior cardiac wall, for at this point it blends with the cardiac silhouette (Fig. 1.26). Occasionally, however, the left leaflet also can be seen in its entirety, and in such cases the usually visible gastric air bubble or inferior vena cava can be used as differentiating aids. The gastric bubble, of course, lies under the left diaphragmatic leaflet while the inferior vena cava, being right-sided, blends with the right diaphragmatic leaflet (Fig. 1.26). All of these findings and relationships may not be present on every lateral chest film, but enough of them usually are present so as to enable one to determine right- or left-sidedness of a diaphragmatic leaflet, and thus, right- or left-sidedness of an adjacent lower lobe pneumonia.

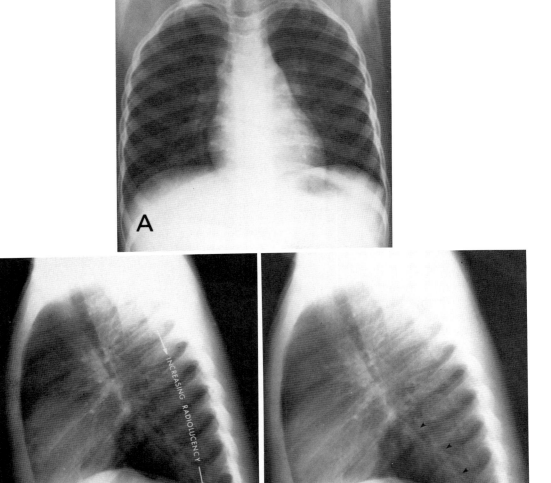

Figure 1.25. *Normal chest—pertinent roentgenographic features.*   (*A*) On this frontal view note that both lungs are of equal density and that the mediastinal, cardiac, and diaphragmatic edges are clearly delineated. In addition note that both sides of the heart are of equal density and that both hilar regions appear equal in density and size. (*B*) Lateral view demonstrating characteristic pattern of increasing radiolucency from top to bottom of the retrocardiac space. Also note how sharp both diaphragmatic leaflets appear. (*C*) Same patient as in (*B*), demonstrating normal lower lobe pulmonary vessels which often are misinterpreted for pulmonary infiltrates (*arrows*). The characteristic sloping configuration of these vessels aids one in proper interpretation.

Picking up Early or Minimal Infiltrates.   Early infiltrates often are so subtle that they are totally overlooked or simply misinterpreted as fortuitous conglomerations of rib and bronchovascular densities. The only way to diagnose such pneumonias is to be suspicious of, and then methodically substantiate, any focal area of increased density, no matter how equivocal (Fig. 1.27). If such infiltrates also happen to be adjacent to a diaphragmatic leaflet or cardiac border, the resulting positive silhouette sign (explained in detail in the next section) can aid one in their detection (Fig. 1.28). In other

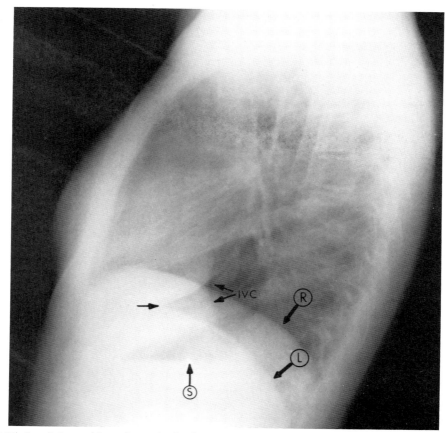

Figure 1.26. *Localizing and lateralizing the diaphragmatic leaflets.* Note that the right diaphragmatic leaflet (*R*) is higher than the left (*L*). Also note that the right diaphragmatic leaflet is seen in its entirety while the anterior third of the left blends with the posterior aspect of the cardiac silhouette (*anteriormost arrow*). The inferior vena cava (*IVC*) blends with the right diaphragmatic leaflet while the stomach bubble (*S*) is located immediately below the left diaphragmatic leaflet.

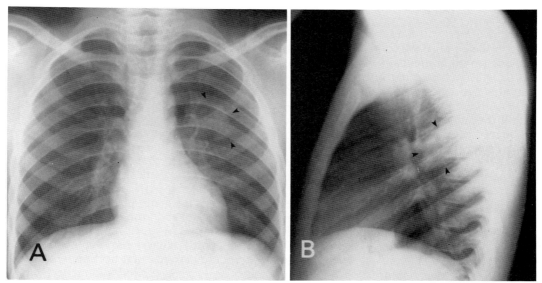

Figure 1.27. *Subtle early infiltrates.* (*A*) There is a vague area of focal infiltration in the left upper lung field, just lateral to the left hilar region (*arrows*). (*B*) Lateral view substantiates the presence of this infitrate as there is a corresponding area of focally increased density in the posterior chest, superimposed over the spine (*arrows*). Early consolidation.

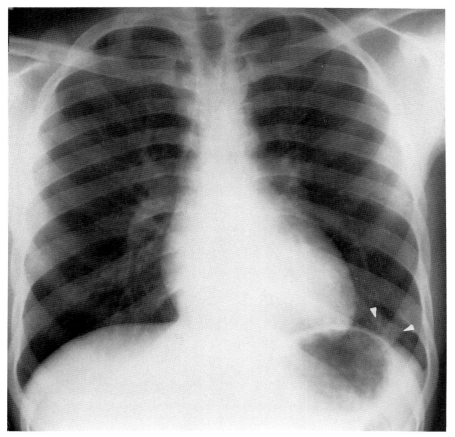

Figure 1.28. *Subtle, early infiltrate along the left diaphragmatic leaflet.*   This chest could pass for normal but on closer inspection note an early, rather subtle, infiltrate in the left lower lung field, just adjacent to the left diaphragmatic leaflet (*arrows*). Early consolidation.

instances, if one still is unsure, it is worthwhile to view the roentgenogram through a reducing (minifying) lens. Such a lens minifies the entire chest roentgenogram and accentuates a previously nebulous, hazy, or questionable infiltrate. Do not underestimate this useful little maneuver. Try it, you will be impressed.

The value of the lateral chest roentgenogram cannot be overstated in diagnosing early pneumonias. Its usefulness is evident in Figure 1.27 and will become repeatedly more evident throughout this chapter. One may be totally surprised as to how well a pneumonia is visible on the lateral view, and yet how poorly demarcated it is on frontal projection (Fig. 1.29). Never neglect to get a lateral chest roentgenogram.

Using Felson's Silhouette Sign.   Felson's silhouette sign (1) is a most useful sign when it comes to detecting an early or subtle infil-

trate. It depends on the fact that, when two structures of equal roentgenographic density are juxtaposed, the interphase between them becomes obliterated. In other words, if an organ such as the heart (water density) is juxtaposed against a pulmonary infiltrate (also water density), then the interphase between them becomes indistinct or frankly obliterated. Normally the heart (water density) lies next to aerated lung (air density) and because they are of such different densities, a sharp line (the cardiac edge) clearly demarcates their interphase. However, once the density of the lung is changed from air to water (i.e., by pneumonia, hemorrhage, edema, or atelectasis), the roentgenographic interphase between that portion of the lung and the adjacent cardiac silhouette is obliterated and you have a positive silhouette sign.

Most often the silhouette sign is applied

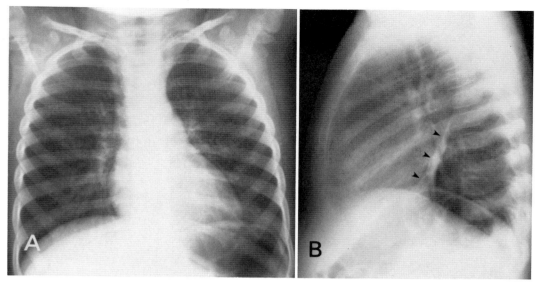

Figure 1.29. *Value of a lateral chest film.* (*A*) The infiltrate is so subtle on this view that it virtually defies identification. However, on close inspection one might note that the left diaphragmatic leaflet is a little indistinct and that it is a little higher than usual (probably secondary to splinting). (*B*) Lateral view. Note how much more clearly the left lower lobe pneumonia is visualized, just behind the left major fissure (*arrows*). The pneumonia, in these cases, is simply not "thick" enough to be clearly seen on frontal view. See a similar pneumonia in Figure 1.31. Both cases represent early consolidation.

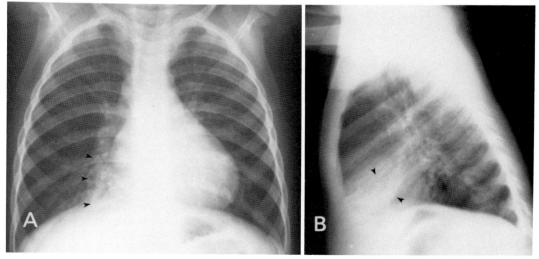

Figure 1.30. *Right middle lobe silhouette sign.* (*A*) Note that the right cardiac border is indistinct and, in fact, obliterated over its lower two-thirds by an adjacent pneumonia in the medial segment of the right middle lobe. The left cardiac border is sharp. (*B*) Lateral view confirms the presence of a right middle lobe pneumonia seen as an area of increased density anterioinferiorly (*arrows*).

to pneumonias in the right middle lobe and lingula. In the right middle lobe the pneumonias which produce a silhouette sign are in the medial segment. Those in the lateral segment are not juxtaposed to the heart, and thus do not produce a positive silhouette sign. In those cases where a medial segment pneumonia is present, the adjacent edge of the heart becomes blurred or obliterated (Fig. 1.30). When the pneumonia is in the lingula it is the left side of the heart which becomes obliterated. Once such blurring of

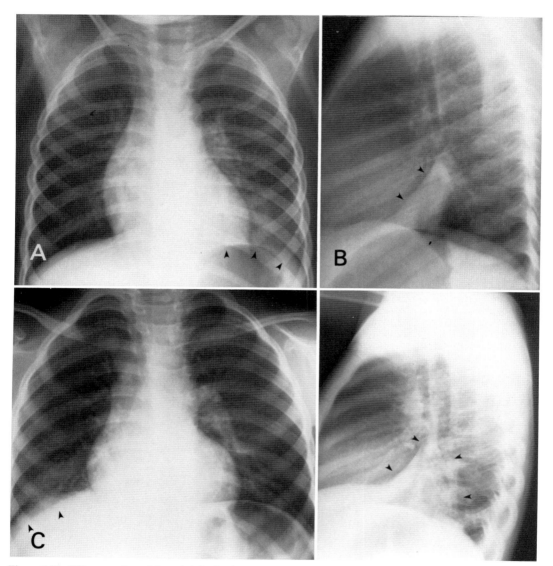

Figure 1.31. *Silhouette signs, left and right diaphragmatic leaflets.* (*A*) The infiltrate in the left lower lung field is difficult to detect on this view, but a strong clue to its presence lies in the fact that the left diaphragmatic leaflet is indistinct (*arrows*). The gastric bubble is seen below the leaflet but the leaflet itself is invisible (positive silhouette sign). This finding localizes the pneumonia to the left lower lobe. (*B*) Lateral view substantiates the presence of the left lower lobe pneumonia lying posterior to the major fissure (*arrows*). The portion of the diaphragmatic leaflet immediately adjacent to the pneumonia is obliterated producing another example of a focally positive silhouette sign. (*C*) Positive silhouette sign right diaphragm (*arrows*). (*D*) Lateral view confirms right lower lobe pneumonia (*arrows*).

the cardiac silhouette is noted on frontal projection, a lateral view should be obtained for confirmation (Fig. 1.30*B*). The silhouette sign, utilized in this fashion, also is useful with pneumonias located adjacent to the superior mediastinal structures or the diaphragmatic leaflets (Fig. 1.31).

In reverse, the silhouette sign also is helpful in localizing lower lobe pulmonary infiltrates. For example, if an infiltrate is present in the lower lobes it lies behind the heart (not in juxtaposition to the lateral edge), and consequently, the heart-lung interphase is preserved (Fig. 1.32). This, then, indicates

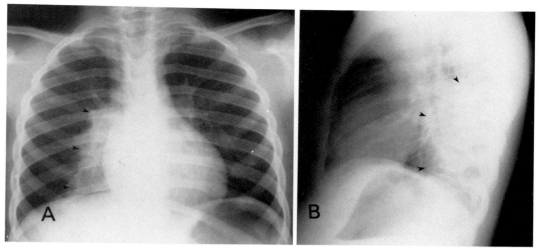

Figure 1.32. *Silhouette sign in reverse, right lower lobe localization.* (*A*) Note the rather extensive pneumonia in the right lower lobe (*arrows*). It is located behind the heart and is causing this portion of the heart to be increased in density (i.e. it is more opaque than the left side). However, because the pneumonia is behind the heart, and not in juxtaposition to its right border, the border remains distinct. If the pneumonia were immediately lateral to the right cardiac border, that is, in the medial segment of the right middle lobe, the cardiac border would be obliterated (i.e., as in Fig. 1.30*A*). (*B*) Lateral view confirms the presence of the extensive right lower lobe pneumonia in that there is a marked increase in density of the entire posterior retrocardiac space (*arrows*). This is completely abnormal and should be compared with the normal radiolucent appearance of the lower retrocardiac space in Figure 1.25.

that the infiltrate is far posterior to the heart, that is, in the lower lobe.

Unfortunately, the silhouette sign also occurs under some normal situations. In this regard the most frequent site is along the right side of the heart. In many children the bronchovascular markings adjacent to the right side of the heart are so prominent that they blend with the cardiac silhouette and result in a positive silhouette sign. *If this normal phenomenon is not appreciated one will continually overcall right middle lobe pneumonia.* Most often this occurs when the inspiratory effort is somewhat shallow and the roentgenogram is obtained with the patient in partial lordotic position. The problem is especially prone to occur in children with parahilar peribronchial infiltrates secondary to viral lower respiratory tract infections (Fig. 1.33*A*). In these latter cases, even though the infection is widespread and the bronchi edematous and thickened throughout both lungs, those along the right cardiac border erroneously appear to be involved most. However, if it is remembered that the bronchovascular markings normally tend to cluster in this area, the resultant silhouette sign is more likely to be considered in its

proper context. In other words, the findings are partially artefactual and do not reflect a focal right middle lobe pneumonia. In reality these patients have typical widespread parahilar peribronchial infiltrates; they only appear to be more prominent and focal in the right middle lobe. This can be verified by obtaining a lateral chest roentgenogram which will show that no middle lobe infiltrate is present (Fig. 1.33*B*). Indeed, it would be most unusual to detect a right middle lobe, medial segment, pneumonia on frontal view and not see even a subtle indication of its presence on lateral view.

Another instance when the silhouette sign can be seen as a normal phenomenon is when a pleural fissure blends with the upper aspect of a diaphragmatic leaflet (Fig. 1.34*A*). This can occur either with a major or accessory fissure, and it is only when a lateral view is obtained that this normally positive silhouette sign can be deciphered and understood (Fig. 1.34*B*). Compare the case illustrated in Figure 1.34 with the one demonstrated in Figure 1.31 where a true left lower lobe pneumonia and a positive left diaphragmatic leaflet silhouette sign are present. Felson's silhouette sign is an excel-

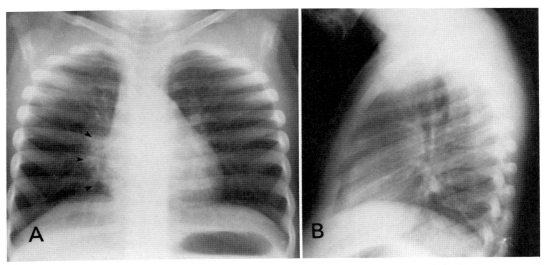

Figure 1.33. *Right middle lobe silhouette sign with parahilar peribronchial infiltrates—pseudofocal pneumonia.* (*A*) This infant has widespread parahilar peribronchial infiltrates. However, the chest film is quite lordotic (the ribs are horizontal posteriorly and slanted downward anteriorly) and this is causing the bronchovascular markings along the right cardiac silhouette to cluster even more than normal (*arrows*). Consequently, the right cardiac border is obliterated and a right middle lobe, medial segment pneumonia is suggested. (*B*) On lateral view, however, there is no evidence of a right middle lobe infiltrate. If an infiltrate were present in the right middle lobe it would be demonstrable on lateral view. Compare this lateral view with the lateral view in Figure 1.30, where a true right middle lobe pneumonia is present.

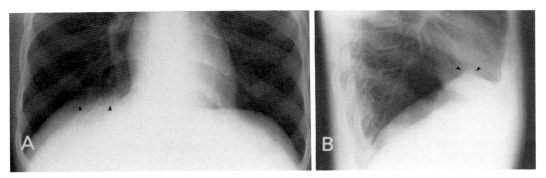

Figure 1.34. *Silhouette sign—normal variation.* (*A*) Note focal obliteration of the right diaphragmatic leaflet (*arrows*). Is this due to an adjacent pneumonia? (*B*) Lateral view shows that the silhouette sign is produced by blending of the lower aspect of the major fissure with the right diaphragmatic leaflet (*arrows*). On frontal view, this area of blending, caught tangentially by the x-ray beam, creates a positive, but normal, silhouette sign. The same phenomenon can occur on the left, and also with accessory fissures.

lent sign, but one must learn to use it properly in children. It is always valid in principle, but at times may not be abnormal.

REFERENCE

1. Felson, B., and Felson, H.: Localization of intrathoracic lesions by means of the posteroanterior roentgenogram: The silhouette sign. Radiology 55: 363–374, 1950.

Favorite Hiding Places of Pneumonia. There are certain areas which are notorious for hiding early pulmonary infiltrates (1). One should become familiar with all of these sites and give them a second look when inspecting the roentgenogram (Fig. 1.35). Unless one becomes thoroughly familiar with these hiding places, pulmonary infiltrates can be totally overlooked.

The first hiding place taught the radiology resident is ***behind the left side of the heart*** (i.e., in the left lower lobe). In most individuals the bulk of the cardiac silhouette extends to the left of the spine and thus can

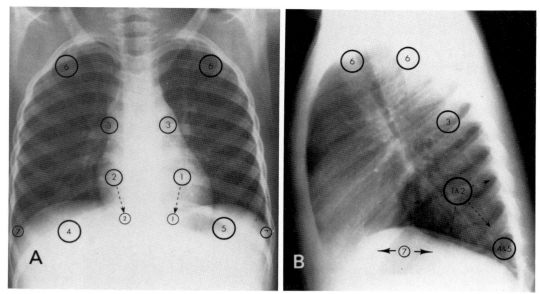

Figure 1.35. *Favorite hiding places of pneumonia.* (*A*) and (*B*) demonstrate common hiding places of pneumonia. (*1*) Behind the left side of the heart in the left lower lobe, often extending into the phrenicovertebral angle, (*2*) behind the right side of the heart in the right lower lobe, also often extending into the phrenicovertebral angle, (*3*) behind the hilar regions, in the superior segment of either lower lobe, (*4*) deep in the posterior costophrenic sulcus behind the liver, (*5*) deep in the costophrenic sulcus behind the stomach, spleen, or left lobe of the liver, (*6*) high in the upper lobes, and (*7*) deep in the lateral costophrenic sulci.

hide a sizeable infiltrate. This is especially true if the film is too light (underpenetrated). In looking for a pneumonia in this location one should first look for an area of focally increased density projected through the left side of the heart. A good way to check for this is to quickly compare the densities of both sides of the heart; in normal individuals they are equal, but with left lower lobe pneumonias they are not. The increase in density in cases where a pneumonia is present is due to the fact that the pneumonia is roentgenographically more dense than normal lung, and thus, when superimposed over the heart, it produces an area of increased density (Fig. 1.36).

Such focal pneumonias are relatively easy to detect, but when the pneumonia is so large that it produces a generalized, rather than focal, increase in density of the entire left side of the heart, it can be missed (Fig. 1.37). In still other cases the infiltrate may be buried deep in the phrenicovertebral sulcus and it is only when both phrenicovertebral sulci are compared that it becomes obvious that one is whiter or denser than normal (Fig. 1.38). The only pitfall to avoid is a normal increase in density in this area

produced by overlapping of the cardiac silhouette and the diaphragmatic leaflet (Fig. 1.38*C*). No such pitfall exists on the right.

So well is it engrained in us to look behind the left side of the heart for hidden pneumonias that we forget to ***look behind the right side of the heart***. Indeed, pneumonias in this area are almost always missed. The best way to recognize a pneumonia in this area is to follow the rule that both sides of the heart should be of equal density. As on the left side, right side pneumonias may produce focal infiltrates (Fig. 1.39*A*) or more generalized infiltrates resulting in a more diffuse increase in density of all of the right side of the cardiac silhouette (Fig. 1.40*A*). Extension into the ipsilateral phrenicovertebral sulcus also is common (Fig. 1.40*B*) and should be kept in mind when perusing roentgenograms in such cases. Confirmation of all these pneumonias is once again readily accomplished with lateral chest roentgenography.

Pneumonias in the superior segment of either lower lobe are notorious for hiding behind one or other of the hilar regions. In this location they cause an increase in density, and at times size, of the ipsilateral hilar

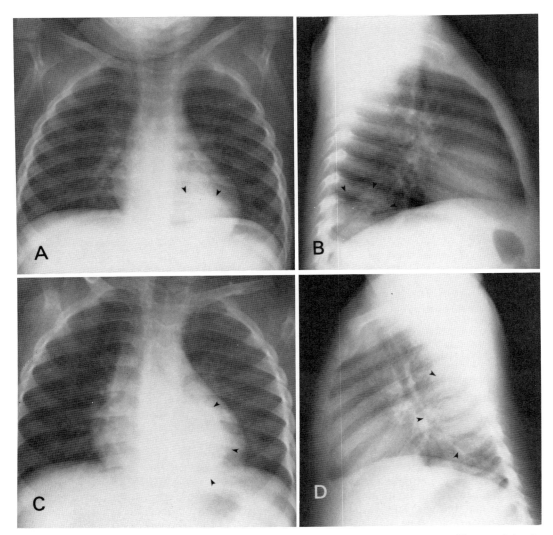

Figure 1.36. *Focal pneumonia in the left lower lobe behind the heart.*   (*A*) Note vague area of increased density projected through the left side of the heart (*arrows*). (*B*) Lateral view clearly localizes the pneumonia to the left lower lobe, deep in the costophrenic sulcus (*arrows*). Note that the adjacent part of the left diaphragmatic leaflet is obliterated, producing a positive silhouette sign. The intact leaflet visualized below this area is the right diaphragmatic leaflet. The left leaflet is higher because of splinting. (*C*) Note large area of increased density behind the left side of the heart (*arrows*). (*D*) Lateral view demonstrates the pneumonia in the left lower lobe but it should be noted that the finding is more subtle on this view and consists only of a diffuse increase in density of the normally radiolucent retrocardiac space (*arrows*).

Figure 1.38. *Left lower lobe pneumonia deep in the phrenicovertebral angle.*   (*A*) Note how the pneumonia in the left lower lobe extends into the phrenicovertebral angle (*arrows*). Compare with normal density of this angle on the other side. Also note that the diaphragmatic leaflet is obliterated in this area. (*B*) Normal chest, somewhat overaerated showing that both phrenicovertebral angles should be of about equal radiolucency (*arrows*). (*C*) *Normal pitfall* wherein the left inferior cardiac border and medial left diaphragmatic leaflet overlap to produce an increase in density in the areas (*arrows*).

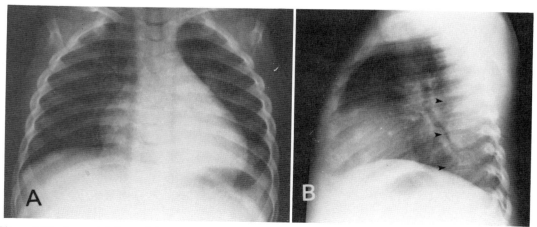

Figure 1.37. *Large left lower lobe consolidation hiding behind the heart.* (*A*) The extensive left lower lobe consolidation causes an increase in density of the entire left side of the cardiac silhouette. In spite of the size of this consolidation it can be missed because the entire left side of the heart, rather than a focal area, shows increased density. A little of the consolidation projects beyond the left cardiac border but this is a subtle finding. Of course, a lateral view should always be obtained and in (*B*) it clearly defines the presence of the left lower lobe consolidating pneumonia (*arrows*).

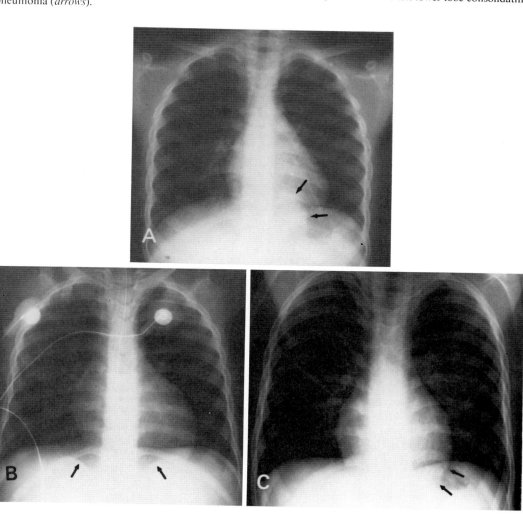

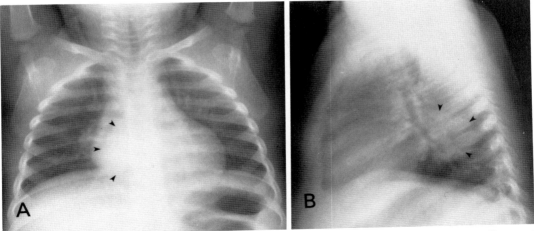

Figure 1.39. *Focal right lower lobe pneumonia behind the right side of the heart.* (*A*) Note focal area of increased density projected through the right side of the cardiac silhouette (*arrows*). (*B*) Lateral view confirms the presence of a right lower lobe pneumonia (*arrows*) located behind the cardiac silhouette.

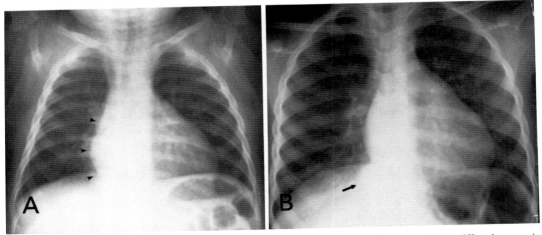

Figure 1.40. *Extensive right lower lobe pneumonia behind the right side of the heart.* (*A*) Note diffuse increase in density of that portion of the cardiac silhouette which lies to the right of the spine. This represents a pneumonia behind the right side of the heart, in the right lower lobe. (*B*) Similar finding in another patient but in this patient there is extension of the pneumonia into the phrenicovertebral sulcus (*arrow*).

region (Figs. 1.41 and 1.42). Indeed, the hilum can be so dense and prominent that lymphadenopathy is suggested, (i.e., as in primary pulmonary tuberculosis). Once again, however, the lateral view clearly elucidates the problem and confirms the presence of a pneumonia in the superior segment of the involved lower lobe (Figs. 1.41 and 1.42).

Lower lobe pneumonias, deep in the posterior costophrenic sulci are also frequently missed on frontal projection. On the right side these pneumonias are projected through the liver silhouette and unless one becomes accustomed to their appearance they are most difficult to recognize (Fig. 1.43). In some cases one may be surprised at the size of a pneumonia so hidden (Fig. 1.44). On

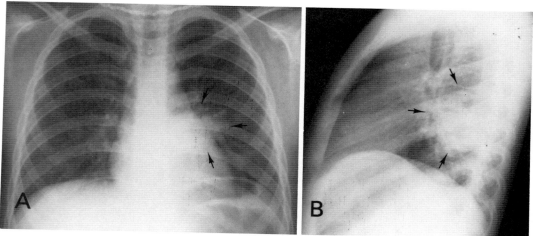

Figure 1.41. *Pneumonia behind the left hilum.* (*A*) Note that the left hilum is denser and larger than the right (*arrows*). (*B*) Lateral view shows that the pneumonia is located in the superior segment of the left lower lobe (*arrows*). If one recalls the normal position of the major fissure it will be clearly apparent that the pneumonia must be in the superior segment of the lower lobe, and not in the upper lobe.

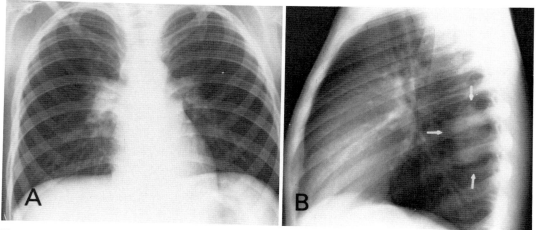

Figure 1.42. *Subtle pneumonia behind the right hilum.* (*A*) Note that the right hilum is much whiter (increased density), and slightly larger than the left hilum. At first this might suggest unilateral hilar adenopathy. (*B*) Lateral view, however, clearly demonstrates the presence of a focal pneumonia in the superior segment of the right lower lobe (*arrows*). (For another case of superior segment pneumonia, occurring in both lungs simultaneously, see Fig. 1.23*B*)

the left side such pneumonias can be projected through the left lobe of the liver, the stomach bubble, or the spleen (Fig. 1.45). On lateral view these pneumonias usually lie deep in the posterior costophrenic sulcus and frequently obliterate the adjacent portion of the diaphragmatic leaflet (i.e., positive silhouette sign).

Two other places where pneumonias can hide are high in the upper lobe and deep in the lateral costophrenic sulcus. In the former instance the pneumonia is often confused with normal overlying soft tissues (Fig. 1.46). In such cases one should compare the densities of both apices (actually one should do this for all areas of the chest) and check

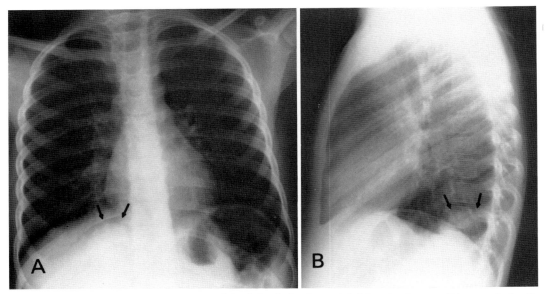

Figure 1.43. *Focal pneumonia, right lower lobe behind the liver.* (*A*) Note focal area of increased density (pneumonia) projected through the medial aspect of the liver silhouette (*arrows*). (*B*) Lateral view showing how deep this pneumonia lies in the posterior costophrenic sulcus (*arrows*). The right diaphragmatic leaflet (*lower leaflet*) is partially obliterated by the adjacent infiltrate (*arrows*) while the left diaphragmatic leaflet is clearly visualized through the infiltrate.

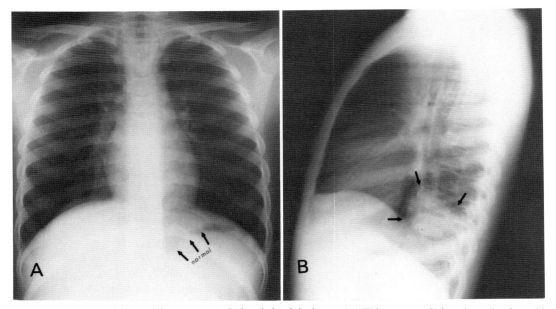

Figure 1.44. *Large right lower lobe pneumonia hiding behind the liver.* (*A*) This pneumonia is so large that it could be missed for this reason. However, note that there is a general increase in density of the entire area below the right diaphragmatic leaflet, but more importantly, that there is increased density of the phrenico-vertebral sulcus. The phrenico-vertebral sulcus on the left (*arrows*) is of normal density. (*B*) Lateral view shows that this increase in density is due to a large consolidating right lower lobe pneumonia (*arrows*). The portion of the right diaphragmatic leaflet just below and adjacent to the infiltrate is completely obliterated (positive silhouette sign).

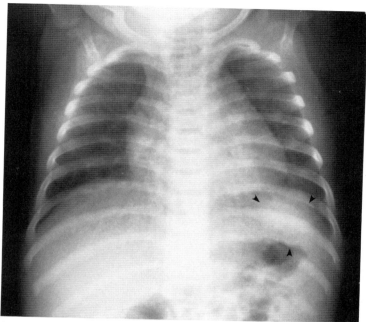

Figure 1.45. *Subtle focal pneumonia behind left diaphragmatic leaflet.* Note vague area of increased density projected through the left diaphragmatic leaflet (*arrows*). This was an early consolidating pneumonia of the left lower lobe, deep in the posterior costophrenic sulcus.

the lateral view for confirmation. In checking the apices for subtle infiltrates, it is worthwhile to "black-out" the remainder of the chest with an opaque piece of cardboard. When this maneuver is performed, comparison of the apices is easier, and subtle infiltrates stand out with more clarity. Pneumonias deep in the lateral costophrenic sulci are usually missed because one simply does not look in this region. These pneumonias are truly subtle and are usually seen on frontal projection only (Fig. 1.47).

REFERENCE

1. Burko, H.: Considerations in the roentgen diagnosis of pneumonia in children. A.J.R. 88: 555–565, 1962.

A Few Peculiarities of Certain Pneumonias. In addition to the preceding discussion of lower respiratory tract infections in children, it might be in order to mention a few peculiarities about certain infections. For example it appears that adenovirus infections, especially type 7 and type 21, produce serious pulmonary infections (i.e., necrotizing bronchitis) in children in general, and in young infants specifically (1, 3, 5, 25,

31). They seem especially prone to produce chronic damage to the lung with eventual development of the so-called Swyer-James lung (9, 15, 22). Measles and pertussis usually produce pulmonary findings not unlike those seen with viral pneumonias (2, 4, 11, 17, 19, 20, 23, 36), and even though the so-called shaggy heart (2) has become synonymous with pertussis, it should be realized that it is not a specifically diagnostic configuration. Actually the shaggy heart is seen more often with viral lower respiratory tract infections (see Fig. 1.5). In addition, it should be noted that not all children with pertussis show abnormal chest roentgenograms; indeed I have been impressed with how many show clear lungs.

Desquamative interstitial pneumonia is not particularly common in children (6, 28) and often produces diffuse interstitial haziness in the lung bases. Varicella (chickenpox), although causing pneumonitis in adults, seldom causes primary pulmonary pneumonia in healthy children (10). Most often it is seen in debilitated or immunologically deficient or suppressed children. Pulmonary involvement in the adolescent with

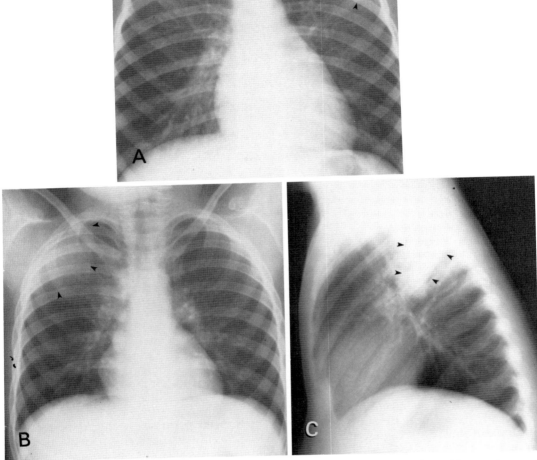

Figure 1.46. *High apical upper lobe pneumonia vs. normal soft tissues.*   (*A*) Normal patient with vague increased density high in the apices due to normal overlying soft tissues (*arrows*). (*B*) Patient with unilateral increase in density in the same area (*arrows*) representing a pneumonia. This pneumonia could easily be overlooked or mistaken for normal soft tissue density. (*C*) On lateral view, however, the pneumonia is clearly visualized in the posterior segment of the right upper lobe (*arrows*).

infectious mononucleosis has been documented (13, 21), but the findings are relatively nonspecific and not unlike those seen with any viral lower respiratory tract infection.

Mycoplasma pneumonias are extremely variable in their clinical and roentgenographic presentation, but two distinct clinical-roentgenographic forms have been suggested (18, 27). The first has acute onset with lobar consolidation, and a clinical picture not unlike that seen with pneumococcal pneumonia; the second is less acute in onset and is associated with diffuse reticulonodular infiltrates (see Fig. 1.21). These are more common, and may take up to 3 months to clear while the lobar consolidation of the first group tends to clear in 2 weeks or so. However, not all patients with *M. pneumoniae* infections fall neatly into one or other

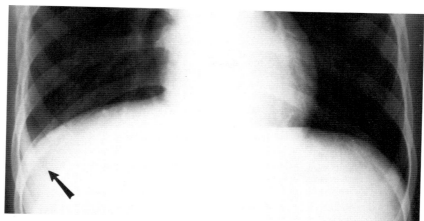

Figure 1.47. *Costophrenic sulcus pneumonia.* Note pneumonia deep in the right costophrenic sulcus (*arrow*) of this patient who had chest pain over the right lower chest, laterally. These pneumonias are commonly overlooked and are not usually seen on lateral view. Consequently they must be picked up on the frontal projection.

of these groups, and indeed, any number of intervening roentgenographic patterns can be seen (7, 8, 14, 16, 32–34).

Bacterial pneumonias such as those due to *S. aureus, H. influenzae* (usually type B), and *D. pneumoniae* have been discussed to some extent in earlier sections, but at this time it should be noted that all three organisms have a distinct propensity to produce complicating empyemas and pleural effusions (see p. 40). Empyema formation is especially common with *S. aureus* infection and as will be seen later pyopneumothorax is the hallmark of infection with this organism.

D. pneumoniae infections, and to some extent *H. influenzae* and *M. pneumoniae* infections seem to be more common in patients with sickle cell anemia, (29, 30), and *H. influenzae* infections are most common under the age of 3 years (26, 35). Friedländer's pneumonia is not at all common in infancy and childhood (24), but when seen it does seem to produce a lobar consolidation which differs from other bacterially induced consolidations in that it tends to expand the lobe and bulge the surrounding fissures outward (12).

Primary pulmonary tuberculosis is still a common problem and can present a variable roentgenographic picture. However, most often one will be confronted with unilateral hilar or paratracheal adenopathy and some other finding in the lung (see p. 57). This other finding can be lobar or segmental atelectasis, pulmonary infiltration, lobar emphysema, or even pleural effusion (at times even massive). Consequently, the rule of thumb for suspecting primary tuberculosis in childhood is as follows: ***unilateral or paratracheal adenopathy, with or without parenchymal change (almost any type) should be presumed tuberculous in origin until proven otherwise.*** Even though these findings can be mimicked by atypical tuberculous infection and *M. pneumoniae* infection, tuberculosis will most often account for the findings and should be the primary diagnosis until proven otherwise.

Fungal infections are not particularly common in childhood, except in a so-called fungus belt. If you reside in such an area, you will soon know that the roentgenographic findings are very variable, ranging from diffuse fluffy pulmonary infiltrates to findings not unlike those seen with primary pulmonary tuberculosis. This being the case, you will soon elevate fungal infections from the bottom of your list of diagnostic possibilities to a higher, more realistic, position.

REFERENCES

1. Angella, J.J., and Connor, J.D.: Neonatal infection caused by adenovirus type 7. J. Pediatr. 72: 474–478, 1968.
2. Barnhard, H.J., and Kniker, W.T.: Roentgenologic findings in pertussis. With particular emphasis on the "shaggy heart" sign. A.J.R. 84: 445–450, 1960.
3. Benyesh-Melnick, M., and Rosenberg, H.S.: The isolation of adenovirus type 7 from a fatal case of pneumonia and disseminated diseases. J. Pediatr. 64: 83–87, 1964.

4. Brooksaler, F., and Nelson, J.D.: Pertussis: A reappraisal and report of 190 confirmed cases. Am. J. Dis. Child. 114: 389–396, 1967.

5. Brown, R.S., Nogrady, M.B., Spence, L., and Wiglesworth, F.W.: Outbreak of adenovirus type 7 infection in children in Montreal. Can. Med. Assoc. J. 108: 434–439, 1973.

6. Buchta, R.M., Park, S., and Giammona, S.T.: Desquamative interstitial pneumonia in a 7-week old infant. Am. J. Dis. Child. 120: 341–343, 1970.

7. Clyde, W.A., Jr., and Denny, M.W.: Mycoplasma infections in childhood. Pediatrics 40: 669–684, 1967.

8. Cordero, L., Cuadrado, R., Hall, C.B., and Horstmann, D.M.: Primary atypical pneumonia: An epidemic caused by *Mycoplasma pneumoniae*. J. Pediatr. 71: 1–12, 1967.

9. Cumming, G.R., MacPherson, R.I., and Chernick, V.: Unilateral hyperlucent lung syndrome in children. J. Pediatr. 78: 250, 1971.

10. Eisenklam, E.J.: Primary varicella pneumonia in a three year old girl. J. Pediatr. 69: 452–454, 1966.

11. Fawcitt, J., and Parry, H.E.: Lung changes in pertussis and measles in childhood. A review of 1894 cases with a followup study of the pulmonary complications. Br. J. Radiol. 30: 76–82, 1957.

12. Felson, B., Rosenberg, L.S., and Hamburger, M.: Roentgen findings in acute Friedländer's pneumonia. Radiology 53: 559–565, 1949.

13. Fermaglich, D.R.: Pulmonary involvement in infectious mononucleosis. J. Pediatr. 86: 93–95, Jan., 1975.

14. Fernald, G.W., Collier, A.M., and Clyde, W.A., Jr.: Respiratory infections due to *Mycoplasma pneumoniae* in infants and children. Pediatrics 55: 327–335, 1975.

15. Gold, R., et al.: Adenoviral pneumonia and its complications in infancy and childhood. J. Can. Assoc. Radiol. 20: 218–224, 1969.

16. Herbert, D.H.: The roentgen features of Eaton agent Pneumonia. A.J.R. 98: 300–304, 1966.

17. Janigan, D.T.: Giant cell pneumonia and measles: An analytical review. Can. Med. Assoc. J., 85: 741–749, 1961.

18. Jensen, P.S., and Putnam, C.E.: Mycoplasma pneumonia: two distinct syndromes. Presented as scientific exhibit, 76th Annual Meeting of the American Roentgen Ray Society. Atlanta, Sept., 1975.

19. Kohn, J.L., and Koiransky, H.: Further roentgenographic studies of chests of children during measles. Am. J. Dis. Child. 46: 40, 1933.

20. Kohn, J.L., Schwartz, I., Greenbaum, J., and Daly, M.M.I.: Roentgenograms of the chest taken during pertussis. Am. J. Dis. Child. 67: 463, 1944.

21. Lander, P., and Palayew, M.J.: Infectious mononucleosis— a review of chest roentgenographic manifestations. J. Can. Assoc. Radiol. 25: 303–306, 1974.

22. Lang, W.R., Howden, C.W., Laws, J., and Burton, J.F.: Bronchopneumonia with serious sequelae in children with evidence of adenovirus type 21 infection. Br. Med. J. 1: 73–79, 1969.

23. MacCarthy, K., Mitus, A., Cheatham, W., and Beebles, T.: Isolation of virus of measles from three fatal cases of giant cell pneumonia. Am. J. Dis. Child. 96: 500–501, 1958.

24. Miller, B.W., Orris, H.W., and Taus, H.H.: Friedländer's pneumonia in infancy. J. Pediatr. 31: 521–527, 1947.

25. Nahmias, A.J., Griffith, D., and Snitzer, J.: Fatal pneumonia associated with adenovirus type 7. Am. J. Dis. Child. 114: 36–41, 1967.

26. Nyhan, W.L., Rectanus, D.R., and Fousek, M.D.: *Haemophilus influenzae* type B pneumonia. Pediatrics 16: 31–41, 1955.

27. Putman, C.E., Curtis, A. McB., Simeone, J.F., and Jensen, P.: Mycoplasma pneumonia: clinical and roentgenographic patterns. A.J.R. 124: 417–422, 1975.

28. Rosenow, E.C., O'Connell, E.J., and Harrison, E.G., Jr.: Desquamative interstitial pneumonia in children. Am. J. Dis. Child. 120: 344–348, 1970.

29. Seeler, R.A., Metzger, W., and Mufson, M.A.: Diplococcus pneumoniae infections in children with sickle cell anemia. Am. J. Dis. Child. 123: 8–10, 1972.

30. Shulman, S.T., et al.: The unusual severity of mycoplasma pneumonia in children with sickle cell disease. N. Engl. J. Med. 287: 164–167, 1972.

31. Simila, S., Ylikorkala, O., and Wasz-Hockert, O.: Type 7 adenovirus pneumonia. J. Pediatr. 79: 605, 1971.

32. Stallings, M.W., and Archer, S.B.: Atypical mycoplasma pneumonia. Am. J. Dis. Child. 126: 837–838, 1973.

33. Stenstrom, R., Jansson, E., and von Essen, R.: Mycoplasma pneumonias. Acta Radiol. [Diagn.] (Stockh.) 12: 833–841, 1972.

34. Sussman, S.J., et al.: Cold agglutinins, Eaton agent and respiratory infections of children. Pediatrics 38: 571, 1966.

35. Vinik, M., Alsman, D.H., and Parks, R.E.: Experience with *Haemophilus influenzae* pneumonia. Radiology 86: 701–706, 1966.

36. Wesley, A.G., and Sutton, J.B.: Measles and its complications. A radiological survey. S. Afr. Med. J. 48: 1001–1003, 1974.

PLEURAL FLUID COLLECTIONS AND EMPYEMA

The types of fluid which can collect in the pleural space include: (a) pus (empyema, pyothorax), (b) serous fluid (hydrothorax), (c) blood (hemothorax), and (d) chyle (chylothorax). **Empyema** is usually a complication of an underlying pneumonia and in this regard is seen most commonly with *S. aureus* infections (8, 11, 13, 15, 27, 30). However, under the age of 3 years, *H. influenzae* must also be considered a common causative organism (12, 19, 24, 34) and in the older child, *D. pneumonia* becomes important. Empyema also can be seen with streptococcal pulmonary infections (16, 17) and secondary to osteomyelitis of the spine or subdiaphragmatic infections such as hepatic or subphrenic abscess. However, most occur secondary to pneumonias caused by *S. aureus, D. pneumoniae,* and *H. influenzae.*

Empyemas can develop rapidly and progression from a subtle pulmonary infiltrate to a full-blow empyema in less than 24 hours is not uncommon. Most of these patients, of course are quite ill and auscultation clearly defines the problem. The roentgenographic changes depend on the size of the pyogenic fluid collection and may range from complete opacification of a hemithorax with massive mediastinal shift, to less striking, and perhaps more puzzling, changes (Fig. 1.48). In this regard, it should be remembered that the empyema must first compress the lung and then shift the mediastinum, and consequently, at certain stages of its development mediastinal shift may be minimal or absent. If one is not aware of this problem, doubt will arise as to whether one should perform a thoracentesis (Fig. 1.48, *B*

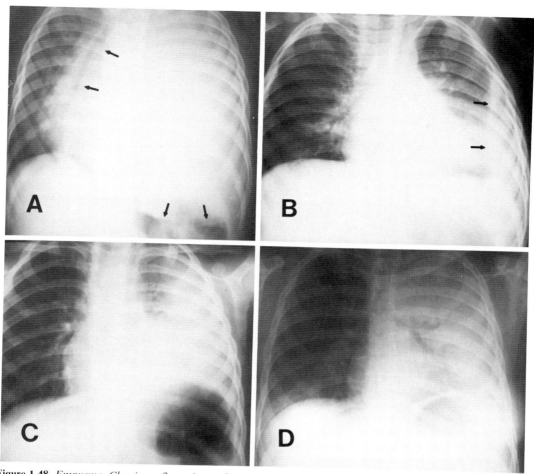

Figure 1.48. *Empyema. Classic configuration and atypical patterns.* (*A*) Classic massive empyema with contralateral mediastinal displacement and ipsilateral diaphragmatic leaflet depression (*arrows*). (*B*) Another typical case, but with a smaller empyema (*arrows*). (*C*) *Empyema with no shift.* The developing empyema is not large enough to produce mediastinal shift. Decubitus views might be helpful here. (*D*) *Pneumonia or empyema?* The air bronchogram would at first suggest consolidating pneumonia. However, one should ask the question, "How many times have I seen a consolidating pneumonia involving the entire lung?" This would be most unusual. The problem here is a developing empyema, partially compressing the lung. Both cases (*C*) and (*D*) might be investigated with ultrasound (see Fig. 1.49).

and *C*). Currently, ultrasound is very useful in delineating the fluid in such cases (Fig.1.49). Ultrasound also is useful in detecting free fluid (see. Fig. 1.68). Underlying pulmonary infiltrates are variable, and in many cases once the purulent fluid is removed, the lungs turn out to be surprisingly clear.

If *empyema is accompanied by pneumothorax* so that pyopneumothorax results, one can be almost completely certain that *S. aureus* is the offending organism. The thick, tenacious secretions characteristic of this infection lead to air trapping secondary

to endobronchial obstruction and as a result complicating pneumothorax is common. In many cases the free air is loculated into numerous compartments, and a multitude of air fluid levels are seen on the upright film (Fig. 1.50). However, whether this occurs or not, the presence of free air and fluid in the pleural space, in the absence of trauma, should suggest *S. aureus* infection with pyopneumothorax. Every so often some other organism will produce the same picture, but in the long run it will be *S. aureus.*

Simple pleural effusions, of course, can be

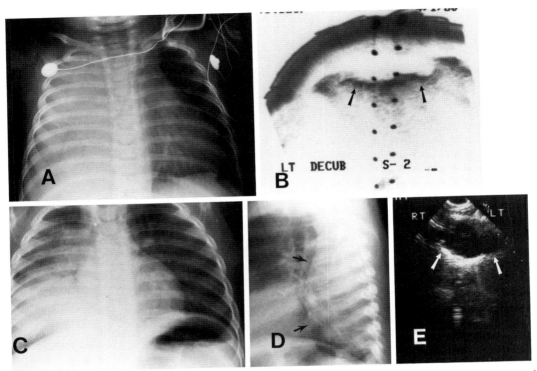

Figure 1.49. *Empyema; ultrasonographic detection.*   (*A*) *Empyema or pneumonia?* Once again it would be unusual to have an entire lung consolidated with pneumonia. (*B*) Ultrasound study clearly demonstrates the presence of pleural fluid (*arrows*). (*C*) Another patient with a problematic infiltrate in the right lower lung. (*D*) Lateral view demonstrating a well defined density posteriorly (*arrows*). Is this an empyema? (*E*) Ultrasound clearly demonstrates the presence of fluid in the empyema (*arrows*).

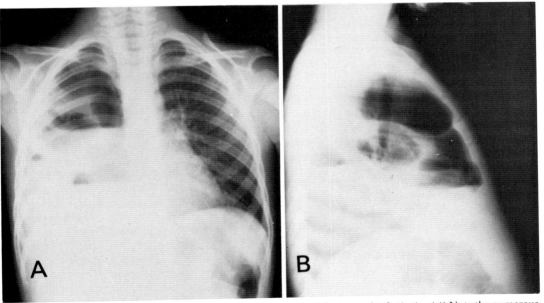

Figure 1.50. *Pyopneumothorax (empyema with pneumothorax in staphylococcal infection).*   (*A*) Note the numerous air-fluid levels on the right. This finding is characteristic of staphylococcal infections. Some of the air collections also could be pneumatoceles. (*B*) Lateral view showing similar findings.

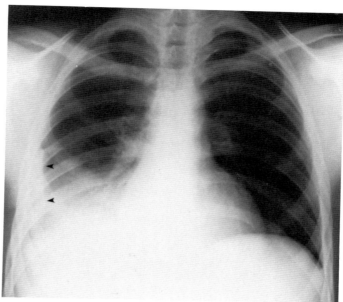

Figure 1.51. *Pneumonia with pleural effusion.* This patient has a right lower lobe consolidating pneumococcal pneumonia but in addition there is a pleural effusion on the right (*arrows*).

seen with pneumonias produced by the same organisms producing empyemas (Fig. 1.51), and occasionally with viral, mycoplasma pneumonia (1, 6), and primary tuberculous infections. In addition, they are commonly seen with kidney disease such as the nephrotic syndrome and acute glomerulonephritis, abdominal tumors such as neuroblastoma and lymphosarcoma, subphrenic or hepatic inflammatory processes, chest wall or spine lesions, pancreatitis, congestive heart failure, and the collagen vascular diseases.

Most often the first sign of a pleural effusion consists of blunting of the costophrenic angles so as to produce wedge-like menisci which extend upward along the lateral chest wall (Fig. 1.52). Similar collections with characteristically curved or sloping menisci are seen in the posterior costophrenic angles on lateral view (Fig. 1.52), while larger volumes of pleural fluid can be seen to extend up the entire lateral chest wall, and eventually over the apex of the lung (Fig. 1.52C). A similar layering phenomenon can occur retrosternally (Fig. 1.53B).

In other instances, early pleural effusions may present with what at first appears to be unusual prominence or thickening of the interlobar fissures, or by wedge-like tapering accumulations of fluid at either end of these fissures (Fig. 1.53). In such cases, one should always obtain anteroposterior and lateral views, for while on one view the wedge-like or thickened fissure configuration is readily appreciated, on the other it may be totally invisible or appear as a focal infiltrate or area of segmental atelectasis (see Fig. 1.54). Fluid accumulations in the right or left major fissures characteristically appear as a thick, sloping line (Fig. 1.55), the so-called vertical fissure (3, 32).

Pleural effusions in the supine position frequently are overlooked or misinterpreted for a consolidating pneumonia. Most often one encounters such effusions in a critically ill or severely injured child whereupon a supine, instead of an upright, chest film is obtained. In these cases, fluid layers beneath the lung (5, 7), and rather than conforming to one of its more typical configurations, it simply produces a generalized increase in density of the involved hemithorax (Fig. 1.56). If this is the only sign present, the pleural effusion usually is missed, especially if its volume is small (i.e., the degree of opacification is minimal). If, on the other hand, other more classic signs of pleural effusion are present, the diagnosis is easier to establish. In this regard, on the left side,

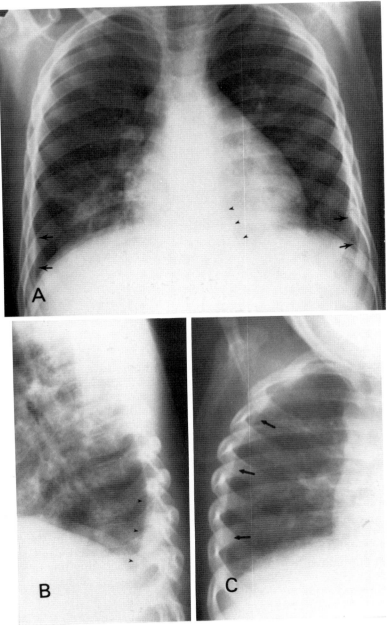

Figure 1.52. *Pleural effusions—common presenting configurations.* (*A*) Note characteristic early accumulations of pleural fluid in both costophrenic angles (*large arrows*). In addition there is accumulation of fluid in the left paraspinal gutter, just barely visible through the cardiac silhouette (*small arrows*). (*B*) Lateral view demonstrating characteristic sloping or curving configuration of fluid in the posterior costophrenic angles (*arrows*). (*C*) Larger volume pleural effusion layered along the entire right lateral chest wall (*arrows*).

on supine position, one may note long paraspinal collections of fluid, paralleling the spine (29).

Subpulmonic pleural effusions also are often difficult to detect and, in fact may completely elude the unwary observer. These effusions are free-flowing (5, 20, 22, 26), and in the upright position collect be-

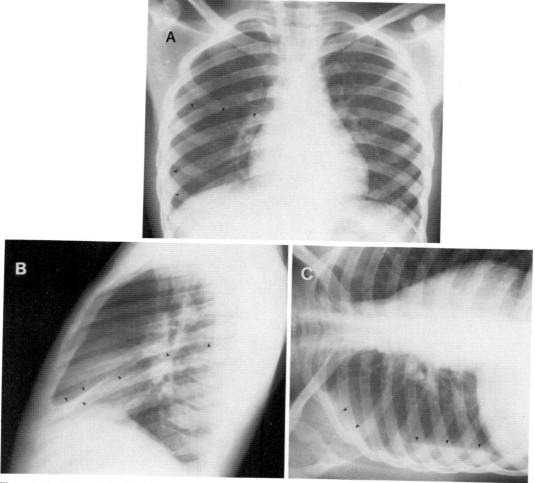

Figure 1.53. *Early, subtle pleural effusions.* (*A*) The pleural effusion on the right might be overlooked in this child who eventually was determined to have a collagen vascular disease. However, note that there is fluid along the right lateral chest wall (*lateral arrows*) and some fluid in the right minor fissure (*upper arrows*). (*B*) Lateral view showing thin layers of fluid in all the interlobar fissures, but note specifically the typical tapering wedge-like configuration of fluid in the anteriormost portion of the right major fissure (*arrows*). A layer of fluid is also present retrosternally. (*C*) Decubitus film with the right side down demonstrates how much fluid actually was present on the right (*arrows*). Decubitus views are invaluable in determining actual volumes of known pleural effusions, and confirming the presence of subtle ones.

tween the lung and the diaphragmatic leaflet. In some cases, the fluid so conforms to the normal curvature of the diaphragm that one is led to believe that the diaphragmatic leaflet is elevated (Fig. 1.57). However, if telltale subtle signs are sought for, these effusions can be detected with greater certainty. Specifically, these signs consist of: (a) unusual flatness of the apparently high diaphragmatic leaflet, (b) a sharp drop-off of the diaphragmatic leaflet laterally, (c) oblit-

eration of the adjacent portion of the cardiac silhouette, (d) increased density of the posterior phrenicovertebral sulcus, (e) paraspinal collections of fluid, especially on the left, (f) peculiar bumps and humps of the apparently high diaphragmatic leaflet, (g) an increase in the space between the top of the apparently elevated diaphragmatic leaflet and stomach bubble, (h) loss of visualization of the normal blood vessels of the lung through the uppermost part of the apparent

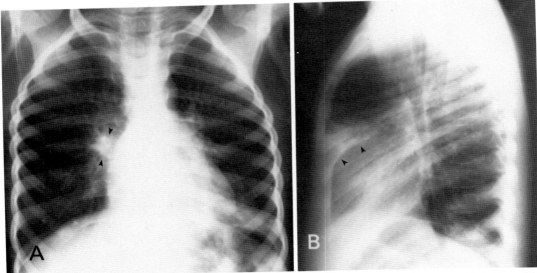

Figure 1.54. *Small interlobar fissure effusion.* (*A*) This patient has a viral lower respiratory tract infection with parahilar peribronchial infiltrates and left lower lobe atelectasis. The right hilum appears dense (*arrows*). (*B*) Lateral view shows that the apparent density of the right hilum is due to superimposition of a small anterior, minor fissure pleural effusion (*arrows*). Note the characteristic triangular shape and the posteriorly tapering, wedge-like configuration of the effusion as it runs into, and along, the minor fissure. Recall that pleural effusions are rare with viral disease.

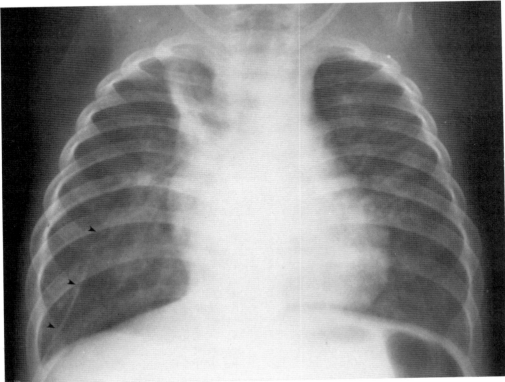

Figure 1.55. *Vertical fissure.* When fluid accumulates in the major fissure its lowermost portion can be seen as a sloping, but basically vertical, line on frontal view (*arrows*). In this case it is on the right but it can also be seen on the left. Usually it is seen with congestive heart failure, clearly present in this patient with congenital heart disease. Atelectasis of the right upper lobe also is present.

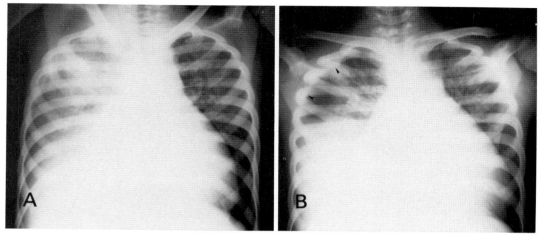

Figure 1.56. *Pleural effusion—supine film findings.* (*A*) Note the generalized increase in density of the right hemithorax. Cardiomegaly and pulmonary edema also are present in this patient who suffered a severe fluid overload. The fact that a large volume of fluid is layered beneath the right lung might be overlooked if this were the only film obtained. (*B*) An upright view, however, shows clearing of the right upper lung field secondary to the fluid shifting downward. It now totally opacifies the lower lung field and mimics a consolidation. Some fluid remains in the apex (*arrows*).

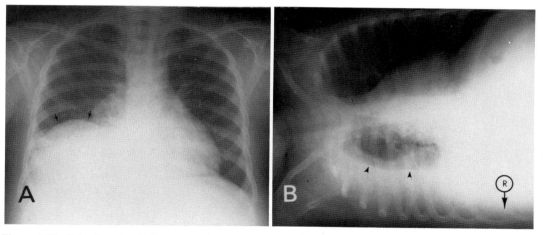

Figure 1.57. *Subpulmonic effusion presenting as an apparently elevated diaphragmatic leaflet.* (*A*) The right diaphragmatic leaflet appears elevated (*arrows*). However, the finding actually represents a subpulmonic effusion. (*B*) Decubitus view with right side down confirms the presence of the large pleural effusion. This patient had nephrotic syndrome.

diaphragmatic leaflet, and (i) evidence of pleural fluid collecting in more familiar sites with more familiar configurations. All of these aspects of subpulmonic effusions are illustrated in Figure 1.58.

In terms of apparent elevation of the diaphragmatic leaflet with subpulmonic effusions, and the sharp drop-off laterally, an explanation involving the pulmonary ligament has been offered (25). Evidently, the pulmonary ligament, more or less tethers the lung medially and does not allow it to

be elevated, to the same degree as its lateral counterpart. Consequently, when fluid collects between the lung and the diaphragm, the lateral portion of the lung is elevated to a greater degree, and the step-off occurs.

In addition to the foregoing considerations in subpulmonic pleural effusions, it should be remembered that right-sided subpulmonic effusions can depress the liver downwardly so as to render it palpable clinically, while those on the left can depress the diaphragm and gastric bubble to such an

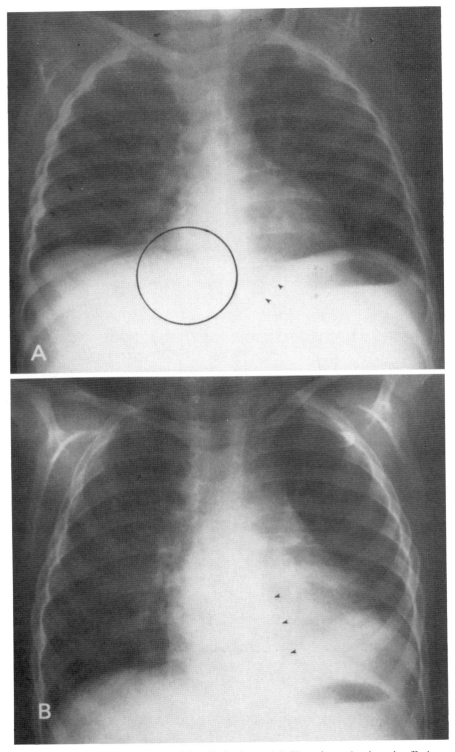

Figure 1.58. *Subpulmonic effusion—some subtle telltale signs.* (*A*) There is a subpulmonic effusion on the right. Telltale signs include: (a) slight elevation and flattening of the right diaphragmatic leaflet, (b) a sharp drop-off of the lateral aspect of the diaphragmatic leaflet, (c) minimal fluid along the lateral chest wall extending into the minor

extent that a mass-like configuration results (Fig. 1.59). Indeed, one may be surprised at how much fluid can accumulate in the subpulmonic space.

On lateral view subpulmonic effusions often are easier to detect for they fill the posterior costophrenic sulcus in the characteristic meniscoid or sloping fashion of any pleural effusion (Fig. 1.60), but of course, if one still is uncertain, a decubitus view almost always clarifies the situation (Fig. 1.60). Indeed, with the decubitus view and with the patient in the Trendelenburg position, effusions as small as 5–25 cc can be demonstrated (2, 5, 18, 23).

Mediastinal and paraspinal gutter effu-

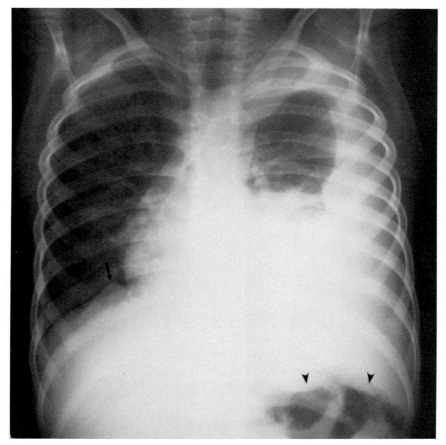

Figure 1.59. *Massive pleural effusion with large subpulmonic component.* Note the large effusion on the left. It virtually encircles the aerated lung. However, there also is a large subpulmonic component which depresses the stomach and splenic flexure to such a degree that a mass might be suggested (*arrows on left*). The *arrow on the right* points to the telltale bump of a subpulmonic effusion, simultaneously present on the right.

fissure (*arrows on the right*), (d) obliteration of the right cardiac border (positive silhouette sign), and (e) opacification of the right phrenicovertebral angle (*circle*). The normal, radiolucent left phrenicovertebral angle is defined by the *arrows* just to the left of the lower thoracic spine. For another case showing similar telltale signs, see Figure 1.59. (*B*) Subpulmonic effusion on the left causes apparent elevation of the diaphragmatic leaflet. However, note the increased distance between the top of the apparent diaphragmatic leaflet and the stomach bubble and the triangular strip of fluid in the paraspinal gutter (*arrows*). Both of these findings should alert one to the presence of a subpulmonic effusion, but in addition it should be noted that while the pulmonary vascular markings can be seen through the top of the right diaphragmatic leaflet, they are not as easily visible through the top of the apparently high left diaphragmatic leaflet. Such obliteration of the vascular markings by the presence of subpulmonic fluid is another subtle telltale finding of such effusions (23). In other cases peculiar bumps along the diaphragmatic leaflets serve to alert one to the presence of a subpulmonic effusion (i.e., Fig. 1.59).

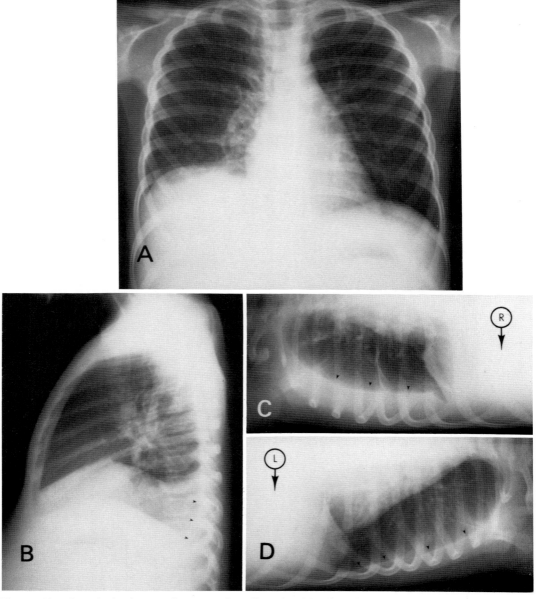

Figure 1.60. *Bilateral subpulmonic effusions—value of lateral and decubitus films.* (*A*) Both diaphragmatic leaflets appear elevated in this patient with nephrotic syndrome. Bilateral subpulmonic pleural effusions are present. (*B*) Lateral view demonstrates characteristic blunting and obliteration of both posterior costophrenic angles, and a typical sloping edge of one of the posterior collections of pleural fluid (*arrows*). (*C*) Right lateral decubitus film shows how the fluid layers along the right lateral wall. (*D*) Left lateral decubitus view shows similar findings (*arrows*).

sions also often elude detection. Posteriorly, in the paraspinal gutter, these effusions usually assume a variably long, tapering, triangular or wedge-like paraspinal configuration (Figs. 1.52*A* and 1.58*B*), while anteriorly or in the middle mediastinum, these effusions may appear mass-like (21) or triangular (Fig. 1.61). Effusions along the minor fissure, such as the one seen in Figure 1.61, must be differentiated from a similar picture produced by normal thymus gland (see Fig. 1.142).

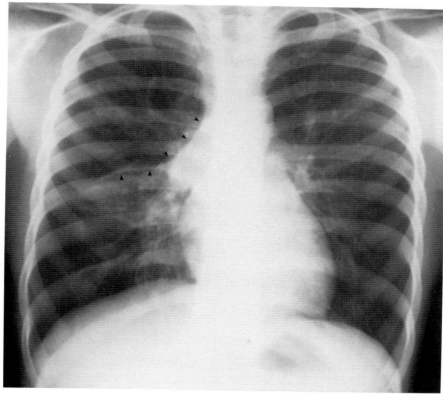

Figure 1.61. *Mediastinal effusion.* Note triangular mediastinal effusion (*upper three arrows*) in this patient with asthma and a viral lower respiratory tract infection. The triangular configuration could be confused with the sail sign of the normal thymus gland in a younger infant (see Fig. 1.142), or an area of segmental atelectasis. However, if it is noted that fluid also extends into the minor fissure (*lower two arrows*) these possibilities can be discounted. Overall, however, one should recall that pleural effusions with viral infections are rare.

Large pleural effusions occasionally can mimic a lobar consolidation (Fig. 1.62), and unquestionably, decubitus views are the answer here. In still other cases pleural effusions, or empyemas, may become loculated in the various interlobar fissures (Fig. 1.63). Characteristically these accumulations are round, oval, or spindle-shaped but some may appear as large pulmonary masses (Fig. 1.64), and others as irregular infiltrates (Fig. 1.65). However, many are more typical and show characteristically tapering ends as they lie along the axis of the involved fissure (Fig. 1.66). In this regard, it might also be noted that while on one projection these effusions may appear characteristic, on the other they usually appear atypical. Pleural effusions or empyemas which loculate laterally or posteriorly are less of a problem (Fig. 1.67). Those effusions or empyemas, which loculate along the lung base and thus become difficult to differentiate from a subphrenic abscess, can be investigated and differentiated with ultrasonography. Indeed, this procedure is becoming extremely useful in differentiating such fluid collections from subphrenic inflammatory problems. The detection of pleural fluid, is relatively easily accomplished with ultrasound (Fig. 1.68).

Before leaving the discussion of pleural effusions, it should be noted that many normal children have minimal collections of pleural fluid in their costophrenic angles (4). This is entirely normal and common (Fig. 1.69*B*), and the findings should not be misinterpreted for a pathologic pleural effusion. A similar problem arises when prominent normal soft tissues over the apex of the lung are misinterpreted for a pleural effusion (Fig. 1.69*A*).

Chylothorax is not a common problem in childhood, but occasionally can be seen with

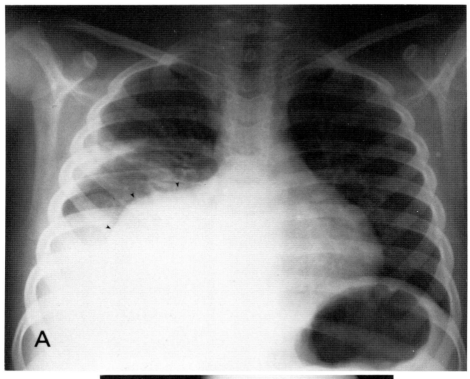

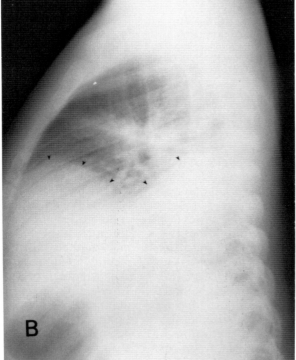

Figure 1.62. *Pleural effusion mimicking lobar pneumonia.* (*A*) The pleural effusion on the right could be misinterpreted for a consolidating pneumonia (*arrows*). Note fluid along the right lateral chest wall and some fluid extending into the minor fissure. (*B*) On lateral view subpulmonic fluid collections are outlined by the *arrows*. Either one of these could be misinterpreted for a consolidating lobar pneumonia.

Figure 1.63. *Loculated interlobar fissure effusions—diagrammatic representations.* (*A*) Large loculated effusion. The characteristic tapering, spindled ends often are not present with effusions this large. (*B*) Classic appearance of loculated interlobar effusion presenting as a rounded or oval mass with characteristic tapering, spindle-shaped ends trailing into the fissure. (*C*) Similar configuration but with a longer, more oval effusion. (*D*) Less characteristic, irregular collection of loculated pleural fluid.

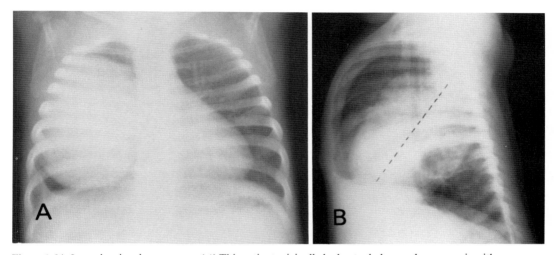

Figure 1.64. *Large loculated empyema.* (*A*) This patient originally had a staphylococcal pneumonia with empyema. This roentgenogram was obtained 3 weeks after treatment and shows how the empyema has loculated into a large, perfectly oval, mass-like lesion. The findings defy distinction from a cyst or tumor. (*B*) Lateral view shows the location of the apparent mass. Although the characteristic tapering ends of a loculated pleural effusion are not present the main axis of the lesion still conforms to the axis of the greater fissure (*dotted line*), and is the clue to correct diagnosis.

rupture of the thoracic duct secondary to blunt chest trauma. It also has been described in the battered child syndrome (9). Otherwise, chylothorax is a problem of newborn and young infants (31, 33), and of the post-thoracotomy patient. Occasionally, the thoracic duct can be obstructed by a hidden mediastinal tumor or cyst and chylothorax can be the presenting problem, but this is a rare situation.

Other pleural fluid collections can be seen with spontaneous or traumatic esophageal rupture (10, 28), bronchial tears following blunt chest trauma, and with bleeding secondary to rib fractures or post-traumatic great vessel rupture. With esophageal perforations and bronchial tears, both air and fluid are seen in the pleural space (i.e., hemopneumothorax or hydropneumothorax).

With esophageal perforations, these changes usually occur on the left side in older children and adults, but on the right in neonates (10). These perforations are believed to result from an acute increase in intraesophageal pressure secondary to traumatic compression of the abdomen and lower chest, or in some cases from profound vomiting. A rare cause of pleural fluid collection is bleeding secondary to rupture of a diverticulum of the ductus arteriosus (14).

Finally, it should be noted that a picture suggesting a large pleural effusion can result in those cases where there is massive unilateral atelectasis and pronounced contralateral compensatory emphysema (see Fig. 1.79). It is most important that this pitfall be appreciated so as to avoid needless thoracentesis. The same precaution should be observed in

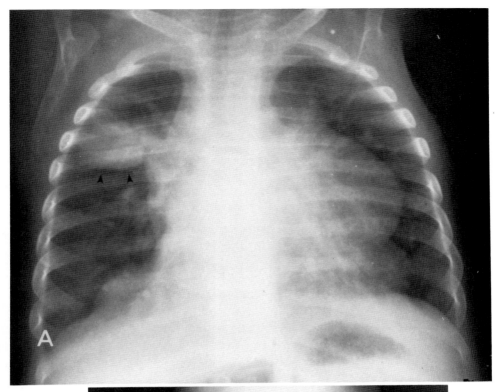

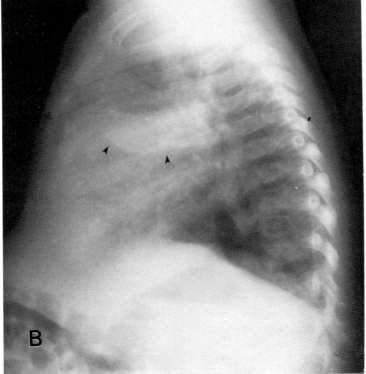

Figure 1.65. *Loculated pleural effusion—irregular configuration.* (*A*) On frontal view this loculated effusion could be misinterpreted for an early consolidating pneumonia (*arrows*). This patient also has an underlying left to right shunt, some congestion, and bilateral eventrations. (*B*) Lateral view delineates the somewhat irregular appearing loculated pleural effusion in the right minor fissure (*arrows*). These less characteristic effusions are often difficult to differentiate from consolidations or areas of segmental atelectasis.

those cases of atypical upper lobe atelectasis mimicking apical pleural effusions (see Fig. 1.81).

REFERENCES

1. Cho, C.T., Hiatt, W.O., and Behbehani, A.M.: Pneumonia and massive pleural effusion associated with adenovirus type 7. Am. J. Dis. Child. 126: 92–94, 1973.
2. Collins, J.D., Burwell, D., Furmanski, S., Lorber, P., and Steckel, R.J.: Minimal detectable pleural effusions. A roentgen pathology model. Radiology 105: 51–53, 1972.
3. Davis, L.A.: Vertical fissure line. A.J.R. 84: 451–453, 1960.
4. Ecklof, O., and Torngren, A.: Pleural fluid in healthy children. Acta Radiol. 11: 346–349, 1971.
5. Felson, B.: Chest Roentgenology, pp. 350–367. W.B. Saunders, Philadelphia, 1973.
6. Fine, N.L., Smith, L.R., and Sheedy, P.F.: Frequency of pleural effusions in mycoplasma and viral pneumonias. N. Engl. J. Med. 283: 790–793, 1970.
7. Fleischner, F.G.: Atypical arrangement of free pleural effusion. Radiol. Clin. North Am. 1: 347–361, 1963.
8. Forbes, G.B., and Emerson, G.L.: Staphylococcal pneumonia and empyema. Pediatr. Clin. North Am. 4: 215–229, 1957.
9. Green, H.G.: Child abuse presenting as chylothorax. Pediatrics 66: 620–621, 1980.
10. Harell, G.S., Friedland, G.W., Daily, W.J., and Cohn, R.B.: Neonatal Boerhaave's syndrome. Radiology 95: 665–668, 1970.
11. Highman, J.H.: Staphylococcal pneumonia and empyema in childhood. A.J.R. 106: 103–108, 1969.
12. Honig, P.J., Pasquariello, P.S., Jr., and Stool, S.E.: H Influenzae pneumonia infants and children. J. Pediatr. 83: 215–219, 1973.
13. Huxtable, K.A., Tucker, A.S., and Wedgewood, R.J.: Staphylococcic pneumonia in childhood: longterm follow-up. Am. J. Dis. Child. 108: 262–269, 1964.
14. Ithuralde, M., Halloran, K.H., Fishbone, G., Brill, S., and Downing, S.E.: Dissecting aneurysm of the ductus arteriosus in the newborn infant. Am. J. Dis. Child. 122: 165–169, 1971.
15. Kanof, A., Epstein, B., Kramer, B., and Mauss, I.: Staphylococcal pneumonia and empyema. Pediatrics 11: 385–392, 1953.
16. Keefer, C.S., Rantz, A., and Rammelkamp, C. H.: Hemolytic streptococcal pneumonia and empyema: a study of 55 cases with special reference of treatment. Ann. Intern. Med. 14: 1533–1550, 1941.
17. Kevy, S.V., and Lowe, B.A.: Streptococcal pneumonia and empyema in childhood. N. Engl. J. Med. 264: 738–743, 1961.
18. Moskowitz, H., Platt, R.T., Schachar, R., and Mellins, H.: Roentgen visualization of minute pleural effusion: experimental study to determine the minimal amount of pleural fluid visible on a radiograph. Radiology 109: 33–35, 1973.
19. Nyhan, W.L., Rectanus, D.R., and Fousek, M.D.: Hae-

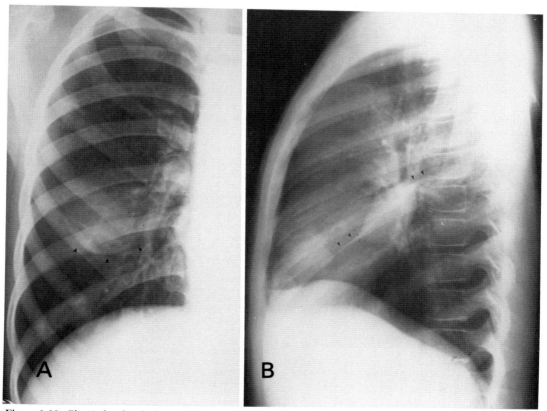

Figure 1.66. *Classic loculated pleural effusion.* (*A*) Note the area of increased density in the right mid-lung field and especially note the sharp rounded lower edge (*arrows*). (*B*) Lateral view clearly establishes that a loculated effusion is present in the right major fissure. Notice the characteristic tapering, spindled ends (*arrows*) of this pseudomass. It lies along the fissure and its tapering ends trail into the fissure. Because these effusions tend to disappear rapidly, and unexpectedly, they have been termed vanishing tumors.

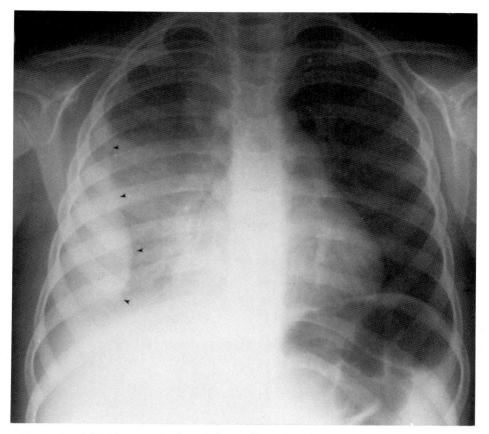

Figure 1.67. *Loculated fluid (empyema)—lateral chest wall.*   This patient had a pneumococcal pneumonia and eventually developed an empyema which then finally loculated laterally (*arrows*). Such loculations are common in the resolving stage of any type of empyema.

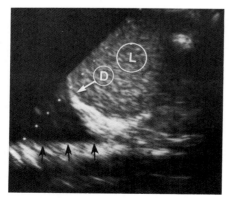

Figure 1.68. *Ultrasound detection of pleural fluid.* Note typical sonolucent fluid in the posterior sulcus (*arrows*). Diaphragm (*D*), liver (*L*).

mophilus influenzae type B pneumonia. Pediatrics 16: 31–41, 1965.

20. Peterson, J.A.: Recognition of infrapulmonary pleural effusion. Radiology 74: 34–41, 1960.

21. Pines, A., Kaplinsky, N., Rubinstein, Z., Bregman, J.,

Meytes, D., and Frankl, O.: Massive loculated pleural effusion simulating mediastinal masses. Br. J. Radiol. 55: 240–242, 1982.

22. Rigler, L.G.: Roentgen diagnosis of small pleural effusions: A new roentgenographic position. J.A.M.A. 96: 104–108, 1931.

23. Rigler, L.G.: Roentgenologic observations of the movement of pleural effusions. A.J.R. 25: 220–230, 1931.

24. Riley, H.D., and Bracken, E.C.: Empyema due to *Haemophilus influenzae* in infants and children. Am. J. Dis. Child. 110: 24–28, 1965.

25. Rudikoff, J.C.: The pulmonary ligament and subpulmonic effusion. Chest 80: 505–507, 1981.

26. Schwartz, M., and Marmorstein, B.: New radiologic sign of subpulmonic effusion. Chest 67: 176–178, 1975.

27. Smith, P.L., and Gerald, B.: Empyema in childhood followed roentgenographically: decortication seldom needed. A.J.R. 106: 114–117, 1969.

28. Tolstedt, G.E., and Tudor, R.B.: Esophagopleural fistula in a newborn infant. Arch. Surg. 97: 780–781, 1968.

29. Trackler, R.T., and Brinker, R.A.: Widening of the left paravertebral pleural line on supine chest roentgenograms in free pleural effusions. A.J.R. 96: 1027–1034, 1966.

30. Turner, J.A.P.: Staphylococcal pneumonia, a contemporary rarity. Clin. Pediatr. 11: 69–71, 1972.

31. Watson, E.G., and Foster, L.F.: Spontaneous chylothorax in infancy: prognosis and management. Am. J. Dis. Child. 72: 89–94, 1946.

32. Webber, M.M., and O'Loughlin, B.J.: Variations of pleural

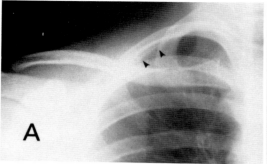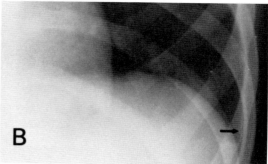

Figure 1.69. *Normal pleural reflections mimicking pleural effusions.* (*A*) Apparent fluid over the apex of the right lung (*arrows*). This finding is commonly seen in children and is due to normal soft tissues between the lung and ribs. (*B*) Pleural reflection in the left costophrenic angle of a normal child (*arrows*). There is some debate as to whether this finding represents the pleural reflection alone, or a minimal amount of normal pleural fluid. Whichever explanation is correct, the finding is normal.

vertical fissure line. Radiology 82: 461–462, 1964.
33. Wessel, M.A.: Chylothorax in two-week-old infant with spontaneous recovery. J. Pediatr. 25:201–210, 1944.
34. Vinik, M., Altman, D.H., and Parks, R.E.: Experience with *Haemophilus influenzae* pneumoniae. Radiology 86: 701–706, 1966.

HILAR AND PARATRACHEAL ADENOPATHY

Enlarged lymph nodes in the hilar or paratracheal regions are most often inflammatory in nature, and in this regard, most often are seen with viral lower respiratory tract infections (see Figs. 1.3 and 1.4). They also can be seen in certain asthmatic children, especially those with superimposed viral lower respiratory tract infections. Of course, bilateral hilar and paratracheal adenopathy also can be seen with conditions such as sarcoidosis, histoplasmosis, histiocytosis X, sinus histiocytosis (2), etc., but a detailed discussion of these entities is not within the scope of this book. Hilar adenopathy secondary to lymphoma or leukemia is not as common a presenting feature in children as is coalescent mediastinal adenopathy (see Fig. 1.139).

Unilateral hilar or paratracheal adenopathy, although occasionally occurring with any of the conditions mentioned in the foregoing paragraph, usually is the hallmark of primary pulmonary tuberculosis in childhood (Fig. 1.70). There is good reason for this to occur, for if one considers the basic pathology in these cases, one will recall that adenopathy is secondary to a peripheral Ghon lesion, and that this lesion usually is single. Because of this, hilar or paratracheal lymph node involvement is usually unilat-

eral and, indeed, a good rule to follow is that unilateral hilar or paratracheal adenopathy, with or without associated change in the lungs, should be considered tuberculous in origin until proven otherwise. Occasionally, mycoplasma pneumonia infections can produce similar findings, but primary pulmonary tuberculosis should be the first consideration in any patient presenting such a picture.

In many cases adenopathy is discrete and smooth-edged (Fig. 1.70). In other cases, however, associated inflammatory changes cause the edge of the enlarged hilar nodes to be fuzzy (Fig. 1.71).

Associated parenchymal changes in primary pulmonary tuberculosis include parenchymal infiltrates, atelectasis, and obstructive emphysema. Atelectasis, however, is the most common of the three (1, 4, 5). Both atelectasis and obstructive emphysema can result from endobrachial obstruction by mucosal inflammation or granuloma formation, or from compression by the adjacent enlarged lymph nodes. However, it is the endobronchial inflammatory change which is probably more important in obstructing the bronchus. Later on segmental bronchial stenosis may be the cause of more persistent atelectasis, and indeed, such atelectasis often develops or becomes more profound after treatment has been instituted (5).

In those cases where atelectasis is the associated finding, its presence may obscure the fact that hilar adenopathy is present, and one must be aware of this pitfall (Fig. 1.72). This is less of a problem when obstructive emphysema is present (Fig. 1.73). Other

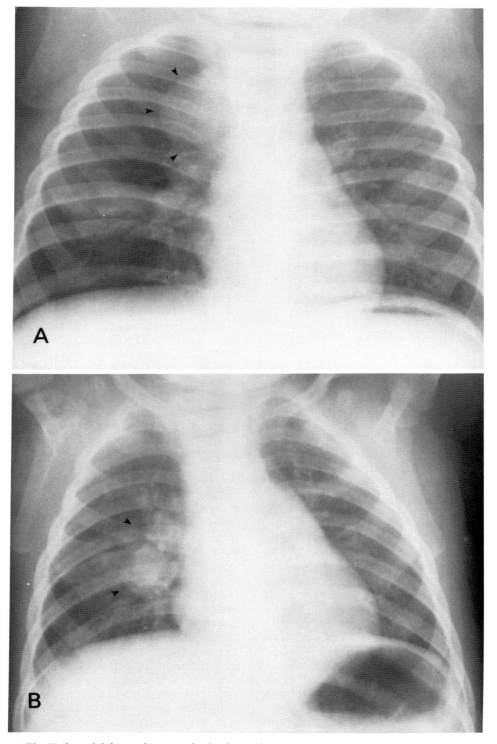

Figure 1.70. *Unilateral hilar and paratracheal adenopathy in tuberculosis.* (*A*) Note extensive paratracheal adenopathy on the right (*arrows*). (*B*) Another case showing unilateral hilar adenopathy on the right (*arrows*). For another case of massive unilateral hilar adenopathy in pulmonary tuberculosis see Figure 1.74, *A* and *B*.

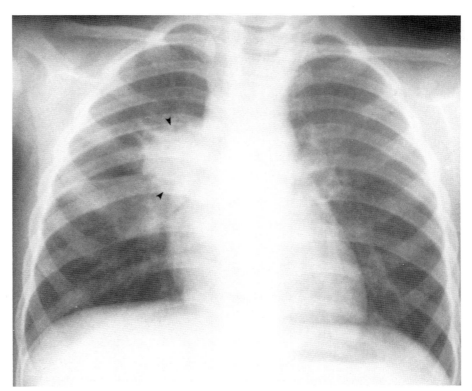

Figure 1.71. *Unilateral hilar adenopathy with fuzzy edges—tuberculosis.*   Note hilar adenopathy (*arrows*), but also note that the edges of the enlarged nodes are hazy due to associated inflammatory change. There also is fluid in the minor fissure.

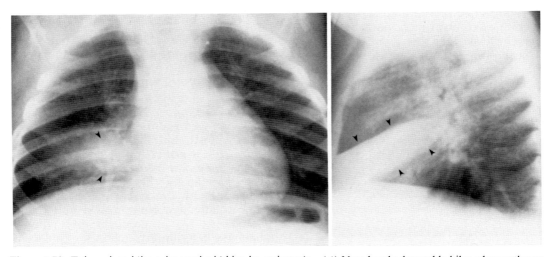

Figure 1.72. *Tuberculous hilar adenopathy hidden by atelectasis.*   (*A*) Note barely detectable hilar adenopathy on the right (*arrows*). It is hidden by the more diffuse density due to associated right middle lobe atelectasis. (*B*) Lateral view clearly demonstrates the triangular, dense configuration of the atelectatic right middle lobe (*arrows*). Also note hilar prominence suggesting adenopathy.

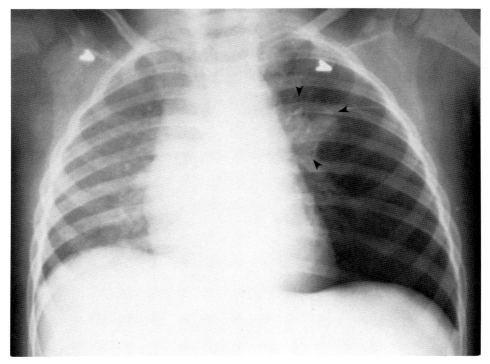

Figure 1.73. *Tuberculous adenopathy with obstructive emphysema.* Patient with left-sided tuberculous adenopathy (*arrows*), and obstructive emphysema of the left lung. Note how large and hyperlucent the left lung is on this expiratory film.

findings seen with primary pulmonary tuberculosis include pleural effusion and pneumatoceles, but frank cavitation, as in reinfection tuberculosis, is rare (3).

Before leaving the subject of hilar adenopathy, one should recall that its presence can be mimicked, on frontal view, by superior segment lower lobe pneumonias. However, no such problem should last for long, for on lateral view it will be clearly seen that hilar adenopathy is central (paracarinal) while superior segment lower lobe pneumonias lie posterior to the carina (Fig.1.74). Large pulmonary arteries, as might be seen with pulmonary hypertension mimicking hilar adenopathy, are not as great a problem in childhood as in the adult.

REFERENCES

1. Matsaniotis, N., et al.: Bullous emphysema in childhood tuberculosis. J. Pediatr. 71: 703, 1967.
2. Siegel, M.J., Shackelford, G.D., and McAlister, W.H.: Sinus histiocytosis: some radiologic observations. A.J.R. 132: 783–785, 1979.
3. Solomon, A., and Rabinowitz, L.: Primary cavitating tuberculosis in childhood. Clin. Radiol. 23: 483–485, 1972.
4. Veneeklas, G.M.H.: Cause and sequela of interpulmonary shadows in primary tuberculosis. Am. J. Dis. Child. 83: 271, 1952.
5. Weber, A.L., Bird, K.T., and Janower, M.L.: Primary tuberculosis in childhood with particular emphasis on changes affecting the tracheobronchial tree. A.J.R. 103: 123–132, 1968.

ATELECTASIS AND EMPHYSEMA

Which Side Is Abnormal? Among the most troublesome problems with unilateral lobar (total lung) atelectasis or emphysema is trying to decide which side of the chest is abnormal. In this regard there is no question that an inspiratory-expiratory sequence of chest roentgenograms is the ultimate answer for diagnosis, but there are *certain rules which can be utilized in determining which side is abnormal* before these are obtained. More specifically, these include: (a) in obstructive emphysema, the large, hyperlucent lung usually shows diminished pulmonary vascularity; (b) in compensatory emphysema, the large emphysematous, radiolucent lung (nonobstructed) usually shows normal or engorged pulmonary vascularity; and (c) an obstructed, emphysematous lung, no

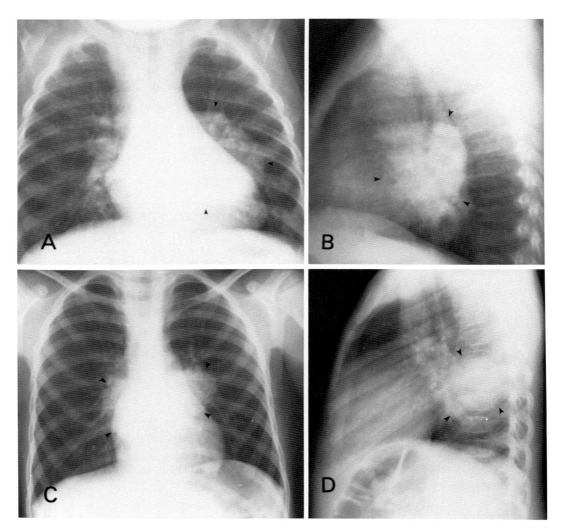

Figure 1.74. *Hilar adenopathy versus superior segment lower lobe pneumonia.* (*A*) Note massive unilateral left hilar adenopathy in this patient with primary pulmonary tuberculosis (*arrows*). (*B*) Lateral view shows typical central, paracarinal location of hilar adenopathy (*arrows*). (*C*) Patient in whom findings might at first suggest bilateral hilar adenopathy or a posterior mediastinal mass (*arrows*). (*D*) Lateral view shows that the findings represent bilateral superior segment lower lobe pneumonias (*arrows*). Characteristically these pneumonias lie high in the lower lobes, behind the major fissure, and unlike enlarged hilar lymph nodes, behind the carina. In most cases they overlie the spine. This patient had pneumococcal "double" pneumonia in that he had consolidations in both lower lobes in the superior segment. After appropriate treatment the pneumonias cleared completely.

matter how large, cannot compress the other lung to the point of total atelectasis or opacity (Fig. 1.75).

Of course, not every initial film reveals the foregoing findings with clarity, but whether the findings are clear or not, an inspiratory-expiratory film sequence should be next. The most important point to note on this study is that, usually, *the abnormal lung, no matter what its appearance, does not significantly change its size from inspiration to expiration.* In other words, the lung which changes size most is the normal lung (Fig. 1.75, *C* and *D*). For the most part these rules suffice for almost any aeration disturbance encountered except, perhaps, with the congenitally hypoplastic lung. Such a lung often is small, hyperlucent (decreased vas-

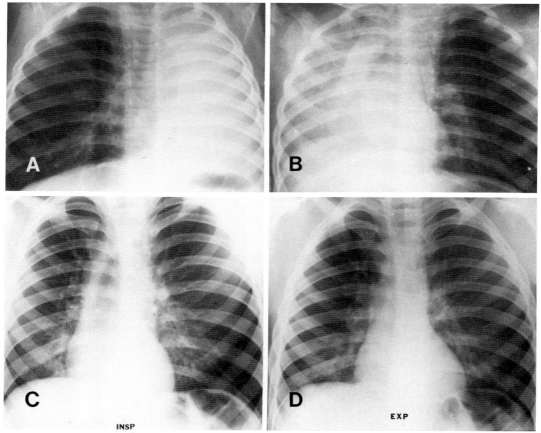

Figure 1.75. *Atelectasis and emphysema; which side is abnormal?.* (*A*) Note complete opacification of the left lung. The right lung shows compensatory emphysema and relatively normal vascularity. The fact that the left lung is totally opacified suggests that the problem is atelectasis on the left. An emphysematously obstructed lung, no matter how large, seldom, if ever, totally compresses the other lung. (*b*) The right lung is markedly deflated, but not totally opacified and airless. The problem here is obstructive emphysema on the left side. Also note that vascularity is relatively sparse in the overdistended left lung. (*C*) Large left lung. Note, that vascularity is normal or even slightly engorged. This should not represent obstructive emphysema. (*D*) Expiratory film shows the left lung to empty well, but the right lung to change little in size. This suggests that it is the right lung which is abnormal, and indeed, it was obstructed by a mucous plug in an asthmatic.

cularity), and yet shows significant change on inspiratory-expiratory film studies.

Atelectasis is a common roentgenographic finding and can involve an entire lung, lobe, or just a portion of it. Indeed, sublobar and segmental atelectases are quite common in children and, for the most part, occur with viral lower respiratory tract infections and asthma. To be sure, they often are confused with true pulmonary infiltrates (Fig. 1.76). The reason for such atelectasis being common in children is that the collateral air drift phenomenon, through the pores of Kohn and ducts of Lambert, is not as efficient in children as in adults (7). Consequently,

whereas in the adult segmental atelectasis does not last very long, it does tend to linger in children. If such segmental atelectasis is widespread and patchy, it is indeed difficult to differentiate it from pulmonary infiltration (see Fig. 1.76). On the other hand, when such atelectasis produces vertical, horizontal, or oblique streaks or wedges, it is easier to appreciate these densities for what they are (Fig. 1.77). Such atelectasis often is referred to as discoid, plate-like, or vertical atelectasis.

Atelectasis also can produce a confusing picture when a lobe is just beginning to collapse. The problem arises when the lobe

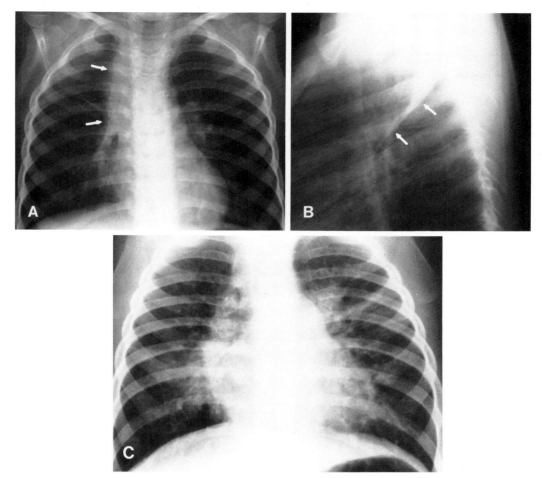

Figure 1.76. *Sublobar and segmental atelectasis.* (*A*) Asthmatic child with acute asthma attack. Note area of apparent consolidation in the right paratracheal region (*arrows*). This represents collapse of one portion of the right upper lobe. A more subtle finding, assisting in one's interpretation is that the minor fissure is slightly elevated. (*B*) Lateral view demonstrates early atelectasis (*arrows*). (*C*). Widespread patchy infiltrates due to segmental atelectasis in viral infection. Note that the infiltrates tend to cluster toward the center of the lung fields. This is characteristic of multiple segmental atelectasis. (For discussion of this problem, see p. 10.)

collapses against a major fissure (Fig. 1.78). In such cases the edge of the slightly elevated, or displaced fissure remains sharp, while the inner edge is somewhat indistinct. Indistinctness results from the fact that aeration of the lung, along the inner aspect of the atelectasis, still occurs. This is accomplished through collateral air drift, which even though less efficient in children still occurs. Overall, then, some aeration of the collapsing lobe occurs, but not in the portion abutting the fissure. Along the fissure, no such collateral aeration occurs, and thus the collapsing lung is outlined by a sharp line. On the other side, because some aeration does

occur, the edge is fuzzy. Overall, these findings often tend to mimic interlobar effusions, or even early consolidations.

Atelectasis of an entire lung, or a lobe thereof, is most often seen with asthma, viral lower respiratory tract infection, primary tuberculosis, or foreign bodies. In the classic case of total lung atelectasis the findings are clearly apparent, for the entire hemithorax becomes opacified, the mediastinum shifts to the ipsilateral side, and the heart virtually disappears into the atelectatic lung (Fig. 1.79*A*). However, because the other lung becomes overaerated (compensatory emphysema), one very often misinterprets the

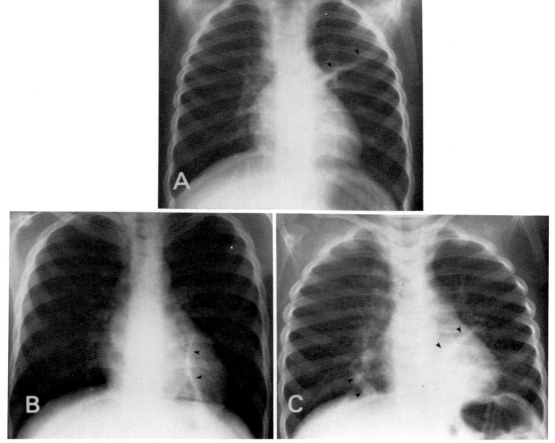

Figure 1.77. *Discoid, "plate-like" or vertical atelectasis.* (*A*) Segmental discoid atelectasis in the left upper lobe (*arrows*). (*B*) Another patient demonstrating so-called vertical discoid atelectasis (*arrows*). (*C*) Multiple oblique densities are seen throughout both lung fields, representing multiple areas of segmental, discoid atelectasis (*arrows*).

findings as being abnormal on the wrong side (i.e., obstructive emphysema with mediastinal shift). Expiratory films are the answer here, but before they are obtained one should also evaluate the pulmonary vascularity. In compensatory emphysema, the vascularity in the overaerated lung is normal or accentuated (Fig. 1.75*C*), while in obstructive emphysema usually it is decreased. Furthermore, it should be noted that in these cases the collapsed lung is totally opaque, even into the costophrenic angle. This can happen only with atelectasis or agenesis, for an overaerated lung alone, no matter how large, cannot compress the other lung to the point of complete opacity. Some aeration will remain.

Another problem which can arise in patients with total lung collapse is that a pleural effusion-like picture can be produced when compensatory emphysema of the other lung is pronounced (Fig. 1.79*B*). Indeed, it is difficult not to consider thoracentesis in these patients, but if the roentgenograms are properly assessed, it should become clear that atelectasis is the only problem.

Classic atelectatic patterns (4,8,10) for collapse of the various lobes are demonstrated in Figure 1.80, but from the onset it should be stressed that while on one view the atelectatic lobe may be clearly visualized, on the other it may be difficult to perceive. This occurs because on one view the lobe is seen on edge (easier to see), while on the other, it

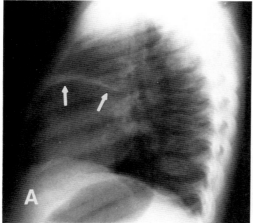

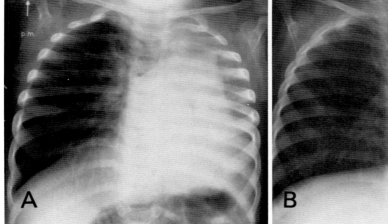

Figure 1.78. *Early lobar atelectasis.* (*A*) Note slight elevation of the minor fissure (*ararows*) and that its inferior edge is sharp, while its superior edge is fuzzy. (*B*) Lateral view showing similar findings (*arrows*).

Without close inspection, these findings often are misinterpreted for small interlobar effusions. Pleural effusions demonstrate sharp edges on both sides (see Fig. 1.101*B*).

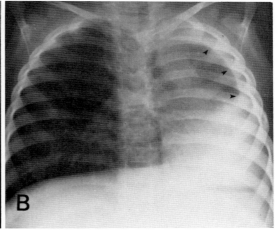

Figure 1.79. *Total atelectasis of a lung.* (*A*) In this infant atelectasis was due to an obstructing mucous plug. Note the marked loss of volume on the left, pronounced shift of the mediastinum to the left, and overexpansion of the right lung. However, the pulmonary vascularity in the right lung is normal, or in fact, a little increased. This rules against obstructive emphysema of the right lung. With obstructive emphysema the vascularity is diminished. (*B*) Another patient with complete atelectasis of the left lung and pronounced compensatory emphysema of the right lung. Indeed, the right lung has herniated across the mediastinum to produce a configuration suggesting a pleural effusion (*arrows*). This is not pleural fluid; it merely represents the overaerated herniated right lung superimposed on the collapsed left lung. The pulmonary vascularity in the right lung is not markedly diminished, and this identifies the problem as one of compensatory, rather than obstructive, emphysema. In other words, blood from the atelectatic left lung is shunted to the right lung. If the right lung were distended because of obstructive emphysema, the vascularity would be diminished.

is seen en face (more difficult to see). Indeed, atelectatic lobes visualized en face often are so ill-defined that they are misinterpreted for pulmonary infiltrates. It is only when one notes associated volume loss, and on the other view a typical lobar collapse pattern, that one comes to the conclusion that atelectasis only is present.

The pattern of collapse of the upper lobes is different from side to side. This is explained by the fact that on the right the minor fissure separates the right and middle

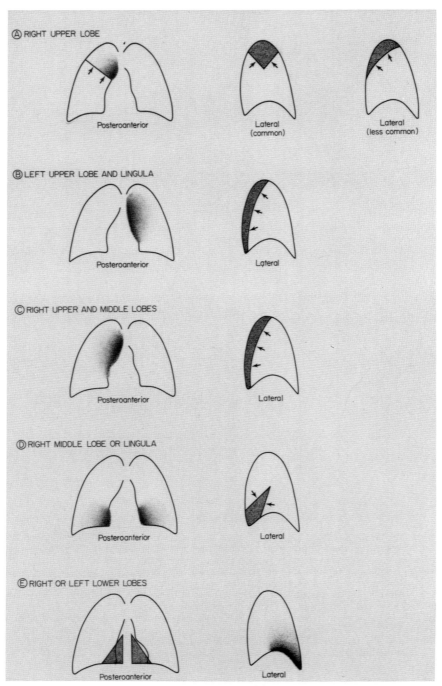

Figure 1.80. *Lobar atelectasis—diagrammatic representation of classic patterns.* (*A*) Right upper lobe atelectasis. (*B*) Left upper lobe and lingular atelectasis. (*C*) Right upper and right middle lobe atelectasis. (*D*) Right middle lobe or lingular atelectasis. (*E*) Right lower lobe or left lower lobe atelectasis. *Arrows* indicate direction of collapse and displacement of the involved major fissures. Roentgenographic examples of the above patterns are presented in Figures 1.81–1.87.

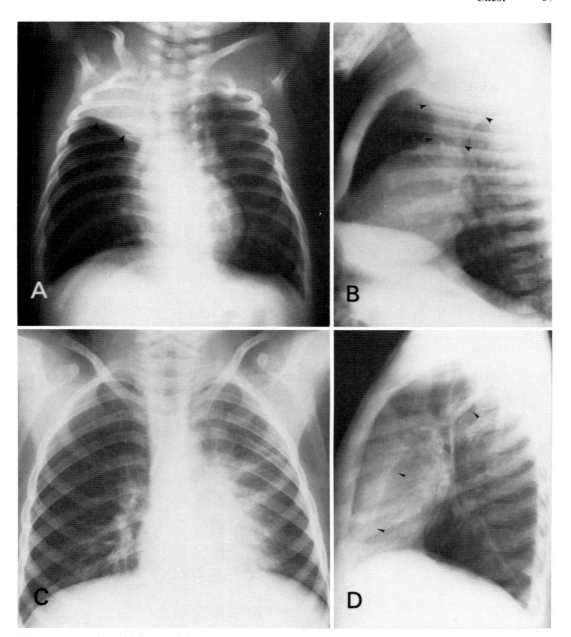

Figure 1.81. *Right and left upper lobe atelectatic patterns.* (*A*) Right upper lobe atelectasis, classic configuration. The minor fissure (*arrows*) is elevated, and the collapsed upper lobe is dense and triangular. In addition, there is some mediastinal shift to the right. This patient had bronchiolotis with a complicating mucous plug in the right upper lobe. (*B*) Lateral view of right upper lobe atelectasis demonstrating characteristic V-shaped configuration (*arrows*). The minor fissure delineates the collapsed lobe anteriorly, and the major fissure, posteriorly. (*C*) Left upper lobe and lingular atelectasis. First note that there is mediastinal shift to the left, and then that the entire left cardiac border is obliterated (positive silhouette sign). In addition note diffuse central haziness in the left lung field. (*D*) Lateral view shows characteristic configuration of the collapsed left upper lobe and lingula. The major fissure is displaced anteriorly and more or less parallels the anterior chest wall (*arrows*).

lobes, while on the left the lingula functions as part of the left upper lobe. On the right, on frontal projection, the elevated minor fissure is characteristic (Fig. 1.81*A*). On lat-eral view, the minor and major fissures often outline the collapsed right upper lobe as a "V" (Fig. 1.81*B*), but it is not always easy to see the "V" in its entirety. On the left side,

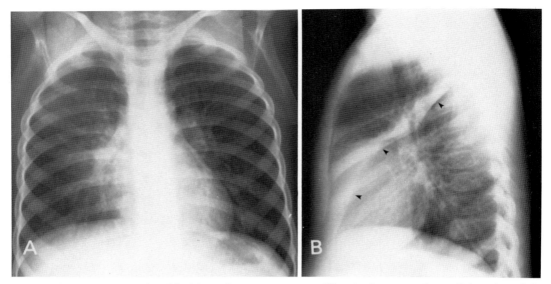

Figure 1.82. *Right upper and middle lobe atelectasis.* (*A*) Note diffuse haziness over the medial portion of the right lung field. An adjacent positive silhouette sign obliterates the entire right mediastinal edge, and the right hemithorax is slightly smaller than the left. There is some ipsilateral mediastinal shift and slight elevation of the right diaphragmatic leaflet (secondary signs of collapse). (*B*) Lateral view showing characteristic forward displacement of the major fissure as it outlines the collapsed upper and middle lobes (*arrows*).

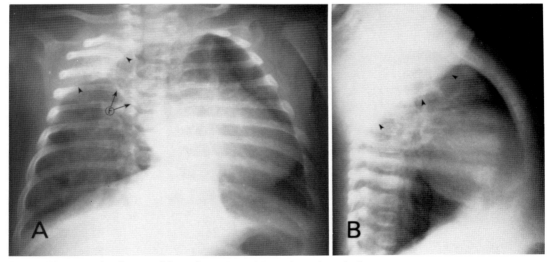

Figure 1.83. *Atypical right upper lobe atelectasis.* (*A*) Note the atelectatic right upper lobe compressed toward the apex of the right hemithorax (*arrows*). The minor fissure (*F*) is barely visible but elevated. Since the right upper lobe has collapsed, the right middle lobe has become overaerated and has herniated across the anterior mediastinum to the left side. This patient also has left lower lobe atelectasis as demonstrated by the dense area behind the left side of the heart. (*B*) Lateral view demonstrating atypically collapsed right upper lobe in the apex of the thorax (*arrows*).

since no minor fissure is present, one sees only a vague area of increased density over the left upper and mid-lung fields (Fig. 1.81*C*). On lateral view, the left upper lobe and lingula collapse anteriorly and are de-

marcated posteriorly by the forwardly displaced major fissure (Fig. 1.81*B*). In most of these cases, the displaced major fissure tends to parallel the anterior chest wall. On the right, a similar configuration results only

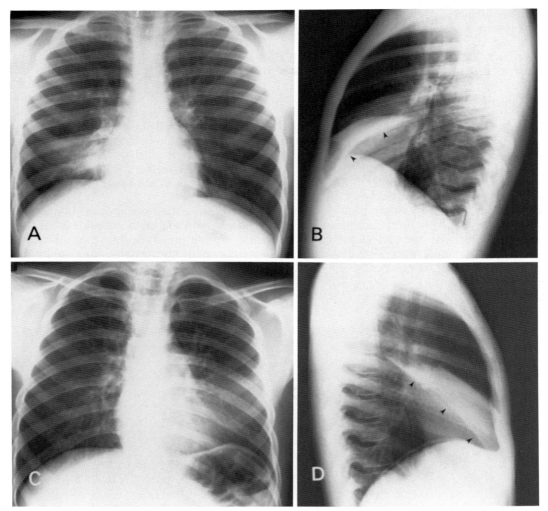

Figure 1.84. *Right middle lobe and lingular atelectasis.* (*A*) Characteristic findings of right middle lobe atelectasis consisting of an area of increased density just to the right of the lower cardiac border, obliteration of the adjacent portion of the cardiac border (positive silhouette sign), elevation of the diaphragmatic leaflet, and depression of the right hilum. The latter two findings, plus the slight mediastinal shift to the right, are secondary signs which indicate that a volume loss problem is present. (*B*) Lateral view shows the typical V-shaped configuration of the collapsed right middle lobe (*arrows*). (*C*) Lingular atelectasis producing findings similar to those of right middle lobe atelectasis but on the left side. (*D*) *Arrows* delineate the characteristically triangular collapsed lingula.

when the middle and upper lobes are collapsed together (Fig. 1.82).

Finally, it should be noted that either the right or left upper lobe can collapse in atypical fashion (5), and in so doing produce a pleural effusion-like picture (Fig. 1.83). To the unwary, the findings will strongly suggest a pleural effusion, and an unwarranted thoracentesis may even be performed. This can be avoided, however, by becoming familiar with this type of upper lobe collapse.

Right middle lobe and lingular collapse produce focal areas of increased density along the lower right or left cardiac borders (Fig. 1.84). In many cases, these findings may at first suggest pneumonia, but the characteristic V-shaped configuration on lateral view should enable one to make the proper diagnosis. However, it should be mentioned that some variation in the discreteness and density of the V-shaped collapse pattern should be expected, for it is dependent entirely on the degree of atelectasis present.

Lower lobe collapse is best appreciated on frontal view (Figs. 1.85 and 1.86), for on lateral view it may be totally invisible. At most, the lateral view will reveal a diffuse increase in density over the lower posterior half of the chest, and in some cases, loss of visualization of the adjacent diaphragmatic leaflet (i.e., positive silhouette sign—see Fig. 1.86*B*). Only rarely will the edge of the major fissure be seen demarcating the lower lobe anteriorly.

On frontal view differentiation of lower lobe collapse from right middle lobe or lingular collapse is accomplished by noting the presence or absence of an adjacent positive silhouette sign. With right middle lobe or lingular atelectasis, the ipsilateral cardiac border is obliterated, while with lower lobe atelectasis it is not (compare Fig. 1.84 with Fig. 1.85). Classically, left lower lobe collapse produces a triangular area of increased density confined more or less to the area behind the left side of the heart (Fig. 1.85). On the right, because there is less cardiac mass, the triangular density of the collapsed right lower lobe often extends beyond the right cardiac border (Fig. 1.86). On the left, if the lower portion of the inferior pulmonary ligament is congenitally defective, anchoring of the left lower lobe is less than normal, and the lobe collapses against the spine in a rounded fashion (6). A paraspinal mass is then suggested, for the characteristic triangular shape of left lower lobe collapse is absent.

When more than one lobe is collapsed in a patient, and the lobes are adjacent, problems in interpretation can arise. Peculiar patterns result and usually reflect a combination of the findings seen when each of the lobes collapses separately (Figs. 1.81, *C* and *D*, and 1.87).

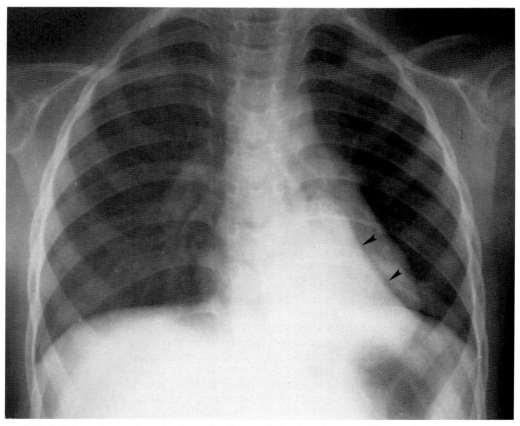

Figure 1.85. *Left lower lobe atelectasis.*   Note the characteristic triangular area of increased density behind the left side of the heart adjacent to the spine (*arrows*). In less pronounced cases the triangular configuration is not as distinct and a vague area of increased density only is seen.

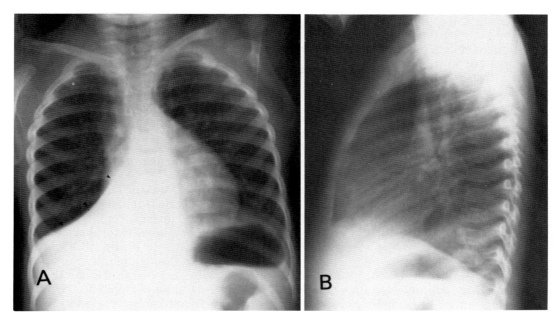

Figure 1.86. *Right lower lobe atelectasis.* (*A*) Note the dense triangular configuration of the collapsed right lower lobe extending beyond the right cardiac border (*arrows*). In addition the right cardiac leaflet is obliterated and elevated and there is slight mediastinal shift to the right. (*B*) Lateral view shows only a vague area of increased density behind the heart. The left diaphragmatic leaflet is clearly visualized (note the stomach bubble beneath it) but the right is obliterated because of a positive silhouette sign.

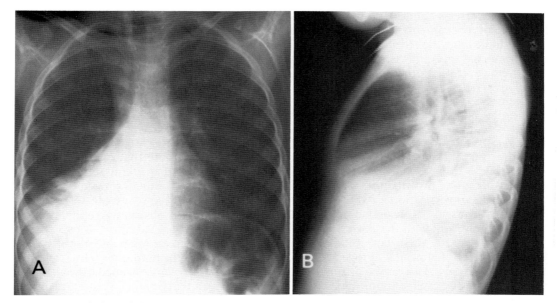

Figure 1.87. *Right lower lobe and middle lobe atelectasis.* (*A*) Frontal view showing characteristic configuration of the collapsed right lower and middle lobes. The triangular configuration suggests lower lobe collapse and the fact that the cardiac border is obliterated indicates that, in addition, the right middle lobe is collapsed. (*B*) Lateral view showing a large area of increased density behind and over the heart due to the atelectatic right lower and middle lobes.

All of the foregoing patterns of lobar atelectasis are understandably somewhat variable from patient to patient, for they depend to a large extent on the degree of atelectasis present. Because of this it is of value to be familiar with certain accessory signs which become useful in subtle cases. For example, elevation or depression of a hilum from its usual location (remember that the left hilum is normally a little higher than the right) suggests that there is atelectasis of the upper (elevated hilum) or lower (depressed hilum) lobe. By the same token, elevation of the ipsilateral diaphragmatic leaflet usually is present with lower lobe atelectasis and with all types of lobar collapse there is the inevitable ipsilateral shift of the mediastinum. This latter finding, however, may not always be striking and often becomes more convincing with inspiratory-expiratory film sequences. So-called "rounded atelectasis" in adults (2, 9) is not commonly seen in children. Atelectasis may appear so round in these patients that a pulmonary nodule or mass is erroneously suggested.

Before leaving the subject of atelectasis, a comment regarding the so-called *right middle lobe syndrome* (1, 3) is worthwhile. This is a poorly defined "syndrome" which simply states that the right middle lobe is chronically or recurrently atelectatic. Because this phenomenon occurs more commonly in the right middle lobe, the term right middle lobe syndrome has been devised. It should be noted, however, that other lobes can be similarly involved.

There is no specificity with regard to etiology in the right middle lobe syndrome, and it can be seen as the aftermath of viral or tuberculous infections, and in some cases be a feature of asthma. The presence of the right middle lobe syndrome suggests a chronic aeration disturbance, and eventually, further investigation is required. Most often this consists of bronchoscopy and bronchography and with these studies proximal narrowing of the right middle lobe bronchus often is delineated. If repeated pulmonary infections are a problem, the right middle lobe may well require surgical removal.

Emphysema can be generalized or lobar. Generalized emphysema is seen with central obstructing lesions such as foreign bodies in the trachea, paratracheal masses, vascular rings, diffuse peripheral small airway disease with air trapping (i.e., viral- or thermal injury-induced bronchiolitis), and with bronchospasm secondary to asthma, cystic fibrosis, and some immunologic disorders (Fig. 1.88). A similar problem has been noted in some children with α_1-antitrypsin deficiency (11).

Emphysema due to tracheal obstruction is often accompanied by expiratory wheezing and stridor. The roentgenographic findings may not be striking for the only feature may be what would initially be considered an apparently "overexuberant" normal inspiration. However, when it is remembered that it is difficult to obtain a film in deep inspiration in young infants, this finding alone should alert one to the fact that generalized air trapping is present. Thereafter, one should look for more specific findings such as: (a) abnormal tracheal deviation, (b) a right-sided aortic arch (indicating a vascular ring problem), (c) a mediastinal mass, or (d) opaque endotracheal foreign bodies.

Lobar emphysema is best known in its congenital form, and in this regard most often involves the left upper lobe (Fig. 1.89*A*). The right upper lobe and right middle lobe also are frequently involved, but lower lobe involvement is rare. Many of these patients present in the newborn period, while others are asymptomatic into adulthood. Still others can come to the attention of the physician when a superimposed lower respiratory tract infection aggravates the air-trapping problem and renders the patient symptomatic. However, before one assumes that the findings in such a patient are the result of congenital lobar emphysema, one should make certain that one is not dealing with transient lobar emphysema secondary to endobronchial mucus plugging as seen in asthma and viral lower respiratory tract infections, or with obstructing endobronchial foreign bodies. In addition, lobar emphysema can be seen with other obstructing lesions such as the pulmonary sling (aberrant left pulmonary artery), mediastinal masses or cysts, and in infants with bronchopulmonary dysplasia. These latter infants may well present in the emergency room with acute respiratory distress after having been previously discharged from the hospital.

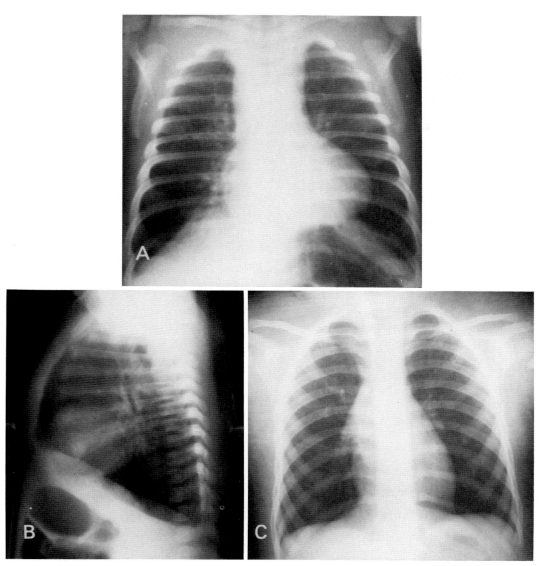

Figure 1.88. *Obstructive emphysema; generalized.* (*A*) Note the overdistended lungs in this patient with a vascular ring producing expiratory air trapping. (*B*) Lateral view showing marked overdistension of the chest with a typical bell-shaped configuration and flat diaphragmatic leaflets. (*C*) Marked overaeration secondary to thermal injury-induced bronchiolitis. This patient suffered from smoke inhalation and expired shortly thereafter. Note how depressed the diaphragmatic leaflets are. The soft tissues of the chest wall show extensive edema secondary to widespread cutaneous burns.

Most instances of well developed lobar emphysema pose no real problem as far as roentgenographic interpretation is concerned, but a modification might be made in those cases where the right middle lobe alone is involved. In such cases, the unwary observer may be fooled and pick the right middle lobe as being normal (but compen- satorily overinflated) and the right upper and right lower lobes as showing primary col- lapse. In these cases, it is only when one realizes that the combination of right upper lobe and lower lobe atelectasis is rather un- common, that one begins to focus attention on the right middle lobe as the one abnor- mally overaerated (Fig. 1.89*B*). Of course, if

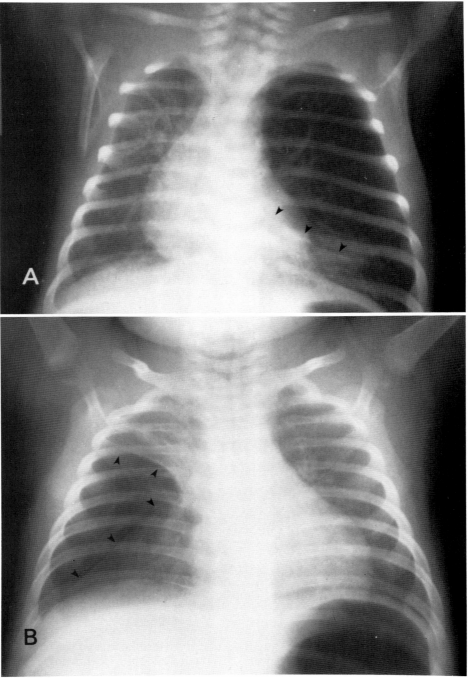

Figure 1.89. *Lobar emphysema.*   (*A*) Classic findings in congenital left upper lobe emphysema. The left upper lobe is hyperlucent, the left lower lobe collapsed in a small triangle (*lower arrows*), and the mediastinum shifted to the right (*B*) Right middle lobe emphysema producing an overaerated right middle lobe defined by the upwardly displaced minor fissure (*upper arrows*), and the downwardly and medially displaced major fissure (*lower arrows*). The right upper and lower lobes show a slight increase in density because they are partially compressed.

still in doubt, and as part of a general policy of confirming a suspected abnormality of aeration, inspiratory-expiratory film sequences are very worthwhile.

In the odd case, congenital lobar emphysema will be mimicked by cystic disease of the lung (i.e., congenital adenomatoid malformation). In these cases, air trapping in the multiple cysts becomes so profound that the septa between the cysts are almost obliterated and a picture of lobar emphysema or even pneumothorax is suggested.

Before leaving the topic of emphysema, a note might be made regarding those times when bilateral obstructive emphysema is mimicked by overaeration of the lungs due to some other nonpulmonary problem. In this regard, the most common situation is that of overaeration of the lungs secondary to the dehydration and acidosis seen with viral gastroenteritis (see Fig. 1.137). The clinical picture in these infants, of course, usually quickly clarifies the situation. The other time when lungs appear overdistended and suggest obstructive emphysema is when a normal child takes an overexuberant inspiration for the roentgenographic examination. All that is required here is that one be aware of this pitfall and remember not to interpret the roentgenograms in the absence of clinical history.

REFERENCES

1. Billig, D.M., and Darling, D.B.: Middle lobe atelectasis in children. Clinical and bronchographic criteria in the selection of patients for surgery. Am. J. Dis. Child. 123: 96–98, 1972.
2. Cho, S.R., Henry, D.A., Beachley, M.C., and Brooks, J.W.: Round (helical) atelectasis. Br. J. Radiol. 54: 643–650, 1981.
3. Dees, S.C., and Spock, A.: Right middle lobe syndrome in children. J.A.M.A. 197: 8–14, 1966.
4. Felson, B.: *Chest Roentgenology*, pp. 92–142. W. B. Saunders, Philadelphia, 1973.
5. Franken, E.A., Jr., and Klatte, B.C.: Atypical (peripheral) upper lobe collapse. Ann. Radiol. 20: 87–93, 1977.
6. Glay, J., and Palayew, M.J.: Unusual pattern of left lower lobe atelectasis. Radiology 141: 331–333, 1981.
7. Griscom, N.T., Wohl, M.E.B., and Kirkpatrick, J.A., Jr.: Lower respiratory infections: how infants differ from adults. Radiol. Clin. North Am. 16: 367–387, 1978.
8. Krause, G.R., and Lupert, M.: Gross anatomicospatial changes occurring in lobar collapse: a demonstration by means of three-dimensional plastic models. A.J.R. 79: 258–268, 1958.
9. Lubert, M., and Krause, G.R.: Patterns of lobar collapse as observed radiographically. Radiology 56: 165–182, 1951.
10. Schneider, H.J., Felson, B., and Gonzalez, L.L.: Rounded atelectasis. A.J.R. 134: 225–232, 1980.
11. Talamo, R.C., Levison, H., Lynch, M.J., Hercz, A., Hyslop, N.E., Jr., and Bain, H.W.: Symptomatic pulmonary emphysema in childhood associated with hereditary α_1-antitrypsin and an elastase inhibitor deficiency. J. Pediatr. 79: 20–26, 1971.

PNEUMATOCELES AND PULMONARY ABSCESS

A *pneumatocele* is an air-filled cyst, variable in size, usually thin-walled, fluid-free, and most frequently seen as a complication of staphylococcal pulmonary infections. They may be single or multiple, but most often rather than being the presenting feature of the pulmonary infection they tend to develop during the course of the disease. Some pneumatoceles are subject to rapid changes in size (Fig. 1.90), and may rupture to produce complicating pneumothoraces, but most remain relatively static for extended periods of time. Eventually, they disappear (3), and overall the vast majority are asymptomatic.

In addition to being seen with *S. aureus* infection, pneumatoceles can be seen with other bacterial pneumonias (1, 9), occasionally with tuberculosis, and in the odd case of viral lower respiratory tract infection. They also have been documented with hydrocarbon pneumonias, hyperimmunoglobulinemia E syndrome (5, 8), and are a common feature of closed, or blunt chest trauma (see Fig. 1.127). For the most part little needs to be done about a pneumatocele, regardless of the cause, for it is only when complications such as pneumothorax or infection arise that definitive therapy is required.

Various etiologies have been considered in the development of pneumatoceles and in this regard it has been suggested that pneumatoceles represent subpleural blebs, rather than intraparenchymal blebs (2). This seems a reasonable explanation but probably does not account for all pneumatoceles, and some most likely are truly intraparenchymal. However, whatever the precise location or terminology, most all agree that pneumatoceles result from alveolar or bronchiolar rupture secondary to air trapping distal to areas of small airway obstruction (4).

Pulmonary abscesses are a complication of lobar pneumonia or chronic bronchial obstructions (7). They are easily recognized by their round or oval configuration, air-fluid levels, and relatively thick walls (Fig. 1.91). Overall, most pulmonary abscesses tend to appear different from pneumatoceles, primarily in that they contain fluid and that their walls are thicker and more irregular. Of course, if infection supervenes in a pneumatocele, differentiation may be

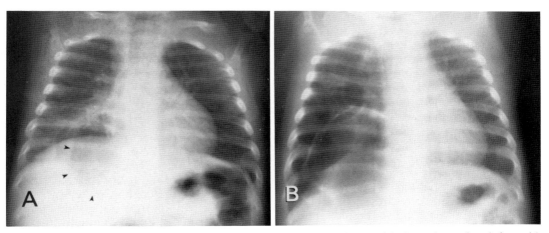

Figure 1.90. *Pneumatocele.* (*A*) Note large pneumatocele developing in the right lower lung of an infant with staphylococcal pneumonia (*arrows*). A smaller pneumatocele is seen just lateral to the large one. (*B*) Seven days later note how large the pneumatoceles have become. Indeed there is a tension phenomenon with the mediastinum being shifted to the left. Eventually, some 30 days later, the chest film in this infant was completely normal.

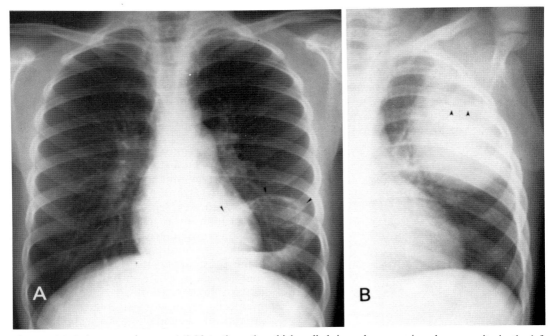

Figure 1.91. *Pulmonary abscess.* (*A*) Note the rather thick-walled, irregular appearing abscess cavity in the left lower lobe (*arrows*). There is an air fluid level in the bottom of the abscess. (*B*) Another patient with an abscess in the left upper lung. Note that it is rounded but its hazy margin reflects adjacent inflammatory change. The abscess is nearly full of fluid with only a small air fluid level noted at the top (*arrows*).

more difficult, but this is not a particularly common occurrence.

Acute cavitating pneumonias usually are bacterial in origin, but have been reported with *M. pneumoniae* infections (6). In any of these cases, it is not always possible to determine whether one is dealing with pneu-

matoceles, infected pneumatoceles, or multiple small abscesses.

REFERENCES

1. Asmar, B.I., Thirumoorthi, M.C., and Dajani, A.S.: Pneumococcal pneumonia with pneumatocele formation. Am. J. Dis. Child. 132: 1091–1093, 1978.
2. Boissett, G.F.: Subpleural emphysema complicating staph-

ylococcal and other pneumonias. J. Pediatr. 8: 259–266, 1972.

3. Caffey, J.: On the natural regression of pulmonary cysts during early infancy. Pediatrics 11: 48, 1953.

4. Conway, D.J.: The origin of lung cysts in childhood. Arch. Dis. Child. 26: 504, 1951.

5. Hill, H.R.: The syndrome of hyperimmunoglobulinemia E and recurrent infections. Am. J. Dis. Child. 136: 767–771, 1982.

6. Johnson, F.: Cavitating lesions in a cold agglutinin positive pneumonia. Pediatr. Radiol. 6: 181–182, 1977.

7. Marks, P.H., and Turner, J.A.P.: Lung abscesses in childhood. Thorax 23: 216, 1968.

8. Merten, D.F., Buckley, R.H., Pratt, P.C., Effmann, E.L., and Grossman, H.: Hyperimmunoglobulinemia E syndrome: radiographic observations. Radiology 132: 71–78, 1979.

9. Warner, J.O., and Gordon, I.: Pneumatoceles following haemophilus pneumonia. Clin. Radiol. 32: 99–105, 1981.

PNEUMOMEDIASTINUM, PNEUMOTHORAX, AND PNEUMOPERICARDIUM

Pneumomediastinum and pneumothorax in childhood can be seen with closed or penetrating chest or neck trauma (1), asthma, pulmonary infections with air trapping (10), airway foreign bodies, and occasionally with other obstructing lesions of the airway. Spontaneous pneumothorax and pneumomediastinum are not as common in children as in adults (3, 12). A rather rare cause of pneumothorax or pneumomediastinum is diabetic ketoacidosis (19, 21). In these cases it is the "overbreathing" associated with acidosis which leads to airway rupture.

Pneumomediastinal air collections are central in location (2) and of an endless assortment of shapes and sizes. They tend to outline the various mediastinal structures such as the thymus, aorta, and pulmonary artery, and in some cases the free air extends upward to outline the great vessels and soft tissues of the superior mediastinum and neck (Fig. 1.92*A*). In other cases the air may outline the heart (Fig. 1.92*A*), and as such should not be confused with a medial pneumothorax (see Fig. 1.94), or pneumopericardium (see Fig. 1.97). In addition, one should be aware of the fact that pneumomediastinal air can collect subpleurally along the diaphragm (9, 14), and may even extend across the mediastinum to result in the "continuous diaphragm sign" of Levin (8). In these latter cases the heart virtually is lifted off the diaphragm so that the diaphragm is seen in its entirety (Fig. 1.92*B*). So gross is the finding that it may be missed for this reason alone. In those cases where air collects subpleurally, that is, beneath the visceral pleura of the diaphragm, a thin strip of air is seen along the diaphragmatic leaflet. Clinically mediastinal air often produces the so-called crunch of Hamman (7), but seldom is a

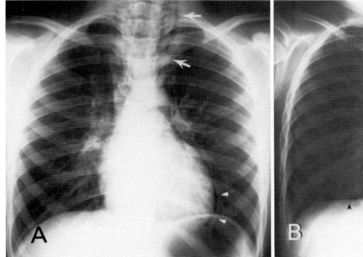
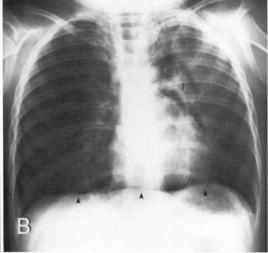

Figure 1.92. *Pneumomediastinum—varying configurations.* (*A*) Asthmatic child with pneumomediastinum showing air: (a) surrounding the small triangular thymus gland (*T*), (b) extending as linear sheaths into the neck and superior mediastinum (*upper arrows*), and (c) extending along the lower left cardiac edge (*lower arrows*). (*B*) Another asthmatic child with pneumomediastinal air outlining the thymic gland on the left (*T*) and producing the continuous diaphragm sign (*arrow*).The diaphragm is seen in its entirety from side to side including that portion just beneath the cardiac silhouette. A similar configuration can be seen on lateral view.

simple pneumomediastinum a cause for alarm, for even extensive air collections are relatively, if not entirely asymptomatic. Only occasionally will one encounter such a severe pneumomediastinum that surgical intervention might be required (16).

Pneumothorax, on the other hand, usually is accompanied by pain on inspiration, and if large enough and under tension, by respiratory distress. Auscultatory findings include decreased air entry or muffled breath sounds on the involved side, contralateral shift of the cardiac apical impulse, and in some cases of left-sided pneumothorax, a "click" which might be confused with the crunch of a pneumomediastinum (20).

The job of the radiologist, in cases of pneumothorax, is not so much to detect the large one, for this is relatively easy, but rather to detect the one under tension, or the one so subtle that it would otherwise be missed. In this regard, in the patient in the supine position, since air collects anterior to the lung, a free lung edge may not be visualized. However, certain telltale signs are usually present (17) and should be sought for. They include: (a) increased lucency, and often, size of the involved hemithorax (air under tension over the anterior surface of the lung); (b) contralateral shift of the mediastinum (tension phenomenon); and (c) increased sharpness or crispness of the ipsilateral mediastinal edge (Fig. 1.93A). The latter finding results from the fact that free

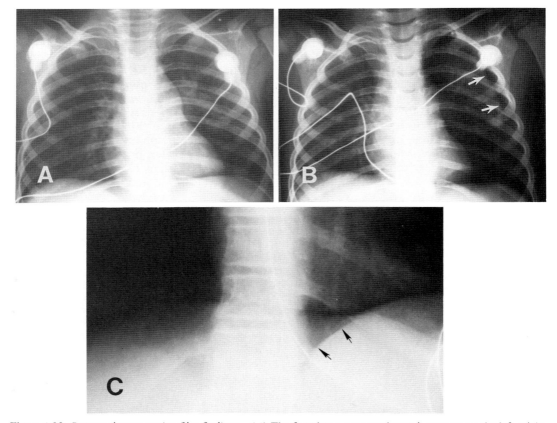

Figure 1.93. *Pneumothorax; supine film findings.* (*A*) The fact that a pneumothorax is present on the left might be missed. A faint free lung edge might be seen in the left apex and a little air might be suggested beneath the left lung. However, the findings are subtle and actually the most important finding is that the entire left mediastinal edge is "sharper" or "crisper" than that on the right. This sign indicates that free air, lying anterior to the lung and against the heart, is present. (*B*) Moments later an expiratory film more clearly demonstrates the pneumothorax. The free lung edge on the left is now clearly visualized (*arrows*) and the compressed left lung, virtually bathed in an envelope of free air, is easy to detect. Note that the trapped air on the left causes the left hemithorax to remain large and hyperlucent, and that the left cardiomediastinal edge is still sharper than its mate on the right. (*C*) *Deep sulcus sign* (6). Note increased radiolucency of the left paravertebral sulcus (*arrows*).

air, rather than aerated lung abuts the heart, and because of this the edge of the heart and other mediastinal structures become more clearly demarcated; i.e., they appear "sharper" or "crisper." The same phenomenon occurs over the diaphragmatic leaflets if air happens to accumulate solely along the bottom of the lung. In addition, the diaphragmatic leaflet may be depressed or show a double contour (15, 22). In still other cases air may accumulate deep in the posterior paravertebral sulcus (6), and produce increased radiolucency in this area (Fig. 1.93C).

For the most part, the foregoing findings are quite dependable in allowing one to detect an anterior pneumothorax, on supine films. However, it should be remembered that increased "sharpness" or "crispness" of the mediastinal edge or diaphragmatic leaflet also can be seen when a lung becomes overdistended, either because of obstruction or because of compensatory emphysema. Consequently, if one suspects an anterior or basal pneumothorax on a supine film, some other film should be obtained for confirmation. For the most part this can be a cross-table lateral (11), regular lateral, decubitus, or expiratory phase roentgenogram. During expiration the lungs empty and become smaller but the free air of the pneumothorax does not (4). One can use any or all of these views as an aid in detecting a subtle pneumothorax, and actually one should not limit oneself to a single additional view.

Another misleading configuration of pneumothorax occurs when air collects along the medial aspect of the lung so as to mimic a pneumomediastinum or pneumopericardium (Fig. 1.94). In such cases, an expiratory, regular or cross-table lateral, or decubitus view once again becomes useful for differentiation (13, 17).

On upright view, large pneumothoraces

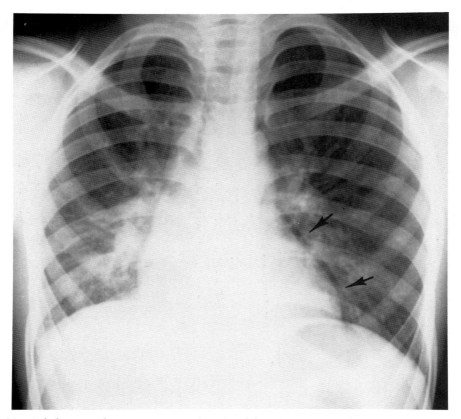

Figure 1.94. *Medial pneumothorax.* Note the thin strip of free air along the left cardiac border (*arrows*). The finding represents a medial pneumothorax and should not be confused with pneumomediastinum or pneumopericardium.

are not difficult to detect; the free lung edge is usually readily discernable, and the area lateral to it appears blacker than usual and free of vascular markings (Fig. 1.95). However, smaller pneumothoraces require astute inspection and careful scrutiny of the lung over its apex and in the costophrenic angle. In the costophrenic angle, one should look for the typical, laterally pointing, V-shaped air fluid level (4). If you see this finding, look harder for a pneumothorax for it will be there (Fig. 1.96). The V-shaped configuration results from the fact that fluid lies both in the anterior and posterior pleural space, and as the x-ray beam travels through the chest, these two fluid levels are traversed at two different angles and appear as the two limbs of the "V." Over the apex of the lung, free air is seen as a slender, radiolucent apical cap.

The key to distinguishing pneumopericardium from these other entities is to actually note the fine white line of the pericardium as it is separated from the heart by air (Fig. 1.97). Unfortunately, this does not always work in distinguishing pneumomediastinum from pneumopericardium, and thus in addition to this finding it should be noted that with pneumomediastinum air usually outlines one side of the heart only (Fig. 1.98*A*), while with pneumopericardium, it usually outlines the entire heart (Fig. 1.97). Nonetheless, in cases where air collections are minimal, if no other signs of pneumomediastinum are present, it may be difficult to make the distinction.

Pneumopericardium usually is traumatic in origin and not particularly difficult to recognize (Fig. 1.97). It can be seen with penetrating chest trauma, or blunt chest trauma. The latter, of course, is less common. In addition it has been noted with airway foreign bodies (18), and it has been suggested that air enters the pericardium

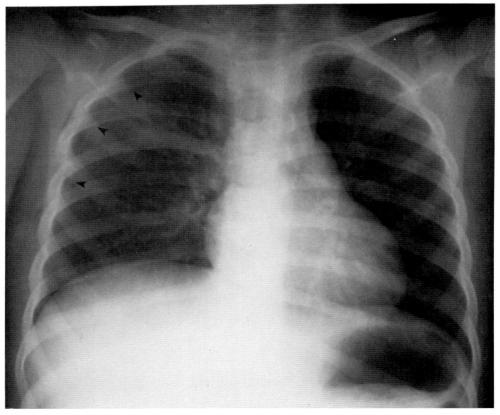

Figure 1.95. *Typical pneumothorax.*   Note the free lung edge on the right (*arrows*). The findings are typical of pneumothorax in that there are no vascular markings beyond the free lung edge.

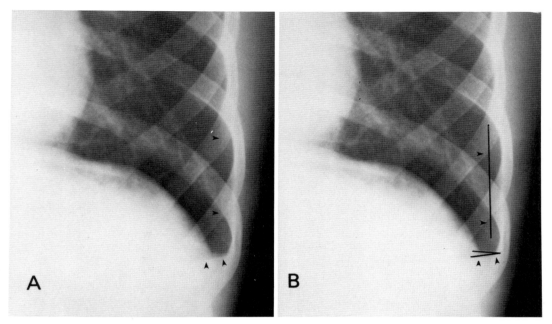

Figure 1.96. *Horizontal V sign in pneumothorax.* (*A*) At first the V-shaped collection of fluid in the left costophrenic angle might be overlooked (*lower two arrows*). The free lung edge, is barely discernable (*upper two arrows*). (*B*) Diagrammatic representation of the horizontal "V" sign and the free lung edge.

through tears between it and the adjacent connective tissue attachments to the pleura. However, more often than not it is some other roentgenographic finding which usually is misinterpreted as being representative of pneumopericardium. This can occur with a medial pneumothorax (Fig. 1.94), pneumomediastinum (Fig. 1.98*A*), and artefactually by Mach effect (5, 17) enhancement of a normal pericardial radiolucency occurring between the cardiac edge and the adjacent lower lobe pulmonary artery branches (Fig. 1.98*B*).

Finally a note regarding air in the inferior pulmonary ligament is in order. Most often seen with blunt chest trauma (see Fig. 1.128), it also can occur with other causes of mediastinal air. Its characteristic location and usually somewhat oval configuration, just along the spine, on frontal view, is the key to proper diagnosis.

REFERENCES

1. Eklof, O., and Thomasson, B.: Subcutaneous emphysema, pneumomediastinum and pneumothorax secondary to blunt injury to the throat. Ann. Radiol. 23: 169–173, 1980.
2. Evans, J., and Smalldon, T.: Mediastinal emphysema. A.J.R. 64: 375–389, 1950.
3. Feldtman, R.W., Oram-Smith, J.C., Manning, L.G., and Buckley, C.J.: Spontaneous mediastinal emphysema. J. Pediatr. Surg. 15: 648–650, 1980.
4. Felson, B.: *Chest Roentgenology*, pp. 366–371 and 392–399. W. B. Saunders, Philadelphia, 1973.
5. Friedman, A.C., Lautin, E.M., and Rothenberg, L.: Mach bands and pneumomediastinum. J. Can. Assoc. Radiol. 32: 232–235, 1981.
6. Gordon, R.: The deep sulcus sign of pneumothorax. Radiology 136: 25–27, 1980.
7. Hamman, L.: Spontaneous mediastinal emphysema. Bull. Johns Hopkins Hosp. 64: 1–22, 1939.
8. Levin, B.: Continuous diaphragm sign: newly recognized sign of pneumomediastinum. Clin. Radiol. 24: 337–338, 1973.
9. Lillard, R.L., and Allen, R.P.: The extrapleural air sign in pneumomediastinum. Radiology 85: 1093–1098, 1965.
10. Lipinski, J.K., and Goodman A.: Pneumothorax complicating bronchiolitis in an infant. Pediatr. Radiol. 9: 244–246, 1980.
11. MacEwan, D.W., Dunbar, J.S., Smith, R.D., St. Brown, B.: Pneumothorax in young infants: recognition and evaluation. J. Can. Assoc. Radiol. 22: 264–269, 1971.
12. McSweeney, W.J., and Stempel, D.A.: Non-iatrogenic pneumomediastinum in infancy and childhood. Pediatr. Radiol. 1: 139–144, 1973.
13. Moskowitz, P.S., and Griscom, N.T.: The medial pneumothorax. Radiology 120: 143–147, 1976.
14. O'Gorman, L.D., Cottingham, R.A., Sargeant, E.N., and O'Laughlin, B.J.: Mediastinal emphysema in the newborn: review and description of the new extrapleural gas sign. Dis. Chest 53: 301–308, 1968.
15. Rhea, J.T., van Sonnenberg E., and McLoud, T.C.: Basilar pneumothorax in the supine adult. Radiology 133: 593–595, 1979.
16. Stiegmann, G.V., Brantigan, C.O., and Hopeman, A.R.: Tension pneumomediastinum. Arch. Surg. 112: 1212–1215, 1977.
17. Swischuk, L.E.: Two lesser known but useful signs of neonatal pneumothorax, A.J.R. 127: 623–627, 1976.
18. Tjen, K.Y., Schmaltz, A.A., Ibrahim, A., and Nolte, K.: Pneumopericardium as a complication of foreign body

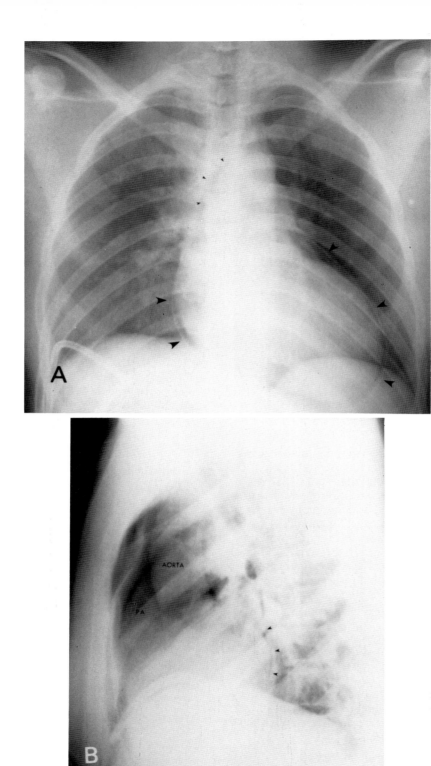

Figure 1.97. *Pneumopericardium.* (*A*) Traumatic pneumopericardium. Note the halo of free air around the heart and the clearly visualized pericardial sac (*large arrows*). Air also extends along the aorta (*small arrows*). (*B*) Note air in the pericardial sac posteriorly (*arrows*), but also note that air clearly outlines both the pulmonary artery (*PA*), and aorta. The pericardium attaches onto the base of the great vessels, and with larger volume pericardial air collections, the aorta and pulmonary artery are outlined by the air.

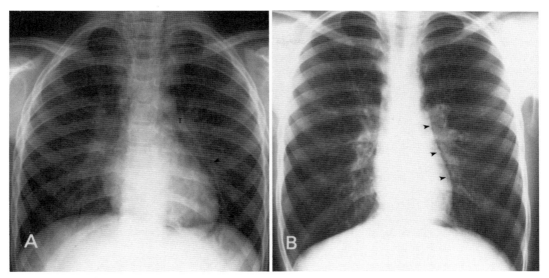

Figure 1.98. *Pseudopneumopericardium.* (*A*) Pneumomediastinum mimicking pneumopericardium. Note what would appear to be the pericardial sac on the left (*arrows*). However, if this truly were the pericardial sac, enough air should be present so that it would surround the entire cardiac silhouette. Furthermore, the thymus gland (*T*) would not be elevated and visualized as a separate structure with pneumopericardium. (*B*) Note what would appear to be free air along the left cardiac border (*arrows*). The artifact is produced by a thin strip of normally aerated lung being projected between the cardiac border and the descending left lower lobe pulmonary artery. In such cases radiolucency of the apparent stripe of pneumopericardial air, is enhanced by the Mach effect.

aspiration. Pediatr. Radiol. 7: 121–123, 1978.
19. Toomey, F.B., and Churnock, R.F.: Subcutaneous mediastinum and pneumothorax in diabetic ketoacidosis. Radiology 116: 543, 1975.
20. Wright, J.T.: The radiological sign of "clicking" pneumothorax. Clin. Radiol. 16: 292–294, 1965.
21. Zahller, M.C., Skoglund, R.R., and Larson, J.M.: Pneumomediastinum associated with diabetic ketoacidosis. J. Pediatr. 93: 529–530, 1978.
22. Ziter, F.M.H., Jr., and Westcott, J.L.: Supine subpulmonary pneumothorax. A.J.R. 137: 699–701, 1981.

PULMONARY CONGESTION AND EDEMA

Pulmonary congestion, and eventually frank pulmonary edema, can arise from a number of cardiac and extracardiac causes. However, before discussing the roentgenographic features of pulmonary congestion and edema, it would be wise to first address oneself to the problem of *pneumonia versus congestion.* Indeed, I suspect that this is the most frequently asked question by the clinician of the roentgenologist. Unfortunately, there is no simple answer to the problem for only through experience comes the solution, but there are one or two points which might be utilized to differentiate the two.

First, one should be aware that problems arising in the differentiation of pulmonary congestion from pneumonia are most frequently encountered in young infants. Almost always the problem is one of differentiating a child with a viral lower respiratory tract infection with an interstitial pattern of infiltration from one with true congestion (25). Indeed, in some of these cases the roentgenographic patterns virtually defy distinction, and if one were to limit the examination to the lung fields alone, it certainly would be nearly impossible to differentiate the two. However, one should look at the heart, too, for if cardiomegaly is present, cardiac disease is most likely, and if it is not, viral pulmonary infection should be one's choice (Fig. 1.99). Of course, it is not quite as simple as this, but the above distinction does represent a good starting point, and thereafter, film reading experience is the answer.

Pulmonary vascular congestion can be divided into two broad groups, active and passive. Active congestion is most often seen with underlying left to right shunts, and thus, its presence virtually assures the possibility that a congenital heart lesion is present. In such cases, more blood flows through the lungs than normal and because of this,

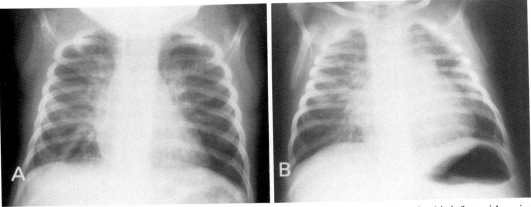

Figure 1.99. *Pneumonitis versus congestion.* (*A*) The parahilar distribution of infiltrates in this infant with a viral lower respiratory tract infection might be mistaken for pulmonary congestion. However, the heart is not enlarged. (*B*) Contrarily the parahilar pattern of pulmonary congestion secondary to heart disease in this patient might be misinterpreted for parahilar peribronchial infiltration, except that the heart is enlarged.

the vessels (the arteries are seen best) enlarge, become more tortuous, and as opposed to normal, are visualized far into the periphery (outer third) of the lung. Once this pattern of pulmonary congestion is appreciated, one can go on to differentiate one lesion from another (37), but a discussion of this is beyond the scope of this book.

Passive congestion, on a purely cardiac basis, infers the presence of a failing left heart and while this can occur with obstructing lesions such as aortic stenosis and coarctation of the aorta, more often it occurs with myocardial dysfunction such as is present with myocarditis, cardiomyopathy, and rheumatic fever. The roentgenographic pattern of passive congestion differs completely from that of active congestion, for as opposed to the latter, the volume of blood flowing through the lungs is not increased. Rather, since pulmonary venous pressures are elevated, blood flow through the lungs is impeded, the pulmonary veins and capillaries distend, fluid (transudate) oozes out into the perivascular interstitium, and an overall fuzzy appearance of the vessels results. Actually, what one is witnessing is the development of interstitial, and then alveolar, pulmonary edema.

Pulmonary edema results from increased permeability of the pulmonary capillaries, either due to increased microvascular pulmonary venous pressures secondary to a failing left heart or direct damage to the vessel wall. In the latter case, pulmonary vascular pressures usually are normal, but in either instance, when fluid first seeps out of the vessels, it accumulates in the pulmonary interstitium. This being the case, one first will note the development of stringy or reticular white lines in the chest, and then, increasing opacity or haziness of the lungs (Fig. 1.100). The white lines represent fluid in the interstitial septa of the lungs and commonly are referred to as Kerley "A" and "B" lines (10). The B lines are the small, transverse lines usually best seen around the costophrenic sulci, while the A lines are the longer lines, generally running outward from the hilar regions. The hazy appearance which eventually develops may at first suggest alveolar fluid accumulation, but actually, it still probably represents fluid in the interstitial space (Fig. 1.101). When diffuse, such haziness must be differentiated from that seen with interstitial viral infections of the lungs (see Fig. 1.6).

Once fluid saturates the interstitium, alveolar pulmonary edema develops. In other words, fluid then oozes out into the alveolar space producing pulmonary consolidations, either patchy and nodular, or lobar (Fig. 1.102*A*). In a few instances, edema fluid collects more in the parahilar regions, leaving the periphery of the lungs relatively clear and producing the typical "butterfly" configuration (Fig. 1.102*B*). In many of these cases, the patchy and asymmetric nature of the infiltrate makes it most difficult to differentiate from widespread pneumonia.

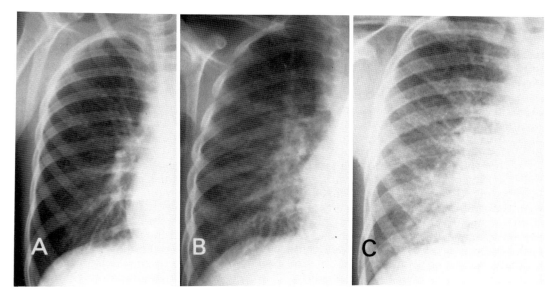

Figure 1.100. *Pulmonary edema—interstitial stage.* (*A*) Note early development of streaky white lines (interstitial septal edema) radiating from the hilar region. In this case, the lines primarily are Kerley "A" lines. This patient had acute glomerulonephritis. (*B*) More extensive reticular pattern of pulmonary interstitial edema in a patient with cardiac failure secondary to aortic stenosis. (*C*) Very extensive interstitial edema producing pronounced reticulation throughout the lung and some underlying parenchymal haziness. Kerley "A" and "B" lines are present. This patient had acute glomerulonephritis.

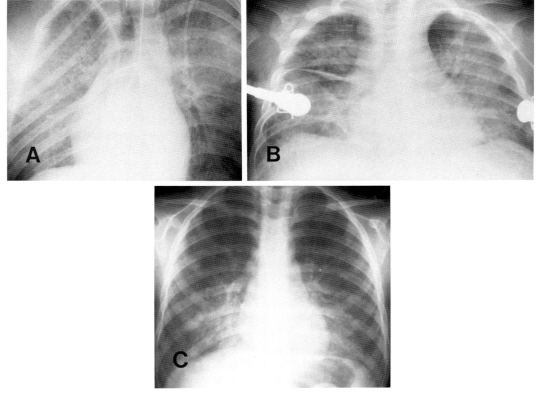

Figure 1.101. *Pulmonary edema; hazy interstitial pattern.* (*A*) Note diffuse haziness throughout both lungs in this patient with diffuse interstitial pulmonary edema. The cause was iatrogenic fluid overload. (*B*) Fluid overload leading to extensively hazy, almost opaque lungs and pleural fluid in the minor fissure on the right. (*C*) Hazy, almost opaque infiltrates confined more to the lung bases. This patient had acute glomerulonephritis.

One of the most common causes of pulmonary edema in childhood is **acute glomerulonephritis** (9, 16, 19, 33). These patients often demonstrate a combination of interstitial and alveolar edema, and overall, the findings frequently first suggest myocarditis with cardiac failure. Indeed, the pattern of congestion, including the presence of Kerley's B lines and pleural effusions, is virtually indistinguishable from that seen with acute myocarditis (Fig. 1.103*A*). At first, this roentgenographic picture may seem a strange one for the disease, but it is more common than generally believed, and actually quite typical. The most likely cause for pulmonary congestion and cardiomegaly in these patients is circulatory overload (hypervolemia) secondary to sodium and fluid retention (19). No cardiac disease has been demonstrated in these patients, and indeed, once the fluid overload is corrected, the chest findings return to normal. Some of these patients may demonstrate a little cardiomegaly, but normal heart size is more the rule (see Fig. 1.101*C*).

It is most important to appreciate this roentgenographic manifestation of glomerulonephritis for not only will it be seen in clinically apparent cases, but it may be the first clue to the diagnosis in clinically atypical patients. I have seen children with little, if any, facial puffiness and peripheral edema, who visit the emergency room for a cough and shortness of breath and whose roentgenograms demonstrate findings typical of glomerulonephritis.

Other causes of pulmonary edema include iatrogenic fluid overload, smoke or hot air inhalation (5, 13, 21, 30, 38), noxious fume inhalation, near drowning (12, 29, 32), neurogenic pulmonary edema secondary to increased intracranial pressure (4, 7, 11, 22), rheumatic pneumonia (33, 34), collagen vascular disease, massive aspiration (17) fat embolism (2, 6, 8, 20), allergic pneumonitis, and the shocked lung syndrome (1, 18, 24–27). In addition, pulmonary edema has been demonstrated with poisoning by the following chemicals or drugs: heroin (15), methadone (38), Librium (31), carbon monoxide (35), and insecticides (3, 14). In many of these conditions, cardiomegaly is minimal or absent, and this finding serves to alert one to the extracardiac origin of the pulmonary edema in these cases. Edema, in such cases, often results from the damaging of capillaries with resultant increased permeability and the extravasation of fluid into the interstitial and alveolar spaces. In other instances, the underlying mechanisms are more complicated or incompletely understood.

Neurogenic pulmonary edema occurs as the aftermath of an acute rise in intracranial pressure, but its precise etiology is incom-

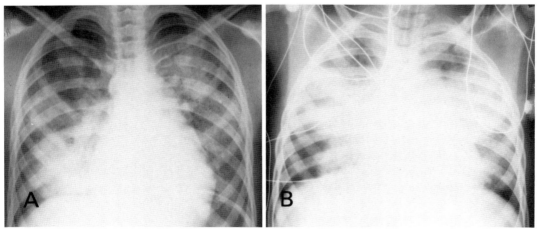

Figure 1.102. *Pulmonary edema—alveolar stage.* (*A*) Note patchy areas of confluent pulmonary alveolar edema throughout both lungs. The apices and costophrenic angles remain relatively clear. The asymmetrical distribution would be difficult to differentiate from widespread pneumonia. (*B*) Another patient demonstrating pronounced parahilar and mid-lung field pulmonary alveolar edema. There is more sparing of the apices and costophrenic angles leading to the typical "butterfly" configuration. This patient was overloaded with fluid during treatment for status asthmaticus.

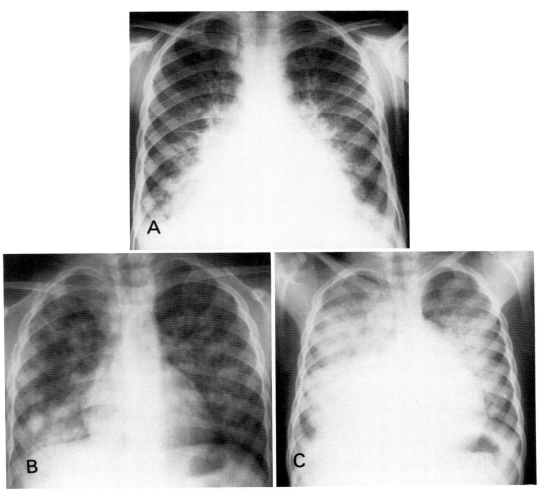

Figure 1.103. *Pulmonary edema—varying causes and configurations.*   *(A) Acute glomerulonephritis.* Note extensive interstitial pulmonary edema, moderate cardiomegaly, and moderate bilateral pleural effusions. The findings would be difficult to differentiate from acute myocarditis with failure. *(B) Near drowning.* Note the extensive fluffy, nodular infiltrates distributed throughout both lung fields. In other patients the infiltrates may be more diffuse or hazy, and less nodular. *(C) Rheumatic pneumonia.* This patient was discharged from the hospital after convalescing from acute rheumatic fever. His heart was near normal in size at that time. Less than 48 hours later he returned with severe dyspnea and this roentgenographic appearance typical of extensive pulmonary interstitial and alveolar edema. Necropsy findings substantiated the diagnosis of rheumatic "pneumonia."

pletely understood. Generally, however, it has been noted that these patients demonstrate bradycardia, peripheral vasoconstriction, lowered cardiac output, and elevated pulmonary venous and arterial pressures (7, 22). Because of this, hydrostatic pressure across the pulmonary capillaries become excessive and fluid extravasates into the surrounding lung tissue. Hyperactivity of the vagus nerve leading to bradycardia and lowered cardiac output has been incriminated as a more basic mechanism in these patients,

but overall, the precise etiology is unclear. Misinterpretation of the roentgenographic findings for aspiration pneumonia is common, for the roentgenographic appearances are similar.

Near drowning is simply a matter of aspirating water into the lungs, and as far as the roentgenographic findings are concerned, it makes little difference as to whether one aspirates salt or fresh water (29). Only the volume is important, for the more water aspirated, the more striking the roentgenographic findings. The chest film in these patients serves as a baseline study, and although it frequently clearly shows the presence of aspirated water and debris (Fig. 1.103*B*), it must be stressed that clinical assessment, with serial blood gas determinations, is more important than judging the patient's condition from the roentgenograms. Fluid aspirated into the lung usually clears quickly.

Pulmonary edema secondary to smoke inhalation or noxious fume inhalation is self-explanatory. However, it should be noted that if smoke or hot air inhalation has caused bronchiolar damage, the chest film may show pronounced air trapping rather than pulmonary edema. These changes may clear after 1 or 2 days and later be replaced by nonspecific infiltrates caused by edema and microatelectasis secondary to pulmonary microembolization (13, 36). In other instances, frank pneumonia may supervene, while yet in other cases, of either hot smoke or noxious fume inhalation, a necrotizing bronchiolitis with widespread infiltrates can develop. Very often these patients go on to rapid demise.

Rheumatic pneumonia often produces startling and widespread changes of pulmonary edema in the lungs (Fig. 1.103*C*) and is a dreaded complication of rheumatic fever. It is presumed to result from local vascular changes and increased capillary permeability secondary to the streptococcal toxin.

Fat embolism with subsequent pulmonary congestion results from the trapping of fat droplets in the pulmonary circulation after they have been dispersed into the blood stream by the fracturing of a long bone such as the femur. However, it is not a common complication in childhood, and overall while many patients with fractures have evidence of fat droplets in the blood stream, only a few develop pulmonary complications.

Shock lung or adult respiratory distress syndrome (18, 26) occurs after profound hypoxia and hypotension and is seen with any number of conditions leading to these complications; i.e., trauma, blood loss, septic shock, neurogenic shock, etc. (18). The roentgenographic findings develop after the shock state has been corrected. The etiology of shock lung is unknown, but a central nervous system origin has been suggested

(23, 24). In addition, local changes such as loss of surfactant, increased cell wall permeability, and small vessel thrombosis also have been considered (28). However, these complications usually occur after the initial episode of pulmonary edema and result in diffuse patchy infiltrates, often misinterpreted for widespread pneumonia. On a chronic basis, interstitial hypercellularity and fibrosis eventually result. Overall, it is the clinical setting and roentgenographic findings which suggest the diagnosis in most cases.

REFERENCES

1. Adrens, J.F.: Shock lung. South. Med. J. 65: 206–208, 1972.
2. Berrigan, T.J., Carsky, E.W., and Heitzman, E.R.: Fat embolism. Roentgenographic-pathologic correlation in 3 cases. A.J.R. 96: 967–971, 1966.
3. Bledsoe, F.H., and Seymour, E.Q.: Acute pulmonary edema associated with parathion poisoning. Radiology 103: 53–56, 1972.
4. Chang, C.H., and Smith, C.A.: Postictal pulmonary edema. Radiology 89: 1087–1089, 1967.
5. Cudmorer, R.E., and Virom, E.: Inhalation injury to respiratory tract of children. Prog. Pediatr. Surg. 14: 173, 1981.
6. Feldman, F., Ellis, K., and Green, W.: Fat embolism syndrome. Radiology 114: 535–542, 1975.
7. Felman, A.H.: Neurogenic pulmonary edema: observations in 6 patients. A.J.R. 112: 393–396, 1971.
8. Goodwin, N.M.: Fat embolus—the post-traumatic syndrome. S. Afr. Med. J. 48: 998–1000, 1976.
9. Gwinn, J.L., and Lee, F.A.: Radiological case of the month. Am. J. Dis. Child. 130: 515–516, 1976.
10. Heitzman, E.R., Ziter, F.M., Markarian, B., McClennan, B.L., and Sherry, H.S.: Kerley's interlobar septal lines: roentgen pathologic correlation. A.J.R. 100: 578–582, 1967.
11. Huff, R.W., and Fred, H.L.: Postictal pulmonary edema. Arch. Intern. Med. 117: 824–825, 1966.
12. Hunter, T.B., and Whitehouse, W.M.: Fresh-water near drowning: radiological aspects. Radiology 112: 51–56, 1974.
13. Kangarloo, H., Beachley, M.C., and Ghahremani, G.G.: The radiographic spectrum of pulmonary complications in burn victims. A.J.R. 128: 441–445, 1977.
14. Kass, J.B., Khamapirad T., and Wagner, M.L.: Pulmonary edema following skin absorption of organo-phosphate insecticide. Pediatr. Radiol. 7: 113–114, 1978.
15. Katz, S., Aberman, A., Frand, U.I., Stein, I.M., and Funlop, M.: Heroin pulmonary edema, evidence for increased pulmonary capillary permeability. Am. Rev. Respir. Dis. 106: 472–474, 1972.
16. Kirkpatrick, J.A., and Fleisher, D.S.: Roentgen appearance of chest in acute glomerulonephritis in children. J. Pediatr. 64: 492–498, 1964.
17. Landay, M.J., Christensen, E.E., and Bynum, L.J.: Pulmonary manifestations of acute aspiration of gastric contents. A.J.R. 131: 587–592, 1978.
18. Lyrene, R.K., and Truog, W.E.: Adult respiratory distress syndrome in a pediatric intensive care unit: predisposing conditions, clinical course, and outcome. Pediatrics 67: 790–795, 1981.
19. Macpherson, R.I., and Banerjee, A.J.: Acute glomerulonephritis: a chest film diagnosis? J. Can. Assoc. Radiol. 25: 58–64, 1974.
20. Marayama, Y., and Little, J.B.: Roentgen manifestations of traumatic pulmonary fat embolism. A.J.R. 79: 945–952, 1962.

21. Mellins, R.B., and Park, S.: Respiratory complications of smoke inhalation in victims of fire. J. Pediatr. 87: 1–7, 1975.
22. Milley, J.R.,Nugent, S.K., and Rogers, M.C.: Neurogenic pulmonary edema in childhood. J. Pediatr. 94: 706–709, May 1979.
23. Moss, G.: The role of the central nervous system in shock: the centroneurogenic etiology of the respiratory distress syndrome. Crit. Care Med. 4: 181–185, 1974.
24. Moss, G., Staunton, C., and Stein, A.A.: Cerebral etiology of the "shock lung syndrome." J. Trauma 12: 885–890, 1972.
25. Munk, J.: The radiological differentiation between acute diffuse interstitial pneumonia and pulmonary interstitial edema in infancy and early childhood. Br. J. Radiol. 47: 752–757, 1974.
26. Ostendorf, P., Birzle, H., Vogel, W., and Mittermayer, C.: Pulmonary radiographic abnormalities in shock: roentgen-clinical-pathological correlation. Radiology 115: 257–263, 1975.
27. Pfenninger, J., Gerber, A., Tshappeler, H., and Zimmerman, A.: Adult respiratory distress syndrome in children. J. Pediatr. 101: 352–357, 1982.
28. Pinet, F., Tabib, A., Clermont, A., Loire, R., Motin, J., and Artru, F.: Post-traumatic-shock lung: post-mortenmicroangiographic and pathologic correlation. A.J.R. 139: 449–454, 1982.
29. Putman, C.E., Tummillo, A.M., Myerson, D.A., and Myerson, P.J.: Drowning: another plunge. A.J.R. 125: 543–548, 1975.
30. Putman, C.E., Loke, J., Matthay, R.A., and Ravin, C.E.: Radiographic manifestations of acute smoke inhalation. A.J.R. 129: 865–870, 1977.
31. Richman, S., and Harris, R.D.: Acute pulmonary edema associated with librium abuse, a case report. Radiology 103: 57–58, 1972.
32. Rosenbaum, H.T., Ghompson, W.L., and Fuller, R.H.: Radiographic pulmonary changes in near-drowning. Radiology 83: 306–312, 1964.
33. Serlin, S.P., Rimza, M.E., and Gay, J.H.: Rheumatic pneumonia: the need for a new approach. Pediatrics 56: 1075–1077, 1975.
34. Singelton, E.B., and Wanger, M.L.: *Radiologic Atlas of Pulmonary Abnormalities in Children*, pp. 237–241. W. B. Saunders, Philadelphia, 1971.
35. Sone, S., Higashihara, T., Kotake, T., Morimoti, S., Miura, T., Ogawa, M., and Sugimoto, T.: Pulmonary manifestations in acute carbon monoxide poisoning. A.J.R. 120: 865–871, 1974.
36. Stone, H.H.: Pulmonary burns in children. J. Pediatr. Surg. 14: 48–52, 1979.
37. Swischuk, L.E.: *Plain Film Interpretation in Congenital Heart Disease*, Ed. 2. Williams & Willkins, Baltimore, 1979.
38. Wilen, S.B., Ulreich, S., and Rabinowitz, J.G.: Roentgenographic manifestations of methadone-induced pulmonary edema. Radiology 114: 51–55, 1975.

PERICARDIAL FLUID AND MYOCARDITIS

Myocarditis and pericardial effusions can occur together, and differentiation of the two may be difficult. However, in their pure forms the major difference between them is that with myocarditis the vascularity is congested, while with pericardial effusion it is not (Fig. 1.104). Of course, if both are present the findings may well overlap. Pericardial fluid accumulations can occur with

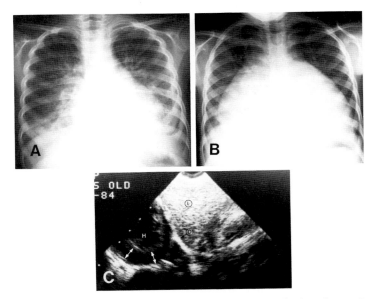

Figure 1.104. *Myocarditis versus pericardial effusion.* (*A*) Moderate generalized cardiomegaly and marked passive congestion of the pulmonary vasculature in this patient with myocarditis. Note, however, that the superior mediastinum, in the region of the aorta and pulmonary artery, is not widened. Bilateral pleural effusions also are present. (*B*) Pericardial effusion producing diffuse globular enlargement of the cardiac silhouette. Note that the superior mediastinum is widened and that the aorta and pulmonary artery are completely obscured. The pulmonary vasculature, however, is not congested. (*C*) Ultrasound study demonstrating pericardial effusion (*arrows*). Heart (*H*), diaphragm (*D*), liver (*L*).

rheumatic fever, viral, bacterial and tuberculous pericarditis, kidney disease (glomerulonephritis and the nephrotic syndrome), collagen vascular diseases, and as hemopericardium with chest trauma (10, 12). Chylopericardium is very rare.

The roentgenographic identification of pericardial effusions of enough volume to cause cardiac enlargement entails the study of the superior mediastinum. When such effusions are present, the great vessel (aorta and pulmonary artery) silhouettes become obliterated, for fluid accumulates in that portion of the pericardial sac which extends over their bases (8). This is, perhaps, the most important roentgenographic finding to detect, for enlargement of the cardiac silhouette is relatively nonspecific. Displacement of the epicardial fat pad has also been described with pericardial effusion (7, 11), but I have found this finding difficult to utilize in most cases, and actually, when one suspects a pericardial effusion one should turn to ultrasonography for diagnosis (1–5, 9). If this modality is not available, isotope studies (6) are helpful, but most often ultrasound equipment is available and diagnostic studies may be readily obtained (Fig. 1.104C).

Myocarditis frequently is of viral origin, but bacterial and even tuberculous infection also can lead to myocardial inflammation. Overall, however, rheumatic myocarditis is the most common form of carditis in childhood. The roentgenographic features of myocarditis with pulmonary vascular congestion are seen in Figure 1.104A.

REFERENCES

1. Abbasi, A.S., Ellis, N., and Flynn, J.J.: Echocardiographic M-scan technique in diagnosis of pericardial effusion. J. Clin. Ultrasound 1: 300–305, 1973.
2. Ellis, K., and King, D.L.: Pericarditis and pericardial effusion. Radiologic and echocardiographic diagnosis. Radiol. Clin. North Am. 11: 393–413, 1973.
3. Feigenbaum, H.: Echocardiographic diagnosis of pericardial effusion. Am. J. Cardiol. 26: 475–479, 1970.
4. Feigenbaum, H., Waldhausen, J.A., and Hyde, L.P.: The ultrasound diagnosis of pericardial effusion. J.A.M.A. 191: 711–714, 1965.
5. Goldberg, B.B., Ostrum, B.J., and Isard, H.J.: Ultrasonic determination of pericardial effusion. J.A.M.A. 202: 927–930, 1967.
6. Kriss, J.P.: Diagnosis of pericardial effusion by radioisotopic angiocardiography. J. Nucl. Med. 10: 233–241, 1969.
7. Lane, E.J., Jr., and Carsky, E.W.: Epicardial fat: lateral plain film analyis in normals and in pericardial effusion. Radiology 91: 1–5, 1968.
8. Soulen, R.L., Lapayowker, M.S., and Cortex, F.M.: Distribution of pericardial fluid: Dynamic and static influences. A.J.R. 103: 583–588, 1968.
9. Soulen, R.L., Lapayowker, M.S., and Gimenez, J.L.: Ech-

ocardiography in the diagnosis of pericardial effusion. Radiology 86: 1047–1051, 1966.
10. Stolz, J.L., Borns, P., and Schwade, J.: The pediatric pericardium. Radiology 112: 159–165, 1974.
11. Torrance, D.J.: Demonstration of subepicardial fat as an aid in diagnosis of pericardial effusion or thickening. A.J.R. 74: 850–855, 1955.
12. Van Reken, D., Strauss, A., Hernandez, A., and Feigin, R.D.: Infectious pericarditis in chidren. J. Pediatr 85: 165–169, 1974.

ASTHMATIC CHILD

The child with asthma comes to the emergency room, not so much for the diagnosis of asthma, but for the diagnosis or exclusion of one of its complications. On a practical basis the problem often boils down to the following: (a) is pneumonia present, and if so, what kind? (b) are there any focal aeration disturbances (i.e., atelectasis or obstructive emphysema), and (c) is there evidence of pneumomediastinum or pneumothorax?

In answer to the first question, that is, "Is pneumonia present?" one should note that, although asthmatic children are more susceptible to lower respiratory tract infections, these more often are viral than bacterial (15, 18–20). This is especially true if increased wheezing accompanies the infections (20), for bacterial infections do not usually cause increased wheezing in asthmatic children (15). There is good reason for this to occur, for bacterial infections usually are parenchymal infections with little in the way of associated bronchitis. Viral lower respiratory tract infections, on the other hand, almost always have a prominent and widespread bronchitic component, and it is this aspect of these infections which predisposes to even more bronchospasm and mucous plug formation, and eventually, more expiratory wheezing. This is not to say that bacterial infections with parenchymal consolidations do not occur in asthma, for indeed they do, but only to emphasize that they are much less common than generally believed. Indeed, most of the time, what is at first suspected to be a parenchymal infiltrate turns out to be an area of segmental atelectasis (Fig. 1.105). Segmental and lobar atelectasis are extremely common in asthma and, once this is appreciated, one will come to the realization that the single most common cause of pulmonary densities on the chest films of asthmatic children is segmental atelectasis secondary to endobronchial mucous plugging and not parenchymal pneu-

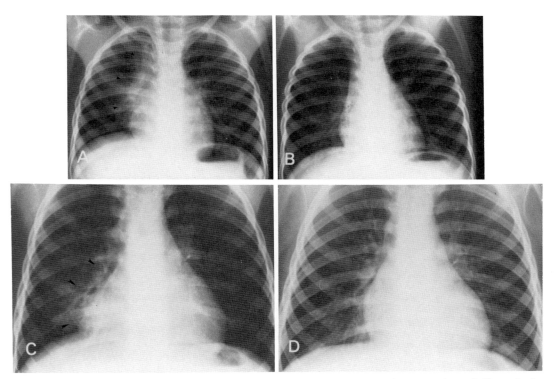

Figure 1.105. *Atelectasis mimicking pneumonia in asthma.* (*A*) Note what would appear to be an infiltrate in the right upper lobe (*arrows*). (*B*) Less than 24 hours later the infiltrate has disappeared. It was due to partial atelectasis of the right upper and middle lobes. Such areas of atelectasis are common in asthma and are frequently misinterpreted for patchy pneumonia. (*C*) Another patient with an apparent right middle lobe infiltrate (*arrows*) which suggests a pneumonia. Also note generalized overaeration. (*D*) Twenty-four hours later the chest film is normal. No pneumonia would clear this rapidly. The findings are due to transient middle lobe atelectasis.

monia (6). Indeed, such changes are much more common in children than adults (30).

In many asthmatic children, a characteristic baseline roentgenogram is seen (6, 8). It consists of widespread overaeration, parahilar peribronchial prominence with bronchial cuffing and overall a picture very similar to that seen with viral lower respiratory tract infections (Fig. 1.106). Indeed, so similar are the findings that it is often difficult to determine whether or not an asthmatic child has a superimposed viral lower respiratory tract infection. All of these findings may at first appear relatively nonspecific, but familiarity with them soon leads to a typical template of the so-called "asthmatic chest" in childhood. Histologically, in these children, there is thickening of the bronchi and peribronchial tissues (9, 10, 24), and bronchographically the following changes have been demonstrated: (a) spasm of the

bronchi at their bifurcations, (b) increased secretions, (c) increased bronchial dilatation, (d) mucosal irregularities and dilated mucous glands, and (e) mucous plugs (25).

It must be noted, however, that not all asthmatic patients show this typical baseline chest appearance. Indeed, there are those who merely show overaeration, and never really develop a pattern of parahilar peribronchial infiltration. It is not completely understood why this should occur, but there is a tendency to ascribe repeated viral lower respiratory tract infections as the cause of the chronic parahilar peribronchial infiltrate. Indeed, so-called chronic bronchitis of childhood (27) may well just be another manifestation of asthma. In addition to these considerations there is the problem of airway hyperactivity (5, 26), a problem at first suggestive of classic asthma, but yet one more of peripheral, small airway broncho-

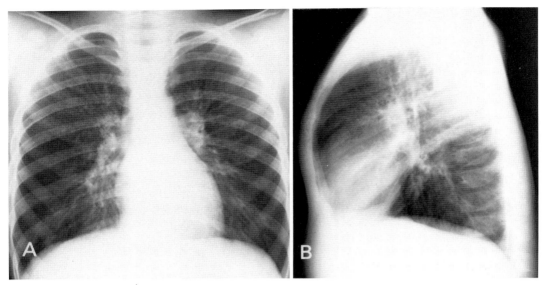

Figure 1.106. *Typical baseline asthmatic chest appearance.* (*A*) Note moderate overaeration, pronounced parahilar peribronchial infiltration, some bronchial cuffing, and hilar adenopathy. (*B*) Lateral view showing overdistended chest. Note how the heart is pushed away from the sternum.

spasm. Indeed, in the long run, often it is difficult to completely separate the two conditions from each other.

The generalized air trapping commonly seen in asthmatic children is, of course, secondary to bronchospasm. During acute attacks such air trapping may be profound, and it is at these times that there is a greater tendency for complications, such as pneumomediastinum and pneumothorax, to occur (2, 11, 12, 14, 16, 17, 21 22). Pneumomediastinum, however, is the much more common of the two (Fig. 1.107, *A* and *B*), and in some of these cases the mediastinal air can leak into the interstitial tissues of the neck and chest wall (Fig. 1.107, *C* and *D*). Most often pneumomediastinum is treated conservatively, but occasionally surgical decompression has been required (16).

Mucous plugs, as has been noted earlier, also are common in asthmatic children and are present whether the children are acutely symptomatic or not (24). However, during acute attacks, or during associated viral lower respiratory tract infections, aeration disturbances produced by these plugs frequently become more striking. Either atelectasis or obstructive emphysema (7) may occur, but atelectasis is probably more common. In their classic forms, neither is difficult to identify, but in other cases the pres-

ence of such problems may not be appreciated until expiratory films are obtained (Figs. 1.108 and 1.109).

Other findings seen in acute asthma include prominence of the pulmonary artery and elongation of the entire cardiac silhouette (Fig. 1.110). The latter finding is explained by the fact that the diaphragm is depressed downward, and the heart is elongated and squeezed by the overdistended lungs. Prominence of the pulmonary artery usually is explained on the basis of pulmonary hypertension secondary to increased pulmonary vascular resistance produced by the profound degree of emphysema and sludging of the blood in the pulmonary arteries (24). In asthma, when the antibody-antigen reaction occurs on the tracheobronchial mucosal surfaces, there is a release of the so-called primary mediators which act on the lung to produce (a) bronchospasm, (b) increased sludging of the blood, and (c) breakdown of the cellular membranes with the exudation of fluid into the interstititium to produce pulmonary edema (24). The various mediators may act in all three ways, but some are better at producing bronchospasm, while others are more effective in promoting sludging of the blood or altering cell wall permeability. This latter manifestation can lead to a picture suggestive of pulmonary

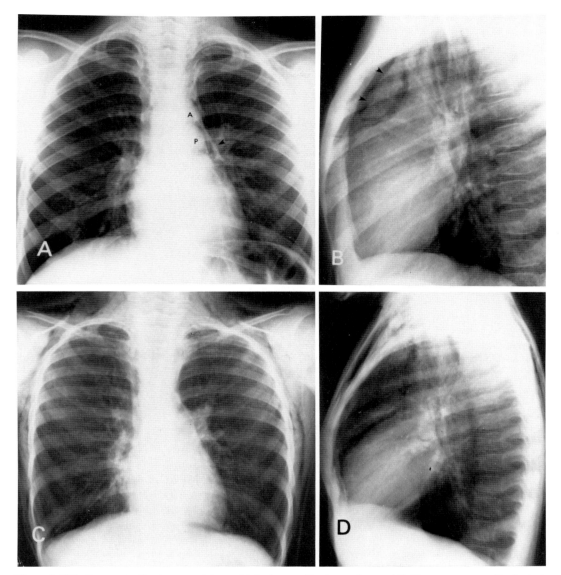

Figure 1.107. *Pneumomediastinum and interstitial air complicating asthma.* (*A*) Note pneumomediastinal air outlining the aorta (*A*), pulmonary artery (*P*), and a slender left thymic lobe (*arrow*). (*B*) Lateral view in another patient demonstrating a small thymus gland (*arrows*) surrounded by pneumomediastinal air. (*C*) Note the typically over distended chest with chronic perihilar peribronchial infiltrates in this child with acute asthmatic attack. A little air is present in the superior mediastinum, but most has escaped into the soft tissues of the neck and chest wall. (*D*) Lateral view—note interstitial air in the soft tissues of the chest wall, both anteriorly and posteriorly. Some air is seen in the mediastinum.

congestion, even to the point of producing Kerley's B lines (23, 24). However, this pattern usually is not seen until initial bronchospasm has been broken, and thus is usually not a presenting picture in the emergency room.

Chronic mucous plugging with superim-posed aspergillosis infection (3, 13, 28) is not particularly common in childhood asthma, but it can occur. In these cases, the mucous plugs can be seen as oval or elongated, sometimes Y-shaped densities in the lung field. Distal to these areas one usually sees focal air trapping and increased lucency of the

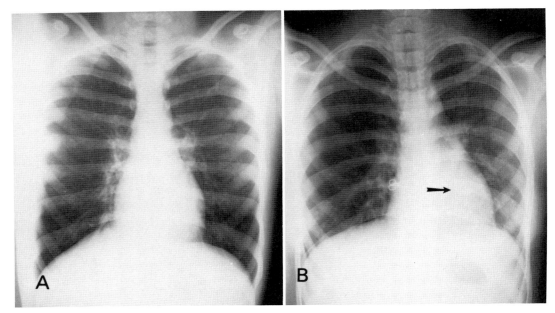

Figure 1.108. *Mucous plug causing unsuspected obstructive emphysema.* (*A*) On this inspiratory chest film, the lungs are markedly overdistended, but apart from this, the roentgenogram would most likely be interpreted as normal. One would not suspect that any focal aeration disturbance was present, and yet as will be seen in (*B*) an obstructing mucous plug is present on the right. (*B*) On expiration, note that the mediastinum has shifted to the left (*arrow*) and that while the left lung has emptied partially, the right lung remains large and radiolucent, attesting to the fact that obstructive emphysema is present. In such cases obstruction is of such a degree that enough air escapes during expiration to keep the obstructed lung from getting overly large.

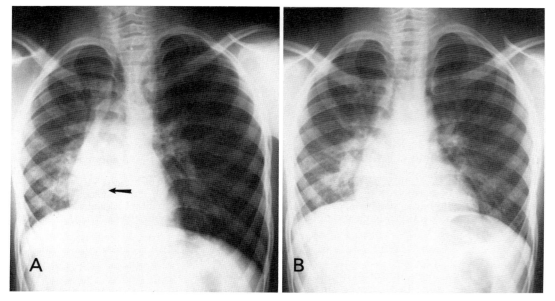

Figure 1.109. *Mucous plug with distracting contralateral compensatory emphysema.* (*A*) On this inspiratory view, there is marked mediastinal shift to the right (*arrow*), and the left lung might be suspected of being the abnormal lung. However, as will be seen in (*B*), it is normal and on this view merely shows compensatory overaeration on inspiration. (*B*) Expiratory films showing that the problem lies on the right. Note that the left lung has emptied but that the right lung has not changed in size on this view. A little mediastinal shoft to the right persists, attesting to the fact that the problem is one of an obstructing mucous plug on the right. The thin radiolucent band outlining the left pericardial border represents a small medial pneumothorax.

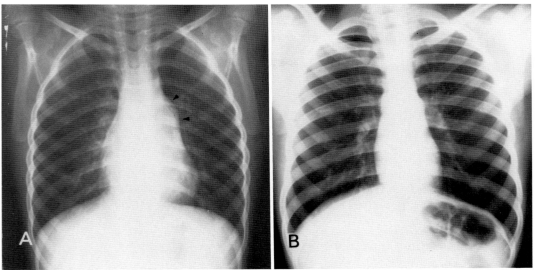

Figure 1.110. *(A) Prominent pulmonary artery in asthma.* Note the prominent pulmonary artery *(arrows)* in this patient with an acute asthmatic attack. This is a common finding in asthmatic children and is a reflection of acute pulmonary hypertension. *(B) Elongated small heart in asthma.* Note the long thin cardiac silhouette in this asthmatic child suffering from status asthmaticus. Such stretching of the heart with resultant smallness of the cardiac silhouette (microcardia) is not uncommon in asthma. If dehydration is present in these patients, it further accentuates the findings of microcardia. Note that in this patient perihilar peribronchial infiltrates are virtually absent and this demonstrates that not all asthmatic children show the degree of perihilar peribronchial infiltration seen in Figure 1.106.

involved lobe. Mucous plugs, without superimposed aspergillosis infection also can be seen (Fig. 1.111). They may be difficult to differentiate from areas of early pneumonia or even small areas of focal atelectasis.

Finally a note might be in order regarding chronic gastroesophageal reflux and asthma (1, 4, 29). Although much publicized in recent years, and probably responsible for a few cases of asthma, the problem probably arises much less frequently than first considered. At any rate, these patients usually are not so much emergency problems as chronic pulmonary problems. On an emergency basis, one is much more likely to see an asthmatic in trouble because of coming into contact with some antigen or contracting a viral lower respiratory tract infection. In addition, there also is the question of hyperactive baroreceptors in the lungs. Indeed this may explain why many asthmatics seem to have more difficulty when barometric pressure is changing rapidly.

REFERENCES

1. Berquist, W.E., Rachelefsky, G.S., Kadden, M., Siegel, S.C., Katz, R.M., Fonkalsrud, E.W., and Ament, M.E.: Gastroesophageal reflux—associated recurrent pneumonia and chronic asthma in children. Pediatrics 68: 29–35, 1981.
2. Bierman, C.W.: Pneumomediastinum and pneumothorax complicating asthma in children. Am. J. Dis. Child. 114: 42–50, 1967.
3. Carlson, V., Martin, J., Keegan, J., and Dailey, J.: Roentgenographic features of mucoid impaction of the bronchi. A.J.R. 96: 947–952, 1966.
4. Christie, D.L., O'Grady, L.R., and Mack, D.V.: Incompetent lower esophageal sphincter and gastroesophageal reflux in recurrent acute pulmonary disease of infancy and childhood. J. Pediatr. 93: 23–27, 1978.
5. Cloutier, M.M., and Loughlin, G.M.: Chronic cough in children: a manifestation of airway hyperreactivity. Pediatrics 67: 6–12, 1981.
6. Eggleston, P.A., Ward, B.H., Pierson, W.E., and Bierman, C.W.: Radiograpic abnormalities in acute asthma in children. Pediatrics 54: 442–449, 1974.
7. Fanburg, B.L., and Mark, E.J.: Hyperinflated right middle lobe in a 15-year-old asthmatic girl. N. Engl. J. Med. 305: 1398–1403, 1981.
8. Gillies, J.D., Reed, M.H., and Simons, F.E.R.: Radiologic assessment of severity of acute asthma in children. J. Can. Assoc. Radiol. 31: 45–47, 1980.
9. Hodson, C.J., and Trickey, S.E.: Bronchial wall thickening in asthma. Clin. Radiol. 11: 183, 1960.
10. Hungerford, G.D., Williams, H.B.L., and Gandevia, B.: Bronchial walls in radiologic diagnosis of asthma. Br. J. Radiol. 50: 783–787, 1977.
11. Jorgensen, J., Falliers, C., and Bukantz, S.: Pneumothorax and mediastinal and subcutaneous emphysema in children with bronchial asthma. Pediatrics 31: 824–832, 1963.
12. Kirsh, M., and Orvald, T.: Mediastinal and subcutaneous emphysema complicating acute bronchial asthma. Chest 57: 580–581, 1970.
13. McCarthy, D., Simon, G., and Hargreave, F.: The radiological appearances in allergic bronchopulmonary aspergillosis. Clin. Radiol. 21: 366–375, 1970.

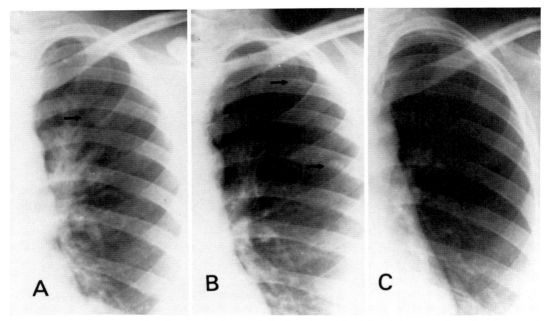

Figure 1.111. *Transient peripheral mucous plugs with focal atelectasis?.* (*A*) Adolescent asthmatic with round nodule in left upper lobe (*arrow*). (B) During another admission the previous nodule disappeared but two new ones appeared (*arrows*). (*C*) At a later date, no nodules are present. These may represent areas of transient peripheral mucous plugging.

14. McGovern, J. P., Ozkaragoz, K., Roett, K., Haywood, T. J., and Hensel, A. E., Jr.: Mediastinal and subcutaneous emphysema complicating atopic asthma in infants and children. Pediatrics 27: 951–960, 1961.
15. McIntosh, K., Ellis, E. F., Hoffman, L. S., Lybass, T. G., Eller, J. J., and Fulginiti, V.A.: The association of viral and bacterial respiratory infections with exacerbations of wheezing in young asthmatic children. J. Pediatr. 82: 578–590, 1973.
16. McNicholl, B.: Pneumomediastinum and subcutaneous emphysema in status asthmaticus, requiring surgical decompression. Arch. Dis. Child. 35: 389–392, 1960.
17. McSweeney, W.J., and Stempel, D.A.: Non-iatrogenic pneumomediastinum in infancy and childhood. Pediatr. Radiol. 1: 139–144, 1973.
18. Minor, T.E., Baker, J.W., Dick, E.C., DeMeo, A.N., Ouellette, J.J., Cohen, M., and Reed, C.E.: Greater frequency of viral respiratory infections in asthmatic children as compared with their non-asthmatic siblings. J. Pediatr. 85: 472–477, 1974.
19. Minor, T.E., Dick, E.C., DeMeo, A.N., Ouellette, J.J., Cohen, M., and Reed, C.E.: Viruses as precipitants of asthmatic attacks in children. J.A.M.A. 227: 292–298, 1974.
20. Mitchell, I., Inglis, H., and Simpson, H.: Viral infection in wheezy bronchitis and asthma in children. Arch. Dis. Child. 51: 707–711, 1976.
21. Ozonoff, M.: Pneumomediastinum associated with asthma and pneumonia in children. A.J.R. 95: 112–117, 1965.
22. Payne, T., and Geppert, L.: Mediastinal and subcutaneous emphysema complicating bronchial asthma in a nine-year-old male. J. Allergy 32: 135–138, 1961.
23. Prossor, I.M., and Thurley, P.: Case report, septal lines in a case of asthma with eosinophilia. Br. J. Radiol. 49: 176, 1976.
24. Reilly, B.J.: Asthma in children. Presented at the Centennial Pediatric Radiology Seminar, Hospital for Sick Children, Toronto, Ontario, Canada, September, 1975.
25. Robinson, A.E., and Campbell, J.B.: Bronchography in childhood asthma. A.J.R. 116: 559–566, 1972.
26. Sibbald, B., Horn, M.E.C., and Gregg, I.: A family study of genetic basis of asthma and wheezy bronchitis. Arch. Dis. Child. 55: 354–357, 1980.
27. Taussig, L.M., Smith, S.M., and Blumenfeld, R.: Chronic bronchitis in childhood: what is it? J. Pediatr. 67: 1–5, 1981.
28. Wang, J.L.F., Patterson, R., Mintzer, R., Roberts, M., Rosenberg, M.: Allergic bronchopulmonary aspergillosis in pediatric practice. J. Pediatr. 94: 376–381, 1979.
29. Winterleitner, H., Eipl, M., Jarisch, R., et al.: Bronchial asthma and gastroesophageal reflux in childhood. Z. Kinderchir. 27: 216–226, 1979.
30. Zieverink, S.E., Harper, A.P., Holden, R.W., Klatte, E.C., and Brittain, H.: Emergency room radiography of asthma: an efficacy study. Radiology 145: 27–29, 1982.

FOREIGN BODIES IN THE LOWER AIRWAY

Small infants are virtual vacuum cleaners, for anything they see goes into the mouth and foreign body aspirations into the airway are as common as ever. Clinically the problem often is clearly apparent, for the aspiration, followed by coughing, gagging, vomiting, varying degrees of respiratory distress, and even cyanosis, all are clearly documented. Interestingly enough, however, these symptoms often subside quickly, and the patient may appear surprisingly well shortly after the acute problem. The reason for this is that the endobronchial receptors, responsible for producing initial symptoms, soon lose their sensitivity and react less to the foreign body (2). However, do not be fooled by this lull in the clinical picture, for the foreign body is still present, and if not detected may lead to the development of recurrent pneumonias or wheezing, suggestive of asthma. Indeed, wheezing in the absence of known pulmonary disease such as asthma should be considered due to a foreign body until proven otherwise.

Once foreign body aspiration is suspected, the roentgenographic workup should be thorough and undertaken immediately. The patterns of aeration disturbance are varied, many are subtle, and many are missed. Indeed, even the experienced observer cannot let his guard down when a foreign body problem is being investigated; every possible clue should be sought for. Of course, if the foreign body is opaque (i.e., teeth, pebbles, metal tacks, etc.), the problem is lessened (11) but most foreign bodies are nonopaque and thus one must rely on an evaluation of disturbances of aeration.

Before embarking on a discussion of these disturbances, a few general considerations might be in order. First it should be noted that there is a difference between tracheal (central) and bronchial (peripheral) foreign bodies. The latter, of course, are much more common (2, 12), and there is a slight preponderance of right bronchial foreign bodies (2, 12). At first, one might expect that the overwhelming majority of aspirated foreign bodies would settle in the right bronchus, but it has been shown that in infants and young children the right and left bronchial angles are rather symmetric, and it is only in the older child and adult that the right bronchus offers a more direct route for aspirated foreign bodies (5). Central foreign bodies located in the trachea, but below the larynx, can be difficult to diagnose and *plain films can be deceptively normal* (Fig. 1.112). The reason for this is that the aeration disturbance is generalized, and not laterized to one or other of the lungs and in this regard the problem more often is underaeration, rather than overaeration, of the chest during inspiration. At the same time there may be paradoxical enlargement of the cardiac and mediastinal silhouettes (4, 8). Ordinarily,

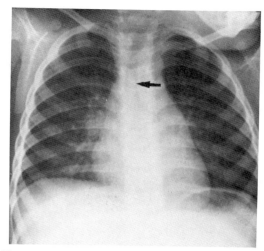

Figure 1.112. *Tracheal foreign body.* This is an inspiratory film and easily could be passed for normal. One might note that the lungs are not as large as one would expect for a full inspiration, but almost always the film would be read as normal. However, a peanut (*arrow*), just barely visible, was present in the trachea. Incidentally, note that the trachea is quite well distended, suggesting that the film is an inspiratory film, and not an expiratory film.

with inspiration, as the lungs deepen and diaphragmatic leaflets become depressed, heart size usually diminishes. However, with central obstruction, be it in the trachea or larynx, intrathoracic pressures become negative during inspiration and the heart and mediastinum enlarge. This certainly is a useful sign, but not one easy to detect on cursory examination.

As far as endobronchial foreign bodies are concerned, a variety of radiologic maneuvers are available for their investigation. These include isotope scanning, xeroradiography, computerized tomography, etc. (1, 7, 9), but plain films usually suffice. Even fluoroscopy usually is not needed. Regarding the plain film changes, the most common roentgenographic finding encountered is obstructive emphysema. In advanced cases such emphysema is not difficult to identify (Fig. 1.113). In such cases, during inspiration, there is enough physiologic dilatation of the bronchus to allow some air to get around the foreign body and enter the lung. On expiration, however, physiologic narrowing of the bronchial tree occurs, and in the presence of an occluding foreign body and associated edema, air is trapped in the lung. These

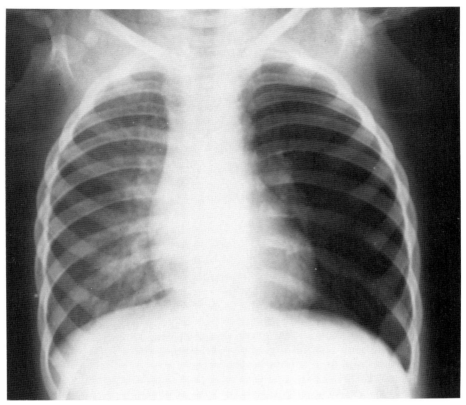

Figure 1.113. *Foreign body in left main stem bronchus with obstructive emphysema.* Note the large hyperlucent, underperfused (oligemic) left lung. Such underperfusion is characteristic with obstructive emphysema and is not seen with compensatory emphysema (i.e., compare with left lung, Fig. 1.109). The mediastinum is shifted to the right, and the left diaphragmatic leaflet is displaced downward. The findings are classic for a check valve foreign body producing obstructive emphysema on the left.

events cycled over and over again eventually lead to obstructive emphysema and overaeration of the involved lung or lobe. In these children, such a lobe or lung appears larger and more radiolucent than the other lung (Fig. 1.113). Largeness is explained on the basis of chronic air trapping, while hyperlucency occurs because more air than normal is present in the lung, and because pulmonary blood flow is diminished in such a lung. Indeed, this latter finding is a hallmark of obstructive, emphysematous overdistention of a lung, and as such can be used to differentiate obstructive emphysema from compensatory emphysema. With compensatory emphysema, although the lung may appear large during inspiration, pulmonary blood flow is not compromised.

In other cases of obstructive emphysema, the findings may not be so obvious. In these

cases, entry and exit of air is abnormal but neither predominates to the point to where frank obstructive emphysema or total atelectasis result. Consequently the lung may be of normal, or near normal size, and it is only during expiration that one notes that the involved lung is not being ventilated. In many of these cases, a clue to the fact that some degree of obstructive emphysema exists is that the pulmonary vascularity, in the involved lung is somewhat diminished (Fig. 1.114). Indeed, a good rule to follow is that the lung with diminished blood flow is the abnormal lung, whether it is large and hyperlucent, or small and hyperlucent. In this regard, another good rule to follow is that the lung which changes shape least, or none at all, between inspiratin and expiration, is the abnormal lung.

Clearly, inspiratory-expiratory film se-

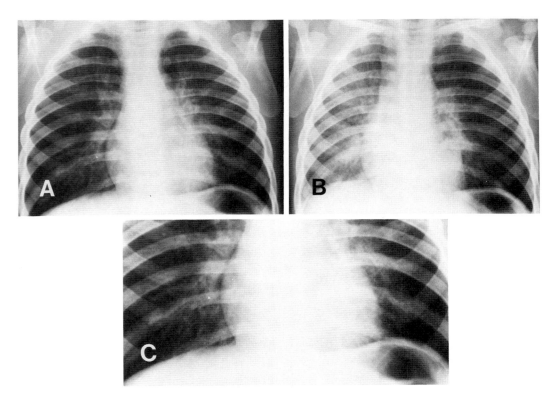

Figure 1.114. *Obstructed lung, subtle findings.* (*A*) On this inspiratory film note that, even though the right lung is a little larger than the left, it is the left lung which shows decreased vascularity. (*B*) Subsequent expiratory film shows that the right lung empties normally (i.e., changes size dramatically), while the left lung retains its original size and does not empty. A foreign body was present in the left main bronchus. (*C*) Coned view of the lung, before the foreign body was removed, demonstrates the decrease in vascularity in the left base to better advantage.

quences are the key to identifying obstructed lungs. However, in some cases one may resort to decubitus films (3), for with lateral decubitus positioning, a normal lung, if it is the dependent lung, empties and becomes smaller (i.e., it is compressed). With an obstructed lung, however, the trapped air prevents it from collapsing and becoming smaller in the dependent, decubitus position (Fig. 1.115). Simply speaking, the obstructed lung acts as an air cushion or inflated balloon, and will not deflate by compression. A somewhat similar mechanism for enhancing visualization of an obstructed lung consists of applying pressure to the pit of the stomach during expiration (13). With this maneuver, termed the assisted expiratory chest radiograph, gentle, but firm pressure to the upper mid-abdomen causes more definitive expiration and tends to bring out the obstructed lung into clearer relief. These points notwithstanding, however, almost always, with

regular inspiratory-expiratory films, one can identify the abnormal lung, and while fluoroscopic examination of the chest may more vividly demonstrate findings such as mediastinal shift away from the obstructed lung, and fixation of the involved diaphragmatic leaflet, seldom is it necessary.

When patchy atelectasis or pneumonic infiltrates are associated with obstructing foreign bodies, they may distract one away from the actual problem. Indeed, it is not unusual for such children to be treated for a presumed pneumonia for a number of days or even weeks, and yet in the final analysis to be determined to have an obstructing foreign body (Fig. 1.116). In other instances, if the foreign body is not recognized, emphysema eventually is replaced by atelectasis (Fig. 1.117), pneumonitis, or even a pulmonary abscess or bronchiectasis. This is especially likely to occur with a foreign body of low irritation such as a piece of plastic,

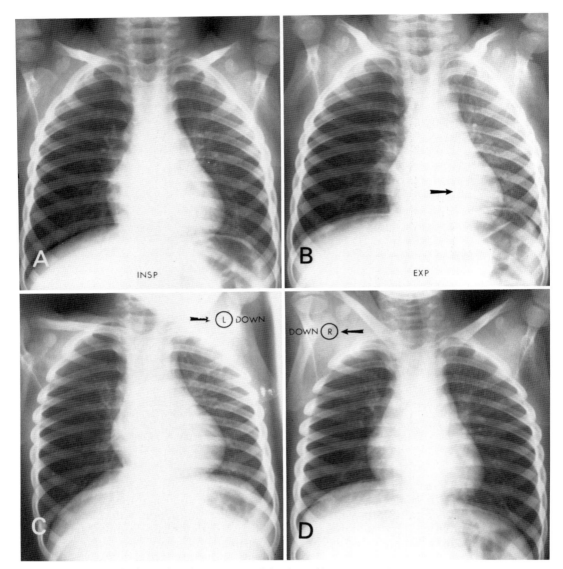

Figure 1.115. *Foreign body—value of expiratory and decubitus films.* (*A*) Inspiratory (*INSP*) view shows a large, hyperlucent right lung. An obstructing foreign body in the right main bronchus should be suspected. (*B*) Expiratory film (*EXP*) accentuates the hyperlucent large right lung. Note how air has emptied from the normal left lung and note also that the mediastinum is now clearly shifted to the left (*arrow*). (*C*) Left lateral decubitus film. The left side is down, and the left lung is partially deflated (compressed). The right lung is relatively overinflated. This is normal in the left side down decubitus position. (*D*) Right lateral decubitus. This time the right side is down and the right lung should have deflated. However, because it is obstructed it remains radiolucent and large (i.e., the presence of obstructive emphysema does not allow it to deflate). Compare its density and size with that of the normally deflated lung in (*C*). The decubitus films in (*C*) and (*D*) are illustrated in the upright position for ease of comparison.

metal, or bone. Peanuts and popcorn, on the other hand, because of their fat content produce a more pronounced and rapidly ensuing local inflammatory reaction. Be-

cause of this, the obstructive problem is accelerated and the patient comes to the attention of the physician sooner.

Foreign bodies which totally occlude a

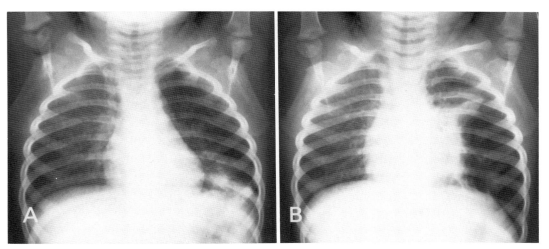

Figure 1.116. *Foreign body disguised as pneumonia.*   (*A*) Note the infiltrate in the left lower lung field. Clinically, pneumonia was suspected. The overaerated left upper lobe was believed to represent compensatory emphysema. (*B*) However, on the next day note how obstructive emphysema has developed in the left lower lobe. There was an underlying foreign body (peanut fragments) in the left lower lobe.

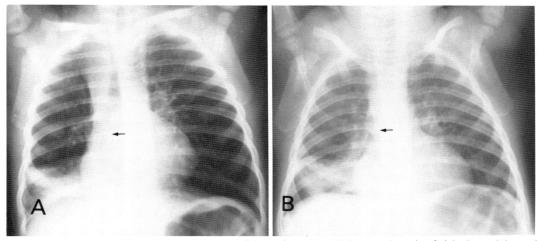

Figure 1.117. *Foreign body producing right lower lobe atelectasis.*   (*A*) Note atelectasis of right lower lobe and compensatory emphysema of the right upper lobe and entire left lung. Also, note tack (*arrow*) in the right main bronchus. If this tack were not seen, a foreign body might not be suspected. (*B*) Expiratory view confirms that compensatory emphysema only was present in the right upper lobe and left lung. Indeed, there is no air trapping anywhere, but atelectasis of the right lower lobe persists, and the tack in the right main bronchus has now moved a little more proximally (*arrow*).

bronchus can produce lobar, or total pulmonary atelectasis (Fig. 1.118). In some of these cases occlusion of the bronchus may occur so rapidly that cyanosis and syncope are surprisingly rapid in onset. In these cases the abrupt mediastinal shift leads to syncope by producing acute kinking and obstruction of the inferior and superior vena cavae, and also by rendering one lung functionless.

Some foreign bodies can produce such gross aeration disturbances that complicating pneumomediastinum and pneumothorax can result. In such cases the roentgenographic findings may be very puzzling for

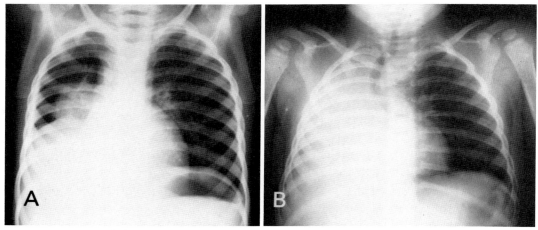

Figure 1.118. *Foreign body causing total massive atelectasis.* (*A*) Note right lower lobe and right middle lobe atelectasis resulting from a long-standing foreign body of low irritation (plastic bottle cap). The findings could be misinterpreted for pneumonia in the right lung. (*B*) Massive, total atelectasis of the right lung. This infant inhaled a pinto bean in the right main bronchus. In less than 60 minutes, total atelectasis of the right lung occurred with pronounced respiratory distress, cyanosis, and syncope.

the presence of mediastinal air often distracts one's attention from the basic underlying problem (Fig. 1.119). These complications can result either from rupture of the lung which is obstructed or rupture of the compensatorily overdistended normal lung.

Finally, it should be noted that not all foreign bodies need remain lodged in any one position for the entire time they are in the tracheobronchial tree. Indeed, some foreign bodies tend to move back and forth at will, and in this regard may even move from one bronchus to another. If this is the case, they will produce confusing clinical and roentgenographic findings. By the same token, one should not be surprised to encounter a patient who, on his own, coughs up the foreign body and becomes symptom-free, even while awaiting initial or further diagnostic studies (Fig. 1.120). Still another peculiarity of endobronchial foreign bodies is that of multiple foreign bodies. Very often the aspirated material has been chewed, or partially chewed and numerous fragments are aspirated. Many times such fragments are small and cause little in the way of additional difficulty, but if the fragments are incompletely chewed, and rather large, diffuse air trapping with numerous peripheral obstructions can be seen (Fig. 1.121).

Most foreign bodies require operative removal, but nonoperative, snare techniques also have been suggested (6, 10).

REFERENCES

1. Berger, P.E., Kuhn, J.P., and Kuhns, L.R.: Computed tomography and the occult tracheobronchial foreign body. Radiology 134: 133–135, 1980.

2. Blazer, S., Naveh, Y., and Friedman, A.: Foreign body in the airway: review of 200 cases. Am. J. Dis. Child. 134: 68–71, 1980.

3. Capitanio, M.A., and Kirkpatrick, J.A.: The lateral decubitus film, and aid in determining air-trapping in children. Radiology 103: 460–462, 1972.

4. Capitanio, M.A., and Kirkpatrick, J.A.: Obstructions of the upper airway in children as reflected on the chest radiograph. Radiology 107: 159–161, 1973.

5. Cleveland, R.H.: Symmetry of bronchial angles in children. Radiology 133: 89–93, 1979.

6. Desautels, J.E.L., Goldstein, A.S., Shaw, D.T., Johns, R.D., and Guichon, D.M.P.: Nonoperative extraction of endobronchial foreign bodies. Radiology 113: 474–475, 1974.

7. Doust, B.D., Ting, Y.M., and Chuang, V.P.: Detection of aspirated foreign bodies with xeroradiography. Radiology 111: 725–727, 1974.

8. Grunebaum, M., Adler, S., and Varsano, I.: The paradoxical movement of the mediastinum. A diagnostic sign of foreign body aspiration during childhood. Pediatr. Radiol. 8: 213–218, 1979.

9. Leonidas, J.C., Stuber, J.L., Rudavsky, A.Z., and Abramson, A.L.: Radionuclide lung scanning in the diagnosis of endobronchial foreign bodies in children. J. Pediatr. 83: 628–631, 1973.

10. Miller, R.E., Cockerill, E.M., and Isch, J.H.: Removal of Intravascular and endobronchial foreign bodies by nonoperative snare technique. Surgery 69: 463–468, 1971.

11. Pochaczevsky, R., Leonidas, J.C., Feldman, F., Naysan, P., and Ratner, H.: Aspirated and ingested teeth in children. Clin. Radiol. 24: 349–353, 1973.

12. Reed, M.H.: Radiology of airway foreign bodies in children. J. Can. Assoc. Radiol. 28: 111–118, 1977.

13. Wesenberg, R.L., and Blumhagen, J.D.: Assisted expiratory chest radiography: an effective technique for the diagnosis of foreign-body aspiration. Radiology 130: 538–539, 1979.

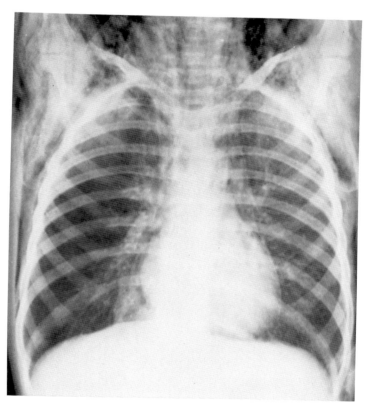

Figure 1.119. *Foreign body with mediastinal and interstitial air.* Note extensive free air in the mediastinum and soft tissues of the neck and chest. So striking are the findings that one might miss the fact that the right lung is a little more radiolucent than the left. The reason for this discrepancy in radiolucency is that a foreign body was present in the right bronchus and the right lung was trapping air. (Courtesy Webster Riggs, M.D.)

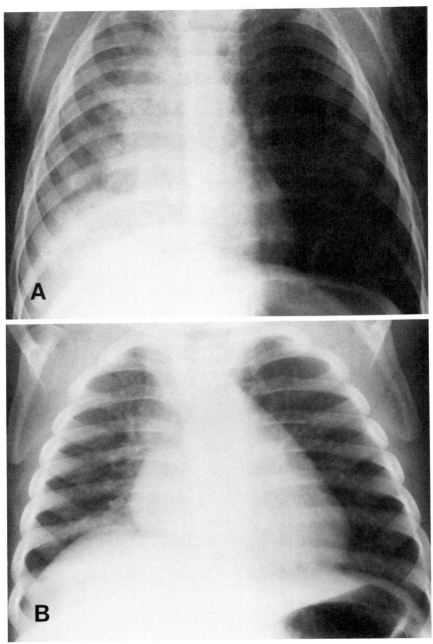

Figure 1.120. *Foreign body—coughed up.* (*A*) Note classic obstructive emphysema of the left lung. (*B*) This patient had a coughing spell and coughed up the foreign body; the left lung now is near normal. However, a little emphysema remains, probably secondary to some residual mucosal edema. This is not an uncommon finding, just after foreign bodies are dislodged or removed.

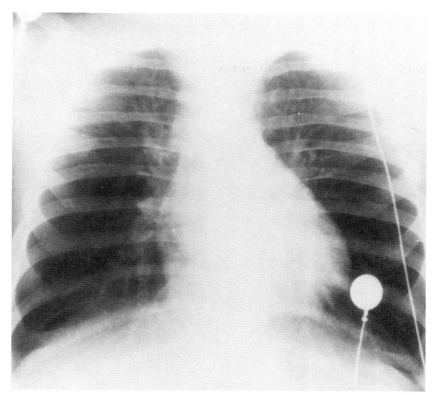

Figure 1.121. *Multiple foreign bodies.* This patient had acute onset of marked generalized wheezing and severe respiratory compromise. History of foreign body aspiration was vague, but the patient's condition deteriorated rapidly and bronchoscopy was performed. Ten or more peanut fragments were found scattered throughout the bronchi of both lungs.

PENETRATING AND NONPENETRATING (BLUNT) CHEST TRAUMA

Blunt chest trauma is more common than penetrating trauma (3), but assessing either is not an easy task. There are many subtle findings to look for, and the thoracic cage, cardiovascular structures, pleural space, and pulmonary parenchyma must be examined quickly and carefully (32). In terms of the thoracic cage, although rib fractures are common, unless they are grossly displaced or multiple, they are not particularly easy to detect on initial films. However, this is not such a great drawback for it is much more important to determine whether complications such as pneumothorax or hemothorax are present (Fig. 1.122, *A* and *B*). In other cases, a rib fracture may be detected by the presence of a local subpleural hematoma (Fig. 1.122 *C*), but most often rib fractures are more easily detected later on, when they are healing.

Rib fractures also aid in directing one's attention to more serious intrathoracic or abdominal injuries. For example, anterior or lateral rib fractures over the lower thoracic area should cause one to look more earnestly for evidence of splenic or liver trauma. Low, posterior rib fractures should alert one to the possibility of underlying renal trauma, and fractures of the first three ribs should obligate one to rule out great vessel injury (11, 13, 25, 41). However, by no means does fracturing of these ribs mean that vascular injury is inevitable, indeed most often it is not present (45). Nonetheless the possibility must be kept in mind, and when searching for rib fractures in this area, one should look for collections of fluid (blood) over the apex of the lung (Fig. 1.123).

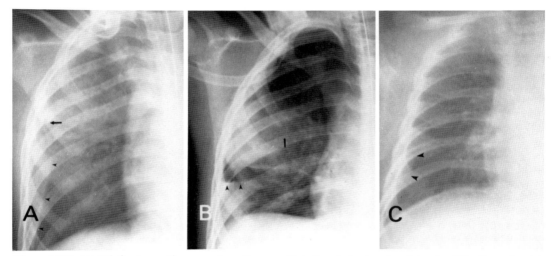

Figure 1.122. *(A) Rib fracture with pneumohemothorax.*   Note the rib fracture involving the fifth rib on the right (*upper large arrow*). Diffuse haziness of the right lung is due to an associated pulmonary contusion. There is blood in the pleural space (*lower small arrows*). (*B*) Upright view showing an air fluid level (*arrows*) substantiating the presence of a pneumohemothroax. The pulmonary contusion is more clearly visualized on this view, and, in addition, fractures of the posterior third, fourth, and fifth ribs now are visible. (*C*) *Rib fracture with subpleural hematoma.* There is a small subpleural hematoma (*arrows*) in this patient who was sat upon by his older sibling. He had chest pain and point tenderness over the area. Although a rib fracture is not visualized, it should be suspected when a subpleural hematoma is identified.

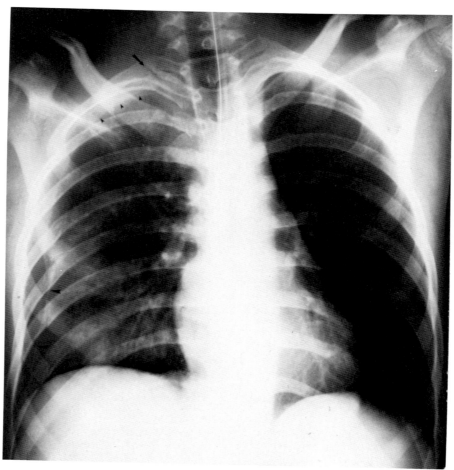

Figure 1.123. *Fracture of the first rib with apical blood.*   Note the fracture of the first rib on the right (*upper large arrow*). Just beneath it note blood over the apex of the right lung (*upper three small arrows*). A pneumothorax also is delineated (*lower arrows*).

Fractures of the sternum are best visualized on the lateral view, and result from blunt trauma to the chest such as occurs with steering wheel injuries or other direct, severe, blows to the chest (Fig. 1.124). Retro- and presternal soft tissue swelling from associated edema and bleeding are commonly noted, but the most important aspect of sternal fractures is that they frequently are associated with underlying cardiac injury. Consequently, if the injury is severe, the cardiac silhouette should be inspected closely, but even more importantly, an ECG should be obtained.

Pulmonary parenchymal manifestations of blunt trauma are numerous and include pulmonary contusion (5, 6, 12, 27, 38, 39, 43, 44), pulmonary hematoma (23, 37, 42), and traumatic pneumatoceles (1, 4, 7–10, 24, 26, 35). Pulmonary contusions produce pneumonic-like areas of homogeneous or nodular infiltrate (Fig. 1.125) which usually become larger and denser during the first 24–48 hours after injury. Pulmonary contusions clear slowly and eventually may contract to the point of suggesting a pulmonary mass. Densities which appear round or oval from the onset probably represent pulmonary hematomas. Usually they are slow to resolve and may cavitate during the course of their resolution (Fig. 1.126).

Traumatic pneumatoceles or air cysts frequently occur with blunt chest trauma and may be seen either in the pulmonary paren-

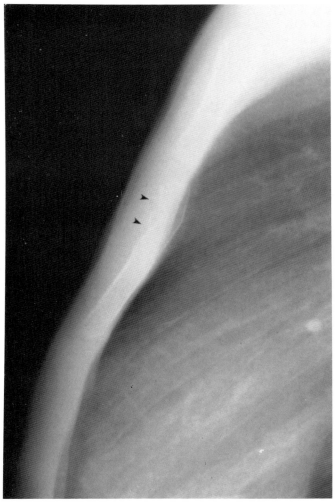

Figure 1.124. *Sternal fracture.*   This patient was wrestling and suffered blunt chest trauma. The sternum is fractured (*arrows*), and there is a little pre- and retrosternal soft tissue swelling.

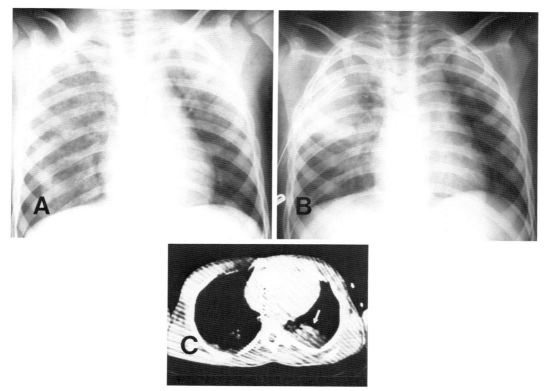

Figure 1.125. *Pulmonary contusion.* (*A*) Note the diffuse nodular infiltrate in the right lung. It is more confluent in the upper lobe. Also note a pneumothorax on the right, and a lesser contusion in the left apex. (*B*) A few hours later note that both contused areas are more consolidated. (*C*) CT scan of pulmonary contusion (*arrows*). A small pleural effusion is present on the other side.

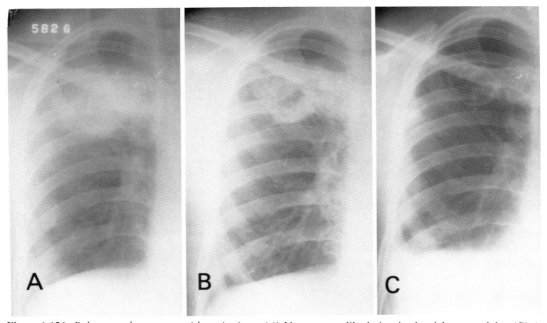

Figure 1.126. *Pulmonary hematoma with cavitation.* (*A*) Note a mass-like lesion in the right upper lobe. (*B*) A few days later, note that a cavity is developing in this hematoma. (*C*) More than a month later, a thin-walled cavity remains. (Reprinted with permission from Fagan, C.J., and Swischuk, L.E.: Traumatic lung and paramediastinal pneumatoceles, Radiology 120: 11–18, 1976.)

chyma or in the mediastinum (7, 9, 10, 19, 26). They usually are seen with other manifestations of pulmonary injury and usually develop within minutes or hours of the injury. These air cysts or pneumatoceles may be round, oval, single, or multiple, and some may contain blood (Fig. 1.127). Generally they are thin-walled and may increase in size rather rapidly after they first appear. Similar air collections in the mediastinum tend to be more elongated and paraspinal in position (Fig. 1.128). These air collections are believed to lie in the inferior pulmonary ligament (9, 10, 26), although similar collections can occur in the retroesophageal ligament. Overall, traumatic pneumatoceles are relatively innocuous for seldom do they rupture or become infected. For the most part, they slowly become smaller and disappear over a 2–3-week period. To the uninitiated, however, they frequently constitute a problem of distraction from other potentially more serious problems which might also be present.

More catastrophic injuries to the respiratory system include bronchial and tracheal fracture or tear, and torsion of the lung (2, 3, 5, 6, 16, 17, 21, 27, 34). Torsion of the lung, with subsequent infarction, is often difficult to diagnose roentgenographically, but it has been pointed out that since such a lung makes a 180° turn around its hilus, the vascular pattern of the upper and lower lobes is inverted (27). This finding, however, first requires awareness of its existence and then close scrutiny of the roentgenogram for its presence.

With *bronchial fracture* one may see massive pneumothorax and/or massive atelectasis (Fig. 1.129*A*), and indeed, with blunt chest trauma, *massive atelectasis should be presumed secondary to bronchial fracture until proven otherwise.* With tracheal lacerations, pneumomediastinum is more common than pneumothorax, and if bleeding occurs into the mediastinum, it will appear widened. When a pneumothorax results from a bronchial tear, it usually is massive, and when the lung is completely detached from its bronchus, upright views will show it to fall to the bottom of the hemithorax (6) (Fig. 1.129*B*). In other cases of bronchial fracture, the air column in the proximal portion of the fractured bronchus appears tapered or beveled, and in still other in-

stances, air may be seen tracking along the bronchial or tracheal wall itself (17, 27). If bleeding also occurs, fluid will be seen in the hemithorax. Unfortunately, however, many cases of fractured bronchi are cases of incomplete fracture, and neither atelectasis nor pneumothorax are present at the onset. It is only later when a frank tear occurs that these complications develop.

Cardiovascular manifestations of blunt chest trauma also are varied and include bloody or serious pericardial effusions, myocardial contusions, and traumatic aneurysms of the heart or aorta. Of course, in the more severe cases, frank tears or ruptures of these latter structures can occur (11, 31, 33, 36). In addition, aortic insufficiency, associated with traumatic aneurysms of the ascending aorta can be encountered (28). Minimial myocardial injuries are best detected with electrocardiograms, or, with myocardial scans using technetium-99m labeled pyro- or polyphosphate (15). Such myocardial injuries are not detectable roentgenographically, but with more extensive contusions nonspecific cardiomegaly will be seen. Pericardial effusions, if large enough, produce enlargement of the cardiac silhouette, but with smaller volume effusions ultrasonography is the diagnostic procedure of choice (see Fig. 1.104*C*).

Injury to the aorta and great vessels is most important to detect, but often the resultant roentgenographic findings have a tendency to elude one's initial observation. Because of this, one must constantly be on guard for signs of superior mediastinal widening (29, 30) or the collecting of blood over the apex of the left lung (Fig. 1.130*A*). This latter finding has been termed the left apical extrapleural cap sign (33), and results from leaking of blood from a ruptured aortic arch into the pleural space over the left lung. There is a normal defect in the pleural covering over the aorta in this area (transverse arch), and mediastinal blood can track directly into the left apical pleural space. The finding is subtle but important, and should be sought for with diligence. Unfortunately, however, it is not always present, and also can be seen with nonaortic trauma. For this reason it is not specific, but in combination with other signs of aortic rupture, especially mediastinal widening (29, 30), should be treated with considerable suspicion. There-

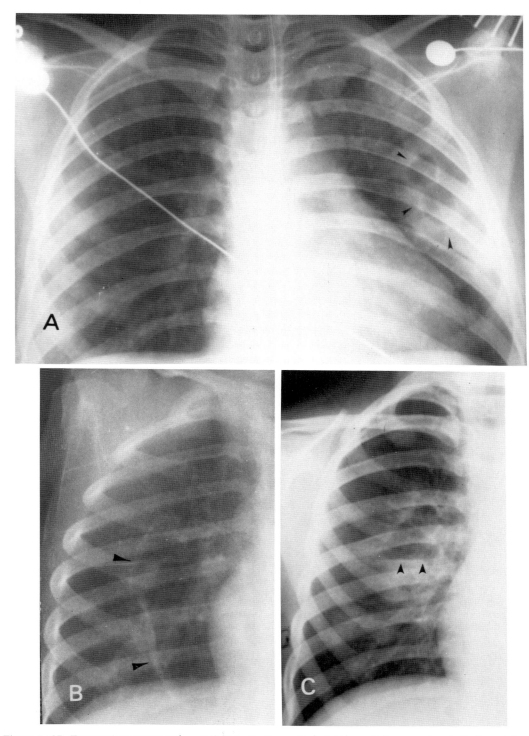

Figure 1.127. *Traumatic pneumatoceles.* (*A*) Note the two spherical, thin-walled pneumatoceles in the contused left lung of this child who was run over by a truck. (*B*) Large post-traumatic pneumatocele on the right side (*arrows*). (*C*) Another patient with a traumatic pneumatocele demonstrating an air-fluid level (*arrows*) on upright view. The air-fluid level represents air and blood in the pneumatocele. (Reprinted with permission from Fagan, C.J., and Swischuk, L.E.: Traumatic lung and paramediastinal pneumatoceles, Radiology 120: 11–18, 1976.)

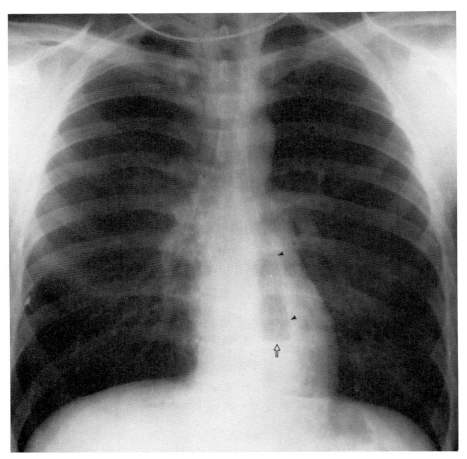

Figure 1.128. *Traumatic pneumatocele in inferior pulmonary ligament.*   Note the characteristic elongated, paraspinal air collection (*small arrows*) characteristic of a pneumatocele in the inferior pulmonary ligament. The *lower arrow* points to an air-fluid (blood) level. (Reprinted with permission from Fagan, C.J., and Swischuk, L.E.: Traumatic lung and paramediastinal pneumatoceles, Radiology 120: 11–18, 1976.)

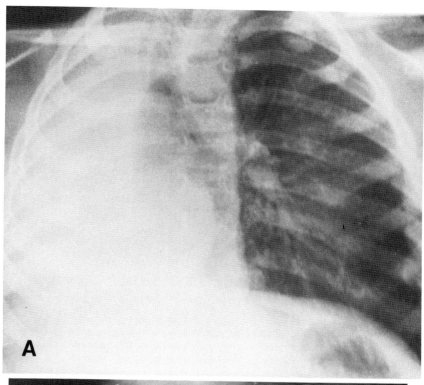

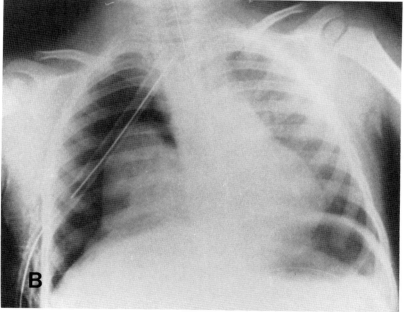

Figure 1.129. *(A) Bronchial rupture.* Note total atelectasis of the right lung. Rib fractures are present on the other side. (Reprinted with permission from Mahboubi, S., and O'Hara, A.E.: Bronchial rupture in children following blunt chest trauma, Pediatr. Radiol. 10: 133–138, 1981.) *(B) Avulsion of the bronchus.* Note the massive pneumothorax and collapsed, dropped right lung. (Reprinted with permission from Grover, F.L., et al.: Diagnosis and management of major tracheobronchial injuries, Ann. Thorac. Surg. 28: 385–391, 1979.)

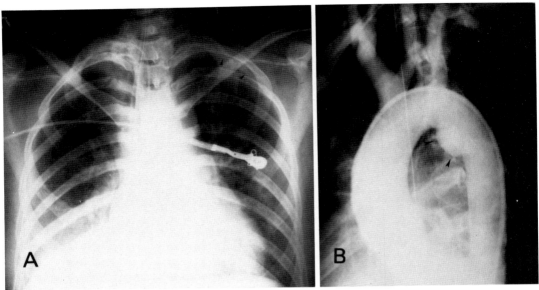

Figure 1.130. *Traumatic aortic aneurysm.* (*A*) Note a collection of fluid over the left lung apex (*arrows*). This is the apical cap sign. The superior mediastinum is widened. Also note rib fractures of the right upper ribs and pleural fluid over the apex of the right lung. There is a fracture through the body of the left scapula. Note that the endotracheal and esophageal tubes are shifted to the right. These findings substantiate the fact that a mediastinal hematoma is present. (*B*) Subsequent aortogram demonstrates traumatic aortic aneurysm (*arrows*).

after, if aortic or great vessel injury is suspected, immediate aortography is required (Fig. 1.130). Mediastinal widening as it is seen with aortic rupture must be differentiated from widening secondary to the presence of normal thymus and supine positioning. Most injured patients are examined in the supine position and the superior mediastinum may appear wide. In this regard it has been noted (14, 40) that with widening due to aortic rupture the trachea and esophagus are displaced to the right (Fig. 1.130). If widening is due to thymus gland and supine positioning, these structures are not displaced to the right (Fig. 1.131). This is an important observation to make and frequently is facilitated by the fact that these patients have indwelling tubes in either the trachea or esophagus, or in both of these structures.

Pneumopericardium is not particularly common with blunt chest trauma but does occur. It is, of course, more common with penetrating wounds to the chest, and roentgenographically it is identified by air surrounding the cardiac silhouette. In these cases the pericardium itself is usually visible, and it is most important than a pneumoper-

icardium not be confused with a medial pneumothorax or pneumomediastinum (see Fig. 1.97). An uncommon injury is rupture of the pericardium. In such cases the heart is displaced or dislocated to the left (20), and because of this the findings resemble those seen with unilateral congenital absence of the left pericardium, or shifting of the heart to the left by a pronounced pectus excavatum deformity of the chest.

Penetrating injuries to the chest, heart, and great vessels can produce all of the findings seen with closed (blunt) chest trauma, but in addition, one can see air in the heart and great vessels (Fig. 1.132). Delayed complications such as cardiac or great vessel tears with hemopericardium also can be encountered (18), and with metallic foreign bodies such as bullets one may see the bullet in one of the chambers of the heart or great vessels. In other instances, the bullet may be lodged in the mediastinum, lung, or spine (Fig. 1.132).

REFERENCES

1. Blane, C.E., White, S.J., Wesley, J.R., et al.: Immediate traumatic pulmonary pseudocyst formation in children. Surgery 90: 872–875, 1981.
2. Burke, J.F.: Early diagnosis of traumatic rupture of the

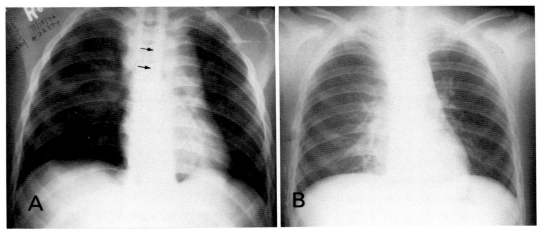

Figure 1.131. *Widened superior mediastinum and pleural fluid but no traumatic aortic aneurysm.* (*A*) Note that there is a pneumothorax on the right and that there is blood layered over the apex of the left lung. The superior mediastinum is widened but note that the tube in the esophagus is in a normal location (*arrows*). It is not shifted to the right, and thus a mediastinal hematoma should not be present. (*B*) Repeat film the next day in upright position shows persistence of the right pneumothorax but a normal appearing superior mediastinum. Some fluid is still present on the left. The findings in (*A*) were due to supine positioning.

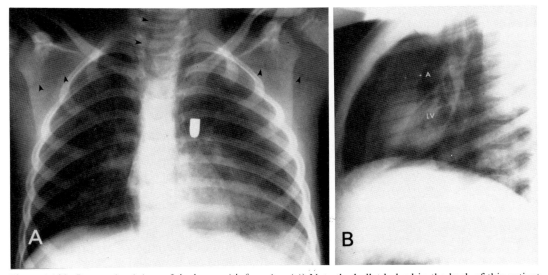

Figure 1.132. *Penetrating injury of the heart with free air.* (*A*) Note the bullet lodged in the back of this patient. Also note; (a) contusion of the left lung, (b) air in the heart, (c) air in the pericardium (best seen on the right), and (d) air in the subclavian and carotid arteries (*upper arrows*). (*B*) Lateral view demonstrates air in the left ventricle (*LV*) and aorta (*A*). The patient expired shortly. The bullet is not seen on this view but was lodged in the soft tissues of the back. (Courtesy of Virgil B. Graves, M.D., Great Falls, Montana.)

bronchus. J.A.M.A. 181: 682–686, 1962.
3. Chesterman, J.T., and Satsangi, P.N.: Rupture of the trachea and bronchi by closed injury. Thorax 21: 21–27, 1966.
4. Cochlin, D.L., and Shaw, M.R.P.: Traumatic lung cysts following minor blunt chest trauma. Clin. Radiol. 29: 151–154, 1978.
5. Cohn, R.: Nonpenetrating wounds of the lungs and bronchi. Surg. Clin. North Am. 52: 585–595, 1972.
6. Crawford, W.: Pulmonary injury in thoracic and nontho-

racic trauma. Radiol. Clin. North Am. 11: 527–541, 1973.
7. Elyaderani, M.K., and Gabriele, O.F.: Traumatic paramediastinal air cysts. Br. J. Radiol 52: 458–460, 1979.
8. Fagan, C.J.: Traumatic lung cyst. A.J.R. 97: 186–193, 1966.
9. Fagan, C.J., and Swischuk, L.E.: Traumatic lung and paramediastinal pneumatoceles. Radiology 120: 11–18, 1976.
10. Felman, A.H., Rogers, B.M., and Talbert, J.L.: Traumatic mediastinal air cyst. A case report. Pediatr. Radiol. 4: 120–121, 1976.
11. Fishbone, G., Robbins, D.I., Osborn, D.J., et al.: Trauma

to the thoracic aorta and great vessels. Radiol. Clin. North Am. 11: 543–554, 1973.

12. Freed, T.A., Neal, M.P., Jr., and Vinik, M.: Roentgenographic findings in extracardiac injury secondary to blunt chest automobile trauma. A.J.R. 104: 424–432, 1968.

13. Galbraith, N.F., Urschel, H.C., Jr., and Wood, R.E., et al.: Fracture of the first rib associated with laceration of the subclavian artery. J. Thorac. Cardiovasc. Surg. 65: 649–652, 1973.

14. Gerlock, A.J., Jr., Muhletaler, C.A., Coulam, C.M., and Hayes, P.T.: Traumatic aortic aneurysm: validity of esophageal tube displacement sign. A.J.R. 135: 713–718, 1980.

15. Go, R.T., Doty, D.B., Chiu, C.L., and Christie, J.H.: A new method of diagnosing myocardial contusion in man by radionuclide imaging. Radiology 116: 107–110, 1975.

16. Grover, F.L., Ellestad, C., Arom, K.V., Root, H.D., Cruz, A.B., and Trinkle, J.K.: Diagnosis and management of major tracheobronchial injuries. Ann. Thorac. Surg. 28: 385–391, 1979.

17. Harvey-Smith W., Bush, W., and Northrop, C.: Traumatic bronchial rupture. A.J.R. 134: 1189–1193, 1980.

18. Hirsch, M., Gueron, M., Moses, S., and Merin, G.: Delayed hemopericardium following penetrating foreign body into the aorta. Pediatr. Radiol. 3: 111–113, 1975.

19. Hyde, I.: Traumatic paramediastinal air cysts. Br. J. Radiol. 44: 380–383, 1971.

20. Kermond, A.J.: The dislocated heart: an unusual complication of major chest injury. Radiology 119: 59–60, 1976.

21. Lynn, R.B., and Iyengar, K.: Traumatic rupture of the bronchus. Chest 61: 81–83, 1972.

22. Mahboubi, S., and O'Hara, A.E.: Bronchial rupture in children following blunt chest trauma. Pediatr. Radiol. 10: 133–138, 1981.

23. Parsai, D., Nussle, D., and Cuendet, A.: Presentation of two cases of pulmonary hematoma in child after closed chest trauma, and review of literature. Ann. Radiol. 17: 831–836, 1974.

24. Pearl, M., Milstein, M., and Rook, G.D.: Pseudocyst of the lung due to traumatic nonpenetrating lung injury. J. Pediatr. Surg. 8: 967–968, 1973.

25. Pierce, G., Maxwell, J., and Boggan, M.: Special hazards of 1st rib fractures. J. Trauma 15: 264–267, 1975.

26. Ravin, C., Smith, G.W., Lester, P.D., McLoud, T.C., and Putman, C.E.: Post-traumatic pneumatocele in the inferior pulmonary ligament. Radiology 121: 39–41, 1976.

27. Reynolds, J., and Davis, J.T.: Injuries of the chest wall, pleura, lungs, bronchi, and esophagus. Radiol. Clin. North Am. 4: 383–401, 1966.

28. Rowland, T.W.: Traumatic aortic insufficiency in children: case report and reviews of the literature. Pediatrics 60: 893–895, 1977.

29. Sefczek, D.M., Sefczek, R.J., and Deeb, Z.L.: Radiographic signs of acute traumatic rupture of the thoracic aorta. A.J.R. 141: 1259–1262, 1983.

30. Seltzer, S.E., Orsi, C.D., Kirshner, R., and DeWeese, J.A.: Traumatic aortic rupture: plain radiographic findings. A.J.R. 137: 1011–1014, 1981.

31. Sherbon, K.J.: Traumatic rupture of the thoracic aorta—the radiologist's responsibility. Aust. Radiol. 19: 164–171, 1975.

32. Shulman, H.S., and Samuels, T.H.: The radiology of blunt chest trauma. J. Can. Assoc. Radiol. 34: 204–217, 1983.

33. Simeone, J.F., Minagi, H., and Putman, C.E.: Traumatic disruption of the thoracic aorta: significance of the left apical extrapleural cap. Radiology 117: 265–268, 1975.

34. Smyth, B.T.: Chest trauma in children. J. Pediatr. Surg. 14: 41–47, 1979.

35. Sorsdahl, O.A., and Powell, J.W.: Cavitary pulmonary lesions following non-penetrating chest trauma in children. A.J.R. 95: 118–124, 1965.

36. Soulen, R.L., and Freeman, E.: Radiologic evaluation of traumatic heart disease. Radiol. Clin. North Am. 19: 285–297, 1971.

37. Specht, D.E.: Pulmonary hematoma. Am. J. Dis. Child. 111: 559–563, 1966.

38. Stephens, E., and Templeton, A.W.: Traumatic nonpenetrating lung contusion. Radiology 85: 247–252, 1965.

39. Ting, Y.M.: Pulmonary parenchymal findings in blunt trauma to the chest. A.J.R. 98: 343–349, 1966.

40. Tisnado, J., Tsai, F.Y., Als, A., and Roach, J.F.: A new radiographic sign of acute traumatic rupture of the thoracic aorta: displacement of the nasogastric tube to the right. Radiology 125: 603–608, 1977.

41. Weiner, D.S., and O'Dell, H.W.: Fractures of the first rib associated with injuries to the clavicle. J. Trauma 9: 412–422, 1969.

42. Williams, J.R., and Bonte, F.J.: Pulmonary hematoma secondary to non-penetrating injury. South. Med. J. 55: 622–625, 1962.

43. Williams, J.R., and Bonte, F.J.: Pulmonary damage in non-penetrating chest injuries. Radiol. Clin. North Am. 1: 439–448, 1963.

44. Williams, J.R., and Stembridge, V.A.: Pulmonary contusion secondary to non-penetrating chest trauma. A.J.R. 91: 284–290, 1964.

45. Woodring, J.H., Fried, A.M., Hatfield, D.R., Stevens, R.K., and Todd, E.P.: Fractures of first and second ribs: predictive value for arterial and bronchial injury. A.J.R. 138: 211–215, 1982.

MISCELLANEOUS CHEST PROBLEMS

Hydrocarbon Pneumonitis. The most commonly ingested hydrocarbons include furniture polish, gasoline, kerosene, and charcoal lighter fluid, and the most important aspect of these hydrocarbons is that, the lower their viscosity and surface tension, the greater is the likelihood that they will be aspirated into the tracheobronchial tree. In this regard, it is mineral seal oil in certain furniture polishes which causes most of the difficulty, for it is one of the lightest of hydrocarbon distillates (13, 14). Consequently, an infant does not have to aspirate a large volume of a hydrocarbon containing mineral seal oil to be in serious difficulty.

There still is some controversy as to whether the pneumonitis resulting from ingestion of hydrocarbons occurs because of aspiration or because of absorption of the hydrocarbon from the stomach, but most authorities now favor aspiration as the major mechanism (6, 12, 14, 15). Although a small amount of the hydrocarbon probably is absorbed from the gastrointestinal tract into the blood stream, it is not enough to explain the pulmonary changes. It may explain the cerebral depression that some of these children demonstrate after such ingestions, but unless the ingestion is massive, damage to the lungs from hydrocarbons circulating in the blood stream is negligible.

Characteristically, in hydrocarbon ingestion, roentgenographic pulmonary changes are absent for the first 6–12 hours, that is, unless massive volumes are aspirated. Consequently, a normal chest film during this lag period can be misleading, and indeed, it is much more important to evaluate the patient clinically and to obtain blood gas values early. Often they will be abnormal, for the local effects of lipid disolution and cell membrane destruction occur rapidly, and hyperemia, edema, bronchial or bronchiolar necrosis, peribronchial edema, small vessel thromboses, and necrotizing bronchopneumonia soon develop (6). It is also likely that the hydrocarbon, because it is a lipid solvent, also destroys surfactant (6, 7), and as such leads to microatelectasis of the al-veoli and further problems with gas exchange.

After the usual clear lung period, infiltrates quickly develop in the lung bases, medially (Fig. 1.133). This characteristic location in itself supports aspiration as the cause of hydrocarbon pneumonitis and the changes can range from minimal fluffy infiltrates to dense, streaky, nodular or confluent infiltrates involving a good portion of the lungs bilaterally. In the latter cases, focal emphysema and pneumatocele formation (Fig. 1.134) are not uncommon and most likely result from air trapping by the damaged small bronchi and bronchioles (1–3, 10, 11). All of these changes are slow to

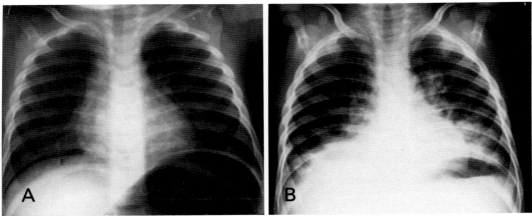

Figure 1.133. *Hydrocarbon pneumonitis.*   (*A*) This patient aspirated red furniture polish, but 2 hours after ingestion, the lungs are clear. (*B*) By 12 hours, note extensive, typical infiltrates in the lung bases medially.

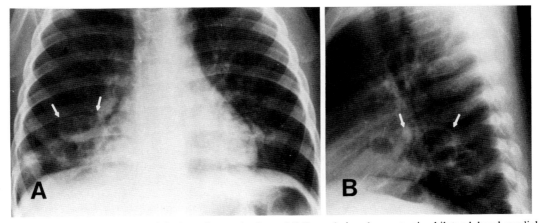

Figure 1.134. *Pneumatoceles with hydrocarbon aspiration.*   (*A*) Frontal view demonstrating bilateral, basal, medial infiltrates and pneumatoceles in the right base (*arrows*). (*B*) Lateral view demonstrates these pneumatoceles to better advantage (*arrows*).

clear, often taking up to 2–3 weeks to completely disappear (4, 6, 8, 14). Indeed long-term pulmonary function abnormalities have been noted in some patients (9).

One other roentgenographic finding has recently been described in the early stages of hydrocarbon ingestion, and that is the double gastric fluid level. This sign was described with kerosene ingestion (5) and results from the fact that kerosene floats on top of the gastric secretions and appears as a more radiolucent fluid layer. Consequently, the presence of both liquids can be identified, but I have not been able to personally witness this finding.

REFERENCES

1. Baghassarian, O.M., and Weiner, S.: Pneumatocele formation complicating hydrocarbon pneumonitis. A.J.R. 95: 104–111, 1965.
2. Bergeson, P.S., Hales, S.W., Lustgarten, M.D., and Lipow, H.W.: Pneumatoceles following hydrocarbon ingestion. Am. J. Dis. Child. 129: 49–54, 1975.
3. Campbell, J.B.: Pneumatocele formation following hydrocarbon ingestion. Am. Rev. Respir. Dis. 101: 414–418, 1970.
4. Daeschner, C.W., Jr., Blattner, R.J., and Collins, V.P.: Hydrocarbon pneumonitis. Pediatr. Clin. North Am. 4: 243–253, 1957.
5. Daffner, R.H., and Jiminez, J.P.: The double gastric fluid level in kerosene poisoning. Radiology 106: 383–384, 1973.
6. Eade, N.R., Taussig, L.M., and Marks, M.I.: Hydrocarbon pneumonitis. Pediatrics 54: 351–357, 1974.
7. Giamonna, S.T.: Effects of furniture polish on pulmonary surfactant. Am. J. Dis. Child. 113:6: 658–663, 1967.
8. Griffin, J.W., Daeschner, C.W., Collins, V.P., and Eaton, W.L.: Hydrocarbon pneumonitis following furniture polish ingestion: Report of fifteen cases. J. Pediatr. 45: 13–26, 1954.
9. Gurwitz, D., Kattan, M., Levison, H., and Culham, J.A.G.: Pulmonary function abnormalities in asymptomatic children after hydrocarbon pneumonitis. Pediatrics 62: 789–794, 1978.
10. Gwinn, J.L., Lee, F.A., Weinberg, H.D., and Beam, C.W.: Radiological case of the month (pneumatocele formation following hydrocarbon pneumonitis). Am. J. Dis. Child. 127: 875–876, 1974.
11. Harris, V.J., and Brown, R.: Pneumatoceles as a complication of chemical pneumonia after hydrocarbon ingestion. A.J.R. 125: 531–537, 1975.
12. Heinisch, H.M., and Levejohann, R.: The pathogenesis of radiological changes in the lungs after ingestion of petroleum distillates: An experimental study in rabbits and extrapolation of the results in children. Ann. Radiol. 16: 263–266, 1973.
13. Huxtable, K.A., Bolande, R.P., and Klaus, M.: Experimental furniture polish pneumonia in rats. Pediatrics 34: 228–235, 1964.
14. Jimenez, J.B., and Lester, R.G.: Pulmonary complications following furniture polish ingestion. A report of 21 cases. A.J.R. 98: 323–333, 1966.
15. Wolfe, B.M., Brodeur, A.E., and Shields, J.B.: The role of gastrointestinal absorption of kerosene in producing pneumonitis in dogs. J. Pediatr. 76: 867–873, 1970.

Other Pulmonary Aspiration Problems.   Aspiration into the tracheobronchial tree with resultant pneumonia can be focal or widespread (6), and the findings depend on the volume of fluid aspirated and the patient's position during the aspiration episode. In small infants, aspiration often occurs into the right upper lobe and results in right upper lobe atelectasis. The findings are rather characteristic and are seen in Figure 1.81. Presumably, aspiration occurs into the right upper lobe of these infants because they are fed in the recumbent position, on their right side. Aspiration in the upright position leads to medial, lower lobe infiltrates, and the roentgenographic findings are not unlike those seen with hydrocarbon pneumonitis (see Fig. 1.133). With massive aspiration, the findings may mimic those of pulmonary edema or widespread bacterial pneumonia. Severe cases are referred to as Mendelson's syndrome (5, 7–9). In these cases, a severe chemical pneumonitis secondary to the aspiration of acid gastric contents occurs, and the roentgenographic findings reflect extensive pulmonary edema. Chronic aspiration problems lead to pulmonary fibrosis, bronchitis, and even bronchiectasis. Infiltrates secondary to significant aspirations usually take weeks, or even months, to completely clear. Chronic aspiration of lipid often leads to very dense, hazy lungs (see Fig. 1.18*B*).

Causes of aspiration are numerous (2) and include swallowing mechanism defects, tracheoesophageal fistulas, aspiration during episodes of seizure activity or unconsciousness, and, as mentioned earlier, incidental aspiration during normal feeding of young infants. In addition, aspiration can occur secondary to gastroesophageal reflux, with or without an underlying hiatus hernia. Indeed, there is now some suggestion that such reflux might explain some cases of the sudden infant death syndrome (3, 4). Massive aspiration of particulate matter, such as dirt and sand (1, 2), usually leads to sudden death. If the foreign material contains calcium carbonate (2), it can be seen to fill the bronchi on chest films.

REFERENCES

1. Bergeson, P.S., Hinchcliffe, W.A., Crawford, R.F., Sorenson, M.J., and Trump, D.S.: Asphyxia secondary to massive dirt aspiration. J. Pediatr. 92: 506–507, 1978.
2. Bonilla-Santiago J., and Fill, W.L.: Sand aspiration in drowning and near drowning. Radiology 128: 301–302, 1978.
3. Herbst, J.J., Book, L.S., and Bray, P.F.: Gastroesophageal reflux in the "near miss" sudden infant death syndrome. J. Pediatr. 92: 73–75, 1978.
4. Leape, L.L., Holder, T.M., Franklin, J.D., Amoury, R.A.,

and Ashcraft, K.W.: Respiratory arrest in infants secondary to gastroesophageal reflux. Pediatrics 60: 924–928, 1977.
5. Mendelson, C.L.: The aspiration of stomach contents into the lungs during obstetric anaesthesia. Am. J. Obstet. Gynecol. 52: 191–204, 1946.
6. Neuhauser, E.B.D., and Griscom, N.T.: Aspiration pneumonitis in children. Prog. Pediatr. Radiol. 1: 265–293, 1967.
7. Richman, H., and Abramson, S.F.: Mendelson's syndrome. Am. J. Surg. 120: 531–536, 1970.
8. Teabeaut, J.R., II: Aspiration of gastric contents. An experimental study. Am. J. Pathol. 28: 51–63, 1952.
9. Wilkins, R.A., Lacey, G.J., Flor, R., and Taylor, S.: Radiology in Mendelson's syndrome. Clin. Radiol. 27: 81–85, 1976.

Delayed Diaphragmatic Hernia. Occasionally, an older child can present with acute respiratory distress secondary to herniation of the abdominal viscera into the thoracic cavity. Indeed, such occurrences in older children are being documented more often (1–3, 5–13). These patients frequently present with acute respiratory distress, which may or may not be preceded by vomiting. The resulting roentgenographic findings may be startling and puzzling, and unless the possibility of delayed diaphragmatic hernia is kept in mind, the proper diagnosis may elude the initial observer. Indeed, mis-

interpretation for a large pneumothorax or pulmonary cyst is usual (Fig. 1.135). In those cases where the stomach contains fluid, the findings may be misinterpreted for an intrathoracic mass.

An upper gastrointestinal (GI) series may be needed for verification that the stomach or other portion of the GI tract is in the chest, but, if gastric volvulus also is present, barium may not pass from the esophagus to the stomach. If volvulus is not present, barium will be seen to pass from the esophagus upward into the stomach which, of course, would be in the chest cavity. Most of these cases are presumed to be instances of delayed herniation through a congenital diaphragmatic defect, but it also should be noted that such hernias can occur after blunt abdominal trauma either on an acute or delayed basis. In addition, rupture of the diaphragm has been documented in association with coughing in pertussis (4).

REFERENCES
1. Booker, P.D., Meerstadt, P.W.D., and Bush, G.H.: Congenital diaphragmatic hernia in the older child. Arch. Dis. Child. 56: 253–257, 1981.

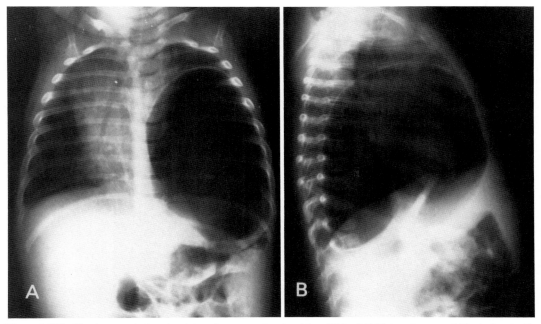

Figure 1.135. *Diaphragmatic hernia, delayed presentation in older child.* (*A*) Note a large cyst-like lesion in the left hemithorax. It displaces the heart and mediastinum to the right. The findings might be misinterpreted for a large lung cyst or pneumothorax. However, note that there is no gastric bubble visualized in the abdomen. (*B*) Lateral view shows the incarcerated, dilated stomach herniated into the chest of this young child who presented with an acute vomiting episode followed by severe respiratory distress. (Courtesy Virgil B. Graves, M.D., Great Falls, Montana.)

2. Brill, P.W., Gershwind, M.E., and Krasna, I.H.: Massive gastric enlargement with delayed presentation of congenital diaphragmatic hernia: Report of three cases and review of the literature. J. Pediatr. Surg. 12: 667–674, 1977.

3. Day, B.: Late appearance of Bochdalek hernia. Br. Med. J. 1: 786, 1976.

4. Dutta, T.: Spontaneous rupture of diaphragm due to pertussis. J. Pediatr. Surg. 10: 147–148, 1975.

5. Faure, C., Sauvegrain, J., and Bomsel, F.: Right-sided congenital diaphragmatic hernia with delayed radiologic manifestations. Ann. Radiol. 14: 305–313, 1971.

6. Gaisie, G., Young, L.W., and Oh, K.S.: Late onset Bochdalek's hernia with obstruction: radiographic spectrum of presentation. Clin. Radiol. 34: 267–270, 1983.

7. Glasson, M.J., Barter, W., Cohen, D.H., and Bowdler, J.D.: Congenital left posterolateral diaphragmatic hernia with previously normal chest x-ray. Pediatr. Radiol. 3: 201–205, 1975.

8. Golladay, E.S., Katz, J.R., Katz, H., and Haller, J.A., Jr.: Delayed presentation of congenital posterolateral diaphragmatic hernia: a dramatic cause of failure to thrive. J. Pediatr. Surg. 16: 503–505, 1981.

9. Hurdiss, L.W., Taybi, H., and Johnson, L.M.: Delayed appearance of left-sided diaphragmatic hernia with infancy. J. Pediatr. 88: 990–992, 1976.

10. Kenny, J.D., Wagner, M.L., Harberg, F.J., Corbet, A.J., and Rudolph, A.J.: Right-sided diaphragmatic hernia of delayed onset in the newborn infant. South. Med. J. 70: 373–374, 1977.

11. Kirchner, S.G., Burko, H., O'Neill, J.A., and Stahlman, M.: Delayed radiographic presentation of congenital right diaphragmatic hernia. Radiology 115: 155–156, 1975.

12. MacPherson, R.I.: "Acquired" congenital diaphragmatic hernia. J. Pediatr. Surg. 12: 657–666, 1977.

13. Woolley, M.M.: Delayed appearance of a left posterolateral diaphragmatic hernia resulting in significant small bowel necrosis. J. Pediatr. Surg. 12: 673–674, 1977.

Delayed Congenital Lobar Emphysema. Congenital lobar emphysema is usually considered a neonatal problem, but this condition occasionally can present at a later point in childhood (1).

REFERENCE

1. Taber, P., Benveniste, H., and Gans, S.L.: Delayed infantile lobar emphysema. J. Pediatr. Surg. 9: 245–246, 1974.

Allergic Pneumonitis. Allergic manifestations in a lung can occur with toxic substances which are either inhaled or ingested (2, 6–9). The resultant infiltrates may be widespread (Fig. 1.136) or focal. When such

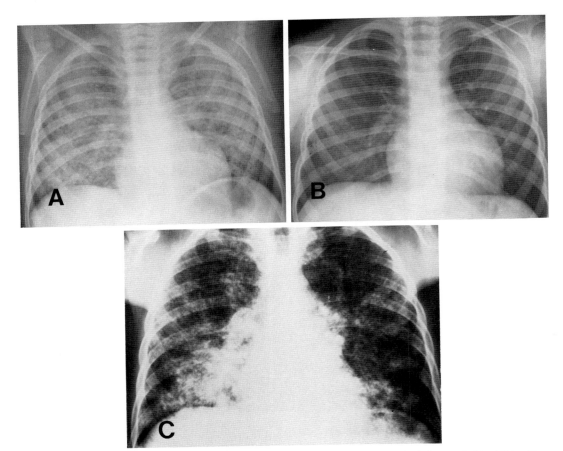

Figure 1.136. *Allergic lung.* (*A*) Note extensive infiltrates scattered throughout both lungs of this child with an allergic manifestation due to cytotoxic drug administration for treatment of leukemia. (*B*) Twenty-four hours later, after steroid adminstration, the lungs are clear. (*C*) Patchy infiltrates in another patient with an "allergic lung" secondary to inhaled fungal antigens. Farmer's lung often is applied to these cases. (Courtesy A. Selke, M.D.)

infiltrates come and go rapidly in different areas of the lung, the terms Löffler's pneumonia or pulmonary infiltrates with eosinophilia (PIE) often are applied (2, 7). A detailed discussion of all of the causes of allergic pneumonitis is beyond the scope of this book, but it should be stressed that proper questioning of the patient regarding the intake of any medication or drugs is mandatory when unexplained infiltrates are seen on chest roentgenograms. Nonspecific pulmonary infiltrates also are seen in the milk allergy or Heiner's syndrome (1, 3–5). In most instances, the findings are nonspecific.

REFERENCES

1. Chang, C.H., and Wittig, H.J.: Heiner's syndrome. Radiology 92: 507–508, 1969.
2. Citro, L.A., Gordon, M.E., and Miller, W.T.: Eosinophilic lung disease (or how to slice P.I.E.). A.J.R. 117: 787–797, 1973.
3. Diner, W.C., Knicker, W.T., and Heiner, D.C.: Roentgenologic manifestations in the lungs in milk allergy. Radiology 77: 564–572, 1961.
4. Heiner, D.C., and Sears, J.W.: Chronic respiratory disease associated with multiple circulating precipitins to cow's milk. Am. J. Dis. Child. 100: 500–502, 1960.
5. Heiner, D.C., Sears, J.W., and Knicker, W.T.: Multiple precipitins to cow's milk in chronic respiratory disease. A syndrome involving poor growth, gastrointestinal symptoms, evidence of allergy, iron deficiency anemia, and pulmonary hemosiderosis. Am. J. Dis. Child. 103: 634–654, 1962.
6. Katz, R.M., and Kniker, W.T.: Infantile hypersensitivity pneumonitis as a reaction to organic antigens. N. Engl. J. Med. 288: 233–237, 1973.
7. Levin, D.C.: The P.I.E. syndrome—pulmonary infiltrates with eosinophilia: a report of 3 cases with lung biopsy. Radiology 89: 461–465, 1967.
8. Singleton, E.B., and Wagner, M.L.: Radiologic Atlas of Pulmonary Abnormalities in Children, pp. 130–131, W. B. Saunders, Philadelphia, 1971.
9. Unger, G.F., Scanlon, G.T., Fink, J.N., and Unger, J.D.: A radiologic approach to hypersensitivity pneumonias. Radiol. Clin. North Am. 11: 339–356, 1973.

Dehydration, Acidosis, Overaeration, and Microcardia. Dehydration with acidosis commonly reflects itself on the chest roentgenograms (3). In childhood, this usually results from dehydration secondary to vomiting and/or diarrhea, and in such cases the lungs appear overaerated and undervascularized (Fig. 1.137). In addition, the cardiac silhouette often is small, and the findings frequently are confused with those of bronchiolitis. Decreased vascularity and smallness of the cardiac silhouette (microcardia) results from hypovolemia, while overaeration results from the metabolic acidosis present. These infants attempt to blow off carbon dioxide, and in so doing, overaerate.

Microcardia, with overdistended lungs, also can be seen with acute, large volume blood loss, and with more severe asthmatic attacks (see Fig. 1.110B). In these latter instances, the overdistended lungs depress the diphragmatic leaflets downward, and this causes the heart to be stretched. In addition, the heart is compressed by the emphysematous lungs.

Other causes of microcardia include Addison's disease, anorexia nervosa, and, of course, a normal long thin heart in an asthenic individual (usually a young female patient). Microcardia secondary to cardiac atrophy, with actual loss of muscle bulk (protein), as a result of long-standing debilitating disease (malignancy, malnutrition, severe burns, chronic infection, etc.) is a less common cause of a small cardiac silhouette (1, 2, 4).

REFERENCES

1. Altemus, L.R.: Malnutrition with microcardia. A.J.R. 99: 674–680, 1967.
2. Hellerstein, H.J., and Santiago-Stevenson, D.: Atrophy of heart; correlative study of eighty-five proved cases. Circulation 1: 93–126, 1950.
3. Nathan, M.H.: Diagnosis of dehydration, acidosis, and gastroenteritis in infants from chest radiograph. Radiology 83: 297–305, 1964.
4. Swischuk, L.E.: Microcardia: An uncommon diagnostic problem. A.J.R. 103: 115–118, 1968.

Hemoptysis in Childhood. Hemoptysis in childhood is not as common as in the adult but it can occur with hemangiomas in the hypopharynx or upper airway, bacterial pneumonias, other acute pulmonary infections (5), chronic pulmonary infections, foreign bodies (5), bronchial adenomas (6), and intrathoracic gastroenteric cysts (1, 2). Pulmonary infections and foreign bodies, however, have been shown to account for approximately half of the cases (5).

With gastroenteric cysts, pulmonary changes may range from discrete cystic masses to nonspecific, consolidative-like lesions. If ulceration of the cysts leads to perforation, blood and free air also will be seen in the thoracic cavity (2). With bronchial adenoma, the findings vary from a solitary pulmonary nodule to focal atelectasis or emphysema caused by airway obstruction by the nodule. In children, however, these adnomas are rare.

Pulmonary hemosiderosis also is a cause of hemoptysis in childhood (3, 4), and then the condition is associated with iron deficiency anemia, variable respiratory distress,

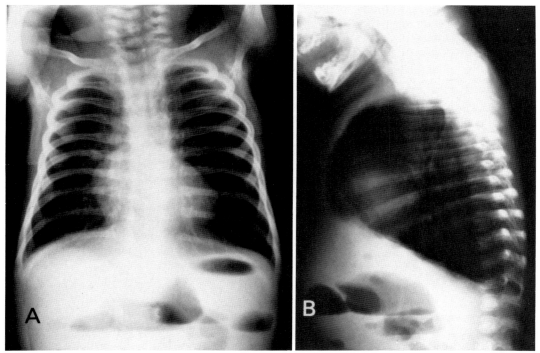

Figure 1.137. *Dehydration and overaeration.* (*A*) Note the overdistended hyperlucent appearance of the lungs in this infant with severe gastroenteritis, diarrhea, and dehydration. The vascularity is diminished and the heart somewhat small in size. Air-fluid levels scattered throughout the abdomen indicate the presence of gastroenteritis. In other cases, the cardiac silhouette is even smaller than in this infant. (*B*) Lateral view showing emphysematous appearance of the lungs, not unlike that seen with bronchiolitis.

oxygen diffusion difficulties, and a wide variety of roentgenographic findings. In acute cases, bleeding leads to fluffy, bilateral parenchymal infiltrates but with repeated bleeding, chronic fibrosis ensues and pulmonary changes may consist of miliary-like nodules (see Fig. 1.138), reticulonodularity, or diffusely hazy lungs. In any given patient the findings may be different from time to time but chronic, progressive fibrosis eventually ensues (3, 4).

REFERENCES

1. Chang, S.H., Morrison, L., Shaffner, L., and Crowe, J.E.: Intrathoracic gastrogenic cysts and hemoptysis. J. Pediatr. 88: 594–596, 1976.
2. Macpherson, R.I., Reed, M.H., and Ferguson, C.C.: Intra-thoracic gastrogenic cysts: Cause of lethal pulmonary hemorrhage in infants. J. Can. Assoc. Radiol. 24: 362–369, 1973.
3. Matsaniotis. N., Karpouzas, J., Apostolopoulou, E., and Messaritakis, J.: Idiopathic pulmonary hemosiderosis in children. Arch. Dis. Child. 43: 307–309, 1968.
4. Repetto, G., Lisboa, C.M., Emparanza, E., Ferretti, R., Neira, N., Etchart, M., and Maneghello, J.: Idiopathic pulmonary hemosiderosis. Pediatrics 40: 24–32, 1967.
5. Tom, L.W.C., Weisman, R.A., and Handler, S.D.: Hemoptysis in children. Ann. Otol. Rhinol. Laryngol. 89: 419–

424, 1980.
6. Wellons, H.A., Eggleston, P., Golden, G.T., and Allen, M.: Bronchial adenoma in childhood. Am. J. Dis. Child. 130: 301–304, 1976.

Anterior Chest Pain. Anterior chest pain is a common complaint of children, but most often it is musculoskeletal and frequently secondary to overexercising or viral infections. Occasionally, it can result from Tietze's syndrome, a costochondritis of the upper costochondral junctions of presumed viral origin. In other cases, it may be pleuritic, but anterior chest pain in children is seldom due to heart disease (1).

REFERENCE

1. Driscoll, D.J., Glicklich, L.B., and Galen, W.J.: Chest pain in children: a prospective study. Pediatrics 57: 648–651, 1976.

Rapidly Expanding Chest Masses and Cysts. A complete discussion of pulmonary mediastinal masses is beyond the scope of this book and not particularly relevant to its theme of emergency medicine. Only one

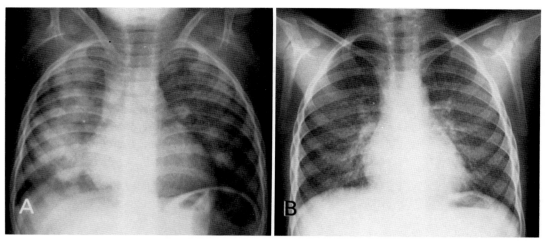

Figure 1.138. *Pulmonary hemosiderosis—varying configurations.* Fluffy, asymmetric infiltrates, resembling widespread pneumonia or even pulmonary edema. (*B*) Another child showing diffuse miliary infiltrates not unlike those seen with miliary tuberculosis.

or two points need be made regarding a child who might present with a chest mass in the emergency room. These children can present with chest pain, respiratory distress, wheezing, or asthma-like symptoms (1). One of the more common masses is a mediastinal lymphoma or a thymus gland infiltrated with leukemic cells. Both have a similar appearance, and the roentgenographic findings are quite characteristic (Fig. 1.139*A*). Other tumors also can be encountered and pulmonary cysts which become infected also can compress the airway and cause respiratory distress (Fig. 1.139, *B* and *C*). Tumors can expand rapidly because of rampant malignant growth or hemorrhage, while pulmonary cysts usually become larger because of supervening infection.

REFERENCE

1. Swischuk, L.E.: Acute respiratory distress in the infant. Radiol. Clin. North Am. 16: 77–90, 1977.

NORMAL FINDINGS CAUSING PROBLEMS

Technically Poor Examination. The fallacy of assessing a chest roentgenogram obtained during expiration is well known, and cannot be overstressed. On the expiratory film, the normal lungs and heart may look totally abnormal (Fig. 1.140*A*), and it is only after a proper inspiration is accomplished that this is appreciated. Rotation of the chest to one side or another causes obvious problems, and lordotic position can throw the heart and pulmonary vessesl into such projection that abnormality is suggested. In this regard, lordotic positioning tends to accentuate the hilar regions and upper lobe vascularity (Fig. 1.140*B*), and cause the heart to assume a right ventricular hypertrophy configuration.

Normal Thymus Gland. The normal thymus gland is notorious for mimicking pathology. Detailed dissertations on the thymus gland are available elsewhere (1–3), and only a few puzzling configurations will be illustrated here. The normal thymus gland usually covers the superior aspect of the heart like an umbrella and blends imperceptibly with the cardiac silhouette (Fig. 1.141*A*). Subtle notches may delineate its inferiormost extent, and on lateral view it will occupy the anterior, superior mediastinal compartment, and be delineated by a straight or undulating line along its inferior border (Fig. 1.141*B*). An important feature of the normal thymus gland is that, no matter how large it is, it does not displace the trachea in an abnormal fashion.

In some cases, the thymus gland is triangular in shape, producing the so-called sail sign (Fig. 1.142*A*). If rotation is present in these patients, the sail-like lobe of the thymus may be thrown into such projection as to suggest a consolidating upper lobe pneumonia (Fig. 1.142*B*). In other instances, the thymus may be of such a peculiar configu-

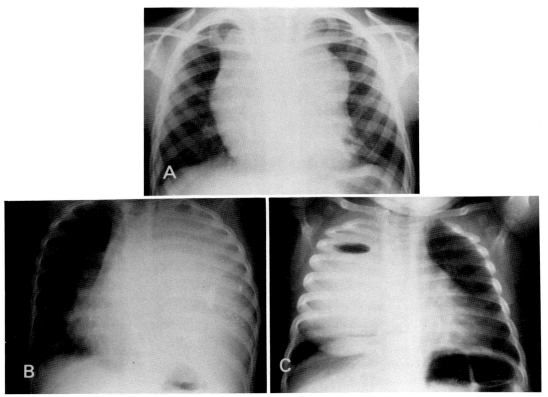

Figure 1.139. *Rapidly expanding masses and cysts.* (*A*) Note the large mediastinal mass in this child presenting with a 4-day history of wheezing and respiratory distress suggesting a pulmonary infection. Biopsy proven lymphoma. (*B*) This child presented with asthma-like symptoms. Note the large mass with calcification in the left chest. It was a teratoma. (*C*) Young infant presenting with respiratory distress. Note the large infected bronchogenic cyst in the right chest. It is compressing the trachea and right bronchus.

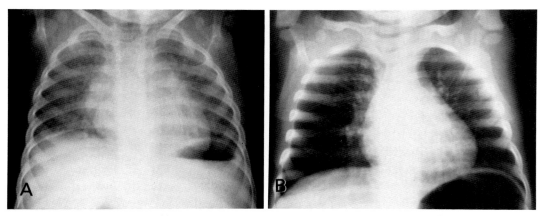

Figure 1.140. *Technically poor films.* (*A*) Expiratory view causes the lungs to appear infiltrated and the heart enlarged. The thymus gland drapes the superior cardiac silhouette, and on the right might suggest hilar adenopathy or a mediastinal mass. (*B*) Same infant with deeper inspiration but lordotic positioning. Lordotic positioning is manifest by horizontal positioning of the posterior ribs, downward pointing anterior ribs, and accentuation of the vascular markings in the upper lobes. This infant was normal.

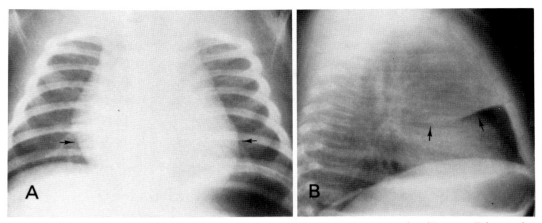

Figure 1.141. *Normal thymus.* (*A*) The normal thymic silhouette blends with the cardiac silhouette. Faint notches are seen at the junction of the thymic lobes and heart (*arrows*). The great vessels are difficult to find. (*B*) Lateral view showing the normal position of the thymus gland, and its undulating lower edge (*arrows*). (From Swischuk, L.E.: *Radiology of the Newborn and Young Infant*, Williams & Wilkins, 1973).

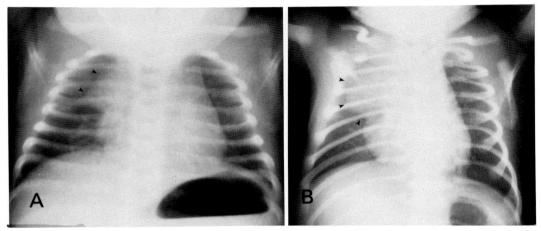

Figure 1.142. *Thymus "sail" sign and pseudopneumonia.* (*A*) Typical sail sign of normal thymus (*arrows*). (*B*) Rotation to the right in another infant causes normal thymus to appear as though it were a consolidating pneumonia of the right upper lobe (*arrows*).

ration that a mediastinal mass is suggested (Fig. 1.143).

One other point about the normal thymus gland is in order: that, although the thymus is most commonly seen in patients under the age of 2 years, it also can be seen in older children. In this regard, one can see normal thymus in children even up to the age of 10–12 years, not routinely, but not so uncommonly that the possibility should be discounted completely. In these cases it is not usually as readily recognizable as normal thymus for it produces tumor-like superior mediastinal widening or prominence (Fig. 1.144). In these cases, one should first ask oneself the question, "Why was this child examined?" and if the answer is because of a possible pneumonia, chest cold, routine chest, preoperative chest, etc., then one should ask oneself the next question, "Could I be dealing with normal thymus?" Many a child has come close to thoracotomy, or has even been subjected to thoracotomy for the erroneous diagnosis of a pathologic chest mass which turned out to be normal thymus.

REFERENCES

1. Caffey, J.: *Pediatric X-Ray Diagnosis.* Ed. 6, p. 443. Year Book, Chicago, 1972.
2. Swischuk, L.E.: *Radiology of the Newborn and Young Infant.* p. 9. Williams & Wilkins, Baltimore, 1973.
3. Tausend, M.E., and Stern, W.Z.: Thymic patterns in the newborn. A.J.R. 95: 125–130, 1965.

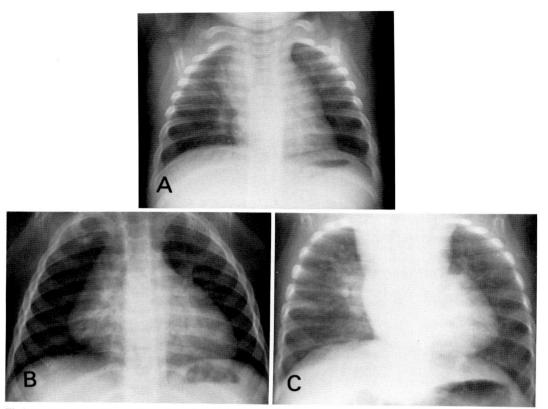

Figure 1.143. *Mass-like configuration of normal thymus gland.* (*A*) Bilateral superior mediastinal fullness caused by normal thymus gland. (*B*) Large right thymic lobe suggesting a mass. (*C*) Peculiar superior medial widening, secondary to incomplete descent of normal thymus gland and lordotic positioning.

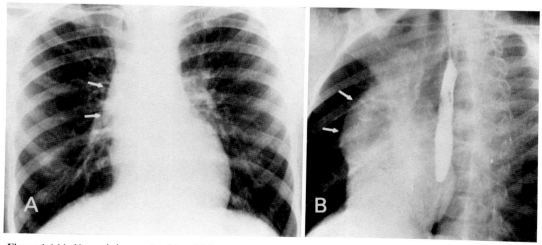

Figure 1.144. *Normal thymus in older child.* (*A*) This 10-year-old child was examined for a possible pneumonia. Incidentally noted was what at first was interpreted to be a superior mediastinal mass (*arrows*). (*B*) Oblique view with barium demonstrates the same mass (*arrows*). It was normal thymus gland.

CHAPTER 2
Upper Airway, Nasal Passages, Sinuses, and Mastoids

NORMAL ANATOMY OF UPPER AIRWAY

One must be thoroughly familiar with the normal anatomy of the upper airway before attempting to identify pathology. Fortunately, this is not too difficult a task, but unless a proper roentgenogram is obtained one will not be able to accomplish it. The upper airway roentgenogram must be obtained during inspiration, in true lateral position, and preferably with neck extended (Fig. 2.1). If the study is obtained during expiration, or with forward flexion of the neck, an endless number of peculiar, misleading, or virtually noninterpretable configurations of the buckled upper airway result (Fig. 2.2). Frontal views of the upper airway also are helpful, but they do not provide as much information as do the lateral views. On lateral view, it is mandatory that the airway be examined in full distension and that the neck be extended, or at least straight. Otherwise, pseudothickening of the retropharyngeal soft tissues will be suggested (Fig. 2.2).

With normal soft tissues, there is an increase in thickness at the level of the larynx, producing a step-off of the airway. The upper airway represents the distended hypopharynx and the lower portion, the subglottic trachea (Fig. 2.2, *B* and *D*). With true retropharyngeal soft tissue thickening this step-off is obliterated and the airway is displaced anteriorly in a smoothly curving fashion (see Fig. 2.17). This does not occur with normal buckling very often (Fig. 2.2*A*), for more often, the step-off is preserved (Fig. 2.2*C*). The findings can be confusing, however, but when the retropharyngeal soft tissues appear lumpy (Fig. 2.2*C*), one should suspect normal lymphoid tissue, rather than a pathologic mass. As noted earlier, masses generally produce smoothly curving deformities and displacements of the upper airway.

Normal adenoidal and tonsilar tissue can pose another problem in evaluation of the upper airway, for in some children the adenoids and tonsils are so large that a pathologic nasopharyngeal mass is suggested (Fig. 2.3). In most such instances, of course, the findings are not abnormal, for adenoidal tissue should be present in the older infant and child, and in some cases is very abundant. Under the age of 3 months, however, adenoidal tissue is normally quite sparse (1).

REFERENCE

1. Capitanio, M.A., and Kirkpatrick, J.A.: Nasopharyngeal lymphoid tissue. Roentgen observations in 257 children two years of age or less. Radiology 96: 389–391, 1970.

UPPER AIRWAY OBSTRUCTION AND ACUTE STRIDOR

Stridor means noisy breathing and usually infers the presence of a lesion in the upper airway. However, before embarking upon the roentgenographic workup, there is some value in reviewing the clinical features of stridor and whether it is: (a) inspiratory or expiratory, (b) associated with wheezing, (c) associated with voice alterations, or (d) as-

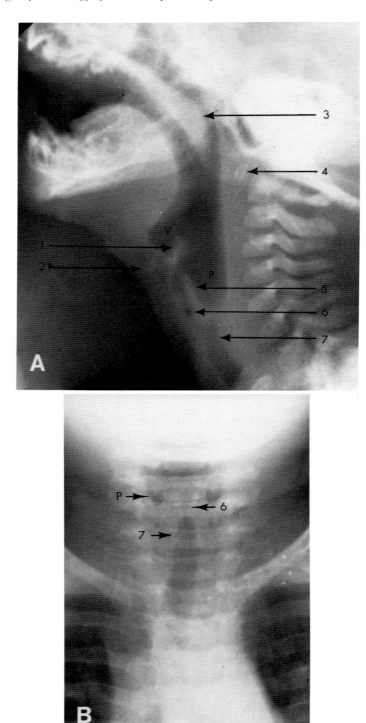

Figure 2.1. *(A and B) Normal upper airway.*   Note the following structures: (*1*) epiglottis, (*2*) body of the hyoid bone, (*3*) uvula, (*4*) anterior arch of C₁, (*5*) aryepiglottic folds, (*6*) ventricle of glottis. (*7*) subglottic portion of trachea, (*V*) vallecula, and (*P*) piriform fossa. (Reprinted from Swischuk, L.E.: *Radiology of the Newborn and Young Infant*, Williams & Wilkins, Baltimore, 1973.)

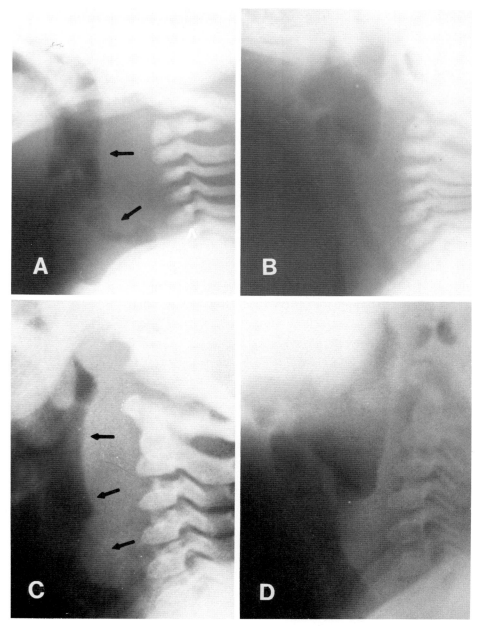

Figure 2.2. *Technically poor film with pseudo-mass configuration.* (*A*) This patient was examined with the neck flexed forward and the airway incompletely distended. A retropharyngeal mass (*arrows*) is suggested. (*B*) With proper positioning, however, note that no mass is present. (*C*) Another patient showing what would appear to be a lumpy retropharyngeal mass (*arrows*). However, note that there is preservation of the step-off between the hypopharynx and subglottic trachea. Furthermore, lumpiness favors adenoidal tissue. (*D*) Properly obtained film with full distension of the airway shows no mass and a normal step-off between the hypopharynx and subglottic trachea.

sociated with dysphagia (Fig. 2.4). If it is inspiratory, or both inspiratory and expiratory, chances are that the lesion is in the glottic or supraglottic regions, but if it is purely expiratory, the lesion probably exists below the glottis, often in the chest. In these latter cases expiratory wheezing also is present. Voice alterations associated with stridor almost always place the lesion in the glottis or immediate paraglottic region, while dys-

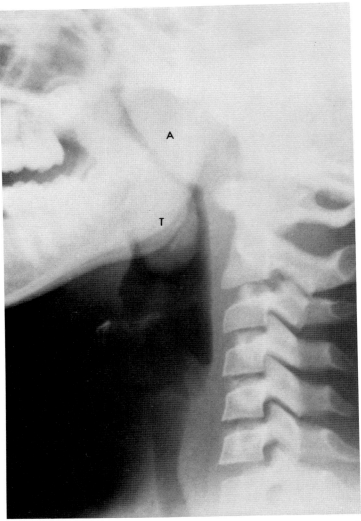

Figure 2.3. *Normal large adenoids and tonsils.* Note the large adenoids (*A*) and palatine tonsils (*T*) in this normal child.

phagia with stridor usually is seen with lesions in the hypopharynx (i.e., epiglottitis, retropharyngeal abscess, hypopharyngeal tumors or cysts), or chest (i.e., vascular rings or mediastinal masses or cysts). After one's clinical assessment of the patient with stridor, the next investigative procedure should be a lateral upper airway roentgenogram, and not endoscopy. With a *proper lateral neck roentgenogram, there hardly is a lesion which will go undetected,* and when a chest film and an occasional barium swallow also are obtained, virtually nothing should escape detection (5, 11, 14, 24, 46). It also has been demonstrated that improved visualization of

the airway, both on frontal and lateral views, can be accomplished by combining increased filtration of the x-ray beam, a higher kilovoltage technique, and magnification (15, 16, 22, 44).

Epiglottitis. Epiglottitis usually affects older children, with the peak incidence occurring between 3 and 6 years. It usually presents abruptly with inspiratory stridor and severe dysphagia, and is caused by *Haemophilus influenzae* infection (10, 20, 29, 36). Dysphagia is secondary to the marked degree of supraglottic edema present, and clinically the cherry red epiglottis is classic. However, most physicians still are cautious

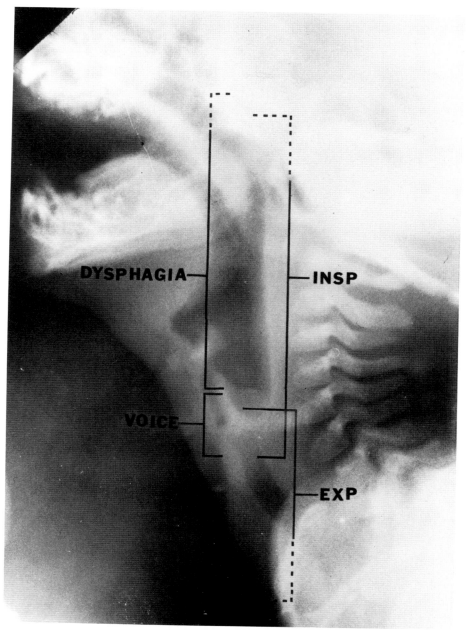

Figure 2.4. *Stridor; location of lesion according to symptoms.* Note zones for predominantly inspiratory or expiratory stridor. Note area of overlap. Also note area for dysphagia and voice problems.

regarding examination of the oropharynx in these patients because of the possibility of inducing glottic spasm. For this reason, the roentgenogram has become a more popular method of diagnosing epiglottitis, and indeed, this relatively innocuous study can clearly demonstrate its presence (4, 10, 11, 14, 25, 36, 37, 47). However, it should be stressed that these patients should not be sent to the x-ray examination room unattended, for the possibility of acute airway obstruction is always present.

On lateral view, the roentgenographic findings of epiglottitis are typical, and con-

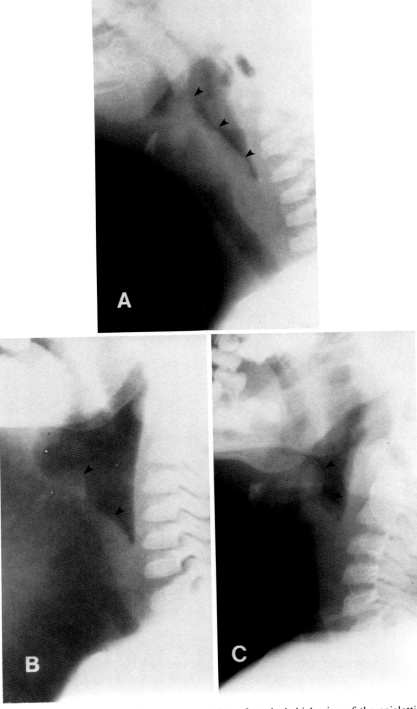

Figure 2.5. *Epiglottitis.* (*A*) Pronounced changes consisting of marked thickening of the epiglottis (*uppermost arrow*), and aryepiglottic folds (*lower two arrows*). Note that the subglottic portion of the trachea is of normal caliber. (*B*) Less pronounced findings in another patient. Again note that the epiglottis is edematous and thickened (*upper arrow*), and that the aryepiglottic folds (*lower arrow*) also are thick and swollen. (*C*) In this patient the

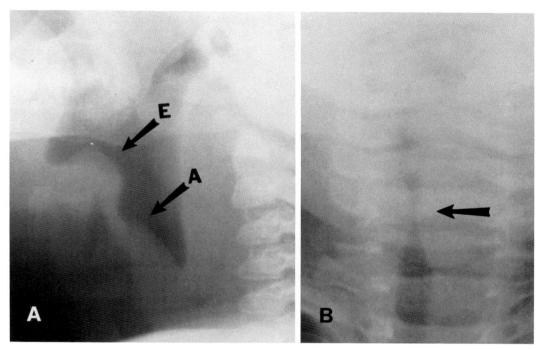

Figure 2.6. *Epiglottitis with subglottic edema.* (*A*) Note typical findings of epiglottitis on lateral view (*arrow*). Note that the subglottic portion of the trachea is of normal diameter. Epiglottis (*E*) and aryepiglottic (*A*) folds. (*B*) Frontal view shows a funnel-shaped glottic and subglottic region (*arrow*), due to subglottic edema. The findings mimic those of croup.

sist of thickening and edema of the aryepiglottic folds and epiglottis (Fig. 2.5). In advanced cases the swollen epiglottis appears as an upward-pointing thumb, and hence, references is made to the "thumb" sign. Mild to moderate hypopharyngeal overdistension also occurs, but seldom is it as marked as in croup. In addition, as opposed to croup, the subglottic portion of the trachea, on lateral view, appears normal. On frontal view, however, some cases of epiglottitis demonstrate subglottic edema and a funnel-shaped glottic area indistinguishable from that seen in croup (Fig. 2.6). In these cases, although the primary problem still is supra- and supraglottic edema, enough edema extends into the subglottic portion of the trachea to produce the funnel deformity (43). In terms of therapy of epiglottitis, while it was once advocated that tracheostomy need be performed in almost all patients (30, 38), currently most centers suggest nasotracheal intubation (2, 27, 32, 39, 49).

It is most important not to misinterpret the normal, so-called omega epiglottis for epiglottitis. In these patients, stridor may be due to croup or some other cause, but the epiglottis may appear a little thickened. This impression is erroneous for it is merely a floppy epiglottis with prominent downward curving lateral flaps. This results in an inverted "U" or omega-shaped epiglottis which on lateral view appears thickened (Fig. 2.7). However, in these cases no thickening of the aryepiglottic folds will be seen, and this should strongly rule against epiglottitis, for in true epiglottitis associated thickening of the aryepiglottic folds is the rule. If one is not able to make this distinction on a lateral neck roentgenogram, it usually is because the inspiratory effort is not deep enough, and the study should be repeated.

Croup. Most cases of croup are of viral origin (9), but bacterial croup, often severe and refractory, can occur. It carries terms such as membranous croup, pseudomem-

findings are more difficult to assess because airway distention is not marked. Because of this the aryepiglottic folds are buckled, but one should still note that they are markedly thickened (*lower arrow*), and in addition that the epiglottis is abnormally swollen (*upper arrow*). (Fig. *A* courtesy Virgil Graves, M.D., Great Falls, Montana.)

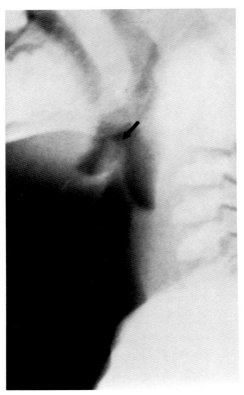

Figure 2.7. *Pseudoepiglottitis (omega epiglottis).* Note that the epiglottis (*arrow*) appears thickened. However, the aryepiglottic folds are not thickened. This case represents an instance of omega epiglottis. If epiglottitis were present, the aryepiglottic folds would be thicker. Compare with the aryepiglottic folds in Figure 2.5.

branous croup, membranous tracheitis, bacterial croup, or refractory croup (8, 12, 13, 15, 21, 28, 35). In these cases symptoms often are more severe, subglottic narrowing more pronounced and response to usual treatment refractory. Associated posterior pharyngeal membranes visualized in these patients can be misinterpreted for the membranes of diphtheria.

Croup also has been demonstrated to be more common in allergic children (51), and this also has been our experience. It pertains especially to those patients with repeated bouts of croup. To be sure, especially in older children, croup can occur on a purely allergic basis, and not be associated with any type of infection at all.

Classically, in croup, stridor primarily is inspiratory, and the entire picture, including the barking cough, is rather typical. Characteristically it is a disease of infants and young children, with the peak age incidence being between 6 months and 3 years (9, 47). Many of these children also have a full-blown viral lower respiratory tract infection, and in the evening, croup develops. Overall, the clinical findings are so typical, that there is question as to why roentgenograms should be obtained in these children. Nonetheless, the study seems to be quite popular and can easily differentiate croup from epiglottitis (4, 7, 10–16, 25, 31, 33, 34, 47). To begin with, there is marked hypopharyngeal overdistention during inspiration, and second, the epiglottis and aryepiglottic folds are normal. The vocal cords, however, usually appear thickened and fuzzy, and the subglottic portion of the trachea narrowed (Fig. 2.8*A*). This narrowing is primarily paradoxical and represents tracheal collapse secondary to negative intraluminal pressures which develop in this area during inspiration (17, 31, 47). This is a nonspecific response which occurs with any glottic obstruction, but in childhood it is most commonly seen with croup, and is an important feature of this condition. On expiration, it should be noted that such narrowing is not as fixed as first it appears (Fig. 2.8*B*). Indeed is usually diminishes or completely disappears, and thus further attests to the fact that in typical viral, spasmodic croup, narrowing is paradoxical in nature and not due so much to fixed edematous stenosis. In more severe cases, however, and especially in bacterial croup, edematous stenosis may be more marked and persistent. Indeed, it may not disappear on expiration. In addition membranes in the trachea may be seen in some of these cases (Fig. 2.9). However, most often only the subglottic tracheal narrowing is seen. This narrowing and swelling of the glottis can produce expiratory airway obstruction and overdistension of the trachea on the expiratory view (17) (Fig. 2.8*B*).

On frontal view, the vocal cords in croup appear thickened and funnel-like in configuration (Fig. 2.10*A*). They appear this way

Figure 2.9. *Membranous croup or bacterial tracheitis.* (*A*) Note the membrane (*arrow*) in the trachea of this patient with severe respiratory stridor. (*B*) Another patient with severe stenosis of the trachea (*arrows*), and an indistinct, subglottic membrane. (fig. *A* courtesy Robin Gaup, M.D.)

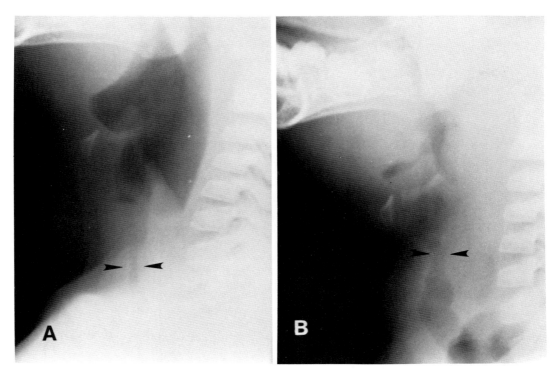

Figure 2.8. *Croup—lateral view.* (*A*) Typical findings include marked overdistention of the hypopharynx and paradoxical narrowing of the subglottic portion of the trachea (*arrows*). The epiglottis and aryepiglottic folds are normal. (*B*) Expiratory film demonstrating that the subglottic narrowing is not fixed, for on this view it appears much wider (*arrows*). In most cases, the narrowing disappears entirely. Also note overdistention of the subglottic trachea.

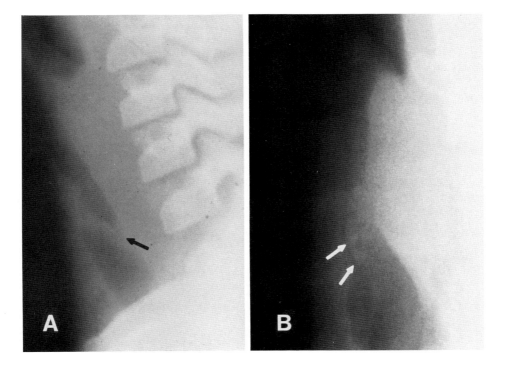

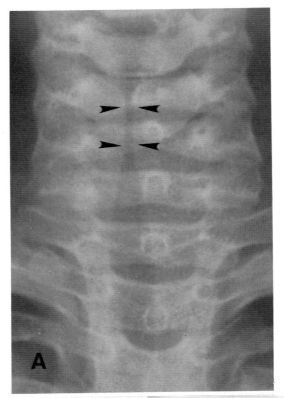

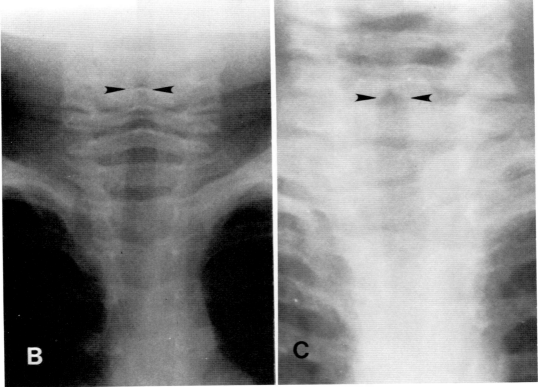

because they are edematous and in spasm. Normally, on inspiration of quiet breathing, the vocal cord should fall away and reveal a wide open airway (Fig. 2.10*B*), while with crying or forced expiration (i.e., Valsalva maneuver) the inferior aspect of the vocal cord should appear shoulder-like or squared-off (Fig. 2.10*C*). With croup, there is little change between inspiration and expiration, and thus the funnel-shaped configuration is almost always present, and interestingly enough often is best seen on standard frontal chest roentgenograms.

Unfortunately, not all children display as classic a picture of croup as just outlined, for if obstruction is less marked, and the inspiratory effort not as deep, less hypopharyngeal overdistention, and paradoxical subglottic tracheal collapse occurs (29). In these patients, the only finding may be thickening or fuzziness of the vocal cords (Fig. 2.11). However, this configuration is just as suggestive of croup as is the one illustrated in Figure 2.10. To be sure, the degree of roentgenographic change in croup is dependent on the degree of inspiration, and not severity of disease (33).

There are one or two other lesions which might present with croupy symptoms, and initially might be misdiagnosed for croup. These include ***congenital subglottic stenosis*** (4, 6, 11, 47), and ***subglottic hemangioma*** (1, 3, 17, 45, 50). In congenital subglottic stenosis, the findings are remarkably similar to those of croup for there is hypopharyngeal overdistention and narrowing of the subglottic portion of the trachea (Fig. 2.12*A*). However, as opposed to most cases of croup, the degree of narrowing does not diminish during expiration for it is truly fixed and stenotic. With subglottic hemangioma, the characteristic finding is an eccentric mass projecting into the subglottic portion of the trachea (Fig. 2.12*B*). These tumors most often are posterior or lateral, but occasionally can be anterior. Hemangiomas may be present elsewhere in the body or on the skin, and under such circumstances, make the diagnosis even more binding. Both congen-

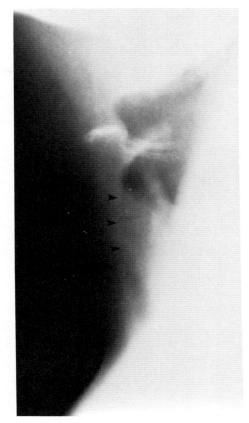

Figure 2.11. *Croup—fuzzy thickened vocal cords.* Lateral view showing moderate hypopharyngeal overdistention and a normal epiglottis and aryepiglottic folds. However, the region of the vocal cords is fuzzy and thickened (*arrows*). This configuration is just as typical for croup as is the one demonstrated in Figure 2.8.

ital subglottic stenosis and subglottic hemangioma are mentioned at this point because, during episodes of viral respiratory tract infection, they may become more symptomatic and lead to a clinical picture suggestive of acute croup.

Another lesion which may mimic the roentgenographic findings of croup is a laryngeal web, and this is the one lesion which is almost impossible to demonstrate roentgenographically. Generally the findings mimic croup, and consequently, endoscopy

Figure 2.10. *Croup—frontal view.* (*A*) Typical funnel-shaped glottic and subglottic narrowing in infant with croup (*arrows*). Edema and spasm of the glottis, and to a lesser extent paradoxical collapse of the subglottic portion of the trachea lead to this typical funnel-shaped upper airway narrowing. (*B*) Normal child, inspiratory film for comparative purposes, showing how normal vocal cords open during inspiration to leave a wider airway (*arrows*). (*C*) Normal child, expiratory film (forced Valsalva maneuver), for comparative purposes showing the normal right angle configuration of the inferior aspects of the vocal cords (*arrows*).

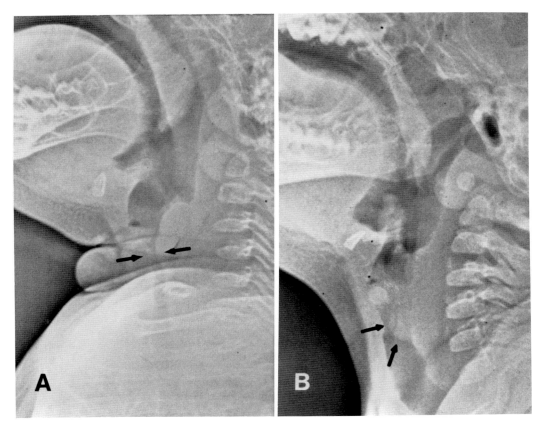

Figure 2.12. *(A) Subglottic stenosis.* Xeroradiogram. Note narrowing of the subglottic portion of the trachea (*arrows*). During expiration this area did not dilate or open up. (*B*) *Subglottic hemangioma.* Xeroradiogram. Characteristic eccentric posterior mass produced by subglottic hemangioma (*arrows*). (Fig. *B* Courtesy Charles J. Fagan, M.D.). Xeroradiography enhances visualization, but is not necessary.

usually is required for its diagnosis. Vocal cord paralysis also can produce findings similar to croup on frontal and lateral views, but of course, hoarseness, or aphonia, also usually is present.

Finally it might be noted that other infections of the larynx, such as candida (19) and herpes (26) can lead to croup or epiglottitis and stridor, and that upper airway obstruction in general has been shown to cause pulmonary edema (18, 23, 33, 41) and systemic hypertension (42, 48). Although of unknown etiology, hypoxia is suspected as the basic trigger for these complications.

Uvulitis. Uvulitis, as a part of pharyngitis (24), or in association with epiglottitis (40), also can cause airway obstruction. In such cases, however, the uvula becomes quite large and swollen and may be a cause of inspiratory stridor, or even dysphagia.

Radiographically the enlarged uvula is readily demonstrable (Fig. 2.13).

REFERENCES

1. Baden, M., Pagageorgious, A., and Joshi, V.V., et al.: Upper airway obstruction in a newborn secondary to hemangiopericytoma. Can. Med. Assoc. J. 107: 1020–1204, 1972.
2. Battaglia, J.D., and Lockhart, C.H.: Management of acute epiglottitis by nasotracheal intubation. Am. J. Dis. Child. 126: 334–336, 1975.
3. Campbell, J.S., Wiglesworth, F.W., and Latarroca, R., et al.: Congenital subglottic hemangiomas of the larynx and trachea in infants. Pediatrics 22: 727–737, 1958.
4. Capitanio, M.A., and Kirkpatrick, J.A., Jr.: Upper respiratory tract obstruction in infants and children. Radiol. Clin. North Am. 6: 265–277, 1968.
5. Christiaens, L., Decroix, G., and Gaudier, B., et al.: Hemangiomas of the larynx and of the trachea in infants: six cases. Arch. Fr. Pediatr. 22: 513–531, 1965.
6. Cuncy, R.L., and Bergstrom, L.B.: Congenital subglottic stenosis. J. Pediatr. 82: 282–284, 1973.
7. Currarino, G., and Williams, B.: Lateral inspiration and expiration radiographs of the neck in children with laryngotracheitis (croup). Radiology 145: 365–366, 1982.
8. Denneny, J.C., III, and Handler, S.D.: Membranous laryngotracheobronchitis. Pediatrics 70: 705–707, 1982.

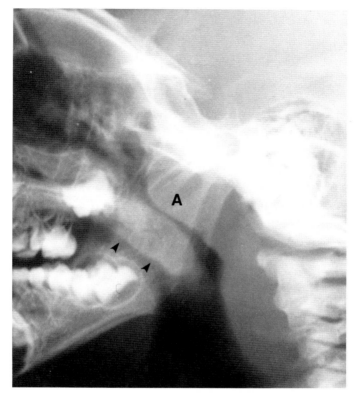

Figure 2.13. *Uvulitis.* Note thickened uvula (*arrows*). Also note prominent, probably inflamed, adenoids (*A*) and retropharyngeal lymphoid tissue.

9. Denny, F.W., Murphy, T.F., Clyde, W.A., Jr., Collier, A.M., and Henderson, F.W.: Croup: an 11-year study in a pediatric practice. Pediatrics 71: 871–876, 1983.
10. Dunbar, J.S.: Epiglottitis and croup. J. Can. Assoc. Radiol. 12: 95–97, 1961.
11. Dunbar, J.S.: Upper respiratory tract obstruction in infants and children. A.J.R. 109: 225–247, 1970.
12. Fearon, B.: Acute laryngotracheobronchitis in infancy and childhood. Pediatr. Clin. North Am. 9: 1095–1112, 1962.
13. Green, R., and Stark, P.: Trauma of the larynx and trachea. Radiol. Clin. North Am. 16: 309–320, 1978.
14. Grünebaum, M.: Respiratory stridor—a challenge for the paediatric radiologist. Clin. Radiol. 24: 485–490, 1973.
15. Henry, R.L., Mellis, C.M., and Benjamin, B.: Pseudomembranous croup. Arch. Dis. Child. 58: 180–183, 1983.
16. Howard, J.B., McCracken, G.H., Jr., and Luby, J.P.: Influenza A2 virus as a cause of croup requiring tracheostomy. J. Pediatr. 81: 1148–1150, 1972.
17. Hudson, H.L., and McAlister, W.H.: Obstructing tracheal hemangioma in infancy. A.J.R. 93: 428–431, 1965.
18. Hurley, R.M., and Kearns, J.R.: Pulmonary edema and croup. Pediatrics 65: 860, 1980.
19. Jacobs, R.F., Yasuda, K., Smith, A.L., and Benjamin, D.R.: Laryngeal candidiasis presenting as inspiratory stridor. Pediatrics 69: 234–236, 1982.
20. Jones, H.M.: Acute epiglottitis and supraglottitis. J. Laryngol. 72: 932–939, 1958.
21. Jones, R., Santos, J.I., and Overall, J.C.: Bacterial tracheitis. J.A.M.A. 242: 721–726, 1979.
22. Joseph, P.M., Berdon, W.E., and Baker, D.H., et al.: Upper airway obstruction in infants and small children: improved

23. radiographic diagnosis by combining filtration, high kilovoltage, and magnification. Radiology 121: 143, 1976.
23. Kanter, R.K., and Watchko, J.F.: Pulmonary edema associated with upper airway obstruction. Am. J. Dis. Child. 138: 356–358, 1984.
24. Kotloff, K.R., and Wald, E.R.: Uvulitis in children. Pediatr. Infect. Dis. 2: 392–393, 1983.
25. Lallemand, D., Sauvegrain, J., and Mareschal, J.L.: Laryngotracheal lesions in infants and children, detection and followup studies using direct radiographic magnification. Ann. Radiol. 16: 293–304, 1973.
26. Lallemand, D., Huault, G., Laboureau, J.P., and Sauvegrain, J.: Lesions of the larynx and esophagus in herpes simplex infection. Ann. Radiol. 17: 317–325, 1974.
27. Lewis, J.R., Gartner, J.C., and Galvis, A.G.: A protocol for management of acute epiglottitis: successful experiences with 27 consecutive instances treated by nasotracheal intubation. Clin. Pediatr. 17: 494–496, 1978.
28. Liston, S.L., Gehrz, R.C., Siegel, L.G., and Tilelli, J.: Bacterial tracheitis. Am. J. Dis. Child. 137: 764–767, 1983.
29. Margolis, C.Z., Colletti, R.B., and Grundy, G.: *Haemophilus influenzae* type B: the etiologic agent in epiglottitis. J. Pediatr. 87: 322–323, 1975.
30. Margolis, C.Z., Ingram, D.O., and Meyer, J.H.: Routine tracheotomy in *Haemophilus influenzae*, type B epiglottitis. J. Pediatr. 81: 1150–1153, 1972.
31. Meine, F.J., Lorenzo, R.L., Lynch, P.F., Capitanio, M.A., and Kirkpatrick, J.A.: Pharyngeal distention associated with upper airway obstruction. Experimental observations in dogs. Radiololgy 111: 395–398, 1974.
32. Milko, D.A., Marshak, G., and Striker, T.W.: Nasotracheal

intubation in the treatment of acute epiglottitis. Pediatrics 53: 674–677, 1974.
33. Mills, J.L., Spackman, T.J., Borns, P., Mandell, G.A., and Schwartz, M.W.: The usefulness of lateral neck roentgenograms in laryngotracheobronchitis. Am. J. Dis. Child. 133: 1140–1142, 1979.
34. Newth, C.J.L., Levison, H., and Bruan, A.C.: The respiratory status of children with croup. J. Pediatr. 81: 1068–1073, 1972.
35. Phelan, P., and Hey, E.: Progressive inflammatory subglottic narrowing responsive to steroids. Arch. Dis. Child. 58: 228–230, 1983.
36. Poole, C.A., and Altman, D.H.: Acute epiglottitis in children. Radiology 80: 798–805, 1963.
37. Rapkin, R.H.: Diagnosis of epiglottitis: simplicity and reliability of radiographs of neck in differential diagnosis of croup syndrome. J. Pediatr. 80: 96–98, 1972.
38. Rapkin, R.H.: Tracheostomy in epiglottitis. Pediatrics 52: 426–429, 1973.
39. Rapkin, R.H.: Nasotracheal intubation in epiglottitis. Pediatrics 56: 110–112, 1975.
40. Rapkin, R.H.: Simultaneous uvulitis and epiglottitis. J.A.M.A. 243: 1843, 1980.
41. Rivera M., Hadlock, F.P., and O'Meara, M.E.: Pulmonary edema secondary to acute epiglottitis. A.J.R. 132: 991–992, 1979.
42. Serratto, M., Harris, V.J., and Carr, I.: Upperairways obstruction. Presentation with systemic hypertension. Arch. Dis. Child. 56: 153–155, 1981.
43. Shackelford, G.D., Siegel, M.J., and McAlister, W.H.: Subglottic edema in acute epiglottitis in children. A.J.R. 131: 603–605, 1978.
44. Slovis, T.L.: Noninvasive evaluation of the pediatric airway: a recent advance. Pediatrics 59: 872–880, 1977.
45. Sutton, T.J., and Nogrady, M.B.: Radiologic diagnosis of subglottic hemangioma in infants. Pediatr. Radiol. 1: 211–216, 1973.
46. Swischuk, L.E.: *Radiology of the Newborn and Young Infant.* Williams & Wilkins, Baltimore, 1973.
47. Swischuk, L.E., Smith, P.C., and Fagan, C.J.: Abnormalities of the pharynx and larynx in childhood. Semin. Roentgenol. 9: 283–300, 1974.
48. Travis, K.W., Todres, I.D., and Shannon, D.C.: Pulmonary edema associated with croup and epiglottitis. Pediatrics 59: 695–698, 1977.
49. Weber, M.L., Desjardins, R., Perreault, G., Rivard, G., and Turmel, Y.: Acute epiglottitis in children: treatment with nasotracheal intubation; report of 14 consecutive cases. Pediatrics 57: 152–155, 1976.
50. Williams, H.E., Phelan, P.D., and Stocks, J.G., et al.: Hemangiomas of the larynx in infants: diagnosis, respiratory mechanics and management. Aust. Paediatr. J. 5: 149–154, 1968.
51. Zach, M., Erben, A., and Olinsky, A.: Croup, recurrent croup, allergy and airways hyper-reactivity. Arch. Dis. Child. 56: 336–341, 1981.

Chest Film in Airway Obstruction. Obstruction of the airway below the glottis manifests itself primarily as an expiratory problem, and although there may be both inspiratory and expiratory breathing difficulty, it is the expiratory air trapping which predominates roentgenographically. Because of this the chest tends to be overaerated, and classic examples of lesions leading to such overaeration include obstructing vascular rings and mediastinal masses and cysts. With obstruction in and around the glottis, however, air cannot enter the chest

in adequate amounts, and thus, the chest often appears underaerated (1). Furthermore, there is a paradoxical increase in heart size during inspiration (1, 2). The reason for this is that, with glottic or supraglottic obstruction, inspiratory intrathoracic pressures become negative, and in so doing, cause the cardiac silhouette to become larger and more prominent. Normally, of course, it would become smaller during inspiration.

REFERENCES

1. Capitanio, M.A., and Kirkpatrick, J.A.: Obstructions of the upper airway in children as reflected on the chest radiograph. Radiology 107: 159–161, 1973.
2. Grunebaum M., Adler, S., and Varsano, I.: The paradoxical movement of the mediastinum. A diagnostic sign of foreign-body aspiration during childhood. Pediatr. Radiol. 8: 213–218, 1979.

Foreign Bodies in the Upper Airway and Hypopharynx. With hypopharyngeal foreign bodies, after the initial coughing episode, the foreign body can remain surprisingly silent. Roentgenographically, if such foreign bodies are opaque, they are readily identified (Fig. 2.14*A*). If, however, they are radiolucent (i.e., aluminum, wood, plastic, etc.) they are almost impossible to detect. If perforation occurs, a retropharyngeal abscess may result (Fig. 2.14*B*). Hypopharyngeal foreign bodies, unless they totally occlude the hypopharynx, seldom result in acute respiratory catastrophies. Laryngeal foreign bodies, on the other hand, commonly present with severe respiratory distress, stridor, and even apnea. Indeed, the problem often is so acute that there is not time for roentgenograms to be obtained (4, 5).

Foreign bodies which lodge in the vocal cords usually are slender and either flat or long. The classic such foreign body is an eggshell fragment (3), but eggshell aspiration is not as common these days. However, if it should occur, the eggshell may be seen on end, located between both vocal cords. In this position, it appears as a thin, opaque, vertical stripe. Occasionally, other opaque foreign bodies such as chicken and turkey bones can be visualized in the same position (Fig. 2.14*C*). Fishbones, however, almost always elude detection (1) for only those which are large and heavily calcified usually are detected. One may have greater success with xeroradiography or CT in these cases. Nonradiopaque foreign bodies can pose

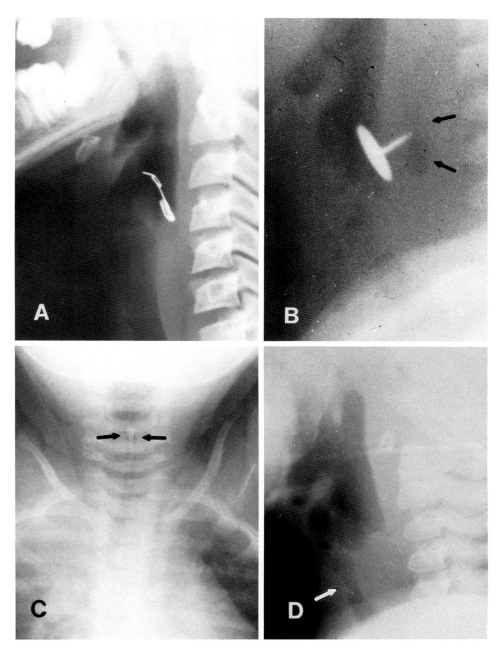

Figure 2.14. *Upper airway foreign bodies.* (*A*) Foreign body in hypopharynx. Note safety pin in this young infant. (*B*) Another infant with a thumbtack in the hypopharynx. Note that the retropharyngeal space is markedly thickened, and that there are air bubbles in it (*arrows*). These findings represent a retropharyngeal abscess secondary to perforation of the posterior pharyngeal wall. (*C*) *Opaque laryngeal foreign body.* A chicken bone is present in the larynx just at the level of the glottis (*arrows*). (*D*). *Radiolucent upper airway foreign body—indirect findings only.* This patient had an acute episode of coughing and hemoptysis, and then persistent stridor for 3 weeks. The only reoentgenographic finding was a persistent soft tissue mass bulging from the anterior tracheal wall, just below the glottis (*arrow*). On subsequent endoscopy, a small piece of aluminum foil was found embedded just below the glottic region.

even more difficulty for often there is nothing more to see than secondary findings. One must correlate these findings with the clinical history to establish the proper diagnosis (Fig. 2.14*D*). The problem of confusing a foreign body with normally calcified laryngeal cartilage (2) is not as great in childhood as it is in adulthood. These calcifications are discussed with upper esophageal foreign bodies in Chapter 3.

REFERENCES

1. Campbell, D. R., Brown, S. J., and Manchester, J. S.: An evaluation of the radio-opacity of various ingested foreign bodies in the pharynx and esophagus. J. Can. Assoc. Radiol. 19: 183–186, 1968.
2. Muroff, L.R., and Seaman, W.B.: Normal anatomy of the larynx and pharynx and the differential diagnosis of foreign bodies. Semin. Roentgenol. 9: 267–272, 1974.
3. Naveh, Y., Friedman, A., and Altmann, M.: Eggshell aspiration in infants. Am. J. Dis. Child. 129: 498–499, 1975.
4. Steichen, F.M., Fellini, A., and Einhorn, A.H.: Acute foreign body laryngotracheal obstruction: A cause of sudden and unexplained death in children. Pediatrics 48: 281–285, 1971.
5. Weston, J.T.: Airway foreign body fatalities in children. Ann. Otol. Rhinol. Laryngol. 74: 1144–1148, 1965.

Other Causes of Upper Airway Obstruction. Edema of the larynx and paraglottic structures can be seen with caustic burns secondary to lye ingestion (Fig. 2.15*A*), laryngeal trauma (Fig. 2.15*B*), and in some cases hot air or smoke inhalation. In such cases, hypopharyngeal overdistention and enlargement or obliteration of the glottic and paraglottic structures is seen. With **trauma to the larynx**, associated fractures of the hyoid bone and laryngeal cartilage also can be seen. In this regard, it is important not to confuse the separate ossification centers of the normal body and wings of the hyoid bone for a fracture (Fig. 2.15*B*). CT scanning now is very valuable in further documenting laryngeal fractures.

Acute stridor occasionally is seen with **angioneurotic (allergic) edema of the epiglottis** or uvula (5). In some of these cases, symptoms may be profound since nearly total airway occlusion may occur. Roentgenographically, the swollen, enlarged epiglottis (Fig. 2.15*C*) or uvula is readily demonstra-

ble. In other cases, a chronically lodged **foreign body in the upper esophagus may lead to tracheal compression** and acute stridor (1–4). These patients often do not present with a history of dysphagia, and roentgenograms may demonstrate compression of the trachea only (see Fig. 3.135).

Vascular rings or other vascular anomalies usually present with chronic airway obstructive problems, but if a superimposed respiratory tract infection is present, acute stridor or wheezing may occur. In such cases, it is most important to identify the presence of a right-sided aortic arch, for this is almost always present with a vascular ring (Fig. 2.16). Of course, tracheal compression may be seen on plain films, but generally speaking the workup of stridor secondary to a vascular ring is not an emergency room procedure. A similar statement can be made regarding mediastinal masses and cysts which might present with airway obstruction.

REFERENCES

1. Lallemand, D., Roussel, B., and Sauvegrain, J.: Narrowing of the cervical trachea following foreign body aspiration. Ann. Radiol. 18: 413–418, 1975.
2. Schidlow, D.V., Palmer, J., Balsara, R.K., Turtz, M.G., and Williams, J.L.: Chronic stridor and anterior cervical "mass" secondary to an esophageal foreign body. Am. J. Dis. Child. 135: 869–870, 1981.
3. Smith, P.C., Swischuk, L.E., and Fagan, C.J.: An elusive and often unsuspected cause of stridor or pneumonia (the esophageal foreign body). 122: 80–89, 1974.
4. Tauscher, J.W.: Esophageal foreign body: an uncommon cause of stridor. Pediatrics 61: 657–658, 1978.
5. Watts, F.B., Jr., and Slovis, T.L.: The enlarged epiglottis. Pediatr. Radiol. 5: 133–136, 1977.

RETROPHARYNGEAL ABSCESS

Retropharyngeal abscess usually presents with fever, neck pain and stiffness, and dysphagia (1–3). Stridor can be seen in these patients, but usually is not a predominant feature. Adenopathy usually is present in the neck, and in some cases may be striking. In most instances, the retropharyngeal abscess results from suppuration of lymphoid tissue in the retropharyngeal space, but occasionally can result from perforation of the hy-

Figure 2.15. (*A*) *Lye burns to larynx.* Note the edematous folds (*arrows*) in this patient who sustained lye burns to the esophagus, hypopharynx, and vocal cords. (*B*) *Trauma to larynx.* This boy was hit in the anterior neck by a fist and became horse. Note the edematous, indistinct vocal cords (*arrows*). The findings mimic those of croup (see Fig. 2.11). Note the separately ossified body and wings of the thyroid bone. These should not be misinterpreted for a fracture. (*C*) *Angioneurotic edema of the epiglottis.* Note the markedly thickened epiglottis, aryepiglottic folds, and retropharynx (*arrows*) in this patient presenting with acute respiratory distress. (Reprinted with permission from Watts, F.B., Jr., and Slovis, T.L.: The enlarged epiglottis. Pediatr. Radiol. 5: 133–316, 1977.)

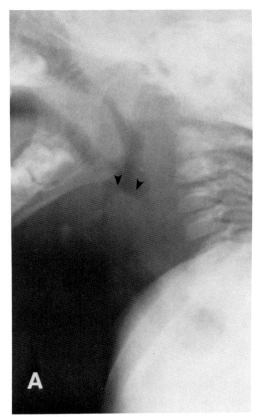

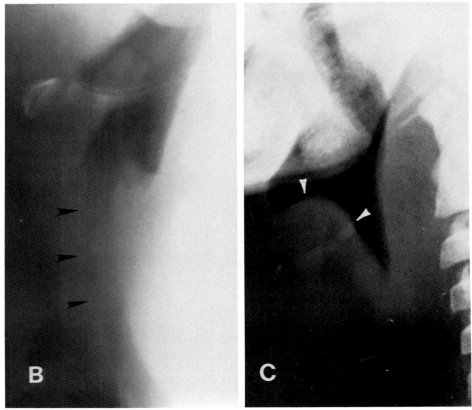

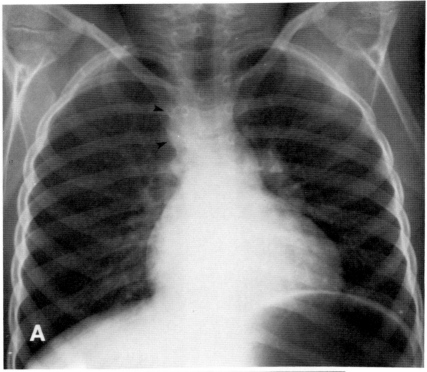

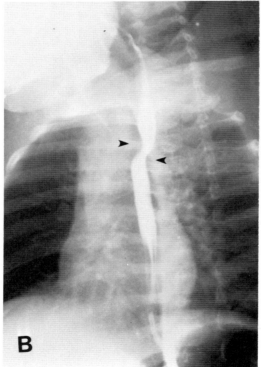

Figure 2.16. *Vascular ring causing stridor.* (*A*) Note the right-sided aortic arch (*arrow*) in this patient with a vascular ring (double aortic arch). The trachea is displaced to the left and indented on the right by the right-sided aortic arch. On lateral view in these patients, one occasionally can see anterior displacement of the trachea. (*B*) Barium swallow demonstrating characteristic reverse "S," double indentation of the esophagus (*arrows*).

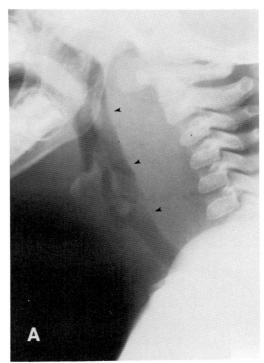

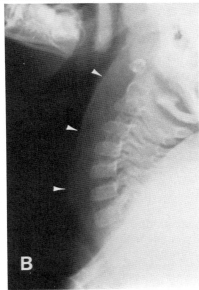

Figure 2.17. *Retropharyngeal abscess.* (*A*) Large retropharyngeal abscess causing thickening of the retropharyngeal space and anterior displacement of the airway (*arrows*). The spine shows mild kyphosis secondary to intense muscle spasm. (*B*) Less striking case showing less thickening of the retropharyngeal tissues (*arrows*). Note, also, that the neck is in its normal extended position. Nonetheless, the prevertebral soft tissues are thickened and the airway displaced anteriorly in a smooth, curving fashion. In addition, the normal step-off of the airway at the level of the larynx is lost.

popharynx by a foreign body (see Fig. 2.14*B*).

Roentgenographically, the findings consist of thickening of the retropharyngeal soft tissues and forward, bulging displacement of the airway (Fig. 2.17). If gas is present in the abscess, the diagnosis is more readily established (see Fig. 2.14*B*). In those cases where findings are minimal, and one is in doubt, a barium swallow is helpful. This study will show the abnormal forward position of the esophagus and more clearly demonstrate the presence of soft tissue swelling in the retropharyngeal space.

The cervical spine usually is straight or flexed in cases of retropharyngeal abscess and often there is some degree of anterior offsetting of C_2 on C_3. This latter finding results from the intense muscle spasm present and does not represent true dislocation. By the same token, C_1 may be displaced forward on C_2, and as a result the space between the anterior arch of C_1 and the dens will become widened. In the past, it has been stated that this finding was due to inflammation-induced laxity of the ligaments in the area, but I do not believe that this is true. The findings probably are due to the intense muscle spasm present in these children, exaggerating normal hypermobility.

REFERENCES

1. Capitanio, M.A., and Kirkpatrick, J.A., Jr.: Upper respiratory tract obstruction in infants and children. Radiol. Clin. North Am. 6: 265–277, 1968.
2. Dunbar, J.S.: Upper respiratory tract obstruction in infants and children. A.J.R. 109: 225–246, 1970.
3. Swischuk, L.E., Smith, P.C., and Fagan, C.J.: Abnormalities of the pharynx and larynx in childhood. Semin. Roentgenol. 9: 283–300, 1974.

SINUSITIS, MASTOIDITIS, AND NASAL PASSAGE ABNORMALITIES

Sinusitis (1, 2, 4–6, 8, 9) and mastoiditis are common afflictions of children, and with sinusitis, in spite of the fact that in the past some authorities have indicated that roentgenographic examination of the sinuses is nearly worthless in children (7), the studies are productive and sinusitis is common in children (1–3, 5, 9).

Part of the problem in recognizing sinus disease in children, especially young infants, arises from the fact that it is generally held that sinuses are not present in infants. This is untrue, for the maxillary and ethmoid sinus cavities are present at birth and can

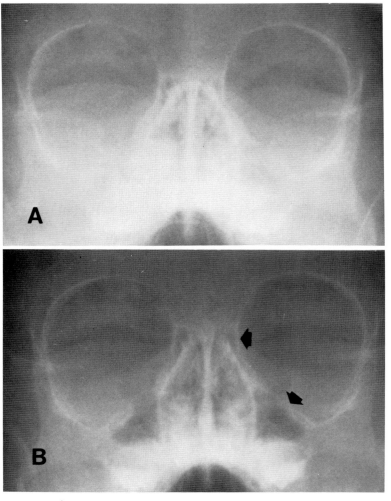

Figure 2.18. *Sinusitis in infancy.* (*A*) Note that the maxillary sinuses are difficult to see in this 11-month-old infant. The reason is that they are completely obliterated by inflammatory changes. However, one might be tempted to erroneously conclude that the maxillary sinuses are not yet developed. (*B*) After treatment, just 3 weeks later, one can see the normally aerated maxillary (*lower arrow*) and ethmoid (*upper arrow*) sinuses.

become infected at ages as early as 3 and 6 months (9). The problem, however, is that roentgenographic examinations of these cavities in this age group is difficult, and interpretation of the findings is even more difficult. Consequently, it is easier to say "the sinuses have not as yet developed" than to try to find them and interpret the findings. In such cases it is only when, with treatment, the sinus cavities clear, that one comes to realize that they were present all the time, and indeed infected (Fig. 2.18).

Another problem is that accomplishing a satisfactory roentgenographic examination

is difficult in infants. Most often the Waters' view, the single most important view in evaluating sinusitis in children, is obtained with too steep an angle (Fig. 2.19). While this problem is not always completely circumvented in very young infants, one's awareness of it can prompt repeat studies.

In addition to these considerations it seems doubtful that, as previously proposed, crying can cause enough mucosal edema and sinus obliteration to mimic disease (1–3, 9). By the same token mucosal redundancy, suggested as a normal phenomenon of young infants causing opacification of si-

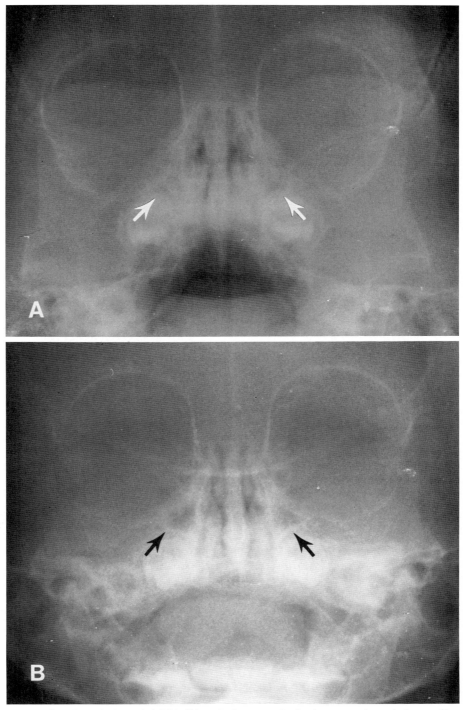

Figure 2.19. *Faulty Waters' view.* (*A*) This Waters' view was obtained too steeply and the maxillary sinuses (*arrows*) appear obliterated. (*B*) With proper angulation (less steep than in adults), the sinuses are seen to be clear (*arrows*).

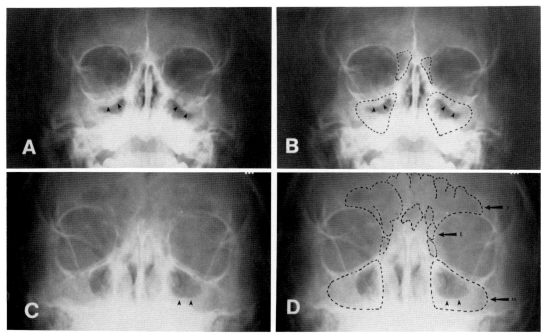

Figure 2.20. *Sinusitis—other configurations.* (*A*) Bilateral mucosal thickening is noted in both maxillary sinuses (*arrows*). This configuration frequently is seen in allergic children. In addition, the ethmoid sinuses, located just along the medial aspect of the orbital rims also are partially obliterated and involved by inflammatory change. (*B*) For comparative purposes the bony cortex of the maxillary and ethmoid sinuses in this patient have been delineated by *dotted lines.* (*C*) Another patient with an air-fluid level in the left maxillary sinus (*arrows*). The right maxillary sinus is almost completely obliterated by inflammatory change (exudate and mucosal thickening) and the ethmoid and frontal sinuses also are involved. Air-fluid levels most often are seen with acute sinusitis of bacterial origin. (*D*) *Dotted lines* once again outline the sinus cavities for comparative purposes. Maxillary sinus (*M*), ethmoid sinus (*E*), frontal sinus (*F*).

nuses in the very young, also seems a doubtful concept. One only has to ask why of all the mucosal surfaces in a newborn infant, would the mucosa in the maxillary sinuses selectively be redundant. Consequently, we have come, more and more, to the conclusion that the only normal sinus cavity is the one completely clear. ***Opacified sinus cavities, no matter what the configuration, are abnormal.*** There is, however, no ability of the roentgenograph to determine how serious the infection may be. Only when air-fluid levels are present can one confidently suggest acute sinusitis, and with circumferential mucosal thickening, allergic sinusitis might be suggested. In this regard, it should be realized that sinusitis is more common in allergic children (1, 5, 9).

The fact that the roentgenograms, for the most part, cannot yield data regarding severity of sinusitis, can explain why various studies have shown that patients with no complaints show opacified sinuses (3, 7). Indeed, most likely if a random adult population were examined, a fair number of individuals would have opacified sinuses, and yet not be overly complaintive of them. Sinusitis is a disease with a wide clinical spectrum and many individuals, including children, can tolerate certain degrees of sinusitis. This does not mean, however, that the sinuses are normal, only that the disease is not very severe, or perhaps, the patient's tolerance is high. ***Overall, then, the roentgenogram is quite sensitive in detecting sinus opacification,*** and we have come to utilize it quite regularly in cases of suspected sinusitis. Furthermore, because it is difficult to differentiate purulent rhinitis from purulent sinusitis on a clinical basis alone, the sinus films have become even more valuable. In terms of which views to obtain, it is the Waters' view which is most beneficial, but we do obtain the lateral view for evaluation of the nasopharynx and sphenoid sinus. The frontal sinuses usually do not develop until the age of 7–10 years.

The roentgenographic manifestations of sinusitis include total opacification of the sinuses, a variably thick rim of mucosal thickening, or air-fluid levels (Fig. 2.20). With circumferential mucosal thickening, it is important not to misinterpret the findings as merely being representative of small sinus cavities (Fig. 2.21). This is a common mis-

take in the pediatric age group and is not without significance, for mucosal thickening is common, especially in allergic children and children with cystic fibrosis. As has been mentioned earlier, air fluid levels suggest an acute bacterial sinusitis, and for their demonstration, upright views are necessary. We attempt to obtain upright views after the age of 1 year. Similar air fluid levels can be seen due to bleeding with facial trauma.

Symptoms of sinusitis in childhood often

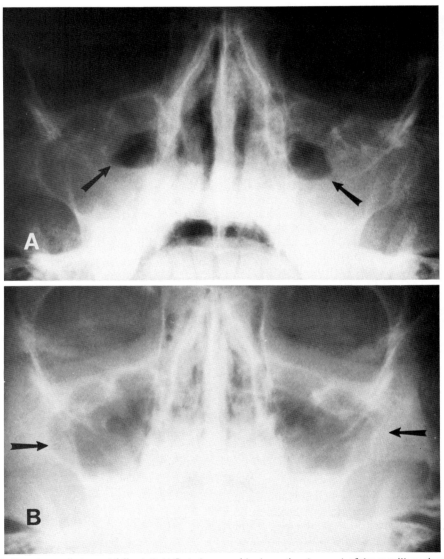

Figure 2.21. *Pseudo small sinus pitfall.*   (*A*) At first glance residual aeration (*arrows*) of the maxillary sinuses might suggest that they are normal, only small. (*B*) After treatment, however, one can see how large the sinus cavities really are. If one looks back at (*A*), one can see the bony margins of the maxillary sinuses which are filled, virtually to their entirety, by mucosal thickening.

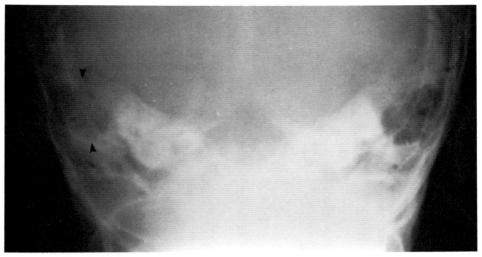

Figure 2.22. *Acute mastoiditis.*   Note the hazy, obliterated right mastoid air cells (*arrows*). The mastoid air cells on the left are normal and well aerated. In such cases often it is difficult to determine whether one is dealing with extensive acute inflammatory disease or early destruction secondary to an abscess.

are not like those in adults (1, 2, 4–6, 8, 9), and while pain and redness can occur over an acutely infected sinus cavity in a child, more often sinusitis is a chronic problem presenting with a persistent cough (due to a postnasal drip and often worse at night) and recurrent bouts of otitis media (2, 3, 9). In other children with maxillary and ethmoid sinusitis, proptosis due to orbital edema may be the presenting problem, and actually, is quite common.

Acute mastoiditis is best demonstrated on Towne's projection of the skull. In these cases one has both mastoid areas to compare and acute mastoiditis will be reflected by haziness or obliteration of the mastoid air cells (Fig. 2.22), and in more acute cases, actual destruction of the bone with abscess formation. Obliteration of the mastoid air cells also occurs with bleeding associated with calvarial trauma, and bone destruction as seen with histiocytosis X, leukemia, and lymphoma.

Aeration of the mastoid antra is present at birth, and mastoid air cell development occurs rapidly thereafter. Consequently, mastoid air cell aeration usually is present in infants as young as 3 months, and thus the diagnosis of acute mastoiditis with obliteration of the air cells can be made roentgenographically at this age. In those patients who suffer chronic repeated bouts of otitis media, overall air cell development is impaired, and bony sclerosis supervenes. Overall, in these patients, there are fewer aerated air cells, and dense or white appearing petrous bones. Currently, CT scanning more clearly delineates many of these problems.

REFERENCES

1. Furukawa, C.T., Shapiro, G.G., and Rachelefsky, G.S.: Children with sinusitis. Pediatrics 71: 133–134, 1983.
2. Kogutt, M.S., and Swischuk, L.E.: Diagnosis of sinusitis in infants and children. Pediatrics 52: 121–124, 1973.
3. Kovatch, A.L., Wald, E.R., Ledesma-Medina, J., Chiponis, D.M., and Bedingfield, B.: Maxillary sinus radiographs in children with nonrespiratory complaints. Pediatrics 73: 306–308, 1984.
4. McLain, D.C.: Sinusitis in children: lessons from 25 patients. Clin. Pediatr. 9:342, 1970.
5. Rachelefsky, G.S., and Shapiro, G.G.: Diseases of the paranasal sinuses in children. In Bierman C.W., and Pearlman, D.S. (eds.): *Allergic Diseases of Infancy, Childhood and Adolescence*, pp. 526–624. W. B. Saunders, Philadelphia, 1980.
6. Rulon, J.T.: Sinusitis in children. Postgrad. Med. 48: 107, 1970.
7. Shopfner, C.E., and Rossi, J.O.: Roentgen evaluation of the paranasal sinuses in children. A.J.R. 118: 176–186, 1973.
8. Smith, C.H.: Sinusitis in children: a simple diagnostic test. Clin. Pediatr. 3: 489, 1964.
9. Swischuk, L.E., Hayden, C.K., Jr., and Dillard R.A.: Sinusitis in children. Radiographics 2: 241–252, 1982.

EPISTAXIS

Epistaxis is a common problem in childhood. Most often it results from a simple

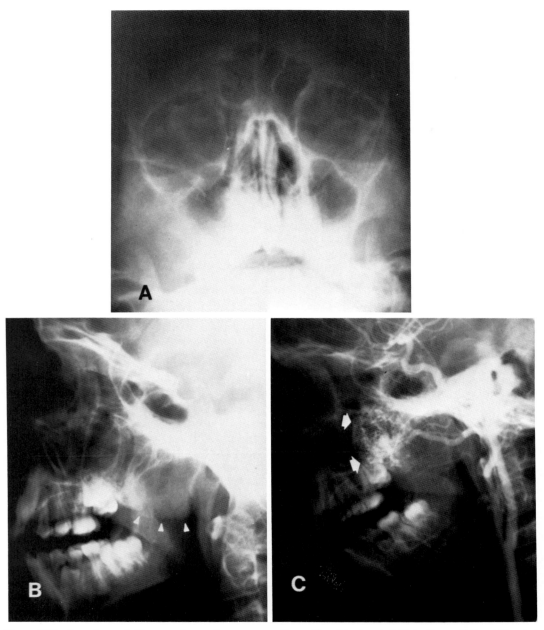

Figure 2.23. *Juvenile angiofibroma of nasopharynx presenting with epistaxis.* (*A*) Note the partially obliterated right maxillary sinus in this patient with epistaxis. (*B*) Lateral view showing large nasopharyngeal mass (*arrows*), which might be mistaken for large adenoids. (*C*) Subsequent arteriogram demonstrates extensive tumor vascularity (*arrows*) characteristic of this lesion. It is being supplied by the external maxillary artery.

nosebleed, and no roentgenograms are obtained. However, one should be aware of the fact that juvenile angiofibromas often present with epistaxis and sinusitis (1–3). These

angiofibromas occur most commonly in adolescent boys, and on the lateral roentgenogram of the paranasal sinuses present as a mass in the nasopharynx (Fig. 2.23). This mass should not be confused with normal adenoidal tissue which often is very abundant in normal children (see Fig. 2.3).

Epistaxis also may result from an acute or chronic foreign body in the nose, and if such a foreign body is radiolucent, it may remain undetected for extended periods of time.

REFERENCES

1. Fitzpatrick, P.J.: The nasopharyngeal angiofibroma. Clin. Radiol. 18: 62–68, 1967.
2. Holman, C.B., and Miller, W.E.: Juvenile nasopharyngeal fibroma: Roentgenologic characteristics. A.J.R. 94:292–298, 1965.
3. Swischuk, L.E., Smith, P.C., and Fagan, C.J.: Abnormalities of the pharynx and larynx in childhood. Semin. Roentgenol. 9: 283–300, 1974.

CHAPTER 3
The Abdomen

Analyzing the abdominal roentgenogram is more difficult and often less rewarding than analyzing the chest roentgenogram, but yet it is an important study. In the chest, symmetry of structures and densities from side to side is of paramount importance, but in the abdomen symmetry is a minor consideration. In the abdomen, it is a matter of becoming familiar with the appearance of relatively fixed organs seen through changing intestinal gas patterns. No one normal configuration looks exactly like another, and the overall "normal" picture comes only through examining many roentgenograms over many years.

In beginning one's assessment of the abdominal roentgenogram, it is worthwhile to localize the stomach, rectum, and both the hepatic and splenic flexures of the colon. These areas of gastrointestinal tract are relatively fixed, usually contain gas, and look much the same from one patient to another. After this one should attempt to define the solid abdominal viscera, and of these the easiest to visualize are the liver, spleen, kidneys, psoas muscles, and urinary bladder (Fig. 3.1). After the abdominal viscera are examined one should cast an eye over the diaphragmatic leaflets and bony structures such as the vertebrae, ribs, and pelvis. This is especially important in abdominal trauma.

Once one has learned to examine the abdominal roentgenogram in some such orderly fashion, one will become more adept at recognizing and assessing the abnormal patterns and findings discussed in the remainder of this chapter.

All of the foregoing points are most pertinent to plain films which, of course, will continue to be obtained for the evaluation of acute abdominal problems in children. However, ultrasonography, even more than computerized tomography (CT), has now come to play a significant role in the evaluation of the acute abdomen in children. Consequently, one must become familiar with normal ultrasonographic landmarks, and also recognize ultrasound's ability to look into corners and crevices not previously amenable to plain films. Indeed, ultrasonography can much more clearly identify the presence of abdominal fluid, abdominal abscesses, masses, and even a surprising variety of gastrointestinal and genitourinary disturbances. CT also can perform these functions, but only in trauma does it routinely excel over ultrasonography in children.

Ultrasonography usually is best performed with real time equipment, and almost invariably the first organs to be imaged are the right kidney and liver (Fig. 3.2). Thereafter the spleen and left kidney are identified and then, primarily in cross-section, one can assess the retroperitoneal structures (Fig. 3.2). The lower abdomen and pelvic regions also can be assessed in longitudinal and cross-section, but to do so, the urinary bladder must be distended, either with urine, or with saline introduced by the examiner.

CT yields cross-sectional anatomical data

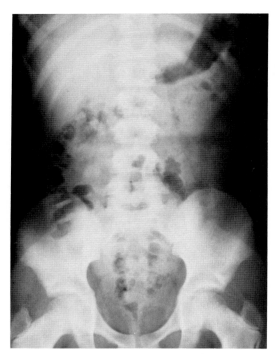

Figure 3.1. *Normal abdomen.* The distribution and volume of gastrointestinal gas is about average. The renal silhouettes are clearly visible and the psoas shadows are seen as broad triangular structures on either side of the spine. A distended urinary bladder is seen in the pelvis.

and while it is quite useful in adults, it is of lesser value in children. The one exception is abdominal trauma, where it is better than ultrasonography. Overall, however, because of the lack of fat in children, separation of the various intra-abdominal structures from one another, is not as rewarding as in adults. This, together with the fact that ultrasonography is noninvasive, does not utilize ionizing radiation, and is so easy to perform, has relegated CT to a lesser role in children.

Nonetheless, one should be familiar with the anatomy, as demonstrated with CT (Fig. 3.3).

ACUTE ABDOMINAL PROBLEMS

Examination of the acute abdomen, regardless of cause, ***requires supine and upright views of the abdomen, and both posteroanterior and lateral views of the chest.*** This combined examination should never be cut short, and if because of the patient's condition upright films are impossible to obtain, then ***cross-table lateral or decubitus views should be substituted. There is no room for a compromise, and he who cuts the examination short will regret it sooner or later.*** With ultrasonography a thorough examination of the abdomen and pelvis, along with the base of the chest, should be accomplished.

ABNORMAL INTRALUMINAL GAS PATTERNS

Airless Abdomen. An airless abdomen usually is abnormal, and most often results from excessive vomiting and/or diarrhea. Many times this occurs with gastroenteritis (1, 3, 5, 9), but an airless abdomen also can be seen in the early stages of acute appendicitis (Fig. 3.4). It is also a feature of the adrenogenital syndrome in young infants (15), and Addison's disease. Less commonly a relatively airless abdomen is seen in those patients with such a degree of cerebral depression that swallowing is markedly impaired (2).

Paralytic Ileus. Generalized paralytic ileus can be seen with gastroenteritis, intestinal ischemia, or as a secondary phenomenon in certain systemic conditions such as sepsis, hypokalemia (12), and neurogenic

Figure 3.2. *Normal abdomen; ultrasound.* (*A*) Longitudinal section, on the right side demonstrates the diaphragm (*D*), right kidney (*K*), and liver (*L*). (*B*) Longitudinal scan somewhat more medial demonstrates the inferior vena cava (*IVC*); liver (*L*). (*C*) Longitudinal scan over the aorta demonstrates the aorta (*a*) and the superior mesenteric artery (*sma*) branching from it. (*D*) Another longitudinal scan demonstrates the liver (*L*) and gallbladder (*gb*). (*E*) Transverse scan demonstrates the spine (*S*), aorta (*a*), celiac artery (*c*), and the hepatic artery (*ha*). In addition, note the inferior vena cava (*ivc*), portal vein confluence (*P*), and the splenic vein (*sv*). (*F*) Another transverse cut demonstrating the spine (*S*), aorta (*a*), and the superior mesenteric artery (*sma*). Characteristically, the superior mesenteric artery is surrounded by a collar of echogenicity. Also note the portal vein confluence (*P*), the inferior vena cava (*ivc*), and the splenic vein (*sv*). The thin sonolucent streak heading medially from the inferior vena cava is the left renal vein. The pancreas lies above the splenic vein but is not clearly delineated here. (*G*) Longitudinal scan in the pelvis demonstrates the bladder (*B*), uterus (*U*), and the vagina (*V*). The thin, sonolucent channel in the vagina is the vaginal lumen. (*H*) Transverse scan in the pelvis demonstrates the urinary bladder (*B*), uterus (*U*), and both ovaries (*o*).

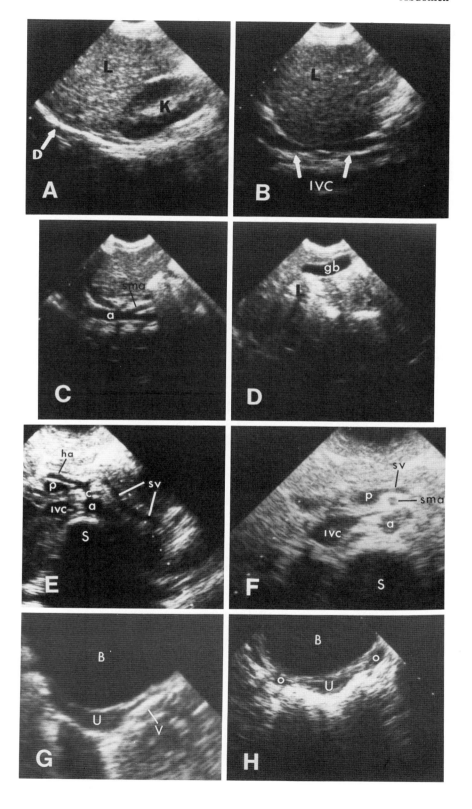

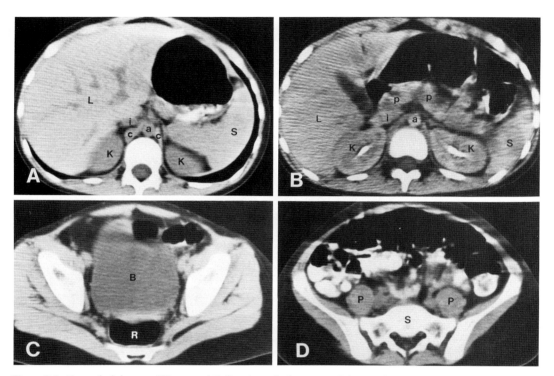

Figure 3.3. *Normal abdomen; CT scan.*   (*A*) Cut through the upper abdomen demonstrates both kidneys (*K*), the liver (*L*), and the spleen (*S*). Also note the inferior vena cava (*i*), aorta (*a*), and both the right and left crura of the diaphragm (*c*). The sonolucent branching structures in the liver represent the portal veins. (*B*) A contrast-enhanced scan, a little lower, demonstrates both kidneys (*K*), the spleen (*S*), and the liver (*L*). The aorta (*a*), now is opacified, but because the inferior vena cava also is opacified (*i*), it becomes more difficult to delineate. Above these structures lies the pancreas (*p*).The white areas in the center of the kidneys represent contrast material in the collecting systems. (*C*) Cut low in the pelvis demonstrates urine-filled bladder (*B*), and the air-filled rectum (*R*). The white structures on either side are the iliac wings. (*D*) Lower cut demonstrates the sacrum (*S*), and both psoas (*P*) muscles. Note the iliac wings, lateral to the sacrum, and in between, the sacroiliac joints.

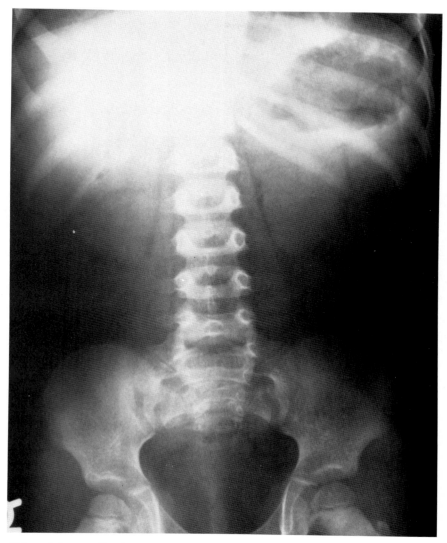

Figure 3.4. *Airless abdomen.* Gas is present in the stomach only (left upper quadrant). Most often an airless abdomen is seen with gastroenteritis or acute appendicitis; this patient had gastroenteritis.

(spinal) shock. It differs from mechanical ileus (mechanical obstruction) in that there is no differential distention of the gastrointestinal tract. In other words, all portions of the gastrointestinal tract dilate in proportion to each other and in the classic case the colon remains larger than the small bowel (Fig. 3.5). Furthermore, the picture of dilated intestinal loops is much less orderly than in mechanical obstruction, for generally speaking, many more loops are dilated. Indeed, in many cases dilated, disorganized, messy, intestinal loops seem to be present from top to bottom and side to side. On upright view, numerous air-fluid levels are seen, but the majority appear rather "inactive" or "sluggish" and tend to extend over long lengths of bowel. In this regard they are quite different from the acute, inverted, hairpin loops of the distended bowel seen with classic mechanical obstruction (see Fig. 3.6).

The preceding description of the roentgenographic appearance of generalized paralytic ileus is more or less classic, but by no means the only one seen. Indeed, paralytic ileus can be quite variable and, in some

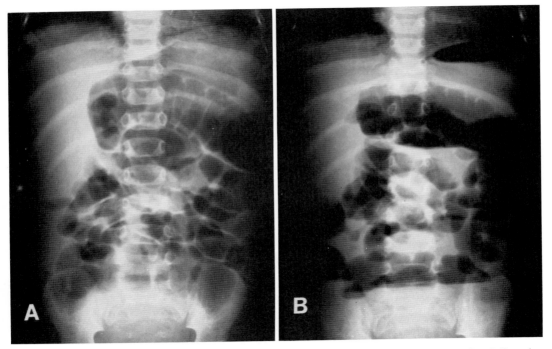

Figure 3.5. *Paralytic ileus.* (*A*) Distended loops of intestine are present everywhere, but proportional distention persists and the transverse colon (uppermost loop of distended intestine) remains larger than the numerous loops of distended small bowel. (*B*) Upright view showing numerous sluggish, long air-fluid levels scattered throughout the abdomen. Compare this adynamic appearance with the dynamic appearance of mechanical obstruction seen in Figure 3.6.

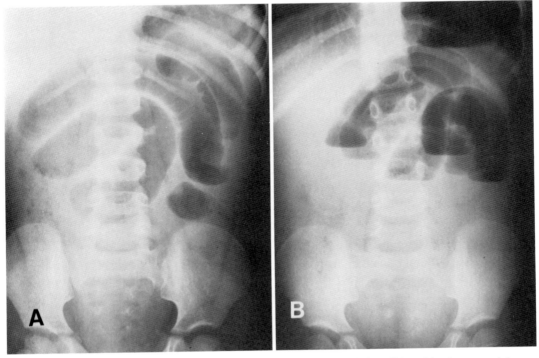

Figure 3.6. *Mechanical ileus.* (*A*) Note the well organized loops of distended small bowel in the upper abdomen. No gas is seen distal to these loops which are arranged in the so-called "stepladder" configuration. (*B*) Upright view showing persistence of the orderly pattern with acute inverted "U" or "hairpin" loops characteristic of mechanically obstructed intestine. Also note that the air-fluid levels within any given loop are at different heights.

cases, so localized and clean that obstruction is suggested. Most often this occurs with gastroenteritis (see Fig. 3.39), and in such cases close clinical-roentgenographic correlation is mandatory, for otherwise, roentgenographic misinterpretations will be common.

Mechanical Ileus. As opposed to paralytic ileus, the pattern of distended intestinal loops in mechanical obstruction is much more orderly, especially when one is dealing with small bowel obstruction (7, 8, 14). With low colonic obstruction, if ileocecal valve incompetence is present, there may be less orderliness and more difficulty in differentiating the findings from those of paralytic ileus, but in the classic case of small bowel obstruction, the findings are rather typical (Fig. 3.6). The number of dilated loops visualized depends on the level of obstruction, but in any case, the loops are discretely visualized and rather orderly in appearance. If, as often occurs on the supine view, the loops are stacked one under the other, the term "stepladder" is applied to the configuration. In those cases where obstruction has existed for a long enough period of time, no gas will be seen distal to the obstruction, but if the duration of obstruction is short, or if the obstruction is incomplete, some gas may be seen in loops of intestine distal to the site of obstruction. Of course, these latter intestinal loops will not be distended, or at least not as distended as the more proximal obstructed loops.

On upright view, the loops of intestine form acute, hairpin loops with short air-fluid levels visible in both limbs of any given loop (Fig. 3.6). In addition these fluid levels usually are at different heights in any two limbs of one loop of intestine. This clearly demonstrates that mechanical obstruction is an active or dynamic process. In other words, in their effort to overcome the obstruction, the loops show hyperperistalsis, and as the intestinal contents churn back and forth, the air-fluid levels are captured at different heights in each limb of a loop.

The classic case of well developed intestinal obstruction is not difficult to recognize, and indeed, the radiologist's real job is to detect obstructions before they reach this stage. This represents a true challenge for in such cases, signs of obstruction are much more subtle. Indeed, in some cases the loop,

or loops, are quite inconspicuous and unless the roentgenogram is closely scrutinized, they will be missed (Fig. 3.7). Such loops can be considered sentinel loops (see p. 161), and their presence may be confirmed with upright films (Fig. 3.7). In those children too ill to be placed in the upright position, decubitus or cross-table views can be helpful.

One other point regarding obstructed loops of intestine is in order. In some cases, very little air is present in the distended intestinal loops, for they are filled with fluid. In some of these cases the loops of intestine may be seen as vague opaque sausage-like structures in the abdomen. On upright views, as the small amount of gas becomes trapped in the valvulae conniventes a "string-of-beads" sign results (Fig. 3.8). On ultrasonography, such fluid-filled loops may be seen as anechoic circular or sausage-like structures (see Fig. 3.29).

After determining that an intestinal obstruction is present, the second job for the roentgenologist is to determine its level. This is relatively easily accomplished with gastric and duodenal obstructions, but with small bowel and colonic obstructions it may be more difficult. Generally speaking, however, the number of loops visualized in these cases is the best clue to the level of obstruction; i.e., the lower the obstruction, the more loops will one see. In those cases of low small bowel obstruction where differentiation from colonic obstruction is difficult, one should not waste time in trying to make the decision from plain films alone. A contrast study of the colon (usually barium) is most helpful in these cases, and should be performed on an emergent basis. With such a study one clearly can identify problems such as sigmoid volvulus, intussusception, Hirschsprung's disease, etc., and later on one might even employ a barium meal for detecting poorly defined or elusive small bowel obstructions (4, 11).

Mixed Paralytic and Mechanical Ileus. In some patients with a mechanical obstruction there is some supervening systemic illness such as sepsis or peritonitis and this may then predispose to a mixed picture of paralytic and mechanical ileus. In these cases, the abdominal film findings may be difficult to interpret and close clinical corelation, along with repeated analysis of the roentgenograms is the only real answer.

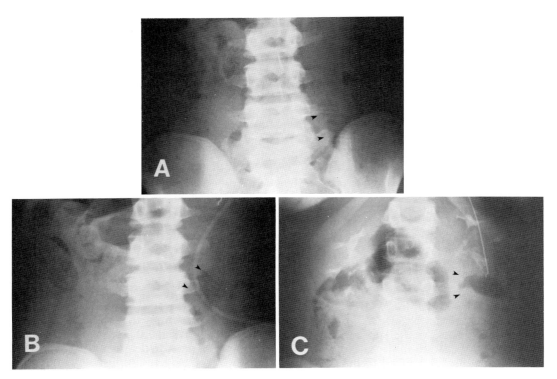

Figure 3.7. *Sentinel loop of early obstruction.*   (*A*) Note the rather innocuous appearance of a minimally dilated loop of small intestine, just to the left of the lumbar spine (*arrows*). Transverse opaque lines representing the valvulae conniventes identify the loop as being dilated jejunum. On any one film this loop probably would be dismissed as an incidental finding. (*B*) However, later in the day the same loop is visible in the same general location (*arrows*). (*C*) The next day on an upright view obtained during an intravenous pyelogram note that the isolated loop is present again (*arrows*). The presence of this one loop of distended jejunum on three separate, well spaced occasions is very significant; this patient had a small bowel obstruction secondary to adhesions from a previous laparotomy.

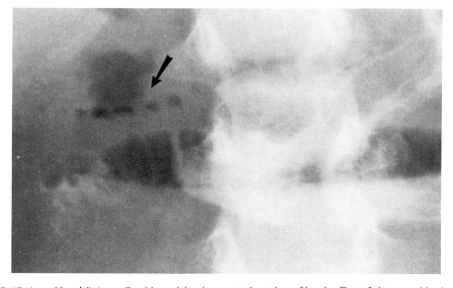

Figure 3.8. *"String-of-beads" sign.*   On this upright view, note the string-of-beads effect of air trapped in the valvulae conniventes (*arrow*).

Most classically, such a problem occurs in perforated appendicitis where a picture of superimposed small bowel obstruction is not uncommon (see Fig. 3.49).

Closed Loop Obstruction. When a loop of intestine is obstructed at both ends, it is termed a closed loop obstruction. In many of these cases, the intestinal loop becomes strangulated and gangrenous before the obstruction is diagnosed. Consequently, a closed loop obstruction is one of the most serious forms of mechanical obstruction of the intestinal tract, and the condition must be recognized early. Closed loop obstructions can occur with colonic or small bowel volvulus, internal hernias, or when loops of intestine twist around congenital peritoneal bands or postoperative adhesions.

Roentgenographically, the hallmark of closed loop obstruction is the presence of a fixed, dilated loop of bowel, frequently assuming the configuration of the letter "U" or a "coffee bean" (10, 13). If such a loop is all that is visualized the diagnosis is relatively easy (Fig. 3.9), but if a more classic small bowel obstruction begins to develop behind the strangulated loop, the loop itself may be more difficult to isolate. In other cases, the loop is full of fluid, and although it still may occasionally retain its "coffee bean" configuration, more often it produces a less specific mass on the abdominal roentgenograms. A similar mass-like configuration results if the loop of intestine becomes ischemic and extremely edematous.

Sentinel Loop. The sentinel loop usually refers to a segment of intestine which becomes paralyzed and dilated as it lies next to an inflamed intra-abdominal organ (16). It represents short segment paralytic ileus, and because it alerts one to the presence of an adjacent inflammatory process, it has been termed the "sentinel" loop. In the *right upper quadrant*, the sentinal loop can be seen with cholecystitis, pyelonephritis, and hepatic inflammatory or traumatic disease, while in the *left upper quadrant*, it is usually seen with pancreatitis, pyelonephritis, or splenic injury. In the *right lower quadrant*, the sentinel loop classically occurs with appendicitis, Meckel's diverticulitis, and regional enteritis. Sentinel loops in the *left lower quadrant* are much less common, but in the lower abdomen, in female patients, salpingitis and cystitis often produce a sen-

tinel loop. In the *upper mid abdomen*, most sentinel loops are seen with pancreatitis or trauma to the duodenum.

Roentgenographically, sentinel loops are visualized as isolated loops of distended intestine (Fig. 3.10*A*). However, it is most important that when a sentinel loop is suspected that it be demonstrated to remain in one general position from film to film, for although the loops of distended intestine in these cases are not absolutely fixed, they should remain in the same general vicinity from film to film. This is most important, for it is not unusual to see isolated loops of dilated intestine fortuitously present on a single film of some patients (Fig. 3.10*B*). Such loops can appear in perfectly normal individuals or in patients with gastroenteritis, and thus it is only when a sentinel loop persists, that it is significant. Because of this, the sentinel loop must be assessed with the utmost of caution and clinical correlation, for on as many occasions as it is helpful, on an equal number it can be misleading.

A special form of the sentinel loop is demonstrated in the so-called *colon "cutoff" sign.* Most often this sign is seen in the left transverse colon with pancreatitis (see Fig. 3.106), but it also can be seen on the right side with appendicitis (see Fig. 3.45). With pancreatitis the finding probably results from the fact that the transverse colon overlying the inflamed pancreas becomes dilated on the basis of paralytic ileus. With appendicitis, however, the sign probably results from the fact that, while the ascending colon and cecum go into spasm (because of adjacent inflammation of the appendix), the transverse colon dilates, probably on a secondary reflex paralytic ileus basis. Consequently, the colon cutoff sign, although similar in appearance, may result from two different mechanisms.

A sentinel loop also can be seen in early intestinal obstruction. In such cases, the visualized loop is the leading (sentinel) loop of an early intestinal obstruction, and as such is quite valuable. However, often it is overlooked, for it is difficult to detect (see Fig. 3.7).

Acute Gastric Dilatation. Acute gastric dilatation can be seen in extremely sick individuals and represents a profound degree of localized paralytic ileus. It can be a lethal condition for it induces a vagal response

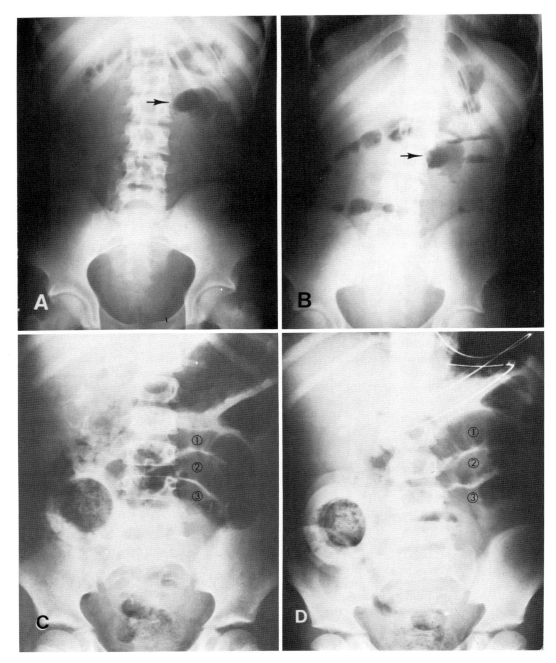

Figure 3.9. *Closed loop obstruction—single and multiple loops.* (*A*) Note a single loop of distended jejunum (*arrow*) in this child with a closed loop obstruction. A nasogastric tube is present in the stomach. (*B*) On upright view, note that the loop does not change position or configuration (*arrow*) and that its tapered end suggests a twisted or volved loop. One or two other loops of distended intestine with air-fluid levels are visualized, but it is the unchanging loop identified by the *arrows* which is most significant in indicating the presence of a closed loop obstruction. (*C*) Another patient with postoperative adhesions leading to a closed loop obstruction. Note the 1–2–3 arrangement of the distended loops of small bowel. (*D*) On upright view this arrangement is essentially the same (i.e., fixed loops). Also note the colostomy bag and calculi in the right kidney.

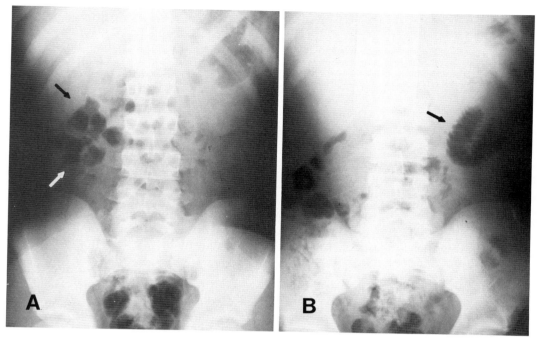

Figure 3.10. *(A) Sentinel loops adjacent to intra-abdominal inflammation.* In this patient with suspected appendicitis, note the presence of a number of dilated loops of intestine in the right flank *(arrows).* These are sentinel loops lying adjacent to an inflamed retrocecal appendix. Right lower quadrant sentinel loops in appendicitis are seen in Figure 3.41. *(B) Pseudosentinel loop—fortuitous demonstration of an isolated loop of distended intestine.* Note the single loop of distended jejunum on the left side of the abdomen *(arrow)* of this patient with gastroenteritis. Such fortuitous demonstration of a transiently dilated loop (or loops) of small bowel is not uncommon in gastroenteritis.

which may result in cardiorespiratory arrest. Consequently, prompt treatment with nasogastric tube decompression is in order. However, not all cases of a grossly dilated stomach represent acute gastric dilatation. Indeed, dilatation of the stomach is commonly seen in gastroenteritis (see Fig. 3.38), some normal infants, and in infants and children with respiratory distress. In these latter cases the finding results from excessive air swallowing commonly present with respiratory difficulty. In addition, it has been noted that acute gastric dilatation can occur in neglected children (6). In these cases, gastric dilatation usually occurs after the first full meal (6). Evidently the stomach is not able to handle this gross overload and part of the reason may be that some atrophy of the gastric muscle is present in these children. Once they get over the acute episode, they usually do not have further problems.

REFERENCES

1. Benson, H.H., and Jacobson, G.: Deficiency of small intestinal gas simulating obstruction. A.J.R. 82: 450–454, 1959.
2. Burko, H.: Toxic depression of the newborn causing deficient intestinal gas pattern. A.J.R. 88: 575–578, 1962.
3. Eklof, O.: Abdominal plain film diagnosis in infants and children. In *Progress in Pediatric Radiology.* H.J. Kaufmann (ed.), p. 3–25. Year Book. Chicago, 1969.
4. Eklof, O., and Ringertz, H.: The value of barium enema in establishing nature and level of intestinal obstruction. Pediatr. Radiol. 3: 6–11, 1975.
5. Feinberg, S.B., et al: Dehydration and deficiency of intestinal gas in infants. A.J.R. 76: 551–554, 1956.
6. Franken, E.A., Jr., Fox, M., Smith, J.A., and Smith, W.L.: Acute gastric dilatation in neglected children. A.J.R. 130: 297–299, 1978.
7. Hodges, P.C., and Miller, R.E.: Intestinal obstruction. A.J.R. 74: 1015–1025, 1955.
8. Levin, B.: Mechanical small bowel obstruction. Semin. Roentgenol. 8: 281–297, 1973.
9. Margulis, A., et al: Deficiency of intestinal gas in infants with diarrhea. Radiology 66: 93–96, 1956.
10. Mellins, H.Z., and Rigler, L.G.: The roentgen signs in strangulating obstructions of the small intestine. A.J.R. 71: 404–415, 1954.
11. Nelson, S.W., and Christoforidis, A.J.: The use of barium sulfate suspensions in the study of suspected mechanical obstruction of the small intestine. A.J.R. 101: 367–378, 1967.
12. Preeyasombat, C., Pitchayayothin, N., and Viravekin, A.: Hypokalemic crisis simulating intestinal obstruction in a 4-year old girl. Am. J. Dis. Child. 130: 1143–1145, 1976.
13. Rigler, L.: Roentgen diagnosis of acute abdominal conditions. Bull. Univ. Minn. Hosp. 16: 120, 1944.
14. Schwartz, S.S.: The differential diagnosis of intestinal obstruction. Semin. Roentgenol. 8: 323–338, 1973.

15. Weens, H.S., and Golden, A.: Adrenal cortical insufficiency in infants simulating high intestinal obstruction. A.J.R. 74: 213–219, 1955.
16. Young, B.R.: Significance of regional or reflex ileus in roentgen diagnosis of cholecystitis, perforated ulcer, pancreatitis and appendiceal abscess, as determined by survey examination of acute abdomen. A.J.R. 78: 581–586, 1957.

ABNORMAL EXTRALUMINAL GAS PATTERNS

Extraluminal air may lie in the intestinal wall itself (intramural) or more often completely outside the intestine. In the latter cases, such air may be seen in the peritoneal cavity or retroperitoneal space, and as such signifies the presence of a gastrointestinal perforation. Extraluminal, intramural air (pneumatosis cystoides intestinalis) usually signifies a loss of intestinal mucosal integrity secondary to intestinal ischemia or severe inflammation (i.e., necrotizing enterocolitis). However, pneumatosis cystoides intestinalis also is seen in the absence of these problems and as such is termed benign pneumatosis.

Portal vein gas most often occurs in association with intestinal infarction or necrotizing enterocolitis, while biliary tree air usually is seen with intestinal obstructions around the duodenum, distal to the ampulla of Vater.

Pneumoperitoneum (Free Peritoneal Air). Pneumoperitoneum signifies the presence of gastrointestinal tract perforation. Such perforations usually occur with duodenal or gastric ulcer disease, ulcerative intestinal disease, Meckel's diverticulitis, appendicitis, abdominal trauma, and foreign body perforations. Roentgenographically the findings are virtually the same as those in adults. However, perforations in general are not nearly as common in childhood as in adults (31).

In the *supine position* it is surprising to see how large a collection of free air may remain undetected. This is most likely to occur in neonates and very young infants with gastric or colonic obstructions, but it also can occur with small intestinal obstruction when the small intestine is grossly distended. In such cases, one may note an extremely clear, almost diagrammatic and hyperlucent appearance to the abdomen (Fig. 3.11). In addition, the falciform ligament (28), urachus (13), or as an inverted "v", the inferior epigastric arteries or lateral umbilical ligaments (3, 35) can be outlined by the air. The overall configuration of massive pneumoperitoneum as it appears on the supine roentgenogram of these infants often receives one or other of the following descriptive terms: "saddlebag" or "football" sign (22).

In addition to the findings just noted, one usually will see loops of intestine with their walls outlined by air on both sides (26); that is, both their serosal and mucosal surfaces (Fig. 3.11A). Indeed, it is this latter finding which becomes most useful in the older child with lesser volumes of free air who is examined in the supine position, but before proceeding to this problem, one or two more points regarding massive pneumoperitoneum in the young infant are in order. In some of these infants air may extend into the scrotum or groin, for the processus vaginalis is patent in male infants of this age, and in other infants, the abdominal viscera, especially the liver and spleen, become compressed toward the center of the abdomen. This latter finding often is more readily appreciated on upright or cross-table lateral views (Fig. 3.11B).

In the older child with lesser volumes of free air in the peritoneal cavity, the most useful finding on the supine film is visualization of both the outer and inner aspects of a dilated loop of intestine (Fig. 3.12). However, a word of caution is in order regarding this sign, for it also can be present in the absence of pneumoperitoneum in the child with grossly distended intestines. In such cases, one loop is visualized through another (6), and because these loops contain so much air, segments of the bowel wall appear to be outlined by air on both sides (Fig. 3.13). In other cases of pneumoperitoneum air will be seen to collect over the anterior surface, or along the inferior aspect of the liver (19), and as such will appear as a variety of formless or linear parahepatic collections of air (Figs. 3.12, 3.14, and 3.15A).

On *upright view*, of course, free air characteristically collects beneath the diaphragmatic leaflets (Fig. 3.15), but if upright positioning is impossible to accomplish because of the patient's condition, *cross-table lateral or decubitus views* will demonstrate

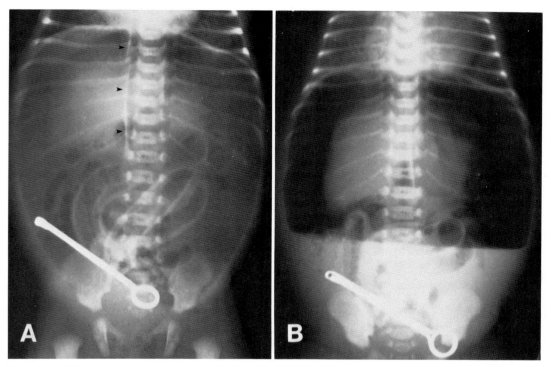

Figure 3.11. *Massive pneumoperitoneum—supine film findings.*   (*A*) Note the hyperlucent appearance of the entire abdomen. Both aspects of the walls of the loops of intestine clustered in the center of the abdomen are well visualized. Because of this they appear as discrete linear and curvilinear white stripes. A similar phenomenon is seen along the falciform ligament (*arrows*). This esthetically pleasing, almost diagrammatic appearance of the roentgenogram is characteristic of massive pneumoperitoneum, but is overlooked with surprising regularity. (*B*) Upright view confirms the presence of a massive volume of free air in the peritoneal cavity. Note how the liver and stomach have been compressed centrally. (Reprinted from Swischuk, L.E.: *Radiology of the Newborn and Young Infant*, Williams & Wilkins, Baltimore, 1973.)

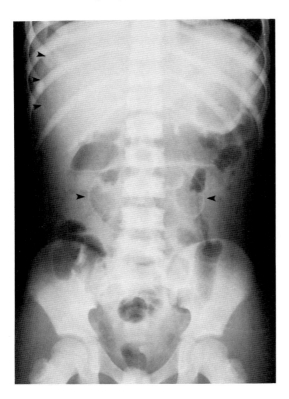

Figure 3.12. *Small volume pneumoperitoneum—supine film findings.* Note the fine white line representing intestinal wall (*lower arrows*) visualized in this manner because air is present both inside the lumen of the intestine, and along its outer surface in the peritoneal space. Also note the presence of free air overlying the liver anteriorly (*upper arrows*). A similar parahepatic collection of air can be seen in Figure 3.15*A*. There also is a pleural effusion in the right costophrenic angle of the patient illustrated above.

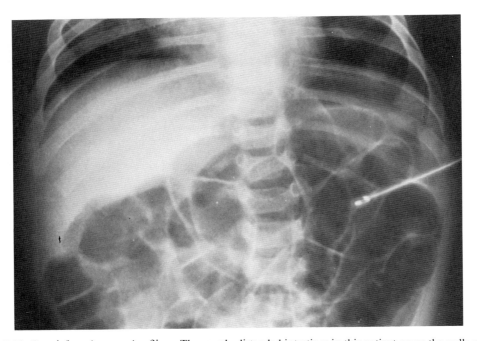

Figure 3.13. *Pseudofree air on supine film.* The grossly distended intestines in this patient cause the walls of each loop to be projected through other loops. This being the case the walls appear to be outlined by air on both sides. However, no free air is present, but the finding is misleading and often misinterpreted for free air.

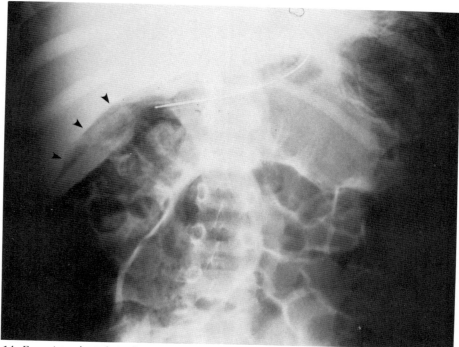

Figure 3.14. *Free air under inferior liver margin.* Note the collection of free air lying just inferior to the lower aspect of the liver (*arrows*). Also note the presence of pneumatosis cystoides intestinalis in this patient. It is visualized best as curvilinear and bubbly collections of intramural gas in the splenic flexure. This patient was severely burned and demonstrated so-called benign pneumatosis cystoides intestinalis secondary to profound distention of the intestines. The free air was a complication of the pneumatosis.

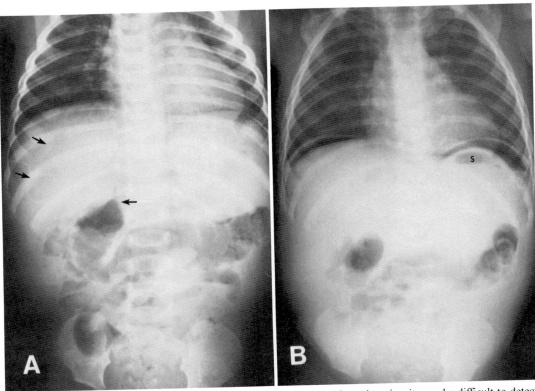

Figure 3.15. *Free peritoneal air—utilizing the upright view.* (*A*) On this supine view it may be difficult to detect that free air is present. However, some is present over the anterior aspect of the liver (*upper arrows*), and some can be seen under the liver, along its inferior medial aspect (*lower arrow*). Actually, the air probably outlines the gallbladder. (*B*) Upright positioning clearly identifies the presence of free air as it accumulates in characteristic fashion under both diaphragmatic leaflets. Stomach air bubble (*S*).

the same findings (Fig. 3.16). Indeed, with proper upright or decubitus positioning, it is said that as little as 1 cc of free air can be detected. Of course, the patient must remain in one of these positions for more than just a few seconds, for otherwise the air will not trickle up to the uppermost portion of the abdomen.

Small volume collections of air beneath the diaphragmatic leaflet (Fig. 3.17A) must be differentiated from certain normal, almost artifactual findings. One of these occurs when a diaphragmatic leaflet is visualized just over the lower edge of a rib (Fig. 3.17B), while the other occurs when the gastric bubble is visualized under the left diaphragmatic leaflet (Fig. 3.17C). In differentiating the stomach bubble from pneumoperitoneum, it should be noted that the combined thickness of the distended stomach and diaphragm usually is thicker than that of the diaphragm alone (Fig. 3.17C).

Most cases of pneumoperitoneum eventually are associated with peritonitis for they result from perforation of the gastrointestinal tract, but occasionally one can encounter pneumoperitoneum without peritonitis. This can occur with pneumatosis cystoides intestinalis, pneumomediastinum, and after laparotomy. With regard to pneumatosis cystoides intestinalis, it is not the intestine which perforates, but merely the outer serosal surface, and thus free air may escape into the peritoneal cavity in the absence of intestinal contents. The mechanism of pneumoperitoneum in cases of pneumomediastinum is poorly understood, but it has been suggested that air may track into the abdomen along the aorta and abdominal vessels, or that there may actually be a congenital pulmonary-peritoneal communication present. At any rate, whatever the precise etiology, massive amounts of peritoneal air can accumulate this way, and it is remarkable that both the pneumomediastinum and pneumoperitoneum so incurred can remain rather silent. In addition, in some of these cases the presence of the initial lesion, that is, pneumomediastinum, may be difficult to detect, and only the pneumoperitoneum will be seen.

Retroperitoneal Free Air. Free air in the retroperitoneal space is much less commonly encountered than is free intraperitoneal air. Often such air layers itself against the psoas muscles or kidneys (Fig. 3.18), and in the more subtle cases can be missed even by the experienced observer. Retroperitoneal free air can be seen with perforation of the duodenum, a retrocecal appendix, or perforation of the rectum (Fig. 3.18B). It also can be seen with pneumomediastinum (Fig. 3.18A).

On supine view, when retroperitoneal air collects beneath the diaphragmatic leaflet, the leaflet itself is outlined (Fig. 3.18A). In addition, in some cases one can see oblique striations, crossing over the liver area, representing the muscle bundles of the diaphragm (5). One also may visualize the inferior aspect of the heart border, as a clear, distinct line (16).

Intramural Air (Pneumatosis Cystoides Intestinalis). Pneumatosis cystoides intestinalis is a term utilized to designate the presence of intramural gas. Most frequently such gas is seen with a loss of mucosal integrity as incurred by extensive inflammatory or ischemic disease of the intestine, and classically it is a feature of necrotizing enterocolitis of the newborn infant (25, 27, 29, 30, 33, 34). In these latter cases, intramural air is believed to represent gas formed by an overgrowth of bacteria in the bowel wall, and often such air first appears in the terminal ileum and ascending colon. Pneumatosis cystoides intestinalis secondary to enterocolitis also is seen in some infants with Hirschsprung's disease, and also is a feature of ischemia induced by mechanical catastrophies such as closed loop strangulation or intestinal volvulus.

So-called benign pneumatosis intestinalis can be seen with intestinal obstruction (27), collagen vascular diseases (8, 9, 21, 23, 24), cystic fibrosis (36, 39), leukemia, steroid or other immunosuppressive therapy (2, 9, 12, 14, 18), and occasionally with perforated duodenal ulcer or jejunal diverticula (4). With intestinal obstruction, simple overdistention is believed to lead to mucosal tears and leakage of intraluminal gas into the bowel wall. Most often this is seen with chronic small bowel obstructions. Dilatation with loss of integrity of the mucosa also is believed to lead to pneumatosis cystoides intestinalis in children with collagen vascular diseases, but it should be noted that some of these patients also may develop pneumatosis cystoides intestinalis secondary to

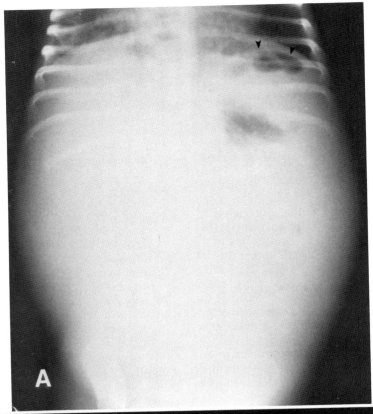

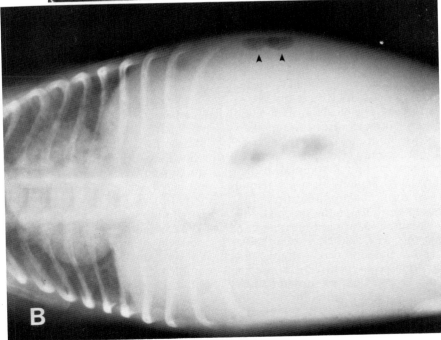

Figure 3.16. *Free peritoneal air—value of decubitus views.* (*A*) In this patient with intestinal perforation and peritonitis the presence of free air in the abdominal cavity may be difficult to detect. However, the air demarcated by the *arrows* will turn out to be free air on the decubitus view. (*B*) Decubitus view demonstrating how the collection of free air has shifted in position and come to lie just below the abdominal wall (*arrows*). (Reprinted from Swischuk, L.E.: *Radiology of the Newborn and Young Infant*, Williams & Wilkins, Baltimore, 1973.)

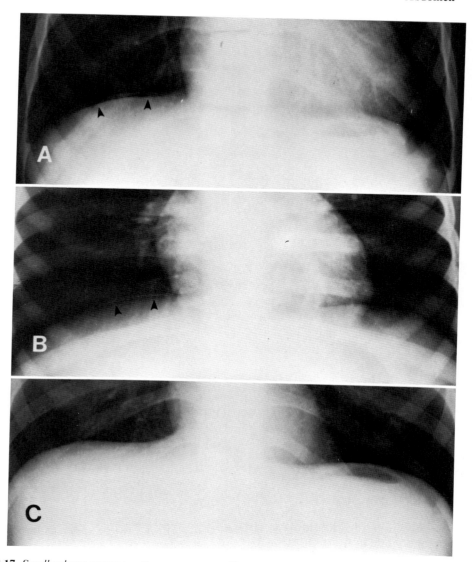

Figure 3.17. *Small volume pneumoperitoneum versus artifact.* (*A*) Note the thin sliver of free air under the right diaphragmatic leaflet (*arrows*). Note how thin the diaphragmatic leaflet appears. (*B*) Pseudo free air resulting from superimposition of the top of the right diaphragmatic leaflet over the lower aspect of the underlying rib (*arrows*). (*C*) Pseudopneumoperitoneum produced by gas in the stomach. Note that the white line (*arrows*) above the collection of gas in the stomach is thicker than that seen in (*A*). It is thicker because it represents both gastric wall and diaphragmatic leaflet. The bolus of food present in the stomach further adds to the illusion that free air is present under the diaphragmatic leaflet.

intestinal ischemia and necrotizing entero-colitis (8, 17). Consequently, in this group of patients, both benign and nonbenign pneumatosis cystoides intestinalis can be seen. Pneumatosis cystoides intestinalis in cystic fibrosis and in children on steroids or other immunosuppressive therapy is of un-known etiology. With immunosuppressive therapy it has been suggested that atrophy

of submucosal lymphoid tissue may render the mucosa prone to tear more easily with overdistention. Pneumatosis cystoides intes-tinalis secondary to pneumomediastinum, with or without obstructive emphysema, is uncommonly seen in children.

The classic roentgenographic appearance of pneumatosis cystoides intestinalis consists of linear or curvilinear collections of gas

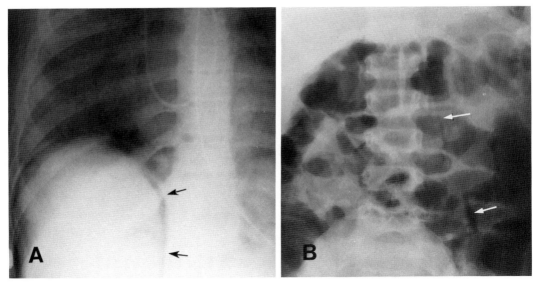

Figure 3.18. *Retroperitoneal air.* (*A*) Note air outlining the liver, right diaphragmatic leaflet, and right kidney (*arrow*). This air tracked from a pneumomediastinum resulting from ventilator therapy in a patient with a closed head injury. (*B*) Another patient with retroperitoneal air along the left psoas muscle (*arrows*). This resulted from a rectal perforation in a battered child.

within the bowel wall (Fig. 3.19). Unfortunately, not all patients present with this configuration, and in others the collection of gas appears so bubbly that it is difficult to differentiate it from food in the stomach, fecal material in the colon, or an intra-abdominal abscess (Fig. 3.19). Linear air collections must be differentiated from the normal properitoneal fat stripe (Fig. 3.19*C*).

Pneumatosis cystoides intestinalis occasionally can be limited to the stomach (10, 11, 20, 32), and while in most of these cases it merely is a part of more generalized, widespread enterocolitis, in others it truly is an isolated phenomenon. In these latter cases, it is believed to result from chronic overdistention of the stomach, such as is seen with infantile pyloric stenosis.

Portal Vein and Biliary Tract Gas. Portal vein gas is a common finding in necrotizing enterocolitis of infancy (1, 32, 34, 37, 38), but can be seen with small bowel necrosis due to any number of causes. For this reason, it usually is seen hand in hand with pneumatosis cystoides intestinalis. Presumably, in these cases, gas enters the portal circulation from the intestinal wall, either through the veins or lymphatics, and then passes into the liver (Fig. 3.20). Biliary tract gas is quite uncommon and usually is seen with duodenal obstructions distal to the entrance of the common bile duct (7, 15).

REFERENCES

1. Arnon, R.G., and Fishbein, J.F.: Portal venous gas in pediatric age group: Review of the literature and report of 12 new cases. J. Pediatr. 79: 255–259, 1971.
2. Bornes, P.F., and Johnston, T.A.: Indolent pneumatosis of the bowel wall associated with immune suppressive therapy. Ann. Radiol. 16: 163–166, 1973.
3. Bray, J.F.: The "inverted V" sign of pneumoperitoneum. Radiology 151: 45–46, 1984.
4. Bryk, D.: Unusual causes of small bowel pneumatosis: Perforated duodenal ulcer and perforated jejunal diverticula. Radiology 106: 299–302, 1973.
5. Christensen, E.E., and Landay, M.J.: Visible muscle of the diaphragm: sign of extraperitoneal air. A.J.R. 135: 521–523, 1980.
6. de Lacey, G., Bloomberg, T., and Wignall, B.K.: Pneumoperitoneum: The misleading double wall sign. Clin. Radiol. 28: 445–448, 1977.
7. Frates, R.E.: Incompetence of sphincter of Oddi in newborn. Radiology 85: 875–879, 1965.
8. Fischer, T.J., Cipel, L., and Stiehm, E.R.: Pneumatosis intestinalis associated with fatal childhood dermatomyositis. Pediatrics 61: 127–129, 1978.
9. Gupta, A.: Pneumatosis intestinalis in children. Br. J. Radiol. 51: 589–595, 1978.
10. Henry, G.W.: Emphysematous gastritis. A.J.R. 68: 15–18, 1952.
11. Holgersen, L.O., Bornes, P.F., and Srouji, M.N.: Isolated gastric pneumatosis. J. Pediatr. Surg. 9: 813–816, 1974.
12. Jaffe, N., Carlson, D.H., and Vawter, F.G.: Pneumatosis cystoides intestinalis in acute leukemia. Cancer 30: 239–243, 1973.

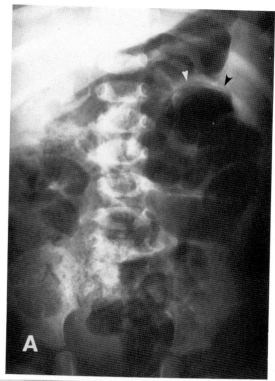

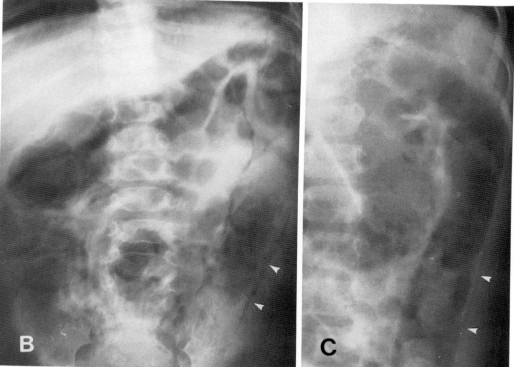

Figure 3.19. *Pneumatosis cystoides intestinalis (intramural air).* (*A*) Note classic curvilinear collections of air within distended loops of intestine (*arrows*). The bubbly pattern over the remainder of the abdomen often is misinterpreted for feces mixed with air, but actually represents another configuration of pneumatosis cystoides intestinalis. (*B*) Typical curvilinear collections of free air are seen in the ascending colon, while linear collections of air are noted in the descending colon (*arrows*). (*C*) *Normal properitoneal fat line mimicking pneumatosis cystoides intestinalis.* In this normal infant, the properitoneal fat line (*arrows*) might be misinterpreted for pneumatosis cystoides intestinalis.

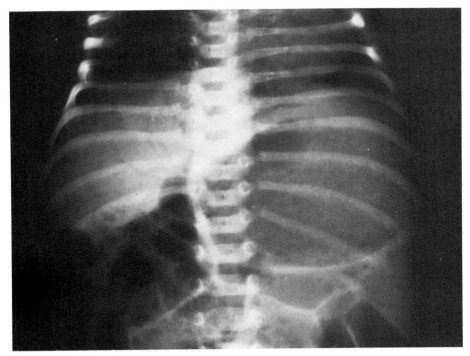

Figure 3.20. *Portal vein gas.*   Note the linear collections of gas in the portal vein radicles of the liver. Characteristically they radiate toward the porta hepatis. This patient had necrotizing enterocolitis.

13. Jelasco, D.V., and Schultz, E.H., Jr.: The uracus—an aid to the diagnosis of pneumoperitoneum. Radiology 92: 295–296, 1969.
14. Keats, T.E., and Smith, T.H.: Benign pneumatosis intestinalis in childhood leukemia. A.J.R. 122: 150–152, 1974.
15. Kirks, D.R., and Baden, M.: Incompetence of the sphincter of Oddi associated with duodenal stenosis. J. Pediatr. 83: 838–843, 1973.
16. Klein, D.L.: Visibility of the inferior heart border in pneumoperitoneum. A.J.R. 137: 622–623, 1981.
17. Kleinman, P., Meyers, M.A., Abbott, G., and Kazam, E.: Necrotizing enterocolitis with pneumatosis intestinalis in systemic lupul erythematosus and polyarteritis. Radiology 121: 595–598, 1976.
18. Kleinman, P.K., Brill, P.W., and Winchester, P.: Pneumatosis intestinalis: its occurrence in the immunologically compromised child. Am. J. Dis. Child. 134: 1149–1151, 1980.
19. Menuck, L., and Siemers, P.T.: Pneumoperitoneum: Importance of right upper quadrant features. A.J.R. 127: 753–756, 1976.
20. Meyes, H.I., and Parker, J.J.: Emphysematous gastritis. Radiology 89: 426–431, 1967.
21. Miercort, R.D., and Merrill, F.G.: Pneumatosis and pseudo-obstruction in scleroderma. Radiology 92: 359–362, 1969.
22. Miller, R.E.: Perforated viscus in infants. A new roentgen sign. Radiology 74: 65–67, 1960.
23. Mueller, C.F., Morehead, R., Alter, A.J., and Michener, W.: Pneumatosis intestinalis in collagen disorders. A.J.R. 115: 300–305, 1972.
24. Oliveros, M.A., Herbst, J.J., Lester, P.D., and Ziter, F. A.: Pneumatosis intestinalis in childhood dermatomyositis. Pediatrics 52: 711–712, 1973.
25. Richmond, J.A., and Mikity, V.: Benign form of necrotizing enterocolitis. A.J.R. 123: 301–306, 1975.
26. Rigler, L.G.: Spontaneous pneumoperitoneum: A roentgenologic sign found in the supine position. Radiology 37: 604–607, 1941.
27. Robinson, A.E., Grossman, H., and Brumley, G.W.: Pneumatosis intestinalis in the neonate. A.J.R. 120: 333–341, 1974.
28. Schultz, E.H., Jr.: An aid to the diagnosis of pneumoperitoneum from supine abdominal films. Radiology 70: 728–731, 1958.
29. Seaman, W.B., Fleming, R.J., and Baker, D.H.: Pneumatosis intestinalis of the small bowel. Semin. Roentgenol. 1: 234, 1966.
30. Touloukian, R.J., Posch, J.N., and Spencer, R.: The pathogenesis of ischemic gastroenterocolitis of the neonate: Selective gut mucosal ischemia in asphyxiated neonatal piglets. J. Pediatr. Surg. 7: 194–205, 1972.
31. Tucker, A.S., Soine, L., and Izant, R.J., Jr.: Gastrointestinal perforations in infancy: anatomic and etiologic gamuts. A.J.R. 123: 755–763, 1975.
32. Vaughan, B.R.: Emphysema of the stomach with portal vein gas. Australas. Radiol. 16: 377–378, 1972.
33. Vicki, G.F., Maggini, M., Moggi, P., Gori, F., and Paoli, F.: Pneumatosis intestinalis in infants: Clinical, radiological and anatomo-pathological study on eighteen patients. Ann. Radiol. 16: 153–161, 1973.
34. Vollman, J.H., Smith, W.L., and Tsang, R.C.: Necrotizing enterocolitis with recurrent hepatic portal vein gas. J. Pediatr. 88: 486–487, 1976.
35. Weiner, C.I., Diaconis, J.N., and Dennis, J.M.: The "inverted V": A new sign of pneumoperitoneum. Radiology 197: 47–48, 1973.
36. White, H., and Rowley, W.F.: Cystic fibrosis of the pancreas: Clinical and roentgenographic manifestations. Radiol. Clin. North Am. 1: 539–556, 1963.
37. Wiot, J.F., and Felson, B.: Gas in the portal venous system. A.J.R. 86: 920, 1961.

38. Wolfe, J.N., and Evans, W.A.: Gas in the portal veins of liver in infant. A.J.R. 74: 186, 1955.
39. Wood, R.E., Herman, C.J., Johnson, K.W., and di Sant Agnese, P.A.: Pneumatosis coli in cystic fibrosis. Am. J. Dis. Child. 129: 246–248, 1975.

THICKENED AND PSEUDOTHICKENED BOWEL WALLS

True thickening of the intestinal wall can be seen with any type of inflammatory disease of the intestine, chronic obstruction, and intestinal ischemia or infarction (Fig. 3.21). Pseudothickening of the bowel wall is seen with ascites or peritonitis, or when loops of distended intestine contain more fluid than air (1, 2). In the first instance, as the loops of air-filled bowel float in the ascitic fluid, they become separated to such a degree that bowel wall thickening is suggested (Fig. 3.22A). In the second case, bowel wall thickening is suggested when small amounts of gas collect at the top of a primarily fluid-filled loop of intestine. The cap of free air in each such loop is so small that an optical illusion suggesting thickened bowel wall is suggested (Fig. 3.22, *B* and *C*). All of these findings are summarized in the

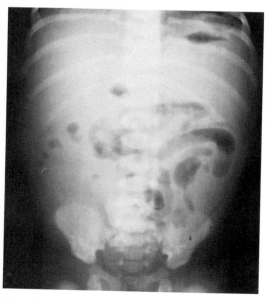

Figure 3.21. *True thickening of intestinal wall.* Note, that on this upright view, the space between the air-filled loops of intestine is increased. This type of thickening would not persist on the upright view if it were pseudothickening. This infant had necrotizing enterocolitis and the intestine was necrotic.

diagram illustrated in Figure 3.23, but it should be noted that if true bowel wall thickening is present it tends to persist on upright view (see Fig. 3.21).

REFERENCES

1. Hoffman, R.B., Wankmuller, R., and Rigler, L.G.: Pseudoseparation of bowel loops: A fallacious sign of intraperitoneal fluid. Radiology 87: 845–847, 1966.
2. Nelson, S.W., and Eggleston, W.: Findings on plain roentgenograms of the abdomen associated with mesenteric vascular occlusion with a possible new sign of mesenteric venous thrombosis. A.J.R. 83: 886–894, 1960.

ABDOMINAL FLUID COLLECTIONS (ASCITES, PERITONITIS, HEMOPERITONEUM)

The roentgenographic findings of fluid in the abdomen are much the same from case to case, and depend primarily on the volume, not the type, of fluid present (5, 11). *Types of fluid which might be encountered include serous effusions, chyle, urine, bile, blood, and pus.* With massive fluid collections the diagnosis is relatively easy, for the abdomen becomes distended and opaque, and the normally visible liver edge and retroperitoneal structures become obscured (Fig. 3.24A). If distended loops of intestine also are present they tend to float toward the center of the abdomen (Fig. 3.24B), and in so doing result in the clinically percussable "tympanic cap." In addition to these findings in many cases one will be able to delineate the edge of the medially displaced liver (Fig. 3.24B). This subtle finding is present more often than generally appreciated and results from the fact that the densities of the liver and adjacent fluid are just different enough that a roentgenographically perceptible interface between them develops (13, 19). This phenomenon is even more dramatically portrayed with CT scanning (see Fig. 3.27B).

With lesser volumes of fluid, the findings on supine views of the abdomen often are subtle, and in this regard it should be noted that fluid first accumulates in the pelvis in the peritoneal cul-de-sac (Fig. 3.25A). When enough fluid accumulates here the cul-de-sac bulges laterally and the term "dog ears" has been assigned this finding (Fig. 3.26A). However, in young infants this finding is almost impossible to detect, and actually, when young infants present with ascites it is usually of considerable volume. In older

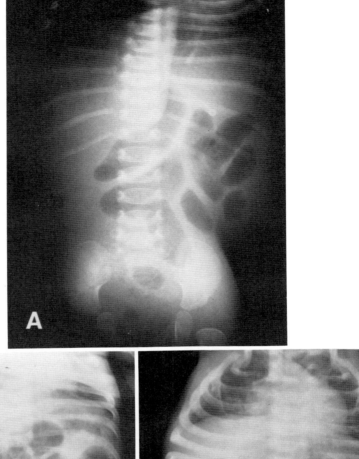

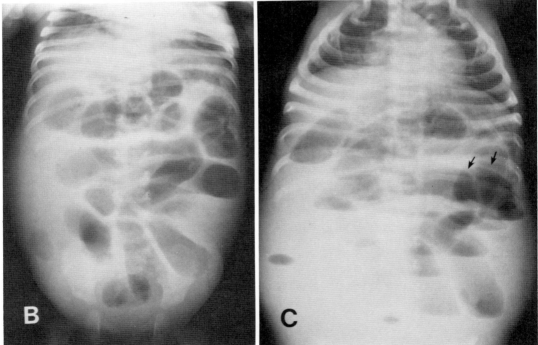

Figure 3.22. *Pseudothickening of bowel walls.* (*A*) In this infant, ascites is causing separation of the distended loops of intestine so as to mimic bowel wall thickening. (*B*) In this infant with low small bowel obstruction, the presence of large volumes of fluid within the dilated loops erroneously suggests bowel wall thickening. However, on upright view (*C*), note that the bowel walls are not thickened (*arrows*), but that the intestinal loops do contain large volumes of fluid. In these cases, the relatively small amount of air in the intestinal loops is so small that on supine view, as this air floats to the top of each loop, the fluid under it causes the space between any two given air collections to be widened. In this manner, bowel wall thickening is suggested, but actually is not present (see Fig. 3.23*A* for diagrammatic depiction of this phenomenon).

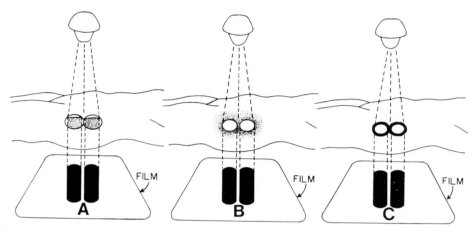

Figure 3.23. *True versus pseudothickening of bowel walls—diagrammatic representation.* (*A*) When large volumes of fluid are present in intestinal loops, and only small amounts of gas float on top of this fluid, the resultant roentgenographic image is such that the space between the loops of intestine appears widened and bowel wall thickening is suggested. The bowel wall, however, is not thickened. (*B*) With ascitic fluid between the bowel loops, the loops themselves are separated, and since the space between them is widened, bowel wall thickening is once again erroneously suggested. (*C*) True thickening of the bowel wall. The widened space between the loops of air-filled intestine truly represents thick intestinal walls. (Reprinted with permission from Hoffman, R.B., et al.: Pseudoseparation of bowel loops: a fallacious sign of intraperitoneal fluid, Radiology 87: 845–847, 1966.)

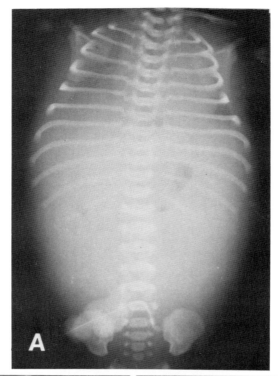

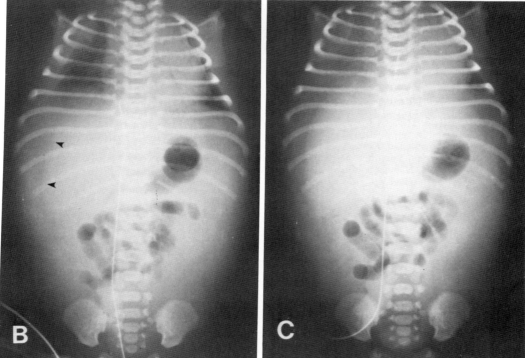

Figure 3.24. *Massive ascites.* (*A*) Massive ascites in a young infant produces marked abdominal distension, marked opacity of the abdomen, obliteration of the inferior liver edge, and obliteration of all the retroperitoneal structures. In the right upper quadrant, one can see a slight difference in density between the medially displaced liver and the adjacent ascitic fluid. (*B*) With more penetration of the abdomen, the interface between the liver and ascitic fluid is more clearly visualized (*arrows*). In addition, note that some air is now present in the intestines, and that the air-filled loops of intestine cluster and float in the center of the abdomen. (*C*) Enhanced visualization of the liver after injection of contrast material for an intravenous pyelogram. The increased density of the liver is secondary to the circulating contrast material and is useful in substantiating that the findings in (*A*) and (*B*) actually were due to the ascitic fluid-liver interface.

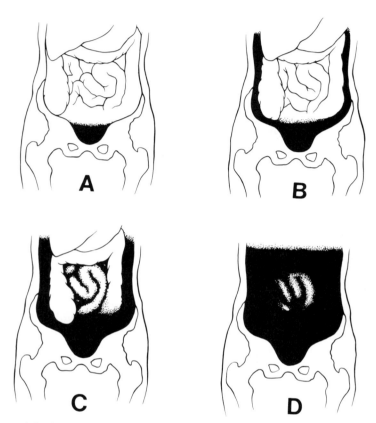

Figure 3.25. *Peritoneal fluid accumulation—sequence of findings.*   (*A*) In early cases, in the supine position fluid accumulates in the cul-de-sac. (*B*) With larger volumes fluid begins to track upward, and accumulates primarily between the abdominal wall and the ascending colon on the right, and the abdominal wall and descending colon on the left. (*C*) With even greater volumes of fluid, displacement of the ascending and descending colon medially becomes more pronounced, and fluid begins to accumulate beneath and around the liver. (*D*) With massive peritoneal fluid accumulations the entire abdomen becomes filled with fluid, gas is compressed out of the ascending and descending colon, and the few remaining air-filled loops of small bowel cluster and float in the center of the abdomen.

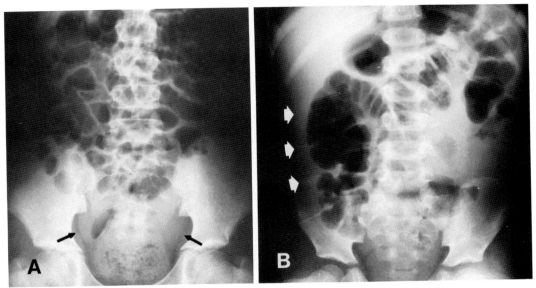

Figure 3.26. *(A) Fluid in peritoneal cul-de-sac—"dog ears" sign.* Fluid first accumulates in the peritoneal cul-de-sac and when the cul-de-sac bulges laterally, a dog ear-like configuration is suggested (*arrows*). (*B*) *Fluid collecting between ascending colon and abdominal wall.* This patient was in an automobile accident and had hemoperitoneum. The best evidence for the presence of peritoneal blood (fluid) lies in the increased distance between the right abdominal wall and the ascending colon (*arrows*).

children, on the other hand, with close inspection of the roentgenogram it often is possible to detect these early fluid accumulations in the peritoneal cul-de-sac. Thereafter, as more fluid accumulates it tends to pass upward between the abdominal wall and both the ascending and descending portions of the colon (Figs. 3.25*B* and 3.26*B*). Eventually fluid reaches the liver, and as it collects along the inferior aspect of this organ, the liver angle (14) and its entire inferior edge become invisible (Figs. 3.24 and 3.25*C*). At the same time fluid accumulates between the abdominal wall and liver, and causes medial displacement of the liver (Figs. 3.24 and 3.25). All the while the accumulating fluid tends to gather in between, and separate, the centrally floating loops of intestine, and as such may at first erroneously suggest that thickening of the intestinal walls is present (Fig. 3.22).

Since ultrasonography has been on the scene, it has become the best tool for detecting the presence of peritoneal fluid of any type. Although it can easily detect large volumes of fluid, is especially useful in detecting small volume fluid collections in and around the liver, and in the peritoneal cul-de-sac

(10). Various configurations of free abdominal fluid are presented in Fig. 3.27.

Serous ascitic effusions in children can be seen with many conditions including: (a) renal disease, (b) liver disease with portal hypertension, (c) portal vein obstruction, (d) hypoproteinemia, (e) protein-losing enteropathy, (f) congestive heart failure, and (g) pancreatitis (5, 21). Chylous ascites usually occurs on a congenital basis and results from congenital defects or obstructions of the thoracic duct (2, 3, 5, 8, 16, 21), but it also can occur on a spontaneous basis, secondary to abdominal trauma (22), and with intestinal lymphangiectasia. In any of these cases, if fat content is high enough, the chylous fluid may appear more radiolucent than the adjacent liver, etc.

Urine ascites is another cause of peritoneal fluid accumulation, and most commonly occurs with urinary tract obstruction (5, 6, 21), but of course, also can be seen with renal or urinary bladder injuries secondary to abdominal trauma. When it is due to urinary tract obstruction, it is believed that there is rupturing of the distended upper urinary tract with extravasation of urine, first into the perirenal space, and then,

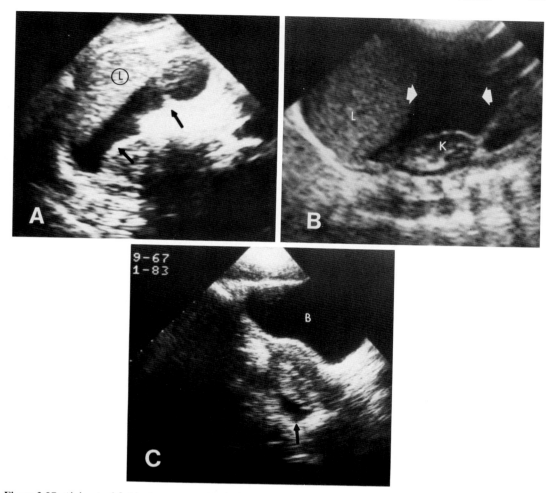

Figure 3.27. *Abdominal fluid; ultrasonographic findings.* (*A*) Note blood (*arrows*) under the liver (*L*) in this patient with abdominal trauma. (*B*) Fluid (*arrows*) between the liver (*L*) and kidney (*K*) in a patient with ascites. (*C*) Fluid in the cul-de-sac (*arrow*) in a patient with a bleeding ovarian cyst.

through normal congenital defects, into the peritoneal cavity. Bile ascites can occur on a congenital basis from obstruction, tears, or congenital defects of the bile ducts (4, 9, 17, 21), but it also can result from bile duct injuries secondary to abdominal trauma.

Peritonitis in childhood may occur secondary to gastrointestinal perforations, or as a primary infection (1, 7, 12, 15). In these latter cases the causative organism often, but not always, is *Diplococcus pneumoniae*, and these primary infections are especially prone to develop in children with the nephrotic syndrome (20). Tuberculous peritonitis is uncommonly seen in childhood, but when it occurs it tends to produce a more adhesive

peritoneal reaction, and consequently, the loops of bowel, instead of floating freely in the fluid, tend to remain more fixed from view to view. Peritonitis secondary to ascaris infection (18), is uncommon in this country, and meconium peritonitis, of course, is a problem of neonates. In these patients, peritoneal calcification frequently is present (21).

In cases of advanced peritonitis, the roentgenographic findings are relatively easy to detect for the presence of fluid (pus), causing separation of the loops of intestine and obliteration of the retroperitoneal structures, is relatively easy to see (Fig. 3.28*A*). However, in early cases where fluid is not very abun-

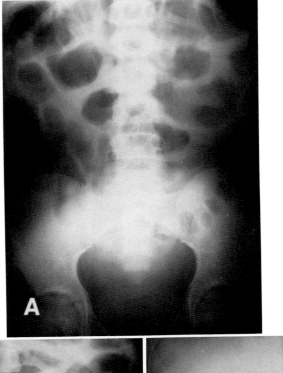

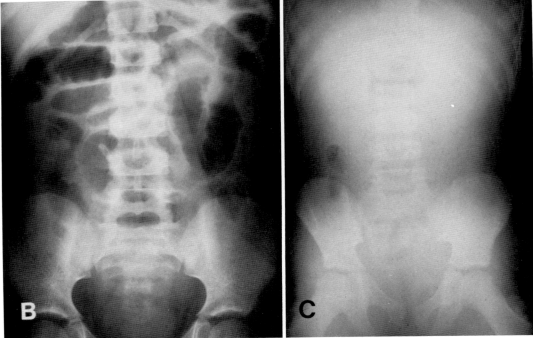

Figure 3.28. *Peritonitis—varying configurations.* (*A*) Peritonitis in this patient has caused marked separation of the loops of small intestine. The retroperitoneal structures are difficult to see. Fluid also is present in the peritoneal cul-de-sac in the pelvis. (*B*) Peritonitis secondary to appendiceal perforation results in inflammation of the serosal surface of the intestine and thickening of the intestinal wall (i.e., the space between the loops of intestine is widened). Note, however, that the retroperitoneal structures (i.e., psoas muscles) are still clearly visible. In this case, although serosal inflammation was present, and clinical findings of peritonitis were clearly present, the absence of large volumes of fluid (pus) allows for the apparently paradoxically persistent visualization of the retroperitoneal structures. (*C*) In this patient, virtually no air is present in the gastrointestinal tract. However, the retroperitoneal structures and inferior liver edge are invisible. They are obliterated by the presence of a massive volume of intraperitoneal pus and overall the entire abdomen assumes a very homogeneous opaque appearance. This patient had peritonitis secondary to appendiceal perforation.

dant, and yet significant peritoneal inflammation is present, the findings may be a little puzzling. Clinically there will be no doubt that peritonitis is present, but roentgenographically one may still be able to see the retroperitoneal structures through the loops of distended, thickened intestine (Fig. 3.28B). The loops of intestine are thickened because of serositis, but because the infection has not advanced to the point of massive production of pus, the retroperitoneal structures still remain visible. Later on these structures become invisible (Fig. 3.28, A and C).

Hemoperitoneum is most often seen secondary to abdominal trauma with splenic or liver injury. However, it also can be seen with injuries to the mesenteric vessels and aorta. The clinical setting, of course, is what alerts one to the diagnosis, for the roentgenographic findings are similar to those of any other abdominal fluid collection. Of course, with liver and splenic injury it is of utmost importance to look for the presence of lower rib fractures.

Very few conditions can mimic the presence of free peritoneal fluid, but in some patients with voluminous collections of fluid in the bowel, the findings at first might suggest free peritoneal fluid. This can occur with severe viral gastroenteritis, shigella infection, or small bowel obstruction, and ultrasonography is excellent in demonstrating the fluid-filled loops (Fig. 3.29).

In addition to these situations, it should be mentioned that in some patients with extremely thin-walled, large, mesenteric or lymphangiectatic cysts, the cysts may be so fluctuant that peritoneal fluid is mimicked both clinically and roentgenographically (5, 21). Indeed, even paracentesis, the ultimate tool in the investigation of any abdominal fluid collection, may not solve the problem. This occurs because as the cyst is drained it becomes so flaccid that no residual "mass" remains, and one believes that ascites was the problem. Of course, such fluid almost always recurs, and it may require numerous paracenteses before one realizes that the real problem is a thin-walled lymphangiectatic-mesenteric cyst.

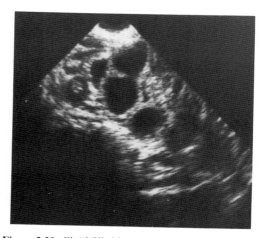

Figure 3.29. *Fluid filled loops—ultrasound.* Note numerous circular, anechoic loops of bowel filled with fluid.

REFERENCES

1. Bose, B., Keir, W.R., and Godberson, C.V.: Primary pneumococcic peritonitis. Can. Med. Assoc. J. 110: 305–307, 1974.
2. Boysen, Bette E.: Chylous ascites. Am. J. Dis. Child. 129: 1338–1339, 1975.
3. Craven, C.E., Goldman, A.S., Larson, D.L., Patterson, M., and Hendrick, C.K.: Congenital chylous ascites: Lymphangiographic demonstration of obstruction of the cisterna chyli and chylous reflux into the peritoneal space and small intestine. J. Pediatr. 70: 340–345, 1967.
4. Esposito, G.: Biliary peritonitis in a child due to spontaneous perforation of the bile duct. Ann. Chir. Inf. 13: 339–346, 1972.
5. Franken, E.A.: Ascites in infants and children. Roentgen diagnosis. Radiology 102: 393–398, 1972.
6. Friedland, G.W., Tune, B., and Mears, E.M.: Ascites due to spontaneous rupture of the renal pelvis in an 11-month-old infant with uretero-pelvic junctional obstruction. Pediatr. Radiol. 2: 263–264, 1974.
7. Geley, L., and Brandesky, G.: Pneumococcic peritonitis in childhood. Z. Kinderchir. 11: 42–49, 1972.
8. Gribetz, D., and Ganog, A.: Chylous ascites in infancy. Pediatrics 7:632–639, 1951.
9. Hansen, R.C., Wasnich, R.D., Devries, P.A., and Sunshine, P.: Bile ascites in infancy: diagnosis with ^{131}I-rose bengal. J. Pediatr. 84: 719–721, 1974.
10. Hunig, R., and Kinser, J.: The diagnosis of ascites by ultrasonic tomography (B-scan). Br. J. Radiol. 46: 325–328, 1973.
11. Keefe, E.J., Gagliardi, R.A., and Pfister, R.C.: The roentgenographic evaluation of ascites. A.J.R. 101: 388–396, 1967.
12. Khan, A.J., Evans, H.E., Macabuhay, M.R., Lee, Y., and Werner, R.: Primary peritonitis due to group G streptococcus: a case report. Pediatrics 56: 1078–1079, 1975.
13. Love, L., Demos, T.C., Reynes, C.J., Williams, V., Shkoinik, A., Gandhi, V., and Zerofos, N.: Visualization of the lateral edge of the liver in ascites. Radiology 122: 619–622, 1977.
14. Margulies, M., and Stoane, L.: Hepatic angle in roentgen evaluation of peritoneal fluid. Radiology 88: 51, 1967.
15. McDougal, W., Izant, R., and Zollinger, R.: Primary peritonitis in infancy and childhood. Ann. Surg. 181: 310–313, 1975.
16. McKendry, J.B.J., Lindsay, W.K., and Gerstein, M.C.: Congenital defects of the lymphatics in infancy. Pediatrics 19: 21–35, 1957.
17. Moore, T.C.: Massive bile peritonitis in infancy due to

spontaneous bile duct perforation with portal vein occlusion. J. Pediatr. Surg. 10: 537–538, 1975.

18. Parashar, S.K., Nadkarni, S.V., and Varma, R.A.: Primary roundworm peritonitis. Indian J. Surg. 36: 200–201, 1974.

19. Porto, A.V., and Lane, E.J.: Visualization of differences in soft-tissue densities. The liver in ascites. Radiology 121: 19–23, 1976.

20. Rubin, M., Blau, E.B., and Michaels, R.H.: Hemophilus and pneumococcal peritonitis in children with the nephrotic syndrome. Pediatrics 56: 598–601, 1975.

21. Swischuk, L.E.: *Radiology of the Newborn and Young Infant*, pp. 386, 349. Williams & Wilkins, Baltimore, 1973.

22. Vollman, R.W., Keenan, W.J., and Eraklis, A.J.: post-traumatic chylous ascites in infancy. N. Engl. J. Med. 275: 875–877, 1966.

ABDOMINAL ABSCESS

In the classic case, an abdominal abscess has a bubbly, amorphous pattern, but in other instances only a mass displacing adjacent intestines is seen (Fig. 3.30). The granular appearance must be differentiated from a somewhat similar appearance seen in normal patients when gas is mixed with: (a) fecal material in the colon, (b) food in the stomach, and (c) a bezoar in the gastrointestinal tract.

Abscesses in the right lower quadrant usually result from perforation of the appendix or a Meckel's diverticulum. In the right upper quadrant, an abscess may be subhepatic or intrahepatic. Intrahepatic abscesses may

be bacterial or amoebic in origin (6, 11, 17, 22, 24, 28), and in those cases where gas-forming organisms flourish, the findings may be striking (Fig. 3.31C). If no gas is present within the abscess, one simply may be presented with a large liver, elevated diaphragmatic leaflet, and associated changes in the right lung base (Fig. 3.31A). Pyogenic abscesses may be encountered in totally normal children, but it also should be noted that one of the classic presentations of children with chronic granulomatous disease of childhood (neutrophil dysfunction) is liver abscess (23, 27). Amoebic liver abscess also can be seen in children, but liver abscess secondary to ascaris infection is uncommon. Subhepatic abscesses can develop after perforation of a retrocecal appendix, a duodenal ulcer, or the gallbladder.

Abscesses in the upper mid abdomen usually are located in the lesser sac or pancreas. Lesser sac abscesses may result from perforation of a duodenal ulcer (4), while pancreatic abscesses result from pancreatitis (1), often from the more fulminant form referred to as emphysematous pancreatitis (see Fig. 3.62). Abscesses in the pelvis may result from appendiceal perforation (most common), salpingitis, or bladder perforations.

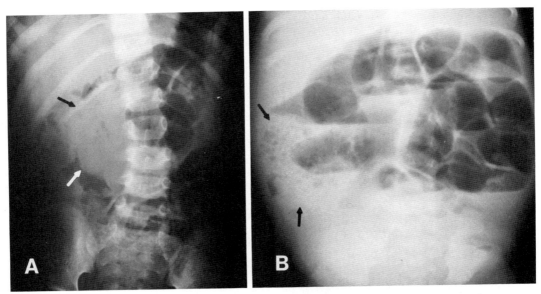

Figure 3.30. *Abdominal abscess; varying configurations.* (*A*) Mass-like effect of abdominal abscess with no granular appearance in patient with perforated appendicitis and "walled off" abscess on the right (*arrows*). Note pronounced ipsilateral scoliosis secondary to spasm of the psoas muscle. (*B*) Typical granular appearance of an abscess in the right lower quadrant (*arrows*) secondary to intestinal perforation in young infant.

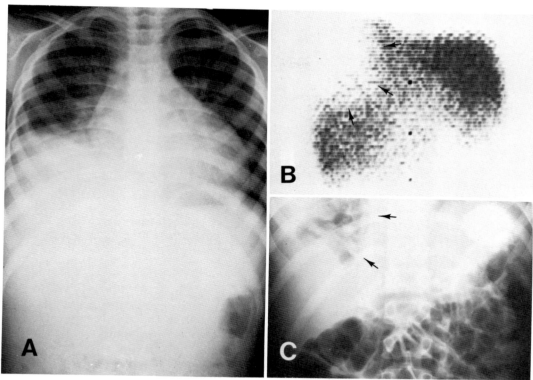

Figure 3.31. *Intrahepatic abscess—varying configurations.* (*A*) Intrahepatic abscess manifesting primarily in enlargement of the liver (note the increased distance between the elevated right diaphragmatic leaflet and the lower liver edge) and secondary changes in the base of the right lung. (*B*) Same patient with liver scan demonstrating area of decreased uptake in the liver (*arrows*). This patient had chronic granulomatous disease (neutrophil dysfunction) of childhood. (*C*) Note gas (*arrows*) in an intrahepatic abscess secondary to liver laceration after an automobile accident.

A subphrenic abscess often will elevate the diaphragmatic leaflet and be associated with pulmonary changes such as atelectasis and pleural effusion (Fig. 3.32). On the right, such an abscess often displaces the liver downward, while on the left it displaces the stomach and splenic flexure medially and/ or downwardly (8, 18, 21). Perinephric abscesses produce mass-like configurations in the retroperitoneal area, obliteration of the retroperitoneal soft tissues, and on intravenous pyelography, decreased function and/ or displacement of the kidney (2, 5, 13–16). They are, however, relatively uncommon in children (26, 29), and so are renal abscesses (19). Abscesses along the psoas muscle may be tuberculous or nontuberculous in origin (7, 9).

More recently ultrasonography has been virtually indispensable in the detection of abdominal abscesses. Characteristically,

with ultrasound, abscesses present with a sonolucent center and an echogenic peripheral rim (Fig. 3.33). Some central echoes may be present within the center of the sonolucency, but generally, the more classic configuration is present. However, in some cases, especially in those where the abscess is older and its central fluid collection is being obliterated, it may appear solid. Such abscesses, of course, can be detected anywhere in the abdomen, including the liver, and here either pyogenic or amebic abscesses can be encountered (3, 10, 12, 20, 25, 28). Amebic abscesses, more than pyogenic liver abscesses, tend to have a strikingly anechoic center and the former may be seen to penetrate the diaphragm, or erode into the pericardial cavity (Fig. 3.34). Demonstration of these complications is extremely import and and when such an abscess is demonstrated to be near the diaphragmatic

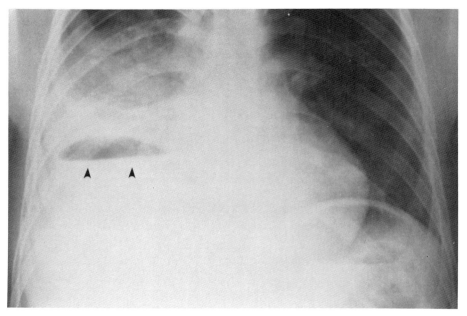

Figure 3.32. *Subphrenic abscess.*   Note the elevated right diaphragmatic leaflet and gas accumulation beneath it (*arrows*). Note associated changes in the right lung base. This patient had a right subphrenic, suprahepatic abscess secondary to a perforated retrocecal appendix.

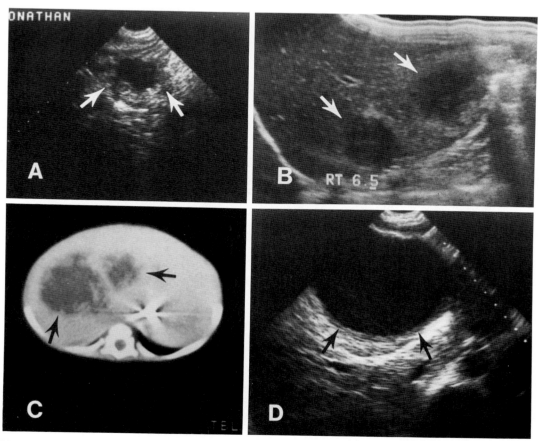

Figure 3.33. *Abdominal abscess—various configurations.* (*A*) Note the sonolucent abscess containing some echogenic debris (*arrows*). Other abscesses may appear more completely solid, especially when they are healing. (*B*) Ultrasound demonstrating two sonolucent abscesses within the liver (*arrows*). (*C*) CT study demonstrating a liver abscess (*arrows*). (*D*) Typical appearance of amebic abscess, in that it is quite sonolucent (*arrows*).

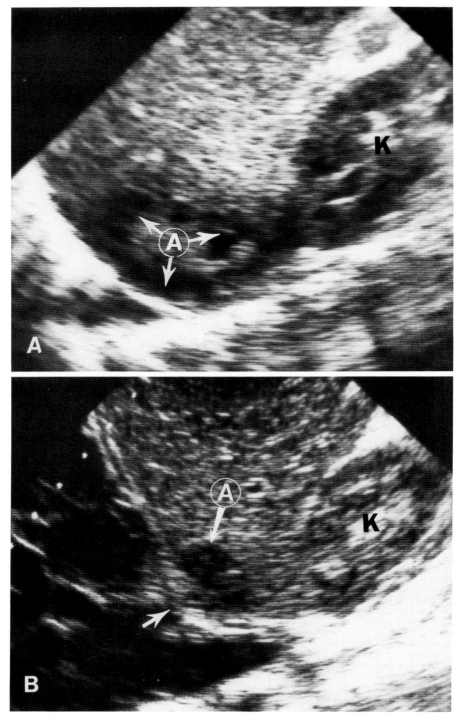

Figure 3.34. *Amebic abscess extending into the chest.* (*A*) Note the sonolucent abscess in the liver (*A*). It lies just below the curvilinear appearing diaphragmatic leaflet; kidney (*K*). (*B*) A little later, note that the abscess (*A*), has become smaller but that there is disruption of the diaphragmatic leaflet (*arrow*), where the abscess has perforated into the chest to produce multiloculated collections of fluid; kidney (*K*).

leaflet, or the pericardium, impending penetration should be considered and the abscess drained immediately.

REFERENCES

1. Agnos, J., and Holmes, R.: Gas in the pancreas as a sign of abscess. A.J.R. 80: 60, 1958.
2. Bliznak, J., and Ramsey, J.: Emphysematous pyelonephritis. Clin. Radiol. 23: 61–64, 1972.
3. Boultbee, J.E., Sinjee, A.E., Rooknooden, F., and Engelbrecht, H.E.: Experiences with gray scale ultrasonography in hepatic amoebiasis. Clin. Radiol. 30: 683–689, 1979.
4. Boyce, M.J., Burwood, J.R., Johnson, M., and Wood, C.B.S.: Chronic duodenal ulcer in infancy complicated by hemorrhage, perforation, and cyst formation in the lesser sac. J. Pediatr. Surg. 8: 323–324, 1973.
5. Evans, J.A., Meyers, M.A., and Bosniak, M.A.: Acute renal and perirenal infections. Semin. Roentgenol. 61: 274–291, 1971.
6. Foster, S.C., Schneider, B., and Seaman, W.B.: Gas-containing pyogenic intrahepatic abscesses. Radiology 94: 613–618, 1970.
7. Graves, V.B., and Schreiber, M.H.: Tuberculous psoas muscle abscess. J. Can. Assoc. Radiol. 24: 268–271, 1973.
8. Gwinn, J.L., and Lee, F.A.: Radiological case of the month (subphrenic abscess). Am. J. Dis. Child. 129: 1333, 1975.
9. Hardcastle, J.D.: Acute non-tuberculous psoas abscess. Br. J. Surg. 57: 10, 1970.
10. Hayden, C. Keith Jr., Toups, M., Swischuk, L.E., and Amparo, E.G.: Sonographic features of hepatic amebiasis in childhood. J. Can. Assoc. Radiol. 35: 279–282, 1984.
11. Isaac, F.: Roentgen findings in amebic disease of liver. Radiology 45: 581–587, 1945.
12. Kuligowska, E., Conners, S.K., and Shapiro, J.H.: Liver abscess: sonography in diagnosis and treatment. A.J.R. 138: 253–257, 1982.
13. Langston, C.S., and Pfister, R.C.: Renal emphysema: a case report and review of the literature. A.J.R. 110: 778–786, 1970.
14. Levy, A.H., and Schwinger, H.N.: Gas containing perinephric abscess. Radiology 60: 720–723, 1953.
15. Lipsett, P.J.: Roentgen ray observations in acute perinephritic abscess. J.A.M.A. 111: 1374–1376, 1928.
16. Love, L., Baker, D., and Ramsey, R.: Gas producing perinephric abscess. A.J.R. 119: 783–792, 1973.
17. McCarty, E., Pathmanand, C., Sunakorn, P., and Scherz, R.G.: Amebic liver abscess in childhood. a case study of a 21-month-old Thai child and a literature review. Am. J. Dis. Child 126: 67–70, 1973.
18. Miller, W.T., and Talman, E.A.: Subphrenic abscess. A.J.R. 101: 961–969, 1967.
19. Moenne-Locloz, J.P., Bomsel, F., Gatti, J.M., and Prot, D.: Renal abscess in children. A rare but important radiological diagnosis. Pediatr. Radiol. 7: 150–154, 1978.
20. Newlin, N., Silder, T.M., Stuck, K.J., and Sandler, M.A.: Ultrasonic features of pyogenic liver abscess. Radiology 139: 155–159, 1981.
21. Pancoast, H.K.: The roentgenological diagnosis of liver abscess with or without subdiaphragmatic abscess. A.J.R. 16: 303–320, 1926.
22. Parodi-Hueck, L.E., Wenger, F., and Montiel-Villasmil, D.: Ascaris hepatic abscess in children. J. Pediatr. Surg. 7: 69, 1972.
23. Preimesberger, K.F., and Goldberg, M.E.: Acute liver abscess in chronic granulomatous disease of childhood. Radiology 110: 147–150, 1974.
24. Rab, S.M., Alam, N., Hoda, A.N., and Yee, A.: Amoebic liver abscess: some unique presentations. Am. J. Med. 43: 811–816, 1967.
25. Ralls, P.W., Colletti, P.M., Quinn, M.F., and Halls, J.: Sonographic findings in a hepatic amebic abscess. Radiology 145: 123–126, 1982.
26. Rote, A.R., Bauer, S.B., and Retik, A.B.: Renal abscess in children. J. Urol. 119: 254–258, 1978.
27. Samuels, L.D.: Liver scans in chronic granulomatous disease of childhood. Pediatrics 48: 41–50, 1971.
28. Schmidt, A.G.: Plain film roentgen diagnosis of amebic hepatic abscess. A.J.R. 107: 47–50, 1969.
29. Sukow, R.J., Cohen, L.J., and Sample, W.F.: Sonography of hepatic amebic abscesses. A.J.R. 134: 911–915, 1980.
30. Vanni, L.A., Lopez, P.B., Porto, S.O., and Brazil, P.A.: Solitary pyogenic liver abscess in children. Am. Dis. Child. 132: 1142, 1978.

ACUTE INFLAMMATORY PROBLEMS

Pneumonia Causing Acute Abdomen. Pneumonia, usually pneumococcal in origin, is notorious for producing symptoms suggesting an acute abdominal problem. Very often (1–3), but not always, the pneumonia is in the base of one or other of the lungs, and interestingly enough these pneumonias often are best seen on abdominal films (Fig. 3.35). The reason for this is that the higher kilovolt technique utilized for abdominal roentgenography tends to accentuate the density of the pneumonia, and in addition, since many of these pneumonias are hidden behind the left or right side of the heart, a relatively overpenetrated roentgenographic technique actually is desirable. On the other hand, it should be remembered that not all such pneumonias are located in this area, and indeed, many are located higher in the lungs, and surely will be missed if a chest roentgenogram is not obtained (Fig. 3.36).

Most often when a pneumonia produces symptoms referable to the abdomen, a condition such as appendicitis is at first suspected, but as opposed to appendicitis, the roentgenographic examination of the abdomen in these children usually is normal. On occasion, however, one will encounter both appendicitis and pneumonia in the same patient (1, 2). We have had two such cases, and it does require close clinical and roentgenographic correlation, maximal objectiveness, and diligence in analysis of the roentgenograms.

REFERENCES

1. Baechli, D., and Braun, P.: Concomitant pneumonia and acute appendicitis in a child. Z. Kinderchir. 23: 409–411, 1978.
2. Gongaware, R.D., Weil, R., III, and Santulli, T.V.: Right lower lobe pneumonia and acute appendicitis in childhood: a therapeutic disorder. J. Pediatr. Surg. 8: 33–35, 1973.
3. Jona, J.Z., and Belin, R.P.: Basilar pneumonia simulating acute appendicitis in children. Arch. Surg. 111: 552–553, 1976.

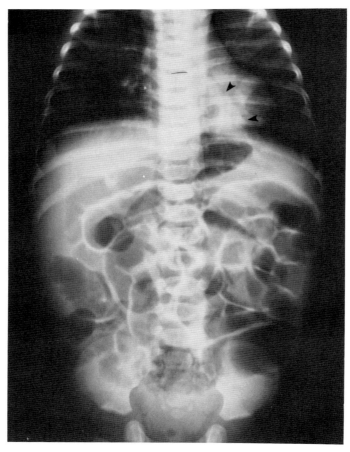

Figure 3.35. *Acute abdomen—pneumonia in the left base.*   Note the extensive paralytic ileus in this patient with an acute abdomen. However, also note the area of increased density behind the left side of the heart (*arrows*) representing a pneumonia in the left lower lobe.

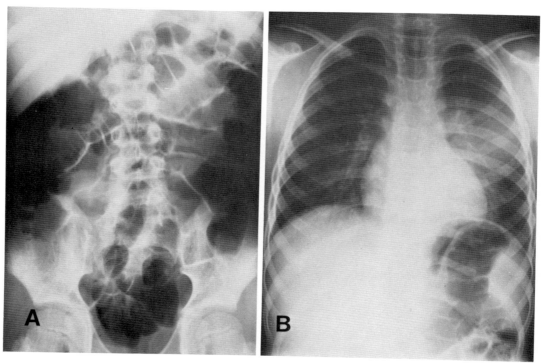

Figure 3.36. *Acute abdomen—value of chest film.* (*A*) Note extensive paralytic ileus in this patient presenting with an acute abdomen and suspected appendicitis. (*B*) Chest film demonstrates a large consolidating pneumonia in the left mid lung.

Acute Gastroenteritis. Gastroenteritis is the single most common abdominal inflammatory problem, and most often one is dealing with a viral infection. The clinical symptoms of vomiting and/or diarrhea are well known, and dehydration, especially in young infants, is a common and potentially serious complication. Roentgenographically dehydration commonly is reflected on the chest films by the presence of markedly overaerated lungs, decreased pulmonary vascularity, and a small cardiac silhouette (see Fig. 1.137).

In the abdomen, the abnormal roentgenographic patterns are extremely numerous, and to say the least, frequently very puzzling. However, the most common pattern is that of many loops of air-filled, distended intestine. Both large and small bowel are involved, but so gross are the findings that frequently it is difficult to define one or the other. Indeed, one frequently first believes that mechanical obstruction is present (Fig. 3.37). In other cases of gastroenteritis, only a portion of the gastrointestinal tract may be

dilated, and in such cases if: (a) the stomach shows predominant dilatation, a gastric outlet obstruction may be suggested (Fig. 3.38); (b) one or two loops of small bowel predominate, a small bowel obstruction may erroneously be diagnosed (Fig. 3.39A); and (c) the findings are confined to the colon, colon obstruction will be suggested (Fig. 3.39B). Finally, it should be noted that early in the course of gastroenteritis, when vomiting is the basic problem, one also may see a totally airless abdomen (see Fig. 3.4). In still other instances a locally dilated loop of small intestine (pseudo sentinel loop) may be encountered (see Fig. 3.10).

Appendicitis. After gastroenteritis, appendicitis is the most common acute abdominal inflammatory problem in childhood and its accurate diagnosis remains as challenging as ever. Indeed, many times the diagnosis is not secured until 24–48 hours have passed, and by that time perforation has occurred (49). In this regard, it has been demonstrated that observation in a hospital environment can significantly remedy this

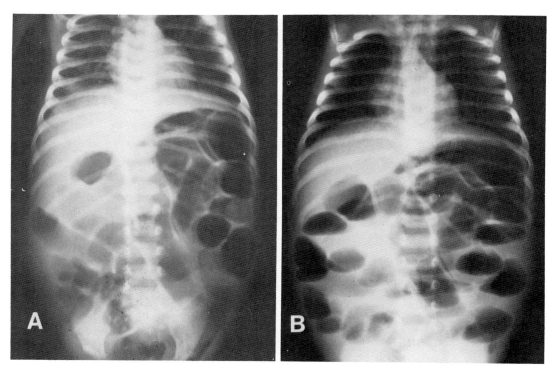

Figure 3.37. *Gastroenteritis.* (*A*) Note extensive dilatation of the intestines in this infant presenting with signs and symptoms of gastroenteritis. (*B*) Upright film demonstrates numerous air-fluid levels in the intestines. Although the characteristic dynamic, inverted "U" or hairpin configuration of obstructed intestinal loops is absent, these findings still often are misinterpreted for intestinal obstruction.

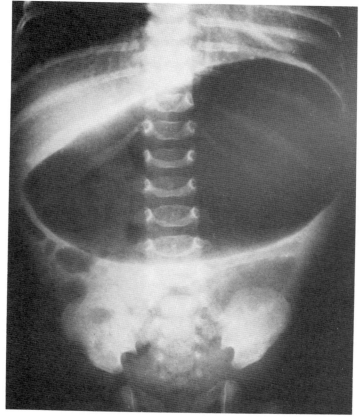

Figure 3.38. *Gastroenteritis—isolated gastric distension.* The isolated gastric distension in this infant with gastroenteritis could be misinterpreted for a gastric outlet obstruction.

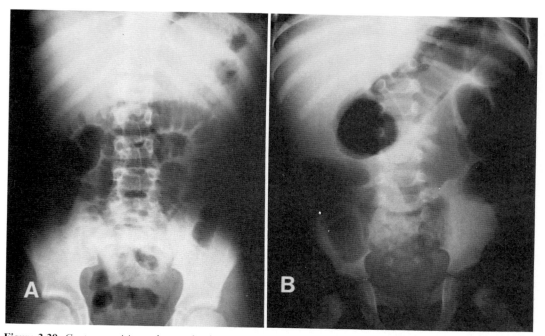

Figure 3.39. *Gastroenteritis—other misleading configurations.* (*A*) Older child with gastroenteritis demonstrating a picture suggesting jejunal obstruction. (*B*) Infant with gastroenteritis showing distension of the colon only. (For a patient with gastroenteritis and an airless abdomen see Figure 3.4, and for a patient with a pseudosentinel loop see Figure 3.10).

problem and also result in a greater yield of positive laparotomies (60). However, the authors of this article underscore the fact that these patients must be observed in the hospital and not on an outpatient basis.

The classic clinical findings of appendicitis are well known, but of course, not all always are present in any one patient. In addition there is the controversial problem of recurrent appendicitis (23), and because of this, the clinician may look for help elsewhere. In this regard, the additional investigative procedures most often obtained are: (a) the white blood cell (WBC) count, (b) the abdominal roentgenogram, and more recently (c) the barium enema. In terms of the WBC count, it has been suggested that a count of under 10,000 WBC/mm of blood is virtually incompatible with the diagnosis of acute appendicitis (29). By the same token, it can be stated that a count of over 20,000 WBC/mm of blood also is unlikely to be due to appendicitis, but of course, neither limit completely excludes the diagnosis.

As far as the abdominal roentgenogram is concerned, although there have been numerous dissertations on the subject (2, 18, 20, 22, 24, 25, 34, 36, 53–55, 58, 61), many still consider it a totally peripheral study, valid only for the demonstration of a fecalith, free air, or some other complication of acute appendicitis. However, there is no question that the study is of far more value that this, but to be of such value the *relationship of the pathology of perforated and nonperforated appendicitis to the roentgenographic findings must be understood.*

In this regard, it should first be noted that *most children with acute nonperforated appendicitis show diminished air in the gastrointestinal tract.* Indeed, in some cases the abdomen is virtually airless (Fig. 3.40), while in others only a few sentinel loops are present in the right lower quadrant (Fig. 3.41). In explaining the paucity of intestinal gas in these children, one must only recall that acute nonperforated appendicitis usually is associated with one or all of the following: (a) anorexia, (b) nausea, (c) vom-

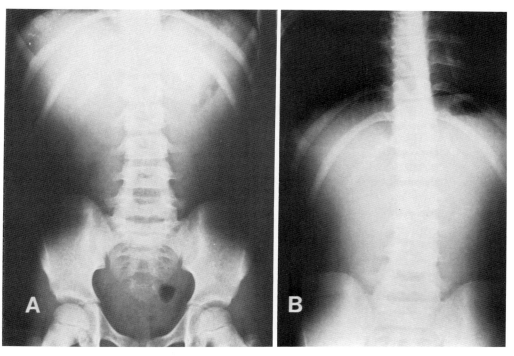

Figure 3.40. *Acute appendicitis—airless abdomen and scoliosis.* (*A*) Supine film showing abdomen in which gas is virtually absent. There is a minimal degree of scoliosis present. (*B*) On the upright film, however, note how much more pronounced the degree of scoliosis has become. Only a little gas is seen in the stomach.

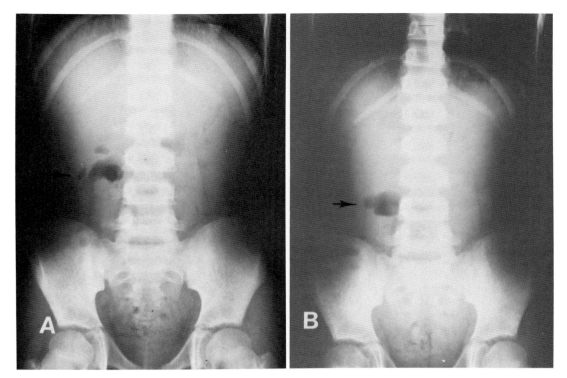

Figure 3.41. *Acute appendicitis—localized right-sided gas collections and indistinct right psoas shadow.* (*A*) Supine film showing a few isolated loops of distended intestine in the right flank (*arrow*). The right psoas shadow is less distinct than the left. (*B*) On upright view air-fluid levels are seen in the isolated loops of distended intestine (*arrow*). Indistinctness of the right psoas muscle is more apparent. No real scoliosis is present.

iting, and (d) diarrhea. In any combination, these findings can lead to little air and fluid getting into, or staying in, the gastrointestinal tract. Of course, in those cases where these symptoms have not been present for a long enough period of time, usually under a day, the airless gas pattern may not have had enough time to develop and the roentgenograms will be normal. On the other hand, seldom if ever is the gas pattern increased, and actually, if in a patient with suspected appendicitis intestinal gas is markedly increased, perforation should be suspected (Fig. 3.42).

The reasons for this change in the intestinal gas pattern with appendiceal perforation are multiple. First of all, just after perforation there is a relatively quiet clinical period, and as the acute anorexia and nausea settle down, more air is swallowed and retained in the gastrointestinal tract. At the same time peritonitis develops, and progressive paralytic ileus in the intestines

is induced. Because of this the swallowed air becomes trapped in the paralyzed intestine, and in many cases the degree of intestinal dilatation and gas accumulation is startling (Fig. 3.42). In such cases, if the findings are considered in the absence of clinical correlation, confusion with gastroenteritis can occur (i.e. compare Fig. 3.42 with Fig. 3.37).

Other roentgenographic signs of acute appendicitis consist of the following: (a) lumbar or lumbosacral scoliosis with concavity to the right, (b) absence or indistinctness of the right psoas margin, (c) localized loops of dilated intestine in the right lower quadrant or flank, (d) air in the appendix, and (e) the presence of a calcified fecalith in the appendix.

Scoliosis with concavity to the right results from splinting of the paraspinal and psoas muscles, and the curve produced usually involves the lumbar spine or the lumbosacral junction. Scoliosis should be as-

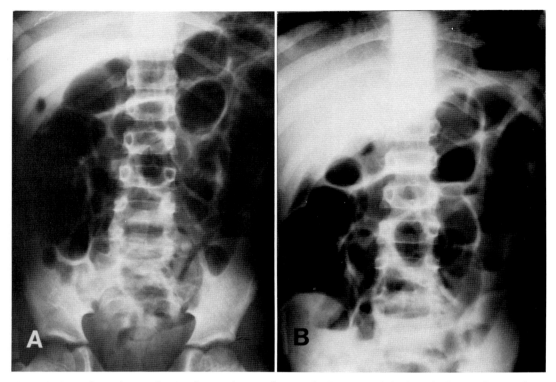

Figure 3.42. *Perforated appendicitis—large volumes of gas in the intestine.* (*A*) Note the large volumes of gas present in both the large and small bowel in this patient with perforated appendicitis. The findings are distinctly different from those seen with non-perforated acute appendicitis as demonstrated in Figures 3.40 and 3.41. (*B*) Upright view showing numerous air-fluid levels scattered throughout both the large and small intestine. On the supine view, there is a small fecalith visualized just to the right of the mid sacral spine, and there may be some suggestion of fluid displacing the cecum medially from the right abdominal wall, but other than this the findings easily could be misinterpreted for gastroenteritis.

sessed on both the supine and upright views for minimal degrees of scoliosis often become more apparent on the upright views (Fig. 3.40). Absence or indistinctness of the right psoas muscle margin also is a common finding in acute appendicitis and is variably explained in terms of obliteration due to adjacent edema and distortion of the muscle edge due to spasm of the muscle. Most likely the latter is the more important, and as with scoliosis it is not uncommon for obliteration of the right psoas margin to be more pronounced on the upright view. Localized right lower quadrant loops are sentinal loops and represent localized paralytic ileus of the terminal ileum and cecum resulting from the adjacent inflammatory process in the appendix (18, 33, 54, 55).

Air in the appendix is a relatively rare finding in acute appendicitis (Fig. 3.43), but generally is believed to be suggestive of the condition (16, 28, 47). On the other hand, it has been pointed out that air may be present in the appendix of patients with profound paralytic ileus or other inflammatory bowel disease (32, 52). Nevertheless, in a case of suspected acute appendicitis, the persistent presence of air in the appendix should be taken as a positive finding. This is especially true if the abdomen is airless, and the appendix overdistended, or its lumen irregular in diameter (Fig. 3.43, *A* and *B*). If these additional criteria are absent, one should be cautious about interpreting air in the appendix.

In acute appendicitis gas accumulates in the appendix because it is occluded and because gas-producing organisms grow in it. Occlusion can be secondary to a fecalith (calcified or uncalcified) inspissated feces, or

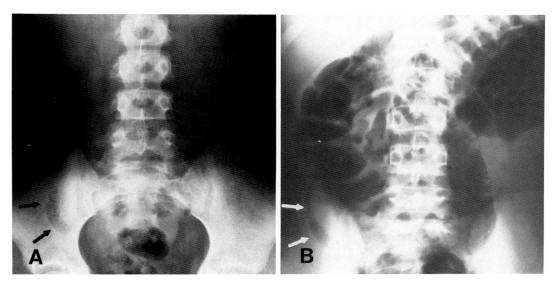

Figure 3.43. *Air in the appendix; acute appendicitis.* (*A*) Note air in an irregular and overdistended appendix (*arrows*). In addition, note absence of the right psoas shadow, and a virtually airless abdomen. (*B*) Another patient with a distended, air-filled appendix (*arrows*), with an irregular lumen. There is proximal narrowing and distal distension. Also note the soft tissue mass effect around the appendix.

rarely, inflammatory lymphadenopathy. Only occasionally will air be seen to persist in a normal appendix, and in such cases the appendix usually is retrocecal and traps air in its upward pointing tip. Pneumatosis cystoides intestinalis of the cecum also has been seen with acute appendicitis, but is very rare (10).

A calcified fecalith in the right lower quadrant, in the pelvis, or on the right side of the abdomen (Figs. 3.44 and 3.50), should virtually assure the diagnosis of acute appendicitis (3, 4, 12–14, 18, 20, 30, 51, 54, 55, 57, 58, 61, 62). This is not to say, however, that calcified fecaliths are seen only in patients with acute appendicitis, for this would be untrue. Indeed, not uncommonly one can encounter a calcified fecalith in a totally asymptomatic child, but since it is generally held that over 50% of cases of perforated appendicitis are accompanied by fecaliths, the presence of this finding certainly does place even the asymptomatic patient in a higher risk category. Indeed, some advocate prophylactic appendectomy in such cases, for the feeling is that appendicitis will develop sooner or later.

Roentgenographic signs of perforated appendicitis may consist of any of the follow-

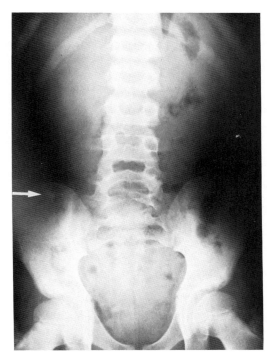

Figure 3.44. *Acute appendicitis with calcified fecalith.* Note that the abdomen shows virtual absence of intestinal gas. In addition, however, note the presence of a calcified fecalith in the right lower quadrant (*arrow*).

ing: (a) right side colon cutoff sign, (b) small bowel obstruction with or without persistent right lower quadrant gas pattern abnormalities, (c) an inflammatory mass or abscess in the right lower quadrant or pelvis, (d) a positive flank stripe sign, (e) obliteration of the properitoneal fat line on the right, and (f) free intraperitioneal air. Many times, more than one of the findings are present at in any one patient, but free air is relatively rare (35, 45). In addition, it should be noted that in most cases of perforated appendicitis there is considerable intestinal gas, quite different from the situation with nonperforated appendicitis.

The right colon cutoff sign (26, 56), often is the first sign of perforation (56). It results from a combination of spasm of the cecum and ascending colon induced by the adjacent inflammatory process, and reflex paralytic ileus of the transverse, or remaining ascend-

ing colon. As a result, the two areas of the colon are demarcated by a sharp cutoff of gas in the right upper quadrant. This finding is best assessed on the supine view, for on upright view shifting gas and fecal material in the colon can totally obscure its presence (Fig. 3.45). It is most important that, when the colon cutoff sign is present, it be determined that right side colon gas is diminished because of spasm and not because the cecum and ascending colon are full of feces. If gas is present in the transverse colon and absent in the ascending colon because it is full of fecal material, the colon cutoff sign is invalid (Fig. 3.46). In any such case, if there is doubt about the validity of the sign, a decubitus film, with right side up, can be employed. If one is dealing with a false cutoff sign then the ascending colon should fill on the decubitus view (Fig. 3.47).

The right colon cutoff sign, of course, is

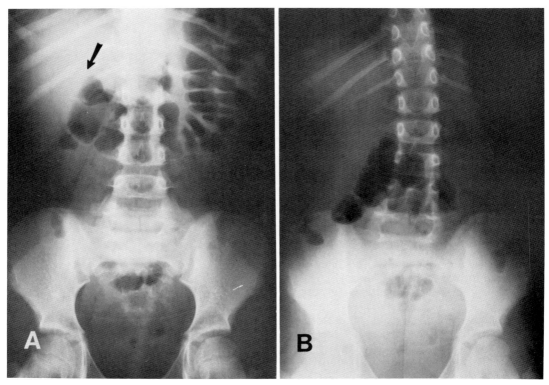

Figure 3.45. *Acute appendicitis—colon cutoff sign.* (*A*) Note gas in the transverse colon. The transverse colon is not unduly dilated, but gas terminates abruptly in the region of the hepatic flexure (*arrow*). This is the colon cutoff sign. In addition, note that the ascending colon and cecum are virtually empty. Also note one or two locally distended sentinel loops of intestine in the right lower quadrant. (*B*) Upright view demonstrating the development of significant scoliosis and confirmation of the presence of locally distended loops of dilated intestine in the right lower quadrant.

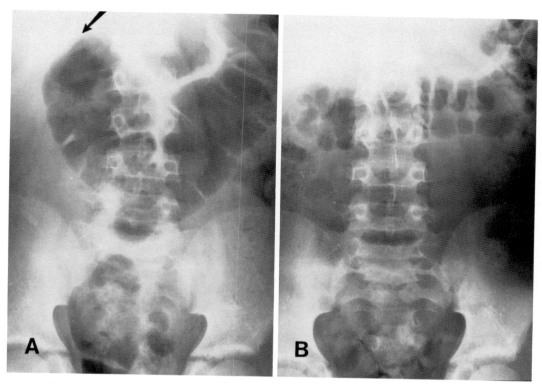

Figure 3.46. *Acute appendicitis; colon cutoff sign.* (*A*) Note the colon cutoff sign (*arrow*), and the presence of a fecalith. (*B*) Two years earlier the patient had symptoms suggestive of appendicitis; the fecalith was present and a colon cutoff sign was suggested. However, note feces in the ascending colon and lack of dilatation of the transverse colon. This negates the colon cutoff sign. The patient was not operated upon at this time, but returned 2 years later with perforated appendicitis as demonstrated in (*A*).

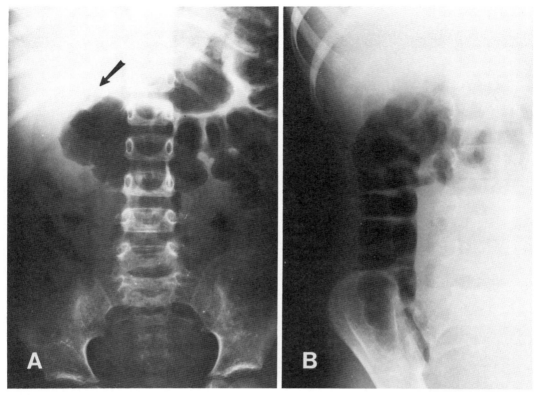

Figure 3.47. *Acute abdomen; pseudo colon cutoff sign.* (*A*) On this supine view, note that a colon cutoff sign is suggested (*arrow*). (*B*) Decubitus film shows the ascending colon to readily fill with air. This negates the original suggestion of a colon cutoff sign.

not seen in all cases of perforated appendicitis and actually, more commonly one will encounter a picture suggestive of low small bowel obstruction (Figs. 3.48 and 3.49). This type of obstruction has been termed "functional obstruction" for it probably represents a combination of mechanical and paralytic ileus (34, 36). The mechanical aspect results from the obstructive effects of the progressive inflammatory process developing in the right lower quadrant, while the paralytic aspect represents reflex paralysis of the small bowel (43). Together these factors lead to varying degrees of obstruction, and in some cases, the picture of obstruction is so distracting that, unless one is cognizant of the phenomenon, one will not consider perforated appendicitis as the primary diagnosis. Other findings associated with perforated appendicitis include signs of peritonitis, a positive flank stripe sign, and obliteration of the properitoneal fat line.

Signs of peritonitis are those of fluid in the abdomen (Fig. 3.50), while a positive flank stripe sign consists of an increase in the soft tissue distance between the abdominal wall and air-filled descending colon or cecum. The soft tissue space is widened by inflammatory edema or frank abscess formation (7). There is no question that when the finding is present it is very useful, but most often so many other findings of perforated appendicitis also are present that its practical value is diminished (Fig. 3.51). Absence of the right properitoneal fat line also is seen in advanced cases of appendiceal perforation, but as with the positive flank stripe sign, absence of the properitoneal fat line often is a superfluous finding, for other findings of perforation usually are present (Fig. 3.51). The presence of free air is the least common finding in appendicitis, and when present, usually is of small volume and more difficult to detect.

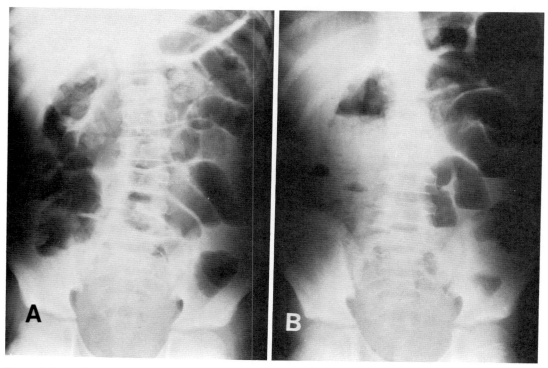

Figure 3.48. *Perforated appendicitis with early functional obstruction.* (*A*) Note moderate scoliosis and three of four loops of distended small bowel, just to the left of the spine. (*B*) Upright view showing the same loops, but this time with air-fluid levels. These findings represent early functional obstruction secondary to perforated appendicitis.

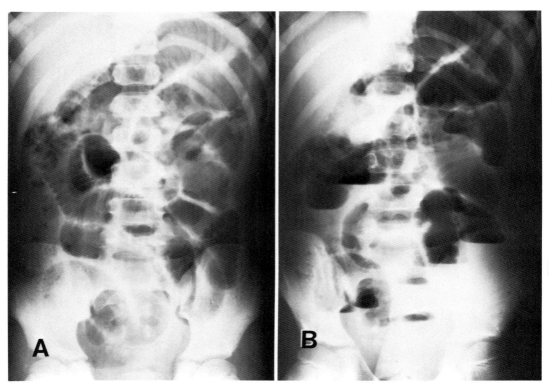

Figure 3.49. *Perforated appendicitis with pronounced functional obstruction.* (*A*) Supine view demonstrating numerous loops of distended intestine. However, note that the loops of jejunum are disproportionately distended when compared to gas in the colon. (*B*) The findings are visualized with greater clarity on the upright view where numerous, acute appearing air-fluid levels are noted within the distended loops of jejunum. These findings represent pronounced functional obstruction secondary to perforation of the appendix.

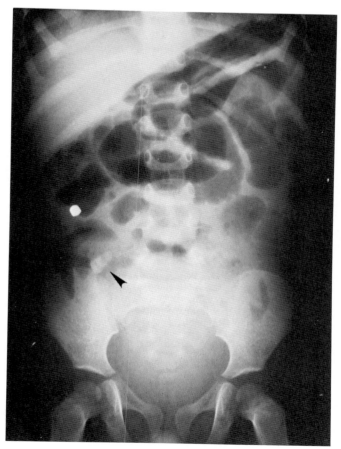

Figure 3.50. *Perforated appendicitis with abscess, fecalith, and peritonitis.*   First note that there are numerous loops of distended intestine in the abdomen (i.e., functional obstruction). However, note that the space between the individual loops is thickened. This indicates the presence of intraperitoneal fluid (pus), and hence, the presence of peritonitis. Also note the calcified fecalith (*arrow*) and surrounding inflammatory mass (abscess). Increased density and whiteness of the lower abdomen and pelvic regions are due to the presence of intraperitoneal pus. An incidental colonic foreign body is seen above the calcified fecalith.

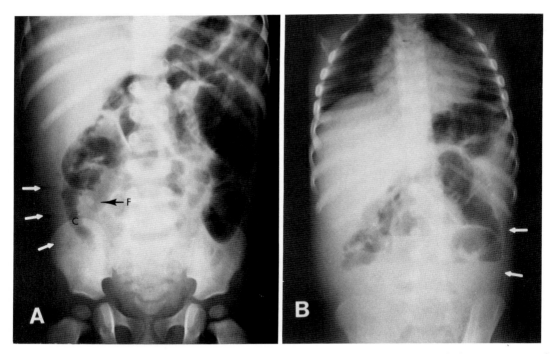

Figure 3.51. *Perforated appendicitis—calcified fecalith, abscess, positive flank stripe sign, and absent properitoneal fat stripe.* (*A*) Supine view demonstrating abundant gas within dilated intestines, a calcified fecalith (*F*), and medial displacement of the contracted cecum (*C*). The cecum is displaced medially because of the presence of fluid and edema between it and the abdominal wall. This constitutes a positive flank stripe sign (*arrows*). (*B*) Upright view showing the presence of a few distended loops of jejunum with air-fluid levels, but in addition clear-cut evidence that the properitoneal fat stripe on the right is absent. The properitoneal fat stripe on the left (*arrows*) is present. In addition, note that the gas-filled intestine on the right continues to be displaced medially from the abdominal wall (i.e., positive flank stripe sign).

An abscess clearly reflects an underlying perforation, and while in some cases the abscess may appear classically granular, or dense and well defined (see Fig. 3.30), more often it is less well organized (Figs. 3.50 and 3.51). In still other instances, fixed, formless air bubbles are present within the generalized opacity of the abscess (Fig. 3.52), and finally, in some cases massive accumulations of air are seen in an abscess cavity (Fig. 3.53).

Ultrasonography is not generally used for the diagnosis of acute appendicitis, although the acutely inflamed appendix can be demonstrated in some patients (19). The findings consist of a sonolucent ring or donut on cross-section, and an oval on longitudinal section (Fig. 3.54). The sonolucent rim, in either projection, represents edema of the appendiceal wall, and the central echoes

come from the mucosa within the lumen (Fig. 3.54). Certainly ultrasonography is not advocated as the diagnostic modality for appendicitis, but one should be familiar with its appearance should the condition be encountered.

With perforated appendicitis, ultrasound is excellent in demonstrating the presence of an appendiceal abscess. Characteristically an echo-free area surrounded by an echogenic rim are seen (Fig. 3.55). Of course, the center of the abscess may be variably anechoic for with debris some echoes may result. In addition, echoes from a fecalith can be seen (17) (Fig. 3.55*D*).

The diagnosis of *retrocecal appendicitis* is more difficult than the diagnosis of appendicitis in its usual location, and in such cases the clinical findings may mimic those of cholecystitis, pancreatitis, hepatitis, or kid-

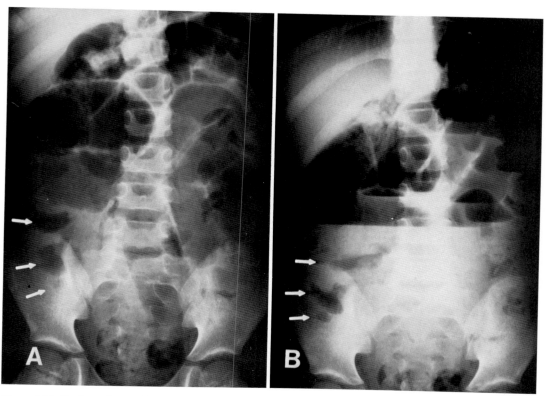

Figure 3.52. *Perforated appendicitis with abscess—fixed bubbles.* (*A*) Supine view demonstrating numerous loops of distended small bowel in the abdomen and two or three formless loops of gas in the right lower quadrant. In addition, a soft tissue, inflammatory mass around these latter air collections is suggested (*arrows*). (*B*) Upright view shows the development of numerous air-fluid levels in the distended loops of small bowel. A functional obstruction is present. However, note that the formless collections of gas in the right lower quadrant (*arrows*) have not changed significantly in configuration or position. This lack of change in the appearance of the bubbles from supine to upright view can be taken as presumptive evidence for the presence of an abscess. (Surgically confirmed.)

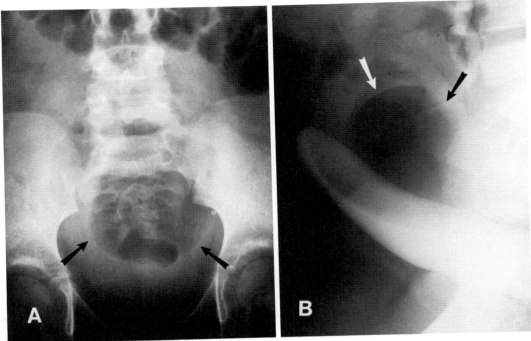

Figure 3.53. *Appendiceal abscess.*   (*A*) Note the large gas-filled abscess (*arrows*). (*B*) Lateral view showing the same abscess (*arrows*), behind the contrast-filled bladder.

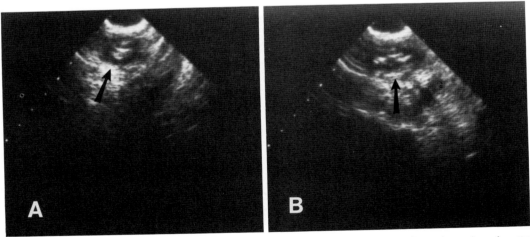

Figure 3.54. *Acute appendicitis; ultrasonographic findings.*   (*A*) Note the sonolucent donut (*arrow*), and central area of echogenicity. This is a cross-sectional view. (*B*) Longitudinal view showing a sausage-like echo-free structure with dense central echoes.

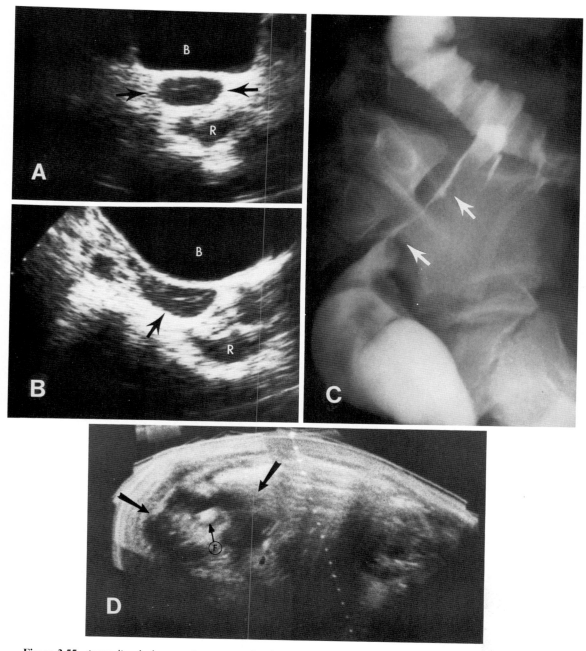

Figure 3.55. *Appendiceal abscess; ultrasonographic findings.* (*A*) Transverse pelvic ultrasonogram demonstrates sonolucency and some echogenic debris within an abscess (*arrows*). The abscess is between the bladder (*B*), and the rectum (*R*). (*B*) Longitudinal sonogram in the same patient demonstrating the abscess (*arrow*), between the bladder (*B*) and the rectum (*R*). (*C*) Barium enema demonstrating the compressed rectum by the large abscess (*arrows*). (*D*) Abscess (*arrows*) with fecalith (*F*).

ney disease. Consequently, a delay in diagnosis is common, and because of this, perforation occurs more often (19, 37, 58). Roentgenographically, in these cases, the findings may be very subtle, and may differ from the usual case of appendicitis in the following ways: (a) scoliosis may be located in the upper lumbar or thorocolumbar spine, (b) sentinel loops may lie more in the right upper quadrant (see Fig. 3.10*A*), (c) a fecalith may lie higher than expected, and (d) the positive flank stripe sign may be located high in the right flank.

The *barium enema* for the diagnosis of acute, nonperforated appendicitis, has now become quite popular (15, 27, 31, 41, 50), and generally is a safe and valuable procedure. It always has been useful in defining abscess formation after perforation, even though indirect findings only generally are available (11, 42). For the most part these

consist of displacement of the involved portions of the colon and edematous involvement of the colonic wall, even to the point of suggesting mucosal disease (Fig. 3.56). Symptoms from such colonic involvement are varied, but may suggest primary colon disease (40).

As far as acute, nonperforated appendicitis is concerned, the barium enema generally is used in cases where considerable uncertainty exists. Recently, it has been suggested that its primary use be restricted to those patients in whom the diagnosis is difficult to ilicit; i.e., obese individuals, immunologically compromised patients, very young infants, adolescent girls, etc. (31). Basically, with the barium enema one is looking for filling or nonfilling of the appendix. It should be noted, however, that approximately 10–15% of normal appendices do not fill on barium enema examination (46)

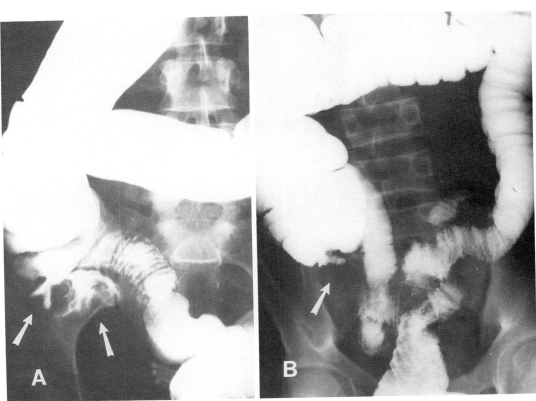

Figure 3.56. *Perforated appendicitis; barium enema findings.*   (*A*) Note the contracted, deformed cecum (*arrows*), and abscence of filling of the appendix even though the terminal ileum is well filled. (*B*) Another patient demonstrating similar findings but a less deformed cecum (*arrow*). Also note changes in the sigmoid colon suggesting pericolonic inflammation. The colon contour is irregular and edema and deformity of the wall is suggested. Also see Figure 3.55*C* for lateral view in perforated appendicitis.

and that one can call the appendix unequivocally normal, only when it is completely filled, fully distended, and demonstrative of a round, bulbous tip (Fig. 3.57). The latter finding is most important for it has been noted that, when the appendix perforates at its tip, most of the appendix still will fill on barium examination (13). Obviously this would not occur very often; and then, the tip probably would not be bulbous, but it does reinforce the fact that one should be totally convinced that the appendix is completely filled before calling it normal.

Abnormalities of the appendix, as seen with appendicitis, include complete or partial lack of filling, a pointed beak of barium the base of the appendix, cobblestoning or other signs of mucosal edema of the appendix, and spasm, irregularity, or deformity of the adjacent cecum (Fig. 3.58). If these findings are not present, one should be cautious regarding one's interpretation of the finding (Fig. 3.59).

Other interesting features of acute appendicitis include the following: (a) appendiceal foreign bodies can lead to appendiceal inflammation (6), (b) appendicitis can be seen with shigellosis (48), (c) urinary tract disease can present as appendicitis or vice versa, (d)

a genitourinary fistula may result (21, 44), and (e) an inflamed or perforated appendix can lie in an inguinal or femoral hernia, or in the scrotum of a young male infant (1, 5, 59). In these latter cases, the infant may present with an acute abdomen, intestinal obstruction (Fig. 3.60), or a mass in the inguinal region or scrotum. With urinary tract involvement, symptoms such as pyuria, hematuria, right flank pain, etc., may make the problem virtually indistinguishable from that of true urinary tract infection. Indeed, even if an intravenous pyelogram is performed, paralytic ileus with apparent obstruction of the ureter may further add to one's erroneous initial impressions (8, 38).

REFERENCES

1. Alvear, D.T., and Rayfield, M.M.: Acute appendicitis presenting as a scrotal mass. J. Pediatr. Surg. 11: 91–92, 1976.
2. Bakhda, R.K., and McNair, M.M.: Useful radiological signs in acute appendicitis in children. Clin. Radiol. 28: 193–196, 1977.
3. Berg, R.M., and Berg, H.M.: Coproliths. Radiology 68: 839, 1957.
4. Brady, B., and Carroll, D.: The significance of the calcified appendiceal enterolith. Radiology 68: 648, 1957.
5. Carey, L.C.: Acute appendicitis occurring in hernias: a report of 10 cases. Surgery 61: 236, 1967.
6. Carey, L.S.: Lead shot appendicitis in northern native people. J. Can. Assoc. Radiol. 28: 171–174, 1977.
7. Casper, R.B.: Fluid in the right flank as a roentgenographic sign of acute appendicitis. A.J.R. 110: 352–354, 1970.
8. Chiu, R., and Gambach, R.: Radiographic ureteral changes with appendicitis. J. Can. Assoc. Radiol. 25: 154–160, 1974.
9. Deutsch, A., and Leopold, G.R.: Ultrasonic demonstration of the inflamed appendix: case report. Radiology 140: 163–164, 1981.
10. DiDonato, L.R.: Radiographic exhibit: pneumatosis coli secondary to acute appendicitis; case report. Radiology 120: 90, 1976.
11. Ekberg, O.: Ileocecal abnormalities in appendiceal abscess. Acta Radiol. 19: 343–347, 1978.
12. Faegenburg, D.: Fecalith of the appendix: incidence and significance. A.J.R. 89: 752–759, 1963.
13. Fee, H.J., Jr., Jones, P.C., Kadell, B., and O'Connell, T.X.: Radiologic diagnosis of appendicitis. Arch. Surg. 112: 742–744, 1977.
14. Felson, B., and Bernhard, C.M.: The roentgenologic diagnosis of appendiceal calculi. Radiology 49: 178–191, 1947.
15. Figiel, L.S., and Figiel, S.J.: Barium examination of cecum in appendicitis. Acta Radiol. 57: 469–480, 1962.
16. Fisher, M.S.: A roentgen sign of gangrenous appendicitis. A.J.R. 81: 637–639, 1959.
17. Forel, F., Filiatrault, D., and Grignon, A.: Ultrasonic demonstration of appendicolith. J. Can. Assoc. Radiol. 34: 66–67, 1983.
18. Graham, A.D., and Johnson, H.F.: The incidence of radiographic findings in acute appendicitis compared to 200 normal abdomens. Milit. Med. 131: 272–276, 1966.
19. Harned, R.K.: Retrocecal appendicitis presenting with air in the subhepatic space. A.J.R. 162: 416–418, 1976.
20. Hatten, L.E., Miller, R.C., Hester, C.L., Jr., and Moynihan, P.C.: Appendicitis and the abdominal roentgenogram in children. South. Med. J. 66: 803–806, 1973.
21. Hoffer, F.A., Ablow, R.C., Gryboski, J.D., and Seashore, J.H.: Primary appendicitis with an appendio-tuboovarian fistula. A.J.R. 138: 742–743, 1982.

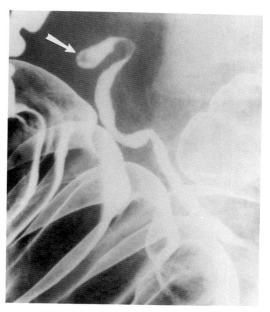

Figure 3.57. *Normal appendix.* Note the well-filled, normal appendix with a bulbous end (*arrow*).

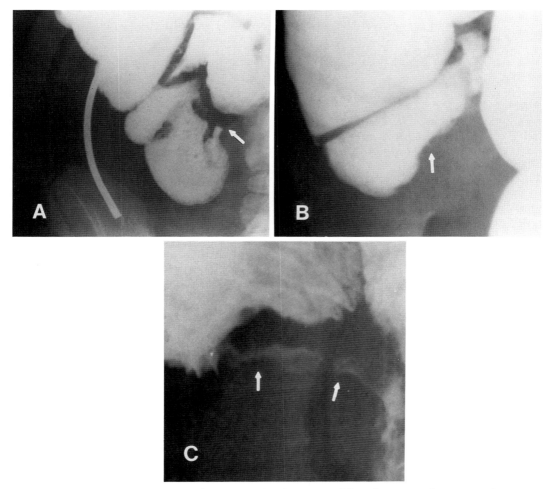

Figure 3.58. *Barium enema; acute appendicitis.*   (*A*) Note incomplete filling of the appendix and lack of a rounded bulbous end (*arrow*). (*B*) Nonfilling of the appendix with a barium-filled pointed beak at its base (*arrow*). Also note minimal associated cecal indentation. (*C*) Incomplete filling of the appendix with mucosal edema causing gross cobblestoning (*arrows*).

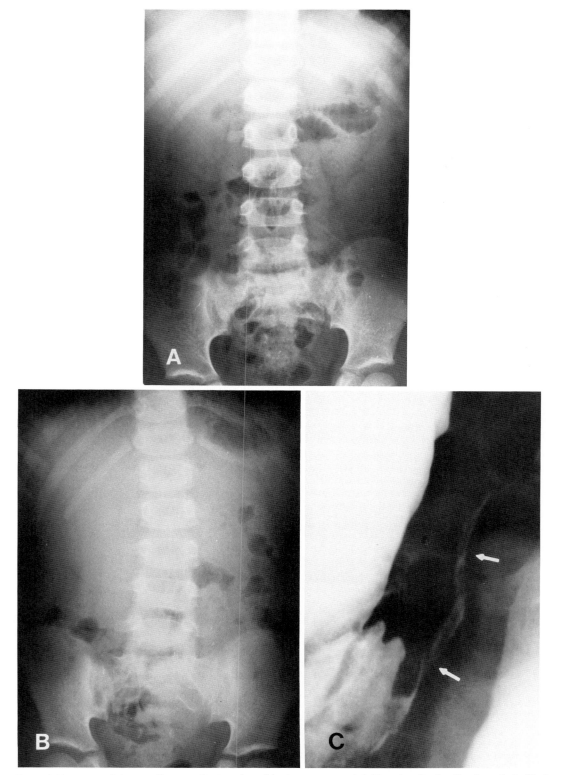

Figure 3.59. *Acute abdomen; (?) appendicitis-value of barium enema.* (*A*) Note localized collection of air-filled loops of intestine in the right lower quadrant. This patient had an acute abdomen somewhat suggestive of appendicitis. (*B*) Upright view demonstrates the development of scoliosis and persistence of the loops of intestine in the right lower quadrant. Does this patient have appendicitis? (*C*) Barium enema demonstrates a normal cecum and complete filling of the appendix (*arrows*). However, the appendix does appear somewhat edematous. Filling of the appendix to its end mitigates against appendicitis, but yet edema of the appendix causes one to equivocate. Eventually this patient was demonstrated to have shigellosis and edema of the appendix may well have been part of the problem.

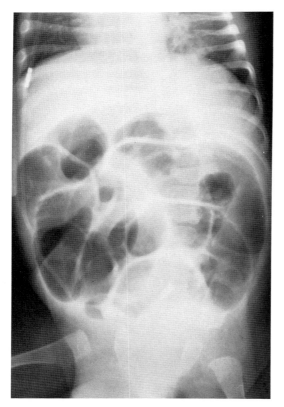

Figure 3.60. *Acute appendicitis presenting in inguinal hernia and producing an associated small bowel obstruction.* This patient had acute appendicitis which had gone on to perforation. He presented with a mass in the inguinal region and a distended abdomen. At surgical exploration the mass was determined to be a perforated appendix in the inguinal canal, and the small bowel obstruction was secondary to this problem.

22. Holgerson, L.O., and Stanley-Brown, E.G.: Acute appendicitis with perforation. Am. J. Dis. Child. 122: 288–293, 1971.
23. Homer, M.J., and Braver, J.M.: Recurrent appendicitis: reexamination of controversial disease. Gastrointest. Radiol. 4: 295–301, 1979.
24. Isdale, J.M.: The radiological signs of acute appendicitis in infancy and childhood. S. Afr. Med. J. 53: 363–364, 1978.
25. Joffe, N.: Some uncommon roentgenologic findings associated with acute perforative appendicitis. Radiology 110: 301–305, 1974.
26. Johnson, J.F., Pickett, W.J., and Enzenauer, R.W.: Contrast enema demonstration of a colon cut-off sign in a baby with perforated appendicitis. Pediatr. Radiol. 12: 150–151, 1982.
27. Jona, J.Z., Belin, R.P., and Selke, A.C.: Barium enema as a diagnostic aid in children with abdominal pain. Surg. Gynecol. Obstet. 144: 351, 1977.
28. Killen, D.A., and Brooks, D.W., Jr.: Gas-filled appendix: a roentgenographic sign of acute appendicitis. Ann. Surg. 161: 474–478, 1965.
29. Lee, P.W.R.: The leukocyte count in acute appendicitis. Br. J. Surg. 60: 618, 1973.
30. Leonidas, J.C., Harris, D.J., and Amoury, R.A.: How accurate is the roentgen diagnosis of acute appendicitis in children. Ann. Radiol. 18: 479–487, 1975.
31. Lewin, G.A., Mikity, V., and Wingert, W.A.: Barium enema: an outpatient procedure in the early diagnosis of acute appendicitis. J. Pediatr. 92: 451–453, 1978.
32. Lim, M.S.: Gas-filled appendix: lack of diagnostic specificity. A.J.R. 128: 209–210, 1977.
33. May, L.M., O'Neill, F.E., and Allen, S.W.: Cecal ileus: an undescribed and helpful sign in acute appendicitis. Tex. J. Med. 54: 92, 1958.
34. Mayson, P.B., Jr., and Rosenthal, S.J.: Roentgen findings in delayed diagnosis of appendicitis. A.J.R. 103: 347–350, 1968.
35. McCort, J.J.: Extra-alimentary gas in perforated appendicitis. A.J.R. 84: 1087–1092, 1960.
36. Melamed, M., Melamed, J.L., and Rabushka, S.E.: Appendicitis: "functional" bowel obstruction associated with perforation of the appendix. A.J.R. 99: 112–117, 1967.
37. Meyers, M.A., and Oliphant, M.: Ascending retrocecal appendicitis. Radiology 110: 295–299, 1974.
38. Moncada, R., Raffensperger, J., Wasserman, D., and Freeark, R.: Hydronephrosis secondary to acute appendicitis in children. Pediatr. Radiol. 2: 121–124, 1974.
39. Movsas, I.: Gas in the hepato-renal space. An unusual radiological sign of perforated appendicitis. S. Afr. J. Radiol. 3: 35–37, 1965.
40. Picus, D., and Shackelford, G.D.: Perforated appendix presenting with severe diarrhea: findings on barium enema examination. Radiology 149: 141–143, 1983.
41. Rajagopalan, A.E., Mason, J.H., Kennedy, M., and Pawlikowski, J.: The value of the barium enema in the diagnosis of acute appendicitis. Arch. Surg. 112: 531–533, 1977.
42. Riddlesberger, Jr., M.M., Afshani, E., Kuhn, J.P., and Duszynski, D.O.: Unusual presentation of appendiceal abscess on barium contrast studies. Pediatr. Radiol. 7: 15–18, 1978.
43. Riggs, W., and Parvey, L.S.: Perforated appendix presenting with disproportionate jejunal distention. Pediatr. Radiol. 5: 47–49, 1976.
44. Rizen, B.K., Itzig, C., and Quinn, P.J.: Case report, appendicovesical fistula in childhood. Am. J. Dis. Child. 130: 530–531, 1976.
45. Saebo, A.: Pneumoperitoneum associated with perforated appendicitis. Acta Chir. Scand. 144: 115–117, 1978.
46. Sakover, R.P., and DelFava, R.L.: Frequency of visualization of the normal appendix with the barium enema examination. A.J.R. 121: 312–317, 1974.
47. Samuel, E.: The gas-filled appendix. Br. J. Radiol. 30: 27–30, 1957.
48. Sanders, D.Y., Cart, C.R., and Stubbs, A.J.: Shigellosis associated with appendicitis. J. Pediatr. Surg. 7: 315–317, 1972.
49. Savrin, R.A., and Clatworthy, W., Jr.: Appendiceal rupture: a continuing diagnostic problem. Pediatrics 63: 37–43, 1979.
50. Schey, W.L.: Use of barium in the diagnosis of appendicitis in children. A.J.R. 118: 95–103, 1973.
51. Shaw, R.: Appendix calculi and acute appendicitis. Br. J. Surg. 52: 451–459, 1955.
52. Shimkin, P.M.: Commentary: radiology of acute appendicitis. A.J.R. 130: 1001–1004, 1978.
53. Sisson, R.G., Ahlvin, R.C., and Harlow, M.C.: Superficial mucosal ulceration and pathogenesis of acute appendicitis. Am. J. Surg. 122: 378–380, 1971.
54. Soter, C.S.: The contribution of the radiologist to the diagnosis of acute appendicitis. Semin. Roentgenol. 8: 375–388, 1973.
55. Soteropoulos, C., and Gilmore, J.H.: Roentgen diagnosis of acute appendicitis. Radiology 71: 246–257, 1958.
56. Swischuk, L.E., and Hayden, C.K., Jr.: Appendicitis with perforation: the dilated transverse colon sign. A.J.R. 135: 687–689, 1980.
57. VanderMolen, R.L., Amoury, R.A., and Haydes, W.G.:

Appendicitis and a calcified fecalith in a five-month-old child. J. Pediatr. Surg. 9: 541–542, 1974.

58. Vaudagna, J.S., and McCort, J.J.: Plain film diagnosis of retrocecal appendicitis. Radiology 117: 533–536, 1975.
59. Voitk, A.J., MacFarlane, J.K., and Estrada, R.L.: Ruptured appendicitis in femoral hernias. Ann. Surg. 179: 24, 1974.
60. White, J.J., Santillana, M., and Haller, J.A., Jr.: Intensive in-hospital observation: a safe way to decrease unnecessary appendectomy. Ann. Surg. 41: 793–798, 1975.
61. Wilkinson, R.H., Bartlet, R.H., and Eraklis, A.J.: Diagnosis of appendicitis in infancy: value of abdominal radiograph. Am. J. Dis. Child. 118: 687–690, 1969.
62. Williams, H.H.: Coproliths in children: recognition and significance. Pediatrics 34: 372–377, 1964.

Conditions Mimicking Acute Appendicitis. The most common conditions mimicking the clinical and roentgenographic findings of acute appendicitis are: (a) mesenteric adenitis, (b) yersinia ileocolitis, (c) Crohn's disease or regional enteritis, (d) Meckel's diverticulitis, (e) the so-called ileocecal syndrome or typhlitis in children with leukemia, and (f) the occasional case of infarction of the appendices epiploicae.

Mesenteric adenitis is considered by many a myth, but I do believe it occurs. Most cases are of viral origin and are common during gastroenteritis (flu) epidemics. However, differentiation of mesenteric adenitis from acute appendicitis often is most difficult, both clinically and roentgenographically, and actually one not uncommonly encounters cases where the initial diagnosis is that of mesenteric adenitis, but yet in a few days the patient returns with perforated appendicitis. This probably occurs much more frequently than is generally believed, and it is my opinion that *many cases of so-called mesenteric adenitis actually are cases of acute appendicitis which fail, at that particular time, to culminate in a classic clinical and roentgenographic picture.* Others, however, probably represent true adenitis due to infection, and differentiating the findings from those of acute appendicitis should be facilitated more and more by the use of the barium enema. With mesenteric adenitis, the barium enema is normal, while with appendicitis, incomplete or nonfilling of the appendix, and other associated findings are seen (see Fig. 3.56).

So-called suppurative mesenteric lymphadenitis (2), is a much more severe illness and laparotomy is difficult to avoid. In these cases, lymph node infection probably is of bacterial origin, and as such, closely parallels the findings of acute appendicitis. A variety of enteric organisms have been found to cause the problem, including yersinia (1, 2, 4, 9). Indeed, yersinia ileocolitis is being recognized more and more as a cause of abdominal symptoms mimicking acute appendicitis. If barium enemas are performed in these patients, one may see extensive edema and nodularity of the ileocecal region (Fig. 3.61) and nonspecific mucosal irregularities. In some cases, the findings might be confused with those of post-perforation appendiceal abscess.

Crohn's disease or regional enteritis is notorious for first presenting with findings suggestive of acute appendicitis (6, 11, 12, 14, 19). There is no real way to get around this dilemma, except to remember that such patients are going to present in the emergency room from time to time. Even then, they probably will be operated upon for acute appendicitis.

Meckel's diverticulitis also can mimic acute appendicitis but to spend a great deal of time on the plain film findings of this condition would not be fruitful. Indeed, in many cases the plain film findings are nor-

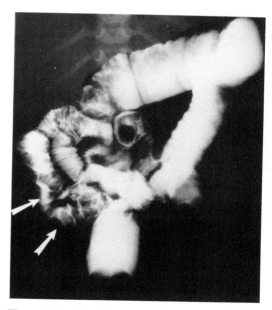

Figure 3.61. *Yersinia enterocolitis.* Note extensive edema and thumbprinting of the cecum and ascending colon (*arrows*). In other cases similar changes are seen in the terminal ileum. (Courtesy Barlow, B., Gandhi, R., and Young, L.W.: Radiological case of the month, Am. J. Dis. Child. 135: 171–172, 1981.)

mal, and even barium studies of the gastrointestinal tract are seldom helpful (16). If inflammation is more pronounced, right lower quadrant findings similar to those seen in acute appendicitis may develop, and if perforation occurs, those associated with perforated appendicitis will be seen (3, 5, 8, 10, 15, 21). Other manifestations of Meckel's diverticulitis include a right lower quadrant or lower abdominal air or fluid-filled mass (with larger diverticula) and stone formation (3, 13).

Typhlitis or the so-called ileocecal syndrome is an affliction of patients with leukemia (1, 7, 18, 20). It is characterized by a profound necrotizing inflammation of the terminal ileum, appendix, and cecum, and usually is a terminal event. However, it is not known just why it occurs. The findings mimic those of acute appendicitis very closely, and the key to proper diagnosis is knowledge that the patient is suffering from leukemia.

Idiopathic infarction or torsion (17) of the appendices epiploicae is not particularly common in childhood, but in some cases can mimic the findings of acute appendicitis.

REFERENCES

1. Abramson, S.J., Berdon, W.E., and Baker, D.H.: Childhood typhlitis: its increasing association with acute myelogenous leukemia. Report of five cases. Radiology 146: 61–64, 1983.
2. Alvear, D.T., and Kain, T.M.: Supurrative mesenteric lymphadenitis, a forgotten clinical entity. J. Pediatr. Surg. 10: 969–970, 1975.
3. Baldero, J.: Calculi in a Meckel's diverticulum. J. Fac. Radiol. 9: 157–160, 1958.
4. Barlow, B., Tandhi, R., and Young, L.W.: Radiological case of the month—suppurative mesenteric adenitis: *Yersinia enterocolitica.* Am. J. Dis. Chlid. 135: 171–172, 1981.
5. Canty, T., Meguid, M.M., and Eraklis, A.J.: Perforation of Meckel's diverticulum in infancy. J. Pediatr. Surg. 10: 189–193, 1975.
6. Cohen, W.N., and Denbesten, L.: Crohn's disease with predominant involvement of the appendix. A.J.R. 113: 361–363, 1970.
7. Cronin, T.G., Jr., Calandra, J.D., and DelFava, R.L.: Typhlitis presenting as toxic cecitis. Radiology 138: 29–30, 1981.
8. Dalinka, M.K., and Wunder, J.F.: Meckel's diverticulum and its complications, with emphasis on roentgenologic demonstration. Radiology 106: 295–298, 1973.
9. Ekberg, O., Sjostrom, B., and Brahme, F.: Radiological findings in yersinia ileitis. Radiology 123: 15–19, 1977.
10. Enge, I., and Frimann-Dahl, J.: Radiology in acute abdominal disorders due to Meckel's diverticulum. Br. J. Radiol. 37: 775–780, 1964.
11. Ewen, S.W.B., Anderson, J., Galloway, J.M.D., et al.: Crohn's disease initially confined to the appendix. Gastroenterology 60: 853–857, 1971.
12. Hall, J.H., and Hellier, M.D.: Crohn's disease of the appendix presenting as acute appendicitis. Br. J. Surg. 56: 390–392, 1969.
13. Hirschy, J.C., Thorpe, J.J., and Cortese, A.F.: Meckel's stones: a case report. Radiology 119: 19–20, 1976.
14. Hollings, R.M.: Crohn's disease of the appendix. Med. J. Aust. 1: 639–641, 1964.
15. Meguid, M., Canty, T., and Eraklis, A.: Complications of Meckel's diverticulum in infants. Surg. Gynecol. Obstet. 139: 541–544, 1974.
16. Meguid, M.M., Wilkinson, R.H., Canty, T., Eraklis, A.J., and Treves, S.: Futility of barium sulfate in diagnosis of bleeding Meckel's diverticulum. Arch. Surg. 108: 361–362, 1974.
17. Schikler, K.N., Nagaraj, H.S., and Hodge, K.M.: Torsion of appendix epiploica in systemic lupus erythematosus. Am. J. Dis. Child. 136: 748–749, 1982.
18. Sherman, N.J., and Woolley, M.W.: Ileocecal syndrome in acute childhood leukemia. Arch. Surg. 107: 39–42, 1973.
19. Threatt, B., and Appelman, H.: Crohn's disease of the appendix presenting as acute appendicitis. Report of 3 cases with a review of the literature. Radiology 110: 313–317, 1974.
20. Wagner, M.L., Harberg, F.J., and Kumbar, A.P.: Typhlitis a complication of leukemia in childhood. A.J.R. 109: 341–450, 1970.
21. White, A.F., Oh, K.S., Weber, A.L., and James, A.E., Jr.: Radiological manifestations of Meckel's diverticulum. A.J.R. 118: 86–94, 1973.

Other Intra-Abdominal Inflammations or Infections. These include pancreatitis, cholecystitis, cholelithiasis, pyelonephritis, cystitis, salpingitis, and a variety of colitis disorders. *Pancreatitis* is not a particularly common problem in childhood (3, 13) but is seen with cholecystitis (1), viral infections, such as mumps and infectious mononucleosis, and after blunt abdominal trauma. The latter is especially common in the battered child syndrome (3, 13, 29). In addition, pancreatitis has been noted with cystic fibrosis (26), juvenile diabetes mellitus (17), hyperparathyroidism, refeeding in malnourished children (12), drug (especially steroid) therapy (3, 13), and on a hereditary basis, in certain families (5, 14, 34).

Abdominal roentgenograms in acute pancreatitis most often are entirely normal, but in other instances, one may see so-called sentinel loops of distended intestine overlying the inflamed pancreas (6). These loops may take the form of: (a) a dilated portion of the transverse colon (colon cutoff sign), (b) a dilated duodenum, or (c) dilated loops of small bowel in the upper mid abdomen or left upper quadrant (2, 6, 11, 27). In all of these cases, the findings represent paralytic ileus of the loop of intestine lying next to the inflamed pancreas (see Fig. 3.106).

In addition to these findings, one may note a generalized increase in soft tissue density over the region of the pancreas, and if inflammation is extensive, there may be an increase in the soft tissue distance between the transverse colon and stomach (18). This latter finding represents edema of the pancreas and inflammation of the adjacent stomach and colon (see Fig. 3.106). In some cases there may be actual necrosis of the transverse colon (32).

If pancreatic inflammation is so severe that pancreatic necrosis occurs, a gas abscess of the pancreas can develop (2, 7, 22). Such an abscess can assume the configuration of one large air and fluid-filled cavity, or numerous small bubbles (Fig. 3.62). If a pseudocyst accompanies pancreatitis, a mass also may be visible, but currently these are best demonstrated with ultrasonography. Very rarely calcifications within the pancreas are seen.

In most cases, pancreatitis is suspected and diagnosed clinically. However, confirmation frequently is sought for with ultrasonography, and while the study is not always abnormal, when enlargement of the pancreas and increased sonolucency is seen, the diagnosis should be suspected (4, 8) (Fig.

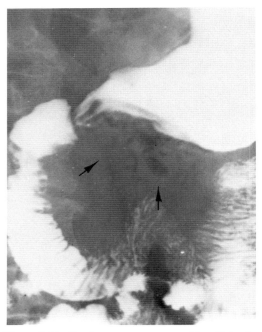

Figure 3.62. *Emphysematous pancreatitis.* Note the widened duodenal loop, elevated antrum of the stomach, and collection of bubbles in the region of the pancreas (*arrows*). These bubbles are gas collections in the pancreas.

3.63). In addition to these findings, one may see increased echogenicity in and around the kidney and liver due to lipolysis (31) of fat (Fig. 3.63C), and of course, if a pseudocyst is present, a large cystic cavity, with or without debris is seen (Fig. 3.64). With ultrasonography now on the scene, seldom is a gastrointestinal series performed for acute pancreatitis, but if one should obtain such a study, one may see widening and compression of the duodenal loop, or the so-called pad sign (Fig. 3.65).

It is important to realize that *although pancreatitis is an abdominal problem, many extra-abdominal clinical and roentgenographic manifestations also can be seen.* Indeed, these findings can distract one's attention from the main problem, and thus one must be aware of them all. Firstly, it should be noted that associated pleural effusions (Fig. 3.66) are very common (2, 19, 20, 22, 33), and that occasionally even pericardial effusions can be seen (20). In addition, when pancreatitic enzymes are liberated into the blood stream, pulmonary edema and profound respiratory insufficiency can result (9, 23). In other instances, hypocalcemia resulting from the binding of calcium to these same pancreatic enzymes (saponification) can lead to electrocardiographic changes suggesting myocardial ischemia (16). Hypocalcemia also can lead to neurologic manifestations.

Fat necrosis from the liberation of lipase into the blood stream can produce subcutaneous nodules (24, 30), widespread necrosis of the fat of the mesentery (18), and in some cases fat necrosis-induced lytic lesions in the bones (10, 15, 21, 29). These latter lesions can mimic osteomyelitis, and usually are seen 2 or 3 weeks after the acute episode of pancreatitis.

Cholecystitis and cholelithiasis are more common in childhood than is generally appreciated (1, 3–7, 10–13, 15, 17), and while it has been generally believed that cholelithiasis most often is secondary to hemolytic blood disorders, it is becoming increasingly apparent that most cases, perhaps two-thirds or more, are due to other causes (4, 7, 14). Indeed, many are idiopathic, and just as in the adult, more cases occur in females than in males.

Clinical features are much the same as in

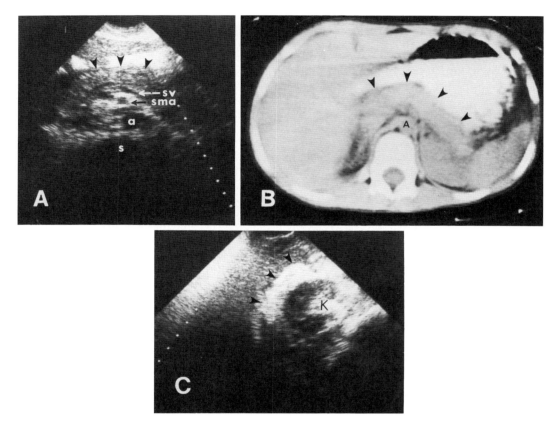

Figure 3.63. *Acute pancreatitis; ultrasonographic findings.*   (*A*) Note the enlarged, but normally echoic pancreas (*arrows*). Aorta (*a*), spine (*s*), superior mesenteric artery (*sma*), and splenic vein (*sv*). (*B*) CT scan in another patient with an enlarged pancreas (*arrows*). Aorta (*A*). (*C*) Fat lipolysis in pancreatitis. Note intense echogenicity surrounding the kidney (*arrows*). This probably is due to lipolysis of fat. Usually, in children, there is not enough fat around the kidney to be visualized ultrasonographically; kidney (*K*). (From L.E. Swischuk et al. (31).)

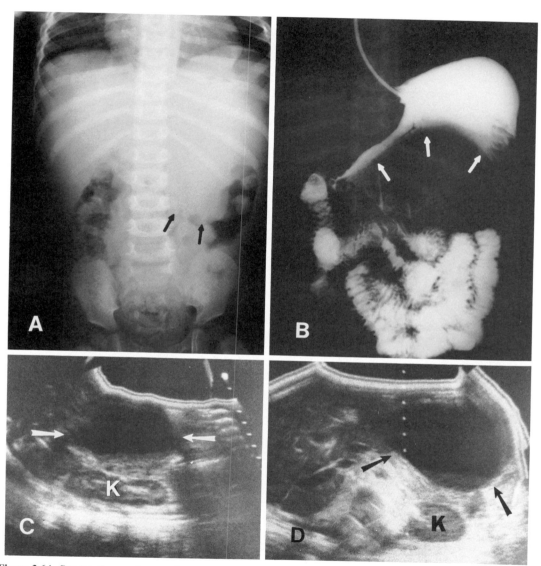

Figure 3.64. *Pancreatic pseudocyst; ultrasonographic findings.* (*A*) Note evidence of an abdominal mass on the left (*arrows*). (*B*) Upper GI series demonstrates displacement of the stomach and duodenum by the mass (*arrows*). (*C*) Longitudinal ultrasound study demonstrates a large anechoic cyst, with debris layered along its base (*arrows*). (*D*) Cross-sectional view showing the same findings (*arrows*); kidney (*K*).

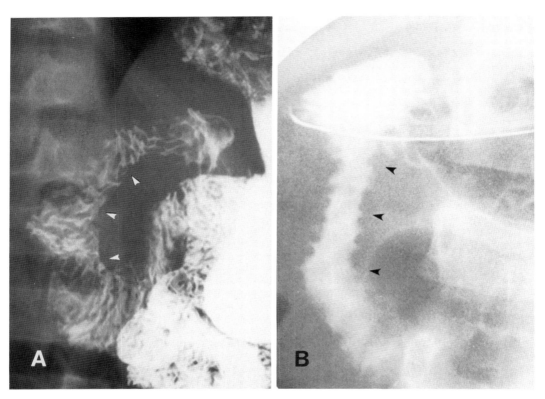

Figure 3.65. *Acute pancreatitis; duodenal loop findings.*   (*A*) Pad sign. Note the pad-like indentation of the inner aspect of the duodenal loop (*arrows*). Although not grossly stretched, the wall demonstrates a rather rigid smooth inner surface. (*B*) Marked edema and spasm of the duodenum (*arrows*). Same patient as in Figure 3.64*B*.

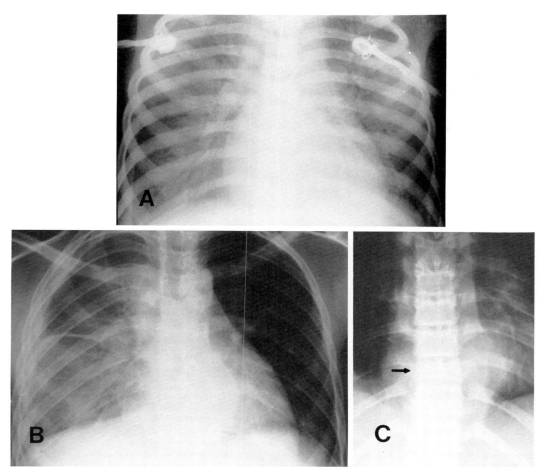

Figure 3.66. *Pancreatitis with chest findings.* (*A*) Note bilateral interstitial pulmonary edema causing haziness of the lungs in this patient with acute pancreatitis. (*B*) Another patient with a semiopacified right hemithorax due to a pleural effusion secondary to pancreatitis. Pulmonary edema of the right lung also probably is present and a paraspinal mass is present on the left . (*C*) A week or two later this paraspinal mass was determined to be due to compression fracture of a thoracic vertebra (*arrows*). The findings were believed to represent vertebral collapse secondary to osteolysis resulting from fat necrosis.

adults, but in infancy the diagnosis may be difficult to make. Jaundice may be present, and in those cases of empyema or hydrops of the gallbladder (2, 3, 8, 9, 16), a mass may be palpable. Indeed, an enlarged gallbladder may be visible roentgenographically (Fig. 3.67*A*), but overall this finding is uncommon. In other cases one may see one or two sentinel loops of dilated bowel in the right upper quadrant, some degree of scoliosis with concavity to the right, and even associated pleural effusions or atelectasis of the right lung. None of these findings, however,

is very specific, nor for that matter, common.

If gallstones are calcified, they may be seen on plain abdominal roentgenograms (Fig. 3.68*A*), and if gangrene or abscess formation develops in the gallbladder, one may see air in the gallbladder or within its wall (i.e., emphysematous cholecystitis). Otherwise, the diagnosis of most acute gallbladder problems now rests with ultrasonography, and to some extent isotope studies. Ultrasound can identify acute cholecystitis, the presence of gallstones, a hydropic gallbladder and di-

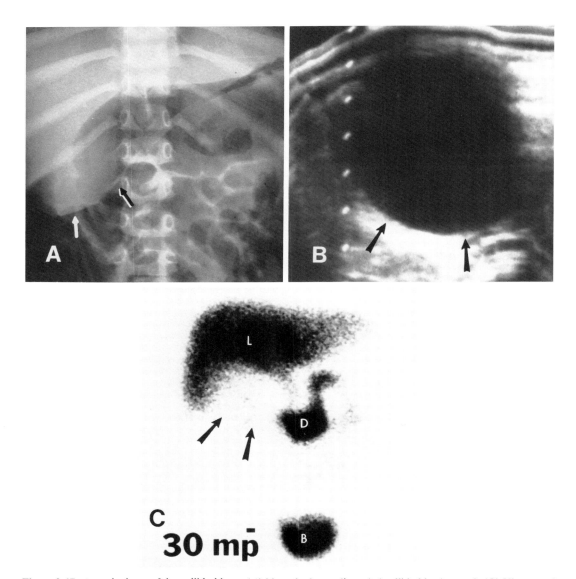

Figure 3.67. *Acute hydrops of the gallbladder..* (*A*) Note the large, distended gallbladder (*arrows*). (*B*) Ultrasound study demonstrating hydropic gallbladder in another patient (*arrows*). (*C*) Isotope Tc-Hida study demonstrates no isotope activity in the gallbladder (*arrows*). Isotope has passed into the duodenum (*D*), and is being excreted into the urinary bladder (*B*).

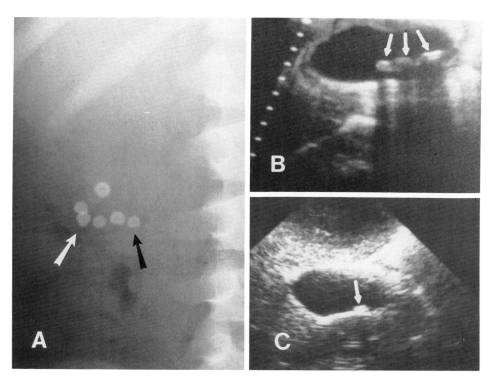

Figure 3.68. *Cholelithiasis.* (*A*) Note calcified gallstones (*arrows*) in this patient with sickle cell disease. (*B*) Ultrasonographic findings demonstrate the gallbladder and numerous hyperechoic gallstones (*arrows*), with distal acoustical shadowing. (*C*) Another patient with a single gallstone (*arrow*).

lated intrahepatic ducts. Isotope studies, utilizing one or the other of the IDA isotopes also is useful and can be utilized to identify acute cholecystitis, a hydropic gallbladder, or an obstructed biliary tract.

Gallstones, on ultrasound, produce increased echoes and usually, distal acoustical shadowing (Fig. 3.68*B*). Shadowing, however, is not always present (Fig. 3.68*C*). Acute cholecystitis may show nothing more than a distended gallbladder but edema of the wall also can be seen (Fig. 3.69*A*). Such edema is not present in every case and also can be seen when there is generalized anasarca. If a hydropic gallbladder is present, it is easily identified as a large, cystic structure (see. Fig. 3.67*B*), and in addition, one will not be able to identify a normal gallbladder. This is important because, with choledochal cysts, the gallbladder usually is identified. Dilated intra- and extrahepatic bile ducts also can be identified with ultrasound (Fig. 3.70).

A normal technetium (Tc)-IDA study identifies the liver, the intra- and extrahepatic biliary ducts, the gallbladder, and excretion of the isotope into the gastrointestinal tract. With acute cholecystitis, because the cystic duct is obstructed, the gallbladder is not visualized (Fig. 3.69*B*). Similar findings are seen with hydrops of the gallbladder (Fig. 3.67*C*), but with choledochal cysts, both the gallbladder and the cyst accumulate isotope.

Acute *pyelonephritis and cystitis* are common in childhood, especially in girls. However, the plain film abdominal findings usually are normal. In a few cases, sentinel loops may be seen over the infected kidney or bladder, and if a unilateral problem such as a renal carbuncle or perinephric abscess exists, evidence of perirenal inflammation or an actual mass with scoliosis to the ipsilateral side may be noted (Fig. 3.71*A*). In these cases, pyelographic findings may demonstrate a displaced kidney with variably de-

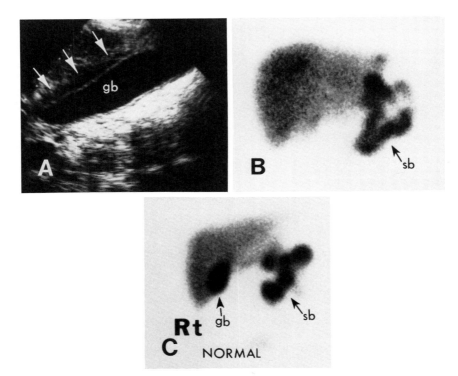

Figure 3.69. *Acute cholecystitis; ultrasonographic and isotope findings.* (*A*) Note the distended gallbladder (*gb*) and thickening of its wall (*arrows*). (*B*) Tc-Hida study demonstrating no isotope in the gallbladder, but isotope does pass into the small bowel (*sb*). (*C*) Normal Tc-Hida study showing isotope in the gallbladder (*gb*) and small bowel (*sb*).

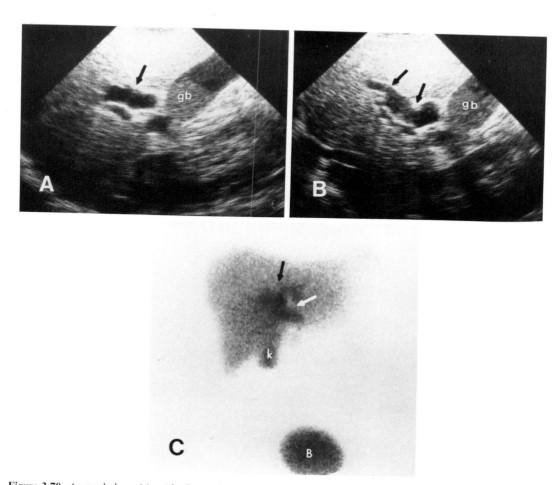

Figure 3.70. *Acute cholecystitis with obstruction.* (*A*) Ultrasonogram demonstrates sludge in the gallbladder (*gb*), and marked dilatation of the bile ducts (*arrow*). The portal vein is seen below the dilated bile duct. (*B*) Another view of the same findings. (*C*) Tc-Hida study demonstrating isotope in the dilated, obstructed bile ducts (*arrows*), but none in the gallbladder. In addition, none has passed into the GI tract. Some is being excreted, as would be expected, into the kidney (*k*) and bladder (*B*).

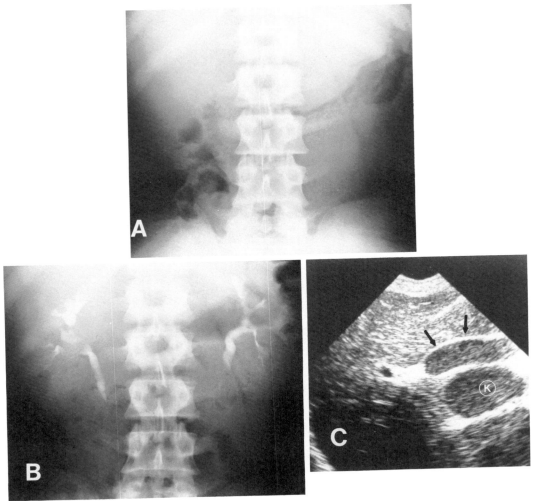

Figure 3.71. *Perinephric abscess.* (*A*) Note sentinel loops and absence of the psoas shadow on the right. The normal psoas shadow is visible on the left. Also note that the inferior edge of the liver is obliterated. (*B*) Intravenous pyelogram demonstrating poorly defined right renal margins and a right kidney which appears a little larger than the left. (*C*) Ultrasonographic findings in another patient demonstrate an echogenic abscess (*arrows*) just above the kidney (*K*).

creased renal function (Fig. 3.71*B*), but in acute pyelonephritis without these complications, the pyelographic findings are minimal. Usually there is nothing more to see than mild to moderate calyceal dilatation and blunting, and dilatation of the ureters secondary to reflex paralytic ileus. Only rarely is spasm and edema of the collecting systems seen.

Getting back to perinephric abscesses, and also, intrarenal abscesses, ultrasound is one's best imaging modality (Fig. 3.71*C*). CT scanning can be used for the same purpose, but ultrasonography usually suffices.

Cystitis usually is seen in combination with pyelonephritis although it can occur as an isolated infection. Most often it is of bacterial origin, but viral infections can occur. In most cases of cystitis, one will note a spastic, irregular bladder, secondary to spasm and mucosal edema (Fig. 3.72*A*). If blood clots are present, they may be seen as radiolucent filling defects in the bladder (Fig. 3.72*B*). Another form of cystitis in children

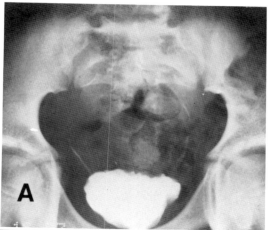

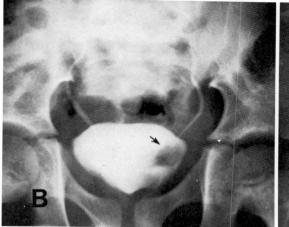

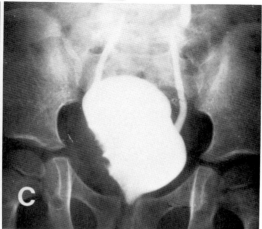

Figure 3.72. *Cystitis—various configurations.* (*A*) Note irregularity over the top of the bladder in this boy with symptoms of cystitis. No bacteria were cultured, and a viral origin was suspected. Symptoms cleared after 10 days to 2 weeks. (*B*) Note the filling defect due to a blood clot in the bladder. This patient had signs and symptoms of cystitis. It was of bacterial origin. (*C*) Note irregularity and mass-like indentation of the right side of the bladder in this patient presenting with bleeding from the urinary tract. This patient had cytoxan cystitis.

is cytoxan cystitis, but this problem is seen exclusively in patients with blood dyscrasias or other tumors requiring Cytoxan therapy (Fig. 3.73*C*).

Generally, urinary bladder abnormalities are best demonstrated with the bladder fully distended, but often edema and irregularity of the mucosa are better demonstrated on the post voiding or partially filled study (Fig. 3.73). In addition, now that ultrasonography is available, advanced cases of inflammatory disease of the bladder can be detected with ultrasound (Fig. 3.73*C*).

Salpingitis occurs in adolescent girls and may produce localizing, sentinel loops over the lower abdomen, profound paralytic ileus mimicking mechanical obstruction (Fig. 3.74), or even mass-like configurations representing pus collections in the lower abdomen and pelvis (1, 2). Such collections, and lesser volumes of purulent exudate are now more clearly defined with ultrasonography (Fig. 3.74).

Colitis, on an acute basis, can be seen with shigellosis (4), ulcerative colitis, granulomatous colitis (Crohn's disease), amebiasis, and the hemolytic uremic syndrome (1, 6, 11). In the latter condition, changes

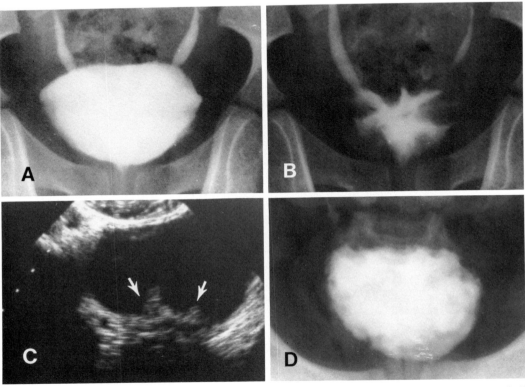

Figure 3.73. *Cystitis; post voiding film.*   (*A*) On this film with the bladder fully filled, no disease is suspected. (*B*) On the post voiding study, note marked mucosal edema. This patient had viral cystitis. (*C*) *Hypertrophic cystitis; ultrasound findings.* Note fronds of thickened mucosa (*arrows*). (*D*) Cystogram demonstrating similar findings.

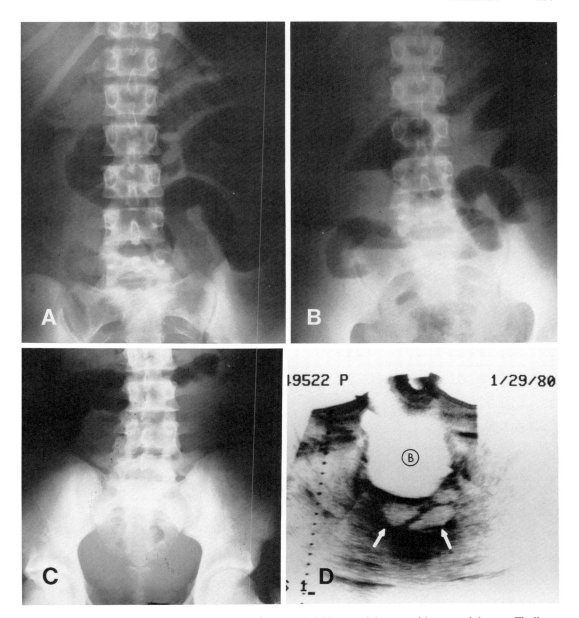

Figure 3.74. *Salpingitis and pelvic inflammatory disease.* (*A*) Young adolescent with acute abdomen. Findings suggest peritonitis and/or obstruction. (*B*) Upright film suggests intestinal obstruction. After antibiotic treatment, these findings disappeared in 24 hours. (*C*) Note fluid in the pelvis of another patient. (*D*) Ultrasonogram demonstrates fluid collections (pus) around the bladder (*arrows*); urinary bladder (*B*).

can be so profound as to lead to colonic necrosis and perforation (5, 9). For the most part, plain film findings in colitis, in general, are lacking, except in those patients with toxic megacolon. Most often this complication is seen with ulcerative colitis and in such cases the colon (usually the transverse colon), is distended and paralyzed. It is void of haustral markings and its wall may be smooth, coarsely serrated, or thumbprinted (Fig. 3.75). The latter configurations result from extensive mucosal inflammation, edema, or pseudopolyp formation. As noted, toxic megacolon classically is seen in ulcer-

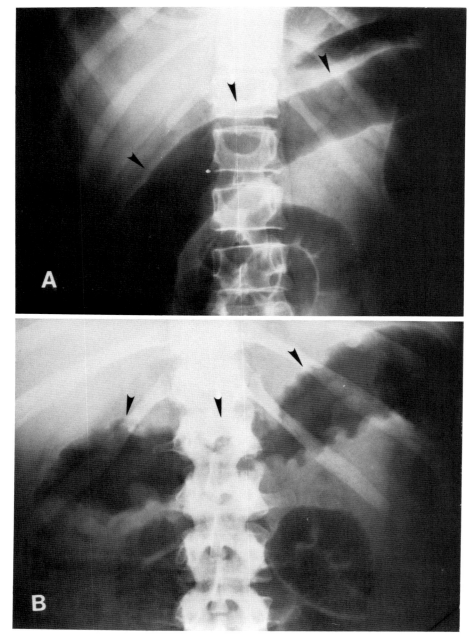

Figure 3.75. *Toxic megacolon.* (*A*) Note the dilated but smooth transverse colon with no haustral markings (*arrows*). (*B*) Another patient with a dilated colon, but in this case, note the nodular projections into the lumen of the dilated colon (*arrows*). The findings represent thickening, edema, and pseudopolyp formation of the colon. (Fig. B courtesy Virgil B. Graves, M.D.)

ative colitis (2, 3, 7, 13), but it also can be seen with granulomatous colitis (8), and amebic colitis (12, 14).

Ultrasonography also can demonstrate an inflamed colon, or indeed, any segment of inflamed intestine. Generally, such a segment of bowel presents as a round (cross-section) or oval (longitudinal section) lesion, with a slightly thickened sonolucent rim (edematous bowel wall) and a relatively large area of central echoes (thickened mucosa) (Fig. 3.76).

Necrotizing enterocolitis is primarily an affliction of premature infants, but also can be seen in older infants (10), and with ischemic disease of the intestine. The findings consist of: (a) pronounced abdominal distension with severe paralytic ileus or locally dilated loops in the right lower quadrant, (b) pneumatosis cystoides intestinalis (Fig. 3.19), (c) portal vein gas (Fig. 3.20), (d) free air in the peritoneal cavity when perforation occurs, and (e) peritonitis.

Finally, a word regarding *shigellosis* is in order. This acute intestinal inflammation represents one of the most severe forms of gastroenteritis, and the volume of fluid loss through the colon is enormous. Indeed, the presence of massive volumes of fluid in the intestines can lead to a variety of plain film findings, some of which may suggest more serious problems, such as ascites, peritonitis,

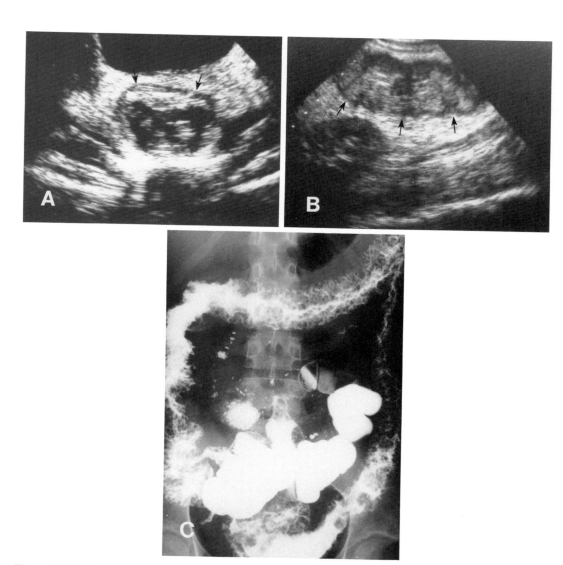

Figure 3.76. *Colitis; ultrasonographic findings.* (*A*) Note the sonolucent rim of thickened rectal wall (*arrows*), in this patient with pseudomembranous colitis. Sonolucent fluid is present in the lumen and there are areas of echogenicity due to debris and thickened mucosa. (*B*) Another patient with ulcerative colitis. Note the sonolucent rim of thickened colon wall (*arrows*), and numerous echoes from the thickened mucosa within. (*C*) Barium enema in the same patient.

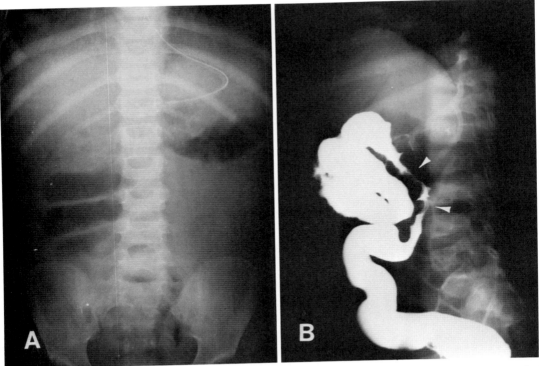

Figure 3.77. *Shigellosis.*. (*A*) Supine film demonstrating diffuse opacity throughout the abdomen and three sentinel loops on the right. The findings could be misinterpreted for peritonitis, small bowel obstruction, or some other intraabdominal problem. However, the patient had shigella infection of the gastrointestinal tract. (*B*) Barium enema in another patient demonstrating extreme spasm with thumbprinting of the descending colon (*arrows*).

or bowel obstruction (Fig. 3.77). In other cases, the abdominal findings are not different from those seen with viral gastroenteritis. Every so often, one is required to perform a barium enema in patients with shigellosis, and the intense colonic spasm demonstrated can be most startling (Fig. 3.77*B*).

REFERENCES

Pancreatitis

1. Auldist, A.W.: Pancreatitis and choledocholithiasis in childhood. J. Pediatr. Surg. 7: 78, 1972.
2. Barry, W.F., Jr.: Roentgen examination of the abdomen in acute pancreatitis. A.J.R. 74: 220–225, 1955.
3. Buntain, W.L., Wood, J.B., and Woolley, M.M.: Pancreatitis in childhood. J. Pediatr. Surg. 13: 143–149, 1978.
4. Cox, K.L., Ament, M.E., Sample, W.F., Sarti, D.A., O'-Donnell, M., Byrne, W.J.: The ultrasonic and biochemical diagnosis of pancreatitis in children. J. Pediatr. 96: 407–411, 1980.
5. Crane, J.M., Amoury, R.A., and Hellerstein, S.: Hereditary pancreatitis: report of a kindred. J. Pediatr. Surg. 8: 893–900, 1973.
6. Davis, S., Parbhoo, S.P., Gibson, M.J.: The Plain abdominal radiograph in acute pancreatitis. Clin. Radiol. 31: 87–93, 1980.
7. Felson, B.: Gas abscess of pancreas. J.A.M.A. 163: 637–641, 1957.
8. Fleischer, A.C., Parker, P., Kirchner, S.G., and James, A.E., Jr.: Sonographic findings of pancreatitis in children. Radiology 146: 151–155, 1983.
9. Goldberg, B.H., and Bergstein, J.M.: Acute respiratory distress in a child after steroid-induced pancreatitis. Pediatrics 61: 317–318, 1978.
10. Goluboff, N., Cram, R., Ramgotra, B., Singh, A., and Wilkinson, G.W.: Polyarthritis and bone lesions complicating traumatic pancreatitis in two children. Can. Med. Assoc. J. 118: 924–928, 1978.
11. Grollman, A.I., Goodman, S., and Fine, A.: Localized paralytic ileus: an early roentgen sign in acute pancreatitis. Surg. Gynecol. Obstet. 91: 65–70, 1950.
12. Gryboski, J., Hillemeier, C., Kocoshis, S., Anyan, W., and Seashore, J.S.: Refeeding pancreatitis in malnourished children. J. Pediatr. 97: 441–443, 1980.
13. Jordan, S.C., and Ament, M.E.: Pancreatitis in children and adolescents. J. Pediatr. 91: 211–216, 1977.
14. Kattwinkel, J., Lapey, A., di Sant'Agnese, P.A., Edwards, W.A., and Huffy, M.P.: Hereditary pancreatitis: three new kindreds and a critical review of the literature. Pediatrics 51: 55–69, 1973.
15. Keating, J.P., Shackelford, G.D., Shackelford, P.G., and Ternberg, J.L.: Pancreatitis and osteolytic lesions. J. Pediatr. 81: 350–353, 1972.
16. Krongrad, E., and Feldman, F.: Acute hemorrhagic pancreatitis: electrolyte and electrocardiographic changes. Am. J. Dis. Child. 119: 143–146, 1970.
17. Malone, J.I.: Juvenile diabetes and acute pancreatitis. J. Pediatr. 85: 825–827, 1974.
18. Meyers, M.A., and Evans, J.A.: Effects of pancreatitis on small bowel and colon: spread along mesenteric planes. A.J.R. 119: 151–165, 1973.
19. Mitchell, C.E.: Relapsing pancreatitis with recurrent pericardial and pleural effusions: a case report and review of the literature. Ann. Intern. Med. 60: 1047–1053, 1964.
20. Morens, D.M., Hammar, S.L., and Heicher, D.A.: Idio-

pathic acute pancreatitis in children. Am. J. Dis. Child. 128: 401–404, 1974.

21. Neuer, F.S., Roberts, F.F., and McCarthy, V.: Osteolytic lesions following traumatic pancreatitis. Am. J. Dis. Child. 131: 738–740, 1977.

22. Poppel, M.H.: The roentgen manifestations of pancreatitis. Semin. Roentgenol. 3: 227–241, 1968.

23. Rovner, A.J., and Westcott, J.L.: Pulmonary edema and respiratory insufficiency in acute pancreatitis. Radiology 118: 513–520, 1976.

24. Schrier, R.W., Melmon, K.L., and Fenster, L.F.: Subcutaneous nodular fat necrosis in pancreatitis. Arch. Intern. Med. 116: 832–836, 1965.

25. Schulz, R.D., Stechele, V., Seitz, K.H., Rettenmaier, G., Weitzel, D., and Mildenberger, H.: Pancreatic pseudocyst in children: echographic and angiographic demonstration. Ann. Radiol. 21: 173–178, 1978.

26. Schwachman, H., Lebenthal, E., and Khaw, K.: Recurrent acute pancreatitis in patients with cystic fibrosis with normal pancreatic enzymes. Pediatrics 55: 86–95, 1975.

27. Schwartz, S., and Nadelhaft, J.: Simulation of colonic obstruction at the splenic flexure by pancreatitis: roentgen features. A.J.R. 78: 607–616, 1957.

28. Siegelman, S.S., Copelande, B.E., Saba, G.P., Cameron, J.L., Sanders, R.C., and Zerhouni, E.A.: CT of fluid collections associated with pancreatitis. A.J.R. 134: 1121–1132, 1980.

29. Slovis, T.L., Berdon, W.E., Haller, J.O., Baker, D.H., and Rosen, L.: Pancreatitis and the battered child syndrome: Report of two cases with skeletal involvement. A.J.R. 125: 456–461, 1975.

30. Swerdlow, A.B., Berman, M.E., Gibbel, M.I., et al.: Subcutaneous fat necrosis associated with acute pancreatitis. J.A.M.A. 173: 765–769, 1960.

31. Swischuk, L.E., and Hayden, C.K.: Pararenal space hyperechogenicity in childhood pancreatitis. A.J.R. (in press).

32. Thompson, W.M., Kelvin, F.M., and Rice, R.P.: Inflammation and necrosis of the transverse colon secondary to pancreatitis. A.J.R. 128: 943–948, 1977.

33. Weens, H.S., and Walker, L.A.: The radiologic diagnosis of acute cholecystitis and pancreatitis. Radiol. Clin. North Am. 2: 89–106, 1964.

34. Whitten, D.M., Feingold, M., and Iesenklam, E.J.: Hereditary pancreatitis. Am. J. Dis. Child. 116: 426–428, 1968.

Cholecystitis and Cholelithiasis

1. Bertin, P., Fortier-Beaulieu, M., Rymer, R., Patrois, R., and Pellerin, D.: Primary biliary lithiasis in children: 18 cases. Ann. Pediatr. 22: 203–212, 1975.

2. Bloom, R.A., and Swain, V.A.J.: Noncalculous distension of gallbladder and childhood. Arch. Dis. Child. 41: 503–508, 1966.

3. Chamberlain, J.W., and Hight, D.W.: Acute hydrops of the gallbladder in childhood. Surgery, 68: 899–905, 1970.

4. Chrichlow, R.W., Seltzer, M.H., and Jannetta, P.J.: Cholecystitis in adolescents. Am. J. Dig. Dis. 17: 68–72, 1972.

5. Fortier-Beaulieu, M., and Rymer, R.: Radiological diagnosis of cholelithiasis in infancy and childhood (21 cases). Ann. Radiol. 16: 167–171, 1973.

6. Hanson, B.A., Mahour, G.H., and Woolley, M.M.: Disease of the gallbladder in infancy and childhood. J. Pediatr. Surg. 6: 277–283, 1971.

7. Harned, R.K., and Babbitt, D.P.: Cholelithiasis in children. Radiology 117: 391–393, 1975.

8. Jamieson, P.N., and Shaw, D.G.: Empyema of gallbladder in an infant. Arch. Dis. Child. 50: 482–484, 1975.

9. Kumari, S., Lee, W.J., and Baron, M.G.: Hydrops of the gallbladder in a child: diagnosis by ultrasonography. Pediatrics 63: 295–297, 1979.

10. Lucus, C.E., and Walt, A.J.: Acute gangrenous acalculous cholecystitis in infancy: report of a case. Surgery 64: 847–849, 1968.

11. Marks, C., Espinosa, J., and Hyman, L.J.: Acute acalculous cholecystitis in childhood. J. Pediatr. Surg. 3: 608–611, 1968.

12. Morales, L., Taboda, E., Toledo, L., and Radrigan, W.: Cholecystitis and cholelithiasis in children. J. Pediatr. Surg.

2: 565–568, 1967.

13. Natar, G.: Gallbladder disease in childhood. Aust. Paediatr. J. 8: 147–151, 1972.

14. Newman, D.E.: Gallstones in children. Pediatr. Radiol. 1: 100–104, 1973.

15. Piretti, R., Auldist, A., and Stephens, C.: Acute cholecystitis in children. Surg. Gynecol. Obstet. 140: 16–18, 1975.

16. Scobie, W.G., and Bentley, J.F.R.: Hydrops of the gallbladder in a newborn infant. J. Pediatr. Surg. 4: 457–459, 1969.

17. Strauss, R.G.: Cholelithiasis in childhood. Am. J. Dis. Child. 117: 689–692, 1969.

Salpingitis

1. Donowitz, L.G., and Lohr, J.A.: Gonococcal disease presenting as right upper quadrant pain (Fitz-Hugh-Curtis syndrome). Clin. Pediatr. 17: 295–296, 1978.

2. Shafer, M.A.B., Irwin, C.E., and Sweet, R.L.: Acute salpingitis in the adolescent female. J. Pediatr. 100: 339–350, 1982.

Acute Colitis

1. Bar-Ziv, J., Ayoub, J., and Fletcher, B.: Hemolytic uremic syndrome; case presenting with acute colitis. Pediatr. Radiol. 2: 203–205, 1974.

2. Diner, W.C., and Barnhard, H.J.: Toxic megacolon. Semin. Roentgenol. 8: 433–436, 1973.

3. Karjoo, M., and McCarthy, B.: Toxic megacolon of ulcerative colitis in infancy. Pediatrics 57: 962–965, 1976.

4. Kelber, M., and Ament, M.E.: Shigella dysenteriae; I. A forgotten cause of pseudomembranous colitis. Pediatrics 89: 595–696, 1976.

5. Liebhaber, M.I., Parker, B.R., Morton, J.A., and Tune, B.M.: Abdominal mass and colonic perforation in a case of the hemolytic-uremic syndrome. Am. J. Dis. Child. 131: 1168–1169, 1977.

6. Peterson, R.B., Meseroll, W.P., Shrago, G.G., et al.: Radiographic features of colitis associated with the hemolytic-uremic syndrome. Radiology 118: 667–671, 1976.

7. Rice, R.P.: Plain abdominal film roentgenographic diagnosis of ulcerative diseases of the colon. A.J.R. 104: 544–550, 1968.

8. Schachter, H., Goldstein, M.J., and Kirsner, J.B.: Toxic dilatation complicating Crohn's disease of colon. Gastroenterology 53: 136–142, 1967.

9. Schwartz, D.L., Becker, J.M., So, H.B., and Schneider, K.M.: Segmental colonic gangrene: a surgical emergency in the hemolytic-uremic syndrome. Pediatrics 62: 54–56, 1978.

10. Takayanagi, K., and Kapila, L.: Necrotising enterocolitis in older infants. Arch. Dis. Child. 56: 468–471, 1981.

11. Tochen, M.L., and Campbell, J.R.: Colitis in children with the hemolytic-uremic syndrome. J. Pediatr. Surg. 12: 213–219, 1977.

12. Vargas, M., and Pena, A.: Toxic amoebic colitis and amoebic colon perforation in children: an improved prognosis. J. Pediatr. Surg. 11: 223–225, 1976.

13. Wolf, B., and Marshak, R.: "Toxic" segmental dilatation of the colon during the course of fulminating ulcerative colitis: roentgen findings. A.J.R. 82: 985–995, 1959.

14. Wruble, L.A., Duckworth, J.K., Duke, D.D., and Rothschild, J.A.: Toxic dilatation of the colon in a case of amebiasis. N. Engl. J. Med. 275: 926–928, 1966.

MISCELLANEOUS ACUTE ABDOMINAL PROBLEMS

Acute abdominal pain can be a presentation in a number of conditions including *diabetes mellitus* (5), *sickle cell anemia, Henoch-Schönlein purpura* (1, 3, 4), *angioneurotic edema of the intestine, abdominal migraine, idiopathic infarction of appendices epiploicae* (2), *and pneumonia.* Most often in diabetes mellitus, sickle cell crisis, pneumonia, and abdominal migraine, the abdominal roentgenograms are normal or show paralytic ileus. In Henoch-Schönlein purpura or angioneurotic edema, one may note locally distended loops of intestine with thickened walls resulting from intramural bleeding or edema. With idiopathic infarction of the appendices epiploicae, acute abdominal symptoms, even to the point of mimicking appendicitis, can occur (2). Abdominal pain associated with duodenal ulcer disease and/or hiatus hernia also is encountered in childhood and is discussed elsewhere.

REFERENCES

1. Byrn, J.R., Fitzgerald, J.F., Northway, J.D., Anand Sudhir, K., and Scott, J.R.: Unusual manifestations of Henoch-Schönlein syndrome. Am. J. Dis. Child. 130: 1335–1337, 1976.
2. Coultre, C. le, and Braum, P.: Idiopathic infarction of appendices epiloica in children: report of 2 cases. Ann. Chir. Inf. 17: 61–64, 1976.
3. Glasier, C.M., Siegel, M.J., MacAlister, W.H., and Schakelford, G.D.: Henoch-Schönlein syndrome in children: gastrointestinal manifestations. A.J.R. 136: 1081–1085, 1981.
4. Macpherson, R.I.: The radiologic manifestations of Henoch-Schönlein purpura. J. Canad. Assoc. Radiol. 25: 275–281, 1974.
5. Valerio, D.: Acute diabetic abdomen in childhood. Lancet 1: 66–67, 1977.

ACUTE MECHANICAL PROBLEMS

Entities to be discussed in this section include intussusception, volvulus, hernias, and visceral torsions. Any of these conditions can present with acute, even catastrophic, clinical pictures, and the radiologist should be aware of them all and the pertinent plain film findings with which they might present.

Intussusception. The clinical findings of classic intussusception are well known and include; (a) crampy abdominal pain, (b) vomiting, (c) bloody (currant jelly) stools, and (d) either a palpable mass, or palpable emptiness in the right flank or lower quadrant. However, not all of these findings need be present at the same time, and furthermore, in many patients they are intermittent. Indeed, it is becoming more and more apparent that many cases of intussusception are atypical in their presentation. For example, the classic triad of clinical findings, in one series, was noted to be present in only 20% of patients (44). Bleeding was present in only 36% of patients in another series (32) and some intussusceptions may be relatively

painless (13, 33). In addition, a palpable abdominal mass has been shown to be present in only 50–60% of cases (32, 44). Altered consciousness and apathy (6, 43), also have been documented as manifestations of intussusception, but it is not known why these phenomena occur. We have, however, seen them in a few of our patients. Overall, then, one should realize that a good many cases of intussusception present with less than classic findings (16, 32, 44, 49, 52).

Intussusception is most common between the ages of 6 months to 2 years, but, of course, can be seen in the older child or even the neonate. In most cases, the cause of intussusception is idiopathic, although mesenteric lymph node enlargement and/or redundant, edematous, intestinal mucosa (i.e., as part of a viral or other gastrointestinal (GI) infection) probably account for the leading point in most cases. A more discrete leading lesion such as polyp, Meckel's diverticulum, duplication cyst, appendix, or hemangioma (2–4, 7, 9, 10, 17, 27, 36, 50), is found in less than 10% of cases and in this regard, usually is found in older children or neonates (15).

Most cases of intussusception are ileocolic (11, 38, 53), with ileo-ileo and ileo-ileocolic intussusceptions accounting for no more than 10–12% of cases (29, 39). Generally speaking, these latter intussusceptions are more difficult to diagnose and tend to be present for longer periods of time before definitive treatment is accomplished. Consequently complications such as bowel necrosis and perforation are more common (20, 29, 37), and because of this, these intussusceptions generally are considered more serious. Back and forth, antegrade and retrograde telescoping of the bowel with multiple layers of intestine encountered within the intussusception is a very rare type of intussusception (23). In addition, occasionally intussusceptions are chronic and may be diagnosed better with upper GI series and small bowel followthrough (30, 48).

Plain film roentgenographic findings of intussusception are variable and depend primarily on the duration of the symptoms and the presence or absence of complications. In early cases, a normal gas pattern is usual, but the longer the intussusception is present, the more likely is one to see a pattern of typical small bowel obstruction (Fig. 3.78).

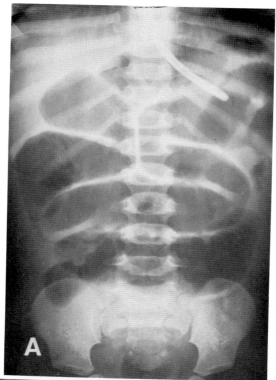

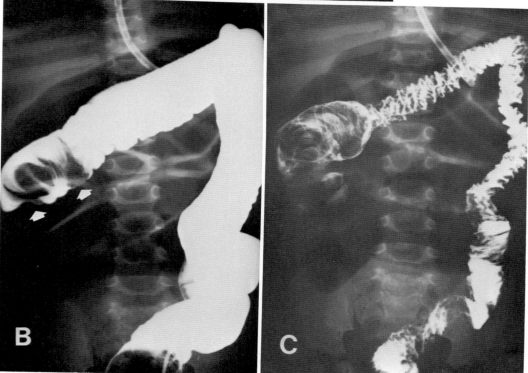

Figure 3.78. *Intussusception with small bowel obstruction.* (*A*) Note typically arranged, distended loops of obstructed small bowel. (*B*) Barium enema demonstrates head of the obstructing intussusception (*arrows*) in the region of the hepatic flexure. Barium enema reduction was not successful. (*C*) Postevacuation film demonstrates persistence of the intussusception and also demonstrates extreme spasticity and irritability of the colon distal to the site of obstruction. This is characteristic when the intussusception is not reduced. Compare with the appearance of the colon in the successfully reduced intussusception demonstrated in Figure 3.80.

In other cases, one can see the actual head of the intussusception on plain films (Fig. 3.79), but this generally occurs in less than 50% of cases. Visualization of the head of the intussusception can be enhanced, with up to 60% visualization, with the use of decubitus views (55), but such views are not generally obtained. Perhaps, more commonly than seeing the head of the intussusception, one sees lack of definition of the inferior aspect of the liver (34), and/or absence of gas in the right lower quadrant or flank (Fig. 3.80). Absence of gas in the right lower quadrant or flank results from the fact that as an intussusception develops, the air is squeezed out of the intestine, and failure of visualization of the liver edge occurs because when right upper quadrant bowel gas is absent, the natural contrasting effect of liver against adjacent air-filled bowel is lost. Of course, if bowel necrosis and perforation ensue, the findings of peritonitis and free peritoneal air supervene. All of these points notwithstanding, however, it should be noted that many cases still demonstrate nor-

mal or near-normal abdominal films and this should not dissuade one from pursuing the diagnosis of intussusception if it is suspected clinically. In this regard, although in some series the plain films are reportedly frequently highly suggestive of the diagnosis (55), our own experience has been less rewarding, and consequently, we have now come to perform ultrasonography in any case, anyway suggestive of intussusception (49). Ultrasound has detected the mass of the intussusception in all our cases, even when it was not palpable clinically or visible roentgenographically (49).

Typically, with ultrasound (5, 26, 40, 41, 49, 54), one can see, on cross-section, a sonolucent donut, and on longitudinal section, a pseudokidney configuration (Fig. 3.81). It is believed that the findings represent edema of the intussusceptum (49), with the sonolucent exterior rim representing the edematous bowel wall and the echoes in the center, the squeezed and crumpled mucosa. With less "tight" intussusceptions, the ring of edema may be thinner and less pro-

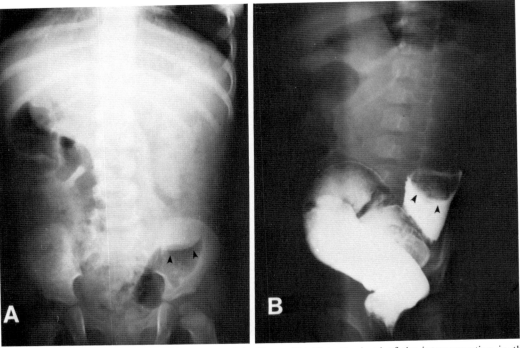

Figure 3.79. *Head of intussusception visible on plain films.* (A) Note the head of the intussusception in the descending colon (*arrows*) of this patient with cystic fibrosis and symptoms of bowel obstruction. More commonly the head is seen in the transverse colon. (*B*) Subsequent barium enema demonstrates the head of the intussusception (*arrows*) corresponding to its plain film location in (*A*).

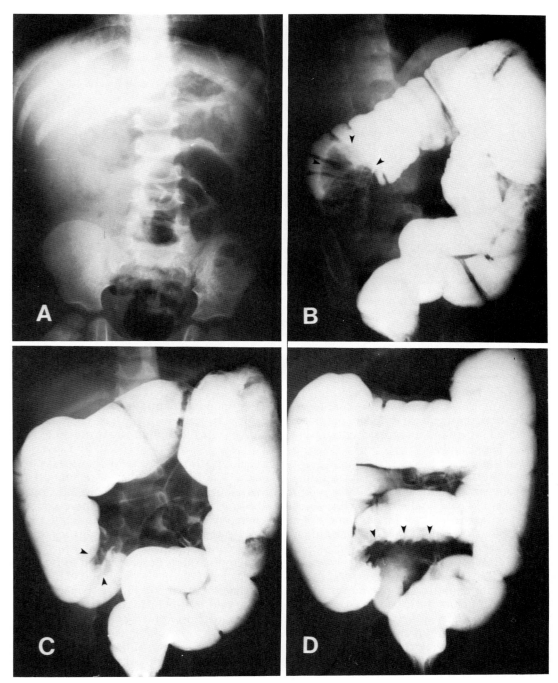

Figure 3.80. *Intussusception, absence of right flank gas,* and *successful barium enema reduction.* (*A*) Note marked paucity of gas in the right flank. A couple of loops of distended (obstructed) small bowel are noted just to the left of the lower lumbar spine, and in addition, a vaguely apparent soft tissue filling defect is seen in the transverse colon, just to the left of the hepatic flexure. Could this be the head of the intussusception? (*B*) Subsequent barium enema demonstrates the head of the intussusception (*arrows*) to correspond to its suspected location on the plain abdominal film. (*C*) Progressive, but incomplete reduction with head of the intussusception visible at the ileocecal valve (*arrows*). (*D*) Complete reduction with filling of the terminal ileum. Note irregularity of the terminal ileum (*arrows*) secondary to persistent edema and spasm. Compare this normal appearing colon with the spastic appearing colon in the nonreduced intussusception illustrated in Figure 3.78.

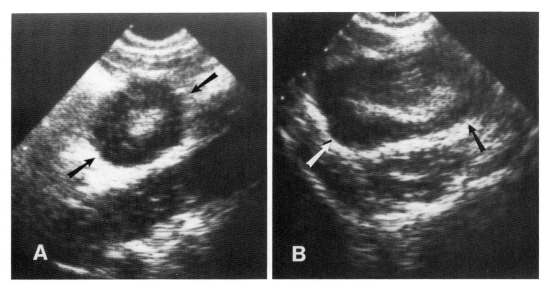

Figure 3.81. *Intussusception; ultrasound findings.* (*A*) Note the typical sonolucent donut (*arrows*) representing the edematous head of the intussusception. Central echoes represent the compressed mucosa. (*B*) Longitudinal view demonstrating a pseudo-kidney appearance (*arrows*). Once again the sonolucent rim represents the edematous head of the intussusceptum and the central echoes the compressed mucosa. This intussusception was not reduced and the leading point was a lymphoma.

nounced (Fig. 3.82). In addition, rather than one sonolucent ring, one may see multiple concentric rings, even with a sonolucent center representing fluid in the incompletely collapsed lumen of the intussusceptum (Fig. 3.82). These multiple rings probably represent the multiple layers of less tightly impacted intussusception and on longitudinal view appear as multiple, wavy layers within the generally oval configuration (Fig. 3.82). From our experience, we have some initial impressions that all of these latter configurations represent less impacted intussusceptions, and hence ones more likely to be reduced by a contrast enema (49). All of these configurations are diagrammatically depicted in Figure 3.83, and the sonolucent donut and pseudo-kidney signs are near pathognomonic of intussusception. Unfortunately, however, they also can be seen with any cause of severe segmental intestinal ischemia, and indeed, are seen with volvulus.

As far as contrast enema reduction of an intussusception is concerned, almost all patients with the disease should be afforded the study. Those patients to be excluded, for the most part, are ones demonstrating signs of peritonitis and/or free peritoneal air. The fact that the intussusception may have been

present for 24 hours or more is no longer generally considered a contraindication to attempted reduction (38, 46).

Success rates with contrast enema reduction of intussusception vary from 45 to 85% (11, 15, 38, 45, 46, 47, 53), and generally speaking, the more recent reviews reflect the higher figures. A number of factors are involved in this increase in success rate, but in the end three stand out: (a) more contrast enema reductions are being attempted now than in previous years, (b) a more aggressive approach to contrast enema reduction is employed, and (c) prereduction sedation of the patient (11, 38, 46, 53), even to the point of general anesthesia (38), is being utilized more and more. The latter factor probably is the most important, but it should be noted that few, if any, patients come to general anesthesia in this country. On the other hand, some form of sedation is indispensable.

In addition to these aspects of barium enema reduction of intussusception, there was, for a short period of time, some enthusiasm for the administration of glucagon in stubborn cases. Glucagon, a well known smooth muscle relaxant, purportedly aided in the reduction of these more stubborn

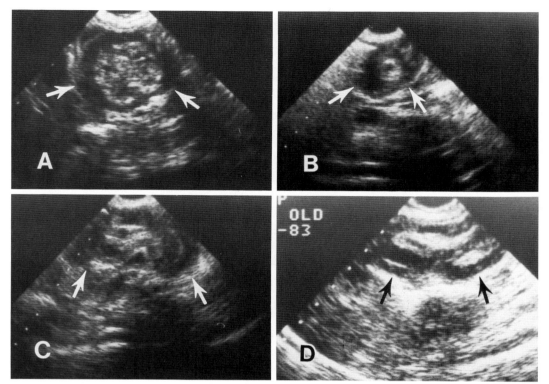

Figure 3.82. *Intussusception; less pronounced findings.* (*A*) Less well developed and thinner, sonolucent donut (*arrows*). The area of central echogenicity also is larger. (*B*) Another patient with a concentric ring effect consisting of a moderately well developed peripheral sonolucent donut, an inner ring of mucosal echoes and a central echo-free area representing fluid in the incompletely compressed intussusceptum. (*C*) Same patient as in (*B*), demonstrating layering within the pseudo-kidney sign (*arrows*). (*D*) Another patient with layering (*arrows*). Reduction was easily accomplished in all these patients.

intussusceptions (18, 28), but more recently it has been demonstrated that glucagon probably has very little effect (21, 22).

The more aggressive approach to the nonoperative reduction of intussusception has led to a slight slackening of the rather rigid and conservative criteria originally established for this procedure (11, 45). For example, while originally 3 feet was suggested for the barium hydrostatic head, the barium container now frequently is raised to 4 feet, and indeed, by some to 5 feet (38). Similarly, while palpation and manipulation of the intussusception once were considered contraindicated, some now suggest it as a standard procedure (38). These latter extensions notwithstanding, however, most radiologists (ourselves included), ***still prefer not to raise the hydrostatic head above 4 feet and not to palpate or manipulate intussusceptions.***

When reducing an intussusception with a contrast enema, the head of the intussusception often will not move easily past the splenic or hepatic flexures, or the ileocecal valve. Obviously, one's overall reduction rate will be influenced by how long one wishes to wait at each one of these sites. Most advocate waiting 15–20 min, but in this regard, 15 min can seem like 15 hours, and because of this there is a tendency for many to cut short the waiting period at each site of prolonged impaction. This, of course, is not so much to advocate such an attitude, but merely to acknowledge that it does occur. On the average, we probably wait 5 min at each site. In addition, we have found it useful to drain the colon in stubborn cases, and to start the reduction again, even up to three times.

It is most important that when contrast enema reduction is attempted, the anus be totally occluded, and usually this is best

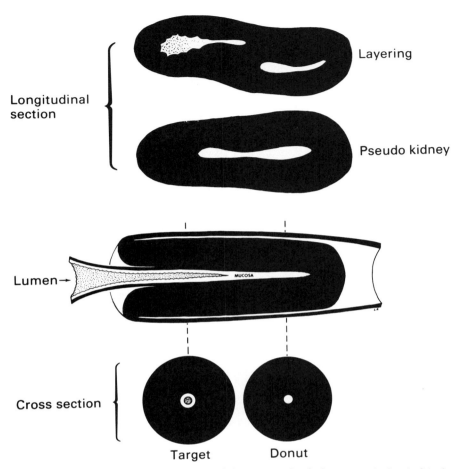

Figure 3.83. *Intussusception; diagrammatic depiction of ultrasonographic findings.*   As the head of the intussusception enters the bowel, it folds upon itself and becomes edematous. This produces the sonolucent rim. Any intervening layers of mucosa or serosa are stretched, and too thin to produce any echoes when impaction is pronounced. The central echoes originate from the compressed mucosa within the intussusceptum. If the intussusceptum is less impacted, filling of the lumen with fluid may be seen, the sonolucent rim is thinner, and concentric rings or layering occur (see Fig. 3.82). (From L.E. Swischuk et al. (49).)

accomplished by tight taping of the buttocks with adhesive tape. In addition, we utilize a Foley bulb in the rectum, and while not all will subscribe to this maneuver, we have found it indispensable. Those who would speak against it are concerned with perforation of the colon, but whatever one's persuasion, *total occlusion of the anus must be accomplished*. Thereafter, one should use a large tube with a free-flowing end to deliver the barium. There should be no kinks in the tubing and the tubing should not drape down to the floor and then up to the examination table; it is best to make sure that one *has a short, straight shot at the colon*.

The configuration of the intussusception on barium enema examination is rather typical and well known to all (Figs. 3.78–3.80). The retrograde progress of the head of the intussusception, as it is pushed around the colon, is easy to detect and document fluoroscopically. However, one must make certain that the head of the intussusception is reduced beyond the ileocecal valve, into the terminal ileum. In most such cases, once this has been accomplished, one still may note narrowing or irregularity of the terminal ileum secondary to residual spasm and edema (Fig. 3.80). However, one is never quite sure that these findings were not present before and in fact represented an inflammatory process or lymphoid hyperplasia which acted as the head of the intussusception. In addition, a lateral wall cecal defect has been demonstrated in some cases (42). This is believed to represent transient invagination of the lateral wall of the cecum between the tinea coli. All of there latter configuration are, on a practical basis, more interesting than important, for they do not influence outcome. One does, however, need to know about their occurence.

A post-evacuation film should be obtained after contrast enema therapy is complete and a 24-hour follow-up film should be taken to determine whether the intussusception has stayed reduced, or has recurred. In this regard, if the intussusception is not fully reduced, the small bowel obstruction will not disappear and in many cases, one may actually see the barium-coated head of the persistent intussusception. Other important points to assess on the post-evacuation and 24-hour follow-up studies are: (a) spasticity of the colon, and (b) effectiveness of evacuation. If the intussusception still is present, the colon distal to the point of obstruction will be more spastic than normal (Fig. 3.78C) and evacuation of the contents of the colon will be explosive (8).

Recurrent rates after contrast enema reduction range from 4 to 11% (12, 35, 53), and the first recurrence should be treated with repeat contrast enema reduction. In this regard, it is not possible to predict which intussusceptions will recur (14), and if after the second attempt, the intussusception does not reduce, or recurs again, most suggest surgical intervention. Recurrent intussusceptions occur more commonly in those cases where a definite leading point is seen (14, 35), and by the same token are more difficult to reduce in the first place (10, 12). In addition, the longer the intussusception remains untreated, or the lower it is in the colon, the more difficult will be the reduction.

Perforations do occur but are relatively uncommon (1, 31). In most cases, perforation results from hydrostatic pressure being transmitted to an already necrotic intestine. There is no way to determine whether such as intestine is present prior to reduction. However, because such perforation can occur, there has been a recent trend to *utilize water contrast agents instead of barium* and we also have made this switch. In addition, it should be understood that it is mandatory that the *surgical service be notified before nonsurgical reduction of an intussusception is contemplated*. The reason for this, of course, is that if perforation should be demonstrated, prompt surgical treatment is required.

In conclusion, it should be mentioned that intussusception can be a presenting feature of cystic fibrosis in older children (19, 25, 51). In these patients, fecal impactions (meconium ileus equivalent) and redundancy and thickening of the intestinal mucosa can predispose to intussusception (see Fig. 3.79). In addition, it should be noted that while the appendix can act as a lead point for intussusception, isolated intussusception of the appendix also can occur, and may be seen in totally asymptomatic individuals (2, 3, 17, 24, 46).

REFERENCES

1. Armstrong, E.A., Dunbar, J.S., Graviss, E.R., Martin, L., and Rosenkrantz, J.: Intussusception complicated by distal perforation of the colon. Radiology 136: 77–81, 1980.
2. Atkinson, G.O., Gay, B.B., and Naffis, D.: Intussusception of the appendix in children. A.J.R. 126: 1164–1168, 1976.
3. Bachman, A.L., and Clemett, A.R.: Roentgen aspects of primary appendiceal intussusception. Radiology 101: 531–538, 1971.
4. Bower, R.J., and Kiesewetter, W.B.: Colo-colic intussusception due to a hemangioma. J. Pediatr. Surg. 12: 777–778, 1977.
5. Bowerman, R.A., Silver, T.M., and Jaffe, M.H.: Real-time ultrasound diagnosis of intussusception in children. Radiology 143: 527–529, 1982.
6. Braun, P., and Germann-Nicod, I.: Altered consciousness as a precocious manifestation of intussusception in infants. Z. Kinderchir. 33: 307–309, 1981.
7. Browne, A.F., Katz, S., Miser, J., and Boles, E.T., Jr.: Blue rubber bleb nevi as a cause of intussusception. J. Pediatr. Surg. 18: 7–9, 1983.
8. Dklog, O., and Hugosson, C.: Post evacuation findings in barium enema-treated intussusceptions. Ann. Radiol. 19:133–139, 1976.
9. Doberneck, R.C., Deane, W.M., and Antoine, J.E.: Ectopic gastric mucosa in the ileum: a cause of intussusception. J. Pediatr. Surg. 11: 99–100, 1976.
10. Ein, S.H.: Leading points in childhood intussusception. J. Pediatr. Surg. 11: 209–211, 1976.
11. Ein, S.H., and Stephens, C.A.: Intussusception: 354 cases in 10 years. J. Pediatr. Surg. 6: 16–27, 1971.
12. Ein, U.: Recurrent intussusception in children. J. Pediatr. Surg. 10: 751–755, 1975.
13. Ein, S.H., Stephens, C.A., and Minor, A.: Painless intussusception. J. Pediatr. Surg. 11: 563–564, 1976.
14. Eklof, O., and Reiter, S.: Recurrent intussusception: analysis of a series treated with hydrostatic reduction. Acta Radiol. 19: 250–258, 1978.
15. Eklof, O.A., Johanson, L., and Lohr, G.: Childhood intussusception: hydrostatic reducibility and incidence of leading points in different age groups. Pediatr. Radiol. 10: 83–86, 1980.
16. Fanconi, S., Berger, D., and Rickham, P.P.: Acute intussusception: a classic clinical picture? Helv. Paediatr. Acta 37: 345–352, 1982.

17. Fink, V.H., Santos, A.L., and Goldberg, S.L.: Intussusception of the appendix: case reports and reviews of the literature. Am. J. Gastroenterol. 42: 431–441, 1964.
18. Fisher, J.K., and Germann, D.R.: Glucagon-aided reduction of intussusception. Radiology 122: 197–198, 1977.
19. Flux, M.: Intussusception in a patient with cystic fibrosis. South. Med. J. 60: 1184–1187, 1967.
20. Foulds, D.M., and Beamish, W.E.: The plain film diagnosis of acute ileo-ileal intussusception. J. Can. Assoc. Radiol. 21: 178–180, 1970.
21. Franken, E.A., Jr., Smith, W.L., Chernish, S.M., Campbell, J.B., Fletcher, B.D., and Goldman, H.S.: The use of glucagon in hydrostatic reduction of intussusception: a double-blind study of 30 patients. Radiology 146: 687–689, 1983.
22. Haase, G.M., and Boles, E.T., Jr.: Glucagon in experimental intussusception. J. Pediatr. Surg. 14: 664–669, 1979.
23. Heymann, A.D.: Compound intussusception consisting of forward and retrograde components. J. Pediatr. Surg. 7: 721–722, 1972.
24. Hill, B.J., Schmidt, K.D., and Economou, S.G.: The "inside out" appendix. A review of the literature and report of two cases. Radiology 95: 613–617, 1970.
25. Holsclaw, D.S., Rocmans, C., and Schwachman, H.: Intussusception in patients with cystic fibrosis. Pediatrics 48: 51–58, 1971.
26. Holt, S., and Samuel, E.: Multiple concentric ring sign in the ultrasonographic diagnosis of intussusception. Gastrointest. Radiol. 3: 307–309, 1978.
27. Howell, J., Pringle, K., Kirschner, B., and Burrington, J.D.: Peutz-Jeghers Polyps causing colocolic intussusception in infancy. J. Pediatr. Surg. 16: 82–84, 1981.
28. Hoy, G.R., Dunbar, D., and Boles, E.T., Jr.: The use of glucagon in the diagnosis and management of ileo-colic intussusception. J. Pediatr. Surg. 12: 939–944, 1977.
29. Humphrey, A. and Reilley, B.J.: Small bowel into small bowel intussusception. J. Can. Assoc. Radiol. 24: 171–177, 1973.
30. Humphry, A., Alton, D.J., and McKendry, J.B.J.: Atypical ileocolic intussusception diagnosed by barium follow-through. Pediatr. Radiol. 12: 65–66, 1982.
31. Humphry, A., Ein, S.H., and Mok, P.M.: Perforation of the intussuscepted colon. A.J.R. 137: 1135–1138, 1981.
32. Hutchinson, I.F., Olayiwola, B., and Young, D.G.: Intussusception in infancy and childhood. Br. J. Surg. 67: 209–212, 1980.
33. Janik, J.S.: Nonischemic intussusception. J. Pediatr. Surg. 12: 567–570, 1977.
34. Jorulf, H.: Tip of the liver in intussusception of the bowel in infancy and childhood. Acta Radiol. [Diagn.] (Stockh.) 14: 26–32, 1974.
35. Keningsberg, K., Lee, J.C., and Stein, H.: Recurrent acute intussusception. Pediatrics 53: 269–270, 1974.
36. Kleinman, P.K.: Intussusception of the appendix: hydrostatic reduction. A.J.R. 134: 1268–1270, 1980.
37. Macpherson, W.A., and Hays, D.M.: The malignant nature of pediatric intussusception secondary to specific etiologic lesions. Am. Surg. 29: 667, 1963.
38. Minami, A., and Fujji, K.: Intussusception in children. Am. J. Dis. Child. 129: 346–348, 1975.
39. Mok, P.M., and Humphry, A.: Ileo-ileocolic intussusception: radiological features and reducibility. Pediatr. Radiol. 12: 127–131, 1982.
40. Montali, G., Croce, F., DePra, L., Solbiati, L.: Intussusception of the bowel: a new sonographic pattern. Br. J. Radiol. 56: 621–623, 1983.
41. Pariety, R.A., Lepreaux, J.F., and Gruson, G.: Sonographic and CT features of ileocolic intussusception. A.J.R. 136: 608–610, 1981.
42. Pokorny, W.J., Wagner, M.L., and Harberg, F.J.: Lateral wall cecal filling defects following successful hydrostatic reduction of cecalcolic intussusceptions. J. Pediatr. Surg. 15: 156–159, 1980.
43. Rachmel, A., Rosenbach, Y., Amir, J., Dinari, G., Shoen-feld, T., and Nitzan, M.: Apathy as an early manifestation of intussusception. Am. J. Dis. Child. 137: 701–702, 1983.
44. Raudkivi, P.J., and Smith, H.L.M.: Intussusception: analysis of 98 cases. Br. J. Surg. 68: 645–648, 1981.
45. Ravitch, M.M.: The non-operative treatment of intussusception—hydrostatic pressure reduction by barium enema. Surg. Clin. North Am. 36: 1495–1500, 1956.
46. Rosenkrantz, J.G., Cox, J.A., Silverman, F.N., and Martin, L.W.: Intussusception in the 1970s: indications for operation. J. Pediatr. Surg. 12: 367–373, 1977.
47. Singleton, E.B.: Hydrostatic reduction of intussusception. Pediatr. Clin. North Am. 10: 175, 1963.
48. Stone, D.N., Kangarloo, H., Graviss, E.R., Danis, R.K., and Silberstein, M.J.: Jejunal intussusception in children. Pediatr. Radiol. 9: 65–68, 1980.
49. Swischuk, L.E., Hayden, C.K., and Boulden, T.: Intussusception: indications for ultrasonography and an explanation of the donut and pseudokidney signs. Pediatr. Radiol. (in press).
50. Tao, H., and Dunbar, J.S.: Intussusception of the appendix. J. Can. Assoc. Radiol. 22: 333–335, 1971.
51. Tucker, A.S., Stern, R.C., Pittman, S.S., and Perrin, E.V.: Intussusception in older children: a complication of cystic fibrosis. Ann. Radiol. 16: 173–176, 1973.
52. Turner, D., Rickwood, A.M.K., and Brereton, R.J.: Intussusception in older children. Arch. Dis. Child. 55: 544–546, 1980.
53. Wayne, E.R., Campbell, J.B., Burrington, J.D., and Davis, W.S.: Management of 344 children with intussusception. Radiology 107: 597–601, 1973.
54. Weissberg, D.L., Scheible, W., and Leopold, G.R.: Ultrasonographic appearance of adult intussusception. Radiology 124: 791–792, 1977.
55. White, S.J., and Blane, C.E.: Intussusception: additional observations on the plain radiograph. A.J.R. 139: 511–513, 1982.

Volvulus. Conditions considered under the broad topic of volvulus include midgut volvulus, volvulus of the colon, gastric volvulus, and segmental small bowel volvulus. *Midgut volvulus* is associated with obstructing duodenal bands and intestinal malrotation. Usually it is a problem of the neonate (14), but it also can present in older infants and children. In such cases, the presentation often is atypical, both clinically and roentgenographically (4,6,7,9,10).

In the classic case of midgut volvulus in the neonate, there is acute onset of bilious vomiting, crampy abdominal pain, and varying degrees of abdominal distension. If vascular compromise is severe, signs of shock also will be evident, and as the bowel undergoes necrosis, perforation with peritonitis may supervene. Most such cases declare themselves in the first month of life, but in the older child, while symptoms occasionally are similar, more often they are atypical and confusing. Indeed, these children frequently first are considered to have chronic malabsorption problems, protein-loosing enteropathy, or simply go on as cases of undiagnosed recurrent abdominal pain. It requires an astute physician to think of the diagnosis under these conditions.

Roentgenographically, a wide spectrum of abnormality is seen in midgut volvulus, and, unfortunately, in some cases the abdominal roentgenograms can appear near normal. However, in those cases demonstrating abnormality, one of the most helpful findings is that of obstruction of the duodenum in its third and fourth portions (Fig. 3.84). In these cases, obstruction usually is due to associated duodenal bands, and is present whether complicating midgut volvulus had occurred or not. With midgut volvulus, however, obstruction often is more pronounced. In those infants where the obstructed duodenum is full of fluid, and a supine film only is obtained, air in the distended stomach erroneously will suggest a gastric outlet obstruction (Fig. 3.85).

Other patients with midgut volvulus may show evidence of a classic small bowel obstruction (Fig. 3.86), or a small bowel obstruction in association with a soft tissue mass (Fig. 3.87). In these latter cases, the mass represents fluid filled, volved bowel, or in other words, a form of closed loop obstruction. The volved mass of intestine frequently is located in the right lower quadrant (10), but in fact can be seen anywhere in the abdomen.

Because of the presence of obstructing duodenal bands in these patients, one would think that almost all of them would show deficient abdominal gas patterns, especially if midgut volvulus also was present. However, this is not so and many children show considerable volumes of gas in distended loops of intestine. The reason for this seeming paradox is that once venous compromise occurs, intestinal gas absorption is severely compromised (3,8). Consequently, the presence of numerous loops of distended intestine in patients with suspected midgut volvulus should be considered an ominous sign.

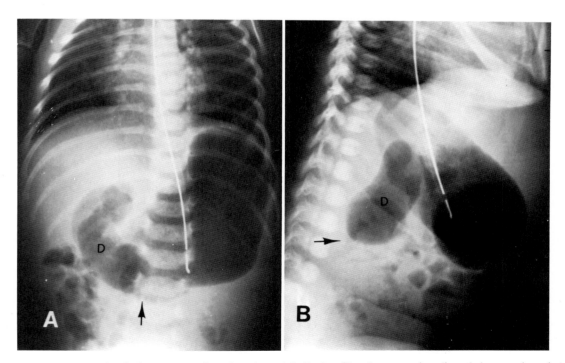

Figure 3.84. *Duodenal obstruction with malrotation.* (*A*) Supine film demonstrating distended stomach and descending duodenum (*D*). The site of obstruction in the third and fourth portions of the duodenum is demarcated by the *arrow*. (*B*) Lateral view demonstrating site of obstruction (*arrow*) in the dilated descending duodenum (*D*) to better advantage. The obstruction is due to compression by the duodenal band, but midgut volvulus could occur at any time in such a patient. (Reprinted from Swischuk, L.E.: *Radiology of the Newborn and Young Infant.* Ed. 2, Williams & Wilkins, Baltimore, 1980.)

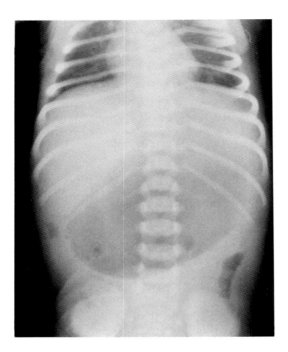

Figure 3.85. *Midgut volvulus appearing as a gastric outlet obstruction.* Note the distended stomach. There is no visible gas in the duodenum and very little is scattered throughout the remainder of the gastrointestinal tract. A gastric outlet obstruction might be suspected, but in actual fact, this patient had midgut volvulus with descending duodenal obstruction. In the supine position, however, the duodenum is filled with fluid and thus, is invisible roentgenographically. (Reprinted from Swischuk, L.E.: *Radiology of the Newborn and Young Infant* Ed. 2, Williams & Wilkins, Baltimore, 1980.)

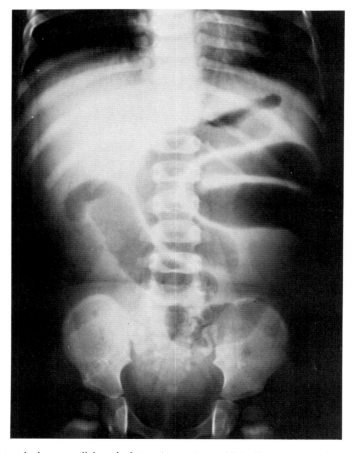

Figure 3.86. *Midgut volvulus—small bowel obstruction pattern.* Note the numerous loops of distended small intestine in this patient with midgut volvulus and obstruction.

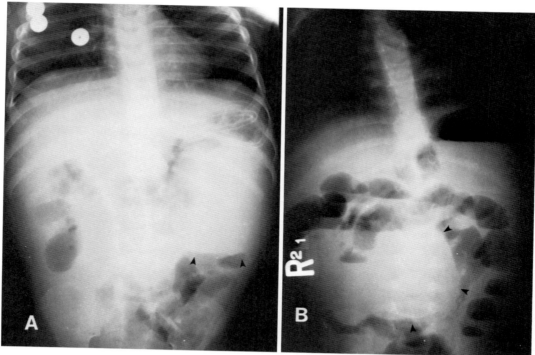

Figure 3.87. *Midgut volvulus with abdominal mass.* (*A*) Note soft tissue mass on the left side of the abdomen (*arrows*). (*B*) Upright view demonstrates that the mass has shifted to a new position (*arrows*). Note also that a small bowel obstruction is suggested. This patient was being investigated for malabsorption and one night developed severe crampy abdominal pain. At laparotomy he had midgut volvulus. The soft tissue mass on the abdominal films represented fluid trapped in some of the volved loops.

Of course, if bowel necrosis occurs, pneumatosis cystoides intestinalis may be seen, and if perforation occurs, signs of peritonitis and free air will develop.

Either the upper GI series or barium enema can confirm the presence of midgut volvulus and should be performed immediately (2,12,14), but most now prefer the upper GI series. With barium enema examinations, one can be totally certain that midgut volvulus is present only if the cecum is misplaced high into the mid abdomen, behind the transverse colon (Fig. 3.88). In such cases, as the intestine volves, the cecum is drawn tightly behind the transverse colon, and the findings are pathognomonic. However, if the cecum simply is out of place, that is, it is medial in position and not in its normal right lower quadrant location (15), then one cannot assume that midgut volvulus is present. Furthermore, a normally placed cecum does not exclude underlying malrotation, and hence, the possibility that midgut volvulus could develop. Because of all these points, the upper GI series has gained popularity as the initial investigative procedure in patients with suspected midgut volvulus.

The upper GI series, in midgut volvulus, will show either: (a) obstruction of the third portion of the duodenum or (b) obstruction of the duodenum and associated, pathognomonic spiraling of the small intestine around the superior mesenteric artery (Fig. 3.89). In addition, the duodenum will lie somewhat further to the right of the spine than normal (i.e. poor fixation due to absence of ligament of Treitz), and as the jejunum fills, it will be seen to lie in an abnormal mid abdominal or right-sided position. If edema of the loops of intestine distal to the area of spiraling also is noted, vascular compromise can be assumed with certainty.

Ultrasonography also can demonstrate findings of midgut volvulus, similar to those seen on upper GI series (5). Although the twisted small intestine (corkscrew configuration) is not demonstrable, the obstructed

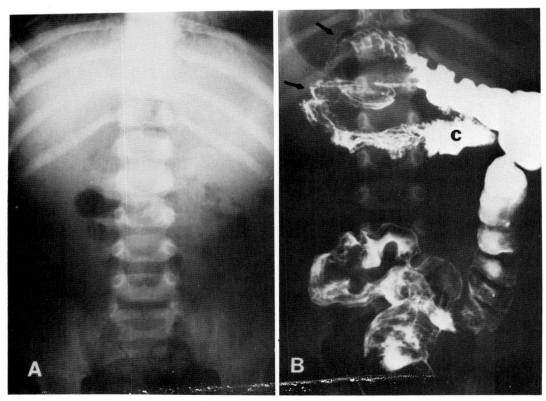

Figure 3.88. *Midgut volvulus, barium enema findings.*   (*A*) Abdominal film revealing a misleadingly near-normal appearance. However, note that although some gas is present in the stomach, the remainder of the abdomen shows a paucity of gas. When these findings are considered with the fact that this patient had acute onset of bilious vomiting and crampy abdominal pain, one should think of some underlying acute mechanical problem. In this case, both midgut volvulus and intussusception were considered and because of this a barium enema was obtained. (*B*) Barium enema demonstrating the typical, totally abnormal position of the volved cecum (*C*) and the twisted colon (*arrows*).

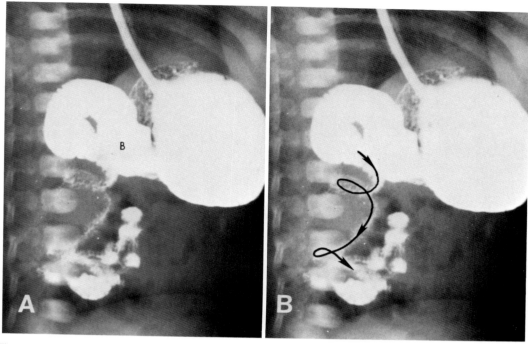

Figure 3.89. *Midgut volvulus, duodenal obstruction, and spiraling of small bowel.* (*A*) Note the distended duodenal bulb (*B*) and descending duodenum. Also note spiraling of the small bowel distal to the site of obstruction of the duodenum. (*B*) Diagrammatic representation of spiraling of the small bowel.

duodenum (full of fluid), and even the beak of the twisted point of an intussusception can be seen (Fig. 3.90).

All of the foregoing changes of midgut volvulus usually are seen in the classic case presenting in the neonate or very young infant. In older children, however, as mentioned earlier, clinical and roentgenographic findings usually are atypical. Indeed, considering that one may have apparently normal intestinal position with poor development of the mesentery (7), and incomplete rotation of the intestine with normal cecal position (13), one can easily understand why such atypia arises. Nonetheless, it is just this type of case which passes into older childhood, and then one must look for every possible clue on the upper GI series, barium enema, or even ultrasound study, for proper diagnosis. In this regard, any bizarre configuration of the duodenum, small bowel, or the cecum should be treated with suspicion (1) (Fig. 3.91).

Segmental volvulus of the small bowel represents a classic cause of closed loop obstruction, and often is associated with anom-

alous peritoneal bands, congenital mesenteric defects, internal hernias, malrotation problems (11), or postoperative adhesions. As with all closed loop obstructions, diagnosis may be late in coming, but it has been noted that if a beaked configuration of the small bowel is seen on barium enema examination, volvulus should be considered the correct diagnosis (11). The beaking is similar to that seen with colon volvulus, a problem discussed in following paragraphs.

Volvulus of the colon is not a common problem in childhood, but it does occur, and in this regard does so most often in the sigmoid colon (1,3–5,7,10). In some of these cases, the U-shaped loop of the volved sigmoid colon appears typical, lying far to the right of the spine and having its apex pointing toward the liver (Fig. 3.92). However, not always does it do this and overall the findings of sigmoid volvulus in children are less specific than in adults. In addition, it should be noted that the normally redundant, but nonvolved sigmoid colon, can present with findings mimicking sigmoid volvulus (Fig. 3.93*A*). If, in such cases, the

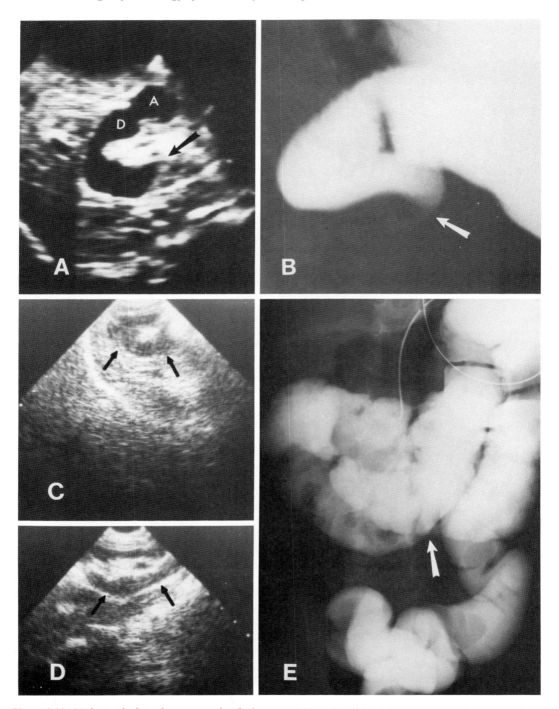

Figure 3.90. *Midgut volvulus; ultrasonographic findings.* (*A*) Note the distended antrum (*A*), duodenal bulb and loop (*D*), and beak (*arrow*). (*B*) Confirmatory upper GI series showing the same findings, including the beak (*arrow*). (*C*) *Edematous intestine in midgut volvulus.* Ultrasonographic cross-section demonstrates sonolucent donut due to edematous segment of intestine (*arrows*). (*D*) Longitudinal view demonstrates a pseudokidney sign (*arrows*). (*E*) Barium enema in same patient, demonstrating the cecum to be in an abnormal position, behind the transverse colon. This was an older patient with midgut volvulus and the segment of edematous intestine was identified surgically. (From C. K. Hayden Jr., et al. (5).)

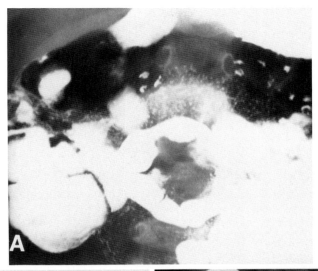

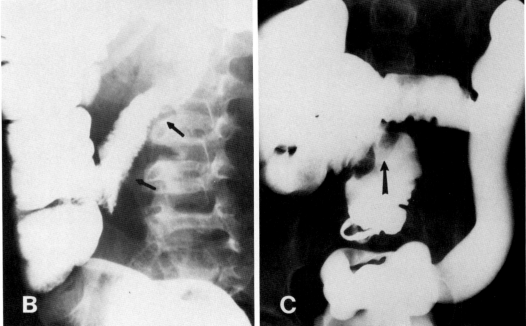

Figure 3.91. *Abnormal fixation of intestine.*   (*A*) In this patient with chronic intermittent abdominal pain, note the peculiarly spiraled, and generally abnormal configuration of the upper small bowel. (*B*) Same patient shows unusual position of terminal ileum (*arrows*). (*C*) Another patient with abnormal positioning of the cecum, and compression by a band (*arrow*). All of these configurations should make one suspect abnormal intestinal fixation. (Fig. *C* courtesy Sue Jacobi, M.D., Austin, Texas.)

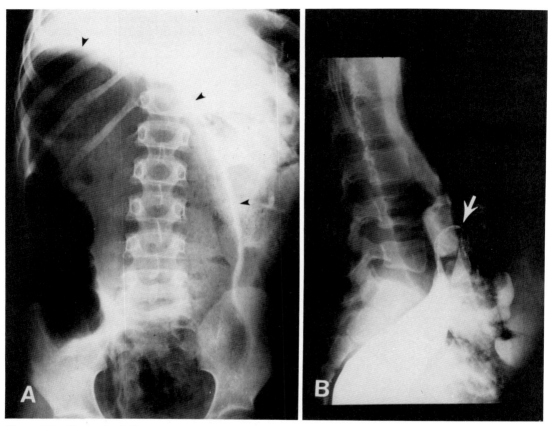

Figure 3.92. *Sigmoid volvulus.* (*A*) Note the large dilated loop of sigmoid colon in its typical right-sided position (*arrows*). (*B*) Barium enema showing narrowing at site of volvulus (*arrow*). (Reprinted with permission from Campbell, J.R., and Blank, E.: Sigmoid volvulus in children, Pediatrics 53: 702–705, 1974.)

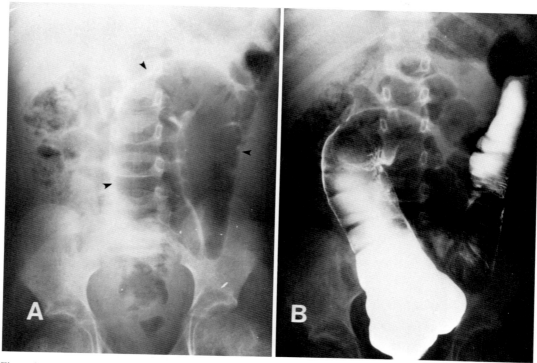

Figure 3.93. *Pseudovolvulus of sigmoid colon.* (*A*) Note the inverted "U" appearance of the sigmoid colon (*arrows*) which in this patient spuriously suggests sigmoid volvulus. However, this patient had no symptoms of obstruction and was being investigated for painless rectal bleeding. (*B*) Subsequent barium enema demonstrates normal, but very redundant, sigmoid colon. This, of course, is not to say that such a loop would not volve, for indeed, it could.

child is asymptomatic and volvulus is not suspected, the finding can be treated as being strictly fortuitous. In other cases, however, it may be difficult to discard the finding without barium enema verification (Fig. 3.93*B*). Cecal volvulus is less common than sigmoid volvulus (6) and the roentgenographic findings are different. With cecal volvulus, the dilated volved cecum is located in the upper mid abdomen, or left upper quadrant (Fig. 3.94). Volvulus of the transverse colon is very rare (2, 9), but when present, demonstrates the volved loop to be more central, and in the upper abdomen. Volvulus of any type is more likely to occur in the bedridden child, and overall, this and normal redundancy of the sigmoid colon are the prime predisposing factors to the development of volvulus.

Once volvulus is suspected, a barium enema examination should be attempted, for not only will it demonstrate the typical beaking, narrowing or twisting deformity of the volved segment of colon (Fig. 3.92*B*),

but also it often is therapeutic. If the barium enema does not relieve the obstruction, proctoscopy with insertion of a decompressing tube should be attempted. After reduction, the colon may show persistent narrowing or thumbprinting as a result of residual edema and spasm (8). The presence of such edema of the intestine also is demonstrable with ultrasound (Fig. 3.95), wherein a sonolucent donut is seen in cross-section and an oval-shaped sonolucency is seen on longitudinal section. The findings, however, are not pathognomonic, and indeed are not unlike those seen with intussusception. Nonetheless, one should become familiar with them, for ultrasound is being used more and more for acute abdominal problems in children.

Gastric volvulus is a true surgical emergency (1–5), and symptoms of vomiting and severe abdominal pain often have sudden onset. Shock may supervene and chest and abdominal films will reveal a large, distended stomach causing the left diaphrag-

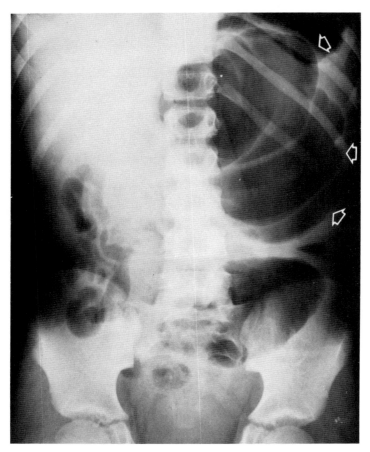

Figure 3.94. *Volvulus of the cecum.*   Note the dilated cecum in its typical left upper quadrant position (*arrows*).

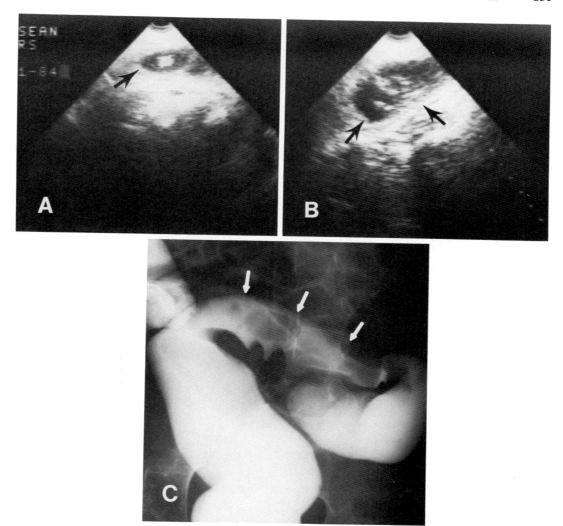

Figure 3.95. *Devolved sigmoid volvulus; ultrasonographic findings.* (*A*) Cross-section demonstrates a sonolucent donut (*arrow*). (*B*) Note an oval mass with a sonolucent rim (*arrows*). These findings represent edema of the intestinal wall. (*C*) Barium enema demonstrating thumbprinting of the involved segment of sigmoid colon (*arrows*).

matic leaflet to be high in position (Fig. 3.96). In addition, one may note two air-fluid levels within the volved stomach (2). If barium is administered it will either stop at the gastroesophageal junction, or pass into the inverted, rotated stomach. If it stops as the gastroesophageal junction, it simply infers that volvulus is so tight that complete obstruction has occurred at this level. Volvulus of the stomach also can be seen with congenital diaphragmatic hernias, and in some cases may be a chronic, recurrent problem (1).

REFERENCES

Midgut Volvulus

1. Ablow, R.C., Hoffer, F.A., Seashore, J.H., and Touloukian, R.J.: Z-shaped duodenojejunal loop: sign of mesenteric fixation anomaly and congenital bands. A.J.R. 141: 461–464, 1983.
2. Berdon, W.E., Baker, D.H., Bull, S., and Santulli, T.V.: Midgut malrotation and volvulus. Which films are most helpful? Radiology 96: 375–383, 1970.
3. Frye, T.R., Mah, C.L., and Schiller, M.: Roentgenographic evidence of gangrenous bowel in midgut volvulus with observations in experimental volvulus. A.J.R. 114: 394–401, 1972.
4. Gwinn, J.L., and Lee, F.A.: Radiological case of the month. Am. J. Dis. Child. 126: 495–496, 1973.
5. Hayden, C.K., Jr., Boulden, T.F., Swischuk, L.E., and

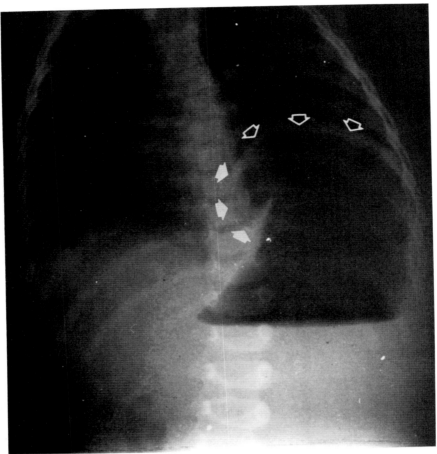

Figure 3.96. *Volvulus of the stomach.* Note the inverted stomach (*upper arrows*). The *solid arrows* demarcate the tapered tip of one end of the volved stomach. (Reprinted with permission from Campbell, J.B., et al.: Acute mesentero-axial volvulus of the stomach, Radiology 103: 153–156, 1972.)

Lobe, T.E.: Sonographic demonstration of duodenal obstruction with midgut volvulus. A.J.R. 143: 9–10, 1984.

6. Houston, C.S., and Wittenborg, M.H.: Roentgen evaluation of anomalies of rotation and fixation of the bowel in children. Radiology 84: 1–17, 1965.

7. Janik, J.S., and Ein, S.H.: Normal intestinal rotation with non-fixation: a cause of chronic abdominal pain. J. Pediatr. Surg. 14: 670–674, 1979.

8. Kassner, E.G., and Kottmeier, P.K.: Absence and retention of small bowel gas in infants with midgut volvulus: mechanisms and significance. Pediatr. Radiol. 4: 28–30, 1975.

9. Pochaczevski, R., Ratner, H., Leonidas, J.C., Naysan, P., and Feraru, F.: Unusual forms of volvulus after the neonatal period. A.J.R. 114: 390–393, 1972.

10. Schaffer, I., and Ferris, I.: The mass sign in primary volvulus of small intestine in adults. A.J.R. 94: 374, 1965.

11. Siegel, M.J., Shackelford, G.D., and McAlister, W.H.: Small bowel volvulus in children: its appearance on the barium enema examination. Pediatr. Radiol. 10: 91–93, 1980.

12. Simpson, A.J., Leonidis, J.C., Krasna, I.H., Becker, J.M., and Schneider, K.M.: Roentgen diagnosis of midgut malrotation: value of upper gastrointestinal radiographic study. J. Pediatr. Surg. 7: 243–252, 1972.

13. Slovis, T.L., Klein, M.D., and Watts, F.B., Jr.: Incomplete

rotation of the intestine with a normal cecal position. Surgery 87: 325–330, 1980.

14. Swischuk, L.E.: *Radiology of the Newborn and Young Infant,* Ed. 2. Williams & Wilkins, Baltimore, 1980.

15. Steiner, G.M.: The misplaced caecum and the root of the mesentery. Br. J. Radiol. 51: 406–413, 1978.

Volvulus of the Colon

1. Allen, R.P., and Nordstrom, J.E.: Volvulus of the sigmoid in children. A.J.R. 91: 690–693, 1964.

2. Asano, S., Konuma, K., Rikimaru, S., et al.: Volvulus of the transverse colon in a four-year-old boy. Z. Kinderchir. 35: 21–23, 1982.

3. Campbell, J.R., and Blank, E.: Sigmoid volvulus in children. Pediatrics 53: 702–705, 1974.

4. Carter, R., and Hinshaw, D. B.: Acute sigmoid volvulus in children. Am. J. Dis. Child. 101: 631–634, 1961.

5. Hunter, J.G., and Keats, T.E.: Sigmoid volvulus in children. A.J.R. 108: 621–623, 1970.

6. Kirks, D.R., Swischuk, L.E., Merten, D.F., and Filston, H.C.: Cecal volvulus in children. A.J.R. 136: 419–422, 1981.

7. Lillard, R.L., Allen, R.P., and Nordstrom, J.E.: Sigmoid

volvulus in children. Case report. A.J.R. 97: 223–226, 1966.
8. Meyers, M.A., Ghahremani, G.G., and Govoni, A.F.: Ischemic colitis associated with sigmoid volvulus: new observations. A.J.R. 128: 591–595, 1977.
9. Newton, N.A., and Reines, H.D.: Transverse colon volvulus: case reports and review. A.J.R. 128: 69–72, 1977.
10. Riddervold, H.O., Keats, T.E., and Son, K.S.: Sigmoid volvulus in children. A case report. J. Can. Assoc. Radiol. 22: 270–271, 1971.
11. van Buch, K., and Schumacher, W.: Torsion of the sigmoid in children. Z. Kinderchir. 15: 168–173, 1974.
12. Wilk, P.J., Ross, M., and Leonidas, J.: Sigmoid volvulus in an 11-year-old girl: case report and literature review. Am. J. Dis. Child. 127: 400–402, 1974.

Gastric Volvulus

1. Ash, M.J., and Sheiman, N.J.: Gastric volvulus in children: report of two cases. J. Pediatr. Surg. 12: 1059–1062, 1977.
2. Campbell, J.B., Rappaport, L.N., and Skerker, L.B.: Acute mesentero-axial volvulus of the stomach. Radiology 103: 153–156, 1972.
3. Cole, B.C., and Dickinson, S.J.: Acute volvulus of the stomach in infants and children. Surgery 70: 707–717, 1971.
4. Kilcoyne, R.F., Babbitt, D.P., and Sakaguchi, S.: Volvulus of the stomach. A case report. Radiology 103: 157–158, 1972.
5. Lorimer, A., and Penn, L.: Acute volvulus of the stomach. A.J.R. 77: 627, 1957.

REFERENCES

1. Currarino, G.: Incarcerated inguinal hernia in infants: Plain films and barium enema. Pediatr. Radiol. 2: 247–250, 1974.
2. Dalinka, M.K., et al.: Internal hernia through the mesentery of a Meckel's diverticulum. Radiology 95: 39–40, 1970.
3. Henisz, A., Matesanz, J., and Westcott, J.: Cecal herniation through the foramen of Winslow. Radiology 112: 575–578, 1974.
4. McKail, R.A.: Hernia through the foramen of Winslow, hernia traversing the lesser sac, and allied conditions. Br. J. Radiol. 34: 611–618, 1961.
5. Meyers, M.A.: Paraduodenal hernias: Radiologic and arteriographic diagnosis. Radiology 95: 29–38, 1970.
6. Parsons, B.: Paraduodenal hernias. A.J.R. 69: 563–589, 1953.
7. Rubin, S.Z., Ayalon, A., and Berlatzky, Y.: The simultaneous occurrence of paraduodenal and paracecal herniae presenting with volvulus of the intervening bowel. J. Pediatr. Surg. 11: 205–208, 1976.
8. St. John, E.G.: Herniation through the foramen of Winslow. A.J.R. 72: 222–228, 1954.
9. Stankey, R.M.: Intestinal herniation through the foramen of Winslow. Radiology 89: 929–930, 1967.
10. Tovar, J., Bertin, P., and Bienayme, J.: Transmesenteric hernias. Ann. Chir. Inf. 17: 113–122, 1976.
11. Zer, M., and Dintsman, M.: Incarcerated "foramen of Winslow" hernia in a newborn. J. Pediatr. Surg. 8: 325, 1973.

Hernias. Internal hernias are difficult to diagnose. The clinical and roentgenographic findings usually are nonspecific, and at most merely suggest an intestinal obstruction. These hernias often are paraduodenal in location (4, 6), but in fact, can be found anywhere along the mesentery or omentum (2, 7, 10). Hernias through the foramen of Winslow frequently involve the cecum, right colon, or terminal small bowel. In such cases, these structures herniate into the lesser sac behind the stomach (3, 5, 7–9, 11), and at first the plain film findings might suggest cecal volvulus. However, with lateral positioning it will be seen that the dilated loop or loops of intestine are located behind the stomach, and not in front as they would be with volvulus of the cecum.

Incarcerated *inguinal hernias* frequently are overlooked during physical examination of an infant with a distended abdomen secondary to the intestinal obstruction caused by the hernia. In such infants, in addition to the pattern of small bowel obstruction, one may see the incarcerated loops of air-filled intestine in the groin or scrotum (Fig. 3.97). If the loops of intestine do not contain air, one may see fullness of the cutaneous inguinal fold (1) on the involved side (Fig. 3.98). Incarcerated umbilical hernias, with obstruction, also occur, but are less common (Fig. 3.97*C*).

Visceral Torsion. Visceral torsion usually involves the spleen or liver, but splenic torsion is more common (1–6, 8, 9–13). Torsion (volvulus) of the stomach and colon have been discussed in previous sections. In *splenic and liver torsion*, the predisposing factor usually is a hypermobile, poorly fixed organ. Clinical findings, with torsion of either the spleen or liver, usually consist of acute, crampy abdominal pain which may or may not refer itself to the expected upper quadrant of the abdomen. Symptoms also may be chronic and intermittent (1, 6, 9).

Abdominal roentgenograms usually show an absence of the normal splenic or liver silhouette, and replacement of the space by gas-filled colon or small bowel. The organ itself may be seen as a soft tissue mass anywhere in the abdomen, but often the spleen lies on the left. Ultrasonographically, clues to the diagnosis consist of absence of the spleen in its normal location and an echogenic mass noted elsewhere (7). Associated intestinal obstruction also may be seen.

Isotope spleen scans with ^{51}Cr-labeled, heat-damaged, red blood cells show either totally absent uptake or partially absent uptake in the spleen (2, 6). In splenic torsion, blood smear findings show Howell-Jolly bodies, burr cells, a leukocytosis with shift to the left, and thrombocytosis (4).

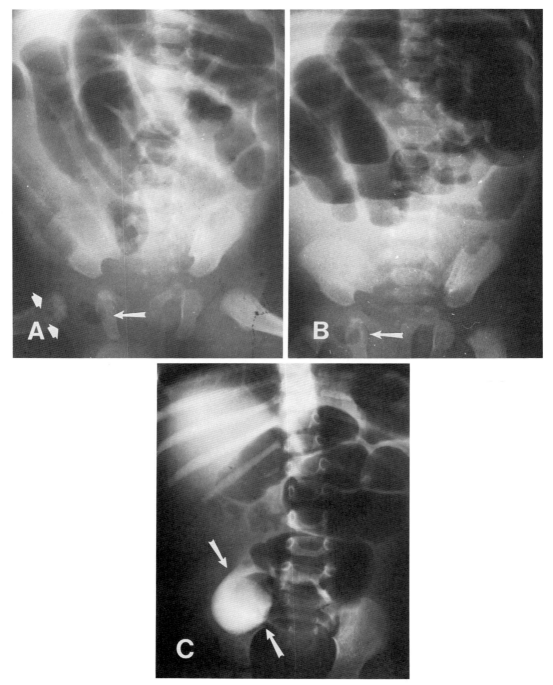

Figure 3.97. *Incarcerated inguinal hernia.* (*A*) Note numerous loops of distended small bowel suggesting a typical small bowel obstruction. In addition, however, note air within the incarcerated right inguinal hernia (*long arrow*). *Short arrows* delineate ipsilateral prominence of the inguinal soft tissue fold commonly seen with incarcerated inguinal hernias. (*B*) Upright view showing same findings. (*C*) *Umbilical hernia with incarceration.* Note obstructed loops of bowel and central umbilical hernia (*arrows*).

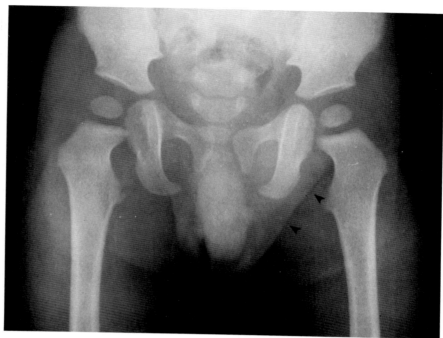

Figure 3.98. *Left incarcerated inguinal hernia; prominent inguinal soft tissue fold only.* Note prominence of the left inguinal soft tissue fold (*arrows*). Compare with the normal appearance of the fold on the right. This patient had an incarcerated inguinal hernia on the left, and presented with hip pain and restricted motion of the left leg.

REFERENCES

1. Bayer, H.P., Joppich, I., and Waag, K.L.: Chronic intermittent torsion of the spleen. Z Kinderchir. 21: 386–391, 1977.
2. Broker, F.H.L., Khettry, J., Filler, R.M., and Traves, S.: Splenic torsion and accessory spleen: a scintigraphic demonstration. J. Pediatr. Surg. 10: 913–915, 1975.
3. Broker, F.H.L., Fellows, K., and Treves, S.: Wandering spleen in three children. Pediatr. Radiol. 6: 211–214, 1978.
4. Dublin, A.B., and Rosenquist, C.F.: Case report. Diagnosis of splenic torsion: a combined radiographic approach. Br. J. Radiol. 49: 1045–1046, 1976.
5. Feins, N.R., and Borger, J.: Torsion of the right lobe of the liver with partial obstruction of the colon. J. Pediatr. Surg. 7: 724–725, 1972.
6. Gordon, D.H., Burrell, M.I., Levin, D.C., Mueller, C.F., and Becker, J.A.: Wandering spleen—the radiological and clinical spectrum. Radiology 125: 39–46, 1977.
7. Hunter, T.B., and Haber, K.: Sonographic diagnosis of a wandering spleen. A.J.R. 129: 925–926, 1977.
8. Isikoff, M.B., White, D.W., and Diaconis, J.N.: Radiographic exhibit: torsion of the wandering spleen, seen as a migratory abdominal mass. Radiology 123: 36, 1977.
9. Muckmel, E., Zer, M., and Dintsman, M.: Wandering spleen with torsion of pedicle in a child presenting as an intermittently appearing abdominal mass. J. Pediatr. Surg. 13: 127–128, 1978.
10. Sequeira, F.W., Weber, T.R., Smith, W.L., Caresky, J.M., and Cairo, M.S.: Budd-Chiari syndrome caused by hepatic torsion. A.J.R. 137: 393–394, 1981.
11. Shende, A., Lanzkowsky, P., and Becker, J.: Torsion of a visceroptosed spleen. Am. J. Dis. Child. 130: 88–91, 1976.
12. Smulewicz, J., and Clemett, A.: Torsion of the wandering spleen. Am. J. Dis. Child. 20: 274–279, 1975.
13. Thompson, J.S., Ross, R.J., and Pizzaro, S.T. The wandering spleen in infancy and childhood. Clin. Pediatr. 19: 221–224, 1980.

Omental Strangulation and Infarction. These problems are quite rare, but do occur (1–3). They are very difficult to diagnose roentgenographically, but with the availability of ultrasound, one may be able to demonstrate an echogenic abdominal mass which then would mitigate toward surgical exploration of the abdomen.

REFERENCES

1. Holden, M.P.: Primary idiopathic segmental infarction of the greater omentum. J. Pediatr. Surg. 7: 77, 1972.
2. Iuchtman, M., Berant, M., and Assa, J.: Transomental strangulation. J. Pediatr. Surg. 13: 439–449, 1978.
3. Rich, R.H., and Filler, R.M.: Segmental infarction of the greater omentum: a cause of acute abdomen in childhood. Can. J. Surg. 26: 241–243, 1983.

ABDOMINAL TRAUMA

General Approach. In abdominal trauma, the abdominal roentgenogram often is used more as a screening examination than one for specific diagnosis (3, 5, 7, 8, 10). In this regard, one should develop some type of general approach to the assessment of the abdominal roentgenogram, for without such an approach significant abnormalities can go undetected. This is especially true in those cases with multiple organ injury and/or associated skeletal trauma.

In beginning one's assessment of the abdomen, one first might scan the lung bases, diaphragmatic leaflets, and larger abdominal viscera. Abnormalities of the lung bases or the diaphragmatic leaflets can focus attention on liver or spleen injury, while any displacement, enlargement or loss of definition of the margins of the abdominal viscera, should serve to focus attention on them. One should also look at the spine for evidence of scoliosis, for scoliosis is very helpful in lateralizing abnormalities to one side or other. Thereafter, one should inspect the abdomen for evidence of free air, peritoneal fluid (blood, bile, etc.), focally distended loops of intestine (i.e., sentinel loops), and fractures of the ribs, bony pelvis, or spine. Fractures in any of these areas should call for closer inspection of the adjacent abdominal viscera.

Currently, both ultrasound and CT are commonly utilized in the investigation of abdominal trauma (1). However, overall CT examination is much more informative and the preferred modality (1, 2, 4, 5). Indeed, some injuries of the spleen can remain occult on ultrasonographic examination. Perhaps the best advantage of CT is that it provides better geography and more clearcut delineation of the injured organ or organs. This is most important since many times multiple injuries are present.

The CT examination usually is performed with contrast enhancement and thus the intravenous pyelogram has come to be used less and less. However, occasionally the intravenous pyelogram (IVP) and cystogram still are utilized for urinary tract injury, but overall CT scanning is one's best screen. Magnetic resonance imaging (MRI) also can provide useful information but generally is more difficult to obtain, and will not readily replace CT in the investigation of abdominal trauma.

Angiography for abdominal trauma (9) occasionally is required on an emergency basis, especially for renal, splenic, and hepatic injuries. However, it is utilized in select cases only.

REFERENCES

1. Babcock, D.S., and Kaufman, R.A.: Ultrasonography and computed tomography in the evaluation of the acutely ill pediatric patient. Radiol. Clin. North Am. 21: 527–550, 1983.
2. Berger, P.E., and Kuhn, J.P.: CT of blunt abdominal trauma in childhood. A.J.R. 13: 105–110, 1981.
3. Burrell, M., Toffler, R., and Lowman, R.: Blunt trauma to the abdomen and gastrointestinal tract. Radiol. Clin. North Am. 11: 561–578, 1973.
4. Federle, M.P.: Computed tomography of blunt abdominal trauma. Radiol. Clin. North Am. 21: 461–475, 1983.
5. Hood, J.M., and Smyth, B.T.: Nonpenetrating intra-abdominal injuries in childhood. J. Pediatr. Surg. 9: 69–77, 1974.
6. Karp, M.P., Cooney, D.R., Berger, P.E., Khun, J.P., and Jewett, T.C., Jr.: The role of computed tomography in the evaluation of blunt abdominal trauma in children. J. Pediatr. Surg. 16: 316–323, 1981.
7. McCort, J.B.: *Radiographic Examination in Blunt Abdominal Trauma.* W. B. Saunders, Philadelphia, 1966.
8. Nelson, J.F.: The roentgenologic evaluation of abdominal trauma. Radiol. Clin. North Am. 4: 415–431, 1966.
9. Osborn, D.J., Glickman, M.G., Grnja, V., and Ramsby, G.: The role of angiography in abdominal nonrenal trauma. Radiol. Clin. North Am. 11: 579–592, 1973.
10. Woodruff, J.H., Jr., Ottoman, R.E., Simonton, J.H., and Averbrook, B.D.: The radiologic differential diagnosis of abdominal trauma. Radiology 72: 641–649, 1959.

Specific Organ Injury. One of the most commonly injured organs is the *spleen*. Clinically, upper abdominal, left upper quadrant, flank, or left shoulder (referred from the diaphragm) pain provides a clue to the diagnosis. The roentgenographic findings associated with splenic injury (2–4, 6, 10) often are difficult to evaluate, but one should look for one or more of the following; (a) medial displacement of the stomach, (b) downward and/or medial displacement of the splenic flexure, (c) elevation of the left diaphragmatic leaflet, (d) scoliosis of the spine with concavity to the left, (e) sentinel loops over the left upper quadrant, (f) pleural effusions or atelectasis in the left lung base, and (g) associated rib fractures in a few cases. Of course, not all these findings are present in any one patient, but being aware of all of them is most important (Fig. 3.99).

If splenic rupture is associated with bleeding into the peritoneal cavity, the roentgenographic findings of peritoneal fluid develop. In such patients, the splenic silhouette often is not visualized as a distinct structure, but yet the splenic "space" is enlarged. In other instances, the spleen may enlarge posteriorly, and as such displace or compress the left kidney, and it may be difficult to determine whether one is dealing with renal or splenic injury. However, if the renal sil-

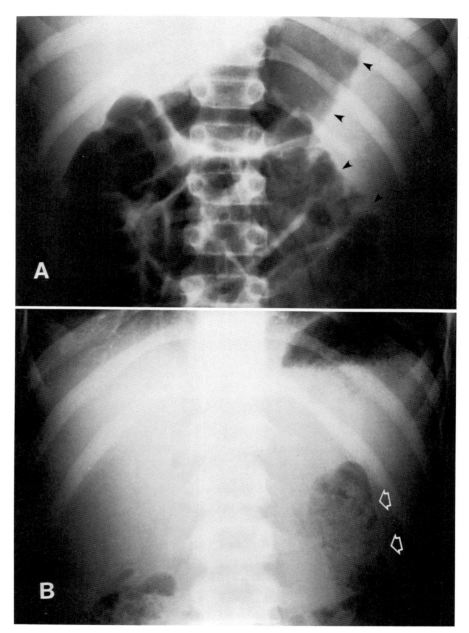

Figure 3.99. *Splenic trauma—plain film findings.* (*A*) Note the enlarged splenic silhouette displacing the stomach and intestines medially (*arrows*). (*B*) Another case showing a medially displaced splenic flexure (*arrows*). The spleen is difficult to identify as such, but the splenic space is increased in width.

houette is intact and kidney function is good, splenic injury is more likely, especially if one notes an enlarged splenic silhouette (Fig. 3.100).

In the past, splenic injuries frequently remained in doubt for a number of days, but currently this should not happen for they can be readily identified with CT scanning and/or radionuclide studies (5, 7–9). Ultrasonography, initially was employed in the investigation of splenic injury (1), but currently we have found that many intrasplenic

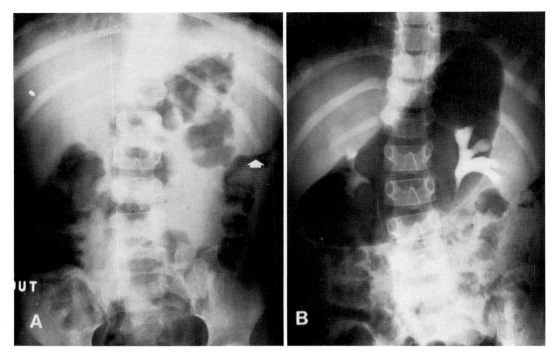

Figure 3.100. *Splenic trauma. Posterior enlargement of spleen causing displacement of kidney.* (*A*) Note the enlarged splenic silhouette (*arrow*) displacing the splenic flexure downward, and the transverse colon and stomach medially. Minimal scoliosis of the spine lateralizes the findings to the left side. (*B*) Note again the enlarged spleen, but also note the deformed calyces of the enlarged left kidney. The kidney was being anteriorly displaced by the enlarging spleen.

hematomas are missed with ultrasound (see Fig. 3.103). Consequently we seldom perform ultrasonography for suspected splenic injury.

CT scanning usually clearly identifies intrasplenic, subcapsular and perisplenic hematomas (Fig. 3.101–3.103). Radionuclide scans also can be employed and are useful, but probably are not required once the CT examination has been performed.

Liver injury with virtual exsanguinating hemorrhage is a true emergency, and often there is barely enough time to obtain abdominal roentgenograms. In such cases, emergency ligation or embolization of the hepatic artery frequently is performed (1, 2, 5, 8, 11, 14). Roentgenographically, intracapsular hematomas lead to enlargement of the liver, upward displacement of the right diaphragmatic leaflet, medial displacement of the duodenum and stomach, downward displacement of the hepatic flexure, and in some cases, downward displacement and compression of the right kidney. Actually,

the findings are similar to those seen with an enlarging spleen, except that they are on the right side (Fig. 3.104). Of course, atelectasis and pleural effusions in the right lung base, along with right rib fractures, also may be noted, and intrahepatic air, probably forced into the liver from the intestinal tract, also has been described (15). If blood escapes into the peritoneal cavity, the findings will be those of peritoneal fluid. Trauma to the hepatic artery also can occur (10).

Currently, however, ultrasonography (6), CT scanning (9), and radionuclide studies almost always delineate the site of injury (Fig. 3.105). Ultrasonography is more rewarding with liver injuries than with splenic injuries, and radionuclide scans certainly can detect hematomas and lacerations of the liver, but once again CT scanning is the procedure of choice. Arteriography usually is not utilized for diagnosis but is necessary when selective artery embolization or ligation is contemplated.

Injury to the **bile ducts** or **gallbladder**

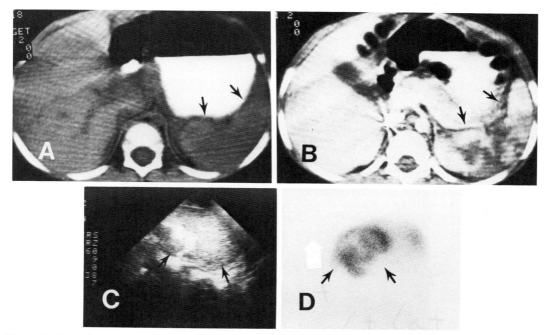

Figure 3.101. *Splenic injury; CT and ultrasonographic findings.* (*A*) Plain CT scan demonstrating indistinct anatomy and lack of delineation of the enlarged spleen (*arrows*). (*B*) Contrast enhanced CT study demonstrates massive fracturing and bursting of the spleen (*arrows*). (*C*) Ultrasound study is less specific and merely demonstrates an inhomogeneous pattern of echogenicity in the poorly defined, enlarged spleen (*arrows*). (*D*) Left lateral isotope scan demonstrating filling defects in the spleen (*arrows*), consistent with multiple hematomas.

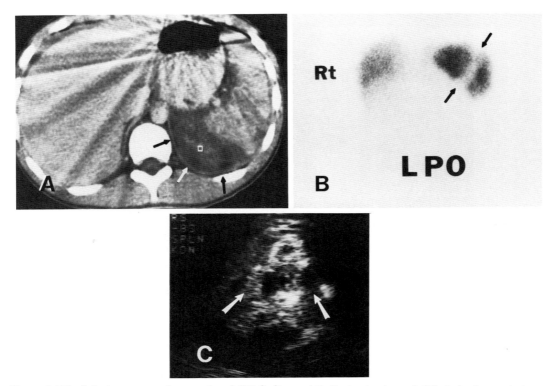

Figure 3.102. *Splenic trauma; ultrasound and CT findings.* (*A*) Contrast-enhanced CT study demonstrates a subcapsular hematoma (*arrows*) and irregular bleeding into the remainder of the enlarged spleen. (*B*) Left posterior oblique isotope study demonstrates defect (laceration) in the spleen (*arrows*). (*C*) Ultrasonography demonstrates nonspecific heterogeneous echogenicity in the splenic bed (*arrows*), but the spleen, itself, is poorly defined.

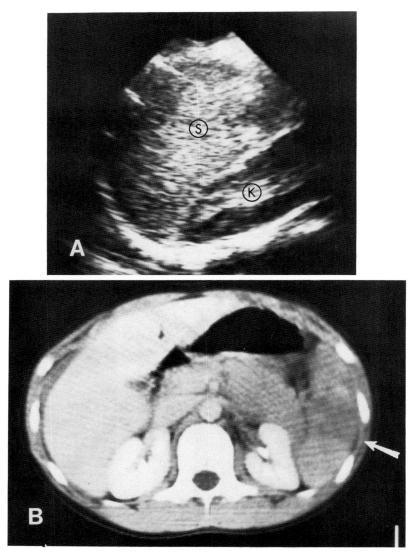

Figure 3.103. *Splenic trauma; ultrasound and CT findings.* (*A*) Misleading ultrasound demonstrates a near normal pattern of echogenicity of the spleen (*S*). Note the left kidney (*K*) below the spleen. (*B*) Contrast enhanced CT scan clearly demonstrates an intrasplenic hematoma (*arrow*). Some blood also is present around the liver.

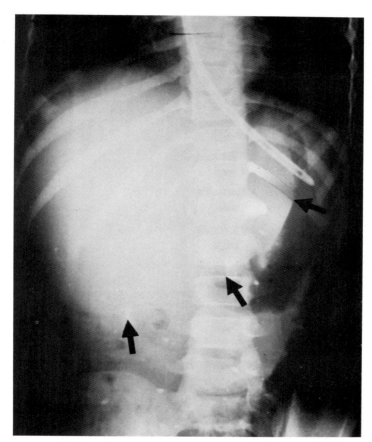

Figure 3.104. *Liver trauma.* Note the markedly enlarged liver (*arrows*) displacing the stomach far to the left, and the intestines downwardly.

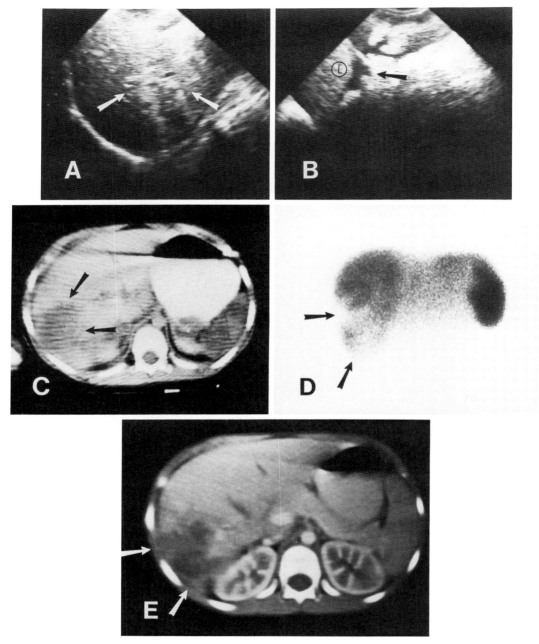

Figure 3.105. *Liver trauma; CT, ultrasound and isotope findings.* (*A*) Ultrasonography demonstrates a few abnormal echoes in the liver (*arrows*). (*B*) A little further to the left, some fluid (*arrow*) is located under the liver (*L*). (*C*) Contrast enhanced CT scan clearly demonstrates the intrahepatic hematoma (*arrows*). (*D*) Liver-spleen scan demonstrating a fractured liver with irregular isotope activity (*arrows*). (*E*) Another patient with CT demonstration of an intrahepatic hematoma (*arrows*).

often is difficult to diagnose and usually is accompanied by injury to other viscera in the area, mainly the liver. If, however, the gallbladder or bile ducts are injured alone, bile peritonitis is the presenting feature (3, 4, 12). In such cases, the peritonitis produced often is of a smouldering nature, and it is not until paracentesis is performed that the diagnosis is substantiated. In the past, direct cholangiography often was employed to detect these leaks but currently radionuclide studies are less invasive and just as rewarding. In such cases a Tc-Hida scan will demonstrate isotope activity outside the hepatobiliary system and gastrointestinal tract (13).

Pancreatic trauma in childhood is relatively common (1–9) and can occur with surprisingly mild injury. Most often it is seen with automobile accidents, bicycle handlebar accidents, blows with the fist to the abdomen, falls on a blunt object, and seat belt injuries in older children. It is also commonly seen in the battered child syndrome.

The roentgenographic findings are variable, and actually most times the abdominal roentgenograms are normal. However, in other cases one may see telltale sentinel loops of dilated intestine over the area of the pancreas. In any given case, these loops may be those of dilated small bowel, duodenum, or transverse colon (Fig. 3.106). When the transverse colon is dilated, it results in the so-called colon cutoff sign (Fig. 3.106). In addition to these findings, one may see widening of the soft tissue space between the stomach and transverse colon as a result of bleeding and/or edema in this area.

Currently, suspected pancreatic injury is best assessed with ultrasound or CT scan-ning. In chronic cases, if a pseudocyst is present, one will see a large cystic structure (2), often containing debris, and identical to that seen with nontraumatic pancreatitis (see Fig. 3.64). In acute cases, the inflamed pancreas appears enlarged, and occasionally more sonolucent than normal. However, in our experience pancreatic echogenicity more often is normal (Fig. 3.107*A*). On CT scanning, the pancreas also is enlarged, but once again, density is not particularly different from normal (Fig. 3.107*B*).

In the past, an upper GI series often was obtained when pancreatitis was suspected, but now, it generally is not required. However, if obtained, it can demonstrate one or more of the following findings: (a) expansion of the duodenal loop, (b) effacement and fixation of the medial duodenal wall, (c) displacement of the antrum of the stomach, or (d) duodenal obstruction.

Trauma to the **duodenum** often is seen in conjunction with pancreatic injury but, of course, can occur alone (5–7). It results from the same type of injury responsible for pancreatic trauma, and also is seen in the battered child syndrome. Trauma to the duodenum may manifest itself in actual duodenal rupture, intramural duodenal tears, or intramural hematoma formation (1–7). The latter injury, however, is most common.

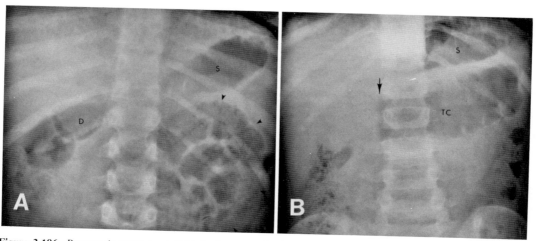

Figure 3.106. *Pancreatic trauma.* (*A*) Note the stomach (*S*), duodenum (*D*), and the sentinel loops of dilated small bowel in the left abdomen (*arrows*). The stomach is displaced upwardly, and the soft tissue space between the stomach and intestines is widened. The duodenal bulb is filled with air secondary to paralytic ileus. (*B*) Another case demonstrating the colon cutoff sign. Note the dilated transverse colon (*TC*) and the abrupt cutoff of gas just to the right of the spine (*arrow*). Also note that the soft tissue space between the stomach (*S*) and the transverse colon is increased. (Reprinted with permission from Young, L. W., and Adams, J. T.: Roentgenographic findings in localized trauma to the pancreas in children, A.J.R. 101:639–648, 1967.)

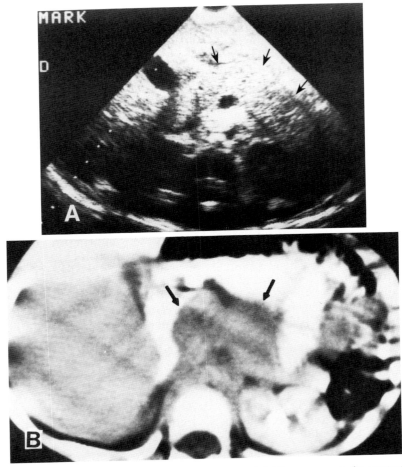

Figure 3.107. *Pancreatic trauma; CT and ultrasound findings.* (*A*) Ultrasonogram demonstrates an enlarged pancreas (*arrows*). (*B*) Contrast-enhanced CT scan with Gastrografin in the stomach and duodenum more adequately demonstrates the enlarged pancreas (*arrows*). Also see Figure 3.63 for additional findings of pancreatitis.

When duodenal rupture occurs, the usual site of perforation is along the posterior duodenal wall, and subsequently, there is leakage of intestinal contents into the retroperitoneal space. Symptoms due to such leakage may not become apparent immediately, and indeed, may take hours or days to develop. When they do develop, they consist of pain in the back or flank, and roentgenographically, if water soluble contrast agents are administered to these patients, retroperitoneal extravasation can be demonstrated. The duodenum, of course, also will be deformed, or even obstructed. Intraperitoneal rupture of the duodenum occurs rarely.

With duodenal intramural hematoma formation, the plain films may show nothing abnormal, or they may show evidence of duodenal or gastric obstruction (Fig. 3.108*A*). Less commonly, the hematoma itself may be seen as an abdominal mass. However, if duodenal injury is suspected, an upper GI series should be performed, for it is likely to demonstrate: (a) duodenal obstruction; (b) an intramural mass (Fig. 3.108); (c) thickened, thumbprinted, or coil-spring duodenal folds; or (d) evidence of an intramural tear. With intramural tears, the barium collection may be seen to remain in place for days. Intramural hematomas eventually disappear, with the blood escaping into the bowel lumen and follow-up GI studies usually showing a complete return to normal. More recently, duodenal hematomas have been demonstrated with ultrasonography or CT scanning. CT findings are

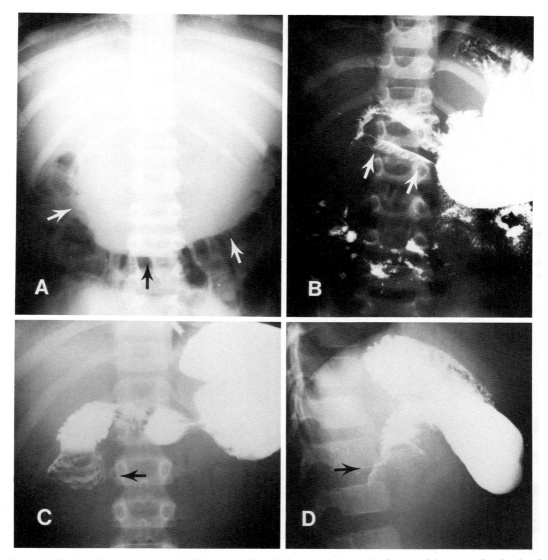

Figure 3.108. *Duodenal trauma.* (*A*) Note large distended stomach (*arrows*) obstructed because of a duodenal hematoma. (*B*) Typical appearance of the duodenal hematoma; an intramural lesion (*arrows*). (*C* and *D*) Another patient with classic findings of an intramural hematoma (*arrows*). (Figs. *C* and *D* courtesy Virgil Graves, M.D., Great Falls, Montana.)

similar to those seen on upper GI series, that is displacement or deformity of the duodenum, and/or obstruction. With ultrasonography one identifies the hematoma as a basically sonolucent mass (see Fig. 3.109). However, with organization of the blood, echoes within the lesion may develop.

Small intestinal injury is becoming more common as seat belt injuries become more common (3, 4), but of course, any type of blunt trauma to the abdomen can cause

small bowel injury. In terms of the specific type of injury incurred, perforation and hematoma formation probably are most common (3–7), and in either case, post-traumatic stenoses with obstruction of the intestine can result (2). In the acute injury, however, abdominal roentgenograms frequently are normal, but in some cases, one or two sentinel loops of dilated, injured small bowel can be seen. If these loops appear thickened, intramural bleeding should be suspected, but often this is a difficult finding to appreciate on plain films and usually is best demonstrated with upper gastrointestinal contrast studies. In some of these cases the hematoma may be in the mesentery or omentum (1), but in either case, if large enough, it may present as an abdominal mass on plain films. In still other cases, it may be associated with intestinal obstruction. Ultrasonography or CAT scanning also can be helpful in the detection of these hematomata (Fig. 3.109).

Perforation of the stomach, small intestine or colon may lead to free air being visualized in the abdomen (6, 7). With gastric or colonic perforations, such air usually is intraperitoneal and of such a volume that it is readily visualized. With small bowel perforations, however, little if any air is seen. Rectal perforations may lead to air accumulations in the pelvic soft tissues, and both

rectal and duodenal perforations can lead to retroperitoneal air collections.

Esophageal perforation can present with widening of the mediastinum, air in the mediastinum, or a hydropneumothorax. Esophageal perforations can be confirmed with the administration of water soluble contrast material. These perforations probably result from acutely increased intraluminal esophageal pressures secondary to blunt trauma to the abdomen and lower chest.

Injury to the **urinary tract** is one of the more common manifestations of abdominal trauma, and renal injury can range from simple renal parencyhmal contusion to complete avulsion of the renal pedicle (3, 4, 6, 7, 9–15, 19, 22). A diagrammatic representation of these injuries is offered in Figure 3.110. Interestingly enough, however, most

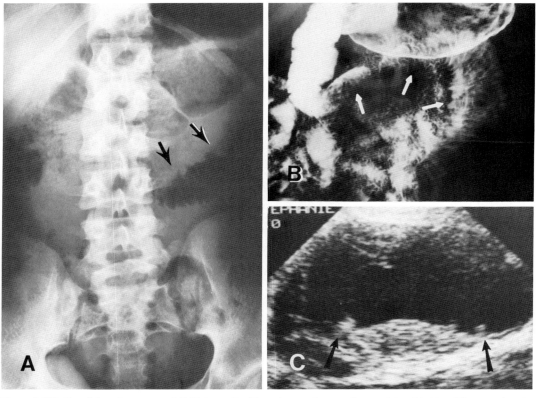

Figure 3.109. *Small bowel trauma.* (*A*) Note sentinel loop (*arrows*), secondary to jejunal injury. The next day the patient developed a classic small bowel obstruction. (*B*) Upper GI series demonstrating large intramural jejunal hematoma (*arrows*). (*C*) Ultrasonogram demonstrates large, sonolucent hematoma (*arrows*). (Figs. *B* and *C* from Kaufman, R. A., Babcock, D. S.: An approach to imaging the upper abdomen in the injured child, Semin. Rentgenol. 14: 308–320, 1984.)

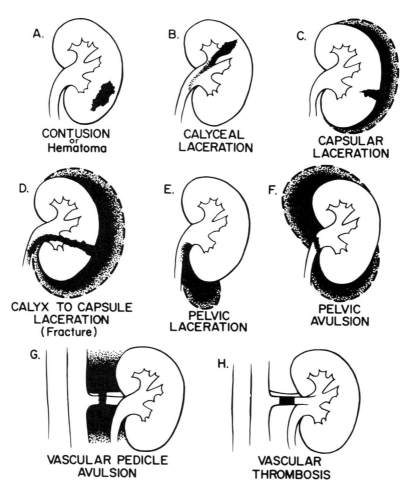

Figure 3.110. *Types of renal injury—diagrammatic representation.*   *Black areas* represent areas of blood accumulation, except in (*H*), where the black area represents the area of thrombosis. (Modified from Macpherson, R. I., and Decter, A.: Pediatric renal trauma, J. Can. Assoc. Radiol. 22: 10–21, 1971.)

of these lesions can be treated conservatively, and it is only the massive injury to the kidney or its blood supply that requires immediate surgical intervention. In addition, McDonald et al. (13) have shown that the emergency urogram doesn't accurately predict the eventual outcome in a patient with renal injury. Indeed, in many instances findings such as scarring and hypertension do not become apparent for weeks or even years (6, 13), and it is difficult to prognosticate, on the basis of the initial studies, which patients will develop these complications.

In the past, one relied almost solely on the intravenous pyelogram for the evaluation of renal trauma and although the study is still quite valuable, CT scanning has provided a more definitive method with which to evaluate renal injury (20, 21). Fractured and lacerated kidneys especially, are more clearly visualized, and extent of perirenal hematoma formation is more accurately assessed. Consequently, whereas in the past, the intravenous pyelogram was the mainstay of the investigation of renal trauma, currently contrast enhanced CT scanning has replaced it. Ultrasonography also can be utilized but the images often are so indistinct around their edges that there is no comparison with what is available with contrast enhanced CT scanning.

With simple ***renal contusions*** or ***intrarenal***

hematomas the renal silhouette is intact, but may be focally or generally enlarged. Intravenous pyelography usually demonstrates a decrease in renal function corresponding to the area of involvement (Fig. 3.111). ***Cortical lacerations*** may extend into the calyces or through the capsule of the kidney into the perirenal space. If the laceration extends through the renal capsule into the perirenal space, and enough bleeding occurs, the renal silhouette will appear enlarged or obliterated. During the nephrographic phase of the intravenous pyelogram in these patients, one may be able to delineate the wedge-like defect corresponding to the cortical laceration (Fig. 3.112). If the cortical laceration extends into a calyx or renal pelvis, extravasation of contrast material into the renal parenchyma will be noted (Fig. 3.113). Finally, if the laceration is such that it extends from the calyx to, and through, the renal capsule (incomplete fracture) then contrast material will extravasate around the kidney (Fig. 3.114).

All of the foregoing abnormalities now usually are more clearly demonstrable with CT scanning (Figs. 3.115–3.117). Ultrasonography, of course, can delineate that some of these injuries have occurred to a kidney (Figs. 3.115–3.117), but the information obtained usually consists of altered renal configuration and a variety of indistinct patterns of increased echo activity in the area of contusion or bleeding. Occasionally a hematoma will produce a sonolucent mass within the kidney, but for practical purposes it is not worth spending one's time examining these kidneys ultrasonographically.

In those instances when the kidney is ***completely fractured***, pyelographic findings usually demonstrate marked impairment of renal function. It is here that CT scanning most dramatically demonstrates its usefulness (Fig. 3.117). With cuts through the entire kidney, one quickly can obtain a composite image of just how severe the injury is.

Injuries to the ***renal pelvis*** lead to extravasation of urine and contrast material around the kidney (Fig. 3.118), and in some cases the urine collection may lead to the development of a so-called urinoma (8, 14). This collection of urine may be visualized as

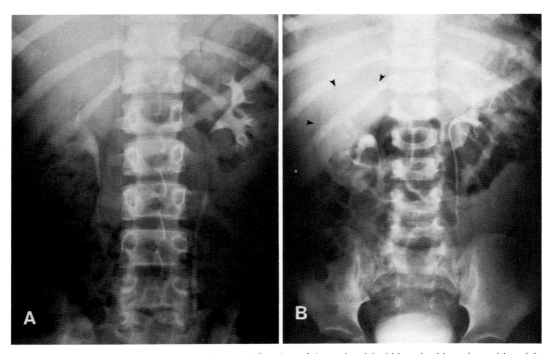

Figure 3.111. *Renal contusion.* (*A*) Note decreased function of the entire right kidney in this patient with a right renal contusion. (*B*) Another patient demonstrating decreased function and slight enlargement of the right upper renal pole only (*arrows*).

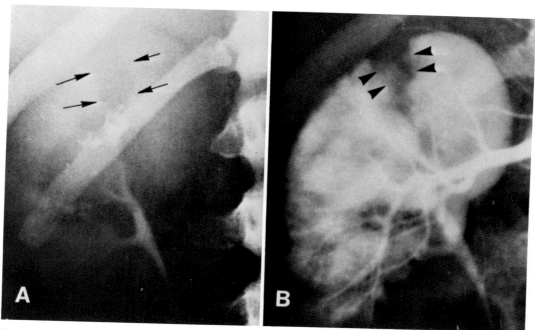

Figure 3.112. *Cortical laceration—nephrographic and angiographic features.* (*A*) Note the wedge-like area of radiolucency (cortical laceration) in the right upper pole (*arrows*). (*B*) Arteriogram demonstrating the wedge-like radiolucency to greater advantage (*arrows*). Compare with Figure 3.110C. (Reprinted with permission from Richter, M. W., Lytton, B., Myerson, D., and Grnja, V.: Radiology of the genitourinary trauma, Radiol. Clin. North Am. 11: 593–631, 1973.)

a soft tissue mass on plain abdominal roentgenograms, and on intravenous pyelography will eventually fill with contrast material (Fig. 3.119). Associated obstruction of the upper urinary tract is common in these cases, and the urine collections may extend into the thorax (2). These urine collections usually are readily demonstrable with ultrasonography, for they are sonolucent. They are, also, readily visualized with CT scanning.

Vascular injury to the renal pedicle may range from traumatic avulsion of both the artery and vein, to renal artery thrombosis (1, 17). With total avulsion of the renal pedicle, perinephric hematoma formation usually is profound, and, of course, during intravenous pyelography, no function of the involved kidney will be seen. With traumatic renal artery thrombosis, the kidney usually is not enlarged on plain films, and arteriography is required for demonstration of the obstructed artery.

Before leaving renal trauma, a note regarding *trauma to a previously unsuspected hydronephrotic kidney* is in order. In some

of these cases, trauma seems to be relatively mild, but pain and hematuria cause the child to seek medical attention. Indeed, one often is surprised at just how large these hydronephrotic kidneys are, and how they remain silent until the time of injury (Fig. 3.120). In these cases, one most often is dealing with an underlying ureteropelvic junction obstruction, but ureteral stenosis at a lower level also can be encountered. When such a kidney is injured, nothing more than hematuria may result, but in other instances, frank tears of the renal pelvis or calices lead to extravasation of urine, blood, and contrast material.

Injuries to the ureter are rare, but *bladder and urethral injury* is rather common, especially in the presence of pelvic fractures (4, 5, 16, 18). *Urethral injury* is most often seen in males, and as such usually involves the posterior urethra, just at its junction with the bladder neck. Tears of the non-distended bladder, around the bladder neck and posterior urethra, lead to extravasation of urine in the extraperitoneal, pelvic soft tissues. In such instances, plain films frequently dem-

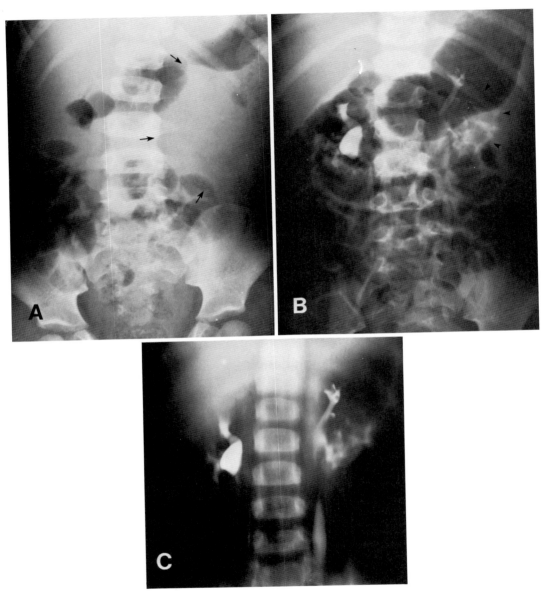

Figure 3.113. *Intrarenal calyceal laceration.* (*A*) Note the enlarged renal silhouette on the left (*arrows*). The intestines are displaced away from the mass. (*B*) Intravenous pyelogram demonstrating extravasation of contrast material into the mid and lower portions of the left kidney. (*C*) Laminography demonstrates the degree of extravasation to greater advantage.

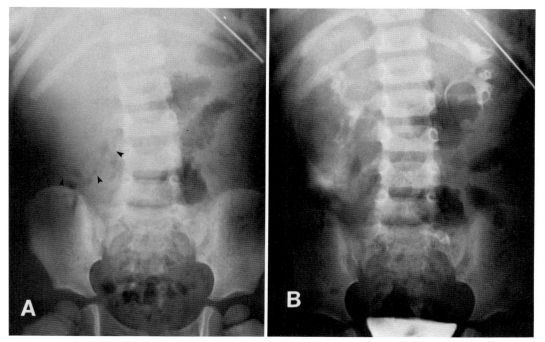

Figure 3.114. *Calyx to capsule laceration (incomplete fracture of kidney).* (*A*) Note the enlarged renal silhouette on the right (*arrows*). Also note that the right psoas margin and inferior edge of the liver are obliterated. Scoliosis with concavity to the right also is present. (*B*) Function of the right kidney is reasonably good, but extravasated contrast material outlines the entire periphery of the right kidney.

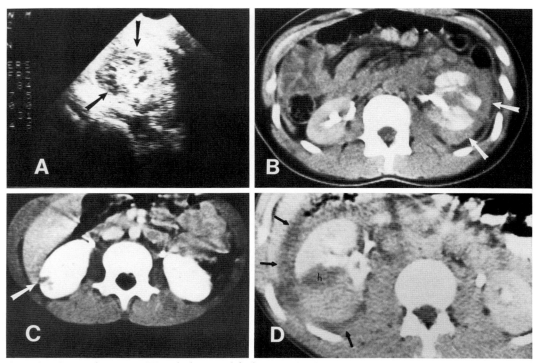

Figure 3.115. *Renal trauma; CT and ultrasound findings.* (*A*) Ultrasonography demonstrates disorganized echo activity in the poorly defined left kidney (*arrows*). (*B*) Contrast-enhanced CT study much more clearly demonstrates the fractured left kidney and blood around it (*arrows*). (*C*) Another patient demonstrating a small intrarenal hematoma or area of contusion (*arrow*). (*D*) Still another patient with a contrast-enhanced CT scan demonstrating a large intrarenal hematoma (*h*), some blood around the kidney (*arrows*), and a contusion over the lower pole. Note that the kidney also is displaced outward.

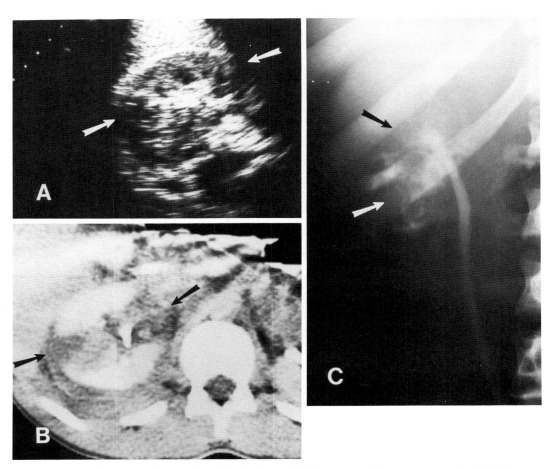

Figure 3.116. *Renal trauma; ultrasound and CT findings.*   (*A*) Ultrasonography demonstrates disturbed, heterogeneous echo activity in the right kidney (*arrows*). There is marked loss of normal architecture. (*B*) Contrast enhanced
CT study, however, more clearly defines the fractured kidney (*arrows*). (*C*) IVP demonstrates extravasation of
contrast material (*arrows*).

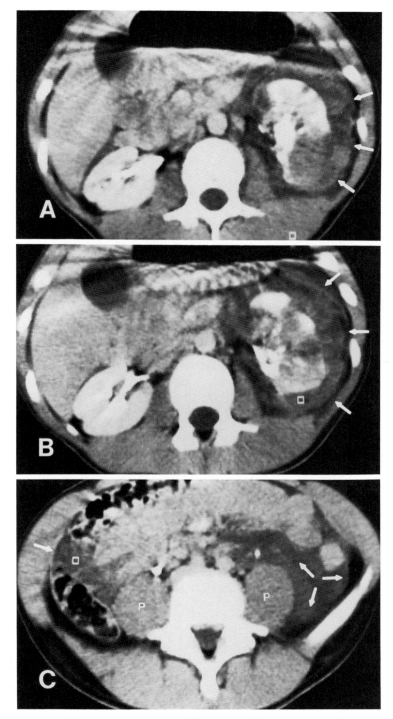

Figure 3.117. *Renal trauma; CT scan showing extent of bleeding.*   (*A*) Note the large left intrarenal hematoma and blood surrounding the kidney (*arrows*). (*B*) A slightly lower slice demonstrates the virtually, totally fractured kidney and blood around it (*arrows*). (*C*) CT scan of pelvis demonstrates extension of blood around the left psoas muscle (*multiple arrows*), and some blood on the other side (*single arrow*); psoas muscle (*P*).

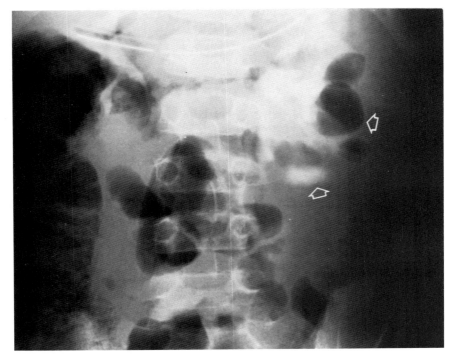

Figure 3.118. *Pelvic laceration.*   Note extravasation of contrast material around the left kidney (*arrows*).

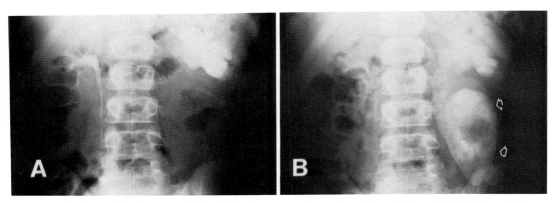

Figure 3.119. *Parapelvic urinoma.*   (*A*) Early film demonstrating an elevated and obstructed left kidney. Note one or two curvilinear collections of contrast material below the left kidney. (*B*) Delayed films demonstrate filling of a large urinoma (*arrows*) which was obstructing the left kidney.

onstrate the presence of an accompanying pelvic fracture and obliteration of the soft tissue planes in the pelvis. Intravenous urography or retrograde cystography will demonstrate extravasation of urine into the pelvic soft tissues (Fig. 3.121). Ultrasonography, and CT scanning, of course, also can demonstrate these fluid collections.

In investigating a potential bladder or urethral injury, it is important to first perform a retrograde urethrogram. This will yield information as to the condition of the urethra. Thereafter, if the urethra and bladder neck are normal a formal retrograde cystogram can be performed. However, if a Foley catheter is being utilized for this procedure, it should be placed in such a position that the inflated bulb does not occlude the bladder neck. This is important, for it occludes the bladder neck, it may also occlude a

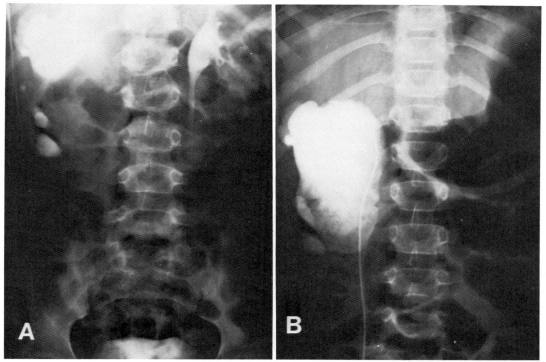

Figure 3.120. *Trauma to hydronephrotic kidney.* (*A*) Note the deformed collecting system of the right kidney. This patient sustained abdominal trauma and presented with pain and hematuria. (*B*) Subsequent retrograde pyelogram demonstrates the degree of hydronephrosis present. Hydronephrosis was secondary to a ureteropelvic junction obstruction which prior to this time was unsuspected. For the ultrasound appearance of a similar kidney, see Figure 3.144.

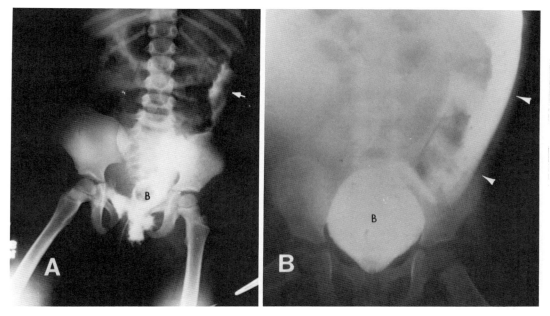

Figure 3.121. *Bladder trauma.* (*A*) Note the displaced urinary bladder (*B*). It is displaced to the left because of intrapelvic blood and urine accumulation. Below the bladder, note extravasation of contrast material into the pelvic soft tissues. Also note that there has been intraperitoneal leakage (*arrow*) of contrast material. (*B*) Intraperitoneal rupture (*arrows*) of the bladder (*B*) in a battered child. (Fig. *A* courtesy Charles J. Fagan, M.D., and Fig. *B* Theresa Stacy, M.D.)

nearby perforation. In cases where a perforation is suspected, but not demonstrated, oblique views of the bladder and bladder neck should be obtained for these views often demonstrated smaller leaks.

Distended urinary bladders, when ruptured, often lead to urine extravasation into the peritoneal cavity. In such cases, plain films will demonstrate the presence of abdominal fluid and subsequent cystography will demonstrate the site and extent of the leak (Fig. 3.121). Trauma to the bladder without perforation also can occur and is especially common with pelvic fractures. Such injury is difficult to document roentgenographically unless a pelvic hematoma surrounds the bladder. In these cases, the bladder may be minimally deformed or elevated, eccentrically deformed or elevated, or deformed in typical pear-shaped fashion (Fig. 3.122).

Once again, ultrasonography and CT

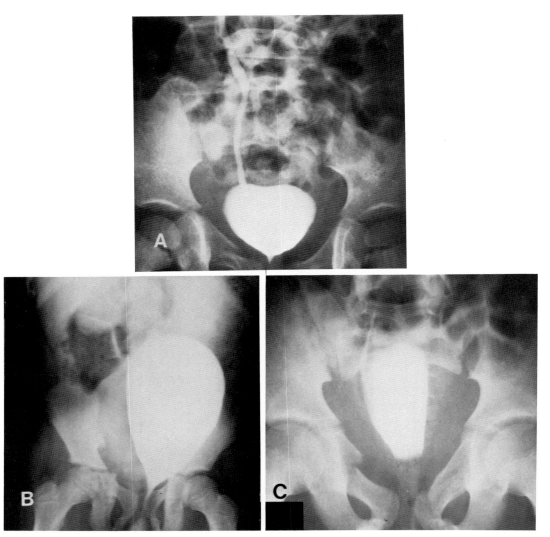

Figure 3.122. *Hematoma around the urinary bladder.*   (*A*) Note the increased soft tissue space between the contrast-filled bladder and surrounding bony pelvis. There is a fracture through the pubic bone on the right. (*B*) Marked displacement and elevation of the urinary bladder upward and to the left by a large pelvic hematoma on the right. Note the fracture through the right triradiate cartilage. (*C*) Typical elongated, almost pear-shaped bladder resulting from extensive perivesical hematoma formation. Note multiple fractures of the pelvis. (Fig. *B* courtesy Charles J. Fagan, M.D.)

scanning can demonstrate these fluid collections around the bladder but these studies have not replaced the cystogram. One of the reasons is that the cystogram is performed under fluoroscopic control and one can determine where the leak has occurred.

Rupture of a diaphragmatic leaflet secondary to blunt abdominal trauma is not exceptionally common in childhood but by the same token frequently is overlooked (1–8). Most often such rupture occurs on the left, but since in many cases there is nothing more to see than a slightly elevated or obscured diaphragmatic leaflet (1, 5, 6), the findings are missed. Of course, if atelectasis or a pleural effusion exists on the ipsilateral side, more attention is focused on the diaphragmatic leaflet, and when loops of distended intestine or stomach are seen in the chest, the diagnosis is virtually assured (Fig. 3.123). In these latter cases, the findings are quite similar to those seen with congenital diaphragmatic hernia and often a nasogastric tube can be seen to head into the chest

(7). On the right side, since the liver protects the right diaphragmatic leaflet, even with tears of the diaphragm, one usually sees only elevation of the right diaphragmatic leaflet. Associated rib fractures can be seen on either side, and contrast studies may be necessary to determine that intestines or stomach are present in the chest. Much more rarely, abdominal contents can herniate into the pericardial sac (4). Delayed herniation, weeks or months after initial injury, also can occur.

Vascular injury often is catastrophic, and there is no time for roentgenograms to be obtained. In those less severe cases where such studies are obtained, the findings often are non-specific and consist of nothing more than one or two loops of isolated, dilated intestine. Angiography, of course, is the procedure of choice in such cases.

Abdominal injury in the battered child syndrome usually is given less attention than it deserves. However, very often these children are dead on arrival in the emergency room and interestingly enough, may show

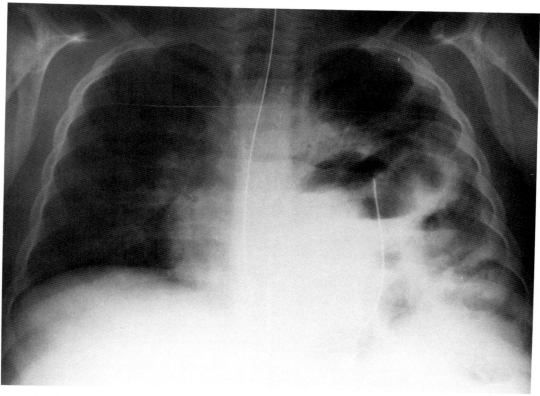

Figure 3.123. *Traumatic diaphragmatic hernia.* Note numerous collections of intestine in the left chest and note the position of the nasogastric tube as it heads into the stomach, herniated into the chest.

little in the way of skeletal injury (Fig. 3.124). One of the most commonly injured organs is the pancreas, and indeed, acute pancreatitis and subsequent pseudocyst formation are becoming more and more common in the battered child syndrome (1, 6, 7, 8). Duodenal trauma, usually with duodenal hematoma formation, also is a common injury in the battered child syndrome and interestingly enough, so is small intestinal trauma. In fact, small intestinal injury is more common in the battered child syndrome than under any other circumstance (4). In addition, colon injuries are probably more common than generally appreciated (Fig. 1.124). These can result from blunt trauma or insertion of various objects into the rectum with perforation (Fig. 3.125). Traumatic mesenteric avulsion also has been reported in a case of presumed battered child (2), and actually, when one encounters a child with any abdominal injury which is inadequately explained, one should suspect that the child has been battered.

Another interesting feature of the battered child syndrome, although not usually seen in the acute phase, is the post-traumatic development of lytic lesions in the long bones secondary to fat necrosis. These lesions, although not particularly common, can be perplexing unless one is aware of the phenomenon (3, 5, 8).

REFERENCES

Spleen

1. Ascher, W., Parvin, S., Virgilio, R., and Haber, K.: Echographic evaluation of splenic injury after blunt trauma. Radiology 118: 411–415, 1976.
2. Brindle, M.J.: Radiological evaluation of splenic injury after blunt trauma. J. Can. Assoc. Radiol. 22: 3–9, 1971.
3. Burrell, M., Toffler, R., and Lowman, R.: Blunt trauma to the abdomen and gastrointestinal tract. Radiol. Clin. North Am. 11: 561–578, 1973.
4. Cimmino, C.V.: Ruptured spleen: some refinements in its roentgenologic diagnosis. Radiology 82: 57–62, 1964.
5. Harris, B.H., Morse, T.S., Weidenmeier, C.H., Jr., Wilkinson, A.H., Jr., and Webb, H.W.: Radioisotope diagnosis of splenic trauma. J. Pediatr. Surg. 12: 385–389, 1977.
6. Kittredge, R.D., and Finby, N.: Infrapulmonary effusion in traumatic rupture of the spleen. A.J.R. 91: 891–895, 1964.
7. Korobkin, M., Moss, A.A., Callen, P.W., DeMartini, W.J., and Kaiser, J.A.: Computed Tomography of subcapsular splenic hematoma: clinical and experimental studies, Radiology 129: 441–445, 1978.

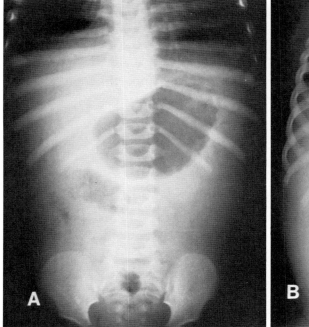
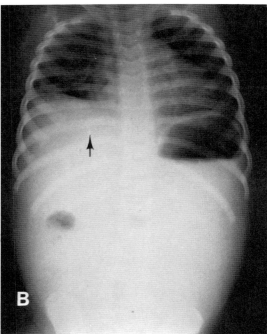

Figure 3.124. *Abdominal trauma—battered child syndrome.* (*A*) Supine film demonstrating generalized opacity of the abdomen and absence of visualization of the psoas shadows and liver edge. The findings suggest peritoneal fluid. (*B*) Upright view demonstrating similar findings and a slightly elevated right diaphragmatic leaflet. There was a small subpulmonic effusion on the right. Also note an almost invisible fresh rib fracture on the right (*arrows*). This was the only sign of skeletal injury in this battered child who had peritonitis secondary to perforation of the colon.

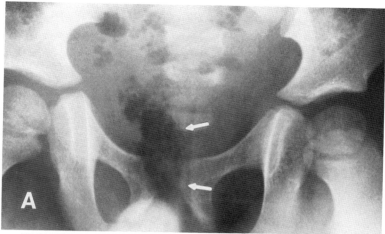

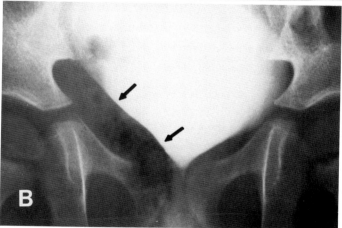

Figure 3.125. *Battered child syndrome: intestinal perforation.* (*A*) Note the bubbles of gas in the right groin region (*arrows*). This resulted from a rectal perforation after insertion of an object into the rectum. (*B*) Cystogram demonstrates displacement of the bladder by the abscess (*arrows*).

8. Mall, J.C., and Kaiser, J.A.: CT diagnosis of splenic laceration. A.J.R. 134: 265–269, 1980.
9. Nebesar, R.A., Rabinov, K.R., and Potsaid, M.S.: Radionuclide imaging of spleen in suspected splenic injury. Radiology 110: 609–614, 1974.
10. Schwartz, S.S., Boley, S.J., and McKinnon, W.M.P.: The roentgen findings in traumatic rupture of the spleen in children. A.J.R. 82: 505–509, 1959.

Liver, Gallbladder, and Bile Ducts

1. Aaron, S., Fulton, R., and Mays, E.: Selective ligation of the hepatic artery for trauma of the liver. Surg. Gynecol. Obstet. 141: 187, 1975.
2. Canty, T.G., and Stephen, A.W.: Hepatic artery ligation for exsanguinating liver injuries in children. J. Pediatr. Surg. 5: 693–700, 1975.
3. Caro, A.M., and Losa, J.M.O.: Complete avulsion of the common bile duct as a result of blunt abdominal trauma: case report of a child. J. Pediatr. Surg. 5: 60–62, 1970.
4. Evans, J.P.: Traumatic rupture of the gallbladder in a three-year-old boy. J. Pediatr. Surg. 11: 1033–1034, 1976.
5. Jander, H.P., Laws, H.L., Kogutt, M.S., and Mihas, A.A.: Emergency embolization in blunt hepatic trauma. A.J.R. 129: 249–252, 1977.

6. Lam, A.H., and Shulman, L.: Ultrasonography in the Management of liver trauma in children. J. Ultrasound Med. 3: 199–203, 1984.
7. Levin, D.C., Watson, R.C., Sos, T.A., and Baltaxe, H.A.: Angiography in blunt trauma. A.J.R. 119: 95–101, 1973.
8. McCort, J.J.: Rupture or laceration of the liver by nonpenetrating trauma. Radiology 78: 49–56, 1962.
9. Moon, K.L., Jr., and Federle, M.P.: Computed tomography in hepatic trauma. A.J.R. 141: 309–314, 1983.
10. Pastershank, S.P., and Wright, C.J.: Blunt trauma to the main hepatic artery. J. Can. Assoc. Radiol. 26: 263–265, 1975.
11. Rubin, B.E., and Katzen, B.T.: Selective hepatic artery embolization to control massive hemorrhage after trauma. A.J.R. 129: 253–256, 1977.
12. Shorthouse A.J., Singh, M.P., Treasure, T., and Franklin, F.H.: Isolated complete transection of the common bile duct by blunt abdominal trauma. Br. J. Surg. 65: 543, 1978.
13. Sty, J.R., Starshak, R.J., and Hubbard, A.M.: Radionuclide hepatobiliary imaging in the detection of traumatic biliary tract disease in children. Pediatr. Radiol. 12: 115–118, 1982.
14. Susan, E.M., Klotz, D., Jr., and Kottmeier, P.K.: Liver

trauma in children. J. Pediatr. Surg. 10: 411–417, 1975.

15. Wolfel, D.A., and Brogdon, B.G.: Intrahepatic air—a sign of trauma. Radiology 91: 952–953, 1968.

Pancreas

1. Berger, J., Sauvage, P., Levy, M., Graf, H., Olive, B., Reinhardt, W., Sauvage, M.R., and Buck, P.: Pancreatic trauma in childhood. Ann. Chir. Inf. 13: 379–390, 1972.
2. Dahman, B., and Stephens, C.A.: Pseudocysts of the pancreas after blunt abdominal trauma in children. J. Pediatr. Surg. 16:17–21, 1981.
3. Ekengren, K., and Soderlund, S.: Radiological findings in traumatic lesions of pancreas in childhood. Ann. Radiol. 9: 279–385, 1966.
4. Harkanyi, Z., Vegh, M., Hittner, I., and Popik, E.: Gray-scale echography of traumatic pancreatic cysts in children. Pediatr. Radiol. 11: 81–82, 1981.
5. Leistyna, J.A., and Macaulay, J.C.: Traumatic pancreatitis in childhood: report of case and review of literature. Am. J. Dis. Child. 107: 644–648, 1964.
6. Pellerin, D., Bertin, P., and Harouchi, A.: Pancreatic trauma in childhood. Ann. Chir. Inf. 13: 391–394, 1972.
7. Stone, H.H.: Pancreatic and duodenal trauma in children. J. Pediatr. Surg. 7: 670–675, 1972.
8. Young, L.W., and Adams, J.T.: Roentgenographic findings in localized trauma to pancreas in children. A.J.R. 101: 639–648, 1967.
9. Young, L.W.: Pancreatic and/or duodenal injury from blunt trauma in childhood: radiopaque examinations and radiological review. Ann. Radiol. 18: 377–390, 1975.

Duodenum

1. Andersson, A., and Bergdahl, L.: Hematoma of the duodenum in children: review of the literature and report of two cases. Am. Surg. 39: 402–405, 1973.
2. Felson, B., and Levin, E.: Intramural hematoma of the duodenum. Radiology 63: 823–831, 1954.
3. Slonim, L.: Duodenal haematoma. Aust. Radiol. 15: 236–242, 1971.
4. Stone, H.H.: Pancreatic and duodenal trauma in children. J. Pediatr. Surg. 7: 670–675, 1972.
5. Wilson, T.S.: Retroperitoneal injuries to duodenum by blunt abdominal trauma: report of 8 cases. Can. J. Surg. 14: 114–120, 1971.
6. Woolley, N.M., Mahour, G.H., and Sloan, T.: Duodenal hematoma in infancy and childhood: changing etiology treatment. Am. J. Surg. 136: 8–14, 1978.
7. Young, L.W.: Pancreatic and/or duodenal injury from blunt trauma in childhood: radiopaque examinations and radiological review. Ann. Radiol. 18: 377–390, 1975.

Stomach, Esophagus, Small Intestines, and Colon

1. Bradpiece, H.A., and Kissin, M.W.: Massive traumatic hemomentocele. J. Pediatr. Surg. 19: 209, 1984.
2. Braun, P., and Dion, Y.: Intestinal stenosis following seat belt injury. J. Pediatr. Surg. 8: 549–550, 1973.
3. Doersch, K.B., and Dosjer, W.E.: The seat belt syndrome. The seat belt sign, intestinal and mesenteric injuries. Am. J. Surg. 116: 831, 1968.
4. Garrett, J.W., and Braunstein, P.W.: The seat belt syndrome. J. Trauma 1: 220, 1962.
5. Shuck, J.M., and Lowe, R.J.: Intestinal disruption due to blunt abdominal trauma. Am. J. Surg. 136: 668–673, 1978.
6. Ting, Y.M., and Reuter, S.R.: Hollow viscus injury in blunt abdominal trauma. A.J.R. 119: 408–413, 1973.
7. Westcott, J., and Smith, J.: Mesentery and colon injuries secondary to blunt trauma. Radiology 114: 597–600, 1975.

Urinary Tract

1. Barlow, B., and Gandhi, R.: Renal artery thrombosis following blunt trauma. J. Trauma 20: 614–617, 1980.
2. Baron, R.L., Stark D.D., McClennan, B.L., Shanes, J.G., Davis, G.L., and Koch, D.D.: Intrathoracic extension of retroperitoneal urine collections. A.J.R. 137: 37–41, 1981.
3. Beckley, D.E., and Walters, E.A.: Avulsion of pelviureteric

junction: rare consequences of nonpenetrating trauma. Brit. J. Radiol. 45: 423–426, 1972.

4. Boston, V.E., and Smyth, B.T.: Bilateral pelviureteric avulsion following closed trauma. Br. J. Urol. 47: 149–151, 1975.
5. Glassberg, K.I., Tolete-Velcek, F., Ashley, R., and Waterhouse, K.: Partial tears of prostatomembranous urethra in children. Urology 13: 500–504, 1979.
6. Holland, M.E., and Hurwitz, L.M., and Nice, C.M.: Traumatic lesions of the urinary tract. Radiol. Clin. North Am. 4: 433–450, 1966.
7. Hutchison, R.J., and Nogrady, M.B.: Late sequelae of renal trauma in the pediatric age group. J. Can. Assoc. Radiol. 24: 3–11, 1973.
8. Itoh, S., Yoshioka, H., Kaeriyama, M., Taguchi, T., Oka, R., Oka, T., and Okamura, Y.: Ultrasonographic diagnosis of uriniferous perirenal pseudocyst. Pediatr. Radiol. 12: 156–158, 1982.
9. Javadpour, N., Guinan, P., and Bush, I.M.: Renal trauma in children. Surg. Gynecol. Obstet. 136: 237–240, 1973.
10. Kokihova, E., Obenbergerova, D., and Apetaurova, B.: Total severance of renal pedicle caused by blunt trauma in children. Pediatr. Radiol. 1: 59–62, 1973.
11. Macpherson, R.I., and Decter, A.: Pediatric renal trauma. J. Can. Assoc. Radiol. 22: 10–21, 1971.
12. Mandour, W.A., Lai, M.K., Linke, C.A., and Frank, I.N.: Blunt renal trauma in the pediatric patient. J. Pediatr. Surg. 16: 669–676, 1981.
13. McDonald, E.J., Korobkin, M., Jacobs, R.P., and Minagi, H.: The role of emergency excretory urography in evaluation of blunt abdominal trauma. A.J.R. 126: 739–742, 1976.
14. McInerney, D., Jones, A., and Roylance, J.: Urinoma. Clin. Radiol. 28: 345–351, 1977.
15. Palavatana, C., Graham, S.R., and Silverman, F.N.: Delayed sequels to renal injury in childhood. A.J.R. 91: 659–665, 1964.
16. Perskey, L.: Childhood urethral trauma. Urology 2: 603–606, 1978.
17. Ready, L.B., Wright, C., and Baltzan, R.B.: Bilateral traumatic renal artery thrombosis. Can. Med. Assoc. J. 109: 885–891, 1973.
18. Reid, I.S.: Renal trauma in children: a ten-year review. Aust. N.Z.J. Surg. 42: 260–266, 1973.
19. Richter, M.W., Lytton, B., Myerson, D., and Grnja, V.: Radiology of genitourinary trauma. Radiol. Clin. North Am. 11: 593–631, 1973.
20. Sandler, C.M., and Toombs, B.D.: Computed tomographic evaluation of blunt renal injuries. Radiology 141: 461–466, 1981.
21. Schaner, E.G., Balow, J.E., and Doppman, J.L.: Computed tomography in the diagnosis of subcapsular and perirenal hematoma. A.J.R. 129: 83–88, 1977.
22. Young, L.W., Wood, B.P., and Linke, C.A.: Renal injury from blunt trauma in childhood. Radiological evaluation and review. Ann. Radiol. 18: 359–376, 1975.

Diaphragm

1. Ball, T., McCrory, R., Smith, J.O., and Clements, J.L., Jr.: Traumatic diaphragmatic hernia: errors in diagnosis. A.J.R. 138: 633–637, 1982.
2. Burrell, M., Toffler, R., and Lowman, R.: Blunt trauma to the abdomen and gastrointestinal tract. Radiol. Clin. North Am. 11: 561–578, 1973.
3. Carter, B.N., Giuseffi, J., and Felson, B.: Traumatic diaphragmatic hernia. A.J.R. 69: 56–72, 1951.
4. Ehrensperger, J., and Genton, N.: Rupture of the diaphragm in the child with multiple injuries. Helv. Chir. Acta 44: 109–110, 1977.
5. Fataar, S., and Schulman, A.: Diagnosis of diaphragmatic tears. Br. J. Radiol. 52: 375–381, 1979.
6. Minagi, H. Brody, W.R., and Laing, F.C.: The variable roentgen appearance of traumatic diaphragmatic hernia. J. Can. Assoc. Radiol. 28: 124–128, 1977.

7. Perlman, S.J., Rogers, L.F., Mintzer, R.A., and Mueller, C.F.: Abnormal course of nasogastric tube in traumatic rupture of left hemidiaphragm. A.J.R. 142: 85–87, 1984.
8. Sharma, L.K., Kennedy, R.F., and Heneghan, W.D.: Rupture of the diaphragm resulting from blunt trauma in children. Can. J. Surg. 20: 553–556, 1977.

Battered Child Syndrome

1. Bonviovi, J.J., and Logosso, R.D.: Pancreatic pseudocyst occurring in the battered child syndrome. J. Pediatr. Surg. 4: 220–226, 1969.
2. Fournemont, E.: Traumatic mesenteric avulsion: case report of presumed battered child. Ann. Radiol. 20: 517–521, 1977.
3. Goluboff, N., Cram, R., Ramgotra, B., Singh, A., and Wilkinson, G.W.: Polyarthritis and bone lesions complicating traumatic pancreatitis in two children. Can. Med. Assoc. J. 118: 924–928, 1978.
4. Gornall, P., Ahmed, A.J., and Cohen, S.J.: Intra-abdominal injuries in the battered baby syndrome. Arch. Dis. Child. 47: 211–214, 1972.
5. Keating, J.P., Shackelford, G.D., Shackelford, P.G., and Ternbert, J.L.: Pancreatitis and osteolytic lesions. J. Pediatr. 81: 350–353, 1972.
6. Kleinman, P.K., Raptopoulos, V.D., and Brill, P.W.: Occult nonskeletal trauma in the battered child syndrome. Radiology 141: 393–396, 1981.
7. Pena, S.D.J., and Medovy, H.: Child abuse and traumatic pseudocyst of the pancreas. J. Pediatr. 83: 1026–1028, 1973.
8. Slovis, T.L., Berdon, W.E., Haller, J.O., Baker, D.H., and Rosen, L.: Pancreatitis and the battered child syndrome. Report of 2 cases with skeletal involvement. A.J.R. 125: 456–461, 1975.

INGESTED AND INSERTED FOREIGN BODIES AND MATERIALS

Corrosive Fluid Ingestion. The most frequently ingested corrosive fluid is lye (sodium hydroxide). Lye results in deep, full thickness thermal burn causing coagulation necrosis of the entire wall of the hypopharynx and/or esophagus (1, 2, 4, 5, 7, 10). With such extensive tissue necrosis, perforation is not uncommon, and in this regard, the most devastating corrosives are the highly concentrated liquid corrosives, some of which also contain potassium hydroxide. These substances produce the severest of burns (2, 7, 10), and because of their high specific gravity and slickness can pass to the stomach with great rapidity. This being the case, it is not uncommon to have the entire esophagus involved, and in addition, to have associated gastric burns. In those cases where granular or pellet corrosives are ingested, focal, upper third esophageal burns are more common.

Hypopharyngeal burns usually are detected clinically and on lateral views of the neck, obliteration of the hypopharynx due to thickening of the pharyngeal soft tissues can be seen. In some cases, lye may spill over onto the vocal cords and produce edema of these structures (see Fig. 2.15). On chest films, one may note a distended (paralyzed) air-filled esophagus (4, 10), or if acute esophageal perforation occurs, mediastinal widening, with or without associated pneumomediastinum, pneumopericardium, or pneumatosis of the esophagus (Fig. 3.126). In other cases, tracheoesophageal fistulas (1) or communications to the pericardial sac can be seen (Fig. 3.126). In those patients with gastric burns, air-filled gastric bullae may be seen on plain films of the abdomen (8). This manifestation is associated with the more severe alkali burns to the stomach, and probably results from gastric air leaking into the wall of the stomach through damaged mucosa.

Other corrosive fluids ingested include ammonium hydroxide and a variety of acids. These substances, however, unlike sodium and potassium hydroxide, usually do not produce a deep thermal burn to the esophagus; their damage is more superficial. In addition, because acids induce less esophageal and hypopharyngeal muscle spasm than does lye, the child is able to drink more, and because of this, gastric burns are more common (6, 11, 12). This is especially true of substances such as sulfuric acid which possess a greater degree of slickness and a higher specific gravity. Often the end result in pyloric scarring and stenosis (6, 12).

Other, less common caustic agent burns to the esophagus are those sustained from the ingestion of Clinitest tablets (3), and more recently, alkaline disk batteries (9, 13). The latter, when impacted for prolonged periods of time, can lead to mucosal ulceration from sheer mechanical erosion, but it also has been detemined that in some of these cases hydroxides within the battery are readily liberated into the esophagus and cause focal caustic burns. Interestingly enough, if these batteries pass into the stomach and distal gastrointestinal tract, little, if any, problem arises (9, 13).

The performance of a contrast study of the esophagus is of debatable value if the acute phase of a corrosive fluid ingestion problem. However, if perforation is suspected, a water-soluble material can be utilized to demonstrate the site of the leak. If no perforation is present, the contrast study

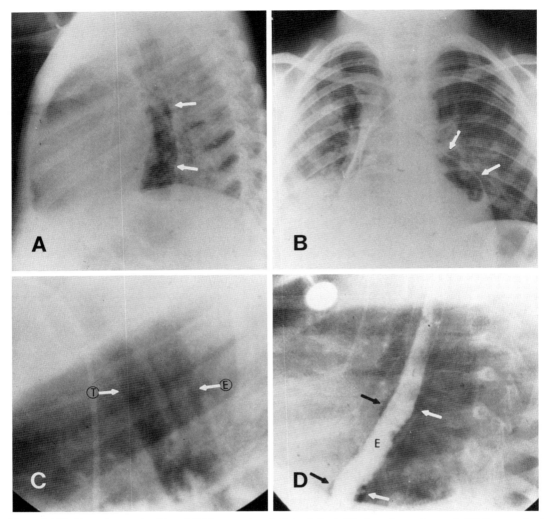

Figure 3.126. *Corrosive esophagitis.* (*A*) Note paralyzed, distended, air-filled esophagus (*arrows*). (*B*) Same patient later on with development of pneumopericardium (*arrows*). Also note that the mediastinum is widened, and that numerous infiltrates, secondary to aspiration are present. (*C*) Preliminary barium swallow film demonstrates the trachea (*T*), and dilated, air-filled esophagus (*E*) (*arrows*). The central, longitudinal density in the esophagus actually is the esophageal mucosa, and the air around it is due to pneumotosis of the esophagus. (*D*) Subsequent barium swallow demonstrates the esophageal lumen (*E*), and the presence of pneumatosis of the esophagus (*arrows*). Some contrast material is in the trachea secondary to aspiration.

of the esophagus shows little more than intense spasm, and in the more severe cases, evidence of mucosal ulceration. After a week or 10 days, the barium swallow can identify potential sites of stricture, for these sites will appear narrow, stiff, and aperistaltic.

REFERENCES

1. Amoury, R.A., Hrabovsky, E.E., Leonidas, J.C., and Holder, T.M.: Tracheoesophageal fistula after lye ingestion. J. Pediatr. Surg. 10: 273–276, 1975.
2. Ashcraft, K.W., and Padula, R.T.: The effect of dilute corrosives on the esophagus. Pediatrics 53: 226–232, 1974.
3. Burrington, J.D.: Clinitest burns of the esophagus. Ann. Thorac. Surg. 20: 400–404, 1975.
4. Franken, E.A., Jr.: Caustic damage of the gastrointestinal tract: roentgen features. A.J.R. 118: 77–85, 1973.
5. Haller, J.A., Jr., Andrews, H.G., White, J.J., Tamer, M.A., and Cleveland, W.W.: Pathophysiology and management of acute corrosive burns of the esophagus: results of treatment in 285 children. J. Pediatr. Surg. 6: 578–584, 1971.
6. Hognestad, J., and Ruud-Hansen, Th. W.: Stenosis of the gastric antrum after sulphric acid ingestion. Z. Kinderchir. 21: 52–55, 1977.
7. Leape, L.L., Ashcraft, K.W., Scarpelli, D.G., et al.: Hazard to health-liquid lye. N. Engl. J. Med. 284: 578–581, 1971.
8. Levitt, R., Stanley, R.J., and Wise, L.: Gastric bullae: an

early roentgen finding in corrosive gastritis following alkali ingestion. Radiology 115: 597–598, 1975.

9. Litovitz, T.V.: Button battery ingestions. A review of 56 cases. J.A.M.A. 249: 2495–2500, 1983.
10. Martel, W.: Radiologic features of esophagogastritis secondary to extremely caustic agents. Radiology 103: 31–36, 1972.
11. Muhletaler, C.A., Gerlock, A.J., Jr., deSoto, L., and Halter, S.A.: Acid corrosive esophagitis: Radiographic findings. A.J.R. 134: 1137–1140, 1980.
12. Pinna, C.D.: Pyloric stenosis from acid burn in a six-year-old girl. Riv. Chir. Pediatr. 9: 384–395, 1967.
13. Votteler, T.P., Nash, J.C., and Rutledge, J.C.: The hazard of ingested alkaline disk batteries in children. J.A.M.A. 249: 2504–2506, 1983.

Ingested Foreign Bodies. Hypopharyngeal foreign bodies have been discussed in Chapter 2, and the discussion of ingested foreign bodies in this section is confined to esophageal, gastric, and intestinal foreign bodies. If such a foreign body is radiolucent, it will not be detected roentgenographically unless secondary signs of inflammation or perforation are present. Most recently, this has become a problem with aluminum pop-top tabs from soft drink cans (5, 13, 16, 17), but it also is a problem with aluminum coins (11), and a wide variety of plastic objects (Fig. 3.127). When one is dealing with such a foreign body, it is worthwhile to remember that xeroradiography can be helpful. Opaque foreign bodies, on the other hand, are readily

detected roentgenographically (Fig. 3.128), and because of this a roentgenographic survey of the neck, chest, and abdomen is in order (1). This is especially true in infants and young children, for unlike the older child, they cannot tell the physician exactly where they think the foreign body has lodged.

Most round or oval foreign bodies pass down the esophagus, into the stomach, and through the intestine to cause little if any problem (1, 23). On the other hand, larger foreign bodies, and those of irregular shape may well become impacted somewhere along the course of the GI tract. In the esophagus, foreign bodies commonly lodge at the level of the: (a) cricopharyngeal muscle, (b) aortic knob, or (c) gastroesophageal junction (Fig. 3.129). The least common site is at the gastroesophageal junction. If these foreign bodies are radiopaque, they are not difficult to detect, but if they are radiolucent, they will go undetected until a barium swallow is obtained (Fig. 3.130). In this regard, many of these children have underlying esophageal strictures secondary to old tracheoesophageal fistula repairs, hiatus hernia problems, or lye burns.

Animal bones impacted in the hypophar-

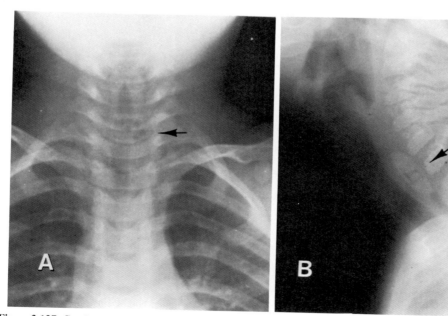

Figure 3.127. *Semiopaque button in upper esophagus.* (*A*) Note the four radiolucent holes in the button (*arrows*), lodged in the upper esophagus. (*B*) Lateral view demonstrates the button (*arrow*) and a mild degree of anterior displacement and compression of the trachea in front of it.

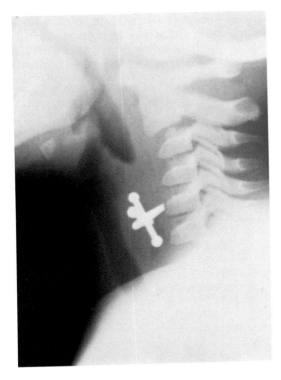

Figure 3.128. *Opaque foreign body (jack) in upper esophagus.* Note the readily visible opaque jack in the upper esophagus of this infant.

ynx or esophagus are not as common in children as in adults. However, they still are encountered, and in this regard, it should be noted that fishbones usually are difficult to visualize (6), although interestingly enough most recently have been shown to be visible roentgenographically (Table 3.1). Chicken and turkey bones, on the other hand, often contain enough calcium to allow them to be visible roentgenographically (Fig. 3.131). In those cases where a foreign body such as a fishbone is not visible, but suspected, one may administer a cotton ball pledget soaked with barium to the patient. In many of these cases, the pledget becomes impaled on the bone, and thus aids in its localization. However, this maneuver does not work as often as one would first believe.

The misinterpretation of normally calcified laryngeal cartilages for a foreign body such as a chicken or fishbone is not a great problem in childhood. Apart from the hyoid bone, which ossifies early, about the only calcified cartilage presenting such a problem is the calcified cartilage triticea (Fig. 3.132). In teenagers and adults, of course, laryngeal calcifications are much more common, and the problem of differentiating them from an opaque foreign body is much greater.

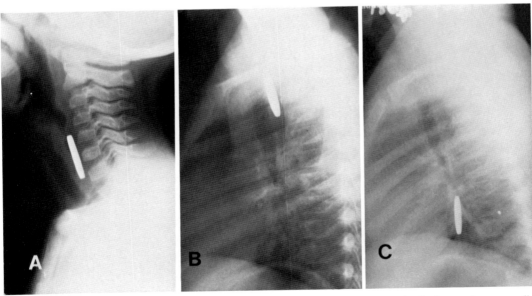

Figure 3.129. *Typical sites of foreign body lodgement in the esophagus.* Foreign bodies in the esophagus usually ledge at one of the following sites: (*A*) just above the level of the cricopharyngeal muscle; (*B*) just above the level of the aortic knob; (*C*) just above the gastroesophageal junction.

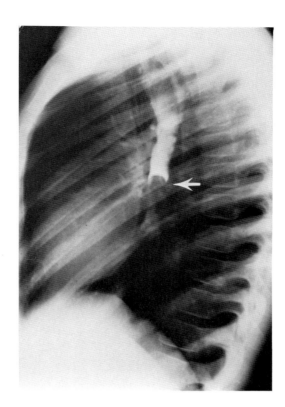

Figure 3.130. *Radiolucent foreign body in the esophagus.* Note the typical curvilinear filling defect (*arrow*) produced by a nonopaque foreign body in this barium-filled esophagus. This patient had underlying esophageal stenosis secondary to an old tracheoesophageal fistula repair. The obstructing foreign body was a kernel of corn.

Table 3.1. *Radiopacity of Bones of Various Fish Species[a]*

Fish	No. Bones X-rayed	Definitely Diagnostic	Visible but Poorly Defined	Invisible
Bass	2	2		
Bluefish	4	3		1
Butterfish	3			3
Codfish	5	5		
Flounder	3	3		
Fluke	2	2		
Fresh salmon	4	4		
Gray sole	2	2		
Haddock	2	2		
Halibut	4	4		
Mackerel	4	1		3
Pompano	5		2	3
Porgie	3	3		
Red snapper	2	2		
Sea bass	2	2		
Smelt	1	1		
Smoked salmon	2	2		
Striped bass	2	2		
Trout	3		2	1
White perch	2	2		
Yellow pike	3	3		

[a] Reproduced from: Bachman, A. L.: Radiology of fish foreign bodies in the hypopharynx and cervical esophagus, Mt. Sinai J. Med. 48: 212-220, 1981 (2).

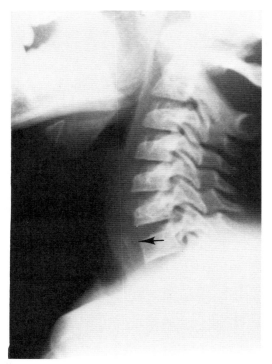

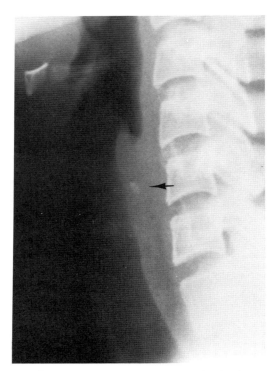

Figure 3.131. *Chicken bone in upper esophagus.* Note faint calcification in a chicken bone (*arrow*) lodged in the upper esophagus of this patient.

Figure 3.132. *Pseudoforeign body.* Calcification in the cartilage triticea (*arrow*) often is mistaken for an opaque foreign body.

In the past, removal of coins and other foreign bodies from the esophagus generally has been acomplished with ordinary esophagoscopy. More recently, however, these foreign bodies have been removed with the aid of flexible fiberoptic panendoscopes (9), and with the use of a Foley catheter (7, 8, 21, 22, 25). When the Foley catheter is utilized, the deflated bulb of the cathether is passed beyond the site of the foreign body, and then the bulb is inflated under fluoroscopic control. Opaque aqueous contrast material is utilized to distend the bulb so that it is visible roentgenographically. After inflation of the bulb, the catheter is withdrawn, and the foreign body is retrieved. One must be careful that the patient does not reswallow or inhale the foreign body, and of course, this procedure should be restricted to foreign bodies of recent impaction and to those which are not pointed or impaled in the esophageal wall (4). In addition, the procedure is not always easy to accomplish first time around, and repeated attempts may be required. Also one should make sure the

mouth is held open with a wrapped tongue depressor.

Those foreign bodies which pass into the stomach can pose a problem in terms of follow-up roentgenograms. However, if the foreign body is small or of such a shape that almost surely it should pass uneventfully, follow-up roentgenograms are not required. On the other hand, should such a foreign body not pass with normal stooling, one might obtain a follow-up roentgenogram on the slight possibility that one might be dealing with an underlying, previously unsuspected, obstructing lesion such as gastric or duodenal web or diverticulum (15, 18) (Fig. 3.133). Obviously, this is a more remote consideration, but still one to be thought of under the proper circumstances.

The problem is quite different with the pointed, jagged, or long foreign body, for impaction of this type of foreign body is more common. Follow-up roentgenograms are most important in these cases, and if the foreign body fails to make progress, or even more significantly, if it does not change its

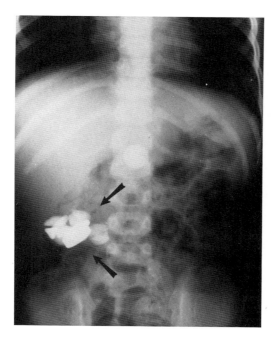

Figure 3.133. *Foreign bodies trapped in duodenal web.* Note numerous opaque foreign bodies on the right (*arrows*). These changed little in position from view to view, and ultimately were demonstrated to be trapped behind a duodenal web. There also is a foreign body in the gastric antrum.

position at all, one should suspect impaction (Fig. 3.134). Another time when a foreign body may cease to make progress is when it lodges in the appendix. In some of these cases, no symptoms arise (14), but in others acute appendicitis eventually may develop.

Finally, it should be noted that ***upper esophageal foreign bodies can present with stridor or pneumonia,*** and little in the way of dysphagia (3, 10, 12, 13, 19, 20, 24, 26–28). Many of these patients are young infants, and they seem to adapt to the esophageal obstruction with deceptive ease. This they do primarily by changing their diet to a more acceptable liquid one. Such a change often is so subtle that it eludes the parent and physician, and overall the presenting symptoms will focus on the respiratory tract (i.e., stridor, wheezing, cough, etc.). It is only with the knowledge that this can occur, and adequate examination of the lateral neck, chest, and esophagus, that many of these foreign bodies are finally discovered (Fig. 3.135).

It is interesting that in these patients periesophageal edema develops so quickly. It is this edema which produces compression of the adjacent trachea, and often is still present

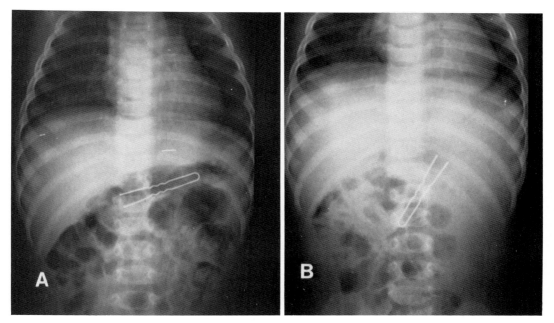

Figure 3.134. *Hairpin in duodenum.* (*A*) Early film showing hairpin in the stomach. (*B*) Later film showing complete change in position of the pin which thereafter remained lodged at this site. At laparotomy this turned out to be the duodenal-jejunal junction.

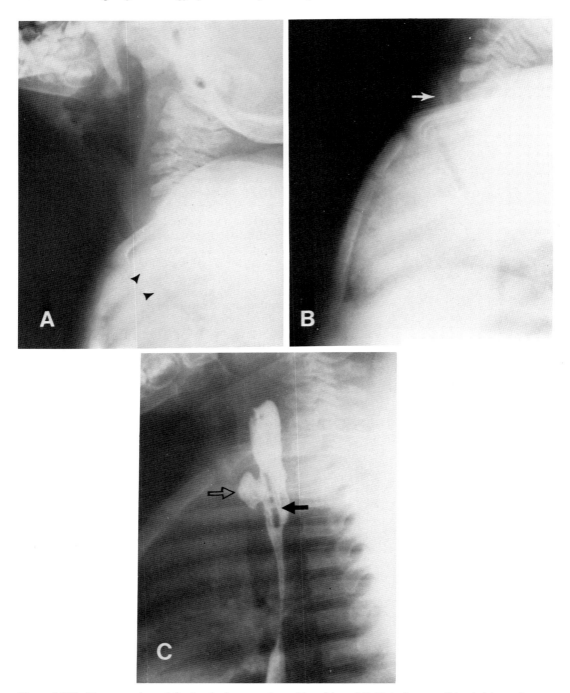

Figure 3.135. *Upper esophageal foreign body presenting with stridor.* (*A*) Note the overdistended hypopharynx and upper trachea in this young infant presenting with stridor. Also note that the trachea below the level of the clavicles is narrowed (*arrows*). (*B*) With the neck fully extended, a semiopaque foreign body is demonstrated in the upper esophagus (*arrow*). The site of this foreign body corresponds to the site of tracheal narrowing noted in (*A*) (*C*) Barium swallow demonstrates the foreign body (*solid arrow*) in the esophagus, and the deep anterior ulcer which it produced (*open arrow*). It is easy to see why this portion of the trachea appeared narrowed on the other studies. (Reprinted with permission from Smith, P.C., Swischuk, L.E., and Fagan, C.J.: An elusive and often unsuspected cause of stridor or pneumonia (the esophageal foreign body), A.J.R. 122: 80–89, 1974).

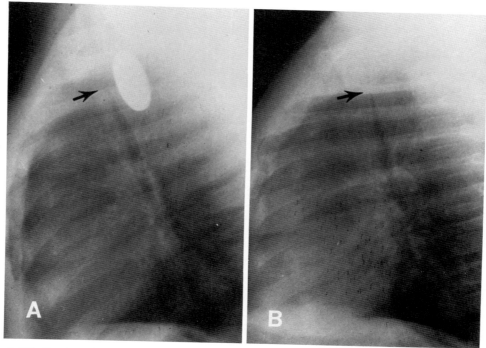

Figure 3.136. *Esophageal foreign body with tracheal compression.* (*A*) Note the coin in the esophagus (*arrow*). Also note that the trachea, just adjacent to it is narrowed. (*B*) After removal of the coin, the trachea still is narrowed (*arrow*).

after the foreign body has been removed (Fig. 3.136).

REFERENCES

1. Alexander, W.J., Kadish, J.A., and Dunbar, J.S.: Ingested foreign bodies in children. In *Progress in Pediatric Radiology*, pp. 256–285. Year Book, Chicago, 1969.
2. Bachman, A.L.: Radiology of fish foreign bodies in the hypopharynx and cervical esophagus. Mt. Sinai J. Med. 48: 212–220, 1981.
3. Beer, S., Avidan, G., Viure, E., and Starinsky, R.: A foreign body in the oesophagus as a cause of respiratory distress. Pediatr. Radiol. 12: 41–42, 1982.
4. Berdon, W.E.: Editorial comment—Foley catheter removal of blunt esophageal foreign bodies. Experience with 100 consecutive children. Pediatr. Radiol. 13: 119, 1983.
5. Burrington, J.D.: Aluminum pop-tops: a hazard to child health. J.A.M.A. 235: 2614–2617, 1976.
6. Campbell, D.R., Brown, S.J., and Manchester, J.A.: An evaluation of the radio-opacity of various ingested foreign bodies in the pharynx and esophagus. J. Can. Assoc. Radiol. 19: 183–186, 1968.
7. Campbell, J.B., Quattromani, F.L., and Foley, L.C.: Foley catheter removal of blunt esophageal foreign bodies. Experience with 100 consecutive children. Pediatr. Radiol. 13: 116–119, 1983.
8. Carlson, D.H.: Removal of coins in the esophagus using a Foley catheter. Pediatrics 50: 475–476, 1972.
9. Christie, D.L., and Ament, M.E.: Removal of foreign bodies from esophagus and stomach with flexible fiberoptic panendoscopes. Pediatrics 57: 931–934, 1976.
10. Glass, W.M., and Goodman, M.: Unsuspected foreign bodies in the young child's esophagus presenting with respiratory symptoms. Laryngoscope 76: 605, 1966.
11. Heller, R.M., Reichelderfer, T.E., Dorst, J.P., and Oh, K.S.: The problem with replacement of copper pennies by aluminum pennies. Pediatrics 54: 684–688, 1974.
12. Humphry, A., and Holland, W.G.: Unsuspected esophageal foreign bodies. J. Can. Assoc. Radiol. 32: 17–20, 1981.
13. Jeffers, R.G., Weir, M.R., Wehunt, W.D., and Carter, S.C.: Pull-tab the foreign body sleeper. J. Pediatr. 92: 1023–1024, 1978.
14. Kassner, E.G., Mutchler, R.W., Jr., Klotz, D.H., Jr., and Rose, J.S.: Uncomplicated foreign bodies of the appendix in children: radiologic observations. J. Pediatr. Surg. 9: 207–277, 1974.
15. Kassner, E.G., Rose, J.S., Kottmeier, P.K., Schneider, M., and Gallow, G.M.: Retention of a small foreign object in the stomach and duodenum. A sign of partial obstruction caused by duodenal anomalies. Radiology 114: 683–686, 1975.
16. Keating, J.P., Weldon, C.S., Connors, J.P., and McAlister, W.H.: The "pop-top" tab. J. Pediatr. 86: 111–112, 1975.
17. Levick, R.K., Spitz, L., and Robinson, A.: The "invisible" can top. Br. J. Radiol. 50: 596, 1977.
18. Mandell, G.A., Rosenberg, H.K., and Schnaufer, L.: Prolonged retention of foreign bodies in the stomach. Pediatrics 60: 460–462, 1977.
19. Naftzger, J.B., and Gittens, T.R.: Foreign bodies in esophagus with respiratory symptoms complicating diagnosis. Laryngoscope 36: 370–376, 1926.
20. Newman, D.E.: The radiolucent esophageal foreign body: an often forgotten cause of respiratory symptoms. J. Pediatr. 92: 60–63, 1978.
21. Nixon, G.W.: Foley catheter method of esophageal foreign body removal: extension of applications. A.J.R. 132: 441–442, 1979.
22. Ong, T.H.: Removal of blunt oesophageal foreign bodies in children using a foley catheter. Aust. Paediatr. J. 18: 60–62, 1982.

23. Pellerin, D., Fortier-Baeulieu, M., and Gueguen, J.: The fate of swallowed foreign bodies. Experience of 1250 instances of sub-diaphragmatic foreign bodies in children. In *Progress in Pediatric Radiology*, H.J. Kaufman (ed.), pp. 286–302. Year Book, Chicago, 1969.
24. Schidlow, D.V., Palmer, J., Balsara, R.K., Trutz, M.G., and Williams, J.L.: Chronic stridor and anterior cervical "mass" secondary to an esophageal foreign body. Am. J. Dis. Child. 135: 869–870, 1981.
25. Shackelford, G.D., McAlister, W.H., and Robertson, C.L.: The use of a Foley catheter for removal of blunt esophageal foreign bodies from children. Radiology 105: 455–456, 1972.
26. Smith, P.C., Swischuk, L.E., and Fagan, C.J.: An elusive and often unsuspected cause of stridor or pneumonia (the esophageal foreign body). A.J.R. 122: 80–89, 1974.
27. Spitz, L., and Hirsig, J.: Prolonged foreign body impaction in the oesophagus. Arch. Dis. Child. 57: 551–553, 1982.
28. Tauscher, J.W.: Esophageal foreign body: an uncommon cause of stridor. Pediatrics 61: 657–658, 1978.

Miscellaneous Ingested Foreign Bodies and Substances. Pills or capsules are usually not identified unless they contain substances such as iron or calcium (1, 6, 7), and in such cases they may well be seen on abdominal films (Fig. 3.137). This is important, for *iron intoxication* is not uncommon in children, and can result in extensive gastrointestinal damage with bleeding, necrosis, and perforation (1, 4–7). *Pica in childhood* most often is accounted for by the eating of dirt or clay (1, 3). In these children, flecks of opaque material can be seen scattered throughout the GI tract, while in other cases actual pebbles may be noted (Fig. 3.138). Of course, fragments of *led paint* also can be seen on roentgenograms, and occasionally, such infants will present in the emergency room with acute lead intoxication. More recently, acute lead intoxication has been seen with a North American Indian medicine known as Azarcon, utilized for a variety of illnesses (2).

Another opaque substance which is sometimes encountered in the emergency room setting is a bismuth-containing antacid. Such medications frequently are administered for gastroenteritis and commonly show up as irregular opacities in the intestines of these children (Fig. 3.139). Other foreign materials include dental fillings, teeth, mercury, plaster, erasers, modeling clay, etc. (1).

REFERENCES

1. Alexander, W.J., Kadish, J.A., and Dunbar, J.S.: Ingested foreign bodies in children. In *Progress in Pediatric Radiology*, H.J. Kaufmann (ed.) pp. 256–285. Year Book, Chicago, 1969.
2. Bose, A., Vashistha, K., and O'Loughlin, B.J., Azarcon por Empacho: another cause of lead toxicity. Pediatrics 72: 106–108, 1983.
3. Clayton, R.S., and Goodman, P.H.: Roentgenographic diagnosis of geophagia (dirt eating). A.J.R. 73: 203, 1955.
4. Gleason, W.A., Jr., de Mello, D.E., de Castro, F.J., and Connors, J.J.: Acute hepatic failure in severe iron poisoning. J. Pediatr. 95: 138–140, 1979.
5. Knott, L.H., and Miller, R.C.: Acute iron intoxication with intestinal infarction. J. Pediatr. Surg. 13: 720–721, 1978.
6. Smith, W.L., Franken, E.A., Jr., Grosfeld, J.L., and Ballantine, T.V.N.: Radiological quiz. Radiology 122: 192, 1977.

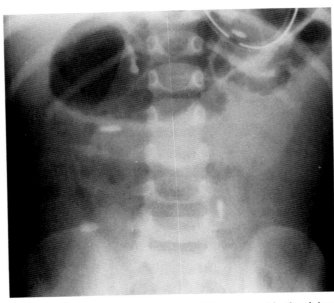

Figure 3.137. *Iron tablet ingestion.* Note numerous, opaque tablets scattered in the abdomen of this toxic infant with iron tablet ingestion.

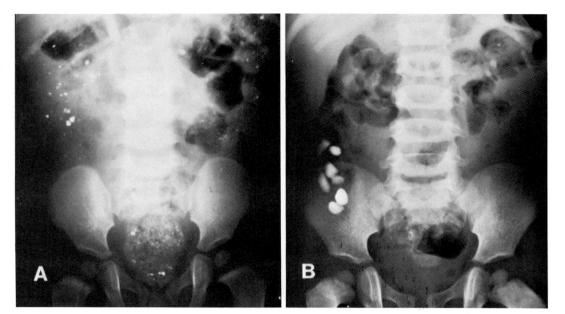

Figure 3.138. *Dirt and pebbles in the GI tract.*   (*A*) Note scattered opacities throughout the GI tract in this patient. A good many of them are mixed with fecal material in the colon. Similar findings can be seen with lead posioning, but most often the findings represent those of dirt eating. (*B*) Note pebbles in the cecum of this patient.

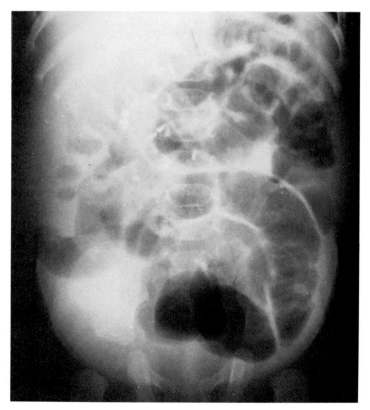

Figure 3.139. *Opacities in the GI tract in a patient with gastroenteritis.*   Note numerous opacities in the distended intestines of this infant with gastroenteritis. Such opacities are common in these patients and represent bismuth in certain antacid preparations.

7. Staple, T.W., and McAlister, W.H.: Roentgenographic visualization of iron preparation in the gastrointestinal tract. Radiology 83: 1051, 1964.

Genitourinary Foreign Bodies. Genitourinary foreign bodies (1, 2), inserted by the patient, are more common than is generally appreciated. In girls, these foreign bodies often are inserted into the vagina, and occasionally they are demonstrable on plain films (Fig. 3.140). Urinary bladder foreign bodies also can be encountered in females, but in males one more often encounters such foreign bodies in the urethra (Fig. 3.140). Patients with these foreign bodies can present with hematuria and/or urinary tract infection.

REFERENCES

1. Prasad, S., Smith, A.M., Uson, A., Melicow, M., and Lattimer, J.K.: Foreign bodies in urinary bladder. Urology 2: 258–264, 1973.
2. Swischuk, L.E.: Acute, non-traumatic, genitourinary pediatric problems. Radiol. Clin. North Am. 16: 147–157, 1978.

MISCELLANEOUS ABDOMINAL PROBLEMS

Bezoars. Bezoars (1–9) most frequently occur in the stomach, but in some cases also may be seen in the small bowel. Most likely

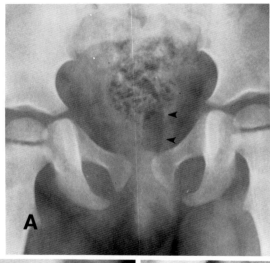

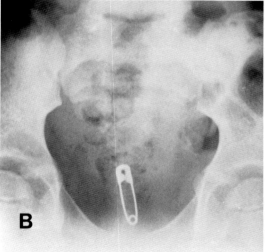

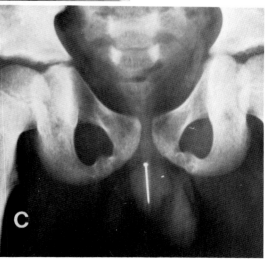

Figure 3.140. *Genitourinary foreign bodies.* (*A*) Note the radiolucent (plastic pen cap) foreign body (*arrows*) in the vagina of this girl. (*B*) Closed safety pin in the bladder of another girl. (*C*) Straight pin in the urethra of a young boy.

these latter instances represent cases wherein portions of the gastric bezoar break off and pass into the small intestine. Once a bezoar enters the small bowel, small bowel obstruction, with or without intussusception (3) may occur (Fig. 3.141).

The most common bezoar in childhood is a trichobezoar resulting from ingestion of hair, usually from the patient's own head. While usually considered to be the result of psychiatric difficulties, pica due to iron deficiency has also been shown to be a potential contributing factor (6). Next most common is a phytobezoar; that is, except for the neonatal period where lactobezoars are becoming more common (2, 3, 5, 7). In these instances, a dense milk coagulum results when powdered milk is mixed with inadequate amounts of water. It is especially likely to occur in premature infants. Bezoars secondary to persimmon seed ingestion are not as common in childhood as in adulthood. In this type of bezoar, the protein material of the persimmon, after being acted upon by gastric acid, is converted to a shellac-like substance.

Plain film findings of a gastric bezoar consist of amorphous, granular, or at times whirlpool-like configurations of solid and gaseous material in the stomach (Fig. 3.141*A*). In other instances, the bezoar is so compact that a layer of air is seen to surround it (Fig. 3.141*B*). Barium studies will confirm the presence of a bezoar and the presence of a gastric ulcer if such a complication is present. On plain films, bezoars must be differentiated from food in the stomach (see Fig. 3.156).

REFERENCES

1. DeBackey, M., and Ochsner, A.: Bezoars and concretions. Surgery 5: 132–160, 1939.
2. Grosfeld, J.L., Schreiner, R.L., Franken, E.A., Lemons, J.A., Ballantine, T.V.N., Weber, T.R., and Gresham, E.L.: The changing pattern of gastrointestinal bezoars in infants and children. Surgery 88: 425–432, 1980.
3. Harris, V.J., and Hanley, G.: Unusual features and complications of bezoars in children. A.J.R. 123: 742–745, 1975.
4. Levkoff, A.H., Gadsden, R.H., Hennigar, G.R., and Webb, C.M.: Lactobezoar and gastric perforation in a neonate. J. Pediatr. 77: 875–877, 1970.
5. Majd, M., and LoPresti, J.M.: Lactobezoar. A.J.R. 116: 575–576, 1972.
6. McGehee, F.T., Jr., and Buchanan, G.R.: Trichophagia and trichobezoar: etiologic role of iron deficiency. J. Pediatr. 97: 946–948, 1980.
7. Wexler, H.A., and Poole, C.A.: Lactobezoar, a complication of overconcentrated mild formula. J. Pediatr. Surg. 11: 261–262, 1976.
8. Wholey, M.H., Zikria, E.A., and Mansoor, M.: Instrument for the removal of a gastric bezoar. Acta Radiol. [Diagn.] (Stockh.) 15: 333–336, 1974.
9. Wolf, R.S., and Bruce, J.: Gastrotomy for lactobezoar in a newborn infant. J. Pediatr. 54: 811–812, 1959.

Abdominal Ascariasis. GI ascariasis may be encountered as an incidental finding, but in some cases intestinal obstruction, or even intestinal perforation can occur (1, 7). In addition, during the early phase of the infection, larvae can pass through the lymphatic system or portal system to the right side of the heart and be filtered out in the lungs causing nonspecific infiltrates. Respiratory distress may be the presenting symptom in these patients (7).

On abdominal roentgenograms (2, 4, 6, 7) the adult Ascaris worm can be seen as a linear or circular filling defect in a loop of dilated bowel, but more commonly infestation is massive and a whirlpool, bezoar-like mass of linear, opaque and radiolucent shadows is seen (Fig. 3.142). If barium is administered the worms will ingest the barium and can be identified by the linear collections of barium in their GI tracts. Ascaris infection of the biliary system also can occur, but is relatively rare (4, 7). Interestingly enough, however, this type of ascaris infection is readily demonstrable with ultrasound (3, 5). The worm, in the dilated bile ducts is echogenic and produces a bull's-eye configuration (Fig. 3.143).

REFERENCES

1. Bar-Maor, J.A., deCarvalho, J.L.A.F., and Chappell, J.: Gastrografin treatment of intestinal obstruction due to Ascaris lumbricoides. J Pediatr. Surg. 19: 174–176, 1984.
2. Bean, W.J.: Recognition of ascariasis by routine chest or abdomen roentgenograms. A.J.R. 94: 379–384, 1965.
3. Cerri, G.G., Leite, G.J., Simoes, J.B., DaRocha, D.J.C., Albuquerque, F.P., Machado, M.C.C., and Magalhaes, A.: Ultrasonographic evaluation of ascaris in the biliary tract. Radiology 146: 753–754, 1983.
4. Cremin, B.J., and Fisher, R.M.: Biliary ascariasis in children. A.J.R. 126: 352–357, 1976.
5. Cremin, B.J.: Ultrasonographic diagnosis of biliary ascariasis: "a bull's eye in the triple O." Br. J. Radiol. 55: 683–684, 1982.
6. Isaacs, I.: Roentgenographic demonstration of intestinal ascariasis in children without using barium. A.J.R. 76: 558–561, 1956.
7. Litt, R.E., Altman, D.H., and Greenberg, L.A.: Radiologic evaluation of the common parasitic diseases of childhood. South. Med. J. 62: 773–778, 1969.

Abdominal Masses, Tumors, and Pseudotumors. Abdominal masses in the emergency setting are not a particularly common problem. However, occasionally, with hemorrhage into a tumor, trauma to a hydronephrotic kidney, etc., acute abdominal pain

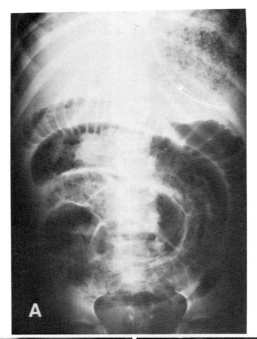

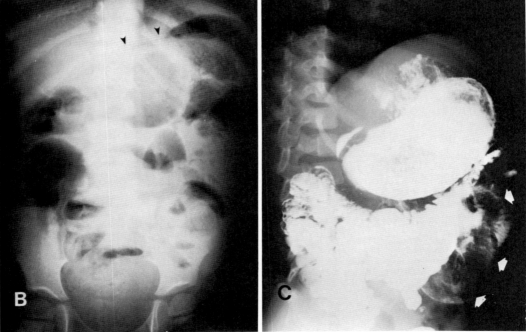

Figure 3.141. *Bezoars.* (*A*) Note the granular appearance of a bezoar in the stomach (*left upper quandrant*). Also note the presence of a classic small bowel obstruction and numerous granular, linear and curvilinear densities within the small bowel. This patient had a large bezoar, part of which had become detached to produce a small bowel obstruction. (*B*) Another bezoar somewhat less well defined. However, note the thin rim of air trapped between it and the gastric wall (*arrows*). (*C*) Subsequent GI series demonstrates the large bezoar in the stomach, but in addition, note that a portion of it has become detached and is present in the distal small bowel (*arrows*). It was causing a moderate degree of obstruction.

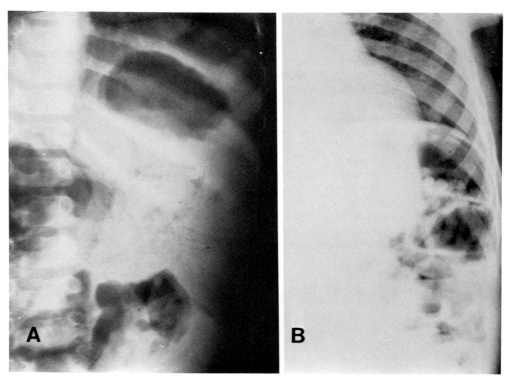

Figure 3.142. *Abdominal ascariasis.*   (*A*) Note the whirlpool-like effect of worms in the intestines on the left side of the abdomen. (*B*) Another patient demonstrating worms visualized in air-filled loops of intestine.

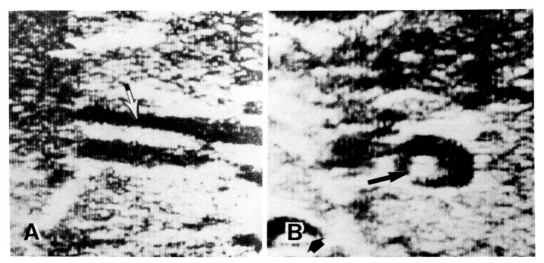

Figure 3.143. *Biliary ascaris; ultrasonographic findings.*   (*A*) Longitudinal section demonstrating dilated common bile duct and worm in the center (*arrow*). (*B*) Cross-section demonstrating the bull's-eye sign with the echogenic worms in the center (*arrows*) of the dilated bile duct. (From Cerri, G.G., Leite, G.J., Simoes, J.B., DaRocha, D.J.C., Albuquerque, F.P., Machado, M.C.C. and Magalhaes, A.: Ultrasonographic evaluation of ascaris in the biliary tract, Radiology 146, 753–754, 1983).

may be the presenting problem and then ultrasonography is the most rewarding screening procedure (2–4). Although certain information can be obtained from plain films, ultrasonography usually provides ready information regarding whether the lesion is solid or cystic, and its precise location (Fig. 3.144). CT body scanning also can be utilized, but ultrasound is easier to use, especially if the ultrasound unit is a portable one.

In the emergency patient, one of the most commonly encountered problems is that of a normal structure presenting as a pseudotumor on abdominal roentgenograms. These so-called pseudotumors are quite common, and among the most common are the distended urinary bladdder (see Fig. 3.1) and the fluid-filled fundus or antrum of the stomach. The fluid-filled fundus appears as a soft tissue "tumor" in the left upper quadrant, while the fluid-filled antrum will produce a similar configuration just to the left of the upper lumbar spine (1). In children, another type of pseudotumor occasionally is produced by a peculiar configuration of the stomach on upright view (Fig. 3.145). Pseudotumors anywhere in the abdomen can be seen as a result of fortuitous visualization of fluid-filled loops of normal intestine, and finally, it should be mentioned that one of the most common pseudotumors in infancy is that produced by an umbilical hernia (Fig. 3.146).

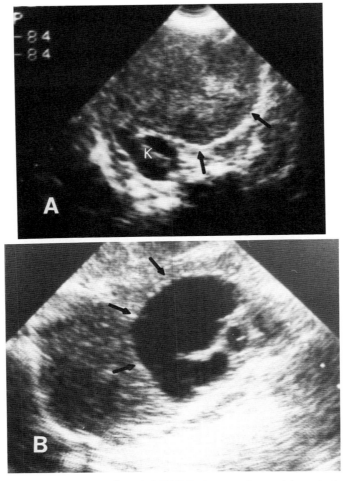

Figure 3.144. *Abdominal masses; ultrasound.* (*A*) Solid Wilm's tumor (*arrows*) in patient with abdominal pain and hematuria; compressed kidney (*K*). (*B*) Classic ureteropelvic junction obstruction (*arrows*), in patient with abdominal trauma and hematuria.

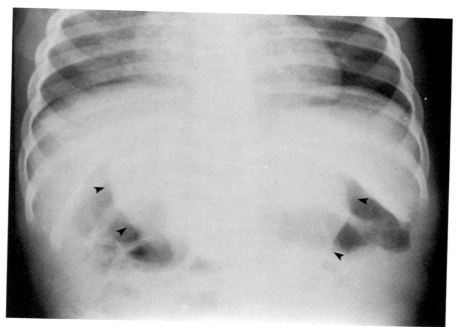

Figure 3.145. *Gastric pseudotumor.* Note the fluid-filled stomach presenting as a peculiar mid abdominal pseudotumor (*arrows*). The *arrows* on the right outline the fluid-filled antrum, while those on the left outline the fluid-filled body. This configuration almost always is seen on upright views.

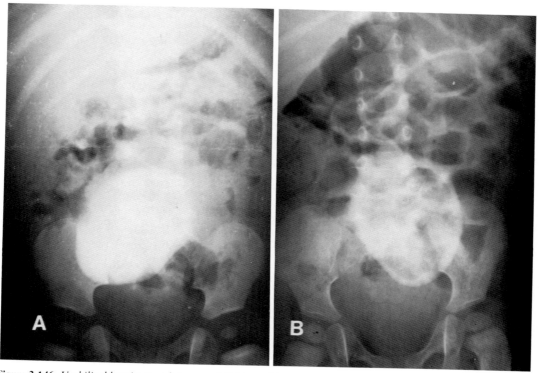

Figure 3.146. *Umbilical hernia, pseudotumor.* (*A*) Note a large opaque umbilical hernia producing a pseudotumor in the mid abdomen. (*B*) Similar appearance in another patient, but this time the umbilical hernia contains air-filled loops of intestine.

REFERENCES

1. Balthazar, E.: Right upper quadrant pseudotumor, a fluid-filled viscus. Radiology 112: 11–12, 1974.
2. Goldberg, B.B., Capitanio, M.A., and Kirkpatrick, J.A.: Ultrasonic evaluation of masses in pediatric patients. A.J.R. 116: 677–684, 1972.
3. Goldberg, B.B., Pollack, H.M., Capitanio, M.A., and Kirkpatrick, J.A.: Ultrasonography: an aid in the diagnosis of masses in pediatric patients. Pediatrics 56: 421–428, 1975.
4. Stuber, J.L., Leonidas, J.C., and Holder, T.M.: Abdominal ultrasonography in pediatrics. Am. J. Dis. Child. 129: 1096–1101, 1975.

Abdominal Wall Hematoma. Hematomas of the abdominal wall, in the rectus muscle, can present with acute abdominal pain and may be mistaken for conditions such as appendicitis or cholecystitis. In other cases, they may be mistaken for an abdominal mass. Because the abdomen often is so tense in these patients that physical examination is difficult to accomplish, ultrasonography has become the best modality with which to demonstrate these hematomas (1, 2) (Fig. 3.147).

REFERENCES

1. Benson, M.: Rectus sheath haematomas simulating pelvic pathology: the ultrasound appearances. Clin. Radiol. 33: 651–655, 1982.
2. Kaftori, J.K., Rosenberger, A., Pollack, S., and Fish, J.H.: Rectus sheath hematoma: ultrasonographic diagnosis. A.J.R. 128: 283–285, 1977.

Abdominal Calcifications. Overall, abdominal calcifications are not particularly common in childhood, but one must realize the significance of those which are seen from time to time. In this regard, one of the most common *incidental calcification* found in the abdomen of a child is that *in the adrenal gland* (5). Such calcifications usually result from a previous, but often undocumented, neonatal adrenal hemorrhage, and when seen in the older child are of no clinical significance. Characteristically, the calcification lies above the kidney and is of triangular or near triangular shape (Fig. 3.148*A*). Another innocuous calcification in the abdomen is the so-called mulberry, or popcorn type calcification of old, inflamed mesenteric or retroperitoneal lymph nodes (Fig. 3.148*B*). Old healed tuberculosis or histoplasmosis often causes round, punctate, frequently multiple, calcifications in the liver or spleen (Fig. 3.148*C*).

Urinary tract calcifications are not as common in children as in adults, but they do occur (1–3, 7, 10, 11). Although in the past such calcifications usually were considered secondary to some type of metabolic disease, it is becoming increasingly apparent that most are due to other causes including

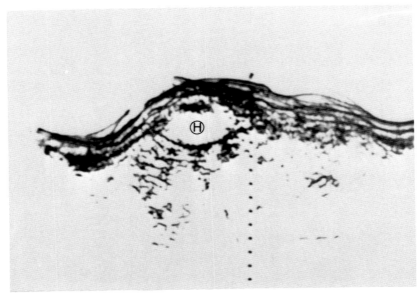

Figure 3.147. *Rectus sheath hematoma.* Ultrasonographic study demonstrating an echo-free hematoma (*H*). This is a cross-section view and the hematoma is located just below the skin. (Courtesy Charles J. Fagan, M.D.).

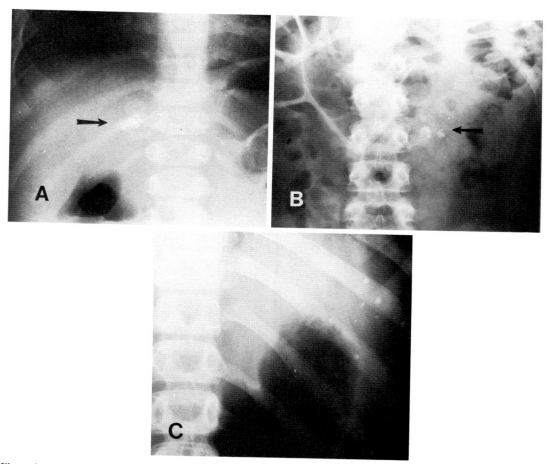

Figure 3.148. *Incidental abdominal calcification.* (*A*) Typical incidental calcification in adrenal gland (*arrow*). (*B*) Typical mulberry calcification in retroperitoneal lymph nodes (*arrow*). (*C*) Typical punctate calcification in the spleen. These calcifications often are secondary to healed histoplasmosis or tuberculosis.

infection and idiopathic (10). Bladder calculi are seen in patients with neurogenic disease and in other chronically immobilized patients. However, in the emergency patient, the urinary tract calcification of most concern is the calcified renal calculus producing *renal colic*. The findings in these patients are no different from those seen in adulthood, and an intravenous pyelogram is mandatory. This study may show decreased renal funtion, an enlarged kidney (ie., acute hydronephrosis), obstruction of the ureter, edema of the ureter around the stone, or the stone itself (Fig. 3.149). If the stone has passed, and an IVP is obtained after, one may see delayed and/or diminished opacification of the kidney (4) and its collecting

system, and even transient residual obstruction due to edema at the site of stone impaction. Ultrasonographically, one can identify renal stones and characteristically one notes dilatation of the collecting system, and then increased echogenicity with acoustical shadowing at the stone site (Fig. 3.149, *C* and *D*).

Diffuse calcifications such as those seen with renal tubular acidosis, oxalosis, and chronic glomerulonephritis, and those resulting from renal cortical and medullary necrosis are seldom encountered other than as incidental findings or in patients presenting with renal failure.

Pancreatic calcifications usually are mid-abdominal and irregular, but on the whole are uncommon in childhood. They can be seen in cystic fibrosis, pancreatitis, and in association with protein malnutrition (6, 9). They usually are stippled and frequently outline the entire pancreas. Calcification of an **_appendiceal fecalith_** is of clear-cut significance and is dealt with under the section on appendicitis. Calcification of a **_stone in a_**

Meckel's diverticulum is uncommon, but can mimic an appendiceal fecalith. **_Other_** abdominal calcifications may occur in teratomas, hemangiomatous tumors of the liver or other organs, hamartomas of the liver, and tumors of the adrenals such as neuroblastomas or adrenal cortical carcinoma. Massive calcification of a large adrenal gland

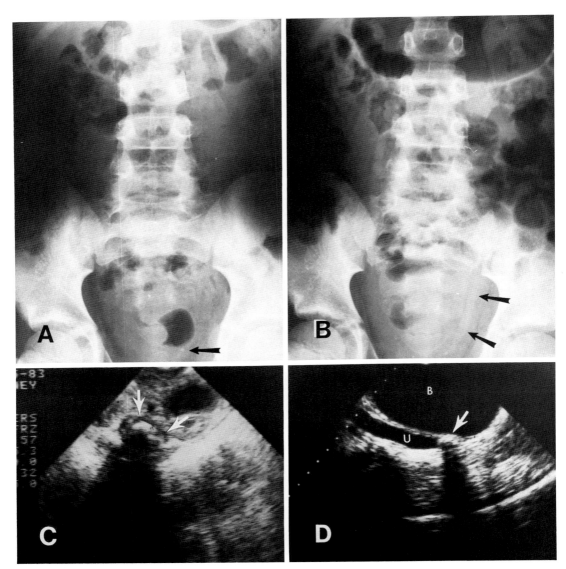

Figure 3.149. *Renal colic—calcified renal calculus.* (*A*) Note the small calcified renal calculus (*arrow*) in the pelvis of this patient who presented with renal colic. (*B*) Subsequent intravenous pyelogram demonstrates moderate dilatation of the distal ureter on the left (*arrows*). The small calcified calculus is visualized again. (*C*) *Ultrasound delineation of renal calculi.* Note echoes with distal shadowing, from multiple renal stones (*arrows*). (*D*) Note echoes, with distal shadowing, from stone impacted in distal ureter (*arrow*); dilated ureter (*U*), bladder (*B*).

is seen in Wolman's disease (8), and curvilinear or amorphous calcifications are seen with meconium peritonitis.

REFERENCES

1. Bennett, A.H., and Colodny, A.H.: Urinary tract calculi in children. J. Urol. 109: 318–320, 1973.
2. Daeschner, C.W., Singleton, E.B., and Curtis, J.C.: Urinary tract calculi and nephrocalcinosis in infants and children. J. Pediatr. 57: 721–732, 1960.
3. Ghazali, S., Barratt, T.M., and Williams, D.I.: Childhood urolithiasis in Britain. Arch. Dis. Child. 48: 291–295, 1973.
4. Hyams, B.B.: The signs of a passed ureteral stone. J. Can. Assoc. Radiol. 28: 270–273, 1977.
5. Jarvis, J.L., and Seaman, W.B.: Idiopathic adrenal calcification in infants and children. A.J.R. 82: 510–520, 1959.
6. Joffe, N.: Pancreatic calcification in childhood associated with protein malnutrition. Br. J. Radiol. 36: 758–761, 1963.
7. Paulson, D.S., Lenn, J.S., Hughes, J., Roberts, L.C., and Coppridge, A.J.: Pediatric urolithiasis. J. Urol. 108: 811–814, 1972.
8. Queloz, J.M., Capitanio, M.A., and Kirkpatrick, J.A.: Wolman's disease. Roentgen observations in 3 siblings. Radiology 104: 357–359, 1972.
9. Rajasuriya, K., Thenabadu, P.N., and Leanage, R.U.: Pancreatic calcification following prolonged malnutrition. Am. J. Dis. Child. 119: 149–151, 1970.
10. Walther, P.C., Lamm, D., and Kaplan, G.W.: Pediatric urolithiases: a ten-year review. Pediatrics 65: 1068–1072, 1980.
11. Wenzl, J.E., Burke, E.C., Strickler, G.B., and Utz, D.C.: Nephrolithiasis and nephrocalcinosis in children. Pediatrics 41: 57–61, 1968.

Peptic Ulcer Disease (1–11) and Hiatus Hernia (1–10).

A thorough, complete discussion of these entities is beyond the scope of this book, but I would like to indicate that both conditions are more common in childhood than is generally appreciated. Consequently, children may come to the emergency room with acute abdominal pain suggestive of duodenal ulcer disease, and indeed may well even go on to perforation. On the other hand, many children with duodenal ulcer disease present with little in the way of abdominal pain, and vomiting is the predominant feature. In still other cases, bleeding may be the problem. All of these aspects of peptic ulcer disease are important, especially if one is to recognize all of the cases with which one might be presented.

The symptoms of a hiatus hernia and gastroesophageal reflux are well known to all, and if one takes the time, a strongly suggestive history can be extracted from an older child if the problem is present. In younger infants, the problem is more difficult, and vomiting may be the only symptom. Associated problems such as resistant asthma (1–4), sudden infant death syndrome (7, 8), and apnea have been attributed to gastroesphageal reflux. While all of these situations probably occur, they are not nearly as common as once believed. This has been demonstrated to be the case with apnea (9), and certainly our experience would suggest that gastroesophageal reflux is not a very common cause of refractory asthma or the sudden infant death syndrome.

REFERENCES

Peptic Ulcer Disease

1. Curci, M.R., Little, K, Sieber, W.K., and Kiesewetter, W.B.: Peptic ulcer disease in childhood reexamined. J. Pediatr. Surg. 11: 329–335, 1976.
2. Deckelbaum, R.L., Roy, C.C., Lussier-Lazaroff, J., and Morin, C.L.: Peptic ulcer disease: a clinical study in 73 children. Can. Med. Assoc. J. 111: 225–228, 1974.
3. Habbick, B.F., Melrose, A.G., and Grant, J.C.: Duodenal ulcer in childhood. Arch. Dis. Child. 43: 23–27, 1968.
4. Johnstone, J.M.S., and Rintoal, R.F.: Perforated duodenal ulcer in childhood. Br. J. Surg. 59: 228–289, 1972.
5. Mohammed, R., and Mackay, C.: Peptic ulceration in adolescence. Br. J. Surg. 69: 525–526, 1982.
6. Ramoz, A.R., Kirsner, J.B., and Palmer, W.L.: Peptic ucler in children. J. Dis. Child. 99: 135–148, 1960.
7. Robb, J.D.A., Thomas, P.S., Orzulok, J., and Odling-Smee, G.W.: Duodenal ulcer in children. Arch. Dis. Child. 47: 688–696, 1972.
8. Rosenlund, M.L., and Koop, C.E.: Duodenal ulcer in childhood. Pediatrics 45: 283–286, 1970.
9. Schuster, S.R., and Gross, R.E.: Peptic ulcer disease in childhood. Am. J. Surg. 105: 324, 1963.
10. Singleton, E.B.: The radiologic incidence of peptic ulcer in infants and children. Radiology 84: 956–957, 1965.
11. White, A., Carachi, R., and Young, D.G.: Duodenal ulceration presenting in childhood. Long-term follow-up. J. Pediatr. Surg. 19: 6–8, 1984.

Hiatus Hernia

1. Danus, O., Casar, C., Larrain, A., and Pope, C.E. II: Esophageal reflux—an unrecognized cause of recurrent obstructive bronchitis in children. J. Pediatrics 89: 220–224, 1976.
2. Darling, D.B., Fisher, J.H., and Gellis, S.S.: Hiatal hernia and gastroesophageal reflux in infants and children: Analysis of the incidence in North American children. Pediatrics 54: 450–455, 1974.
3. Filler, R.M., Randolph, J.G., and Gross, R.E.: Esophageal hiatus hernia in infants and children. J. Thorac. Cardiovasc. Surg. 4: 551, 1964.
4. Friedland, G.W., Yamate, M., and Marinkovich, V.A.: Hiatal hernia and chronic unremitting asthma. Pediatr. Radiol. 1: 156–160, 1973.
5. Friedland, F.W., Dodds, W.J., Sunshine, P., and Zboralske, F.F.: The apparent disparity in incidence of hiatal herniae in infants and children in Britain and the United States. A.J.R. 120: 305–314, 1974.
6. Friedland, G.W., Sunshine, P., and Zboralske, F.F.: Hiatal hernia in infants and young children: A 2 to 3 year followup study. J. Pediatr. 87: 71–74, 1975.
7. Herbst, J.J., Book, L.S., and Bray, P.F.: Gastroesophageal reflux in the "near miss" sudden infant death syndrome. J. Pediatr. 92: 73–75, 1978.
8. Leape, L.L., Holder, T.M., Franklin, J.D., Amoury, R.A., and Ashcraft, K.W.: Respiratory arrest in infants secondary to gastroesophageal reflux. Pediatrics 60: 924–928, 1977.
9. McNamara, J.J., Paulson, D.L., and Urschel, H.C., Jr.:

Hiatus hernia and gastroesophageal reflux in children. Pediatrics 43: 527–532, 1969.

10. Walsh, J.K., Farrell, M.K., Kennan, W.J., Lucas, M., and Kramer, M.: Gastroesophageal reflux in infants: relation to apnea. J. Pediatr. 99: 197–201, 1981.

GI Bleeding.

GI bleeding is not as common in childhood as in adulthood, but by no means is it rare (8). Unfortunately, however, up to 30% of cases remain undiagnosed (6). Arteriography in acute bleeders is often helpful and should be performed on an emergency basis when required. However, bleeding must be brisk, probably at a rate of over 1 ml/minute for the study to be fruitful.

Upper GI bleeding, of a massive nature, is usually due to portal hypertension (1), but also can be seen with esophagitis, peptic ulcer disease, and hemangiomas of the hypopharynx or GI tract. Bleeding from the rectum is very frequently secondary to juvenile polyps of the colon, either single or multiple (2, 9). In other instances, bleeding may result from colonic tumors (7) and conditions such as ulcerative colitis and the hemolytic uremic syndrome. Indeed, colonic bleeding may be the presenting problem in the hemolytic uremic syndrome.

Bleeding in the form of red currant jelly stools is a classic feature of intussusception, but in some of these cases bright red bleeding, or indeed, no bleeding may be seen. Meckel's diverticula are notorious for presenting with painless lower GI bleeding as are so-called benign colonic or small intestinal ulcers of unknown etiology (3–6). Bright red rectal bleeding also occasionally is seen in peptic ulcer disease, especially in young infants where GI transit times may be rapid.

REFERENCES

1. Buonocore, E., Collmann, I.R., Kerley, H.E., and Lester, T.L.: Massive upper gastrointestinal hemorrhage in children. A.J.R. 115: 289–296, 1972.
2. Franken, E.A., Bixler, D., Fitzgerald, J.F., Gamet, D.J., and Russ, M.A.: Juvenile polyposis of the colon. Ann. Radiol. 18: 499–504, 1975.
3. Grosfeld, J.L., Schiller, M., Weinberger, M., and Clatworthy, H.W., Jr.: Primary nonspecific ileal ulcers in children. Am. J. Dis. Child. 120: 447–450, 1970.
4. Harrison, H.E., Spear, G.S., and Dorst, J.P.: Chronic idiopathic ulcerative ileitis in infancy. J. Pediatr. 78: 538–546, 1971.
5. Howard, E.R., and Whimster, W.F.: Benign rectal ulceration of unknown origin: An unusual cause of rectal bleeding. Arch. Dis. Child. 51: 156–157, 1976.
6. Shah, M.J.: Primary nonspecific ulcer in ileum presenting with massive rectal hemorrhage. Br. Med. J. 3: 474, 1968.
7. Skovgaard, S., and Sorensen, F.H.: Bleeding hemangioma

of the colon diagnosed by coloscopy. J. Pediatr. Surg. 11: 83–84, 1976.
8. Spencer, R.: Gastrointestinal hemorrhage in infancy and childhood. 476 cases. Surgery 55: 718, 1961.
9. Toccalino, H., Guastavino, E., dePinni, F., ODonnell, J.C., and Williams, M.: Juvenile polyps of rectum and colon. Acta Paediatr. Scand. 62: 337–340, 1973.

Intramural Intestinal Bleeding or Edema.

Bleeding into the intestinal wall can occur in hemophilia, in Henoch-Schönlein purpura, and after trauma. Edema can occur with hypoproteinemia, portal hypertension, and with angioneurotic edema. Usually there is little to see on plain films of these patients, but if the bleeding or edema is extensive, thumbprinting or a mass-like configuration of the intestine can be noted. Most often these changes are demonstrated more clearly with barium studies of the GI tract (1).

REFERENCE

1. Grossman, H., Berdon, W.E., and Baker, D.H.: Reversible gastrointestinal sign of hemorrhage and edema in the pediatric age group. Radiology 84: 33, 1965.

Intestinal Infarction.

Intestinal infarction in children is uncommon except as seen with mechanical problems such as volvulus or intussusception, or after blunt abdominal trauma causing injury to the blood vessels of the gut. Plain films may show sentinel loops, generalized paralytic ileus, or edematous loops of infarcted intestine (1). Extremely edematous loops may appear as soft tissue masses on the plain film of the abdomen. If an upper GI series is obtained, the edematous loops of the intestine are more clearly visualized and show so-called thumbprinting of the bowel wall.

REFERENCE

1. Tomchik, F.S., Wittenberg, J., and Ottinger, L.W.: The roentgenographic spectrum of bowel infarction. Radiology 96: 249, 1970.

Acute Urinary Retention.

Acute urinary retention problems are uncommon in infancy and childhood. Occasionally, however, one can encounter a patient with a lower urinary tract obstruction and acute distention of the bladder so as to have it present as an abdominal mass. Acute urinary retention also can be seen in severely injured children and those who might be comatosed.

REFERENCE

1. Swischuk, L.E.: Acute, non-traumatic, genitorinary pediatric problems. Radiol. Clin. North Am. 16: 147–157, 1978.

Renal Colic. This subject has been discussed previously on p. 299.

Ovarian Cysts. Most often ovarian cysts present with abdominal pain secondary to bleeding or torsion. If the cyst is small, no mass will be palpable, but if it is large it may be palpable clinically and visible roentgenographically. In a very few instances, torsion of the cyst may be associated with small bowel obstruction (2). In these cases, as the cysts twist, a portion of the intestine is caught up in the twisting, and obstruction results.

With the recent advent of ultrasonographic imaging of patients with acute abdominal problems, it is becoming more apparent that some girls with ovarian cysts are prone to cyst rupture and bleeding. While it is not uncommon to find cysts in the ovaries of adult women, and even some older children, when these are associated with fluid in the cul-de-sac (Fig. 3.150), a presumptive diagnosis of ovarian cyst rupture with bleeding can be suggested.

Internal Genital Torsion in Girls. Although not common, torsion of the normal uterine adnexa (1), along with torsion of ovarian cysts and tumors can occur. Under such circumstances the presenting problem is acute abdominal pain, with or without a palpable abdominal mass. Of course, if the culprit is an ovarian cyst, a sonolucent structure is identified, while with a tumor a solid lesion with or without associated cystic areas is seen (Fig. 3.151), and with normal uterine torsion a solid mass behind the bladder is visualized (1).

REFERENCES

1. Farrell, T.P., Boal, D.K., Teele, R.L., Ballantine, T.V.: Acute torsion of normal uterine adnexa in children: sonographic demonstration. A.J.R. 139: 1223–1225, 1982.
2. Swischuk, L.E.: Acute, non-traumatic, genitourinary pediatric problems. Radiol. Clin. North Am. 16: 147–157, 1978.

Hydrometrocolpos. Although not a common cause of acute abdominal pain in girls, the condition does occur every so often. Classically it presents either in the neonatal period or in adolescence. Two types exist, simple inperforate hymen or actual vaginal atresia. The former is more likely to be the problem in the adolescent, but is not the exclusive cause. With the onset of menses, blood accumulates in the obstructed uterus and a painful abdominal mass develops. It can be seen on intravenous pyelography but is more specifically diagnosed with ultrasonography, where usually a sonolucent, elongated mass is seen behind the bladder (Fig. 3.152). Occasionally the mass is more solid as uterine and vaginal secretions predominate (Fig. 3.152).

Acute Scrotal Problems. Acute scrotal problems include epidydimo-orchitis, orchitis, testicular abscess, and testicular torsion. Testicular torsion occurs abruptly and may at first mimic testicular inflammation. At the present, these problems are best assessed with technetium-99 pertechnetate nuclide imaging (2–4). With epidydimo-orchitis increased perfusion and activity of the involved testicle is seen (Fig. 3.153A), while with testicular torsion, in the early stages, decreased flow to the involved testes is noted (Fig. 3.153B). After a few days, in the so-called missed torsion, the involved testicle shows a cold center, and increased activity around the rim of the testicle (Fig. 3.153C). Testicular abscesses are rather rare but also produce cold spots on the isotope scan. Similar cold spots can be seen after trauma.

Ultrasound also has been utilized for acute testicular problems. With testicular torsion, decreased echogenicity of the testicle in the early stages of the disease is seen (1). The epidydimus, a highly echogenic structure, also will be noted to be displaced into an abnormal position. However, ultrasound is not used for the detection of this entity as much as for the evaluation of trauma to the testicle (1, 5, 6). With trauma, ultrasound usually demonstrates disorganization of the normally uniform echogenicity of the testicle. In addition, there is loss of the testicular margins, demonstration of an associated hematocele (sonolucent area), and thickening of the scrotal wall (5, 6).

REFERENCES

1. Bird, K., Rosenfield, A.T., and Taylor, K.J.: Ultrasonography in testicular torsion. Radiology 147: 527–534, 1983.
2. Boedecker, R.A., Sty, J.R., and Jona, J.Z.: Testicular scanning as diagnostic aid in evaluating scrotal pain. J. Pediatr. 94: 760–762, 1979.

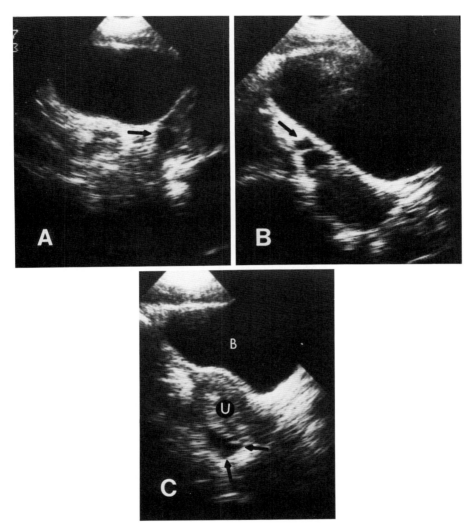

Figure 3.150. *Ovarian cyst with bleeding.*   (*A*) Transverse ultrasound scan demonstrating an ovarian cyst (*arrow*). (*B*) Sagittal section just off midline again demonstrates the ovarian cyst (*arrow*). (*C*) Mid-line sagittal view demonstrates fluid in the cul-de-sac (*arrows*). The fluid is presumed to be blood secondary to a cyst rupture; uterus (*U*), urinary bladder (*B*).

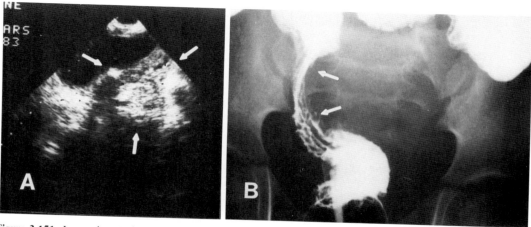

Figure 3.151. *Internal genitalia torsion in girls.* (*A*) Transverse sonogram demonstrates a solid pelvic mass with mixed echoes and some cystic areas (*arrows*) just below and to the left of the sonolucent bladder. (*B*) Barium enema demonstrates nonspecific findings of a pelvic mass. This was an ovarian teratoma which had undergone torsion.

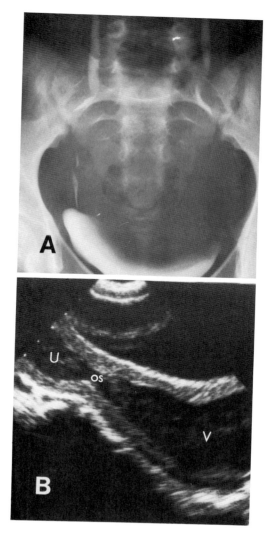

Figure 3.152. *Hydrometrocolpos.* (*A*) Note typical central pelvic mass displacing the ureters and bladder. (*B*) Sagittal sonogram demonstrating fluid and debris in an enlarged vagina (*V*) and uterus (*U*). Note the position of the cervical os (*os*).

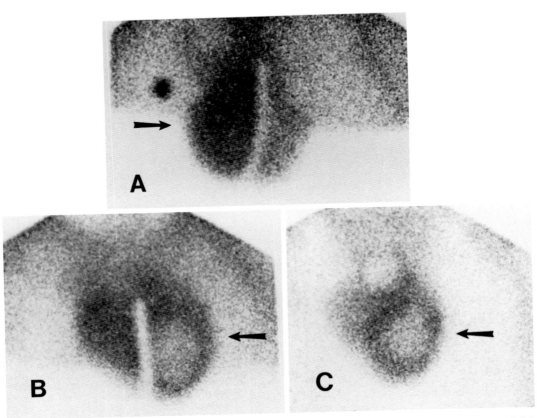

Figure 3.153. *Acute scrotal problems.* (*A*) Epidydimo-orchitis. Note increased isotope activity in the enlarged right testicle (*arrows*). (*B*) Early testicular torsion. Note decreased isotope uptake in the left testicle (*arrows*). A scrotal rim is present, but it is not hyperemic. (*C*) Missed torsion. Characteristically with missed torsion, a similar cold testicular center is seen, but the scrotal wall becomes hyperemic around it (*arrow*). (Courtesy D. Fawcett, M.D., Galveston, Texas.)

3. Gelfand, M.J., Williams, P.J., and Rosenkrantz, J.G.: Pinhole imaging: utility in testicular imaging in children. Clin. Nucl. Med. 5: 237–240, 1980.
4. Hitch, D.C., Gilday, D.L., Shandling, B., and Savage, J.P.: New approach to diagnosis of testicular torsion. J. Pediatr. Surg. 11: 537–541, 1976.
5. Hricak, H., and Jeffrey, R.B.: Sonography of acute scrotal abnormalities. Radiol. Clin. North Am. 21: 595–603, 1983.
6. Jeffrey, R.B., Laing, F.C., Hricak, H., and McAninch, J.W.: Sonography of testicular trauma. A.J.R. 141: 993–995, 1983.

Pregnancy. Of course, it is well known that GI upsets are common in pregnancy, but often one does not think of pregnancy being present in the pediatric age group. Nevertheless, one should be aware of this possibility for the first indication that a pregnancy is present may come from the abdominal roentgenogram wherein a pelvic mass, or even a formed fetus, will be demonstrated. Confirmation now is readily accomplished with ultrasonography (Fig. 3.154) and pregnancy tests.

NORMAL FINDINGS CAUSING PROBLEMS

Gastric and Colon Contents Mimicking Abscesses and Bezoars. This point seems straightforward and yet in some cases, if gastric or colonic contents are visualized in just the right place, it is most difficult to differentiate them from the findings of an abdominal abscess or gastric bezoar (Fig. 3.155). Contents in the right side of the colon are especially problematic in patients with appendicitis and suspected perforation. Indeed, in some cases it is most difficult to determine whether one is dealing with an appendiceal abscess or fortuitous visualization of feces in the colon. In young infants, milk curds can conglomerate in the stomach to produce a bezoar or even mass-like configuration (Fig. 3.156)

Abdominal Pseudotumors. These are discussed with abdominal masses on p. 293.

Chilaiditi's Syndrome (Hepatodiaphragmatic Interposition). This condition usually is considered a normal variation and it consists of interposition of the colon between the liver and the diaphragm. Most often it is seen on the right, but it can be seen bilaterally. The findings should not be misinterpreted for free peritoneal air (Fig. 3.157).

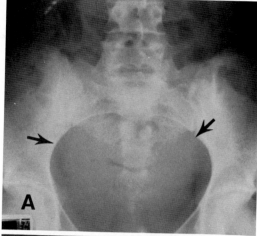

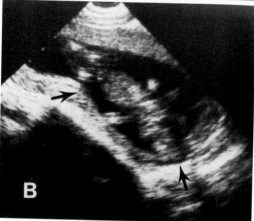

Figure 3.154. *Pregnancy.* (*A*) Note fullness, or a mass in the pelvis (*arrows*). (*B*) Ultrasonogram demonstrating well-developed fetus (*arrows*).

REFERENCES

1. Behlke, F.M.: Hepatodiaphragmatic interposition in children. A.J.R. 91: 669, 1964.
2. Jackson, A.D.M., and Hudson, C.J.: Interposition of colon between liver and diaphragm (Chilaiditi's syndrome) in children. Arch. Dis. Child. 32: 151, 1957.
3. Vessal, K., and Borhanmanesh, F.: Hepatodiaphragmatic interposition of the intestine (Chilaiditi's syndrome). Clin. Radiol. 27: 113–116, 1976.

Duodenal Air Mimicking Air Under the Liver. In some cases, air trapped in the partially collapsed duodenal bulb is virtually indistinguishable from free air trapped under the liver. Only familiarity with this normal configuration will avoid misinterpretation (Fig. 3.158).

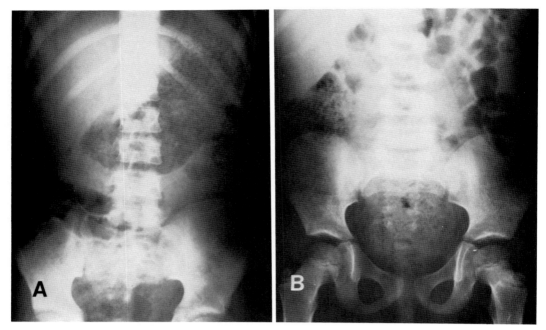

Figure 3.155. *Pseudo-abscess or pseudo-bezoar appearance of gastric and colonic contents.* (*A*) Note the granular appearance of food and air mixed within the stomach of this patient. The pattern is similar to that seen with abdominal abscesses or gastric bezoars. (*B*) Another patient with fecal material mixed with air in the rectum and hepatic flexure. Either of these collections, alone, could be misinterpreted for an abscess.

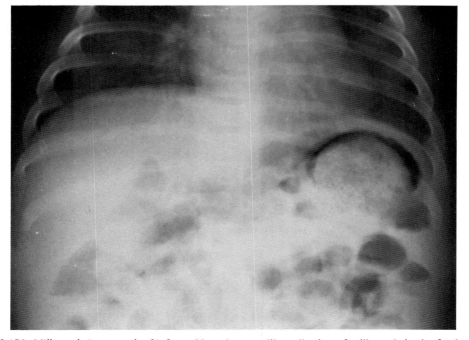

Figure 3.156. *Milk curds in stomach of infant.* Note the mass-like collection of milk curds in the fundus of the stomach of this young infant. The findings mimic those of a gastric bezoar, but they are normal and common.

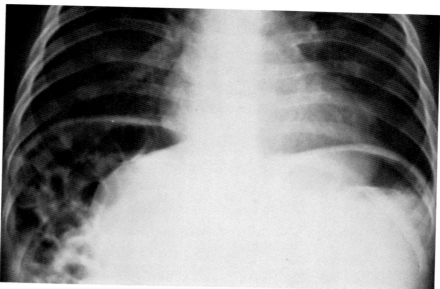

Figure 3.157. *Chilaiditi's syndrome.* Note interposition of slightly dilated loops of colon between the liver and the right diaphragmatic leaflet. The findings should not be misinterpreted for free air under the diaphragmatic leaflet, especially on chest films where the top of the abdomen only is included on the study.

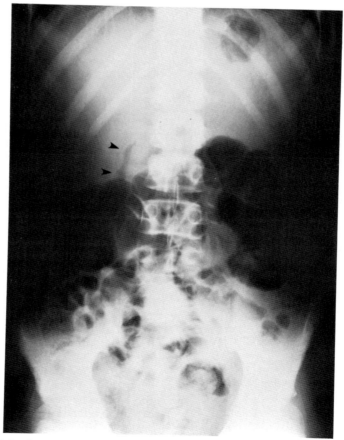

Figure 3.158. *Normal duodenal air mimicking free air under the liver.* Note the linear collection of air in the duodenum (*arrows*). Such configurations usually are best visualized on upright views, and can mimic the appearance of free air under the liver.

CHAPTER 4
The Extremities

This chapter addresses itself primarily to the detection of *the more subtle and frequently missed fractures and inflammatory lesions of the extremities*. There is no attempt to cover all fractures, especially those which require roentgenographic examination merely to confirm their presence or visualize the precise position of the fractured fragments. Although many of these injuries represent significant management problems, they offer no real problems in roentgenographic diagnosis. Furthermore, they are dealt with in whole or part in a number of excellent publications on the subject (1–3).

In addition to these aspects, *there also will be a greater than usual emphasis on evaluation of the soft tissues and periarticular fat pads.* These structures generally are underutilized and underestimated in importance. They are, however, invaluable in yielding data regarding the specific location and nature of a lesion, and their special usefulness in infants and young children will be stressed.

REFERENCES

1. Blount, W.P.: *Fractures in Children*, Ed. 2. Williams & Wilkins, Baltimore, 1980.
2. Pollen, A.G.: *Fractures and Dislocations in Children.* Williams & Wilkins, Baltimore, 1973.
3. Rang, M.: *Children's Fractures*, Ed. 2. J. B. Lippincott, Philadelphia, 1982.

GENERAL CONSIDERATIONS

What Views Should Be Obtained? At least two views, usually at right angles to each other, are necessary. Most often these views consist of a *frontal* and *lateral* projection of the involved extremity, and in this regard it cannot be stated too forcefully that *true frontal and lateral projections are required. One cannot settle for a "sort of" frontal or lateral view,* for if one does, one will come to regret it. If these views fail to yield useful information *oblique* or other *special views* should be obtained. In this regard, *stereoscopic views* are useful but generally underutilized. This is unfortunate for they are readily obtained and especially useful in the detection of shoulder, hip, pelvic, and facial fractures. Recently, however, they have been supplanted by CT scanning.

In addition, it is of the utmost benefit to obtain **comparative views** of the other (normal) side, especially in cases where abnormal findings are subtle. These views are extremely useful, for generally speaking, symmetry from side to side in the normal patient is very consistent, and because of this, any asymmetry, no matter how subtle, should be treated with the greatest suspicion.

Recently, there has been some movement toward discouraging the routine use of comparative views (1–3). These publications all deliver the message that such views, on a generalized basis, are not required. While there is some merit to this attitude, most experienced radiologists, especially those not sustained on a steady diet of pediatric films, still probably prefer to obtain comparative views. Indeed, we at our institution, even though a pediatric facility, obtain comparative views rather liberally, for we do not feel we can detect subtle bony injury, or evaluate the soft tissues satisfactorily without them.

In terms of the publications which speak in opposition of obtaining comparative views, it might be noted, that, in a summary report, the Committee on Radiology of the American Academy of Pediatrics provided so many loopholes in the premise that comparative views are not required, that the loopholes virtually destroyed the original premise. For example, with direct quotation from their report (3), we have the following statements (reproduced by permission of *Pediatrics*, 65: 646–647, 1980):

Injury to the hip joint is a notable exception to the selective approach; at least one view should routinely include the normal hip, with the gonads shielded. Hip injuries in children are most frequently associated with joint effusion, which can be detected only with comparing similar measurements of the opposite joint space.

Other specific areas of appendicular skeleton may require more comparative views. The elbow, with a relatively large number of ossification centers appearing at widely varying times, may prove confusing even to the experienced radiologist; comparison view of this joint may be requested frequently. Detection of joint effusion in the knee and ankle may necessitate a comparison view, in at least one projection. Comparison views may also be helpful in evaluating the tissue planes and subcutaneous fat in suspected inflammatory conditions of the soft tissues or bones.

And finally, a conclusion from another of these communications (1), suggests that no one uniform policy can be expected for all individuals dealing with pediatric trauma. A quotation from this communication is as follows:

A number of theoretical and practical considerations will continue to determine the use of comparison views. Personal conviction based on experience and training is the major theoretical consideration. Practical considerations include the availability of radiologic consultation, the expertise of the physician who initially interprets the study and clinical demands. An individual's policy toward the use of comparison images is a balance of these considerations.

The latter paragraph probably is the most important in this ongoing controversy. Do what you have to do, but be sure in your mind that you will not miss any fractures when you obtain views of the injured side only. In this regard one might ask, "How sure are you that you would not miss a bending fracture, a subtle Salter-Harris type I injury, or a minimal buckle fracture?"

REFERENCES

1. Committee on Radiology: Comparison radiographs of extremities in childhood: recommended usage. Pediatrics 65: 646–647, 1980.
2. McCauley, R.G.K., Schwartz, A.M., Leonidas, J.C., Darling, D.B., Bankoff, M.S., and Swan, C.S., II: Comparison views in extremity injury in children: an efficacy study. Radiology 131: 95–97, 1979.
3. Merten, D.F.: Comparison radiographs in extremity injuries of childhood: current application in radiological practice. Radiology 126: 209–210, 1978.

Utilizing the Soft Tissues. Evaluating soft tissue changes in trauma and infection of the extremities in childhood is invaluable, and the findings one should look for include: (a) localized or generalized swelling of the soft tissues, (b) obliteration of the muscle-fat interfaces, and (c) displacement or obliteration of the periarticular fat pads. These latter structures are displaced when fluid accumulates within the joint and obliterated when edema surrounds the joint. Evaluating the soft tissues in this manner can serve to localize the site of injury or infection, and such an evaluation should be undertaken before the bones themselves are examined (Fig. 4.1). Of course, the changes will differ a little from joint to joint and bone to bone, but basically abnormality can be assessed under one of the three categories just proposed. A more detailed discussion of the soft tissue changes for each joint of the body is presented at subsequent points throughout this chapter.

Significance of Intra-articular Fluid. Intra-articular fluid is readily detected in almost all of the large joints of the body. As a general rule, in children, fluid in the joints should be presumed pus until proven otherwise. In the elbow and ankle, fluid in the joint is manifest by outward displacement of the anterior and posterior fat pads, while in the shoulder and hip, fluid accumulation causes lateral displacement of the humerus or femur, and concomitant joint space widening. Knee fluid produces bulging of the suprapatellar bursa, just behind the quadriceps tendon, while in the wrist, joint fluid is manifest simply by the presence of swelling around the wrist.

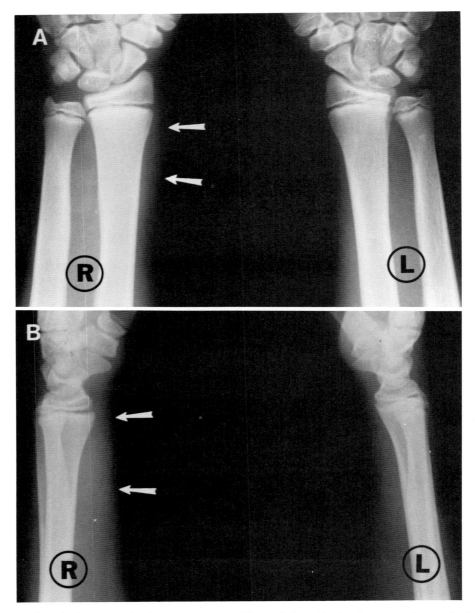

Figure 4.1. *Value of soft tissues in localizing an injury.*   (*A*) Frontal view of both wrists. Bony abnormality is subtle and consists primarily of a little widening of the distal right radial epiphyseal line. This should signify the presence of a Salter-Harris type I epiphyseal-metaphyseal injury, but the finding is subtle and could be missed. However, when it is noted that soft tissue swelling also is present (*arrows*) the finding becomes easier to assess. (*B*) Soft tissue swelling also is noted on the lateral view (*arrows*). Note that not only are the soft tissues thicker, but that edema and swelling have obliterated the normal fat-muscle interfaces. Compare with the normal appearance of the left wrist.

In the presence of trauma, fluid in the joint should cause one to look more diligently at the bones for evidence of a fracture in this area. However, not always will one see such a fracture, and indeed in our recent study (1), the incidence of missed fracture was surprisingly low (Table 4.1). It is important to emphasize, however, that *these figures were compiled on the basis of liberal use of compared views, and close scrutiny of the*

Table 4.1. *Occult Fracture—Percent Probability*[a]

Fracture	Total No. of Cases	Total Cases with No X-ray Follow-up	Total Cases with X-ray Follow-up	No. of Cases with Fracture Detected	Percent Fracture Probability
Shoulder	0	0	0	0	0
Elbow	46	20	26	4	15.8
Wrist	5	2	3	2	67
Hip	0	0	0	0	0
Knee	16	9	7	0	0
Ankle	61	34	27	3	11
Total	128	65	63	8	12.6

[a] Reproduced from: Swischuk, L.E., Hayden, C.K., and Kupfer, M.C.: Significance of intraarticular fluid without visible fracture in children, A.J.R. 142: 1261–1262, 1984.

bones for subtle fractures, frequently missed by the inexperienced observer.

REFERENCE

1. Swischuk, L.E., Hayden, C.K., and Kupfer, M.C.: Significance of intrarticular fluid without visible fracture in children. A.J.R. 142: 1261–1262, 1984.

What Type of Bony Injuries Are Seen in Children? The types of fractures most peculiar to childhood are: (a) cortical, buckle, or torus fractures; (b) greenstick fractures; (c) bent or bowed bones without a visible fracture line (i.e., acute plastic, bending fractures); and (d) epiphyseal-metaphyseal fractures (Fig. 4.2). Of course, typical midshaft, transverse, spiral, oblique, and comminuted fractures also occur in children, but none are especially peculiar to childhood, and most are not difficult to detect. One might make some excpetion when these fractures are of the so-called "hairline" variety (Fig. 4.3), but other than this these fractures are readily demonstrable roentgenographically and not difficult to diagnose.

Buckle or torus fractures are simple compression fractures which manifest themselves by buckling or kinking of the cortex. They occur most frequently in the metaphyseal regions of long bones for this is where the cortex is weakest. However, they also can be seen in the clavicles, pubic bones, and even the scapulae. Some of these buckle or torus fractures are quite subtle, but if one follows the rule that the distal ends of the long bones should possess smooth, continuous curves, then one will not accept even the slightest bump, dent, buckle, or cortical irregularity as normal (Fig. 4.4). Nonetheless, some of these fractures do elude initial

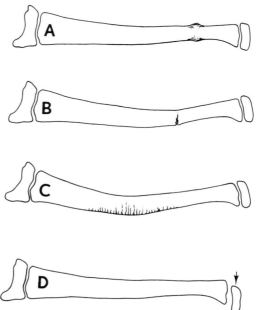

Figure 4.2. *Fractures peculiar to children.* (*A*) Typical torus or buckle fracture with buckling of the cortex. (*B*) Greenstick fracture with fracture visible through one aspect of the cortex only. The fracture is incomplete and a certain degree of bending coexists. (*C*) Bending or plastic bowing fracture of long bone. No fracture line is visible roentgenographically but numerous microfractures exist along the outer aspect of the bent bone. (*D*) Epiphyseal-metaphyseal injury with or without displacement of the epiphysis (*arrow*).

detection, and when follow-up films are obtained, signs of healing in the form of sclerosis along the fracture line and periosteal new bone deposition can be seen (Fig. 4.5).

Greenstick fractures are bending fractures with a fracture line extending through one cortex of the bone only (Fig. 4.6). The term greenstick comes from the comparison of

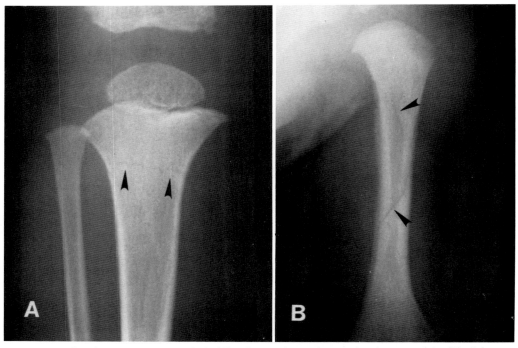

Figure 4.3. *Hairline fractures.*   (*A*) Note the hairline fracture (*arrows*) traversing the upper right tibia. It is not easy to see. (*B*) Spiral hairline fracture (*arrows*) in a battered infant. The presence of periosteal new bone indicates early healing. Hairline fractures often become more readily visible at this stage.

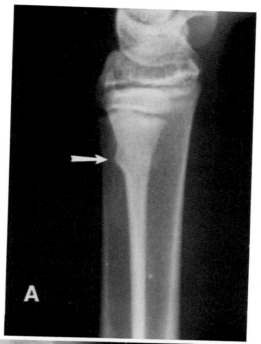

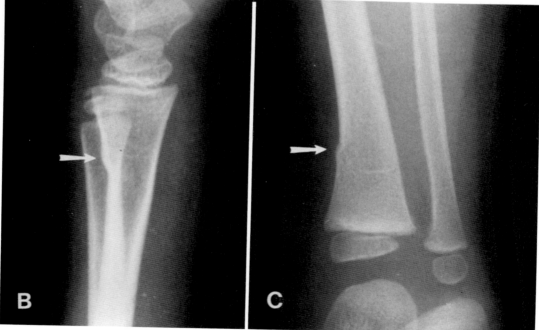

Figure 4.4. *Buckle or torus fractures—various types.*   Note varying degrees of cortical buckling or kinking (*arrows*) in these typical torus fractures of the wrist (*A* and *B*) and ankle (*C*).

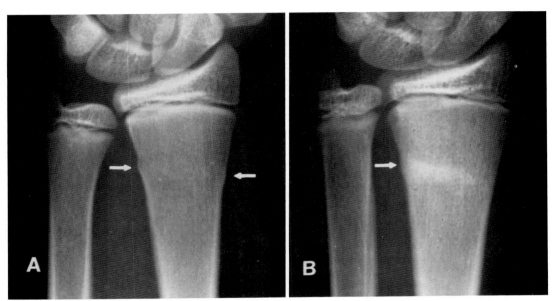

Figure 4.5. *Healing buckle or torus fracture.* (*A*) Note typical, but subtle, bulging of the cortex (*arrows*). Also note that the trabecular pattern along the fracture line has been disturbed. (*B*) Two weeks later note sclerosis along the fracture line. (*arrow*).

this type of fracture to the manner in which a "green," supple tree branch breaks when it is bent. True ***bending or bowing (plastic) fractures, without a visible fracture line*** (2–5, 14) can be considered the precursor of the classic greenstick fractures (i.e., the greenest of greenstick fractures). These fractures frequently are missed unless comparative views of the normal extremity are obtained, and although no fracture line is visible roentgenographically, numerous microfractures exist along the outer surface of the bent bone. In these cases, the fracture force is not dissipated at any one site, and thus a single fracture line is not visualized. Eventually, however, if enough bending occurs, a single fracture line will develop, but until this occurs, only bending will be seen (Fig. 4.6). Most often these fractures occur in the forearm (2–5, 13), but also can be seen in the lower extremity (4, 12), clavical, and indeed almost any bone in the child's body. These fractures are discussed in more detail as they

come up in later sections, but it might be noted at this point that seldom, if ever, do they show classic signs of healing. In other words, whereas with a greenstick fracture one will see sclerosis and periosteal new bone formation, with the usual bending fracture, nothing but the deformity persists (Fig. 4.7).

Epiphyseal-metaphyseal fractures are very common in childhood, and, of course, occur exclusively in the child. Because the junction between the epiphysis and metaphysis is a weak area, if a shearing force is applied to the end of a long bone, it is quite natural that it would result in an epiphyseal-metaphyseal slippage or separation. A variety of injuries can be sustained at this junction, and to facilitate their understanding and categorization, the Salter-Harris classification (11) of five types usually is employed (Fig. 4.8).

As far as the radiologist is concerned, the greatest challenge comes from the Salter-Harris types I and II injuries (10). The reason

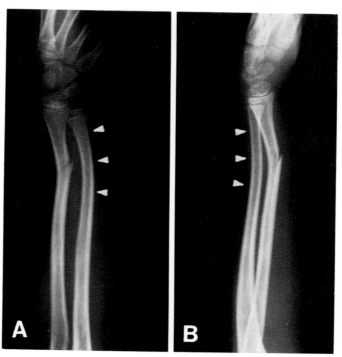

Figure 4.6. *Greenstick fracture of radius and plastic bowing fracture of ulna.* Anteroposterior (*A*) and lateral (*B*) views. Note the greenstick fracture of the distal radius. In addition, however, note bending of the ulna (*arrows*). This latter finding represents an acute plastic bending fracture of the ulna. Some concomitant bending of the fractured radius also is present.

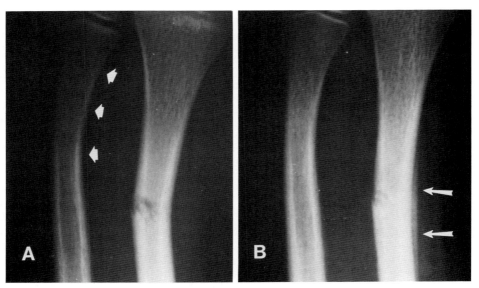

Figure 4.7. *Plastic bending fracture; healing phase..*   (*A*) Note the greenstick fracture of the distal radius. In addition, notice bending of the ulna (*arrows*). (*B*) Follow-up films demonstrate classic healing of the radial fracture (*arrows*), but in the ulna, nothing but residual bending is seen.

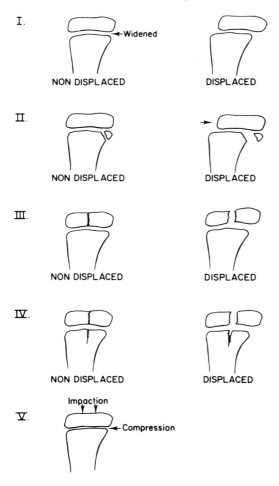

for this is that if in these cases the epiphysis is not displaced, bony changes are subtle, and one must rely more on soft tissue changes and widening of the radiolucent epiphyseal line. Salter-Harris types I and II fractures heal in characteristic fashion, and thus, should they not be detected in their acute phase, repeat roentgenograms 10 days to 2 weerks later will show sclerosis and irregularity of the epiphyseal-metaphyseal junction and periosteal new bone deposition along the metaphysis (Fig. 4.9). Salter-Harris types III and IV fractures usually are relatively easy to detect, for often some degree of epiphyseal displacement exists, and in any

Figure 4.8. *Salter-Harris classification of epiphyseal-metaphyseal fractures. Type I:* the epiphyseal line (physis) is widened secondary to some degree of epiphyseal separation. The epiphysis may or may not be displaced. *Type II:* there is a small or large metaphyseal fracture fragment in association with widening of the epiphyseal line. The epiphysis and fracture fragment may or may not be visibly displaced. *Type III:* in this type, the fracture occurs through the epiphysis and the fracture may or may not be displaced. When displacement occurs, often only part of the fractured epiphysis is displaced. *Type IV:* a fracture exists through the epiphysis and the metaphysis; displacement of the fragments may or may not be present. *Type V:* an impaction fracture with injury of the epiphyseal plate only is present. No roentgenographic findings other than swelling around the involved epiphyseal-metaphyseal junction usually are present.

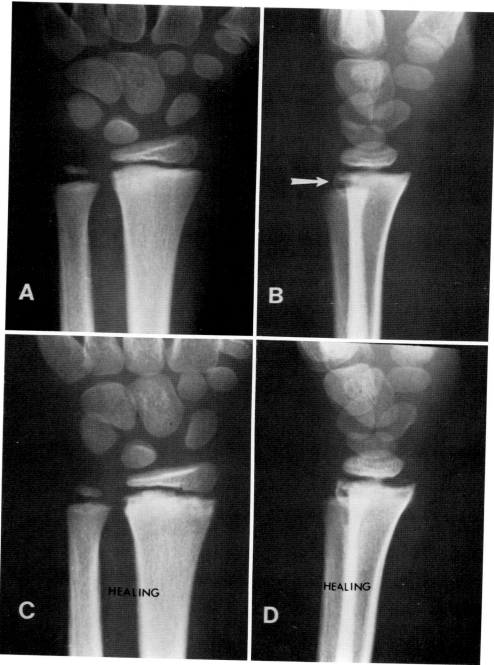

Figure 4.9. *Healing epiphyseal-metaphyseal injury.* (*A*) Frontal view demonstrating little if any abnormality of the epiphyseal-metaphyseal junction. (*B*) Lateral view demonstrates posterior displacement of the radial epiphysis and a corner fracture of the posterior metaphysis (*arrow*). These findings are consistent with a Salter-Harris type II injury. (*C*) Two weeks later note how sclerotic and irregular the radial metaphyseal margin has become. This is characteristic of the healing phase of these fractures. (*D*) Lateral view showing similar findings.

case, the fracture lines are more readily visible.

The type V Salter-Harris injury, that is, the one in which epiphyseal plate compression only occurs, is the least common of all. A question has been raised as to whether it occurs at all (8), and certainly it is not a common injury. It is, however, considered one of the more serious injuries a child can sustain, for epiphyseal plate damage and subsequent impaired epiphyseal growth are common (9, 11). Growth abnormalities also are a significant complication of the type IV fracture, but are a lesser problem with the other Salter-Harris epiphyseal-metaphyseal injuries. Roentgenographically, in the type V fracture the films usually are void of bony abnormality.

Although the fractures just outlined constitute the major portion of childhood fractures, one also can see *stress fractures* with considerable frequency (1, 5, 7, 12, 15), and in addition, *pathologic fractures* can be encountered. Stress fractures usually, but not always, occur in perfectly normal individuals, and the most common site for such a fracture to occur in a child is the upper tibia. However, they can occur in almost any bone of the lower extremity. Stress fractures of the second metatarsal usually are referred to as march fractures.

It is unusual to detect stress fractures in their initial stages, for unless a fracture line is seen through the involved cortex, one will not even suspect that such an injury is present. Consequently, these fractures frequently go undetected for days or weeks, and finally come to the attention of the physician in their healing phase, replete with sclerosis along the fracture line and periosteal new bone deposition over the fracture site (Fig. 4.10*A*). Indeed, so striking are these changes (Fig. 4.10*B*) that very often they are misinterpreted for more serious lesions such as a bone tumor.

In addition, it might be noted that isotope bone scanning is very useful in the detection of stress fractures (6, 9, 14). Although the findings are nonspecific, they do localize the site of injury.

The classic *pathologic fracture* in childhood is the one occurring through a unicameral bone cyst. Unicameral bone cysts are commonly seen in children, and most often

are located in the metaphyses of long bones, especially the humerus. Indeed, in the spring when baseball practice begins, many a child has come to the emergency room with a pathologic fracture through such a cyst (Fig. 4.10*C*). Not as common, but nonetheless quite important, is the pathologic fracture through a malignant bone lesion (Fig. 4.10*D*). Most often the underlying lesion is one of the so-called "round cell" tumors, i.e., Ewing's sarcoma, lymphoma, leukemia, or metastatic neuroblastoma. Pathologic fractures through dysplastic bones such as those seen with osteopetrosis, osteogenesis imperfecta, hyperparathyroidism, rickets, hypophosphatasia, etc., also occur but are not within the scope of this book.

REFERENCES

1. Berkebile, R.D.: Stress fractures of the tibia in children. A.J.R. 91: 588–596, 1964.
2. Borden, S., IV: Traumatic bowing of the forearm in children. J. Bone Joint Surg. 56A: 611–616, 1974.
3. Borden, S., IV: Roentgen recognition of acute plastic bowing of the forearm in children. A.J.R. 125: 524–530, 1975.
4. Cail, W.S., Keats, T.E., and Sussman, M.D.: Plastic bowing fracture of the femur in a child. A.J.R. 130: 780–782, 1978.
5. Crowe, J.E., and Swischuk, L.E.: Acute bowing fractures of the forearm in children: a frequently missed injury. A.J.R. 128: 981–984, 1977.
6. Geslien, G.E., Thrall, J.H., Espinosa, J.L., and Older, R.A.: Early detection of stress fracture using ⁹⁹ᵐTc-polyphosphate. Radiology 121: 683–687, 1976.
7. Kroening, P.M., and Shelton, M.L.: Stress fractures. A.J.R. 89: 1281–1286, 1963.
8. Peterson, H.A., and Burkhart, S.S.: Compression injury of the epiphyseal growth plate: fact or fiction? J. Pediatr. Orthop. 1: 377–384, 1981.
9. Prather, J.L., Nusynowitz, M.L., Snowdy, H.A., Hughes, A.D., McCartney, W.H., and Bagg, R.J.: Scintigraphic findings in stress fractures. J. Bone Joint Surg. 59: 869–874, 1977.
10. Rogers, L.F.: The radiography of epiphyseal injuries. Radiology 96: 289–299, 1970.
11. Salter, R.B., and Harris, W.R.: Injuries involving the epiphyseal plate. J. Bone Joint Surg. 45A: 587–622, 1963.
12. Savoca, C.J.: Stress fractures. A classification of the earliest radiographic signs. Radiology 100: 519–524, 1971.
13. Strenstrom, R., Gripenberg, L., and Bergius, A.R.: Traumatic bowing of forearm and lower leg in children. Acta Radiol. 19: 243–249, 1978.
14. Wilcox, J.R., Jr., Moniot, A.L., and Green, J.P.: Bone scanning in the evaluation of exercise-related stress injuries. Radiology 123: 699–702, 1977.
15. Wilson, E.S., Jr., and Katz, F.N.: Stress fractures. An analysis of 250 consecutive cases. Radiology 92: 481–486, 1969.

What to Look for in Acute Osteomyelitis. The bony changes of acute osteomyelitis are late in onset, taking at least 10 days to 2 weeks to develop. Consequently, if one is to detect osteomyelitis in its earliest stages, one must examine the surrounding soft tis-

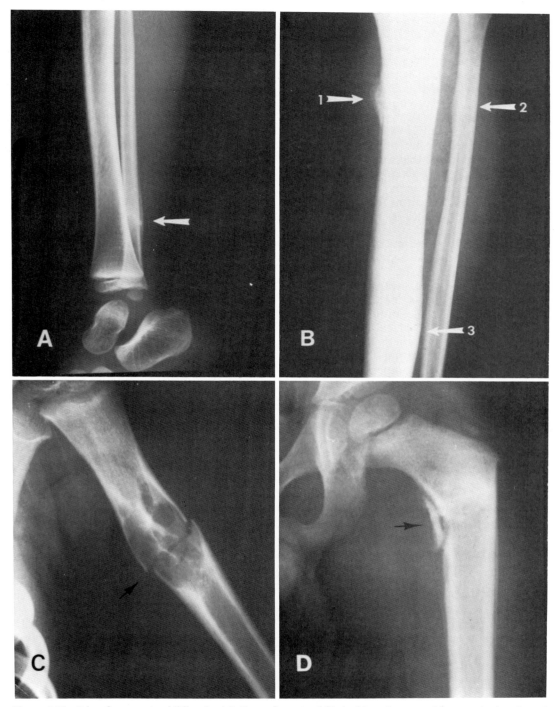

Figure 4.10. *Other fractures in childhood.* (*A*) *Stress fracture of fibula.* Note the area of increased sclerosis and periosteal new bone deposition in the lower fibula (*arrow*). (*B*) Another patient demonstrating *multiple stress fractures.* First note the large "lump" of periosteal new bone adjacent to the tibial fracture (*1*). Then note a similar, but much less pronounced, finding in the fibula just across from the tibia (*2*), and finally note the old healed stress fracture of the lower tibia (*3*). (*C*) *Pathologic fracture through unicameral bone cyst* of the humerus (*arrow*). (*D*) *Pathologic fracture in Ewing's sarcoma* with avulsion of the lesser trochanter (*arrow*). Note that there is destruction of the medullary portion of the bone, and that reactive periosteal new bone is present circumferentially. This patient experienced acute hip pain while running and was brought to the emergency room for evaluation.

sues with great dexterity (1–4). In this regard, one must be thoroughly familiar with the normal tendons, fat pads, joint capsules, etc., around each of the joints, for often it is in the examination of these structures only that osteomyelitis first is detected. More detailed discussions of osteomyelitis in its early stages will be undertaken with each of the joints of the extremities when each of them is discussed individually, but at this point it might be emphasized that soft tissue changes in osteomyelitis occur deep. In other words, they occur next to the bone and in this way can be differentiated from the more superficial soft tissue changes occurring with cellulitis, and the intra-articular soft tissue changes occurring with septic arthritis.

What to Look for in Septic Arthritis and Traumatic Hemarthrosis. The roentgenographic assessment of septic arthritis and traumatic hemarthrosis centers around the detection of fluid in the joint. For the most part this is accomplished by: (a) noting increased width of the joint space, (b) noting displacement or obliteration of the periarticular fat pads, and (c) comparing the suspicious findings on the abnormal side to those on the normal side. Assessment of all of the bony and soft tissue structures is especially important in the very young infant in whom little in the way of systemic response to infection often is present. In other words, fever is not high, a leukocytosis is not striking, toxicity is not marked, and the only finding may be an inability to move the involved extremity. However, with properly positioned roentgenograms, and an evaluation of the joint space and soft tissues, one most always will detect where the problem is located. In this regard, in the absence of trauma, a good rule to follow is: ***fluid in the joint should be considered pus until proven otherwise.*** More detailed discussions of the findings of septic arthritis for each joint are undertaken at later points.

REFERENCES

1. Capitanio, M.A., and Kirkpatrick, J.A.: Early roentgen observation in acute osteomyelitis. A.J.R. 108: 488–496, 1970.
2. Hayden, C.K., Jr., and Swischuk, L.E.: Para-articular soft tissue changes in infections and trauma of the lower extremity in children. A.J.R. 134: 307–311, 1980.
3. Moyson, F., Brombart, J.C., and Wittek, F.: Early radiologic signs of childhood osteomyelitis. J. Belge Radiol. 55: 645–653, 1972.
4. Nixon, G.W.: Acute hematogenous osteomyelitis. Pediatr. Ann. 5: 64–81, 1976.

Isotope, Computed Tomography (CT), and Magnetic Resonance Imaging (MRI) Scanning in Acute Trauma and Infection. Isotope bone scanning can be of considerable aid in the detection of occult fractures, and early infections (4–6, 10, 11, 14, 16, 17) (Fig. 4.11). However, its use in the early detection and differentiation of osteomyelitis from cellulitis, or septic arthritis, is less rewarding. To be sure, numerous documentations of false negative (i.e., normal) technetium bone scans with acute osteomyelitis have come to the forefront (1, 3, 7, 8, 15). The usual explanation for this phenomenon is that, in the early stages of osteomyelitis, there is so much intraosseous pressure and/or venous thrombosis, due to pus accumulation, that blood, and hence, isotope cannot get to the bone. Whatever the explanation, we have had the same experience and have come to delay obtaining the bone scan for 24–48 hours in many cases. In addition, we use either an indium or gallium scan to supplement the technetium scan in many cases (2, 8). Indium-labeled white blood cell scans also can be utilized (13), and in terms of the isotope bone scan, one should utilize blood flow, blood pool, and static scan data.

In the average infection, be it soft tissue, joint or bone, blood flow and blood pool, studies demonstrate early delivery and excessive accumulation of isotope. With delayed scanning, osteomyelitis usually shows a focal area of increased isotope activity in the bone (Fig. 4.12), while septic arthritis produces generalized, but rather nonspecific increased activity around the bones of the joint. With severe cellulitis, some localized uptake in the adjacent bone may be seen, but usually it is not as intense as when the problem is osteomyelitis. The same is true of pyomyositis.

A further problem arises in patients with sickle cell disease where often one is uncertain as to whether one is dealing with infection or infarction. Radionuclide imaging may be helpful in this regard (9), but once again, since both infarcts and osteomyelitis produce positive scans after a few days, differentiation of one from the other may not be so easy. In the very early stages, however, one may see decreased isotope delivery and a "cold spot" in the bone and in older cases, alternating hot and cold areas are common

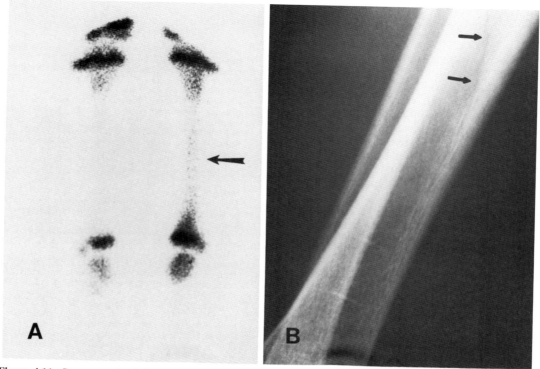

Figure 4.11. *Bone scan in skeletal trauma.* (*A*) Note area of increased activity in the left tibia (*arrows*). (*B*) Subsequent x-ray demonstrates a spiral (toddler's) fracture of the tibia (*arrows*).

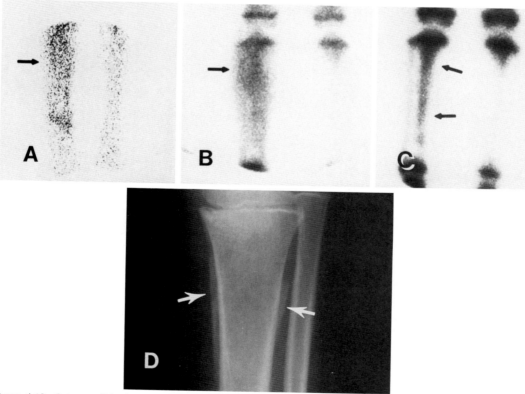

Figure 4.12. *Osteomyelitis; isotope studies.* (*A*) Flow study demonstrates increased flow to the right lower leg (*arrow*). (*B*) Blood pool study demonstrates pooling of isotope in the right lower extremity (*arrow*). (*C*) Static scan demonstrates diffusely increased isotope uptake over the entire right tibia (*arrows*). (*D*) X-ray 2 weeks later demonstrates bone destruction and periosteal new bone deposition. Initially the x-rays were normal.

because of numerous infarcts seen at different stages of evolution (Fig. 4.13).

CT scanning also has been utilized in the diagnosis of osteomyelitis (9, 12), but is not as commonly utilized as regular x-rays and isotope studies. Generally, with CT scanning, the earliest change one can detect is an increase in density of the bone marrow (Fig. 4.14) (9). Thereafter, actual bone destruction and periosteal new bone deposition are seen (Fig. 4.15) and gas in the bone also has been noted (12). MRI scanning may be more sensitive in the future (4), but one is not able to make this determination from data available today.

REFERENCES

1. Berkwitz, I.D., and Wenzel, W.: "Normal" technetium bone scans in patients with acute osteomyelitis. Am. J. Dis. Child. 134: 828–830, 1980.
2. Cox, F., and Hughes, W.T.: Gallium-67 scanning for the diagnosis of infection in children. Am. J. Dis. Child. 133: 1171–1173, 1979.
3. Fleisher, G.R., Paradise, J.E., Plotkin, S.A., and Borden, S., IV.: Falsely normal radionuclide scans for osteomyelitis. Am. J. Dis. Child. 134: 499–502, 1980.
4. Fletcher, B.D., Scoles, P.V., and Nelson, A.D.: Osteomyelitis in children: detection by magnetic resonance. Pediatr. Radiol. 150: 57–60, 1984.
5. Gilday, D.L., and Paul, D.J.: The differentiation of osteo-
myelitis and cellulitis in children using a combined blood pool and bone scan. J. Nucl. Med. 15: 494, 1974.
6. Handmaker, H., and Leonard, R.: The bone scan in inflammatory osseous disease. Semin. Nucl. Med. 6: 95–105, 1976.
7. Handmaker, H.: Acute hematogenous osteomyelitis: has the bone scan betrayed us? Radiology 135: 787–789, 1980.
8. Jones, D.C., and Cady, R.B.: "Cold" bone scans in acute osteomyelitis. J. Bone Joint Surg. 63B: 376–378, 1981.
9. Kuhn, J.P., and Berger, P.E.: Computed tomographic diagnosis of osteomyelitis. Radiology 130: 503–506, 1979.
10. Majd, M., and Frenkel, R.S.: Radionuclide imaging in skeletal inflammatory and ischemic disease in children. A.J.R. 126: 832–841, 1976.
11. Marty, R., Denney, J.D., McKamey, M.R., and Rowley, M.J.: Bone trauma and related benign disease: assessment by bone scanning. Semin. Nucl. Med. 6: 197–220, 1976.
12. Ram, P.C., Martinez, S., Korobkin, M., Breiman, R.S., Gallis, H.R., and Harrelson, J.M.: CT detection of intraosseous gas: a new sign of osteomyelitis. A.J.R. 137: 721, 1981.
13. Raptopoulos, V., Dohery, P.W., Goss, T.P., King, M.A., Johnson, K., and Gantz, N.M.: Acute osteomyelitis: advantage of white cell scans in early detection. A.J.R. 139: 1077–1082, 1982.
14. Rosenthall, L., Hill, R.O., and Chuang, S.: Observation on the use of ^{99m}Tc-phosphate imaging in peripheral bone trauma. Radiology 119: 637–641, 1976.
15. Sullivan, D.C., Rosenfield, N.S., Ogden, J., and Gottschalk, A.: Problems in the scintigraphic detection of osteomyelitis in children. Radiology 135: 731–736, 1980.
16. Treves, S., Khettry, J., Broker, F.H., Wilkinson, R.H., and Watts, H.: Osteomyelitis: early scintigraphic detection in children. Pediatrics 57: 173–186, 1976.
17. Wilcox, J.R., Jr., Moniot, A.L., and Green, J.P.: Bone scanning in the evaluation of exercise-related injuries. Radiology 123: 699–702, 1977.

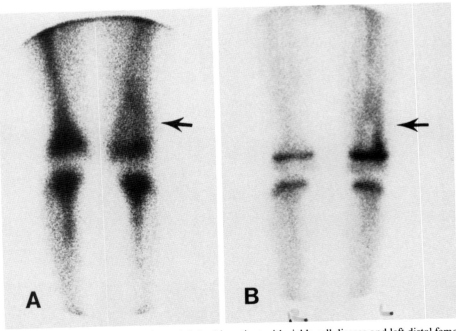

Figure 4.13. *Bone infarction; isotope studies.* (*A*) In this patient with sickle cell disease and left distal femoral pain, note increased isotope activity (*arrow*) on the blood pool study. (*B*) Static scans, however, show irregular uptake of isotope consistent with infarction.

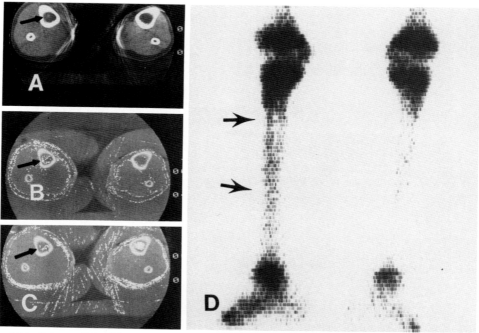

Figure 4.14. *Osteomyelitis; CT examination.* (*A*) CT scan demonstrates slightly increased attenuation of bone marrow in the right tibia (*arrow*). (*B*) With settings to accentuate muscle, note increased attenuation (edema, pus) in the right tibial marrow cavity (*arrow*). (*C*) With settings to accentuate fat, note concomitant decreased attenuation of fat in the right tibial marrow cavity (*arrow*). (*D*) Isotope bone scan demonstrates diffuse uptake of isotope in the right tibia. This patient had surgically proven osteomyelitis.

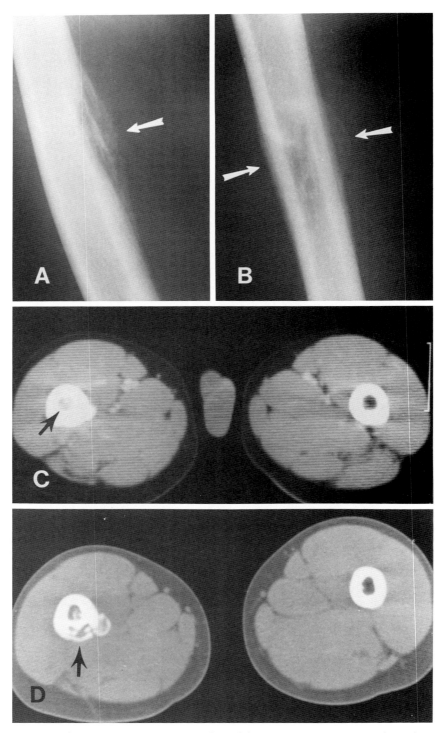

Figure 4.15. *Osteomyelitis; CT scan.* (*A*) Lateral view of femur demonstrates destructive lesion (*arrow*). (*B*) Frontal view demonstrates periosteal new bone with a bubble-like appearance (*arrows*). This patient had pain but very little systemic reaction and bone tumor was entertained. (*C*) CT scan demonstrates markedly increased attenuation in the right femoral marrow cavity (*arrow*). (*D*) A slice, slightly lower, demonstrates bone destruction, two sequestra, and periosteal new bone deposition. Compare the findings with the plain film findings. Surgically proven osteomyelitis.

UPPER EXTREMITY PROBLEMS
SHOULDER

Normal Soft Tissues of the Shoulder.
There are no specific fat pads to evaluate
around the shoulder, but over the clavicle
the companion shadow can be of some use.
This shadow represents the edge of the skin
and subcutaneous tissues as they pass over
the clavicle, and the edge can become obliterated by the edema associated with clavicular fractures (see Fig. 4.17). Other than this,
evaluation of the soft tissues of the shoulder
is nonspecific.

Detecting Fluid in the Shoulder Joint.
Fluid in the shoulder joints (i.e., pus or
blood) causes the humerus to be displaced
laterally and the joint space to be widened
(Fig. 4.16). Associated swelling, edema, and
bulging of the soft tissues around the shoulder may or may not be present, and the joint
capsule may bulge outwardly. These latter
findings are more prone to occur in the
young infants.

As far as positioning the shoulder in these
cases, one can accept almost any reasonable
anteroposterior position, just as long as both
the involved and noninvolved extremities
are examined in the same position. In other
words, one wants to avoid the situation
where one extremity is examined in internal
rotation while the other is examined in ex-

ternal rotation. On a practical basis, it often
is best to examine the involved extremity in
whichever position the patient holds that
extremity, and then to match that position
in the normal extremity.

Clavicular Injuries. Overall the clavicle
is the most commonly injured bone of the
shoulder in infants and young children, and
injury usually results from: (a) falling on an
outstretched extremity, (b) falling directly
on the shoulder, or (c) a direct blow to the
clavicle. By far the most common location
for a clavicular fracture is the midshaft, and
while many are easy to identify (Fig. 4.17A),
others are more elusive. One reason for this
is that many *clavicular fractures are greenstick or plastic bowing fractures or fractures
with a poorly visible fracture line.* In all of
these cases, one should learn to look first for
abnormal angulation or curvature of the
injured clavicle. This is best accomplished
by comparing one clavicle with the other,
and any discrepancy should be treated with
suspicion. In addition, one also should assess
the soft tissues for: (a) a general increase in
density due to edema and bleeding, (b) obliteration of the companion shadow of the
clavicle, and (c) obliteration of the supraclavicular fat-muscle interfaces (Fig. 4.17, *B*
and *C*).

Complete fractures through the midshaft
of the clavicle, with displacement of the

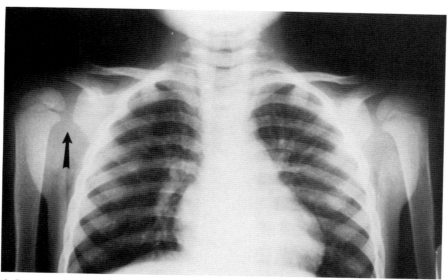

Figure 4.16. *Detecting fluid in the shoulder joint.* Note widening of the joint space on the right (*arrow*). The upper
humerus and humeral head are displaced laterally from the glenoid fossa. This signifies the presence of intra-
articular fluid. This child had *Haemophilus influenzae* septic arthritis.

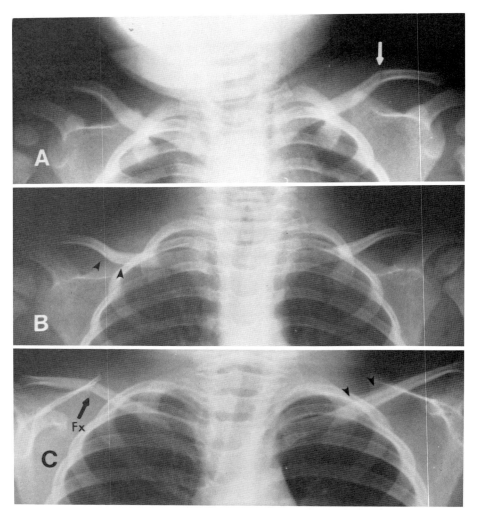

Figure 4.17. *Clavicular fractures.* (*A*) *Typical fracture* of clavicle. Note the easily identified fracture (*arrow*) of the bent left clavicle. (*B*) *Subtle bending fracture.* The only signs of a clavicular injury in this patient are those of unusual downward bending of the right clavicle (*arrows*) and a generalized increase in soft tissue density (edema) of the soft tissues around it. (*C*) *Subtle bending fracture with soft tissue changes.* In this patient, there is an unusual bending of the right clavicle, but the fracture line (*Fx*) is difficult to see because it is obscured by the overlying scapular tip. However, note that there is a generalized increase in soft tissue density of the soft tissues in the right supraclavicular region, and that the companion shadow on the right is absent. Compare these findings with the normal findings on the left, including the presence of a normal companion shadow (*arrows*). The companion shadow represents the skin and subcutaneous tissues overlying the clavicle. With edema and swelling, these soft tissues thicken and bulge and the companion shadow is lost.

fracture fragments, also are common but are not a problem as far as roentgenographic detection is concerned. However, even in these cases, very often the position of the fracture is such that it is hidden behind the first or second ribs. It is only with oblique or lordotic views that one can actually see the fracture (Fig. 4.18).

The most important pitfall in the evaluation of suspected clavicular fractures lies in

the misinterpretation of a clavicle distorted by poor positioning or patient rotation, for a fractured clavicle (Fig. 4.19).

Acromioclavicular separations (3) are not particularly common in infancy, but do occur in the older child and adolescent. In such cases, one should first look for soft tissue prominence over the acromioclavicular joint, and then for separation of the joint itself. In this regard, although the acromio-

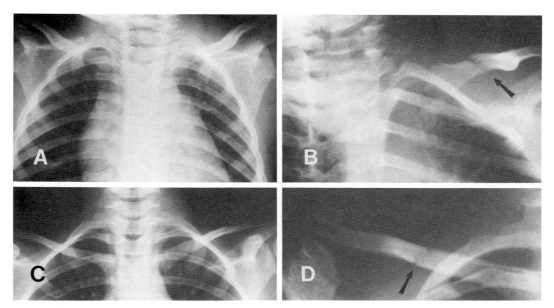

Figure 4.18. *Occult clavicular fractures.* (*A*) The clavicles are quite symmetric but note soft tissue swelling over the left clavicle. Also note that it might be more bent than the right. (*B*) Oblique view demonstrates clear-cut fracture through the medial portion of the left clavicle (*arrow*). (*C*) Curvature of the clavicles is asymmetric. This is important. This patient had injury to the right shoulder, but one cannot see the fracture behind the second rib. (*D*) Another view, however, demonstrates the fracture (*arrow*).

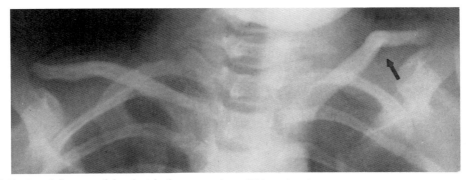

Figure 4.19. *Pseudofracture of the clavicle due to rotation.* This patient is rotated to the left, and this causes the left clavicle to telescope and appear bent (*arrow*).

clavicular joint will be widened, one often also will note widening between the clavicle and the coracoid process of the scapula (Fig. 4.20). Indeed, separation at this site due to ligamentous sprain often is easier to detect than is acromioclavicular separation. Furthermore, in some of these cases it has been noted that an associated coracoid process fracture can occur (6). In the infant and young child, rather than acromioclavicular separation, an isolated fracture through the lateral end of the clavicle usually is sustained. However, even in some of these

cases, a certain degree of acromioclavicular separation and coracoclavicular ligament sprain exists (Fig. 4.21).

Medical clavicular injuries usually consist of ***anterior or posterior dislocations***, for fracturing in this area is relatively uncommon. With anterior displacement, a clinically visible and palpable bulge is present over the involved sternoclavicular joint. With posterior displacement, such a bulge is not present but a more serious problem arises in that tracheal compression occurs (Fig. 4.22). On frontal view, dislocation of the medial end

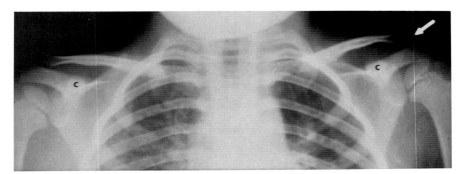

Figure 4.20. *Acromioclavicular separation.*   First note that the left clavicle is higher than the right, and then note that the acromioclavicular joint on the left is widened (*arrow*). However, in addition, note that the space between the clavicle and the coracoid process (*c*) also is increased (coracoclavicular ligament sprain).

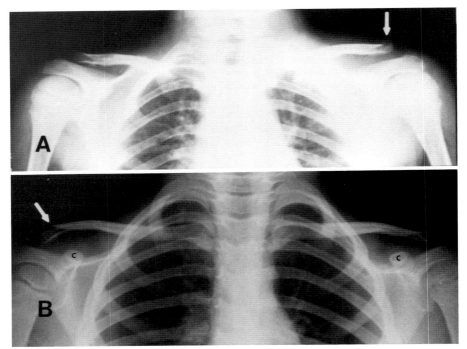

Figure 4.21. *Lateral clavicular fracture with varying degrees of acromioclavicular separation.*   (*A*) Note the fracture of the lateral end of the left clavicle (*arrow*). The space between the fracture fragment and acromial process of the scapula is barely widened. Minimal if any associated acromioclavicular separation exists. (*B*) Note the fracture of the lateral end of the right clavicle (*arrow*). However, also note that the space between the clavicle and coracoid process (*c*) is widened secondary to associated coracoclavicular ligament sprain. Although not visible on this illustration, a mild degree of acromioclavicular separation also was present in this patient.

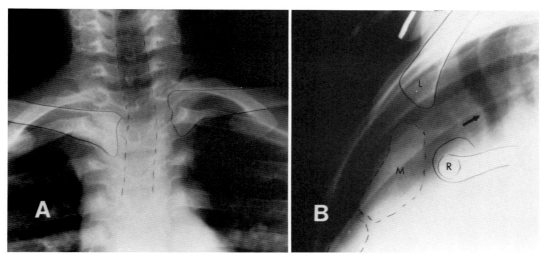

Figure 4.22. *Medial clavicular dislocation.* (*A*) Frontal view demonstrating typical downward displacement of the medial end of the right clavicle. This can occur with either posterior or anterior dislocations. (*B*) Oblique view demonstrating the posteriorly displaced right clavicle (*R*), and normally aligned left clavicle (*L*). Note associated anterior identation of the trachea (*arrow*). Manubrium, *M*. (Reprinted with permission from Lee, F.A., and Gwinn, J.L.: Retrosternal dislocation of the clavicle, Radiology 110: 631–634, 1974.)

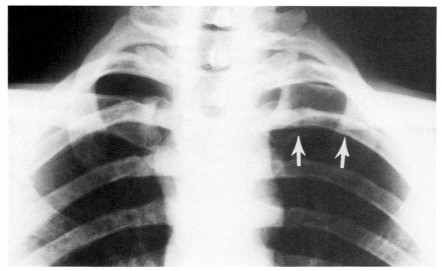

Figure 4.23. *Superior medial dislocation of clavicle.* Note superior displacement of the medially dislocated left clavicle (*arrows*).

of the clavicle, either anterior or posterior, can be suspected when it is noted that the medial end of the involved clavicle is lower than the medial end of the normal clavicle (Fig. 4.22). Occasionally the clavicle is displaced upward (Fig. 4.23). Thereafter, special views may be required for further delineation of the dislocation, and in this regard, the Heinig view illustrated in Fig. 4.24 has been suggested as the view of choice (5).

Injuries of the Upper Humerus. In childhood, one of the more common injuries of the upper humerus is the Salter-Harris type I or II *epiphyseal-metaphyseal injury (Figs. 4.25–4.27). Salter-Harris type III epiphyseal injuries are less common (Fig. 4.27C),* and types IV and V are quite uncommon in the shoulder. In those type I and II injuries where the epiphysis is completely separated, the diagnosis never is in doubt

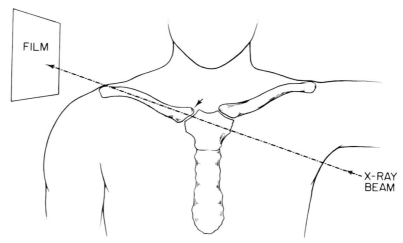

Figure 4.24. *Special view (Heinig view) for demonstration of medial clavicular dislocation.*   The right clavicle is dislocated and downwardly displaced (*arrow*). Note direction of the x-ray beam. The resulting image is seen in Figure 4.22*B*.

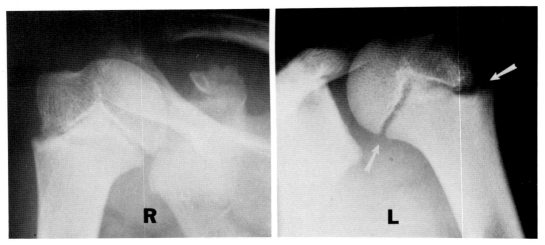

Figure 4.25. *Epiphyseal-metaphyseal fracture of the upper left humerus.*   Note that the epiphyseal line on the left is wider and more radiolucent (*arrows*) than the one on the right. Such widening of the epiphyseal line denotes the presence of a Salter-Harris type injury, either I or II. The findings above are those of a Salter-Harris type I injury. In addition, note that on the normal side the humeral head, along its lateral aspect, appears offset or displaced on the metaphysis. This is normal and should not be misinterpreted for a displaced epiphyseal fracture.

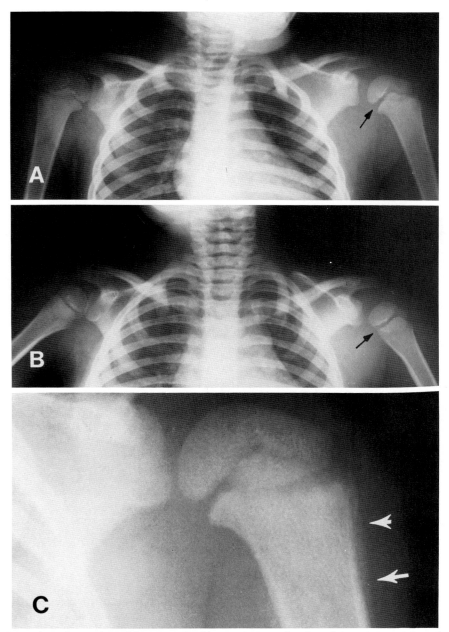

Figure 4.26. *Epiphyseal-metaphyseal fracture—shoulder.* (*A*) Note widening of the epiphyseal line of the upper left humerus (*arrow*). Also note that the joint space is widened, suggesting fluid (blood) in the joint. (*B*) Another view demonstrating similar findings. Note especially, that the epiphyseal line remains widened (*arrow*). (*C*) Follow-up film 2 weeks later demonstrates healing of the fracture with periosteal new bone along the upper humeral shaft (*arrows*).

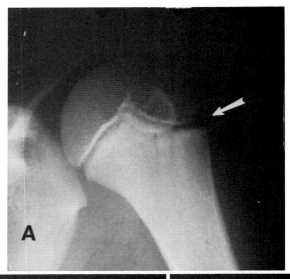

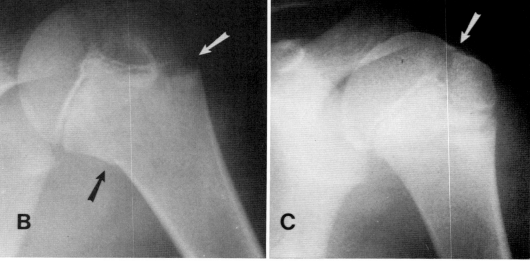

Figure 4.27. *Other epiphyseal-metaphyseal fractures of the upper humerus.* (*A*) Salter-Harris type II injury with a widened epiphyseal line laterally (*arrow*), and two poorly defined vertical fracture lines extending into the upper humeral shaft. (*B*) Salter-Harris type II injury with a widened epiphyseal line laterally (*white arrow*) and a cortical break medially (*black arrow*). The metaphyseal fracture fragment is rather large in this patient. (*C*) Salter-Harris type III injury. Note the fracture (*arrow*) through the nondisplaced epiphysis.

(6), but in the more subtle cases, one should look for widening of the epiphyseal line and/or the presence of a metaphyseal corner fracture. In chronic form, this same injury is the one seen in young boys (excuse me, and girls) playing baseball and partaking in overexuberant pitching. It is termed the *little leaguer's shoulder* (1, 2, 4, 9).

Other fractures occurring through the upper humerus include the easily identified surgical neck fracture, transverse or oblique

upper humeral shaft fractures, and the more subtle buckle or torus fractures (Fig. 4.28). In addition, it should be noted that fractures through unicameral bone cysts quite commonly occur in the upper humerus (see Fig. 4.10*C*).

A major pitfall in the evaluation of the upper humeral fractures is to misinterpret the normal epiphyseal line for a fracture. This can occur when the epiphyseal line is open and wide, or when it is closing and

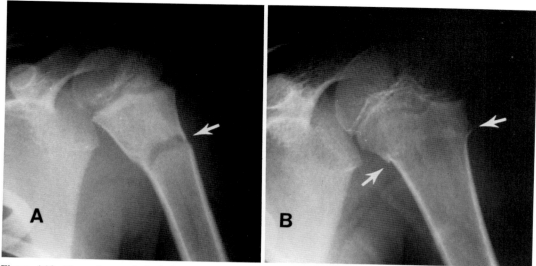

Figure 4.28. *Upper humeral shaft fractures.* (*A*) *Typical* transverse surgical neck fracture (*arrow*). (*B*) Buckle compression type fracture of the upper humerus (*arrows*). This type of fracture is quite common in infants and young children, for the cortex in this area is still relatively weak.

narrow (Fig. 4.29). Of course, when comparative views of the normal extremity are obtained, almost always the line appears exactly the same, and the problem is solved. However, this simple solution notwithstanding, it is still very common to miscall this normal finding for a fracture.

Dislocations of the shoulder are not common in the young infant and child for it is only after the epiphysis closes that it becomes a problem. The dislocations, of course, can be either anterior (i.e., subglenoid or subcoracoid), or posterior. The posterior dislocations are more difficult to detect, for overlapping of the humeral head and the glenoid fossa can be subtle. Anterior dislocations usually present a rather characteristic appearance with the humeral head being displaced downward and resting under the coracoid process or glenoid fossa (Fig. 4.30). In any case, and especially with posterior dislocations, transaxillary views of the shoulder should be obtained for clearer definition (Fig. 4.30).

Scapular Fractures. These can occur through the body of the scapula or the acromial or coracoid processes of the scapula. Fractures through the body of the scapula usually result from direct blows and can be linear, curvilinear (Fig. 4.31), or stellate. Fractures through the acromial and coracoid processes of the scapula can result from direct blows or falls on the outstretched extremity and may be difficult to detect (Fig. 4.31). Comparative views are of the utmost importance here, especially with the more peculiar fractures (Fig. 4.32).

Normal findings in the scapula misinterpreted for fractures include vascular grooves, and an almost endless assortment of bizarre appearing secondary centers of the acromion, coracoid process, and glenoid fossa (see Figs. 4.36 and 4.37).

Septic Arthritis, Osteomyelitis, and Cellulitis of the Shoulder. With septic arthritis, the most important roentgenographic feature is joint space widening and lateral displacement of the upper humerus (Fig. 4.33, *A* and *B*). These findings denote the presence of pus in the shoulder joint (8) and in the very young infant, the adjacent soft tissues may appear edematous and cause the whole shoulder to bulge. In the older child, however, the only finding usually is joint space widening.

When osteomyelitis or cellulitis of the shoulder is present, there usually is little in the way of joint space widening, except in the young infant, where septic arthritis and osteomyelitis frequently occur together. In such cases, of course, features of both conditions will be present (Fig. 4.33, *C* and *D*). With osteomyelitis alone, however, early stage findings usually consist of nothing

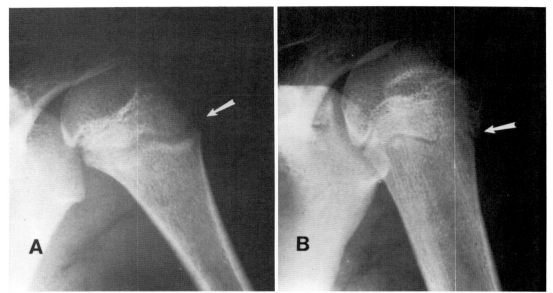

Figure 4.29. *Pseudofracture upper humerus—normal epiphyseal line.*   (*A*) Normal appearance of a wide epiphyseal line (*arrow*) often misinterpreted for a fracture. (*B*) Older child with narrower epiphyseal line mimicking a fracture (*arrow*).

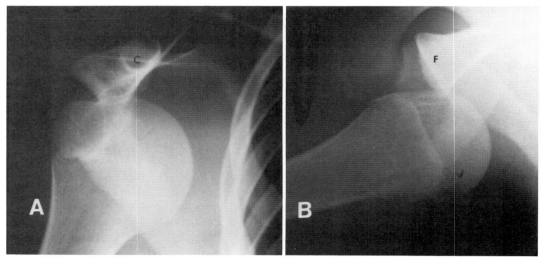

Figure 4.30. *Anterior dislocation of the shoulder.*   (*A*) Note abnormal position of the upper humerus. It is located below the coracoid process (*C*). This is a subcoracoid dislocation. (*B*) Transaxillary view showing dislocated humerus anterior to the glenoid fossa (*F*). With subglenoid dislocations, the humeral head lies under the glenoid fossa, while with posterior dislocations it lies posterior to the scapula.

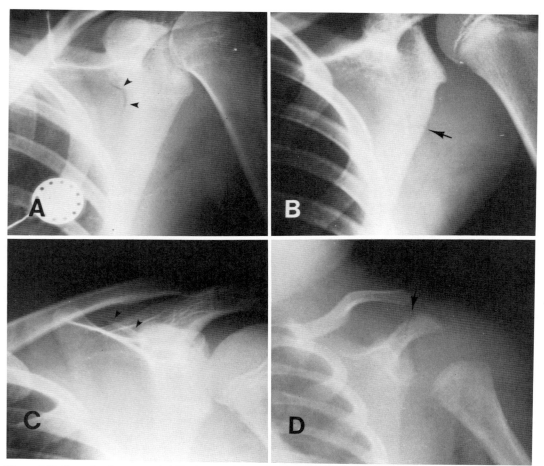

Figure 4.31. *Scapular fractures.* (*A*) Typical curvilinear fracture (*arrows*) of the body of the scapula. (*B*) Transverse, linear fracture (*arrow*) of the scapula. (*C*) Avulsion fracture (*arrows*) of the upper scapular edge in an older child. (*D*) Acromial fracture (*arrow*) in a battered infant.

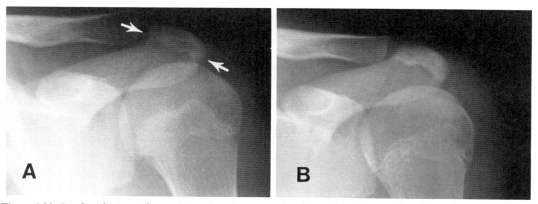

Figure 4.32. *Bending fracture of acromion; value of comparative views.* (*A*) Note peculiar shape of acromial process (*arrows*). This was a bending fracture of the acromion resulting from a direct fall on the tip of the shoulder. (*B*) Normal side for comparison.

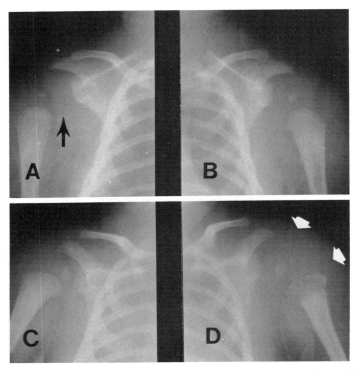

Figure 4.33. *Septic arthritis.* (*A*) Note widening of the joint space (*arrow*), due to pus in the joint. (*B*) Normal left side for comparison. *Septic arthritis and osteomyelitis.* (*C*) Normal right shoulder. (*D*) On the left, note bulging of the soft tissues of the left shoulder (*arrows*), and widening of the joint space due to pus in the joint. Destruction of the upper humerus also is present. If this patient had osteomyelitis alone, little, if any, joint space widening would occur. Contrarily, if septic arthritis were the only problem, no bone destruction of the metaphysis would be seen and soft tissue swelling would be less pronounced.

more than soft tissue edema and obliteration of the normal fat-muscle tissue planes. This causes the soft tissues to appear more homogeneously opaque than normal (Fig. 4.34), and later on, bony destruction can be seen. Cellulitis is more difficult to differentiate from osteomyelitis, but usually soft tissue swelling is more superficial. Fortunately, however, cellulitis around the shoulder is not a particularly common problem in children.

Subacute osteomyelitis, either of the upper metaphysis or epiphysis of the humerus can be a problem for diagnosis. In such cases a radiolucent defect, surrounded by a vague margin of osteosclerosis, is seen. Often the findings are misinterpreted for those of a bone cyst or a benign cortical defect.

Miscellaneous Shoulder Problems. Occasionally, one can encounter a patient who does not move his or her upper extremity because of: (a) scapular or clavicular involvement by Caffey's disease (infantile cortical hyperostosis), (b) osteomyelitis of the scapula or clavicle, or (c) histiocytosis X of the bones of the shoulder, but a discussion of these entities is beyond the scope of this book.

Normal Findings Causing Problems. Misinterpretation of the upper humeral epiphyseal line for a fracture has been dealt with earlier and is demonstrated in Figure 4.29. Other normal structures frequently misinterpreted for abnormalities include a bony exostosis along the inferior aspect of the clavicle just at the site of the costoclavicular ligament (Fig. 4.35*A*), and a normal accessory ossification center at the medial end of the clavicle (Fig. 4.35*B*). Still other normal structures causing problems include the various ossification centers of the scapula (Fig. 4.36), and in this regard, the secondary center for the coracoid process can be very large and surely suggestive of a fracture in

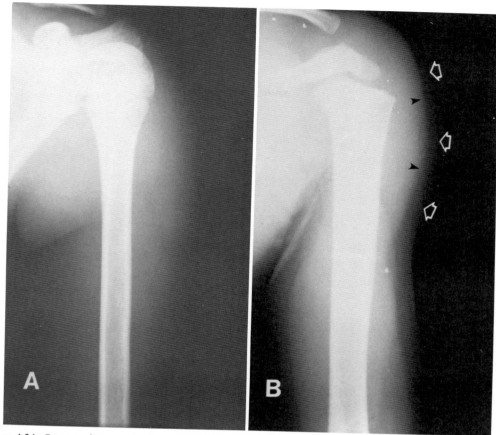

Figure 4.34. *Osteomyelitis—early changes in older child.* (*A*) Note that the humerus is intact, but that there is extensive edema of the adjacent soft tissues. No muscle-fat planes are identified, and the soft tissues are of homogeneous density. (*B*) Normal shoulder for comparison demonstrating the normal interface between the muscle (*black arrows*), and the subcutaneous fat (*white arrows*). Note that the other fat-muscle interfaces also are clearly visible.

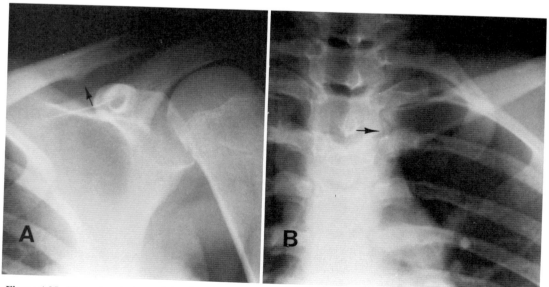

Figure 4.35. *Normal variations of the clavicle.* (*A*) Note the bony exostosis (*arrow*) at the site of the insertion of the costoclavicular ligament. (*B*) Normal medial accessory ossification center (*arrow*). The wire loop just below and medial to it is a wire suture in the sternum from a prior thoracotomy.

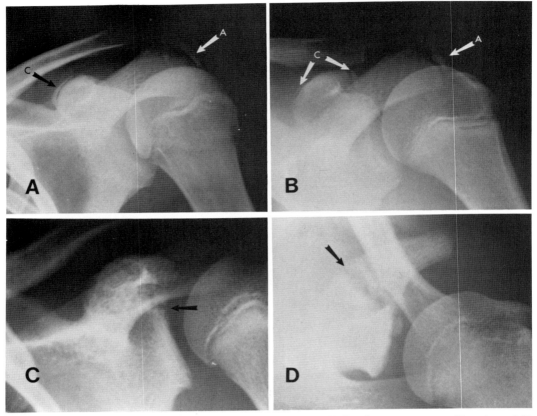

Figure 4.36. *Normal findings—scapular ossification centers.* (*A* and *B*) *Usual accessory centers.* Note the variable appearance of the accessory ossification centers of the acromion (*A*) and coracoid (*C*) process. (*C*) *Large coracoid secondary center.* Note the junction between the large coracoid secondary center and the scapula (*arrow*) simulating a fracture. (*D*) Special oblique view demonstrating that the fracture fragment actually is a large coracoid secondary center, and that the junction between it and the scapula produces a pseudofracture line (*arrow*). These large secondary centers should not be misinterpreted for fractures. This patient had a similar center in the other scapula.

some individuals (Fig. 4.36, *C* and *D*). Vascular grooves in the scapula also can create problems and be misinterpreted for fractures (Fig. 4.37). Finally, one might mention the normal deltoid notch, a finding frequently misinterpreted for a destructive lesion, and the vacuum joint phenomenon around the shoulder, as examples of other findings causing uncertainties in interpretation (Fig. 4.38).

REFERENCES

1. Adams, J.E.: Little league shoulder: osteochondrosis of proximal humeral epiphysis in boy baseball pitchers. Calif. Med. 105: 22–25, 1966.
2. Bowerman, J.W., and McDonnell, E.J.: Radiology of athletic injuries: baseball. Radiology 116: 611–615, 1975.
3. Decloux, P., Bonte, G., and Ducloux, M.: Acromioclavicular dislocation. Radiological, therapeutic and anatomophysiological study. Ann. Radiol. 15: 609–621, 1972.
4. Dotter, W.E.: Little leaguer's shoulder—a fracture of the proximal epiphyseal cartilage of the humerus due to baseball pitching. Guthrie Clin. Bull. 23: 68, 1953.
5. Lee, F.A., and Gwinn, J.L.: Retrosternal dislocation of the clavicle. Radiology 110: 631–634, 1974.
6. Nicastro, J.F., and Adair, D.M.: Fracture-dislocation of the shoulder in a 32-month-old child. J. Pediatr. Orthop. 2: 427–429, 1982.
7. Protass, J.J., Stampfli, F.V., and Osmer, J.C.: Coracoid process fracture diagnosis in acromioclavicular separation. Radiology 116: 61–64, 1975.
8. Schmidt, D., Mubarak, S., and Gelberman, R.: Septic shoulders in children. J. Pediatr. Orthop. 1: 67–72, 1981.
9. Torg, J.S., Pollack, H., and Sweterlitsch, P.: The effect of competitive pitching on the shoulders and elbows of preadolescent baseball players. Pediatrics 49: 267–272, 1972.

HUMERAL SHAFT

Midshaft fractures of the humerus commonly occur in infancy and childhood. The most common is the spiral or oblique fracture, but transverse fractures also are seen. Usually these fractures are so obvious that

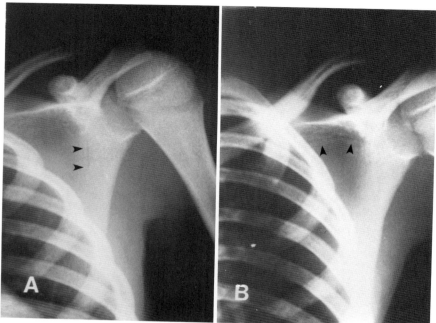

Figure 4.37. *Normal vascular grooves of scapula.* (*A* and *B*) Demonstration of vascular grooves of the scapula (*arrows*), frequently misinterpreted for fractures.

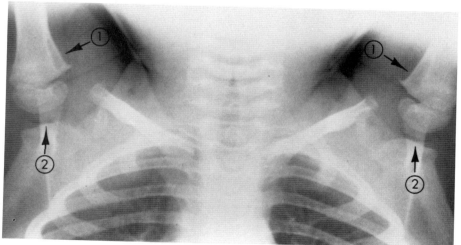

Figure 4.38. *Normal humeral notch and vacuum joint phenomenon.* Note bilateral humeral notches (*1*) often misinterpreted for destructive lesions of the proximal humerus. These notches represent a normal defect in the bone in the region of insertion of the deltoid muscle. They characteristically are visualized when the extremities are upwardly extended. Also note the normal vacuum joint phenomenon in both shoulders (*2*). This phenomenon occurs when the upper extremities are stretched and is normal. Although the term "vacuum joint" is used to describe this finding, there is debate as to whether the radiolucent area actually represents a vacuum, or a space filled with nitrogen or water vapor.

there is no problem in their roentgeno-graphic detection, but occasionally they are hairline and undisplaced and more difficult to detect (see Fig. 4.3*B*). Cortical buckling or torus fractures do not usually occur in the midshaft of the humerus, for the cortex is thick in this area, and the only normal finding which can be misinterpreted for a fracture is a normal vascular groove (Fig. 4.39).

ELBOW

Normal Soft Tissues and Fat Pads. In the elbow, the most important fat pads to assess are the anterior and posterior fat pads (1, 2, 12, 13, 16, 17). The anterior fat pad is located in the coronoid fossa while the posterior fat pad is located in the olecranon fossa. These fat pads must be evaluated on true lateral, flexed views of the elbow, for with any degree of rotation, their usefulness diminishes or is totally invalidated. Normally, on the true lateral flexed view of the elbow, the anterior fat pad is visible, but the

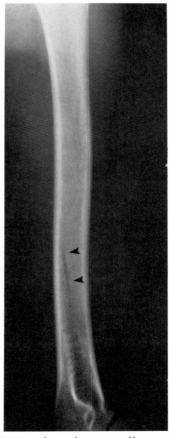

Figure 4.39. *Normal vascular groove of humerus.* Note the vascular groove (*arrows*) in the distal humerus. These vascular grooves can be confused with linear or spiral fractures. However, when one notes that the radiolucent line is rather wide and that there is slight sclerosis along either edge, one should make the diagnosis of normal vascular groove.

posterior fat pad is not (Fig. 4.40). The reason for the lack of visualization of the posterior fat pad is that it lies deep in the olecranon fossa. It becomes visible only when fluid in the joint displaces it posteriorly. On extension, however, it may be visible normally, but never on a flexed view. These fat pad configurations are very consistent, and consequently, any deviation from the configurations illustrated in Figure 4.40 should be considered abnormal.

The supinator fat pad (20) is another normal fat pad around the elbow. It also is seen on true lateral views and overlies the anterior aspect of the supinator muscle (Fig. 4.40). Overall, however, this fat pad is less useful than the other elbow fat pads, for it is less consistently visualized, especially in infants and young children. Nonetheless, it can be displaced with fractures of the proximal radius and obliterated with edema around the elbow.

Evaluation of the soft tissues around the elbow, other than the fat pads, is nonspecific. Basically, it consists of noting whether the fat-muscle interfaces are distinct or indistinct. If they are indistinct, edema is present.

Detecting Fluid in the Elbow Joint—Displaced Fat Pads. Fluid in the elbow joint usually produces upward and outward displacement of the anterior and posterior fat pads (Fig. 4.41*A*). These fat pads overlie the capsule of the elbow joint, and their displacement is very accurate in reflecting the presence of intra-articular fluid. Indeed, evaluation of the fat pads is the only way to roentgenographically determine whether fluid is present in the elbow joint, for the ligaments and muscles around the elbow are too strong to allow distraction of the articulating bones. Consequently, significant joint space widening seldom, if ever, is seen.

Other Abnormal Fat Pad Configurations. As has been noted in the preceding paragraph, both fat pads are displaced when fluid accumulates in the elbow joint (Fig. 4.41*A*). However, if edema surrounds the elbow joint, the fat pads, rather than being displaced, are obliterated. In addition, both of these changes can occur together and consequently a number of abnormal fat pad configurations around the elbow can exist (Fig. 4.41).

Injuries of the Distal Humerus. Injuries

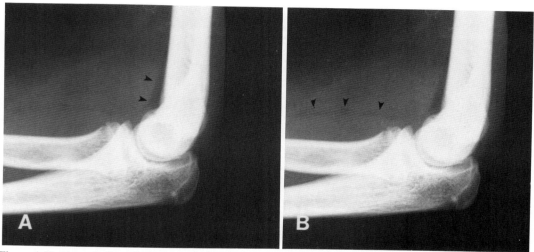

Figure 4.40. *Normal elbow fat pads.* (*A*) The anterior fat pad (*arrows*) normally is visible as a thin, triangular radiolucency anterior to the humerus. The posterior fat pad, on true lateral flexed views of the elbow, is not visible under normal circumstances. (*B*) The supinator fat pad (*arrows*) is thin and more often visible in older children.

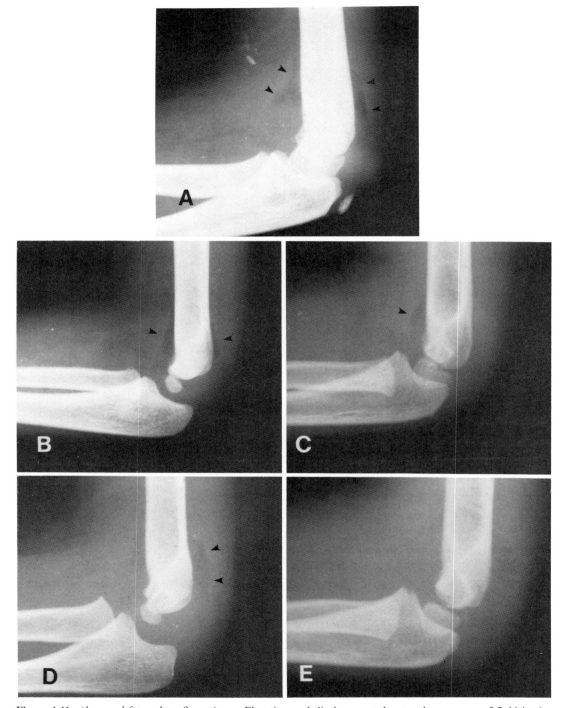

Figure 4.41. *Abnormal fat pad configurations.*   Elevation and displacement denotes the presence of fluid in the joint; obliteration denotes periarticular edema and swelling. Both can occur together. (*A*) *Elevation and displacement only.* Note that both the anterior and posterior fat pads are visible and displaced upward and outward (*arrows*). This patient had an occult supracondylar fracture of the humerus. (*B*) *Less pronounced displacement* of the fat pads. The fact that the posterior fat pad is even visible is abnormal in itself, for when it is visible, it is displaced. (*C*) *Anterior fat pad displacement only.* The anterior fat pad is displaced and elevated (*arrow*) while the posterior fat pad is not displaced and not visible. This patient had a minimal fracture of the lateral condyle. (*D*) *Displacement and obliteration.* The posterior fat pad is markedly displaced (*arrows*) and a little hazy (obliterated) because of

of the distal end of the humerus most commonly include: (a) supracondylar fractures, (b) lateral condylar fractures, and (c) medial epicondylar fractures. The most common of these, however, is the ***supracondylar fracture*** and generally this fracture results from a fall on the outstretched upper extremity. The classic, clearly visible, supracondylar fracture with angulation and posterior displacement of the distal fragment is not difficult to recognize (Fig. 4.42). However, when the fracture is hairline or merely a plastic, bending fracture, little angulation occurs. In such cases, one must rely more on fat pad abnormalities and an abnormal anterior humeral line. The anterior humeral line is a line drawn along the anterior aspect of the distal humerus and should be applied on true lateral views. Under normal circumstances it intersects the ossified capitellum somewhere through its middle third (22). If it intersects the capitellum through the anterior third, or if it misses it entirely, a posteriorly angulated supracondylar fracture should be present (Fig. 4.43). The anterior humeral line is a little more difficult to apply in the young

infant where the capitellum is incompletely ossified, but even in these cases if the findings are compared to those on the normal side, posterior displacement will be detected if present. In addition, in almost every instance, the fat pads are elevated and/or obliterated in these patients, and if they are, one should assume that an elbow injury has occurred. Not always will it be a supracondylar fracture but since this fracture is so common, in the absence of other visible fractures, one should assume that it is present. In many of these cases, on follow-up healing phase films, one's original suspicions will be confirmed (Fig. 4.44). There will, of course, be cases where no such evidence of healing is present, and in such cases one assumes that a traumatic joint effusion only was present. However, it is better to have a few of these cases than to miss those with occult supracondylar fractures.

Although most fractures through the supracondylar region are of the type demonstrated in Figures 4.42 through 4.44, in the young infant where the cortex is relatively thin and weak, one can encounter buckle

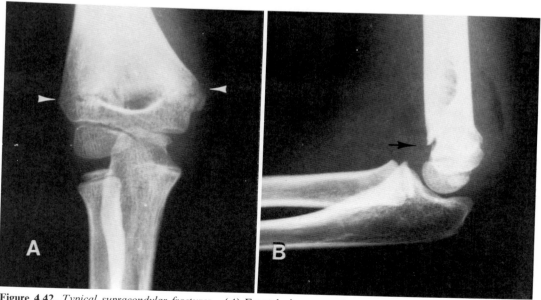

Figure 4.42. *Typical supracondylar fractures.* (*A*) Frontal view; note the transverse fracture line (*arrows*). (*B*) Lateral view; note the anterior fracture (*arrow*), and posterior tilting of the distal fracture fragment. In addition, note that the anterior fat pad is elevated and obliterated, and that the posterior fat pad is markedly elevated.

edema around the elbow. The anterior fat pad also is displaced, but because of edema, also is obliterated. Only a subtle suggestion of its presence, in its abnormally elevated position, is noted. (*E*) *Displacement and marked obliteration.* Both fat pads are displaced and elevated, but both are barely visible because of extensive edema around the elbow. Both this patient and the patient in (*D*) had subtle distal humerus fractures.

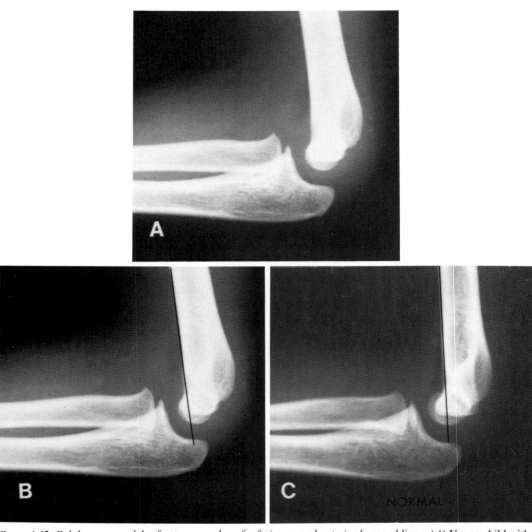

Figure 4.43. *Subtle supracondylar fractures—value of soft tissues and anterior humeral line.*   (*A*) Young child with elbow injury. Note soft tissue swelling around the elbow and a partially obliterated and elevated anterior fat pad. (*B*) Same elbow. The anterior humeral line intersects the capitellum through its anterior third. An occult, greenstick or bending fracture should be suspected. (*C*) Normal elbow for comparison. Note the position of the normal anterior fat pad and the normal position of the anterior humeral line. It intersects the capitellum through its posterior two-thirds.

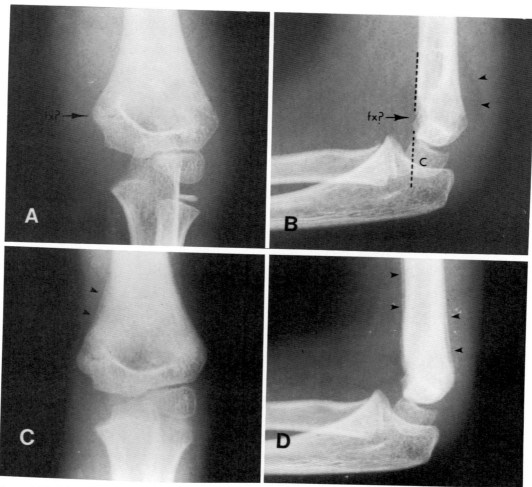

Figure 4.44. *Subtle supracondylar fracture with healing.* (*A*) Frontal view demonstrating little or no abnormality. A subtle fracture line (*fx*) is suggested medially. (*B*) Lateral view demonstrating abnormal fat pads and an anterior humeral line which intersects the capitellum (*c*) through its anterior third. This should suggest posterior displacement of the capitellum and an underlying supracondylar fracture. A fracture line (*arrow*) also is suggested, but it is not definitely visible. (*C*) Two weeks later note periosteal new bone deposition along both sides of the distal humerus (*arrows*). The fracture line is more clearly visible. (*D*) Lateral view demonstrating periosteal new bone deposition along the shaft of the humerus (*arrows*). Also note that the fat pads have returned to normal, but that the capitellum still is posteriorly displaced.

fractures in this region (Fig. 4.45). Of course, as with any buckle type fracture, one view may be better than the other in terms of fracture visualization, and indeed, one often requires oblique views for full demonstration of these fractures. Finally, it should be noted that in some cases a supracondylar fracture results in a cubitus varus (gunstock) deformity of the elbow (14).

In terms of *condylar* and *epicondylar* injuries of the distal humerus, it is the medial epicondyle and lateral condyle which most commonly are injured (5, 19). Unfortunately, however, many of these fractures are rather subtle, and once again examination of the soft tissues becomes most important. In this regard, an abnormality of the fat pads of the elbow usually is present, but more importantly, there will be tell tale unilateral swelling and edema of the soft tissues. With medial epicondylar fractures, of course, such swelling occurs medially while with lateral condylar fractures, it occurs laterally. The presence of such unilateral soft tissue change is especially important in the assessment of those medial epicondylar injuries where minimal or no displacement of the epicondyle occurs (Fig. 4.46), or in children under 5–7 years of age where the epicondyle is not yet ossified.

A wide range of medial epicondylar injuries occur, and one can see patients who demonstrate simple separation of the epicondyle to those who demonstrate complete dislocation and/or joint space entrapment of the epicondyle (Fig. 4.47). Medial epicondylar injuries result from avulsion secondary to the pull of the flexor pronator tendon, and thus, the more severe the wrenching injury, the more severe the displacement. In some cases minimal or no displacement is seen (Fig. 4.48*A*), while in others not only will displacement be present, but the medial epicondyle also will be rotated (Fig. 4.48*B*). When entrapment of the medial epicondyle occurs, the medial epicondyle is not visible in its normal position (Fig. 4.49). In addition to these injuries of the medial epicondyle, it should be noted that avulsion of this secondary center frequently accompanies dislocations of the elbow. In these cases, the fact that the medial epicondyle is displaced can elude detection until postreduction films are obtained (Fig. 4.50).

With lateral condylar injuries, it is most important to determine whether they are displaced or undisplaced. When displacement occurs, it occurs upward and outward, and does so when the fracture extends through the articular cartilage of the distal humerus. In these cases, the stabilizing, hinge-like function of the nondisplaced fracture fragment is lost and the injury becomes unstable (Fig. 4.51). Such fractures require

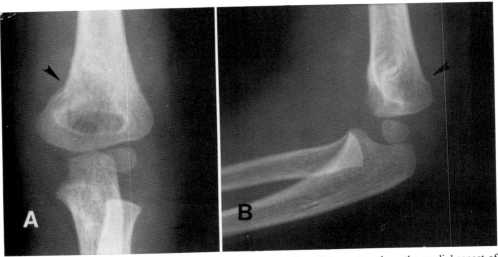

Figure 4.45. *Buckle fracture of the distal humerus.* (*A*) Note buckling of the cortex along the medial aspect of the distal humerus (*arrow*). (*B*) Lateral view demonstrating buckling of the cortex posteriorly and posterior displacement of the capitellum. Also note the faintly visible, but definitely displaced posterior fat pad. The anterior fat pad is, for the most part, obliterated.

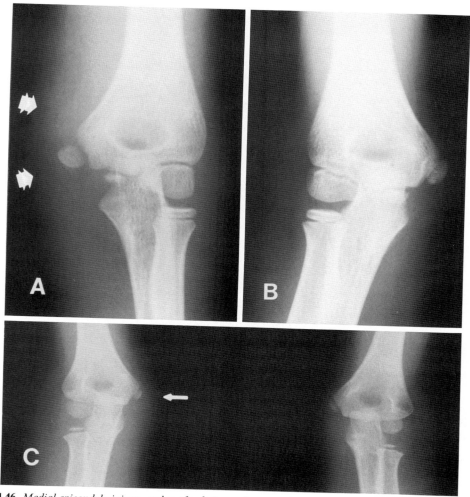

Figure 4.46. *Medial epicondyle injury—value of soft tissue changes.* (*A*) Note prominence of the soft tissues over the medial epicondyle (*arrows*) and that the medial epicondyle appears displaced. (*B*) Comparative view of other side demonstrates normal position of medial epicondyle and lack of soft tissue swelling. (*C*) *More subtle case.* Note swelling over the right medial epicondyle (*arrow*). However, the epicondyle itself does not appear particularly displaced. On the normal side, note that there is no soft tissue swelling over the medial epicondyle. In addition, in this patient, note that there is a small, cortical, corner fracture of the head of the radius on the right.

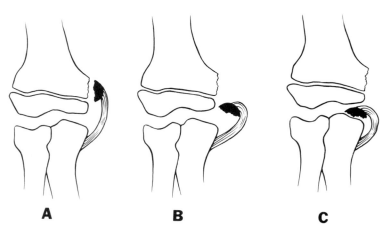

Figure 4.47. *Range of medial epicondylar injuries—diagramatic representation.* (*A*) Simple separation. (*B*) Separation with rotation. (*C*) Separation with entrapment in joint space.

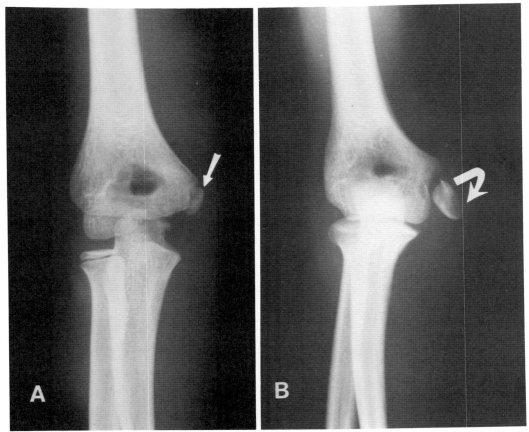

Figure 4.48. *Medial epicondylar avulsions—varying degrees.* (*A*) Minimal separation of the medial epicondyle with slight downward displacement (*arrow*). Note that the soft tissues over the area are a little thickened. (*B*) Markedly displaced and completely rotated medial epicondyle (*arrow*).

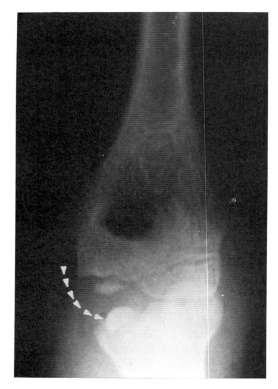

Figure 4.49. *Medial epicondylar entrapment.* Note the abnormal position of the entrapped medial epicondyle. It has been displaced from its normal position, and now lies in the intra-articular space (*arrows*). (Courtesy Lee Rogers, M.D., and Harvey White, M.D.)

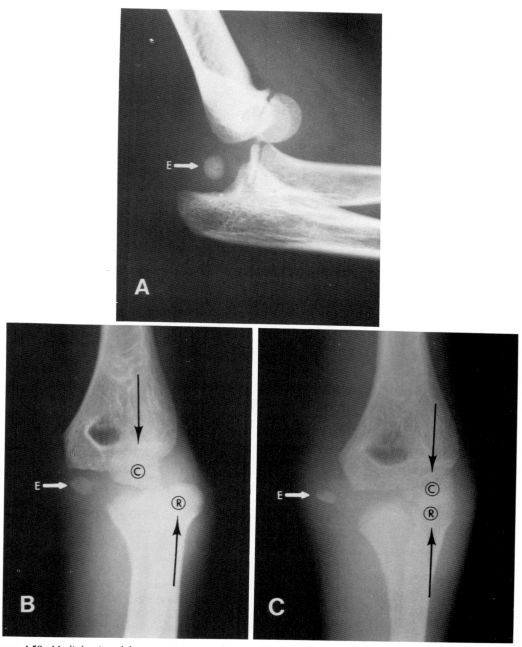

Figure 4.50. *Medial epicondyle separation secondary to elbow dislocation.* (*A*) Lateral view; total dislocation of the elbow. Note position of the medial epicondyle (*E*). (*B*) Frontal view demonstrating complete dislocation of the elbow. Note that the capitellum (*C*) does not line up with the proximal radial head (*R*). However, also note the position of the displaced medial epicondyle (*E*). Just beneath it is a small avulsed sliver-like metaphyseal bony fragment. (*C*) Postreduction film demonstrates extensive edema of the elbow and persistent separation of the medial epicondyle (*E*). Now note that the capitellum (*C*) is in a straight line relationship with the head of the radius (*R*).

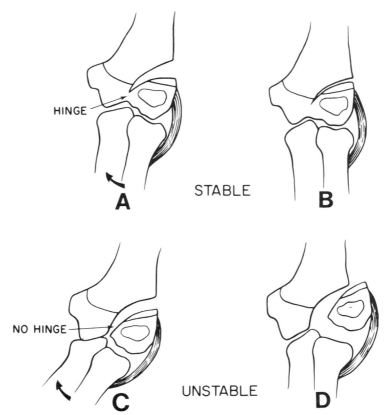

Figure 4.51. *Lateral condyle fractures—mechanics of stability and instability.* (*A*) *Stable fracture.* Twisting forces (*arrow*) cause separation of the lateral condyle from the humeral metaphysis. The articular cartilage, however, is incompletely broken and a stabilizing hinge remains. (*B*) When the fracture-causing forces are removed, the fracture fragment returns to a near normal position. It is stable. (*C*) *Unstable fracture.* Same twisting forces (*curved large arrow*) causing complete fracture through the articular cartilage with no residual hinge. (*D*) With removal of the forces, the totally separated lateral condyle rotates upward and outward. Because there is no hinge remaining, the fracture is unstable. (Redrawn from Rang, M.: *Children's Fractures,* J. B. Lippincott Co., Philadelphia, 1974.)

internal fixation, and thus it is most important to identify them accurately. Examples of displaced and nondisplaced lateral condylar fractures are presented in Fig. 4.52. Another variation of the lateral condylar fracture occurs in young infants where only a small sliver of the metaphysis is avulsed. In these cases, close inspection of roentgenograms and assessment of the fat pads and adjacent soft tissues is most worthwhile (Fig. 4.53), but in other cases oblique views become more important (Fig. 4.54).

Lateral epicondylar and medial condylar fractures are much less common than the fractures just discussed, but in those cases where they occur, similar subtle bony and unilateral soft tissue changes should serve to alert one to their presence. *Total fractures*

through the condylar regions of the humerus can present clinically with apparent dislocation of the elbow (8, 15, 21). Roentgenographically, however, the misconception is readily corrected, for the findings are completely different from those of true dislocation of the elbow (Fig. 4.55).

The *little leaguer's elbow* usually is devoid of significant soft tissue or bony abnormalities on the roentgenograms (3, 4, 23). It is a traumatic lesion resulting from too much pitching at too young an age, and if bony changes occur, they consist of fragmentation and enlargement of the medial epicondyle. However, if such stress on the elbow continues, overgrowth and fragmentation of various epiphyses and secondary centers around the elbow (10), chronic anterior angulation

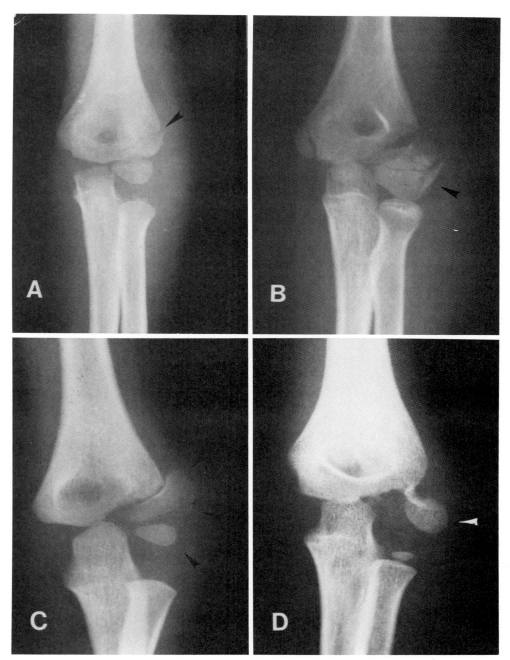

Figure 4.52. *Range of lateral condylar fractures—roentgenographic appearance.* (*A*) Stable fracture—hinge intact. Note the undisplaced lateral condylar fracture (*arrow*). Also note the presence of adjacent unilateral edema of the soft tissues. (*B*) Stable fracture hinge intact. In this case, however, there is more downward displacement of the fractured fragment (*arrow*). (*C*) Unstable fracture—hinge not intact. Note pronounced lateral and upward displacement of the fractured lateral condyle (*arrows*). (*D*) Unstable fracture—hinge not intact. Note complete rotation and marked upward displacement of the lateral condyle (*arrow*).

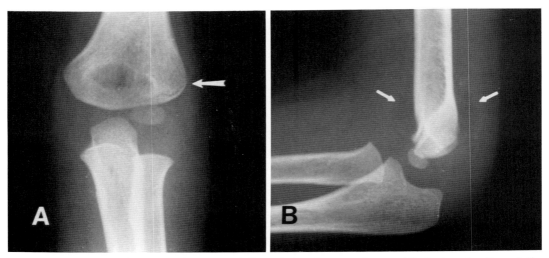

Figure 4.53. *Subtle lateral condylar fracture.* (*A*) Frontal view demonstrating a subtle fracture line through the lateral condyle (*arrow*). (*B*) Lateral view demonstrating abnormal displacement of both the anterior and posterior fat pads (*arrows*). This is a stable fracture.

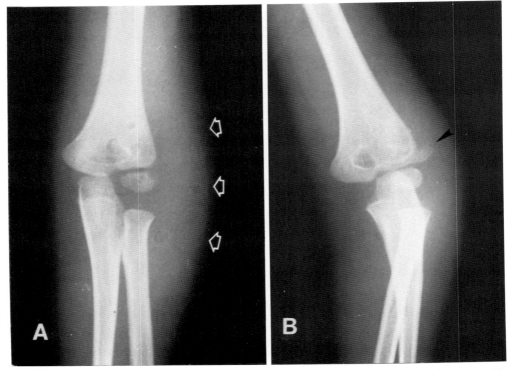

Figure 4.54. *Lateral condylar fracture—value of oblique film.* (*A*) Frontal view demonstrating no significant abnormality in the bones. However, note prominent unilateral swelling of the soft tissues over the lateral condyle (*arrows*). This should signify the presence of an injury to the lateral condyle. (*B*) Oblique view demonstrates the displaced fracture fragment with greater clarity (*arrow*).

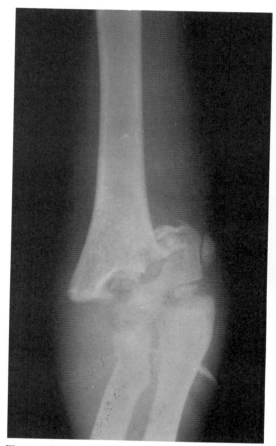

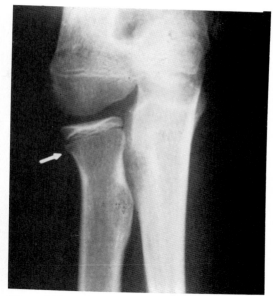

Figure 4.56. *Radial head corner fracture.* Note the minimally impacted corner fracture of the radial head (*arrow*).

Figure 4.55. *Complete fracture distal elbow—clinical pseudodislocation.* Note the completely displaced fracture of the distal humerus. Clinically, this type of injury can cause the elbow to appear dislocated, but in actual fact, no dislocation is present. Note that the displaced distal humeral fracture fragment is in normal alignment with both the radius and ulna. Compare with true dislocation of the elbow in Figure 4.50.

of the radial head (9, 10), and nonunion of the olecranon epiphysis (18) can occur.

Injuries of the Radial Head. Gross, fragmented or displaced fractures of the radial head are not difficult to detect, but the more *subtle corner fracture* frequently is missed (Fig. 4.56). Of course, in most cases, abnormalities of the soft tissues and fat pads around the elbow can alert one to the presence of this fracture, but still, the fracture commonly remains elusive. Equally important as not missing the fracture, however, is not misinterpreting a normal defect in the radial head of many young infants for an

actual fracture (Fig. 4.57). The notch defect in question usually is seen in infants and young children where the radial head epiphysis is not ossified. In the older child, it usually is not a problem.

Impaction fractures of the radial head also can be difficult to detect. In such cases, it is of the utmost importance to obtain comparative views of the normal extremity, and then to look for any subtle evidence of cortical buckling, radial head tilting, or cortical fracturing (Fig. 4.58). Even then, the most subtle of these fractures will elude one's initial detection, and only when follow-up films are obtained will it come to one's attention that such a fracture existed in the first place (Fig. 4.59).

Dislocation of the radius (radial head) obviously occurs when the entire elbow is dislocated, but *dislocation of the radius alone* usually occurs in association with a fracture of the ulna (i.e., Monteggia fracture). The ulnar fracture can occur through the proximal end of the ulna (Fig. 4.60) or the midshaft of the ulna (see Fig. 4.73). In assessing the radius for dislocation, one should determine whether the radial head and capitellum line up in a straight line. If they do not, the

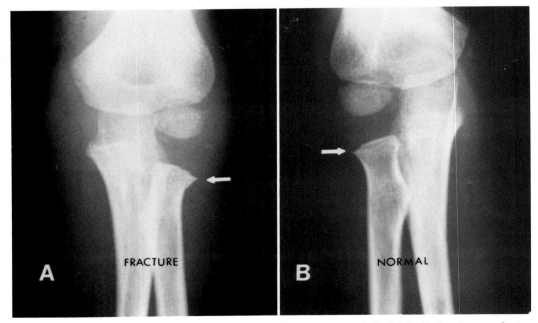

Figure 4.57. *Radial head corner fracture versus normal notch.* (*A*) Note typical, slightly displaced corner fracture of the proximal radial head (*arrow*). (*B*) Normal side for comparison. Note normal notch in radial head (*arrow*), frequently misinterpreted for a fracture. Also note that the soft tissues in (*A*) (fracture side) are fatter and more opaque due to edema and swelling.

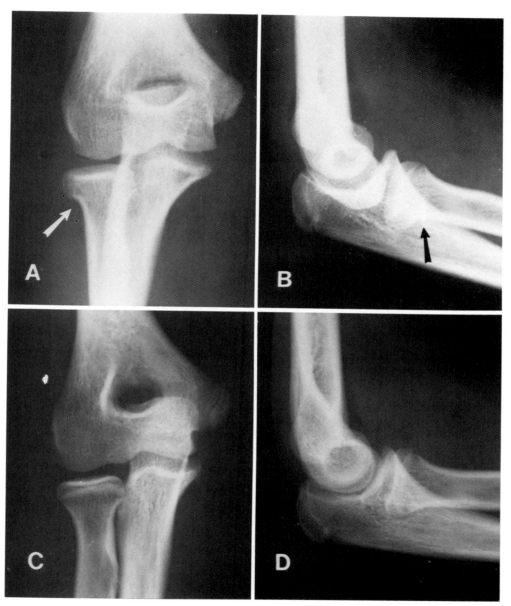

Figure 4.58. *Impacted radial head fracture.* (*A*) Note the minimal cortical break in the radial head (*arrow*). (*B*) Lateral view demonstrating displaced fat pads and subtle suggestion of the same fracture in the radial head (*arrow*). The findings on both views might be overlooked unless compared with the same area on the normal side. (*C*) Normal frontal view for comparison. Compare the configuration of the normal radial head with the tilted and slightly impacted head in (*A*). (*D*) Normal lateral view for comparison. Compare again this normal radial head with the slightly impacted and tilted head in (*B*).

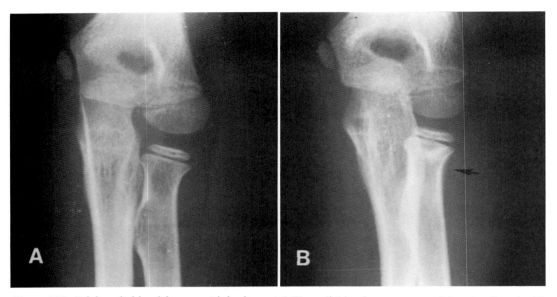

Figure 4.59. *Subtle radial head fracture with healing.* (*A*) The radial head appears normal, but the elbow in this patient was painful. (*B*) Two weeks later note periosteal new bone deposition (*arrow*), and sclerosis of the metaphysis indicating the presence of a healing, impacted radial head fracture.

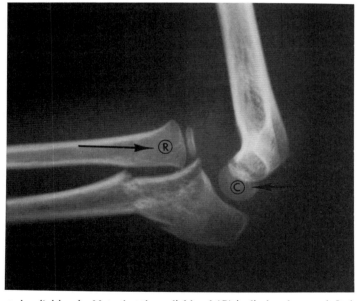

Figure 4.60. *Dislocated radial head.* Note that the radial head (*R*) is displaced upward. It does not line up in a straight line relationship with the capitellum (*C*). Also note the angulated fracture of the proximal ulna. The ulna is not dislocated.

radius is dislocated (Fig. 4.60). This rule is valid on both lateral and anteroposterior views.

Dislocation of the radial head from the annular ligament, or the so-called "*pulled*,"

"*curbstone*," or "*nursemaid's*" elbow, is not a true dislocation (11, 19). Rather, there is subluxation of the radial head from the annular ligament, incomplete tearing of the ligament, and subsequent entrapment of a portion of the ligament in the joint space (Fig. 4.61). This is a very common elbow injury in infancy and early childhood and results from a brisk pull on the elbow such as occurs when lifting the child by one arm. The condition produces exquisite pain and a most unhappy child. The clinical picture is absolutely characteristic: a previously well child suddenly refuses to move the involved extremity. Clinical examination is not productive, for any way you move the arm, or indeed, even touch the arm, the child seems to hurt. The arm is held in slight flexion and pronation, and supination is impossible without great pain.

The roentgenographic findings in "pulled" elbow usually are negative, both in terms of bony and soft tissue abnormality. There is no true dislocation of the radial head, and consequently the radial head and capitellum line up in their normal straight line relationship. Usually, it is very difficult to position these patients for adequate roentgenograms, but on the other hand, many times while trying to position the arm properly, such manipulation leads to reduction of the sub-

luxation. Indeed, almost as if by magic, there is an immediate full return to normal movement of the extremity, and a previously crying, tormented child is all smiles. Actually, if one is cognizant of this injury, it can be reduced before roentgenograms ever are obtained, for with the thumb over the radial head, supination and slight flexion of the elbow will result in a palpable click and subsequent reduction of the radial head (19). After reduction, one can encounter, in some cases, some evidence of fat pad displacement suggesting minimal fluid accumulation in the joint.

Fractures of the Proximal Ulna and Olecranon.   Fractures of the proximal ulna can occur with elbow dislocations, falls on the outstretched extremity, or direct blows to the olecranon. Gross fractures of the olecranon are not difficult to detect, but more subtle fractures may elude one's initial inspection. Fortunately, most of these fractures are associated with some abnormality of the elbow fat pads (Fig. 4.62). However, one should remember that the ulna is prone to a number of peculiar fractures, many of

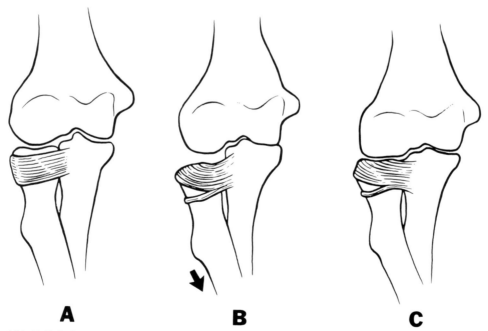

A   **B**   **C**

Figure 4.61. *Pulled elbow mechanics.* (*A*) Note position of the normal annular ligament. It is wrapped around the radial head. (*B*) With pulling on the elbow, the annular ligament is torn, and some of the fibers roll over the radial head. (*C*) When pulling stops, the fibers which rolled over the radial head remain in that position and the elbow becomes painful. (Redrawn and modified from Rang, M.: *Children's Fractures*, J. B. Lippincott Co., Philadelphia, 1974.)

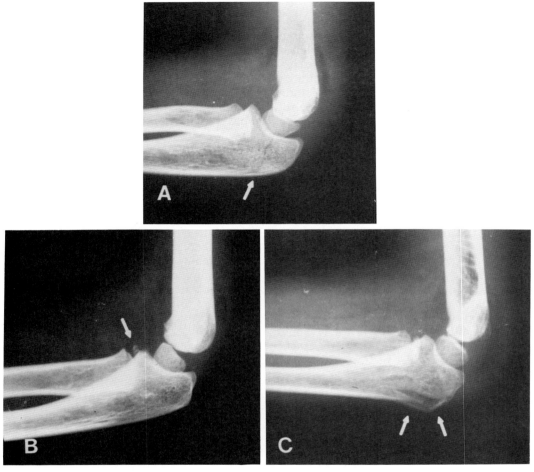

Figure 4.62. *Proximal ulnar fractures.* (*A*) Note linear fracture (*arrow*) through the olecranon. There is no bony displacement, but both fat pads are displaced outward. (*B*) Avulsion fracture of the coronoid process of the ulna (*arrow*). Once again note that both elbow fat pads are displaced. (*C*) Cortical buckling, impaction fracture of the proximal ulna (*arrows*). The fat pads are elevated, indicating the presence of interarticular bleeding.

which are linear and not easy to detect (Fig. 4.63).

Dislocation of the Elbow. Total dislocation of the elbow is not particularly common and usually is associated with a fracture of one or more of the bones of the elbow. Occasionally no fractures exist, but more often one will see transverse or spiral fractures of one of the bones of the elbow or avulsion fractures of the condyles and epicondyles (see Fig. 4.50, p. 000). The clinical deformity in these patients is striking, but a similar deformity can occur with completely displaced fractures through the distal humerus. In these cases, there is no dislocation of the elbow, but the markedly displaced fracture causes the clinical findings to suggest true dislocation. Roentgenographically, however, the two conditions usually are readily differentiated (see Fig. 4.55, and compare with Fig. 4.50).

Osteochondritis of the Elbow. Although not a common problem, osteochondritis of the elbow can involve the capitellum, trochlear epiphysis, or radial head (6). Involvement of the capitellum perhaps is most common and produces a bony defect with subtle adjacent sclerosis (Fig. 4.64).

Septic Arthritis, Osteomyelitis, and Cellulitis of the Elbow. Septic arthritis of the elbow is not as common as is septic arthritis of the shoulder and hip. However, when it

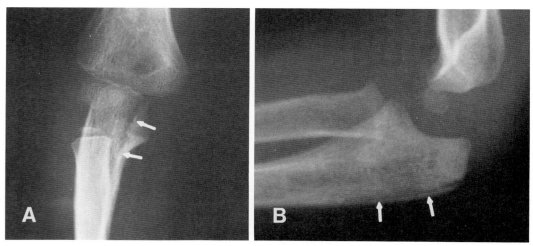

Figure 4.63. *Linear fractures of olecranon process.* (*A*) Note linear fracture of olecranon (*arrows*). (*B*) Another patient with a peculiar linear fracture of the olecranon (*arrows*).

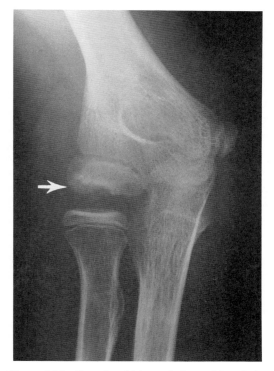

Figure 4.64. *Osteochondritis capitellum.* Note lytic defect with sclerotic border in capitellum (*arrow*).

occurs, it produces marked swelling around the elbow and displacement or obliteration of the elbow fat pads (Fig. 4.65, *A* and *B*). Usually, however, there is little in the way of joint space widening. Osteomyelitis of the

bones around the elbow usually produces extensive deep soft tissue swelling and obliteration of the normal soft tissues and fat pads (Fig. 4.65, *C* and *D*). If fat pad displacement occurs it is more posterior than upward (Fig. 4.65*D*). In the early stages, there is little in the way of bony destruction, but after 10 days or so bone destruction and periosteal new bone deposition will be seen.

With cellulitis of the elbow, if edema is circumferential, the findings are difficult to differentiate from those of early osteomyelitis. However, if edema is superficial, and localized to one side of the elbow, the diagnosis of localized cellulitis can be made with greater confidence (Fig. 4.66). In many such cases, one actually is dealing with an acute epitrochlear lymphadenitis (7).

Normal Variations Causing Problems. The most common normal variations misinterpreted for a fracture are the various secondary ossification centers around the elbow (Fig. 4.67). Of these, the sliver-like lateral epicondyle and the frequently, irregularly ossified medial condyle are the two most problematic bones. However, they are followed in short order by the accessory center of the olecranon (Fig. 4.67*B*). Another normal finding misinterpreted for abnormality is the circular radiolucency in the distal humerus, representing an area of normal thinning of the floor of the olecranon fossa (Fig. 4.67). In young infants, this radiolucency can suggest osteo-

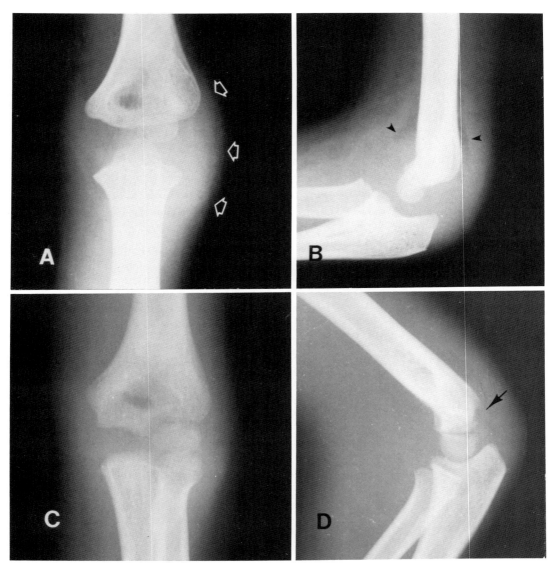

Figure 4.65. *Septic arthritis.* (*A*) Frontal view demonstrating extensive swelling around the elbow (*arrows*). (*B*) Lateral view demonstrating elevation of both the anterior and posterior fat pads (*arrows*). This indicates the presence of fluid (pus) in the elbow joint. (*C*) *Osteomyelitis of the distal humerus.* Frontal view. Note extensive circumferential deep swelling around the elbow. The soft tissues are homogeneously opaque and no normal muscle-fat interfaces are seen. (*D*) Lateral view demonstrating extensive deep edema around the elbow and an area of destruction in the distal humerus (*arrow*). Note that the anterior fat pad has been totally obliterated by edema, and that the indistinct posterior fat pad is displaced. This type of pure posterior displacement (i.e., no elevation) is more indicative of bone, rather than, joint disease. Compare with the fat pad configuration in (*B*) where joint disease is present.

myelitis. Finally, it should be reiterated that the normal radial head notch demonstrated in Figure 4.57 should not be misinterpreted for a radial head corner fracture.

REFERENCES

1. Bledsoe, R.C., and Izenstark, J.L.: Displacement of fat pads in disease and injury of the elbow. Radiology 73: 717–724, 1959.
2. Bohrer, S.P.: The fat pad sign following elbow trauma. Its usefulness and reliability in suspecting "invisible" fractures. Clin. Radiol. 21: 90–94, 1970.
3. Bowerman, J.W., and McDonnell, E.J.: Radiology of athletic injuries: baseball. Radiology 116: 611–615, 1975.
4. Brogden, B.G., Crow, N.E.: Little leaguer's elbow. A.J.R. 83: 671–675, 1960.
5. Chessare, J.W., Rogers, L.F., White, H., and Tachdjian, M.O.: Injuries of the medial epicondylar ossification center to the humerus. A.J.R. 129: 49–55, 1977.
6. Clarke, N.M.P., Blakemore, M.E., and Thompson, A.G.: Osteochondritis of the trochlear epiphysis. J. Pediatr. Orthop. 3: 601–604, 1983.
7. Currarino, G.: Acute epitrochlear lymphadenitis. Pediatr. Radiol. 6: 160–163, 1977.
8. DeLee, J.C., Wilkins, K.E., Rogers, L.F., et al.: Fracture-separation of the distal humeral epiphysis. J. Bone Joint Surg. 62A: 46–51, 1980.
9. Ellman, H.: Anterior angulation deformity of the radial head: an unusual lesion occurring in juvenile baseball players. J. Bone Joint Surg. 11: 281, 1976.
10. Gore, R.M., Rogers, L.F., Bowerman, J., Suker, J., and Compere, C.L.: Osseous manifestations of elbow stress associated with sports activities. A.J.R. 134: 971–977, 1980.
11. Illingworth, C.M.: Pulled elbow: Study of 100 patients. Br. Med. J. 2: 672–674, 1975.
12. Jackman, R.J., and Pugh, D.G.: The positive elbow fat pad sign in rheumatoid arthritis. A.J.R. 108: 812–818, 1970.
13. Kohn, A.M.: Soft tissue alteration in elbow trauma. A.J.R. 82: 867–875, 1959.
14. Labelle, H., Bunnell, W.P., Duhaime, M., and Poitras, B.: Cubtius varus deformity following supracondylar fracture of the humerus in children. J. Pediatr. Orthop. 2: 539–546, 1982.

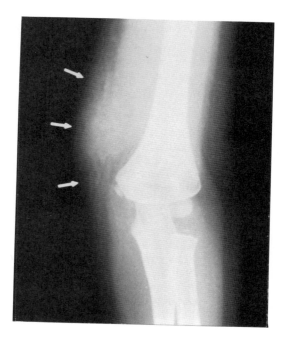

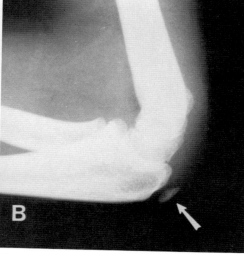

Figure 4.66. *Localized cellulitis of the elbow.* Note the localized area of superficial edema (*arrows*) and reticulation of the subcutaneous fat. These findings are secondary to adenopathy (i.e., epitrachlear adenitis) and soft tissue inflammation in this area. They are quite different from the pattern of generalized soft tissue swelling seen in the patient with osteomyelitis in Figure 4.65, *C* and *D*.

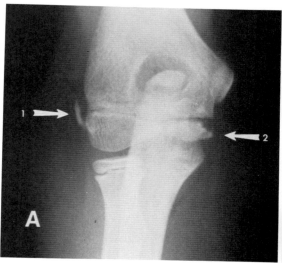

Figure 4.67. *Normal secondary ossification centers of the elbow.* (*A*) The accessory centers most commonly misinterpreted for fractures are the lateral epicondyle (*1*) and the irregularly ossified medial condyle (*2*). The central radiolucency in the humerus is due to normal thinning of the base of the olecranon fossa. (*B*) The accessory ossification center of the olecranon (*arrow*) also often is misinterpreted for a fracture.

15. Mizuno, K., Hirohata, K., and Kashiwagi, D.: Fracture-separation of the distal humeral epiphysis in young children. J. Bone Joint Surg. 61A: 570–573, 1979.
16. Murphy, W.A., and Siegel, M.J.: Elbow fat pads with new signs and extended differential diagnosis. Radiology 124: 659–665, 1977.
17. Norell, H.G.: Roentgenologic visualization of the extracapsular fat: its importance in the diagnosis of traumatic injuries to the elbow. Acta Radiol. 42: 205–210, 1954.
18. Pavlov, H., Torg, J.S., Jacobs, B., and Vigorita, V.: Nonunion of olecranon epiphysis: two cases in adolescent baseball pitchers. A.J.R. 136: 819–829, 1981.
19. Rang, M.: *Children's Fractures*, pp. 93–123. J. B. Lippincott, Philadelphia, 1974.
20. Rogers, S.L., and MacEwan, D.W.: Changes due to trauma in the fat plane overlying the supinator muscle: a radiologic sign. Radiology 92: 954–958, 1969.
21. Rogers, L.F., and Rockwood, C.A.: Separation of the entire distal humerus epiphysis. Radiology 106: 393–399, 1973.
22. Rogers, L.F., Malave, Jr. S., White, H., and Tachdjian, M.O.: Plastic bowing, torus and greenstick supracondylar fractures of the humerus: radiographic clues to obscure fractures of the elbow in children. Radiology 128: 145–150, 1978.
23. Torg, J.S., Pollack, H., and Sweterlitsch, P.: The effect of competitive pitching on the shoulders and elbows of preadolescent baseball players. Pediatrics 49: 267–272, 1972.

FOREARM

Injuries of the Forearm. Fractures through the midshaft of the radius and ulna are common, and either both bones or one bone only can be fractured. In this regard, *when a midshaft fracture is encountered in one bone, it is worthwhile to look for a fracture in the other bone*; not only in its midshaft, but at either end (Fig. 4.68). The types of fractures which can occur through the midshaft of the bones of the forearm include clearly visible transverse, spiral, and oblique fractures; and the more subtle hairline, greenstick, and plastic bending or bowing fractures. Buckle or torus fractures are uncommon in the midshaft of these bones, for as opposed to the metaphyseal regions, the cortex of the midshaft is rather sturdy and not prone to buckling.

Acute, *plastic or bowing* fractures of the forearm are commonly missed in spite of the fact that pain and deformity are present clinically (1, 2, 5, 7). In these patients, there often is loss of supination-pronation function, but when roentgenograms are obtained, a classic fracture with a visible fracture line is not detected. Rather, one notes only a variable degree of bowing of one or another of the bones of the forearm (Figs. 4.69 and 4.70). In this regard, one should note that the entire bone or just one part of it can be bent. These fractures can be considered the *"greenest of greenstick"* fractures, and although numerous microfractures exist along the outer surface of the bones (2–4), none are large enough to be visualized as a single fracture roentgenographically (1, 3, 4). Because of this, the entire injury may go undetected unless comparative views of the other arm are obtained, and when they are, the curvature of the involved bone should be compared inch for inch with the normal contralateral bone

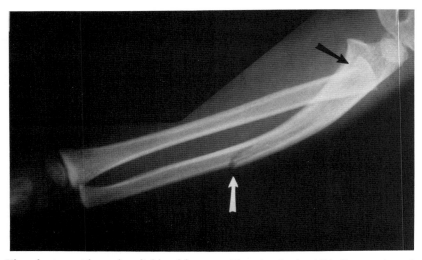

Figure 4.68. *Ulnar fracture with occult radial head fracture.*   Note the clearly visible fracture through the midshaft of the ulna (*white arrow*). It is a greenstick fracture with considerable bending of the ulna. In addition, note that there has been a metaphyseal fracture of the proximal radius (*black arrow*). The radial head is not dislocated in this patient, but the fracture could be overlooked because of the potentially distracting ulnar fracture.

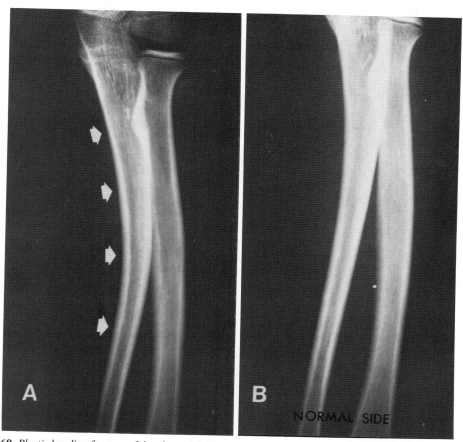

Figure 4.69. *Plastic bending fracture of the ulna.*   (*A*) Note the marked degree of bending of the entire ulna (*arrows*). No fracture line is visible and unless a comparative view of the normal side is examined, the bony deformity could be missed. (*B*) Normal side for comparison. Note the configuration of the normal ulna and compare it with the bent ulna in (*A*).

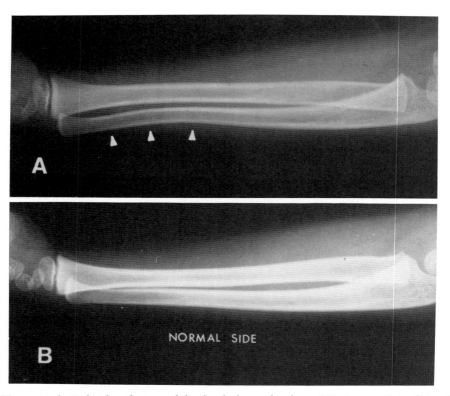

Figure 4.70. *Acute plastic bending fracture of the distal ulna and radius.* (*A*) Note bending of the distal ulna (*arrows*), and to a lesser extent, of the distal radius. (*B*) Normal side for comparison. Although the views are not exactly the same, in terms of positioning, one still can see that the normal ulna and radius are not bent.

(Fig. 4.71). This is most important for, if only one extremity is examined, normal bowing can be misinterpreted for a plastic bending fracture (Fig. 4.72).

Overall, acute plastic bowing or bending fractures of the forearm are more common than generally believed, and at the same time, are quite variable. In some cases, both bones are involved in the bending process, while in others only one is involved. In still other cases, one bone may be bent and the other frankly fractured (5). Another interesting feature of these fractures is that, unlike other fractures of the forearm, when they heal they usually produce little in the way of periosteal bone reaction. Furthermore, because it is difficult to reduce them, residual bowing with supination-pronation motion impairment can persist.

The other noteworthy fracture of the bones of the forearm is the *Monteggia* fracture. This fracture consists of a fracture of the ulna and a dislocation of the radial head (Fig. 4.73). Both anterior and posterior Monteggia fractures occur, and in either case, it is the associated dislocation of the radial head which is the missed portion of this injury (6). In this regard, it cannot be restated often enough that one always should line up the radial head and capitellum to

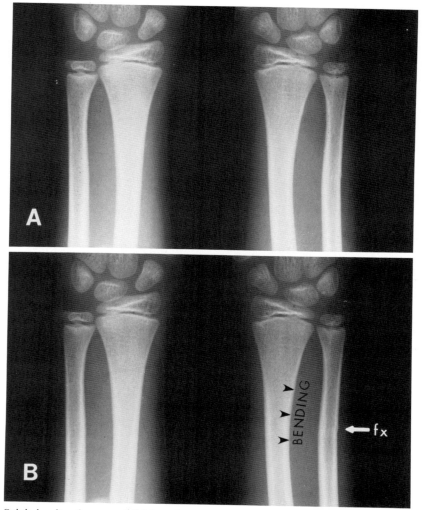

Figure 4.71. *Subtle bending fracture.* (*A*) Note slight bending of the left radius. There also is a subtle greenstick fracture of the distal ulna. (*B*) Fractures are labeled. Bending fracture of radius (*black arrows*). Fracture of ulna (*fx*).

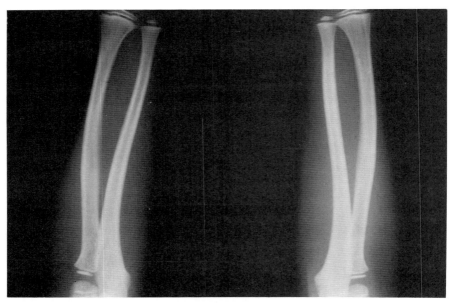

Figure 4.72. *Normal bowing of bones of the forearm.*   Note the normal degree of bowing of the bones of the forearm on both sides. This is the reason why comparative views should always be obtained when a bending fracture is suspected. Only with comparative views will one be certain that such a fracture exists. If only one of these extremities were examined, the degree of bending could be misconstrued as being abnormal.

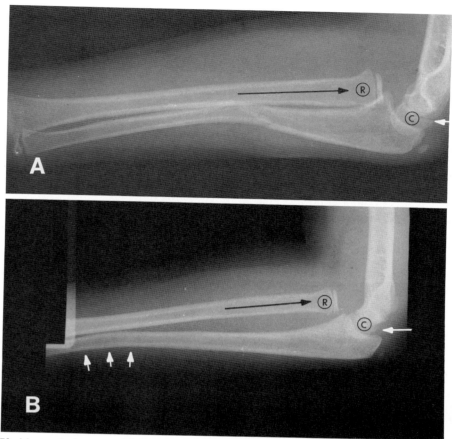

Figure 4.73. *Monteggia fracture.* (*A*) Note the fracture through the midshaft of the ulna. There is considerable associated bending of the ulna. Also note that the radial head (*R*) is dislocated and does not line up in a straight line with the capitellum (*C*). (*B*) Another patient with a dislocated radial head (*R*). This time, however, the only other fracture is a subtle bending fracture of the ulna (*arrows*). Capitellum (*C*).

determine whether they are in a straight line relationship. If they are not, dislocation of the radial head is present.

Normal Variations Causing Problems. The only normal finding in the midshaft of the radius and ulna which can be misinterpreted for a fracture is a vascular groove in either bone. These vascular grooves are diaphyseal and appear no different from those in other long bones.

REFERENCES

1. Borden, S.: Traumatic bowing of the forearm in children. J. Bone Joint Surg. 56A: 611–616, 1974.
2. Borden, S.: Roentgen recognition of acute plastic bowing of the forearm in children. A.J.R. 125: 524–530, 1975.
3. Chamay, A.: Mechanical and morphological aspects of experimental overload and fatigue in bone. J. Biomech. 3: 263–270, 1970.
4. Chamay, A., and Tschantz, P.: Mechanical influences in bone remodeling, experimental research on Wolff's law. J. Biomech. 5: 173–180, 1972.
5. Crowe, J.E., and Swischuk, L.E.: Acute bowing fractures of the forearm in children. A frequently missed injury. A.J.R. 128: 981–984, 1977.
6. Giustra, P.E., Killoran, P.J., Furman, R.S., and Root, J.A.: Missed Monteggia fracture. Radiology 110: 45–47, 1974.
7. Stenstrom, R., Gripenberg, L., and Bergius, A.-R.: Traumatic bowing of forearm and lower leg in children. Acta Radiol. 19: 243–249, 1978.

Wringer Injuries. For the most part, washing machine wringer arm injuries are uncommon in this day and age; but some still do occur (1). However, bone injury is very uncommon, and although an occasional epiphyseal dislocation may be encountered, these injuries are mainly soft tissue injuries.

REFERENCE

1. Stone, H.H., Cantwell, D.V., and Fullenwider, J.T.: Wringer arm injuries. J. Pediatr. Surg. 11: 375–379, 1976.

WRIST

Normal Fat Pads. There are two fat pads around the wrist which can be utilized in the assessmet of wrist injuries. The first is the pronator quadratus fat pad, and the second is the navicular fat pad (3, 7). The pronator quadratus fat pad is seen on lateral views of the wrist and lies along the pronator quadratus muscle (Fig. 4.74). The navicular fat stripe lies just medial to the navicular bone and is seen on posteroanterior views of the wrist (Fig. 4.75). In young infants, this latter fat stripe is not visualized with as much consistency as it is in older children. This is not so unfortunate, however, for the navicular fat pad is utilized primarily in the detection of navicular fractures, and these fractures are not particularly common in infancy. Distal, radial, and ulnar fractures, on the other hand, are quite common, and it is in this regard that the pronator quadratus fat pad becomes most useful.

Determining the Presence of Fluid in the Wrist Joint. Determining the presence of fluid in the wrist joint simply amounts to noting whether the soft tissues around the

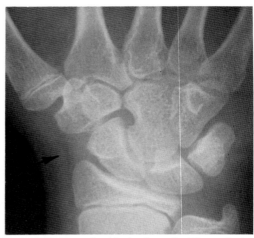

Figure 4.75. *Normal navicular fat pad.* The navicular fat pad (*arrow*) is best visualized in older children. It can be obliterated or displaced with navicular bone injuries.

wrist are swollen or not (see Fig. 4.84). Apart from this, there is little else to look for, for the joint space seldom becomes widened, and except for the navicular fat pad, no other useful fat pads are present.

Injuries of the Distal Radius and Ulna. Although a variety of *transverse* and *oblique fractures*, with or without angulation or displacement, commonly occur through the distal third of the radius and ulna, these fractures usually are not difficult to detect (Fig. 4.76). On the other hand, if they are hairline or subtle *greenstick fractures*, they may elude early diagnosis unless one studies the soft tissues first (Fig. 4.77). The same can be said for subtle bending fractures (see Fig. 4.71).

Cortical buckle or torus fractures and epiphyseal-metaphyseal injuries also are common in this area, and most often are sustained from falls on the outstretched extremity. The cortical buckles and kinks are of an almost endless variety of configurations, and often are more clearly visible on one view than another (Fig. 4.78). This is especially true of posterior buckle fractures of the distal radius where the fracture and associated posterior tilting of the articular surface frequently are seen on the lateral view only (Fig. 4.79). With regard to Salter-Harris epiphyseal-metaphyseal injuries, the type I and II injuries are most common. Types III and IV, and even the type V injury are relatively

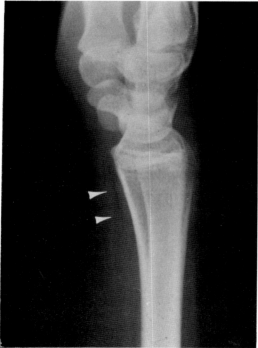

Figure 4.74. *Normal pronator quadratus fat pad.* Note the normal appearance and location of the quadratus pronator fat pad (*arrows*).

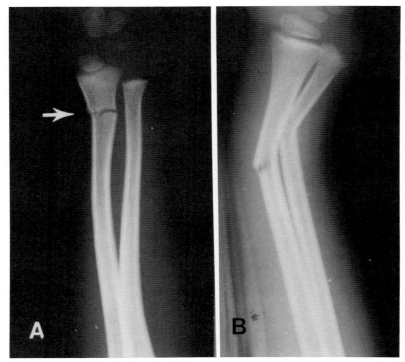

Figure 4.76. *Distal radial and ulnar fractures—varying configurations.* (*A*) Note the transverse, slightly angulated fracture through the distal radius (*arrow*). (*B*) Markedly angulated fractures through both bones of the forearm.

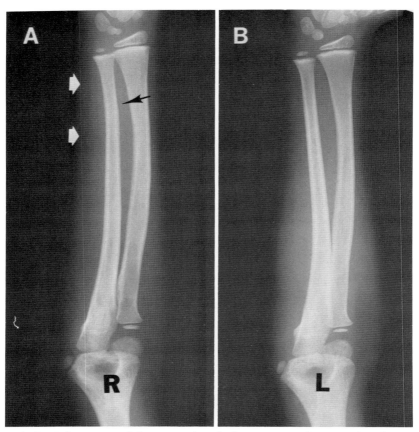

Figure 4.77. *Subtle distal ulnar greenstick fracture—value of soft tissues.*   (*A*) First note thickening and prominence of the soft tissues along the distal ulna (*white arrows*). The greenstick fracture through the distal ulna is barely visible (*black arrow*), and without the soft tissue changes to focus attention on the fracture, it might be missed. (*B*) Normal side for comparison. Note the normal appearance of the soft tissues. Also note that the normal ulna is straighter than the broken ulna, further attesting to the presence of the ulnar fracture on the right.

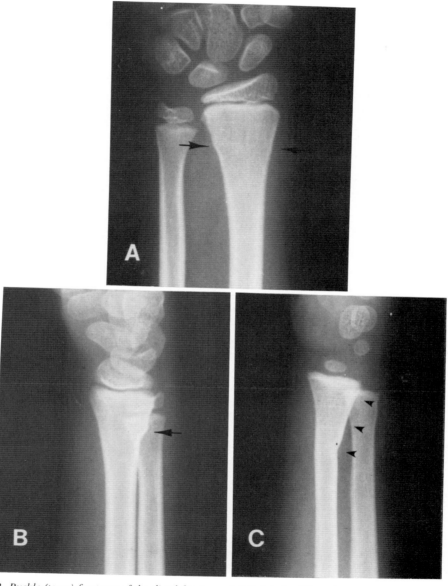

Figure 4.78. *Buckle (torus) fractures of the distal forearm.* (*A*) Subtle buckling of the cortex is seen in the distal radius (*arrows*). (*B*) Lateral view more clearly demonstrating the buckling. Note that the soft tissues are swollen and that the pronator quadratus fat pad has been obliterated. (*C*) Another infant with a buckle fracture of the distal radius (*arrows*).

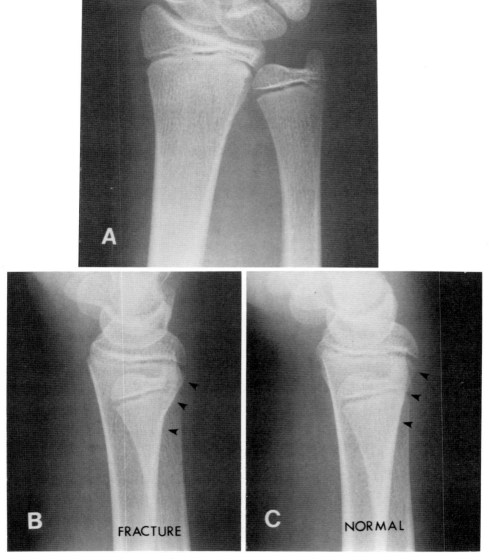

Figure 4.79. *Buckle fracture of posterior distal radius—value of lateral film.* (*A*) On frontal view, no abnormality is seen. (*B*) On lateral view, however, note the subtle buckle fracture of the distal radius (*arrows*). There is slight posterior tilting of the articular surface of the distal radius. (*C*) Normal side for comparison. Compare the normal smooth curve of the posterior aspect of the distal radius (*arrows*).

uncommon. Most often the Salter-Harris type I or II fracture involves the epiphyseal-metaphyseal junction of the radius, but occasionally the ulna also is similarly involved. In detecting these injuries, one should look for one or more of the following changes: (a) soft tissue edema, (b) obliteration or displacement of the pronator quadratus fat pad, (c) widening of the involved epiphyseal line, (d) an associated metaphyseal corner fracture, and (e) displacement of the epiphysis (Figs. 4.80–4.82).

When the ulna is involved in these injuries, very often rather than an epiphyseal-metaphyseal injury, there is a *fracture of the ulnar styloid process*. Indeed, if the radial epiphyseal-metaphyseal fracture is subtle, there is a distinct tendency for the more readily visible styloid fracture to distract one's attention. One should avoid this trap, for almost always, when an ulnar styloid process fracture is present, a radial fracture also is present (Fig. 4.83).

Injuries of the Carpal Bones. Fractures and/or dislocations of the carpal bones in infants and young children are quite uncommon. In the older child, one may encounter *fractures of the navicular*, but even this injury is relatively uncommon. Nonetheless, it can occur, and when it does the clinical findings are similar to those seen in adults. Roentgenographically, this fracture can be suspected when there is: (a) localized soft tissue swelling and/or obliteration of the navicular fat pad (1, 3), (b) shortening or telescoping of the navicular bone, (c) rotation and resultant increase in density of one of the fracture fragments, or (d) a visible fracture line (Figs. 4.84–4.86). In some cases, oblique (navicular) views may be necessary for clearer visualization of the suspected fracture and in those cases where the fracture is in doubt, isotope bone scanning can be of value (4). Aseptic necrosis in these fractures also can occur in children (5).

The only other bones in the wrist to fracture with any frequency in childhood are the pisiform and triquetrum. These injuries usually result from direct blows to the bones, and with the pisiform it is quite important to realize that it tends to ossify irregularly, and as such should not be mistaken for a fracture (see Fig. 4.90).

The occasional case of *lunate or perilunate dislocation* of the wrist in the older child presents with malalignment of the proximal

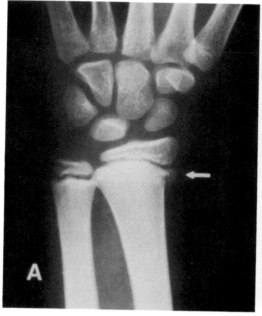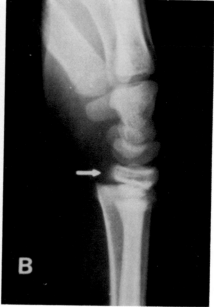

Figure 4.80. *Displaced Salter-Harris type II epiphyseal-metaphyseal fracture of the radius.* (*A*) Note that the distal radial epiphysis is displaced laterally, and that there is a small metaphyseal corner fracture (*arrow*). (*B*) Lateral view demonstrates the marked degree of posterior displacement of the distal radial epiphysis (*arrow*). There is slight impaction of the posterior corner of the distal radial metaphysis.

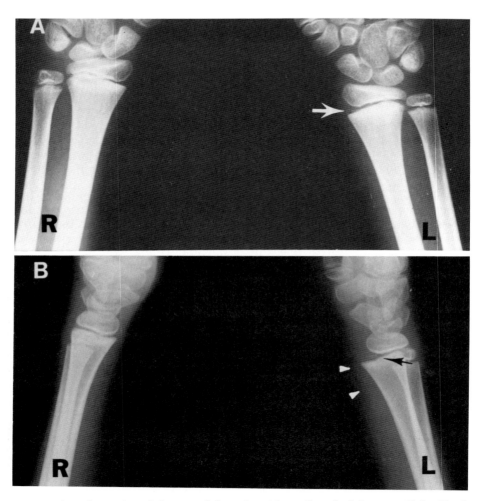

Figure 4.81. *Epiphyseal-metaphyseal fracture of the wrist with small avulsed fragment (Salter-Harris type II injury).* (*A*) On frontal view, note that the left distal radial epiphysis is slightly displaced, and that the epiphyseal line is a little wider than the normal epiphyseal line on the right. Also note the thin sliver-like avulsed metaphyseal fragment (*arrow*). (*B*) Lateral view demonstrating swelling of the soft tissues around the left wrist, anterior displacement of the pronator quadratus fat pad (*white arrows*), posterior displacement of the distal radial epiphysis, and the sliver-like avulsed metaphyseal fragment (*black arrow*).

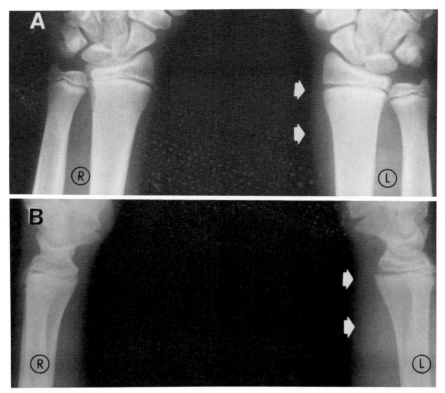

Figure 4.82. *Salter-Harris type I epiphyseal-metaphyseal fracture of the wrist: value of soft tissues.* (*A*) On frontal view, one might suspect that the epiphyseal line through the distal left radius is a little wider than the one on the right, but if one first notes that soft tissue swelling in the area also is present (*arrows*), then the finding becomes even more suspicious. (*B*) Confirmation is present on the lateral view where one can see marked swelling of the soft tissues anterior to the wrist (*arrows*), and complete obliteration of the pronator quadratus fat pad. In addition, the distal radial epiphysis probably is slightly posteriorly displaced.

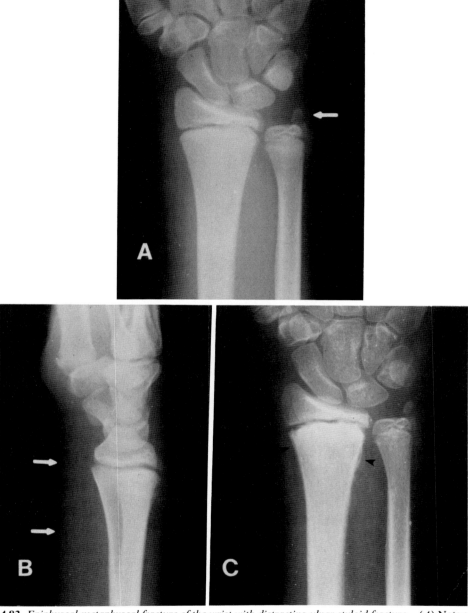

Figure 4.83. *Epiphyseal-metaphyseal fracture of the wrist with distracting ulnar styloid fracture.* (*A*) Note swelling around the wrist and a fractured ulnar styloid process (*arrow*). At first one might think this is the only injury present. However, on lateral view, (*B*), one can see that there is considerable swelling anterior to the wrist (*arrows*), and that the pronator quadratus fat pad is totally obliterated. Under these circumstances, one should suspect an underlying epiphyseal-metaphyseal injury of the radius, for an isolated ulnar styloid process fracture would not result in this much swelling. In (*C*), 2 weeks later, note evidence of healing of the occult epiphyseal-metaphyseal fracture of the distal radius. Some periosteal new bone is seen along the distal radial shaft (*arrows*), and sclerosis along the epiphyseal-metaphyseal junction is clearly evident. The ununited ulnar styloid process fracture is noted again.

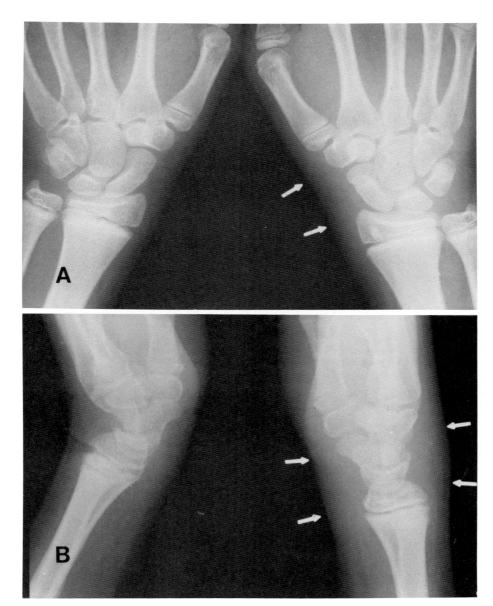

Figure 4.84. *Navicular fracture.* (*A*) First note that the soft tissues adjacent to the navicular bone are thickened and edematous (*arrows*). In addition, note that the navicular bone on the left is shorter (impacted) than the normal one on the right. A subtle fracture line through its upper third also is suggested. (*B*) Lateral view demonstrating extensive swelling around the wrist. Swelling extends both anteriorly and posteriorly (*arrows*). Note that the site of the swelling is located primarily around the carpal bones. With distal radial injuries, it usually is located more proximally and there is more displacement of the pronator quadratus fat pad (i.e., see Fig. 4.82*B*).

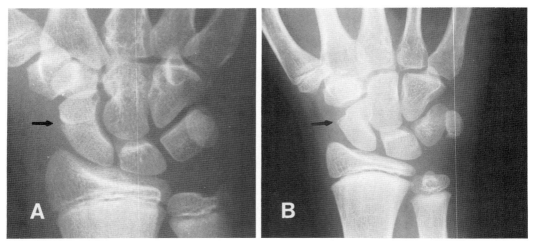

Figure 4.85. *Navicular fractures.* (*A*) Note the line of increased density (*arrow*), through the fracture. (*B*) Another patient with an angulated navicular fracture (*arrow*).

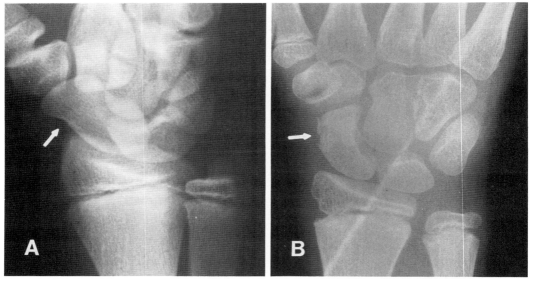

Figure 4.86. *Atypical navicular fractures.* (*A*) Subtle buckle or bending fracture of the navicular (*arrow*). This fracture could be overlooked unless oblique, comparative views are obtained (*B*). Another fracture with an avulsed fragment (*arrow*).

row of carpal bones and associated discrepancy in the width of the perilunate joint spaces. In other words, the joint space will be narrower or completely obliterated on one side, and wider on the other (Fig. 4.87). Obliteration of the joint space is due to overlap of the dislocated carpal bones, and widening, of course, is due to distraction of the involved bones. On lateral view, the normal vertical, sequential arrangement of the capitate, lunate, and distal radial epiphysis is lost in these cases (Fig. 4.87 *B*). This latter point is most important, for any deviation from this arrangement of the carpal bones should indicate an underlying dislocation. Of course, with a lunate dislocation, the lunate will lie anterior to the capitate and distal radial epiphysis while with a perilunate dislocation both the lunate and distal radius and its epiphysis move forward and lie anterior to the other bones of the wrist.

Other dislocations in the wrist are quite

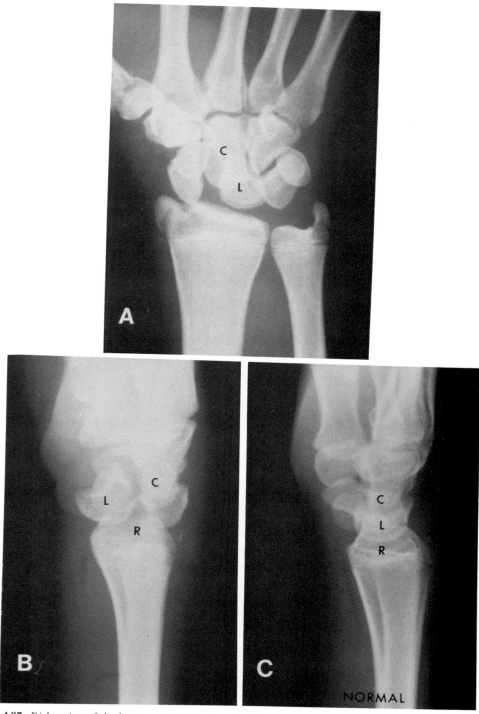

Figure 4.87. *Dislocation of the lunate.* (*A*) Note that the joint spaces to either side of the lunate bone (*L*) are unequal. This should alert one to the dislocation. In addition, note that the lunate bone overlies the capitate (*C*) and that the wrist is foreshortened. Also note fractures of the ulnar styloid process, distal radial epiphysis, proximal thumb, and navicular bone (foreshortening and rotation). (*B*) Lateral view demonstrating abnormal anterior location of the lunate bone (*L*). The capitate (*C*) and distal radial epiphysis (*R*) lie behind the lunate bone. (*C*) Normal view for comparison showing the normal vertical, sequential arrangement of the capitate (*C*), lunate (*L*), and distal radial epiphysis (*R*).

uncommon. These include isolated rotatory subluxation of the navicular (2) (Fig. 4.88), and dislocation of the carpal-metacarpal joints. However, **when assessing the wrist for a suspected underlying dislocation of any of the bones, one should follow two rules.** First, one should identify each of the carpal bones with clarity, and second, one should note whether the individual joint spaces are uniform and delineated by parallel lines. In other words, one should try to determine whether any overlap or widening is present. If any of the individual bones are not clearly visualized and if any of the joint spaces appear suspiciously narrow or wide one should turn to oblique and lateral views for further delineation and verification.

Sprained Wrist. There is a good rule to follow with wrist injuries, and it goes as follows: *"a sprained wrist is a fractured wrist until proven otherwise."* This rule taught to me by Dr. Bill Miller, an orthopaedic surgeon in Oklahoma City, has proven most trustworthy. This is not to say that simple sprains of the wrist do not occur, but rather that many so-called "sprains" actually turn out to be Salter-Harris type I, II, or V injuries. Even in those cases where the radiographic findings are confined to soft tissue swelling and obliteration of the quadratus

pronator fat pad, clinical tenderness along the epiphyseal line will belie the presence of an epiphyseal-metaphyseal injury. It is quite a different problem from the one encountered in the ankle, where a sprained ankle more often than not turns out to be just a sprained ankle.

Septic Arthritis, Osteomyelitis, and Cellulitis of the Wrist. Generally speaking, all of these conditions lead to pronounced swelling in and around the wrist joint. The various normal soft tissue structures are obliterated, and, in early cases, soft tissue swelling will be most pronounced around the area of primary involvement. In less advanced cases, less bone destruction is seen (Fig. 4.89), and isotope imaging often is required.

Normal Findings Causing Problems. For the most part, the carpal bones ossify reasonably regularly, but occasionally irregular ossification of one or another of the carpal bones can be misinterpreted for a fracture. This occurs with the pisiform bone more that any other (Fig. 4.90*A*). Another problem in the wrist, although far less common, is that of misinterpreting a bipartite navicular bone for a fractured navicular bone (Fig. 4.90*B*). In the distal radius and ulna, an incompletely obliterated, but normally closing epiphyseal line (6) can be misinterpreted

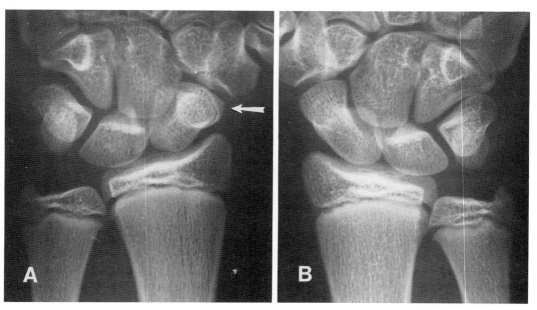

Figure 4.88. *Rotatory subluxation of navicular.* (*A*) Note slight increase in the navicular-lunate joint space and also telescoping (due to rotation) of the navicular resulting in the circle sign (*arrow*). (*B*) Normal side for comparison.

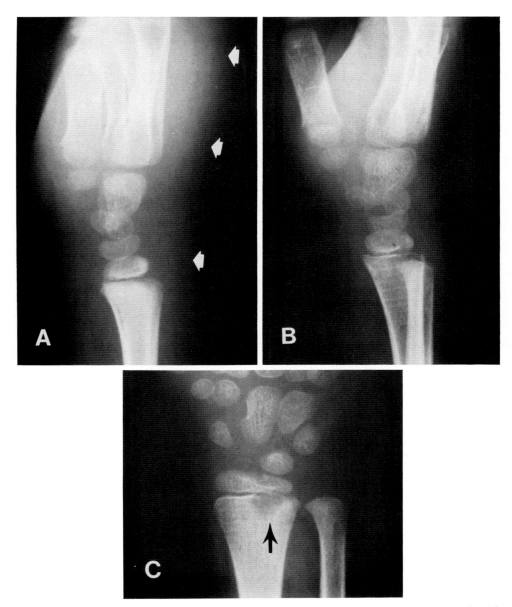

Figure 4.89. *Osteomyelitis—distal radius.* (*A*) Note extensive swelling of the hand, wrist, and distal forarm (*arrows*). (*B*) Normal side for comparison. (*C*) Frontal view demonstrating metaphyseal defect due to osteomyelitis (*arrow*).

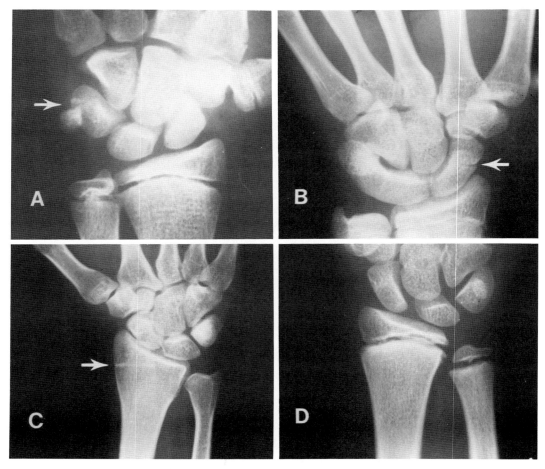

Figure 4.90. *Normal variations in the wrist.* (*A*) *Irregular ossification of the pisiform (arrow).* This should not be misinterpreted for a fracture of the pisiform. (*B*) *Bipartite navicular.* Note the bipartite navicular (*arrow*). Also note that the lunate and triquetral bones are fused. The bipartite navicular should not be misinterpreted for a fracture. (*C*) *Incompletely obliterated epiphysis.* Note the incompletely obliterated epiphysis of the distal radius (*arrow*), often misinterpreted for a fracture. (*D*) *Epiphyseal-metaphyseal spicules.* Note normal spicules extending from the ulnar epiphysis and normal metaphyseal spicules along the inner aspect of the distal radial metaphysis. Both of these bony spicules are normal.

for a fracture (Fig. 4.90*C*), and occasionally normal bony spicules extending into the epiphyseal line can suggest an epiphyseal-metaphyseal injury (Fig. 4.90*D*).

REFERENCES

1. Haverling, M., and Sylven, M.: Soft tissue abnormalities at fracture of the scaphoid. Acta Radiol. 19: 497–501, 1978.
2. Hudson, T.M., Caragol, W.J., and Kaye, J.J.: Isolated rotatory subluxation of the carpal navicular. A.J.R. 126: 601–611, 1976.
3. MacEwan, D.W.: Changes due to trauma in the fat plane overlying the pronator quadratus muscle: a radiologic sign. Radiology 82: 879–886, 1964.
4. Rolfe, E.B., Garvie, N.W., Khan, M.A., and Ackery, D.M.: Isotope bone imaging in suspected scaphoid trauma. Br. J. Radiol. 54: 762–767, 1981.
5. Southcott, R., and Rosman, M.A.: Nonunion of carpal scaphoid fractures in children. J. Bone Joint Surg. 59B: 20–23, 1977.
6. Teates, C.D.: Distal radial growth plate remnant simulating fracture. A.J.R. 110: 578–581, 1970.
7. Terry, D.W., Jr., and Ramin, J.E.: The navicular fat stripe: a useful roentgen feature for evaluating wrist trauma. A.J.R. 124: 25–28, 1975.

HAND

Evaluation of the Fat Pads and Soft Tissues. There are no specific fat pads to evaluate in the hand and evaluation of the soft tissues consists primarily of noting whether localized soft tissue edema and swelling are present. However, this latter finding, as nonspecific as it is, is very helpful in localizing the site of injury in the fingers (Fig. 4.91).

Detecting Fluid in the Small Joints of the Hand. The detection of fluid in the small joints of the hand depends primarily on noting the presence of swelling around the joint. In some cases, the joint space may be widened (4), but this finding often is subtle. There are no specific fat pads to evaluate, and thus, in most cases, one is left only with generalized swelling around a knuckle (Fig. 4.91).

Injuries of the Metacarpals and Phalanges. Crush injuries to the terminal phalanges are hardly worth obtaining roentgenograms for, because unless the fracture is a compound fracture, little needs to be done for these injuries. The typically comminuted terminal phalangeal tuft is not difficult to detect roentgenographically, and even if it is missed, no dire sequelae develop. Other injuries to the fingers and thumb result from hyperextension, twisting, or direct blows to the digits. The *types of fractures* sustained include buckle (torus) fractures, epiphyseal-metaphyseal injuries, fracture dislocations, and linear, transverse, or spiral fractures. They come in an almost endless assortment of configurations, and some are illustrated

in Figure 4.92. In addition, although rare, plastic bending fractures can occur (Fig. 4.93).

An important point regarding cortical buckle (torus) fractures occurring at the proximal end of the phalanges or distal ends of the metacarpals is that if one sees one such fracture, then one should look at the neighboring fingers for other similar fractures for very often they will be there. Furthermore, usually they are more clearly defined on oblique views (Fig. 4.94). Direct blows to the dorsum of the hand resulting in transverse fractures through the metacarpal bones often elude initial observation. The reason for this is that many times the fracture line is barely visible, and little or no displacement of the fracture fragments occurs. In such cases, it is of great benefit to examine the soft tissues first, and then, when edema and swelling are noted, to focus one's attention on the underlying bones (Fig. 4.95).

Dislocations of the fingers and thumb are not particularly common in childhood, for rather than a dislocation, an epiphyseal-metaphyseal separation occurs (see Fig. 4.92*B*). However, clinically these separations often appear to be true dislocations. The classic

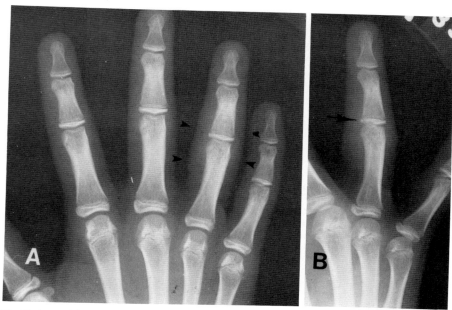

Figure 4.91. *Phalangeal fracture—value of soft tissues.* (*A*) Note soft tissue swelling localizing the site of injury to the proximal interphalangeal joint of the ring finger (*arrows*). (*B*) Oblique view demonstrates the swelling again, but in addition also demonstrates the presence of a small chip fracture of the epiphysis (*arrow*). This is a Salter-Harris type III injury with bleeding into the joint and associated periarticular soft tissue swelling.

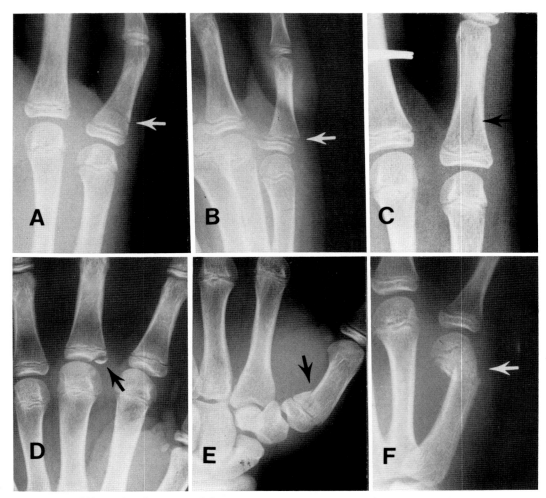

Figure 4.92. *Phalangeal and metacarpal fractures—various types.* (*A*) Typical transverse fracture (*arrow*). (*B*) Epiphyseal-metaphyseal fracture with displacement (*arrow*). Clinically, this type of fracture can be mistaken for a true dislocation (*C*). Longitudinal fracture through phalanx (*arrow*). (*D*) Epiphyseal chip fracture (*arrow*). (*E*) Epiphyseal-metaphyseal fracture (Salter-Harris type II injury) of the base of the first metacarpal (*arrow*). (*F*) Typical angulated fracture (*arrow*) through the head of the fifth metacarpal. This fracture usually is sustained by punching someone or something and often is termed the "boxers" fracture.

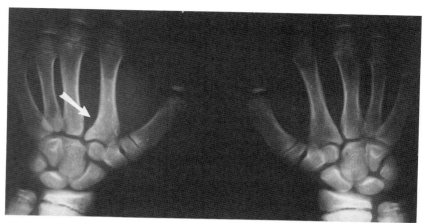

Figure 4.93. *Plastic bending fracture—metacarpal.* Note swelling over the left hand and a wavy, bent appearance of the first metacarpal (*arrow*). Compare with its normal, straight appearance on the other side.

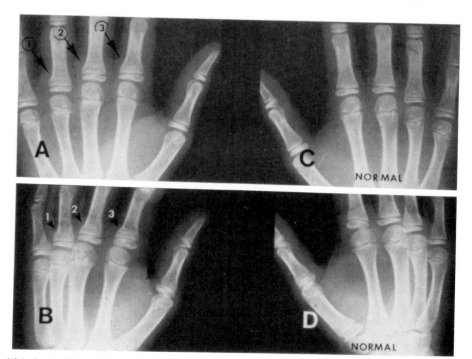

Figure 4.94. *Cortical (torus) fractures of the base of the phalanges.* (*A*) Frontal view demonstrating a buckle fracture through the base of the proximal phalanx of the fourth digit (*1*). A more subtle, but similar, fracture is present through the base of the proximal phalanx of the third digit (*2*). An even more subtle fracture is present through the base of the proximal phalanx of the secnd digit (*3*). This latter fracture is most subtle and might not be appreciated on this view alone. (*B*) Oblique view more clearly demonstrates all three fractures. (*C* and *D*) Normal frontal and oblique views for comparison. Specifically, compare the contour of the cortices of the involved bones.

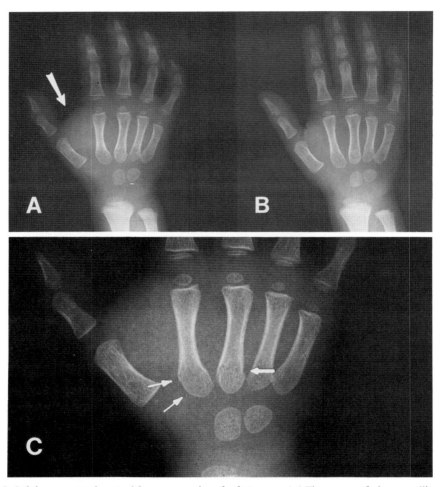

Figure 4.95. *Subtle metacarpal cortical fractures—value of soft tissues.*   (*A*) First, note soft tissue swelling (increased thickness and density of the soft tissues, between thumb and index finger) (*arrow*). (*B*) Normal side for comparison. Look back at the right hand in (*A*) and note that there is a subtle bending-buckle fracture through the base of the second metatarsal and a transverse fracture through the base of the third metatarsal. (*C*) Closeup view demonstrating the buckle-bending fracture of the second metacarpal and the transverse fracture through the base of the third metacarpal (*arrows*).

fracture dislocation of the base of the first metacarpal (Bennett's fracture) occurs only after the epiphysis of the thumb has fused. Until this time, the equivalent of this fracture is a Salter-Harris type I or II injury (Fig. 4.92E). This, however, is not to say that the thumb never dislocates in childhood, for indeed it does, but usually it occurs at the metacarpal-phalangeal joint. Frequently, this dislocation is associated with an epiphyseal-metaphyseal fracture (Fig. 4.96), and in the older child where the epiphysis has fused, or is near fusion, the same injury can result in the so-called "gamekeepers thumb." In this injury, an avulsion fracture indicates the presence of a severe collateral ligament injury leading to instability and an inability to grasp objects with the thumb. Unless surgically corrected, the injury is quite disabling. Roentgenographically, the presence of this injury can be detected when the avulsed fragment is noted (Fig. 4.97).

In assessing the thumb for the presence of a dislocation, it is important to note that when the thumb is examined in oblique position, it can erroneously appear dislo-

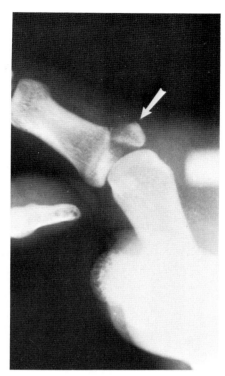

Figure 4.97. *Gamekeeper's thumb.* Note the avulsed epiphyseal-metaphyseal fragment (*arrow*). In this condition, there is an associated injury of the medial joint capsule and ligament, and the injury is unstable. The patient is unable to grasp anything with the thumb.

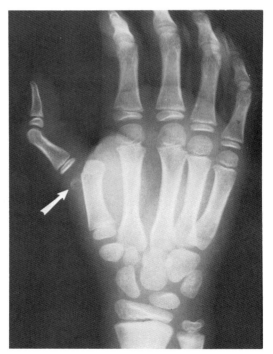

Figure 4.96. *Fracture dislocation of the thumb.* Note the dislocated metacarpal phalangeal joint of the first digit, and the avulsed bony fragment (*arrow*).

cated. This ***pseudodislocated appearance of the thumb*** is a common finding, for almost always the thumb is in oblique position when the remainder of the hand is being examined in true frontal projection. Under such circumstances, the first metacarpal joint appears dislocated, but with proper positioning one will soon see that the joint is normal (Fig. 4.98).

Septic Arthritis, Osteomyelitis, and Cellulitis of the Hand. Cellulitis of the fingers is very common and produces generalized soft tissue swelling without joint or bone abnormalities. Osteomyelitis of the small bones of the hands also produces soft tissue swelling, virtually indistinguishable from that seen with cellulitis. Of course, if bone destruction is present, the diagnosis becomes relatively easy. With septic arthritis, pronounced swelling around the involved joint will be noted, and if enough pus has accumulated in the joint space, one may see some widening of the joint space.

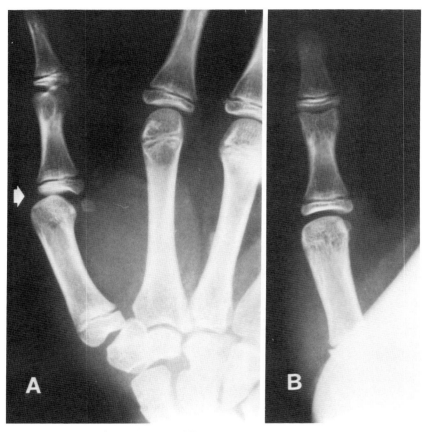

Figure 4.98. *Pseudodislocation of the thumb—pitfall.*   (*A*) Note that the first metacarpal-phalangeal joint appears dislocated (*arrow*). The small bony ossicle along the inner aspect of the joint is a normal sesamoid bone. (*B*) With proper anteroposterior positioning, one can see that the joint is not dislocated.

A note regarding the ***hand-foot syndrome in sickle cell disease*** is probably in order at this point. In these cases, edema and swelling of the soft tissues of the hand can be extensive, and in some cases one may note the presence of healing changes resulting from similar episodes in the past (Fig. 4.99). The bony changes are indistinguishable from those of osteomyelitis.

Frostbite. Frostbite injuries, on an acute basis, produce nothing more than soft tissue swelling. However, later on resorption of the involved bones and eventual autoamputation and deformity can be seen (1–3).

Normal Findings Causing Problems. The small bones of the hand have numerous epiphyses and pseudoepiphyses (apophyses) which commonly are misinterpreted for fractures (Fig. 4.100). Bipartite epiphyses also can be misinterpreted for epiphyseal fractures but are not particularly common in the hand. A number of sesamoid bones also can be seen in the hand but seldom are they misinterpreted for fractures. Only if they are bipartite is there a tendency to make such a misinterpretation, and, actually the problem is more common in the foot (see Fig. 4.210). The most common

sesamoids of the hand are those located just over the heads of the first and second metacarpals (see Fig. 4.98).

REFERENCES

1. Brown, F.E., Spiegel, P.K., and Boyle, W.E., Jr.: Digital deformity: an effect of frostbite in children. Pediatrics 71: 955–959, 1983.
2. Sweet, E.M., and Smith, M.G.H.: "Winter fingers!" Bone infarction in Scottish children as a manifestation of cold injury. Ann. Radiol. 22: 71–75, 1979.
3. Tishler, J.M.: The soft tissue and bone changes in frostbite injuries. Radiology 102: 511–513, 1972.
4. Weston, W.J.: Joint space widening with intracapsular fractures in joint of the fingers and toes of children. Australas. Radiol. 15: 367–371, 1971.

LOWER EXTREMITY PROBLEMS PELVIS AND SACRUM

Injuries of the Pelvis. These frequently are multiple and can range from simple buckle or torus cortical fractures to extensive fracture-dislocations associated with internal organ or vascular injury (10, 13, 17, 19–21, 24). Most often these latter fractures are sustained in automobile accidents. Pelvic fractures resulting in separation of the symphysis pubis, fractures through the acetabulum, and so-called diametric fractures of the pelvis are considered unstable while other fractures are not (20).

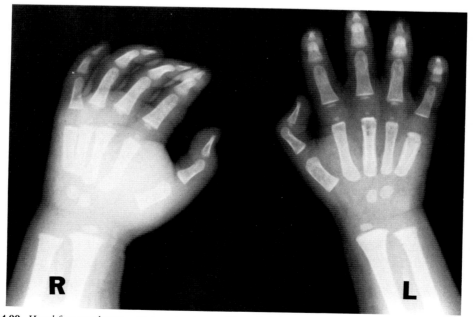

Figure 4.99. *Hand-foot syndrome.* Note extensive swelling of the entire hand on the right. These are acute soft tissue changes of the hand-foot syndrome. The bones are intact. On the left, however, note periosteal new bone deposition along the third and fifth metatarsals, providing evidence of previous infarcts. In addition, lytic lesions are noted through the distal ends of these bones. The findings are similar to those of osteomyelitis.

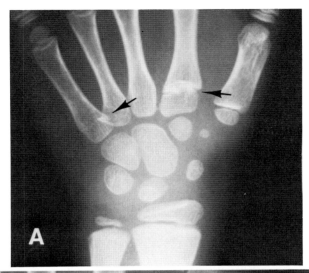

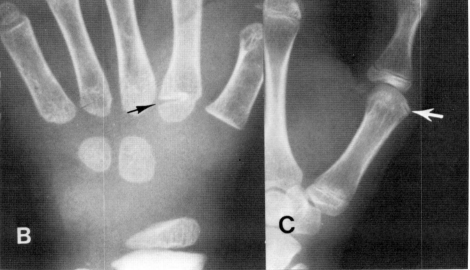

Figure 4.100. *Normal secondary ossification centers—pseudofractures.* (*A*) Note pseudofractures through the base of the fifth and second metatarsals (*arrows*). (*B*) Another infant with an incompletely fused secondary center at the base of the second metacarpal (*arrow*). (*C*) Incompletely fused accessory secondary center producing fracture-like appearance through the distal end of the first metacarpal (*arrow*).

Separation of the Symphysis Pubis. Gross separation of the symphysis pubis leading to instability often is associated with dislocation at the sacroiliac joints and is not difficult to detect. With lesser degrees of diastasis, however, it may be more difficult to appreciate the problem initially, especially in young infants where underossification of the pubic bones leads to a normally wide space between them and a picture suggestive of separation (see Fig. 4.117). However,

when looking for true separation, one should look for asymmetric alignment (offsetting) and fractures of the pubic bones (Fig. 4.101).

Diametric Fractures. In this type of injury, fractures exist both anteriorly and posteriorly, and they may be on the same side or on opposite sides of the pelvis. When they occur on opposite sides, the term ring fracture is applied. The more severe diametric fractures tend to be unstable (19), and oblique views of the pelvis may be required for demonstration of all the individual fractures present. Posteriorly, these can occur through the iliac bone, sacrum, or sacroiliac joint while anteriorly they occur through the pubic bone and/or anterior portion of the ischium (Fig. 4.102).

Isolated Pelvic Fractures. Most often isolated fractures of the pelvis occur through the pubic bone or iliac wing (Fig. 4.103), but

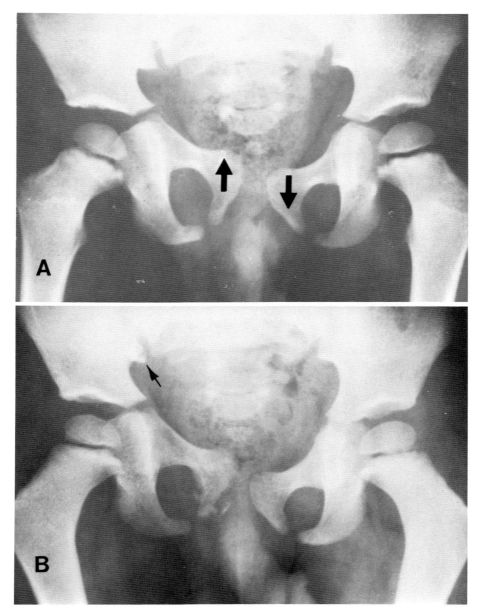

Figure 4.101. *Pubic separation.* (*A*) Note on this well positioned pelvic film that the right pubic bone rides higher than the left (*arrows*). This boy was run over by a farm wagon and complained of right hip pain. (*B*) One month later, note persistent malalignment of pubic bones and signs of healing around the inferior right pubic ramus. Also note development of an osteophyte along the inferior aspect of the right sacroiliac joint (*arrow*), belying a previously suspected injury at this site. Most likely there was a mild degree of sacroiliac joint separation sustained at the time of initial injury.

occasionally they can occur through the ischium or even the ischiopubic synchondrosis (Fig. 4.104). Isolated torus or buckle fractures of the cortex of the pubic bone also are common in childhood, and one can avoid missing them if one looks for subtle bends or kinks in the cortex and adjacent soft tissue edema (Fig. 4.105).

Acetabular Fractures. Acetublar rim fractures are not particularly common in childhood, but can be seen in association with posterior hip dislocations (Fig. 4.106). Fractures through the center of the acetabulum usually occur in older children and result from the femoral head being impacted into the acetabulum. Often they are difficult to detect (21), and indeed, may present with nothing more than widening of the joint space (hemarthrosis) and obliteration of the soft tissues along the obturator internus fat pad (edema and bleeding). In the infant and young child, these fractures tend to occur through the triradiate cartilage (Fig. 4.107), but generally speaking they are not overly common. Furthermore, care should be taken not to confuse the normal triradiate cartilage distorted by faulty positioning of the pelvis for one rendered abnormal by a fracture (Fig. 4.108). Most often such faulty positioning is due to rotation but it also can result from a combination of rotation and utilization of the angled inlet view (26).

Many times, the first clue to the presence of an otherwise occult triradiate cartilage fracture is the presence of edema and soft tissue thickening along the inner aspect of the pelvis (Fig. 4.107). Then, when one notes this finding, one may also note that the triradiate cartilage is wider than normal, or that the bones are displaced (Fig. 4.107).

Finally, it should be noted, that nowadays evaluation of pelvic and upper femoral fractures often is best accomplished with CT scanning (11, 22). Indeed, often the combination of a plain film and a CT scan yields extremely valuable three-dimensional data regarding the fracture (Fig. 4.109).

Avulsion Fractures. Avulsion fractures of the pelvic bones occur most commonly in children and most often they occur along the outer aspect of the iliac wing (Fig. 4.110) and ischium (Fig. 4.111). Less commonly they occur over the upper portion of the superior pubic ramus (Fig. 4.110D), the top of the iliac wing, and in the hip, over the greater and lesser trochanters (see Fig. 4.124).

With most pelvic avulsion fractures, ac-

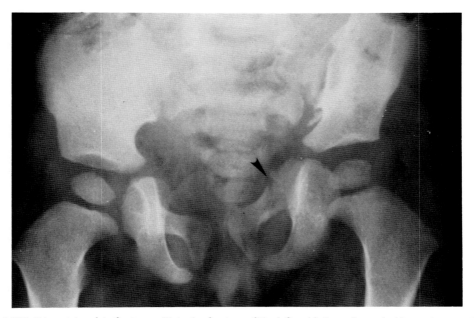

Figure 4.102. *Diametric pelvic fracture.*   Note the fracture of the left pubic bone (*arrow*). Also note separation of the left sacroiliac joint and a small chip fracture along the inferior aspect of the joint. The left iliac wing is abnormally rotated and appears smaller than the right.

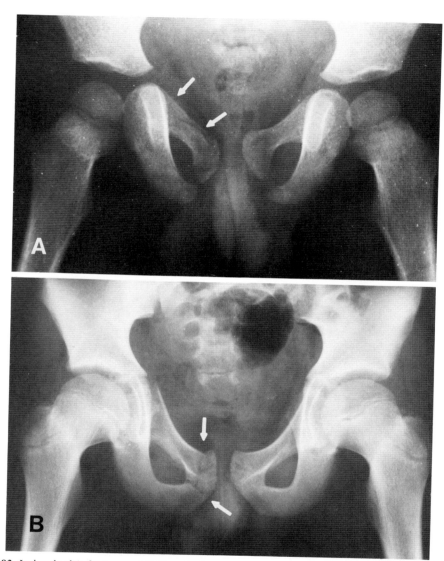

Figure 4.103. *Isolated pelvic fractures.*   (*A*) Note the fracture of the right pubic bone (*arrows*). (*B*) Note the buckled fracture through the left pubic bone (*upper arrow*). Also note soft tissue swelling causing obliteration of the obturator fat pad along the inner margin of the bony pelvis, and a nondisplaced fracture through the ischiopubic synchondrosis (*lower arrow*).

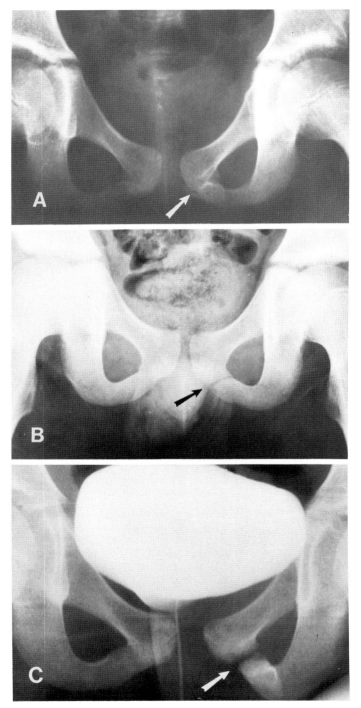

Figure 4.104. *Ischiopubic synchondrosis fractures.* (*A*) Note the fracture through the ischiopubic synchondrosis on the left (*arrow*). It is most important to differentiate this fracture from the normal ischiopubic synchondrosis (see Fig. 4.117). (*B*) Another, more subtle fracture through the ischiopubic synchondrosis (*arrow*). A similar fracture is seen in Figure 4.103*B*. (*C*) A displaced fracture through the ischiopubic synchondrosis (*arrow*). Separation of the symphysis also is present.

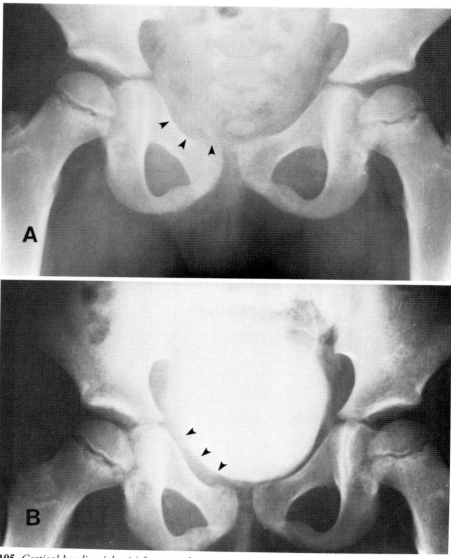

Figure 4.105. *Cortical-bending (plastic) fracture of superior pubic ramus.* (*A*) Note the abnormal curvature of the superior aspect of the right pubic ramus (*arrows*), as compared to the normal left pubic ramus. Also note the increase in soft tissue density over the right pubic ramus and obliteration of the fat pads and soft tissues in the area. (*B*) Follow-up cystogram demonstrates increased soft tissue thickness between the right pubic ramus and contrast filled bladder (*arrows*). This is due to bleeding and edema secondary to the cortical-bending fracture of the right pubic ramus.

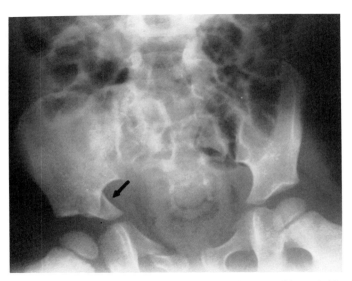

Figure 4.106. *Acetabular fracture.*   Note the fracture through the acetabular roof (*arrow*). The fracture fragment is rotated and there is associated soft tissue thickening medially. The joint space also is widened due to blood in the joint.

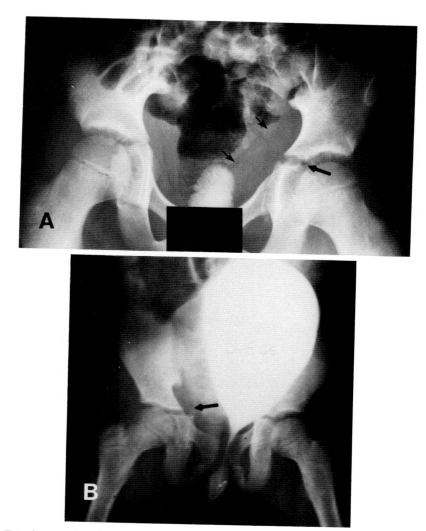

Figure 4.107. *Triradiate cartilage fractures.*   (*A*) Note soft tissue swelling along the left inner pelvic margin (*multiple arrows*). Also note that the triradiate cartilage is wider (*single arrow*) than the one on the right. (*B*) Note the dislocated triradiate cartilage on the right (*arrow*). Also note that on this well-positioned anteroposterior view the joint space on the right is distorted and narrower than that on the left. Also note that the bladder has been displaced and elevated by a large intrapelvic hematoma. (Courtesy Charles J. Fagan, M.D.).

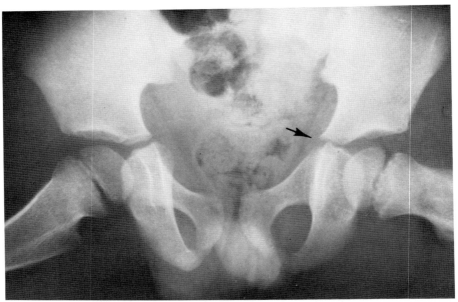

Figure 4.108. *Pseudotriradiate cartilage fracture-dislocation.*   Note that the pelvis is rotated in this patient (i.e., compare the size of the foramina outlined by the pubic and ischial bones on either side; if they are unequal rotation is present). Rotation causes apparent offsetting or pseudodislocation of the bones about the triradiate cartilage on the left (*arrow*).

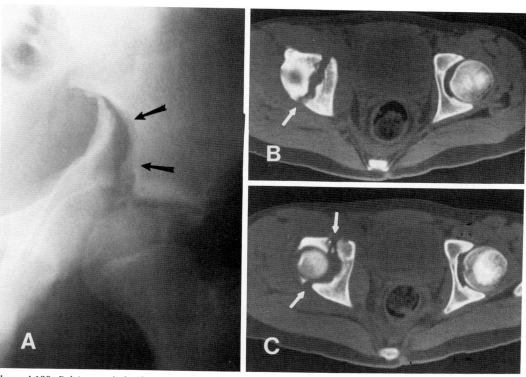

Figure 4.109. *Pelvic acetabular fracture; value of CT.* (*A*) Note the gross fracture through the acetabulum (*arrows*). (*B*) High CT cut demonstrates the fracture through the iliac bone, above the acetabulum (*arrow*). (*C*) Lower CT cut demonstrates the fracture (*arrows*), and even more clearly, its relationship to the femoral head. Overall, the two studies provide a very accurate three-dimensional picture of the fracture.

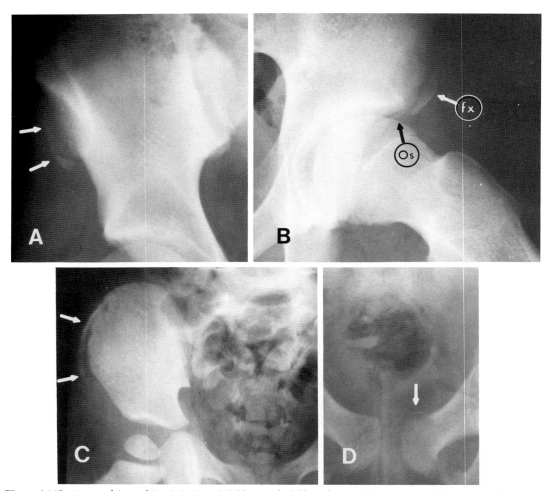

Figure 4.110. *Acute pelvic avulsion injuries.* (*A*) Note typical iliac wing avulsion (*arrows*). (*B*) Another iliac bone avulsion fracture (*fx*). The normal os acetabulae (*Os*) should not be confused with these fractures. The os acetabulae ossicles lie under the acetabular roof while fractures are lateral to the acetabulum. (*C*) Long, linear avulsion of iliac wing (*arrows*). (*D*) Small pubic bone avulsion (*arrow*).

tual fracture fragments are seen, but in some cases not enough bone is avulsed for this to occur. This is especially common over the ischium, where often only bone resorption, causing a cortical defect, is seen in the early stages (Fig. 4.111A). Later on, as this fracture heals, considerable intermixed bony resorption and osteoblastic reparative change occurs, and bizarre roentgenographic configurations result (Figs. 4.111 and 4.112). These healing avulsion fractures also can occur at other sites (Fig. 4.112) and it has always been cautioned, and rightly so, that these bizarre configurations not be misinterpreted for those of a more serious lesion such as a bone tumor or osteomyelitis (3–7, 24, 25, 27, 28). The key, here, is to keep in mind just where these very predictable avulsions occur.

Before leaving the topic of pelvic avulsion fractures, it should be noted that the normal apophyses, along the inferior aspect of the ischium and superior aspect of the iliac wing, can mimic nondisplaced avulsion fractures (see Fig. 4.118). Of course, this is not to say that the apophyses themselves are never avulsed, for this would be untrue, but it does mean that one will see many more normal apophyses than those which are avulsed.

Stress fractures of the pelvic bones are quite uncommon in children, and are more likely to occur in adolescents and adults (12). The key findings include an area of sclerosis, with associated periosteal new bone (Fig. 4.113). They are positive on isotope bone

scans and the main differential diagnosis is osteoid osteoma, which unfortunately also is positive on regular bone scans. On indium bone scans, however, osteoid osteoma usually is not positive.

Fractures of the Sacrum. Sacral fractures commonly are associated with pelvic injuries, and overall, may be difficult to detect. However, if one systematically compares the cortical margins of the sacral foramina on one side to those on the other, disruption of their margins (arcuate lines) (9, 15) will provide a clue to the presence of a fracture (Fig. 4.114A). In addition to sacral fractures, many of these patients demonstrated associated sacroiliac joint separations (Fig. 4.114A). *Other injuries associated with pelvic fractures* include fractures of the femur, or injuries to the bladder (Fig. 4.114B), urethra, and pelvic blood vessels. Indeed, rapid demise secondary to exsanguination associated with vascular injury is not uncommon at all (5, 13, 17).

Osteomyelitis of the Pelvic Bones and Sacroiliac Joints. Osteomyelitis of the pelvic bones is more common than generally appreciated but very often its diagnosis is delayed (1, 2, 8, 14, 23). In the early stages one may see nothing more than nonspecific, but often extensive, soft tissue swelling around the area of bone involvement. Bone scans are invaluable in such cases and should be utilized whenever the possibility of osteomyelitis is even remotely suspected (Fig. 4.115). This is doubly important since de-

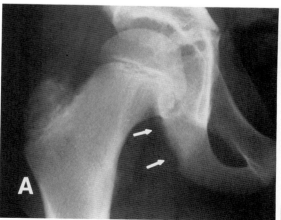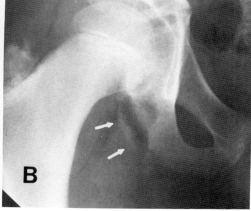

Figure 4.111. *Ischial avulsion with healing.* (*A*) Early phase shows nothing more than bone resorption (*arrows*). (*B*) Later on with healing, the avulsed fracture fragment is visible (*arrows*), and hypertrophic bone is beginning to form.

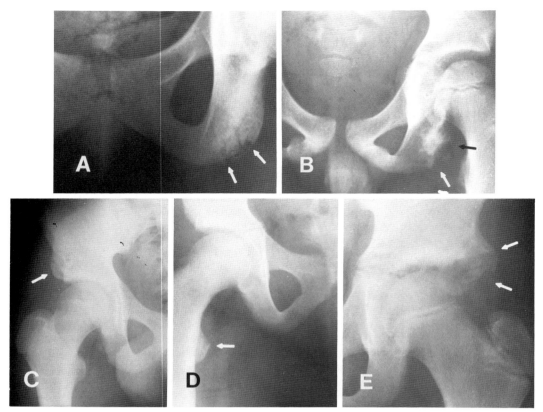

Figure 4.112. *Chronic avulsion injuries.* (*A*) Expanded ischium with irregular new bone formation (*arrows*). (*B*) Tumor-like appearance of a healing ischial avulsion fracture (*arrows*). (Courtesy Ben Allen, M.D.) (*C*) Chronic avulsion of lower iliac wing (*arrow*). (*D*) Chronic avulsion of lesser trochanter (*arrow*). (*E*) Marked hyperostosis due to chronic avulsion over lower iliac wing (*arrows*). All of these patients had hip pain.

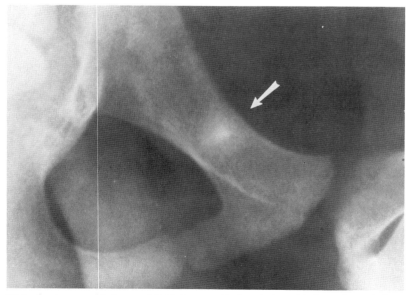

Figure 4.113. *Stress fracture—pubic bone.* (*A*) Note area of sclerosis in pubic bone (*arrow*). Later on periosteal new bone was seen and the bone scan was positive in this patient. (Courtesy Jack Riley, M.D., Denver, Colorado.)

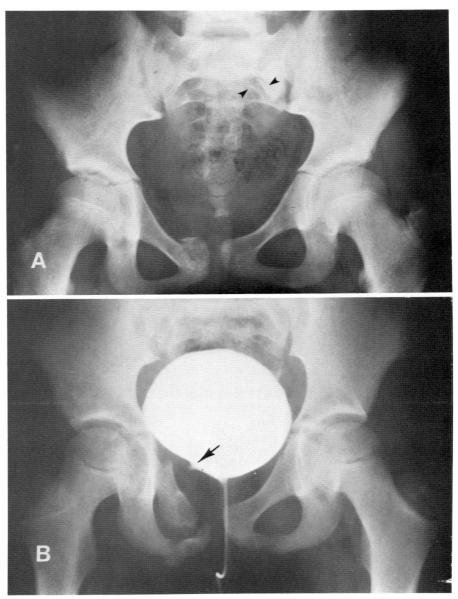

Figure 4.114. *(A) Sacral fracture with pubic bone fracture.* Note the disrupted intervertebral foramina on the left. Two disrupted cortices are seen on edge (*arrows*). In addition, note the pubic bone fracture on the right. (*B*) *Bladder injury with pelvic fracture.* Note the clearly visible extensive fracture of the ischium and pubis on the right, but in addition, note elevation and displacement of the right bladder floor (edema and bleeding) and a small traumatic diverticulum (*arrow*).

struction of the bones of the pelvis may be very subtle in the early stages (Fig. 4.116*A*).

Osteomyelitis of the sacroiliac joint (1, 18, 23), also can be very elusive, and once again is more readily diagnosed in its early stages with bone scans (18) (Fig. 4.116, *C–E*). Patients with sacroiliac joint infection can present with acute back pain, referred pain down the leg, a limp, or symptoms suggestive of an intra-abdominal problem. As with osteomyelitis of the flat bones of the pelvis, initial roentgenographic findings often are

very subtle or nonexistent. Later on, destruction along the sacroiliac joint becomes apparent, but in the meantime it is the isotope bone scan which delivers the most useful information (Fig. 4.116*E*).

In addition to osteomyelitis of the pelvis and sacrum, one occasionally can encounter deep soft tissue abscesses, not associated with bone infection (16). These lesions usually are best demonstrated with CT scanning, ultrasonography, or indium or gallium isotope scanning (see Fig. 4.219).

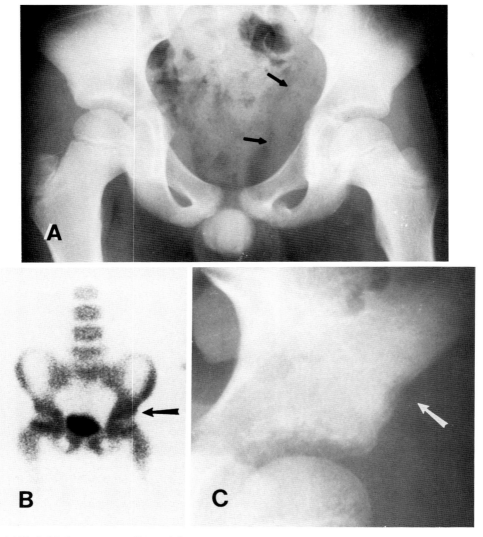

Figure 4.115. *Pelvic bone osteomyelitis with bone scan.*   (*A*) Note soft tissue thickening along the inner left pelvic margin (*arrows*). Bone changes are virtually nonexistent. (*B*) Anterior bone scan, however, demonstrates increased uptake in the left iliac bone (*arrow*). (*C*) Film of the iliac wing obtained 2 weeks later shows bone destruction (*arrow*).

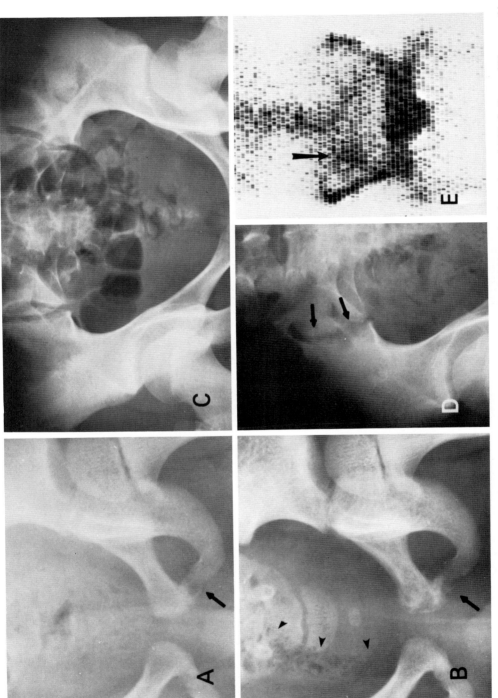

Figure 4.116. *Osetomyelitis of the pelvic bones.* Note faint radiolucency in the region of the left ischiopubic synchondroses (*arrow*). This finding could be normal but was the early lesion in this case. Also note that the obturator fat pad on the left is a little less distinct than the one on the right. This patient presented with acute left hip pain. (*B*) A few weeks later, note destruction of the pubic bone on the left (*lower arrow*), secondary to osteomyelitis. Also note the extensive soft tissue mass in the pelvis causing displacement of the gas- and feces-filled rectum to the right (*upper arrows*). (*C*) *Osteomyelitis of the sacroiliac joint.* This patient presented with back pain and a right limp. No abnormalities are noted, especially in the right sacroiliac joint. (*D*) Two weeks later, note complete destruction of the right sacroiliac joint (*arrows*). (*E*) Bone scan obtained earlier demonstrates increased activity over the sacroiliac joint (*arrow*).

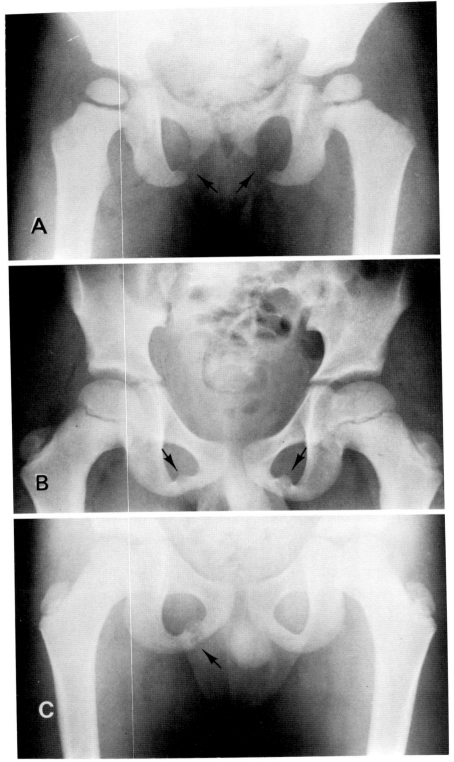

Figure 4.117. *Normal symphysis pubis and ischiopubic synchondroses.* (*A*) Note the normal width between the pubic bones in this young infant. Also note the normal width of the ischiopubic synchondroses (*arrows*). (*B*) Older patient showing normal appearance of the ischiopubic synchondroses (*arrows*). Also note that the space between the pubic bones still is wider than in adults. (*C*) Unilateral ischiopubic synchondrosis on the right (*arrow*).

Normal Findings Causing Problems.

There are a number of normal findings in the pelvis which frequently are misinterpreted for pathology. First of all, the normally wide space between the pubic bones in the infant and young child frequently is mistaken for a pubic bone separation (Fig. 4.117), and second, the exceedingly variable and "pathology suggesting" appearance of the ischial pubic synchondrosis is misinterpreted for a lesion (Fig. 4.117).

The apophyses along the superior aspect of the iliac bone and inferior aspect of the ischial bone are another source of erroneous interpretation (Fig. 4.118), and so are the numerous normal fragments of the normally ossifying acetabulum (Fig. 4.119). All of these normal bony fragments and apophyses can be misinterpreted for fractures, especially avulsion type fractures. In the older child, one of the ossicles, just lateral to the acetabular margin, can remain isolated and is then termed the "os acetabulae." Finally, the nearly obliterated triradiate cartilage remnant must not be misinterpreted for a central acetabular fracture (Fig. 4.119).

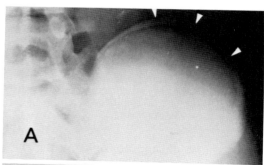

Figure 4.118. *Normal iliac and ischial apophyses.* (*A*) Note the normal iliac wing apophysis (*arrows*). (*B*) Normal ischial apophysis (*arrows*).

REFERENCES

1. Coy, J.T., Wolf, C.R., Brower, T.D., and Winter, W.G.: Pyogenic arthritis of the sacro-iliac joint. J. Bone Joint Surg. 58: 845–849, 1976.
2. Edwards, M.S., Baker, C.J., Granberry, W.M., and Barrett, F.F.: Pelvic osteomyelitis in children. Pediatrics 61: 62–67, 1978.
3. Eklof, O., Hugosson, C., and Lindham, S.: Normal variations and posttraumatic appearance of the tuberosity of ischium in adolescence. Ann. Radiol. 22: 77–84, 1979.
4. Ellis, R.E., and Green, A.G.: Ischial apophyseolysis. Radiology 87: 646–648, 1966.
5. Finby, N., and Begg, C.: Traumatic avulsion of ischial epiphysis simulating neoplasm. N.Y. State J. Med. 67: 2488–2490, 1967.
6. Freiberger, R.H.: Skeletal lesions simulating tumor. In A.R. Margulis and C.A. Gooding (eds.): *Diagnostic Radiology*, pp. 307–318. University of California Press, San Francisco, 1975.
7. Goergen, T.G., Resnick, D., and Riley, R.R.: Post-traumatic abnormalities of the pubic bone simulating malignancy. Radiology 126: 85–87, 1978.
8. Greenstone, G., and Greensides, R.: Osteomyelitis of the pelvis. Am. J. Dis. Child. 132: 581–582, 1978.
9. Jackson, H., Kam, J., Harris, J.H., Jr., and Harle, T.S.: The sacral arcuate lines in upper sacral fractures. Radiology 145: 35–39, 1982.
10. Levine, J.I., and Crampton, R.S.: Major abdominal injuries associated with pelvic fractures. Surg. Gynecol. Obstet. 116: 223–226, 1963.
11. Mack, L.A., Harley, J.D., and Winquist, R.A.: CT of acetabular fractures: analysis of fracture patterns. A.J.R. 138: 407–412, 1982.
12. Meurman, K.O.A.: Stress fracture of the pubic arch in military recruits. Br. J. Radiol. 53: 521–524, 1980.
13. Motsay, E.J., Manlove, C., and Perry, J.F.: Major venous injury with pelvic fracture. J. Trauma 9: 343–346, 1969.
14. Nixon, G.W.: Hematogenous osteomyelitis of metaphyseal-equivalent locations. A.J.R. 130: 123–129, 1978.
15. Northrop, C.H., Eto, R.T., and Loop, J.W.: Vertical fracture of the sacral ala: significance of non-continuity of the anterior superior sacral foraminal line. A.J.R. 124: 102–106, 1975.
16. Oliff, M., and Chuang, V.P.: Retroperitoneal iliac fossa pyogenic abscess. Radiology 126: 647–652, 1978.
17. Patternson, F.K., and Morten, K.S.: The cause of death in fractures of the pelvis. J. Trauma 13: 849–856, 1973.
18. Pope, T.L., Jr., Teague, W.G., Jr., Kossack, R., Bray, S.T., and Flannery, D.B.: Pseudomonas sacroiliac osteomyelitis: diagnosis by gallium citrate ^{67}Ga scan. Am. J. Dis. Child. 136: 649–650, 1982.
19. Quinby, W.C., Jr.: Fractures of the pelvis and associated injuries in children. J. Pediatr. Surg. 1: 353–364, 1966.
20. Reed, M.H.: Pelvic fractures in children. J. Can. Assoc. Radiol. 27: 255–261, 1976.
21. Rogers, L.F., Novy, S.B., and Harris, N.F.: Occult central fractures of the acetabulum. A.J.R. 124: 96–101, 1975.
22. Sauser, D.D., Billimoria, P.E., Rouse, G.A., and Mudge, K.: CT evaluation of hip trauma. A.J.R. 135: 269–274, 1980.
23. Schaad, U.B., McCracken, G.H., Jr., and Nelson, J.D.: Pyogenic arthritis of the sacroiliac joint in pediatric patients. Pediatrics 66: 375–379, 1980.
24. Schlonsky, J., and Olix, M.L.: Functional disability following avulsion fracture of the ischial epiphysis. J. Bone Joint Surg. 54A: 641–644, 1972.
25. Schneider, R., Kay, J.J., and Ghelman, B.: Abductor avulsive injuries near the symphysis pubis. Radiology 120: 567–569, 1976.
26. Shipley, R.T., Griscom, N.T., Kirkpatrick, J.A., and Gross, G.: Artifact of projection simulating a pelvic fracture. A.J.R. 141: 479–480, 1983.

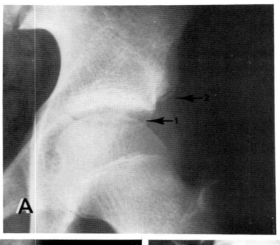

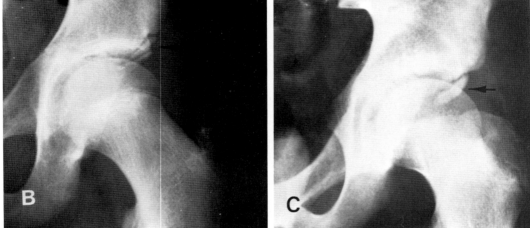

Figure 4.119. *Normal triradiate cartilage remnant and acetabular ossicles.* (*A*) Note the incompletely obliterated triradiate cartilage remnant (*1*) which might be misinterpreted for a central acetabular fracture. Also note the normal, small acetabular ossicle or accessory ossification center (*2*). (*B*) Multiple acetabular ossicles (*arrow*). (*C*) Large acetabular ossicle (*arrow*) which might be misinterpreted for an acetabular rim fracture.

27. Slayton, C.A.: Ischial epiphysiolysis. A.J.R. 76: 1161–1162, 1956.
28. Young, L.W., and Tan, K.M.: Radiological case of the month—traumatic ischial apophyseolysis. Am. J. Dis. Child. 134: 885–886, 1980.

HIP

Normal Fat Pads and Joint Space. The two views generally obtained for evaluating the hip are the straight anteoposterior and anteroposterior frogleg views. The fat pads surrounding the hip and the joint space are best assessed on the straight anteroposterior view (Fig. 4.120). The fat pads around the hip include the obturator internus, iliopsoas, and gluteus (Fig. 4.120). These fat pads do not lie against the joint capsule directly, and thus are not displaced outwardly when fluid accumulates within the joint. The only exception occurs with the gluteus fat pad which can be displaced outwardly with the femur. With soft tissue edema, of course, the fat pads become obliterated.

Detecting Fluid in the Hip Joint. When fluid (blood, pus, serous fluid) accumulates in the hip joint, the femoral head is displaced laterally (Fig. 4.121). This is a natural and easily accomplished decompressive maneuver, for this is the avenue of least resistance in the joint. When such decompression occurs, it causes the joint space to become widened medially, and this is the most im-

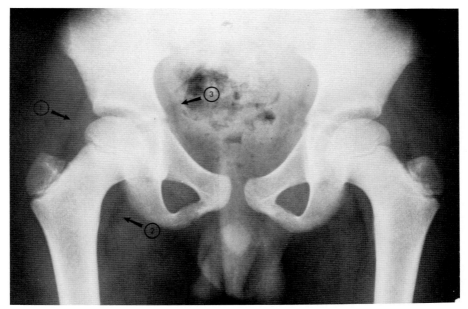

Figure 4.120. *Normal hip joint: soft tissues and fat pads.* Note that the joint space both superiorly and medially is of equal width on both sides. The visible fat pads include the gluteus (*1*), iliopsoas (*2*), and the obturator internus (*3*).

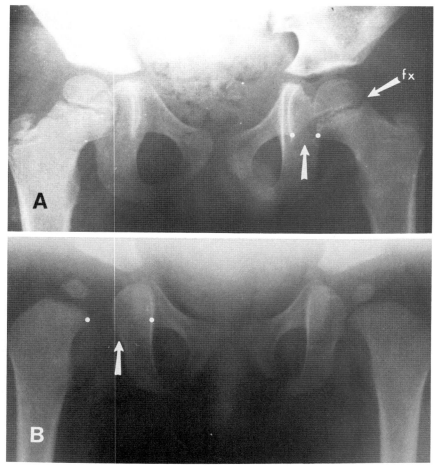

Figure 4.121. *Detecting fluid in the hip joint.* (*A*) Note that the left joint space is wider (*arrow*) than the right. Such lateral displacement of the femoral head with widening of the joint space medially is indicative of fluid in the joint. This patient sustained a mild Salter-Harris type I epiphyseal-metaphyseal injury (i.e., note subtle widening of the epiphyseal line on the left (*fx*)). The fluid, of course, was blood. (*B*) Young infant with septic arthritis on the right. Note marked widening of the joint space (*arrow*). *Dots* mark the best place to make one's measurements.

portant roentgenographic finding in the detection of fluid in the hip joint. In addition, one may note displacement or bulging of the gluteus fat pad, but this latter finding is less consistent and dependable.

Proper positioning of the hips is mandatory for the evaluation of joint space widening, for any deviation from normal positioning can lead to erroneous interpretations. In this regard, the best positioning of the hips is accomplished when the legs are internally rotated (i.e., the toes point towards each other and the kneecaps point upwards). If pelvic rotation occurs, or if one leg is out of position, erroneous measurements surely will result.

Recently it has been demonstrated that widening of the joint space, secondary to the accumulation of joint fluid, is less likely to occur in older children (33). This also has been our experience and most likely this occurs because the ligaments are tighter in older children. In young children, and infants, however, the femur is readily displaced laterally when joint fluid accumulation occurs, and thus, joint space widening in this age group is a reliable finding for the presence of fluid in the hip joint (33).

Injuries of the Upper Femur. Fractures through the femoral neck and intertrochanteric region of the femur are distinctly less common in children than in adults (3, 11,

14, 17, 19). *Epiphyseal-metaphyseal injuries*, on the other hand, are more common and most often are Salter-Harris type I or II injuries. In assessing the upper femur for the presence of these latter fractures, one first should look for an increase in the width and radiolucency of the involved epiphyseal line, and then for widening of the medial joint space (Fig. 4.122*A*). The first finding indicates the presence of an epiphyseal-metaphyseal separation while the second indicates the presence of associated bleeding into the joint. Of course, if dislocation of the femoral capital epiphysis (27) also is present, the injury is not difficult to detect (Fig. 4.122*B*). With Salter-Harris type II injuries, an associated metaphyseal corner fracture also will be present.

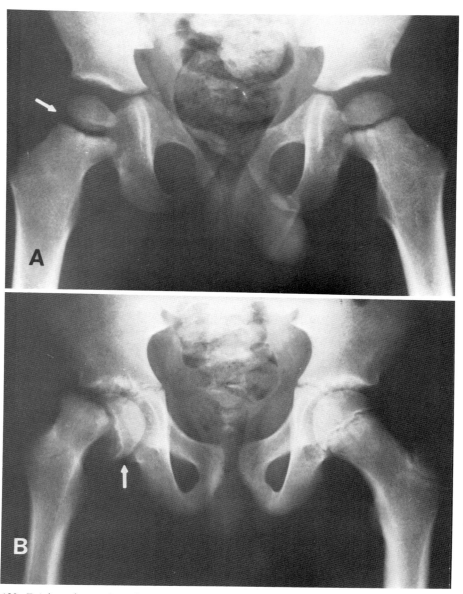

Figure 4.122. *Epiphyseal-metaphyseal injuries of the hip.* (*A*) Note the markedly widened epiphyseal line on the right (*arrow*). The joint space is minimally widened due to associated hemarthrosis. This is a Salter-Harris type I injury, undisplaced. Also see Figure 4.121*A*. (*B*) Note the clearly dispatched epiphysis on the right (*arrow*). This is a displaced Salter-Harris type I epiphyseal-metaphyseal injury.

Anterior or posterior **dislocation of the hip** is not particularly common in childhood (24, 25, 28). The reason for this is that since the epiphysis is still open, it represents the weakest area of the bone, and thus, Salter-Harris type I or II injuries are more likely to result. Of course, in the older child, a dislocation is more likely, and as in adults, posterior dislocations are much more the common (Fig. 4.123). Acetabular rim fractures are a frequent associated injury, and indeed, a fragment of the acetabulum can become trapped in the joint space. Roentgenographically, this complication can be suspected when the joint space fails to return to its normal width after reduction. This can be a most important observation, for the fragment frequently is cartilaginous and not visible, and thus, only a high index of suspicion will lead to subsequent arthrography or CT scanning for definitive diagnosis.

Trochanteric Avulsion Fractures. Avulsion fractures of the trochanteric apophyses, especially of the lesser trochanter, are common (Fig. 4.124*A*). These latter avulsions, however, often are difficult to diagnose and/or to differentiate from the normal lesser trochanter apophysis which is not avulsed. In this regard, an important point to remember is that if the lesser trochanter apophysis is visible and appears avulsed on the normal anteroposterior view of the hips (i.e., with the hips in internal rotation), then an avulsion probably is present. The reason for this is that with the hip in this attitude, the lesser trochanter apophysis usually is not visualized in a tangential, fracture-suggesting position. However, if the femur is externally rotated, or held in the frogleg position, the apophysis of the lesser trochanter is visualized on edge and then erroneously "appears" avulsed (Fig. 4.124*B*).

Septic Arthritis, Toxic Synovitis, Osteomyelitis, and Cellulitis of the Hip. The differentiation of these conditions often is a difficult task (15, 32), for the clinical and roentgenographic findings can be very similar. However, with toxic synovitis systemic symptoms usually are less pronounced. Indeed these infants often "smile" as they limp and hobble along, but with septic arthritis, well established pain rules. The precise etiology of toxic synovitis is unknown, but it probably is a viral joint infection, and usually it is an affliction of older infants and children. It seldom occurs below the age of 2 years. Roentgenographically, the findings are normal in most cases, but in a few, more pronounced cases, there will be widening of the joint space, bulging of the gluteus fat

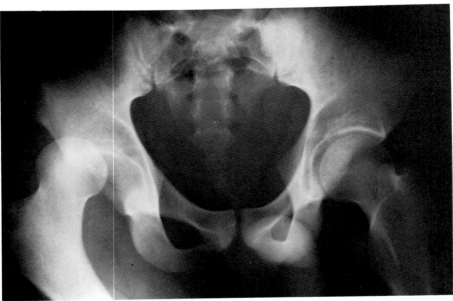

Figure 4.123. *Posterior dislocation of the hip.* Note the typical position of a posteriorly dislocated hip in this teenager. The injury was sustained in an automobile accident. The radiolucent line through the posterior acetabular rim is not a fracture; it is a normal irregularity.

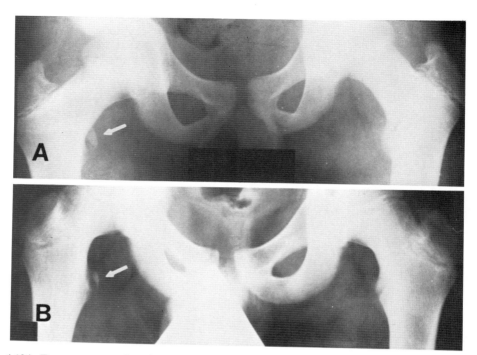

Figure 4.124. *True versus pseudoavulsion of the lesser trochanter.* (*A*) *True avulsion.* Note the avulsed lesser trochanter on the right (*arrow*). Compare the position of both hips. Both are held in internal rotation. In this position, the lesser trochanter should not be visualized on edge; it should appear as it does on the left. (*B*) *Pseudoavulsion.* Note the avulsed appearance of the lesser trochanter on the right (*arrow*). However, note that the position of the right hip is different from that on the left. The left is in internal rotation while the right is an external rotation. External rotation causes the hip to assume a coxa valga configuration and under such circumstances the lesser trochanter is seen on edge and can appear avulsed.

pad, and obliteration of the obturator fat pad (5, 8, 10, 13, 21, 30, 32) (Fig. 4.125). As will be seen in the next paragraph, these latter findings are very similar, if not identical, to those of septic arthritis.

In the classic case of septic arthritis of the hip, there is considerable pain secondary to capsular distention, marked diminution in the range of motion of the hip, and in some cases swelling and redness over the hip. The systemic reaction usually is pronounced and both fever and a marked leukocytosis are common (15, 20, 32). An exception to the latter statement occurs in the very young infant, in whom the lesion may be surprisingly silent. Indeed, in these patients the systemic reaction may be very mild, a leukocytosis may not be present, and the only problem may be a loss of motion of the hip. It is in these cases that the roentgenographic examination of the hip becomes of paramount importance.

Roentgenographically, the hallmark of septic arthritis of the hip is widening of the joint space due to lateral displacement of the femoral head and upper femur (Fig. 4.126). This occurs sooner and more often in infants and young children. In older children pus may be present but due to tighter ligaments the joint is not widened (33). With larger collections of pus in the hip joint, the obturator fat pad often is obliterated, and in younger infants and children there also will be a generalized increase in the density of the soft tissues around the hip secondary to associated edema.

Acute, fulminant, osteomyelitis of the upper femur is common in children, and in very young infants, often is accompanied by septic arthritis. This occurs because in the young infant the blood supply to the femoral metaphysis and epiphysis is contiguous, and thus, spread of infection from one side of the epiphyseal cartilage to the other is readily accomplished. This is not unique to the hip joint, of course, but definitely unique to the

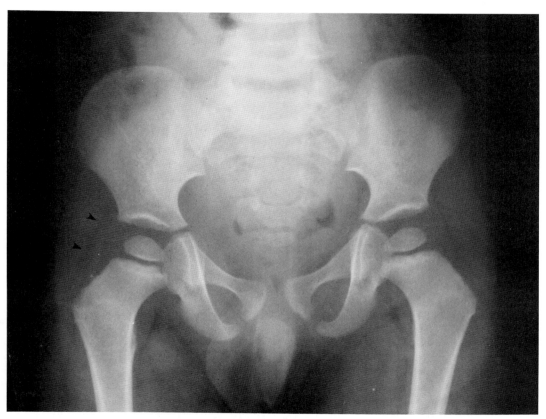

Figure 4.125. *Toxic synovitis—right hip.*   First note that the joint space on the right is a little wider than on the left (fluid). Then, note that the right gluteus fat pad shows slight bulging (*arrows*). In addition, there is complete obliteration of the obturator internus fat pad (edema). Compare these findings with those on the normal left side. Also recall that in most cases of this disease the films are normal.

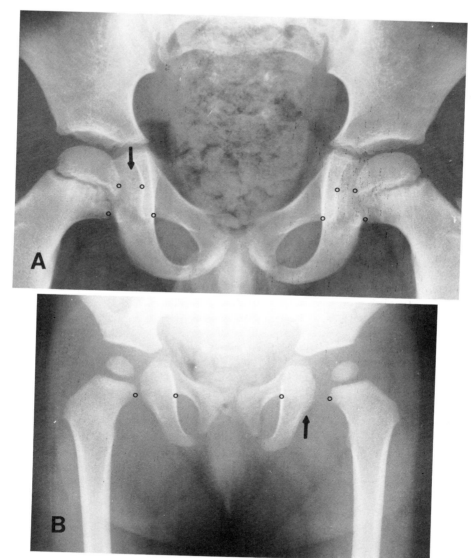

Figure 4.126. *Septic arthritis.* (*A*) Note widening of the joint space on the right (*arrow*). In this older child, widening is more apparent through the *upper dots*. Compare with the normal left side. (*B*) Infant with more pronounced widening of the left joint (*arrow*). The distance between the *dots* is more easily assessed. Also note that there is increased density of the soft tissues along the inner aspect of the acetabulum. This has caused obliteration of the obturator internus fat pad area, characteristic of more advanced cases of septic arthritis.

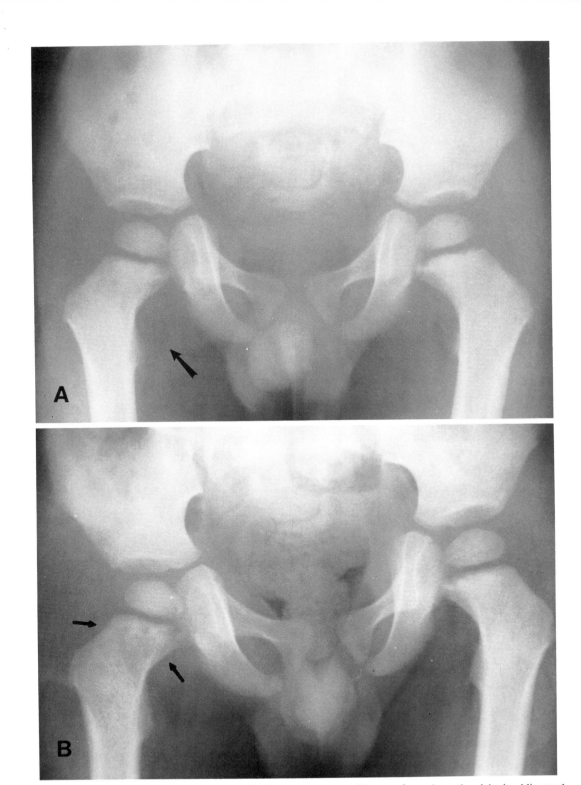

Figure 4.127. *Osteomyelitis, upper femur.* (*A*) First note that the iliopsoas fat pad on the right is obliterated (*arrow*). Compare with the normal fat pad on the left. The joint space is only minimally widened, and is due to a small sympathetic effusion. The fact that septic arthritis (i.e., joint space widening) is not the primary problem can be deduced from the roentgenographic findings. It would be most unusual for septic arthritis to cause enough edema to obliterate the iliopsoas fat pad and yet not cause any more widening of the joint space. In addition, the obturator internus fat pad is intact. (*B*) Follow-up films demonstrate irregular lytic lesions in the upper femur (*arrows*), consistent with osteomyelitis (surgically confirmed).

young infant. In such cases, roentgeno-graphic changes of both conditions are present, but in the older child, where osteomyelitis alone exists, there usually is no joint space widening. This finding, plus obliteration of the iliopsoas fat pad, serve to differentiate septic arthritis from osteomyelitis, even in those cases of osteomyelitis where a small sympathetic joint effusion occurs. In these cases, periarticular soft tissue changes so outweigh the slight degree of joint space widening, that one is forced to conclude that septic arthritis could not be the primary problem. If it were, and were causing so much soft tissue change, joint space widening would be pronounced. Later on, of course, bony destruction of the metaphysis occurs and the diagnosis is more readily established (Fig. 4.127). Low-grade osteomyelitis also can occur in the upper femur, and in some cases, it will take on the appearance of a frank Brodie's abscess, but in the area of the greater trochanter, it often

has a less specific and more subtle appearance (Fig. 4.128). Indeed, because the infection often is so low grade, it may elude initial detection (6, 22, 32).

Cellulitis of the soft tissues around the hip, in the absence of underlying bone infection, also frequently occurs in childhood. Most often such infection is due to inflammation of the inguinal lymph nodes, and roentgenographically, the findings are difficult to differentiate from the early swelling of osteomyelitis. Differentiation from septic arthritis is easier, for with cellulitis no joint space widening should be present.

Isotope studies also can be utilized to differentiate one type of infection from another. However, as with other joints, often they are difficult to interpret and frequently are of limited differentiating value.

Miscellaneous Hip Problems. Occasionally, one can be presented, on an acute basis, with a painful hip due to monoarticular rheumatoid arthritis, nonspecific

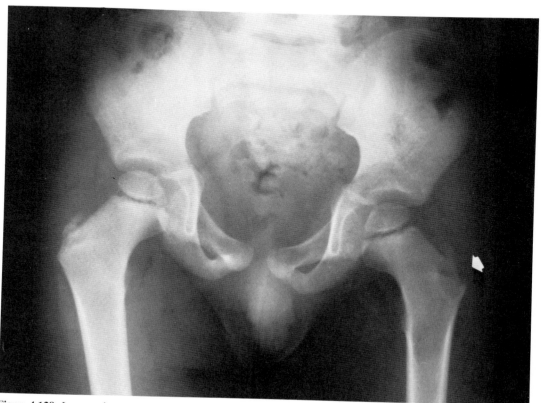

Figure 4.128. *Low-grade osteomyelitis of the femur.* This patient presented with a limp on the left. Roentgenograms demonstrated a large lytic lesion just below the greater trochanter (*arrow*). (Surgically proven low-grade osteomyelitis.)

synovitis, and early Legg-Perthes disease. Any of these conditions can present with findings resembling toxic synovitis or septic arthritis, and indeed, it is generally held that as many as 10% of patients with so-called toxic synovitis eventually are determined to have *Legg-Perthes* disease. This is not to say that the two are related, nor that one is necessarily a precursor of the other, but only to indicate that their initial presentations may be very similar (Fig. 4.129*A*). Later on, in Legg-Perthes disease, one will note demineralization and smallness of the involved femoral head, subchondral avulsions with associated intraepiphyseal gas (3, 23), and eventually, sclerosis and fragmentation of the femoral head (Fig. 4.129*B*).

In many cases irregularities of the metaphysis also are seen (29), and currently early cases often can be diagnosed utilizing iso-

tope bone scanning (1, 4, 31). In such cases one looks for a cold area of isotope activity in the femoral head, usually located laterally (Fig. 4.129*C*).

The so-called *slipped capital femoral epiphysis* of childhood is another lesion which may occasionally present on an acute basis. More often, however, these patients have a history of chronic hip pain or limp for a number of months (2, 7, 12, 16, 26, 32). The classic roentgenographic findings are those of widening and irregularity of the epiphyseal line of the involved femur, and medial tilting of the epiphysis (Fig. 4.130*A*). On frontal view, a line drawn along the outer aspect of the femoral neck can aid in determining whether the epiphysis has slipped medially, for in those cases where such slippage has occurred, the line does not intersect the femoral capital epiphysis (Fig. 4.130*A*).

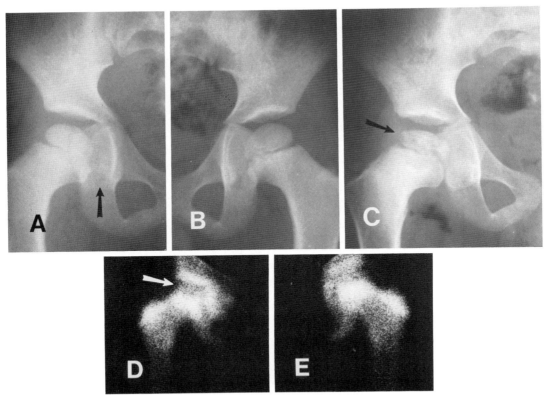

Figure 4.129. *Legg-Perthes disease mimicking acute arthritis.* (*A*) This patient presented with an acute limp and hip pain on the right. The roentgenographic findings suggest slight widening of the joint space on the right (*arrow*), and a general increase in soft tissue density due to edema. The findings would be impossible to differentiate from toxic synovitis or early septic arthritis. (*B*) Normal side for comparison. (*C*) Months later note typical changes of advanced Legg-Perthes disease, consisting of a small sclerotic femoral head and metaphyseal irregularity (*arrow*). (*D*) Isotope study in another patient shows characteristic cold area (*arrow*) in the epiphysis. (*E*) Normal side for comparison.

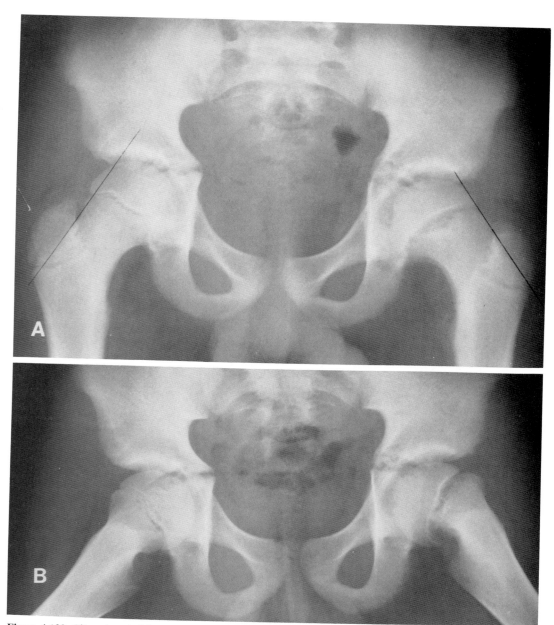

Figure 4.130. *Slipped capital femoral epiphysis.* (*A*) Note that on the left the epiphyseal line between the capital femoral epiphysis and femoral neck is wider than on the right. In addition, note that the line applied along the outer aspect of the femoral neck fails to intersect the femoral capital epiphysis. On the normal right side, it intersects the epiphysis. (*B*) Frogleg view demonstrating posterior slippage of the left femoral head. In addition, note how much wider the epiphyseal line is when compared to its normal counterpart on the right.

Posterior slippage of the femoral head usually accompanies medial slippage, and actually, often predominates. It is best detected on frogleg views of the hips (Fig. 130*B*). The precise etiology of the slipped capital femoral epiphysis in childhood is unknown, but it probably represents a subclinical Salter-Harris type I epiphyseal-metaphyseal injury. In this regard, it has been suggested that in many of these patients, usually somewhat overweight boys, the epiphyseal-metaphyseal junction is more vertical than normal,

and because of this, the epiphysis is more prone to such slippage. An increased incidence of slipped epiphysis also has been noted in hypothyroidism (9).

Normal Variations Causing Problems. In and around the hip, irregularity of the acetabulum and femoral head are the most common normal variations to be misinterpreted for fractures or other abnormalities. Irregularity of femoral head ossification can be pronounced in children, and indeed, the normal femoral head can appear quite frag-

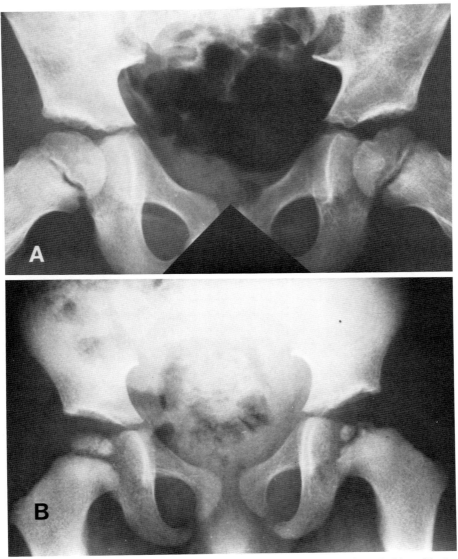

Figure 4.131. *Normal femoral head and acetabular roof irregularities.* (*A*) The irregularities of both acetabular roofs and of the femoral head on the left are normal. (*B*) Normal irregular and asymmetric ossification of the femoral heads.

mented (Fig. 4.131). These findings often are misinterpreted for Legg-Perthes disease (18).

The normal apophysis of the lesser tro-

chanter being mistaken for an avulsion fracture has been dealt with earlier (see Fig. 4.124), but it also should be noted that the normal greater trochanter, because of its frequently very irregular appearance, also can be subject to such misinterpretation (see Fig. 4.132*B*). Similarly, the cartilage remnant between the greater trochanter and femur, as visualized on frogleg views, can be mistaken for a fracture (Fig. 4.132). The vacuum joint phenomenon demonstrated in the shoulder (see Fig. 4.38) also is common in the hip. It is especially prone to occur with stretching of the hips for the frogleg views.

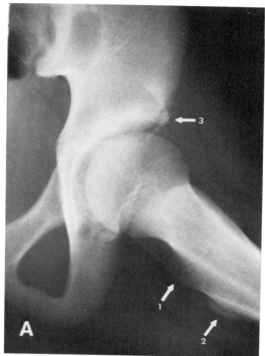

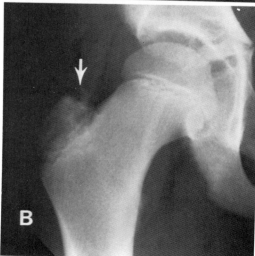

Figure 4.132. *Other normal upper femoral findings causing problems.* (*A*) Note: (*1*) the fracture-like cartilaginous remnant between the greater trochanter and femur; (*2*) normal lesser trochanter apophysis; and (*3*) normal acetabular ossicles. The lesser trochanter apophysis should not be misinterpreted for a fracture (see Fig. 4.124). (*B*) Normal irregular greater trochanter (*arrow*).

REFERENCES

1. Bensahel, H., Bok, B., Cavailloles, F., and Csukonyi, Z.: Bone scintigraphy in Perthes disease. J. Pediatr. Orthop. 3: 302–305, 1983.
2. Bloomberg, T.J., Nuttall, J., and Stoker, D.J.: Radiology in early slipped femoral capital epiphysis. Clin. Radiol. 29: 667, 1978.
3. Caffey, J.: The early roentgenographic changes in essential coxa plana. A. J. R. 103: 620–634, 1968.
4. Canale, S.T., and Bourland, W.L.: Fracture of the neck and intertrochanteric region of the femur in children. J. Bone Joint Surg. 59A: 431–443, 1977.
5. Danigelis, J.A.: Pinhole imaging in Legg-Perthes disease: further observations. Semin. Nucl. Med. 6: 69–82, 1976.
6. Frazier, J.K., and Anzel, S.H.: Osteomyelitis of the greater trochanter in children. J. Bone Joint Surg. 63A: 833–836, 1981.
7. Ghelman, B.: Slipped capital femoral epiphysis. Curr. Probl. Radiol. 3: 40, 1973.
8. Hardinge, K.: The etiology of transient synovitis of the hip in childhood. J. Bone Joint Surg. 52B: 100–107, 1970.
9. Hirano, T., Stamelos, S., Harris, V., and Dumbovic, N.: Association of primary hypothyroidism and slipped capital femoral epiphysis. J. Pediatr. 93: 262–264, 1978.
10. Illingworth, C.M.: Recurrences of transient synovitis of the hip. Arch. Dis. Child. 58: 620–623, 1983.
11. Ingram, A.J., and Bachynski, B.: Fractures of the hip in children. J. Bone Joint Surg. 35A: 867–887, 1953.
12. Jacobs, B.: Diagnosis and natural history of slipped femoral capital epiphysis. Instruct. Course Lect. Am. Acad. Orthop. Surg. 21: 167–173, 1972.
13. Jacobs, B.W.: Synovitis of the hip in children and its significance. Pediatrics 47: 558–566, 1971.
14. Kay, S.P., and Hall, J.E.: Fracture of the femoral neck in children and its complications. Clin. Orthop. 80: 53–71, 1971.
15. Kaye, J.J.: Bacterial infections of the hips in infancy and childhood. Curr. Probl. Radiol. 3: 17–29, 1973.
16. Klein, A., Joplin, R.J., Reidy, J.A., and Hanelin, J.: Roentgenographic features of slipped capital femoral epiphyses. A. J. R. 66: 361–374, 1951.
17. Lam, S.F.: Fractures of the neck of the femur in children. J. Bone Joint Surg. 53A: 1165–1179, 1971.
18. Meyer, J.: Dysplasia epiphysealis capitis femoris. Acta Orthop. Scand. 34: 183–197, 1964.
19. Miller, W.E.: Fractures of the hip in children from birth to adolescence. Clin. Orthop. 92: 155–188, 1973.
20. Morrey, B.F., Bianco, A.J., and Rhodes, K.H.: Suppurative arthritis of the hip in children. J. Bone Joint Surg. 58A: 388–392, 1976.
21. Neuhauser, E.B.D., and Wittenborg, M.H.: Synovitis of the hip in infancy and childhood. Radiol. Clin. North Am. 1: 13–16, 1963.
22. Nixon, G.W.: Hematogous osteomyelitis of metaphyseal-equivalent locations. A. J. R. 130: 123–129, 1978.

23. Norman, A., and Bullough, P.: The radiolucent crescent line—an early diagnostic sign of avascular necrosis of the femoral head. Bull. Hosp. Joint Dis. 24: 99–104, 1963.
24. Offerski, C.M.: Traumatic dislocation of the hip in children. J. Bone Joint Surg. 63B: 194–197, 1981.
25. Pearson, D.E., and Mann, R.J.: Traumatic hip dislocation in children. Clin. Orthop. 92: 189–194, 1973.
26. Ponseti, I.V., and McClintock, R.: Pathology of slipping of the upper femoral epiphysis. J. Bone Joint Surg. 38A: 71–83, 1956.
27. Ratliff, A.H.C.: Traumatic separation of the upper femoral epiphysis in young children. J. Bone Joint Surg. 50B: 757–770, 1968.
28. Schlonsky, J., and Miller, P.R.: Traumatic hip dislocations in children. J. Bone Joint Surg. 55A: 1056–1063, 1973.
29. Smith, S.R., Ions, G.K., and Gregg, P.J.: The radiological features of the metaphysis in Perthes disease. J. Pediatr. Orthop. 2: 401–404, 1982.
30. Spock, H.: Transient synovitis of the hip joint in children. Pediatrics 24: 1042–1049, 1959.
31. Sutherland, A.D., Savage, J.P., Paterson, D.C., et al.: The nuclide bone-scan in the diagnosis and management of Perthes disease. J. Bone Joint Surg. 61B: 300–306, 1980.
32. Swischuk, L.E.: Childhood limp: early diagnosis of his problem. In A.R. Margulis and C.A. Gooding (eds.): *Diagnostic Radiology*, pp. 61–80. University of California Press, San Francisco, 1975.
33. Volberg, F.M., Sumner, T.E., Abramson, J.S., and Winchester, P.H.: Unreliability of radiographic diagnosis of septic hip in children. Pediatrics 74: 118–120, 1984.

FEMORAL SHAFT

Fractures of the femoral shaft are common in childhood, but generally not difficult to detect. Usually they result from serious, known injuries and are of the transverse, spiral, or oblique varieties. Greenstick, buckle (torus), and plastic bending fractures are distinctly uncommon in the femur in any age group. However, they can occur (3). Stress fractures of the midshaft of the femur can occasionally be encountered in children (2), but more often they occur in the femoral neck.

Recently, some note has been made of the fact that many times what appears to be an ordinary fractured femur in an infant is actually part of the battered child syndrome (1, 4). The main gist of these reports is that in young infants, where one might not expect to see femoral shaft fractures with any degree of frequency, if any suspicion regarding the fracture arises, the possibility of the infant being battered should be entertained, and the yield, indeed, is relatively high.

REFERENCES

1. Beals, R.K., Tufts, E.: Fractured femur in infancy: the role of child abuse. J. Pediatr. Orthop. 3: 583–586, 1983.
2. Burks, R.T., and Sutherland, D.H.: Stress fracture of the femoral shaft in children: report of two cases and discussion. J. Pediatr. Orthop. 4: 614–616, 1984.
3. Cail, S.S., Keats, T.E., and Sussman, M.D.: Plastic bowing fracture of the femur in a child. A. J. R. 130: 780–782, 1978.
4. Gross, R.H., and Stranger, M.: Causative factors responsible for femoral fractures in infants and young children. J. Pediatr. Orthop. 3: 341–343, 1983.

KNEE

Normal Fat Pads and Soft Tissues. There are numerous normal fat pads around the knee, and all can be useful. However, those demonstrable on lateral view are the most beneficial (Fig. 4.133). Indeed, one of the best ways to determine whether fluid is present in the knee joint is to assess the soft tissues and fat pads on the lateral view of the knee (see next section).

Detection of Fluid in the Knee Joint. The knee joint does not widen significantly with accumulations of fluid, and thus one must depend on soft tissue and fat pad changes for the detection of fluid in the knee joint (14, 16). In this regard, it is the lateral view of the knee which is most useful. On this view, fluid almost always first accumulates in the suprapatellar bursa, which lies behind the quadriceps tendon and in front of the prefemoral fat pad. When this occurs, the quadriceps tendon is displaced anteriorly and the fat pad posteriorly. Early on, just the neck of the suprapatellar bursa may be distended (Fig. 4.134A), but this finding, almost always, is seen in older children.

With greater fluid accumulations the bursa itself can be identified as a discrete structure (Fig. 4.134B), and once again, this most often occurs in older children, after trauma. In infants and young children, especially if the fluid is pus, the discrete nature of the distended suprapatellar bursa may be lost and the confluent soft tissue density of the quadriceps tendon and distended bursa erroneously suggests that the entire tendon is thickened (Fig. 4.134, C and D). While fluid accumulates in the suprapatellar bursa, it also begins to accumulate in the posterior popliteal bursa (Fig. 4.134C), but one always should look at the suprapatellar bursa first, for fluid accumulates here before it does so in the posterior popliteal bursa. Seldom, then, will one use the posterior popliteal bursa for fluid detection.

Injuries of the Distal Femur and Proximal Tibia. Corticle buckle (torus) fractures around the knee are uncommon for the cortex in both the distal femur and proximal tibia is sturdy. On the other hand, epiphyseal-metaphyseal injuries, transverse frac-

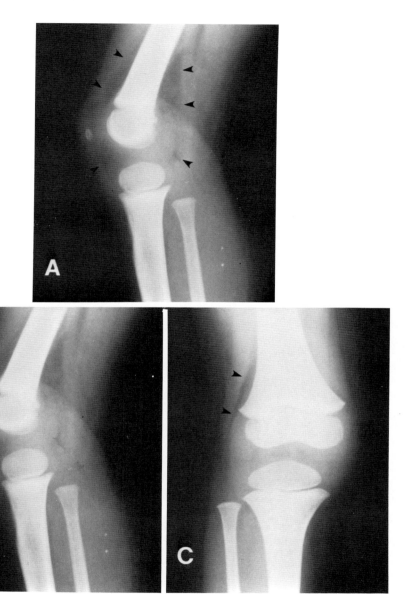

Figure 4.133. *Normal soft tissues and fat pads of the knee.* (*A*) Lateral view. This is the most useful view for evaluation of the joint space and fat pads. The *anterior upper arrows* delineate the prefemoral fat pad while the fat pad posterior to the distal femur is outlined by the *posterior upper arrows*. The *lower anterior arrow* delineates the infrapatellar fat pad, while the fat pad over the cartilaginous tibial epiphysis is outlined by the *posterior lower arrow.* (*B*) Same knee; other findings. Note the small ossification center of the basically cartilaginous patella (*P*) and the easily visualized quadriceps tendon (*Q*), just anterior to the prefemoral fat pad. (*C*) Frontal view demonstrating the most frequently visible fat pad (*arrows*).

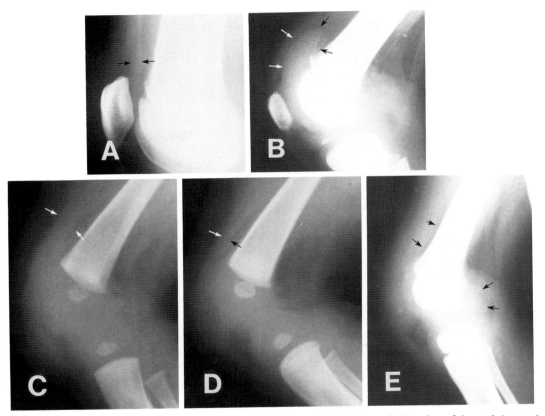

Figure 4.134. *Detecting fluid in the knee joint.*   (*A*) Lateral view. Early findings of distension of the neck (*arrows*) of the suprapatellar bursa. (*B*) Another patient with discrete distention of the suprapatellar bursa (*arrows*). (*C*) This time fluid in the suprapatellar bursa blends in with the quadriceps tendon and causes subtle pseudothickening of the tendon (*arrows*). (*D*) Normal side for comparison. Note normal quadriceps tendon (*arrows*). (*E*) More extensive fluid collection in the suprapatellar bursa leads to marked pseudothickening of the quadriceps tendon. Also note that the prefemoral fat pad is compressed against the femur (*upper arrows*), and that there is early accumulation of fluid in the posterior popliteal bursa (*posterior arrows*). Also see Figure 4.152.

tures of the upper tibia, patellar fractures, and cruciate ligament avulsions are quite common. Meniscal injuries also occur, but more so in the older child, and in any event, usually produce normal roentgenograms. Other injuries sustained around the knee include acute and chronic tibial tubercle and inferior patellar avulsions.

Epiphyseal-metaphyseal injuries are common about the knee and in gross form are not difficult to detect (Fig. 4.135). The more subtle, nondisplaced Salter-Harris type I or II injuries, on the other hand, frequently elude initial observation. In these cases, one must, once again, learn to study the soft tissues first, and then to suspect the slightest degree of widening of the epiphyseal line (Fig. 4.136). In other cases, additional oblique (Fig. 4.137) or stress views may be required to confirm or further delineate the injury. Epiphyseal-metaphyseal injuries of the knee can be sustained in a number of ways: i.e., automobile accidents, athletic injuries (29), etc., and most often the stresses applied to the knee are dissipated through the epiphyseal-metaphyseal junctions. However, in some cases rather than the forces being dissipated through this area, collateral ligament strains cause small, marginal avulsions of either the epiphysis or metaphysis (Fig. 4.138).

Cruciate ligament avulsions most often involve the anterior cruciate ligament at its bony insertion onto the anterior aspect of the tibial epiphysis. With large fragment avulsions, the findings are straightforward, and it is difficult to miss the fragment (Fig. 4.139). With smaller avulsions, however, it is easy to miss the fragment on initial studies (Fig. 4.140*A*). A similar problem can arise with the less common avulsions of the femoral condyle (Fig. 4.140*B*), and in either case, tunnel views of the knee usually more clearly delineate the avulsed fragment (Fig. 4.140*C*).

Supracondylar fractures of the distal femur are not difficult to identify for most often they are gross. However, seldom do they occur in healthy bones, for in such bones the weakest area is the epiphyseal-metaphyseal junction, and fractures occur here. On the other hand, in a severely demineralized or otherwise weakened bone, this is not true, and consequently it is in this type of patient that supracondylar fractures occur. Contrarily, in the **proximal tibia** one commonly sees *transverse metaphyseal fractures* in normal bones (Fig. 4.141), and when these fractures are hairline, they are difficult to detect (see Fig. 4.3*A*). Another interesting feature of these fractures is that if there is associated inbending deformity, it must be

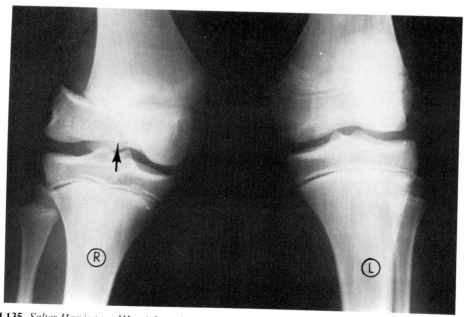

Figure 4.135. *Salter-Harris type III epiphyseal-metaphyseal injury.* Note the grossly displaced epiphysis and the fracture through the middle of the epiphysis (*arrow*) of the distal right femur.

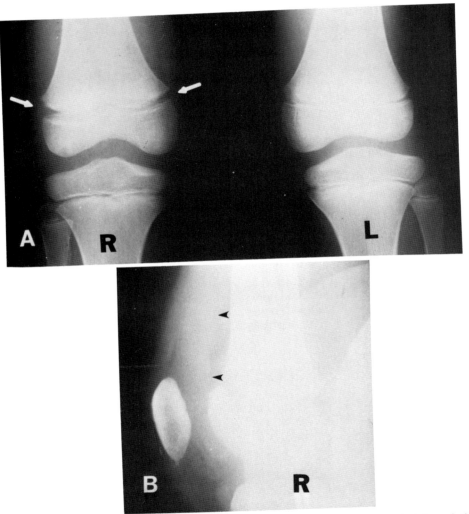

Figure 4.136. *Subtle Salter-Harris type I epiphyseal-metaphyseal injury.* (*A*) First note that the soft tissues are more opaque around the right knee. This indicates the presence of edema. In addition, however, note that the epiphyseal line of the distal right femur is wider (*arrows*) than its counterpart on the normal left side. The findings represent a nondisplaced epiphyseal-metaphyseal separation. (*B*) Lateral view showing associated hemarthrosis manifesting in distention of the suprapatellar bursa.

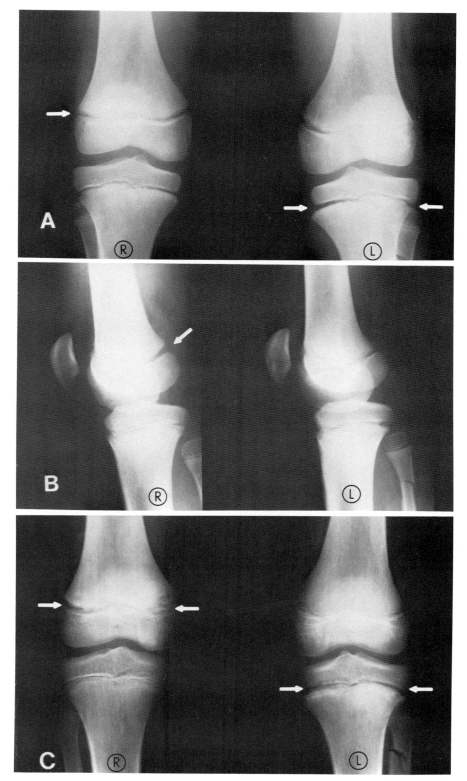

Figure 4.137. *Multiple, more subtle, Salter-Harris type I epiphyseal-metaphyseal injuries.* (*A*) Note widening of the epiphyseal line of the distal right femur and proximal left tibia (*arrows*). Compare these epiphyseal lines with their normal counterparts on the other side. Also note a fracture in the upper left fibula. (*B*) Oblique view demonstrating widening of the right distal femoral and left proximal tibial epiphyseal lines (*arrows*). The left fibular fracture is noted again. (*C*) Two weeks later note evidence of healing of the previously noted epiphyseal-metaphyseal fractures. There is irregular sclerosis along the distal right femoral epiphyseal-metaphyseal junction (*right arrows*), and along the upper left tibial epiphyseal-metaphyseal line (*left arrows*). The fibular fracture is noted again.

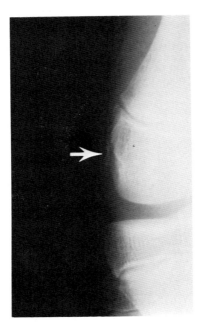

Figure 4.138. *Subtle lateral epiphyseal avulsion.* Note the barely visible avulsed bony epiphyseal fragment (*arrow*). This patient sustained a lateral knee strain injury.

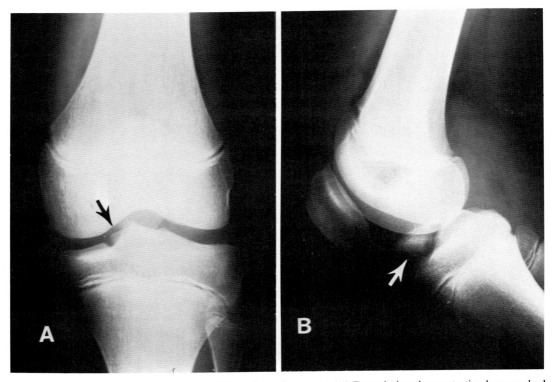

Figure 4.139. *Anterior cruciate ligament avulsion—large fragment.* (*A*) Frontal view demonstrating large avulsed bony fragment (*arrow*). (*B*) Lateral view demonstrating the same avulsed bony fragment (*arrow*). Also note distention of the suprapatellar bursa (hemarthrosis).

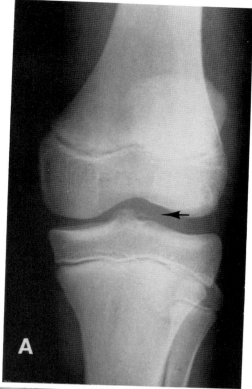

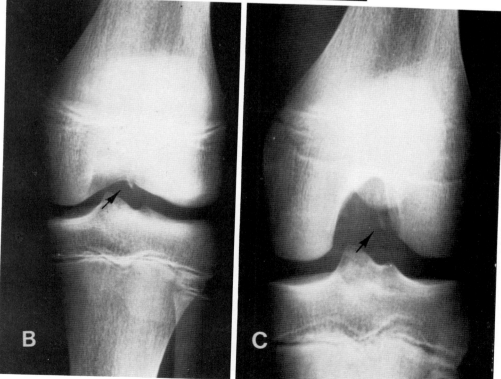

Figure 4.140. *Cruciate ligament avulsions—more subtle changes.* (*A*) Note the thin, sliver-like avulsed bony fragment (*arrow*) in this patient with an anterior cruciate ligament avulsion. (*B*) Another patient with a small avulsed bony fragment (*arrow*) from the lateral femoral condyle. (*C*) Tunnel view in same patient demonstrating the avulsed bony fragment (*arrow*) to greater advantage.

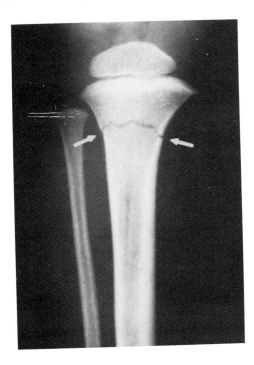

Figure 4.141. *Transverse fracture, upper tibia.* Note the clearly visible transverse fracture through the upper left tibia (*arrow*). There is no angulation through the fracture site.

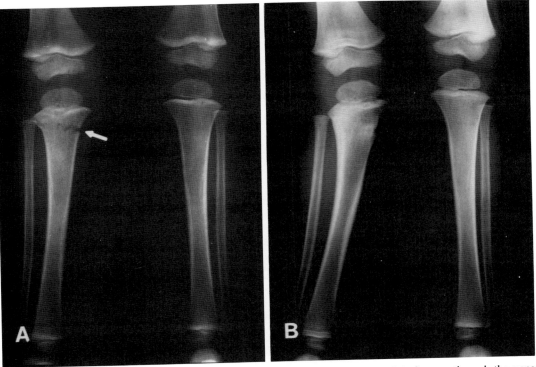

Figure 4.142. *Upper tibial fracture with inward bending.* (*A*) Note the clearly visible fracture through the upper right tibia (*arrow*). Also note that the fracture line is wider medially and that there is slight inward angulation of the tibia. (*B*) Late healing phase demonstrating pronounced angulation.

corrected at the time of initial reduction, for otherwise, it will persist and result in a problematic knock-knee deformity (20, 30) (Fig. 4.142). Most likely the deformity results from the initial inbending deformity, and the subsequent abnormal distribution of vertical forces. However, it also has been suggested that the problem arises because of an occult bending fracture of the tibia, below the transverse fracture (6), or because of overgrowth of the healing bone through the medial aspect of the epiphyseal line (12). These suggestions are intriguing but probably the problem arises simply from the fact that the fracture is angled to begin with.

Compression fractures of the tibial plateau are less common in children than in adults, but upper fibular fractures occur rather frequently both with knee injuries (see Fig. 4.137) and ankle injuries.

Another type of fracture which is quite common about the knee is the **stress fracture**. Most commonly, this fracture occurs in an older child, and although some can be seen in the distal femur, most occur in the proximal tibia. In the acute phase, the fracture line usually is not visible, and it is only after healing begins that the fracture and typical sclerosis and periosteal new bone deposition are seen (Fig. 4.143). In the early stages, these changes can be quite subtle, but later on periosteal new bone deposition is profound and often a more serious lesion such as a bone tumor erroneously is suggested. Periosteal newbone typically is deposited posteriorly.

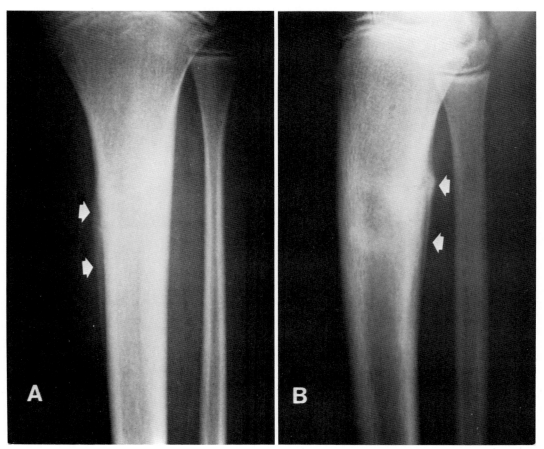

Figure 4.143. *Stress fracture of upper tibia.* (*A*) Frontal view demonstrating periosteal deposition along the upper inner aspect of the tibia (*arrows*). (*B*) Lateral view demonstrating typical posterior deposition of periosteal new bone along the fracture site (*arrows*). In addition, note sclerosis through the medullary cavity indicating the location of the healing stress fracture.

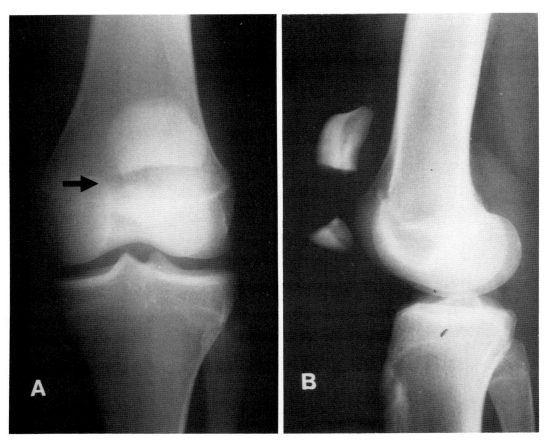

Figure 4.144. *Overt patellar fracture.*   (*A*) Note the clear-cut patellar fracture (*arrow*). (*B*) Lateral view demonstrating marked separation of the bony fragments.

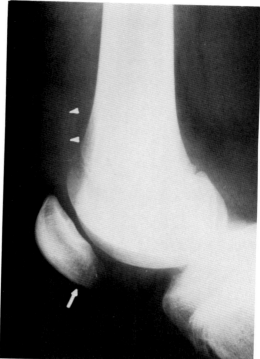

Figure 4.145. *Subtle patellar fracture.* First note the presence of fluid in the suprapatellar bursa (*upper arrows*). Then note the barely detectible transverse fracture through the inferior aspect of the patella (*lower arrow*).

Patellar Fractures and Dislocations. Fractures of the patella usually occur with direct blows to the patella or with injuries producing quadriceps tendon stresses. When these fractures are gross, they are not difficult to detect (Fig. 4.144), but with lesser injuries, the fracture may be difficult to visualize, and one may be left with soft tissue and joint effusion changes only (Fig. 4.145). This is especially true of small avulsion injuries of the patella (Figs. 4.146 and 4.147). In interpreting these chip fractures, the greatest pitfall lies in the misinterpretation of the so-called bipartite or tripartite patella, or a normal irregularly ossified patella, for a fracture (see Fig. 4.146).

Chronic, recurrent, dislocation of the patella is reasonably common in childhood, but in most cases the patella relocates before roentgenograms are obtained. In some cases, a residual telltale sign consisting of a medial avulsion fracture of the patella can be seen (11) (Fig. 4.146*B*), but most often the x-rays are totally normal. If a fracture is present, it is best demonstrated on tangential or so-called skyline views of the patella. Another finding that is said to be present in these patients is a patella higher than normal in position; i.e., the so-called "patella alta" (19, 21, 23, 26).

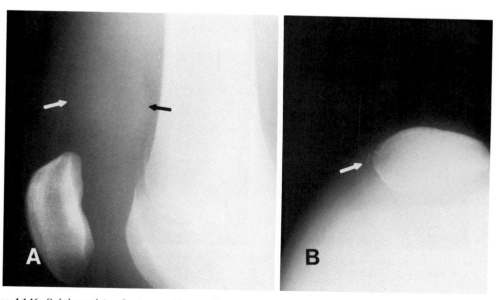

Figure 4.146. *Subtle avulsion fractures of the patella.* (*A*) Note only fluid in the suprapatellar bursa (*arrows*). (*B*) Two weeks later note small fracture fragment (*arrow*). (Also see Fig. 4.147*C*.)

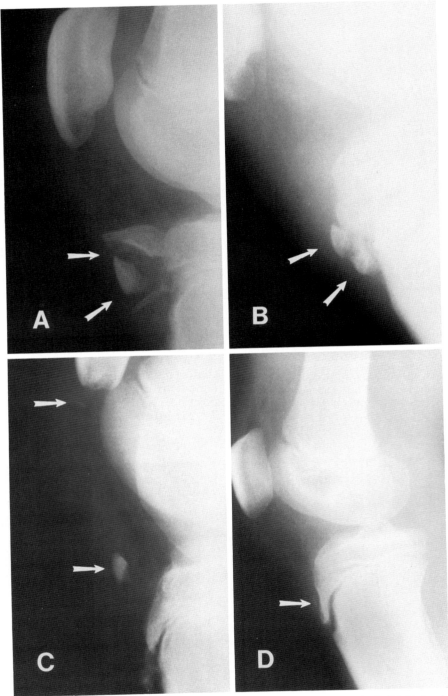

Figure 4.147. *Acute tibial tubercle avulsions.*   (*A*) Note the grossly disorganized, avulsed, tibial tubercle; basketball injury. (*B*) Another patient with a more subtle tibial tubercle avulsion (*arrow*). Also note soft tissue edema extending into, and obliterating the infrapatellar fat pad. (*C*) Note the avulsed tibial tubercle fragment (*lower arrow*), and the small sliver of avulsed bone from the patella (*upper arrow*). (*D*) Very subtle tibial tubercle avulsion consisting of a small sliver of bone (*arrow*). Note again that the infrapatellar fat pad is obliterated.

Miscellaneous Knee Injuries. Miscellaneous knee injuries include acute and chronic tibial tubercle and inferior patellar avulsions, osteochondritis dissecans, and meniscus injuries. *Acute total tibial tubercle avulsions* are relatively uncommon (4, 15, 24, 25). Clinically and roentgenographically, these fractures are not difficult to detect (Fig. 4.147A–C), but the more subtle minimal avulsion can pose a greater problem (Fig. 4.147D). *Osgood-Schlatter's disease* results from repeated, subclinical avulsions of the tibial tubercle (5, 15, 33, 35), and the findings consist of pretubercular swelling and tubercular fragmentation (Fig. 4.148). A similar lesion, occurring along the inferior aspect of the patella (Fig. 4.149), is termed *Sinding-Larsen-Johansson* disease (18, 32, 34). Occasionally, this latter injury can be acute, and must be differentiated from normal irregularity of the inferior aspect of the patella (see Fig. 4.164). The irregularity of Osgood-Schlatter's disease can be mimicked by the very rare periosteal chondroma of the tibial tubercle (22). This lesion is more bulky, mostly lytic, and is associated with destruction of the upper tibia, under the tibial tubercle.

Another cause of knee pain in childhood is *osteochondritis dissecans* of the distal femoral epiphysis, and less often the patella.

Most often these lesions occur in older children and adolescents (13) and while many cases are symptomatic, other individuals are asymptomatic. Roentgenographically, typical findings are those of a bony defect along the anteromedial aspect of the medial femoral condyle (Fig. 4.150). This should be differentiated from normal irregularity which often occurs along the posterior aspect of the lateral femoral condyle. In the patella, osteochondritis dissecans produces an irregular defect on the posterior aspect of the patella (Fig. 4.151). All of these lesions probably represent subchondral fractures.

Meniscus injuries are not as common in childhood as in the young adult, but they do occur. Plain film findings usually are absent and most cases are diagnosed by clinical examination, arthroscopy, and/or arthrography (7). In this regard, a note about the lateral meniscus in children is in order. Often this meniscus is very large, and rather than being disk-shaped, it assumes a semicircular shape. Consequently, the medial aspect extends almost to the intercondylar notch (7, 8, 12, 21), and because of this, the cartilage is very prone to tearing. It is termed the discoid lateral meniscus.

Septic Arthritis, Osteomyelitis, and Cellulitis of the Knee. In the knee, one of the more common clinical problems is that of

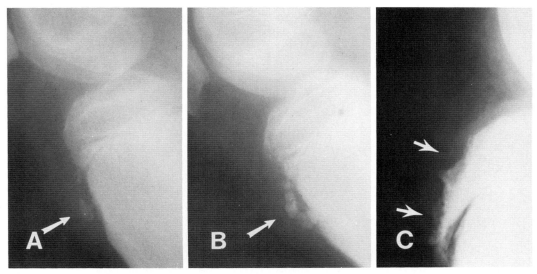

Figure 4.148. *Osgood-Schlatter's disease.* (*A*) Minimal changes consisting of slight irregularity of the tibial tubercle and a little overlying edema (*arrow*). (*B*) More pronounced changes in the same patient, in the other knee (*arrow*). (*C*) Another patient with very gross irregularity of the tibial tubercle (*arrows*).

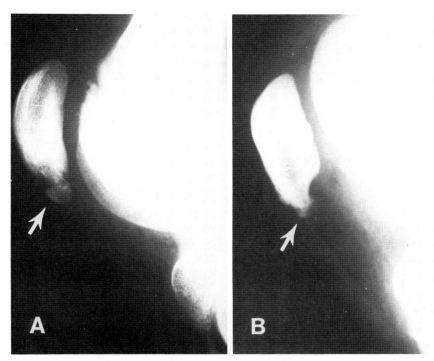

Figure 4.149. *Sinding-Larsen-Johansson disease of the patella.* (*A*) Note the large bony fragment just below the inferior aspect of the patella (*arrow*). (*B*) Less pronounced changes in another patient (*arrow*).

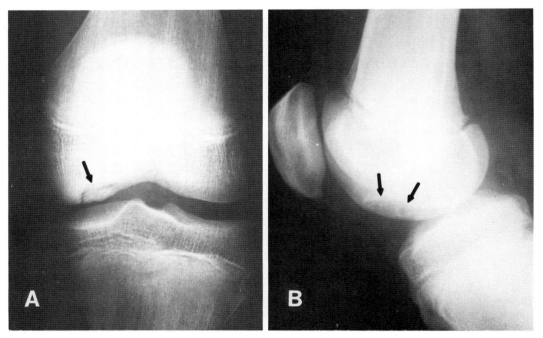

Figure 4.150. *Osteochondritis dissecans.* (*A*) Typical condylar defect in the medial femoral condyle (*arrow*). (*B*) Characteristic location and appearance on lateral view (*arrows*).

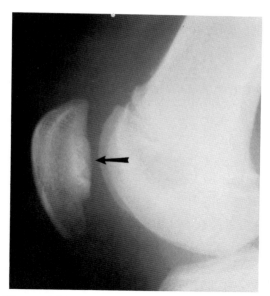

Figure 4.151. *Osteochondritis dissecans of patella.* Note irregularity along the posterior aspect of the patella (*arrow*). Also note distention of the suprapatellar bursa and its neck due to an associated effusion.

differentiating septic arthritis from simple cellulitis. Indeed, this comes up far more often than does the differentiation of septic arthritis from osteomyelitis, for soft tissue infections (cellulitis) are especially prone to develop over the patella, and many times it is difficult to determine clinically whether the joint space is involved. This is especially true in the young child and infant. However, the problem must be resolved, for with septic arthritis, arthrocentesis is required, while with cellulitis it is contraindicated. Although not well appreciated, the lateral view of the knee can solve this dilemma in almost every instance.

With septic arthritis, fluid (pus) accumulates in the various bursae, but first it always accumulates in the suprapatellar bursa (Fig. 4.152A). When it does so, it displaces the quadriceps tendon anteriorly, and the prefemoral fat pad posteriorly. As a result, the soft tissue space between the anterior aspect of the quadriceps tendon and the prefemoral fat pad becomes thickened (Fig. 4.152B). At first the findings might suggest that the entire quadriceps tendon is thickened, but actually they represent the confluent images of the normal quadriceps tendon and abnormal, pus-filled suprapatellar bursa. In addition to

this finding, sooner or later there is bulging of the posterior popliteal bursa, and the greater the accumulation of pus, the greater the bulging (Fig. 4.152). With more extensive collections, the suprapatellar and posterior popliteal bursae can show enormous bulging, and indeed, even the infrapatellar fat pad can become obliterated. However, no matter how extensive the accumulation of pus in the joint, the soft tissues anterior to the patella remain normal and distinct. They do not become edematous, and this is most important in differentiating septic arthritis from prepatellar cellulitis. In advanced cases, however, the posterior soft tissues may become edematous, but distention of the suprapatellar bursa should identify the problem as septic arthritis and not osteomyelitis (Fig. 4.152B).

With prepatellar cellulitis, as opposed to septic arthritis, the suprapatellar bursa does not become distended, but rather, the soft tissues anterior to the quadriceps tendon and patella become thickened and/or edematous (Fig. 4.153). Of course, if soft tissue edema is extensive, the suprapatellar and infrapatellar fat pads may become hazy and the soft tissues behind the femur also may become indistinct (Fig. 4.153B). This then can mimic severe septic arthritis or osteomyelitis, but with septic arthritis bursal distention occurs and with both septic arthritis and osteomyelitis, no prepatellar edema is seen (see Figs. 4.152B and 4.154B).

With osteomyelitis of the distal femur, early stage findings consist only of soft tissue edema and obliteration or displacement of the fat pads (3, 16) around the distal femur (Figs. 4.154 and 4.155). As opposed to septic arthritis, there is no filling of the suprapatellar bursa with pus, and as opposed to prepatellar cellulitis, prepatellar edema is absent (Fig. 4.155). Of course, once again one must make an exception in the young child or infant, for in this age group osteomyelitis and septic arthritis often occur together and present features of both conditions.

In more advanced cases of osteomyelitis, frank bony destruction and periosteal new bone deposition are seen, and then the diagnosis is no problem. However, in early cases, the area of bone destruction may be small and subtle, and may cause confusion with a benign cortical defect (Fig. 4.156).

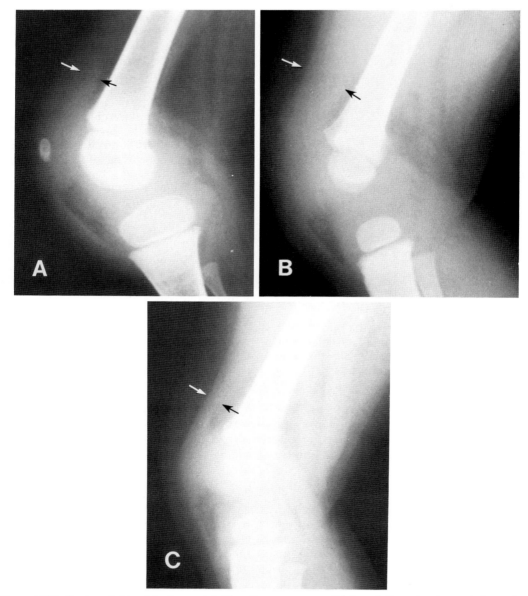

Figure 4.152. *Septic arthritis of the knee.* (*A*) Note discrete suprapatellar bursal distension (*arrows*). Some fluid also is present in the posterior popliteal bursa. (*B*) The distended suprapatellar bursa blends with the quadriceps tendon to produce subtle pseudo-thickening of the tendon (*arrows*). (*C*) Normal side for comparison. Note normal thickness of quadriceps tendon (*arrows*).

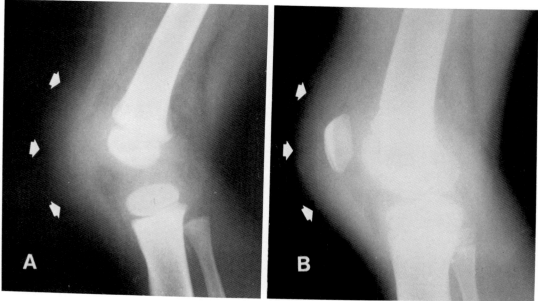

Figure 4.153. *Cellulitis of the knee.* (*A*) First note that swelling is present in the soft tissues anterior to the quadriceps tendon and unossified cartilaginous patella only (*arrows*). The quadriceps tendon is still clearly visible, and there is no evidence of accumulation of fluid in the suprapatellar bursa. (*B*) Another patient demonstrating extensive swelling of the soft tissues anterior to the patella and quadriceps tendon (*arrows*). This time soft tissue swelling is so pronounced that there is associated obliteration of the quadriceps tendon and suprapatellar fat pad. The findings, however, are not those of septic arthritis, for edema of the soft tissues anterior to the patella and quadriceps tendon does not occur with septic arthritis. Also note edema posterior to the femur.

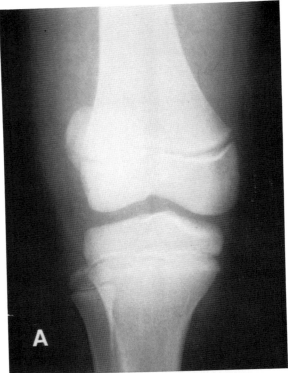

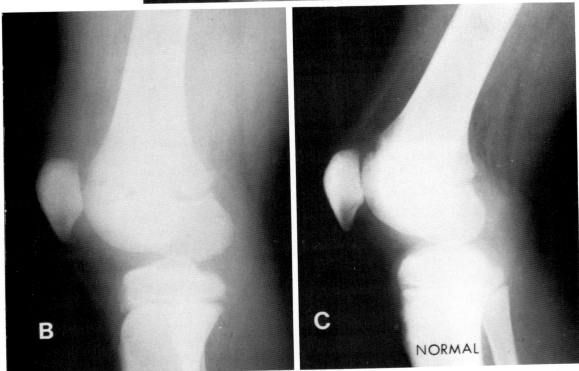

Figure 4.154. *Osteomyelitis—deep soft tissue changes.* (*A*) Note extensive swelling of all the soft tissues around the distal femur. No normal fat-muscle interfaces remain. (*B*) Lateral view demonstrating similar findings. Note that the suprapatellar fat pad and the fat pads posterior to the distal femur have been totally obliterated. Obliteration of these fat pads, especially the ones posterior to the distal femur is a most important finding, for it is not seen with septic arthritis. (*C*) Normal knee of the same patient for comparison. Note the clearly identified fat-muscle interfaces and the various normal fat pads, both anterior and posterior to the distal femur.

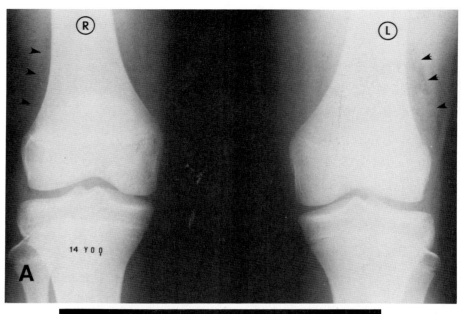

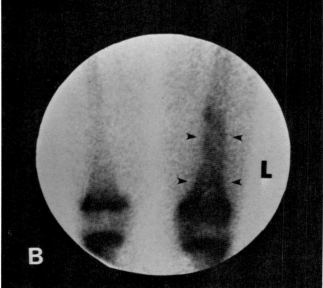

Figure 4.155. *Osteomyelitis—early displacement of the fat pads.* (*A*) First note the generalized increase in soft tissue density and thickness around the distal left femur. Then note displacement of the lateral fat pad outwardly (*arrows*). Compare with the same fat pad on the normal right side (*arrows*) (*B*) Isotope study demonstrating increased uptake of isotope, in the distal left femur (*arrows*), characteristic of osteomyelitis. (Courtesy M. Capitanio, M.D.)

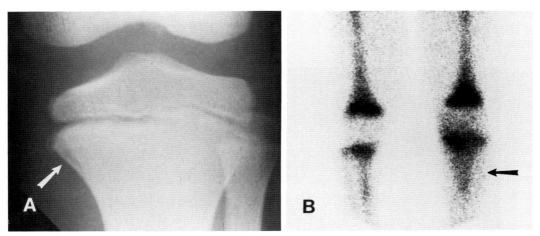

Figure 4.156. *Osteomyelitis—subtle findings.* (*A*) Note the subtle lytic lesion in the upper tibia (*arrow*). This could be confused with a benign cortical defect. (*B*) Bone scan, however, demonstrates increased isotope activity in the upper tibia (*arrow*). This does not occur with benign cortical defects. The patient had surgically proven osteomyelitis.

Normal Findings Causing Problems. One of the more common normal findings around the knee is *irregularity of the distal femur*, just along the *medial supracondylar ridge*. It occurs most commonly in older children and adolescents and should not be misinterpreted for an area of osteomyelitis or a bone tumor (1, 31, 36). The irregularity occurs along the line of muscle insertion, recently suggested to be that of the adductor magnus (28). In terms of etiology, there is histologic support for the concept that this lesion results from chronic avulsion (9, 28), and depending on the degree of healing, the lesion can appear quite ragged or somewhat scalloped (Fig. 4.157). Confusing this concept, however, is the fact that benign cortical defects also occur here, with or without avulsion, and this may be why technetium-99 pyrophosphate bone scanning shows no increased isotope activity in some of these lesions (2, 10). Most important, however, is that one remember that these lesions are not a serious finding. Nonetheless, it is very tempting to assign a causative role to these irregularities in patients with nonspecific knee pain.

Benign cortical (fibrous) defects can be found in any of the long bones and frequently are multiple. However, they most commonly occur in the distal femur and proximal tibia, and characteristically are eccentric and very peripheral (cortical) in location. They seldom extend beyond a half

centimeter or so into the medullary cavity of the bone (Fig. 4.158). When seen en face, they can resemble a lytic lesion of the bone, and should not be mistaken for low-grade osteomyelitis (i.e., Brodie's abscess) or a bone tumor (Fig. 4.159). Benign cortical defects are related to the somewhat larger benign nonossifying fibroma. This latter lesion also is eccentric but often more definitely corticated and larger than a benign cortical defect (Fig. 4.158*B*). Benign cortical defects proper have variably sclerotic margins.

In a few cases, *benign cortical defects appear very cystic* and possess a thin cortex. In such cases, normal muscle pull on the cortex can cause acute avulsion and fragmentation. In these patients, the roentgenographic findings often first suggest malignancy (Fig. 4.160).

In older children, the *tibial tubercle has a normal defect along its inferior aspect*. On lateral view, this defect is not difficult to interpret, but on frontal view, it can be taken for a lytic lesion of the knee (Fig. 4.161). In young infants, the tibial tubercle is not ossified at all, and a scoop-like bony defect in the area can present a problem (Fig. 4.162).

The *patella is very prone to irregular ossification* (Fig. 4.163). Furthermore, when it finally does ossify, a number of peculiar irregularities and deformities can persist. Some of these are so fracture-like in appearance that it is almost impossible to differ-

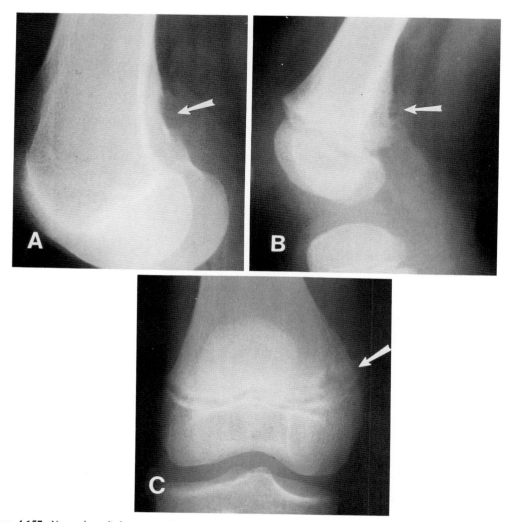

Figure 4.157. *Normal medial supracondylar ridge irregularity.* (*A*) Well-heeled, benign appearing scalloped out area (*arrow*). (*B*) Another patient with more worrisome irregularity (*arrow*). (*C*) Another patient demonstrating similar, worrisome findings on frontal view (*arrow*).

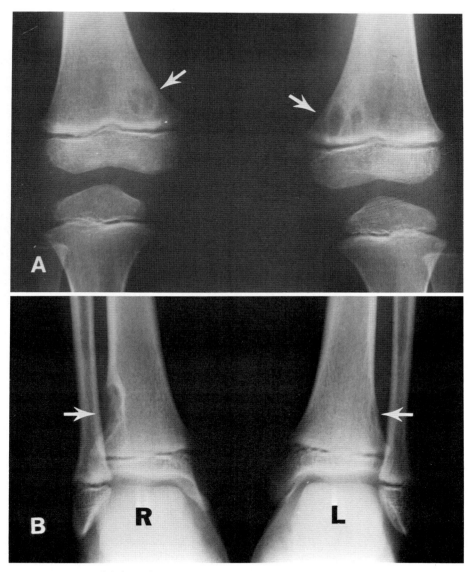

Figure 4.158. *Benign cortical defects, classic appearance.* (*A*) Note typical oval or round, slightly sclerotic, benign cortical defects in both distal femurs (*arrows*). (*B*) Large benign cortical defect in distal right tibia (*arrow*). This lesion is large enough to be considered a small nonossifying fibroma. The two lesions probably are related. On the left, a very small benign cortical defect is noted in the distal tibia (*arrow*).

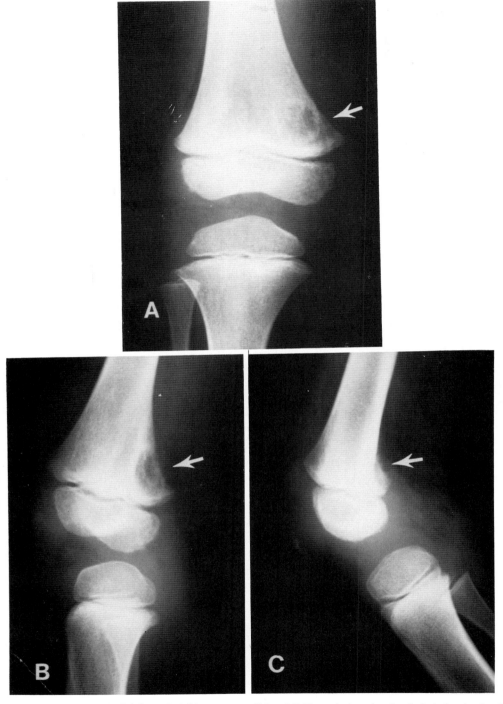

Figure 4.159. *Benign cortical defect mimicking osteomyelitis.* (*A*) Frontal view showing lytic lesion in the distal femur (*arrow*). This patient presented with a swollen, hot knee. (*B*) Oblique view demonstrates the "pseudo" lytic, destructive appearance of this lesion (*arrow*). (*C*) Lateral view demonstrating the irregular lesion (*arrow*). This was misinterpreted for osteomyelitis, where in fact it was a benign cortical defect. The knee was swollen because of cellulitis of the soft tissues anterior to the patella.

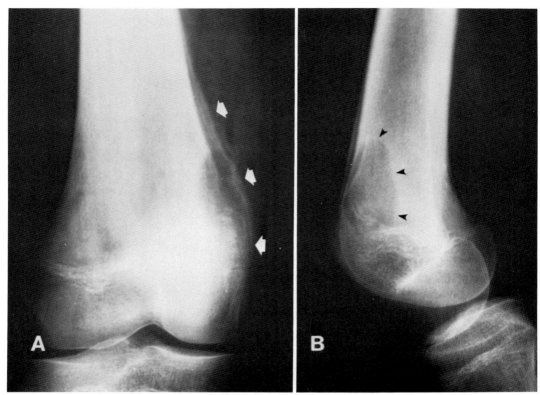

Figure 4.160. *Cystic benign cortical defect with periosteal new bone.* (*A*) Note the layered periosteal new bone over the cystic lesion of the distal femur (*arrows*). This young boy presented with recent onset of knee pain. (*B*) Lateral view demonstrating lytic nature of the lesion and periosteal new bone anterior to it. The findings represent avulsion of the thin cortex of this benign cortical defect with subsequent periosteal new bone formation. (Histologically proven).

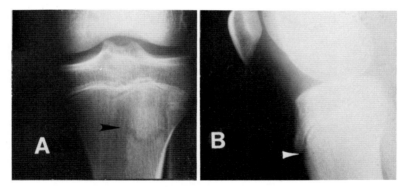

Figure 4.161. *Normal tibial tubercle defect.* (*A*) On frontal view, note the radiolucent line (*arrow*) just beneath an area of transverse sclerosis. The area of sclerosis represents the inferior aspect of the tibial tubercle while the radiolucent line is the normal defect just beneath it. (*B*) Lateral view demonstrating site of radiolucent defect (*arrow*) under the normal tibial tubercle.

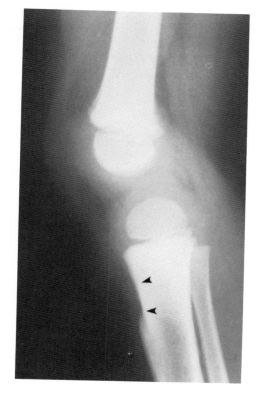

Figure 4.162. *Normal upper tibial notch.* In young infants, the tibial tubercle does not ossify and a normal notch is noted at its site (*arrows*). This notch should not be misinterpreted for a destructive lesion.

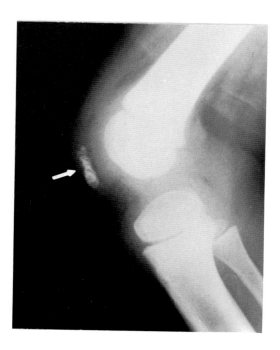

Figure 4.163. *Normal irregular patellar ossification.* Note the normal, irregularly ossified patella (*arrow*). The patella usually begins to ossify at about 5 years of age.

entiate them from a true fracture (Fig. 4.164). However, very often the same configuration is present on the other side, and this sovles the problem. Another common normal ossification anomaly of the patella is the bipartite or tripartite patella. In these cases, the extra portion of the patella usually lies in the upper outer quadrant (Fig. 4.165),

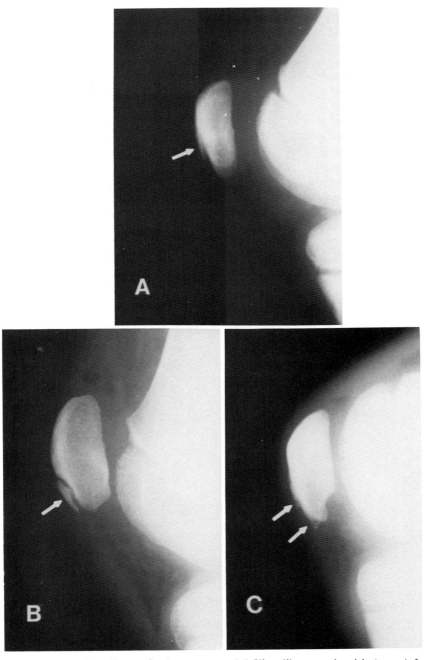

Figure 4.164. *Various normal patellar ossification patterns.* (*A*) Sliver-like normal ossicle (*arrow*). In some cases, this thin sliver-like piece of bone can appear completely detached from the patella. (*B*) Larger accessory ossification center of the patella (*arrow*). (*C*) Normal irregular ossification of the anterior-inferior aspect of the patella (*arrows*). This should not be confused with Sinding-Larsen-Johannson disease where similar fragmentation, associated with pain and local swelling, can be seen.

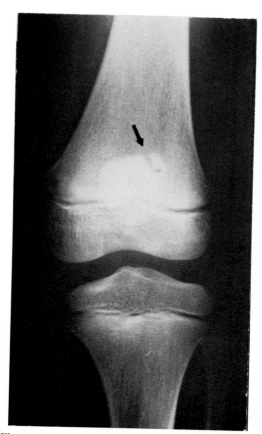

Figure 4.165. *Bipartite patella.* Note typical appearance and location of a bipartite patella (*arrow*).

REFERENCES

1. Barnes, G.R., Jr., and Gwinn, J.L.: Distal irregularities of the femur simulating malignancy. A.J.R. 122: 180–185, 1974.
2. Burrows, P.E., Greenberg, I.D., and Reed, M.H.: The distal femoral defect: technetium-99m pyrophosphate bone scan results. J. Can. Assoc. Radiol. 33: 91–93, 1982.
3. Capitanio, M.A., and Kirkpatrick, J.A.: Early roentgen observation in acute osteomyelitis. A.J.R. 108: 488–497, 1970.
4. Christie, M.J., and Dvonch, V.M.: Tibial tuberosity avulsion fracture in adolescents. J. Pediatr. Orthop. 1: 391–394, 1981.
5. Cohen, B., and Wilkinson, R.W.: The Osgood-Schlatter lesion: a radiological and histological study. Am. J. Surg. 95: 731, 1958.
6. Currarino, G., and Pinckney, L.E.: Genu valgum after proximal tibial fractures in children. A.J.R. 136: 915–918, 1981.
7. Dalinka, M.K., Lally, J.F., and Gohel, V.K.: Arthrography of the lateral meniscus. A.J.R. 121: 79–85, 1974.
8. Dashefsky, J.H.: Discoid lateral meniscus in three members of family. J. Bone Joint Surg. 53A: 1208–1210, 1971.
9. Dunham, W.K., Marcus, N.W., Enneking, W.F., and Haun, C.: Developmental defects of the distal femoral metaphysis. J. Bone Joint Surg. 62A: 801–806, 1980.
10. Feine, U., and Ahlemann, L.M.: Differentiation of the periosteal desmoid of the metaphysis from malignant tumors using bone scanning. R.O.F.O. 135: 193–196, 1981.
11. Freiberg, R.H., and Kotzen, L.M.: Fracture of the medial margin of the patella, a finding diagnostic of lateral dislocation. Radiology 88: 902, 1967.
12. Green, N.E.: Tibia valga caused by asymmetrical overgrowth following a nondisplaced fracture of the proximal tibial metaphysis. J. Pediatr. Orthop. 3: 235–237, 1983.

and very often the anomaly is bilateral. There has been a suggestion that occasionally the bipartite patella can be painful (27). In such cases it has been suggested that the bipartite patella actually represents an incompetely united stress fracture, and that it is positive on isotope bone scanning (27). However, most bipartite patellae are asymptomatic.

The fabella is a normal ossicle occurring in the lateral limb of the gastrocnemius tendon and is best visualized on lateral view (Fig. 4.166).

The ***distal femoral epiphysis frequently ossifies irregularly*** and can appear very disturbing to the uninitiated (Fig. 4.167). However, these irregularities are common, especially in infants and young children where the epiphysis may appear irregular, all around its periphery. In older children, normal irregularities tend to occur in the lateral condyle, posteriorly (Fig. 4.168).

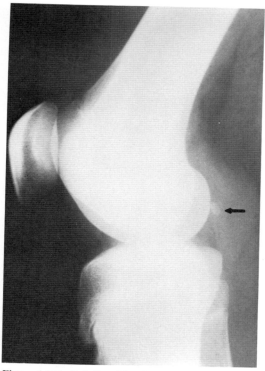

Figure 4.166. *Fabella.* The fabella is a normal sesamoid bone occurring in the gastrocnemius tendon (*arrow*).

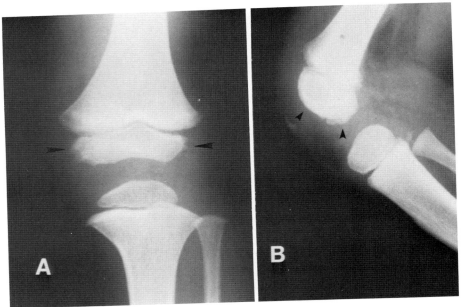

Figure 4.167. *Normal distal femoral epiphyseal irregularities.* (*A*) Frontal view showing normal irregularity of the distal femoral epiphysis (*arrows*). Radiolucencies in the metaphyseal corners also are normal. (*B*) Lateral view showing normal irregular ossification pattern of distal femoral epiphysis (*arrows*).

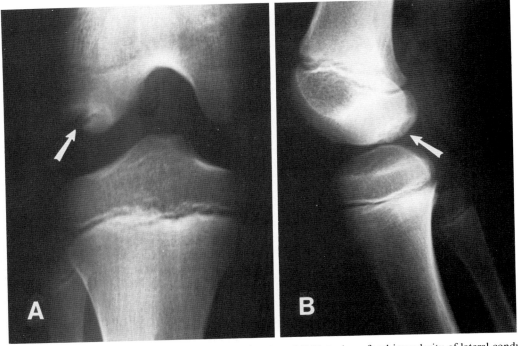

Figure 4.168. *Normal distal femoral epiphyseal irregularities.* (*A*) Note deep, focal irregularity of lateral condyle (*arrow*). (*B*) Lateral view demonstrating the irregularity to be posterior (*arrow*). This patient was asymptomatic. (Courtesy Virgil Graves, M.D., Great Falls, Montana.)

13. Green, W.T., and Banks, H.H.: Osteochondritis dissecans in children. J. Bone Joint Surg. 35A: 26, 1953.
14. Hall, F.: Radiographic diagnosis and accuracy in knee joint effusions. Radiology 115: 49–54, 1975.
15. Hand, W.L., Hand, C.R., and Dunn, A.N.: Avulsion fractures of the tibial tubercle. J. Bone Joint Surg. 53A: 1579, 1971.
16. Hayden, C.K., Jr., and Swischuk, L.E.: Para-articular soft tissue changes in infants and trauma of the lower extremity in children. A.J.R. 134: 307–311, 1980.
17. Haverson, S.B., and Rein, B.J.: Lateral discoid meniscus of knee: arthrographic diagnosis. A.J.R. 109: 581–586, 1970.
18. Holstein, E.R., Lewis, G.B., and Schulze, E.R.: Heterotopic ossification of patella tendon. J. Bone Joint Surg. 45A: 656, 1963.
19. Insall, J., and Salvati, E.: Patella position in the normal knee joint. Radiology 101: 101–104, 1971.
20. Jackson, D.W., and Cozen, L.: Genu valgum as a complication of proximal tibial metaphyseal fractures in children. J. Bone Joint Surg. 53A: 1571, 1971.
21. Kay, J.J.: Roentgenographic evaluation of children with acute onset of a limp. Pediatr. Ann. 5: 11–31, 1976.
22. Kirchner, S.G., Pavlov, H., Heller, R.M., and Kay, J.J.: Periosteal chondromas of the anterior tibial tubercle: two cases. A.J.R. 131: 1088–1089, 1978.
23. Lancourt, J.E., and Cristini, J.A.: Patella alta and patella infera: their etiologic role in patellar dislocation, chondromalacia and apophysitis of the tibial tubercle. J. Bone Joint Surg. 57: 1112–1115, 1975.
24. Levi, J.H., and Coleman, C.R.: Fracture of the tibial tubercle. Am. J. Sports Med. 4: 254–263, 1976.
25. Mayba, I.I.: Avulsion fracture of the tibial tubercle apophysis with avulsion of patellar ligament. J. Pediatr. Orthop. 2: 303–305, 1982.
26. McNab, I.: Recurrent dislocation of the patella. J. Bone Joint Surg. 34A: 957–967, 1952.
27. Ogden, J.A., McCarthy, S.M., and Jokl, P.: The painful bipartite patella. J. Pediatr. Orthop. 2: 263–269, 1982.
28. Resnick, D., and Greenway, G.: Distal femoral cortical defects, irregularities and excavations: a critical review of the literature with the addition of histologic and paleopathologic data. Radiology 143: 345–354, 1982.
29. Rogers, L.F., Jones, S., Davis, A.R., and Dietz, G.: "Clipping injury" fracture of the epiphysis in the adolescent football player: an occult lesion of the knee. A.J.R. 121: 69–78, 1974.
30. Salter, R.B., and Best, T.: The pathogenesis and prevention of valgus deformity following fractures of the proximal metaphyseal region of the tibia in children. J. Bone Joint Surg. 55A: 1324, 1973.
31. Simon, H.: Medial distal metaphyseal femoral irregularity in children. Radiology 90: 258–260, 1968.
32. Sinding-Larson, M.F.: A hitherto unknown affection of the patella in children. Acta Radiol. [Diagn.] (Stockh) 1: 171–173, 1921.
33. Willner, P.: Osgood-Schlatter's disease: etiology and treatment. Clin. Orthop. 62: 178–179, 1969.
34. Wolf, J.: Larsen-Johansson disease of patella: 7 new case records; its relationship to other forms of osteochondritis; use of male sex hormones as a new form of treatment. Br. J. Radiol. 23: 335–347, 1950.
35. Woolfrey, B.F., and Chandler, E.F.: Manifestations of Osgood-Schlatter's disease in late teen age and early adulthood. J. Bone Joint Surg. 42A: 327–332, 1960.
36. Young, D.W., Nogardy, M.B., Dunbar, J.S., and Wiglesworth, F.W.: Benign cortical irregularities in the distal femur of children. J. Can. Assoc. Radiol. 23: 107–115, 1972.

LOWER LEG (MIDSHAFTS OF THE TIBIA AND FIBULA)

Injuries of the Lower Leg. Overt fractures of the midshafts of the tibia and fibula

are not difficult to recognize. However, it might be noted that such fractures show a distinct tendency to fracturing of the tibia but not of the fibula. At least this might be one's initial impression, but with closer perusal of the films, often it will be noted that the fibula actually is bent (Fig. 4.169). In other words, the overt fracture of the tibia is accompanied by an associated acute, bending, plastic fracture of the fibula which occurs at the same level as the transverse fracture of the tibia. These plastic bending fractures of the fibula probably are more common than is generally appreciated (5), and in some cases the fibula may be bent outward (Fig. 4.169c).

In young infants, a very common fracture of the tibia is the so-called *"toddlers fracture"* (1, 2, 4). This fracture characteristically is spiral, hairline, and often invisible, or nearly invisible, on initial roentgenograms. It almost behaves as a stress fracture and even in those cases where it is visible, it often appears clearer on one view than the other (Fig. 4.170). In other cases, soft tissue swelling of the muscles around the tibia will bring attention to the fracture, but it cannot be overstressed that many of these children present with normal roentgenograms. Because of this, the situation can become quite puzzling, for these children will not walk, or if they walk they do so with a limp, and yet on physical examination the findings are relatively negative. When this is coupled with the fact that no fracture is visible roentgenographically, one has a definite diagnostic puzzle. However, if torque stress is placed on the tibia, pain will be evoked and the diagnosis clarified. A somewhat similar fracture has been recorded in ballet dancers. These individuals, in general, are prone to stress injuries of the lower extremities (3). Of course, as with any stress fracture, if these tibial fractures are identified in their advanced healing phases, the pronounced periosteal new bone deposition may erroneously suggest the presence of a bone tumor.

Normal Findings Causing Problems. About the only normal finding in the midshaft of the tibia or fibula which can be confused with an underlying lesion is a normal vascular groove (Fig. 4.171). These vascular grooves appear no different from those in other long bones, but in the tibia can be misinterpreted for a spiral, toddlers type fracture.

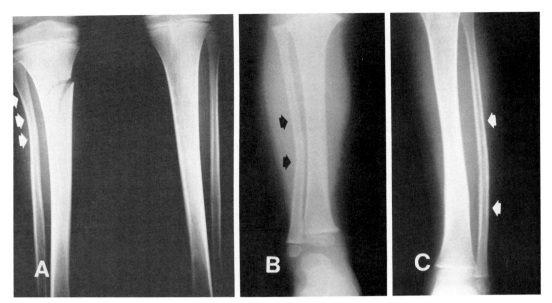

Figure 4.169. *Bending fractures of the fibula.*   (*A*) Note the clear-cut fracture of the tibia, but also note localized bending of the upper fibula (*arrows*). (*B*) Marked inward bending of the right fibula (*arrows*). This is the common direction of bending. (*C*) Unusual outward bending of the fibula (*arrows*). (Fig. *A* courtesy of J. Bjelland, M.D.)

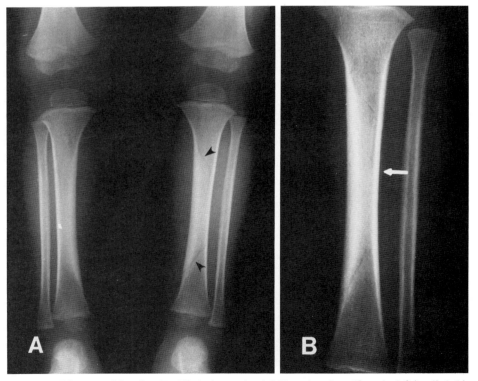

Figure 4.170. *Spiral fracture of the tibia (Toddler's fracture).*   (*A*) Note that the calf on the left is a little bigger and slightly more opaque than on the right. This is due to edema. Then note the two limbs of the typical spiral fracture of the tibia (*arrows*). (*B*) Follow-up film 2 weeks later again demonstrates the fracture line but this time early periosteal new bone is visible (*arrow*— lower medial aspect of tibia).

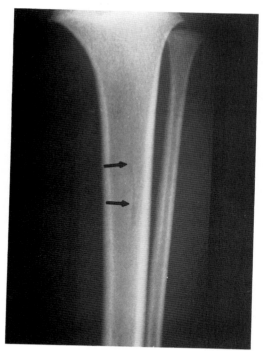

Figure 4.171. *Tibial vascular groove—pseudofracture.* Note the vascular groove (*arrows*) in the upper tibia. This vascular groove is quite common and should not be misinterpreted for a spiral fracture of the tibia.

REFERENCES

1. Condon, V.R.: Radiology of practical orthopedic problems. Radiol. Clin. North Am. 10: 203–223, 1972.
2. Dunbar, J.S., Owen, H.F., Nogrady, M.B., and McLeese, R.: Obscure tibial fracture of infants—the toddler's fracture. J. Can. Assoc. Radiol. 15: 136–144, 1964.
3. Schneider, H.J., King, A.Y., Bronson, J.L., and Miller, E.H.: Stress injuries and developmental change of lower extremities in ballet dancers. Radiology 113: 627–632, 1974.
4. Singer, J., and Towbin, R.: Occult fractures in production of gait disturbance in childhood. Pediatrics 64: 192–196, 1979.
5. Stenstrom, R., Gripenberg, L., and Bergius, A.R.: Traumatic bowing of forearm and lower leg in children. Acta Radiol. 19: 243–249, 1978.

ANKLE

Normal Soft Tissues and Fat Pads of the Ankle. In the infant and child, three fat pads around the ankle usually are visualized on lateral view. The largest is the pre-Achilles fat pad, located just anterior to the Achilles tendon, but this fat pad is not utilized for the detection of joint fluid. Rather, the anterior and posterior fat pads, lying against the joint capsule, are the ones to be assessed for joint fluid detection (Fig. 4.172). In the older child, the anterior fat pad may

be comprised of two fat pads but it is the inner one that should be assessed. With soft tissue edema both the anterior and posterior fat pads are obliterated, while with joint fluid accumulations they are displaced outwardly (Fig. 4.173).

Detecting Fluid in the Ankle Joint. In determining whether fluid is present in the ankle joint, it is best to study the lateral view (2, 12). On frontal view, only soft tissue swelling around the ankle is seen, but on lateral view outward displacement of the anterior or posterior fat pads is seen (Fig. 4.173). In older children, bulging of the capsule, in more discrete fashion, has led to the "teardrop" sign (10) (Fig. 4.174). No joint space widening is seen for the ligaments around the ankle joint are very sturdy and usually do not allow for much in the way of joint distraction.

Injuries of the Distal Tibia and Fibula. A variety of injuries can be sustained in the distal tibia and fibula, and most often these result from a combination of inversion, eversion, and rotational forces. In the young

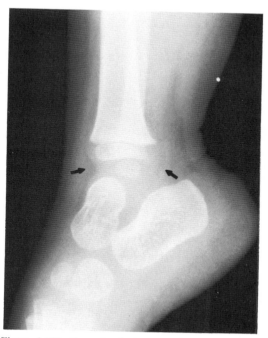

Figure 4.172. *Normal soft tissues and fat pads of the ankle.* The pre-Achilles fat pad is clearly visible but seldom utilized for joint fluid detection. The anterior (*anterior arrow*) and posterior (*posterior arrow*) fat pads are readily visualized and normally are tucked tightly against the joint capsule. With joint fluid they are displaced outwardly (see Fig. 4.173).

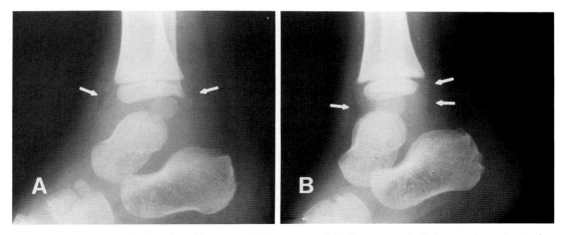

Figure 4.173. *Detecting fluid in the ankle joint.* (*A*) Note outward displacement of both the anterior and posterior fat pads (*arrows*). (*B*) Normal side for comparison. Note normal position of the fat pads (*arrows*).

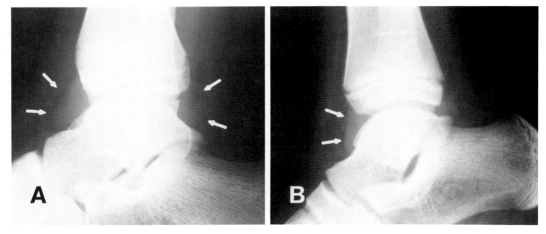

Figure 4.174. *Teardrop configuration of ankle fluid.* (*A*) Note typical teardrop anteriorly (*anterior arrows*). A similar configuration exists posteriorly (*posterior arrows*). (*B*) Another patient with a less prounounced teardrop sign anteriorly (*arrows*). Similar, subtle findings are present posteriorly.

infant, ***cortical buckle (torus)*** fractures through the distal tibia and fibula are very common (Fig. 4.175). In the older child, however, the more common injury is some type of a Salter-Harris ***epiphyseal-metaphyseal fracture***. In the ankle, all of the Salter-Harris type injuries, with the exception of the type V injury, are common. Salter-Harris type III and IV injuries often are associated with some degree of epiphyseal displacement and generally are not difficult to identify (Fig. 4.176), but if displacement of the epiphysis is not present, they may be just as difficult to identify as Salter-Harris type I and II injuries. In this regard, the key to

detecting these more subtle fractures lies in comparing the width of the epiphyseal lines in the injured ankle to those on the normal side, and in assessing the soft tissues for evidence of swelling (Fig. 4.177).

The Salter-Harris type III injury is quite common in the distal tibia and often is missed on initial inspection. Indeed, oblique views may be required for its delineation (3). The reason for this is that the distal tibial epiphysis fuses earlier medially, than laterally. Consequently, with an inversion injury of the ankle there is separation of the epiphysis laterally, but not medially (Fig. 4.176*B*).

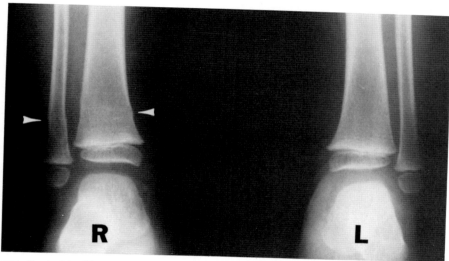

Figure 4.175. *Cortical buckle (torus) fractures of distal tibia.*   Note the cortical buckle fracture along the inner aspect of the distal right tibia (*arrow*). A more subtle cortical buckle fracture is present on the opposite side of the tibia. Also note the acute bending fracture of the distal fibula at the same level (*arrow*).

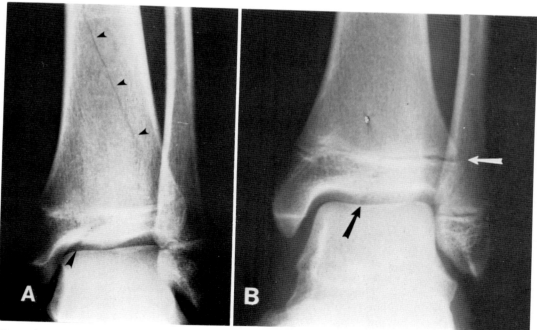

Figure 4.176. *Salter-Harris type III and IV injuries of the ankle.*   (*A*) Note the fracture through the distal tibial epiphysis (*lower arrow*) and the fracture through the metaphysis (*upper arrows*). This is a Salter-Harris type IV injury. (*B*) Note the fracture through the distal tibial epiphysis (*lower arrow*). Also note slight separation of the lateral epiphyseal fragment from the metaphysis (*lateral arrow*). This is a Salter-Harris type III injury.

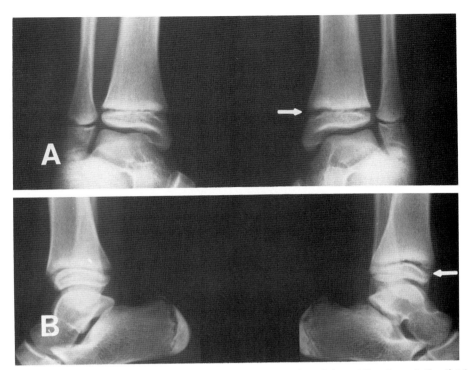

Figure 4.177. *Salter-Harris type I injury of the ankle.* (*A*) Note that the epiphyseal line through the distal tibia is wider on the left (*arrow*) than on the right. (*B*) Lateral view confirms widening of the epiphyseal line on the left (*arrow*). These findings are those of a Salter-Harris type I injury.

Inversion-rotation injuries of the ankle are very common, and while many times they result only in a sprained ankle, in other instances a Salter-Harris injury such as demonstrated in Figure 4.177 results. In other instances, one may encounter an epiphyseal-metaphyseal separation of the distal fibular epiphysis and an associated fracture through the medial malleolus of the distal tibial epiphysis (Fig. 4.178*A*). In these cases, the distal fibular fracture is a Salter-Harris type I or II injury, while the medial malleolar fracture is a type III injury. Less commonly one may encounter only a small sliver-like cortical avulsion of the distal fibular metaphysis or epiphysis (Fig. 4.178*B*). These latter fractures must be differentiated from normal accessory ossicles occurring in this area (see Fig. 4.192*B*). In all of these injuries, there will be a certain degree of soft tissue swelling over the lateral malleolus. Obviously, if an underlying fracture is visualized, the soft tissue thickening is easily evaluated, but many times there is nothing more to see than soft tissue thickening. In these cases, I

have found it useful to assume that an occult Salter-Harris epiphyseal-metaphyseal injury has been sustained if soft tissue thickening is greater than 1 cm.

With eversion injuries, the ankle mortise often is seriously disturbed and a wide range of relatively severe injuries can be encountered (Fig. 4.179). So-called *posterior malleolar fractures* actually are Salter-Harris type II epiphyseal-metaphyseal fractures (Fig. 4.180), and many times the fracture is visible only on lateral view. When these fractures occur with fractures through the medial and lateral maleoli, the term trimalleolar fracture is applied. Finally, a word regarding stress veiws of the ankle is in order. Many times with equivocal bony changes, one can elicit the presence of an occult epiphyseal-metaphyseal separation with views obtained while applying stress on the ankle. Stress views are not required in all cases, but when one is in doubt regarding the presence of such a fracture, they can be employed.

Injuries of the Tarsal Bones. Fractures and dislocations of the tarsal bones are gen-

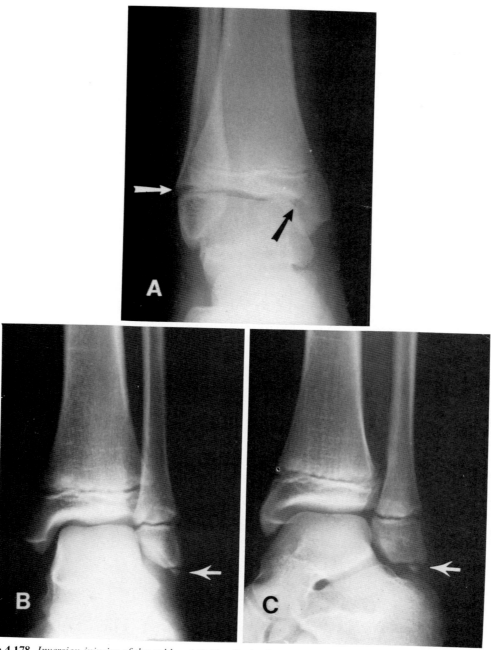

Figure 4.178. *Inversion injuries of the ankle.* (*A*) Bimalleolar fracture. First note the fracture through the medial malleolus (*black arrow*), and then note that the distal fibular epiphysis has been separated from the meatphysis (i.e., there is widening of the epiphyseal line and a small metaphyseal avulsion fracture—*white arrow*). The fibular fracture is Salter-Harris type II injury while the medial malleolar fracture is Salter-Harris type III injury. (*B*) Small avulsion fracture of the distal fibula. Note the small avulsed distal fibular bony fragment (*arrow*). (*C*) Oblique view demonstrates the fragment (*arrow*) to better advantage. There is no epiphyseal-metaphyseal injury of either the tibia or fibula in this patient. The small avulsion fracture should be differentiated from the normal ossicle (os subfibulare) commonly occurring in this area (Fig. 4.191).

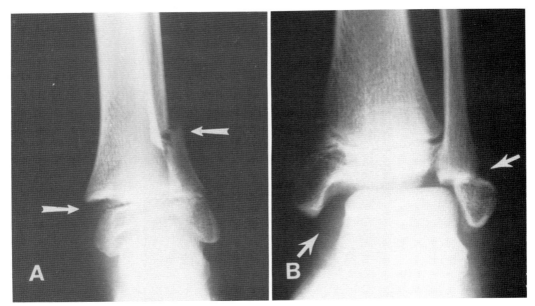

Figure 4.179. *Eversion injuries of the ankle.* (*A*) Note the displaced fracture of the distal fibula (*upper arrow*), and the displaced Salter-Harris type II epiphyseal-metaphyseal injury of the distal tibia (*lower arrow*). The ankle mortise is not disturbed. (*B*) Note the displaced Salter-Harris type I injury of the distal fibula (*lateral arrow*), and the widely opened joint space medially (*medial arrow*). The ankle is dislocated and the ankle mortise grossly disturbed. Note, however, that there is no epiphyseal-metaphyseal injury of the distal tibia.

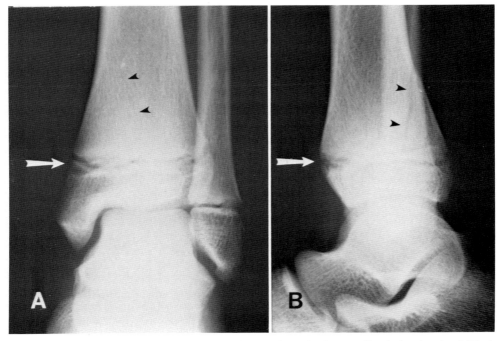

Figure 4.180. *Posterior malleolar fracture.* (*A*) On frontal view, the fracture line is just barely visible (*upper arrows*). However, note that the epiphyseal line is a little wider medially (*lower arrow*) than laterally. (*B*) Lateral view demonstrating the posterior malleolar metaphyseal fracture with greater clarity (*upper arrows*). The epiphyseal line is slightly wider than normal anteriorly (*lower arrow*), and overall the findings constitute a Salter-Harris type II epiphyseal-metaphyseal injury.

erally less common in childhood than in adulthood (6). This is especially true in the infant and young child. In the older child, one can encounter fractures of bones such as the navicular and talus (Figs. 4.181 and 4.182), but the most commonly fractured bone is the calcaneus. With fractures through the talus, dislocation of one of the fragments can occur (Fig. 4.182*A*), and in addition, subsequent aseptic necrosis is a known complication.

Fractures of the calcaneus usually result from the patient jumping or falling on his or her heels, and because one often is not thinking of these fractures, they may remain occult (4, 9). Isotope bone scans are helpful in detecting some of these fractures but in other cases a clear-cut fracture line may be visible (Fig. 4.182). Otherwise, one may have to look for indirect findings such as soft tissue swelling, loss of Boehler's angle, decreased height of the calcaneus, or increased density (impaction) of the calcaneus through the fracture area (Fig. 4.183). In addition, when a calcaneal fracture is suspected, it is mandatory to obtain tangential views of the calcaneus. On this view, the most productive in calcaneal injuries, compression fractures

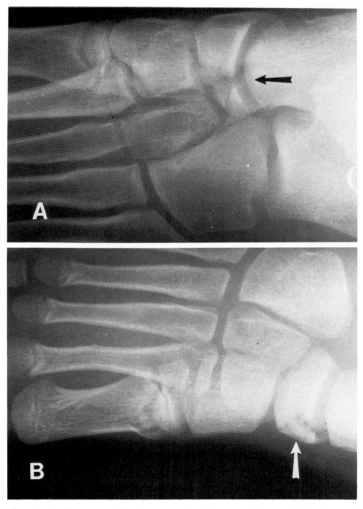

Figure 4.181. *Tarsal navicular fractures.* Note compression fracture of the navicular (*arrow*). (*A*) An impaction-compression fracture of the base of the first metatarsal also is present and there is an angulated cortical fracture through the midshaft of the second metatarsal. (*B*) Another patient with a compression fracture of the navicular (*arrow*).

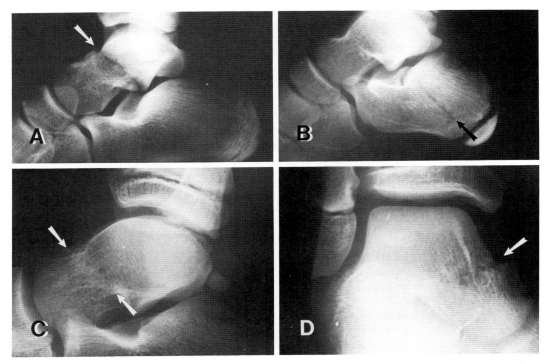

Figure 4.182. *Talar and calcaneal fractures.* (*A*) Note the clear-cut talar fracture (*arrow*), and associated talocalcaneal dislocation. (*B*) Linear fracture through the calcaneus (*arrow*). (*C*) Subtle fracture through the neck of the talus (*arrows*). (*D*) Oblique view demonstrates offsetting of the fracture (*arrow*).

almost always are visualized with clarity, and indeed, previously unsuspected fractures also may become visible (Fig. 4.183). Finally, with calcaneal fractures, it is most important that the normally sclerotic and irregular calcaneal apophyses or the radiolucent defects they produce, not be misinterpreted for such fractures (see Fig. 4.192*A*).

Small avulsion fractures of the various tarsal bones and other bones around the ankle also can be encountered. These are more common than generally appreciated and while they may be visible on standard views, very often oblique views bring the fracture to light (Fig. 4.184). Indeed, in some cases visualization of these fractures is strictly fortuitous, and all of them must be differentiated from normal secondary ossification centers of the various bones around the ankle (see Fig. 4.191).

Sprained Ankle. As opposed to the wrist, *a sprained ankle most often turns out to be nothing more than a sprained ankle.* Of course, this is not to say that fractures never occur, but only to point out that the high incidence of underlying fracture which accompanies wrist sprains is not present with ankle sprains. Another important aspect of a sprained ankle when due to a medial inversion injury, is that very often there is an associated fracture of the base of the fifth metatarsal. The peroneus brevis muscle inserts onto this bone, and with inversion injuries, an avulsion fracture frequently occurs. This fracture usually is overlooked clinically, but almost always is detectable roentgenographically (see Fig. 4.203).

Achilles Tendonitis (1, 7). Children very commonly develop acute, or chronic pain over the insertion of the Achilles tendon onto the calcaneus. Actually, the condition reprsents a bursitis or tenosynovitis and usually is considered to be the result of subclinical injury in the active child. Some children are more prone to develop this problem than others, and frequently it is recurrent. Conserative measures are in order, and there are no roentgenographic findings except perhaps for localized swelling over the area.

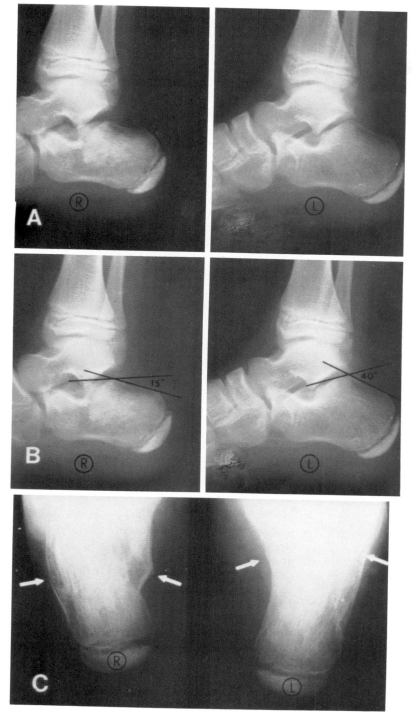

Figure 4.183. *Calcaneal fracture—indirect signs.* (*A*) On the right note that the calcaneus has lost considerable height, and that there is an area of central sclerosis due to impaction. The left ankle appears normal. (*B*) Boehler's angle on the right has been markedly reduced, while on the left it is within normal range. Normally, it measures between 30 and 40°. Anything under 28° is considered abnormal. (*C*) Tangential view of the calcanei demonstrates the previously documented compression fracture of the calcaneus on the right (*arrows*), but in addition detects the presence of a previously unsuspected noncompressed, calcaneal fracture on the left (*arrows*).

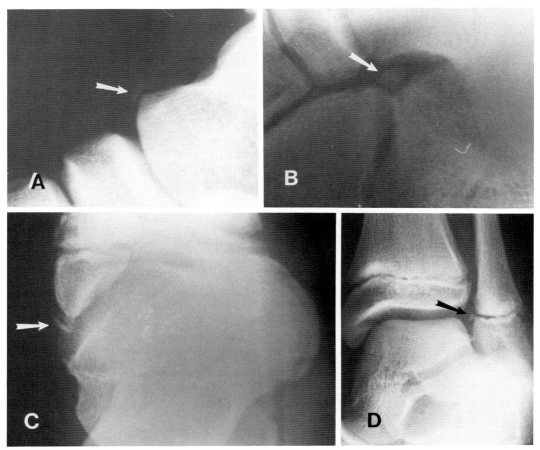

Figure 4.184. *Small avulsion fractures around the ankle.* (*A*) Note small avulsion of the talus (*arrow*). This is a common fracture. (*B*) Small corner avulsion of the calcaneus (*arrow*), seen only on oblique view. (*C*) Avulsion fracture of the distal fibular epiphysis (*arrow*). (*D*) Another avulsion fracture of the fibula (*arrow*), seen only on oblique view.

However, there is a great temptation to erroneously attribute the problem to the nearby, normally sclerotic and irregular, but abnormal appearing, calcaneal apophysis. Such a diagnosis should be avoided for this is the expected appearance of the normal calcaneus (see Fig. 4.192), and never is it involved in Achilles tendonitis.

Osteochondritis of the Tarsal Bones. Osteochondritis of the tarsal bones is not particularly common in childhood, but does occur, and most often involves the talus (5). The findings are similar to those of osteochondritis dissecans elsewhere in that there is a bony defect, with slight peripheral sclerosis (Fig. 4.185). An intra-articular piece of bone, may or may not be visualized. It might be noted, however, that as with osteochon-

dritis dissecans elsewhere, the lesion may or may not be symptomatic at the time of detection.

Aseptic Necrosis of the Tarsal Bones. Aseptic necrosis of the various tarsal bones can be a cause of foot pain, and in this regard, the tarsal navicular is the most commonly involved bone. Köhler's disease (11) is the term applied to aseptic necrosis of the navicular and the roentgenographic features consist of irregularity and sclerosis (Fig. 4.186, *A* and *B*). In addition, one can utilize the soft tissues (13) for detection of less than classic Köhler's disease. The soft tissues, over the aseptically necrotic bone are edematous (Fig. 4.186*C*), whereas, when normal irregular ossification mimics Köhler's disease, the soft tissues are normal.

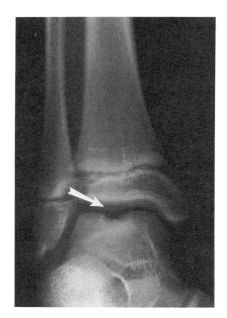

Figure 4.185. *Osteochondritis dissecans of talus.*   Note defect (*arrow*) in the articular surface of the talus.

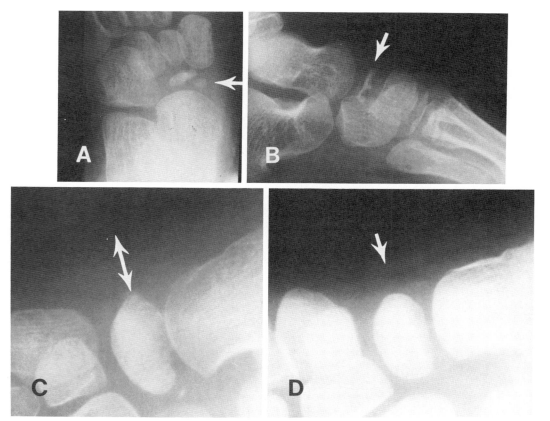

Figure 4.186. *Köhler's disease—tarsal navicular.*   (*A*) Note small, irregular navicular bone (*arrow*). (*B*) Lateral view showing similar fragmentation and compression. (*C*) The navicular bone is a little sclerotic but note mostly that the soft tissues over the bone are thickened due to edema (*arrows*). (*D*) Normal side for comparison. Note the normal appearance of the navicular bone and lack of swelling of the soft tissues.

Septic Arthritis, Osteomyelitis, and Cellulitis. Septic arthritis of the ankle manifests primarily in joint space distention causing displacement of the fat pads (Fig. 4.187). Cellulitis around the ankle is manifest primarily in edema of the soft tissues and obliteration of the various fat pads. The fat pads are not displaced outwardly unless there is pus in the joint (i.e., septic arthritis). With osteomyelitis of the distal tibia and fibula, there also is deep soft tissue swelling and disruption or obliteration of the fat-muscle interfaces but no joint space distention. Of course, if septic arthritis accompanies the problem, fluid in the joint will be present.

The deep soft tissue changes of osteomyelitis, are not particularly different from the soft tissue swelling seen with cellulitis. To be sure, in the ankle, differentiation of superficial, from deep, edema is more difficult than around the other large joints of the body. However, whatever the cause of edema, the anterior and posterior fat pads remain in normal position (Fig. 4.188).

Eventually, with osteomyelitis, bone destruction is seen (Fig. 4.189), but the disease may be present for some time before this becomes evident. This is especially true of the tarsal bones, and consequently, bone scans are indispensable when looking for early osteomyelitis in and around the ankle (Fig. 4.189).

Normal Variations Causing Problems. Numerous accessory ossicles occur in the ankle and to illustrate all of them would be a definite overkill. The most common are those occurring at the distal ends of the lateral and medial malleoli and the posterior aspect of the talus (Fig. 4.190). However, many more commonly occur in the ankle, and a diagrammatic representation of these accessory ossicles is presented in Fig. 4.191. It is most important not to misinterpret these secondary ossification centers and accessory ossicles for avulsion fractures.

The normal, sclerotic, irregular calcaneal apophysis (8) notoriously is misinterpreted for aseptic necrosis of the calcaneus. Indeed, its normal appearance is often so frightening

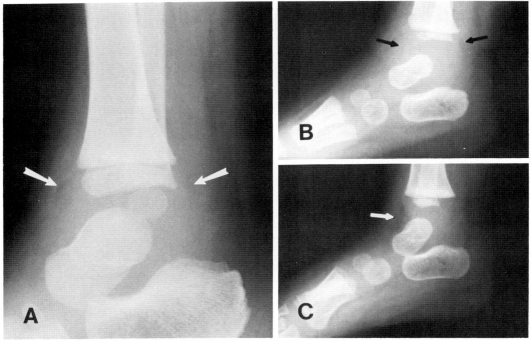

Figure 4.187. *Septic arthritis of ankle.* (*A*) Note outward displacement of the anterior and posterior fat pads. (*arrows*). (*B*) Another patient with outwardly displaced fat pads just barely visible (*arrows*). The reason for poor visualization is that there is marked associated edema of the soft tissues. Note also that the pre-Achilles fat pad, behind the posterior fat pad, is outwardly displaced and curved. (*C*) Normal side for comparison. Note especially, the normal anterior fat pad (*arrow*).

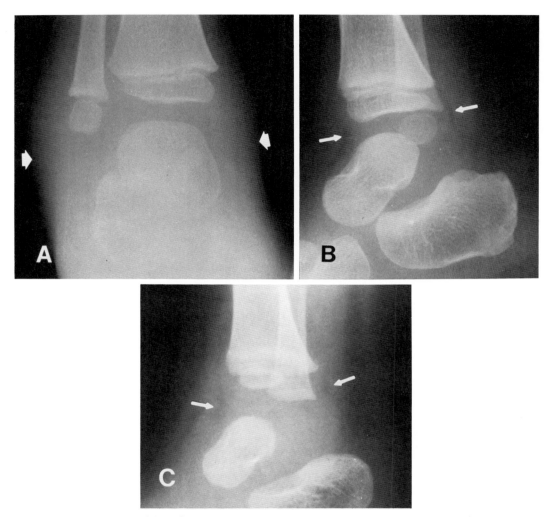

Figure 4.188. *Deep edema of the soft tissues.*   (*A*) Note marked swelling of the ankle (*arrows*). (*B*) Lateral view, however, demonstrates normal position of the anterior and posterior fat pads (*arrows*). This excludes fluid in the joint and suggests the findings are due to soft tissue edema alone. (*C*) Another patient with edema around the ankle and persistent visualization of the anterior and posterior fat pads in their normal location (*arrows*). It is important in these cases to note that the fat pads are in normal position. If they were outwardly displaced, fluid (pus) in the joints should be suspected (see Fig. 4.187).

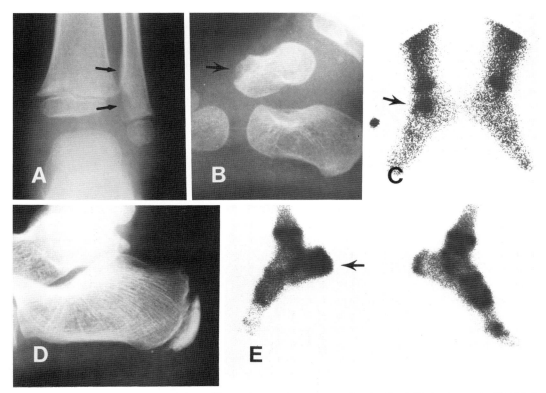

Figure 4.189. *Osteomyelitis around the ankle.* (*A*) Note bone destruction in distal fibula (*arrows*). (*B*) Subtle destruction of the talus (*arrow*) in an infant. (*C*) Bone scan in same patient shows clear-cut hot area in right talus (*arrow*). (*D*) Patient with calcaneal pain. The x-ray is normal. (*E*) Isotope bone scan, however, shows clear-cut increased uptake in the calcaneus (*arrow*).

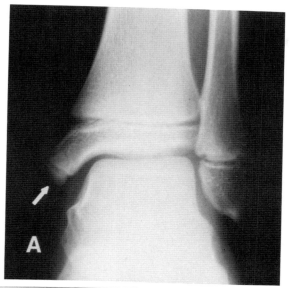

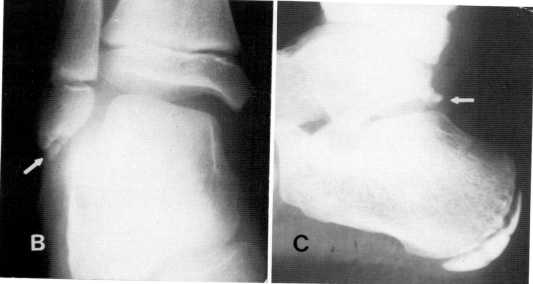

Figure 4.190. *Common accessory ossicles about the ankle.* (*A*) Accessory ossicle (os subtibiale) of medial malleolus (*arrow*). (*B*) Accessory ossicles (os subfibulare) of the distal fibular epiphysis (*arrow*). (*C*) Os trigonum (*arrow*) of talus.

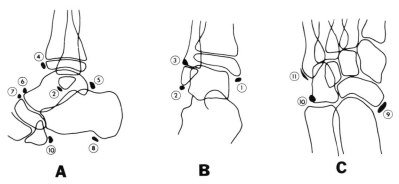

A   **B**   **C**

Figure 4.191. *(A–C) Accessory ossicles about the ankle—diagrammatic representation.* (*1*) Accessory center of medial malleolus or os subtibiale, (*2*) accessory center of distal fibular epiphysis or os subfibulare, (*3*) accessory metaphyseal fibular ossicle, (*4*) os talotibulale, (*5*) os trigonum, (*6*) os supratalare, (*7*) os supranaviculare, (*8*), os subcalcis, (*9*) os subtibiale externum, (*10*) os peroneum, (*11*) os vesalianum.

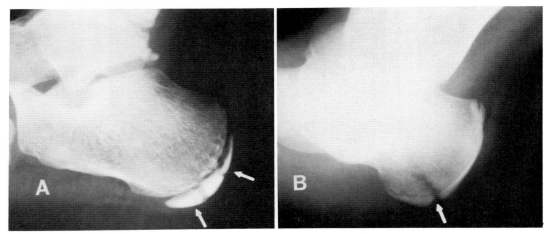

Figure 4.192. *Normal calcaneal apophysis.* (*A*) Note the typical sclerotic, irregular appearance of the often fragmented calcaneal apophysis (*arrows*). (*B*) With obliquity, the normal defects through the calcaneal apophysis can suggest a calcaneal fracture (*arrow*).

that it is almost impossible not to assign some type of pathologic condition to the bone. This is especially true in cases of Achilles tendonitis. Another problem with the calcaneal apophysis is that with certain degrees of obliquity, its fragmented appearance can suggest a calcaneal fracture (Fig. 4.192).

Another normal finding frequently misinterpreted for abnormality is the apparently offset distal fibular epiphysis on oblique views of the ankle (Fig. 4.193). This is a normal finding on this view. In addition, the distal tibial epiphyseal-metaphyseal junction tends to be very irregular in normal children, and can suggest a fracture (Fig. 4.193). Finally, it should be noted that tarsal bones

are especially prone to irregular ossification which should not be misinterpreted for fracturing or aseptic necrosis (Fig. 4.194).

REFERENCES

1. Dickinson, P.H., Coutts, M.B., Woodward, E.P., et al.: Tendo Achilli bursitis. J. Bone Joint Surg. 48A: 77–81, 1966.
2. Hayden, C.K., Jr., and Swischuk, L.E., Para-articular soft tissue changes in infections and trauma of the lower extremity in children. A.J.R. 134: 307–311, 1980.
3. Letts, R.M.: The hidden adolescent ankle fracture. J. Pediatr. Orthop. 2; 161–164, 1982.
4. Matteri, R.E., and Frymoier, J.W.: Fracture of the calcaneus in three children. J. Bone Joint Surg. 55A: 1091–1094, 1973.
5. Newberg, A.H.: Osteochondral fractures of the dome of the talus. Br. J. Radiol. 52: 105–109, 1979.
6. Rang, M.: *Children's Fractures.* J.B. Lippincott, Philadelphia, 1974.
7. Shapiro, J.R., Fallat, R.W., Tsang, R.C., and Glueck,C.J.:

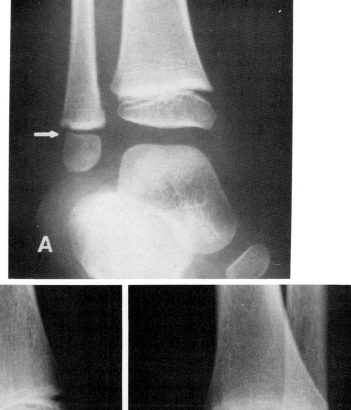

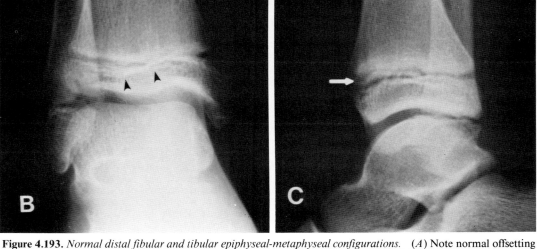

Figure 4.193. *Normal distal fibular and tibular epiphyseal-metaphyseal configurations.*   (*A*) Note normal offsetting of the distal fibular epiphysis (*arrow*). This is a common finding on oblique views of the normal ankle. It should not be misinterpreted for a displaced epiphyseal fracture. Also note slight irregularity along the inner aspect of the fibula. This also is normal. (*B*) Note the typically irregular appearance of the epiphyseal-metaphyseal junction of the normal distal tibia. Also note normal pseudofracture lines produced by unevenness of the normal epiphysis (*arrows*). These should not be misinterpreted for Salter-Harris epiphyseal-metaphyseal fractures. (*C*) Lateral view of another ankle demonstrating what would appear to be a metaphyseal avulsion (*arrow*). However, the finding is normal. Of all the epiphyseal-metaphyseal junctions in the body, the one through the distal tibia is most prone to such normal variations.

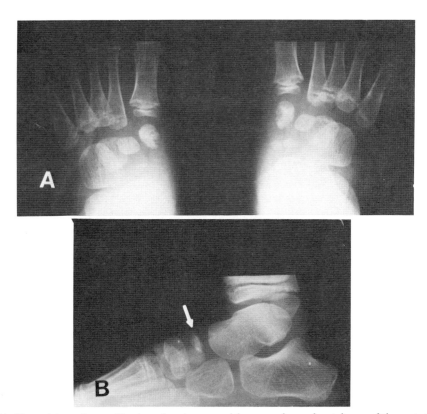

Figure 4.194. *Normal irregular ossification of various tarsal bones and pseudoepiphyses of the metatarsals.* (*A*) Note the various irregular configurations of the tarsal bones and the pseudoepiphyses of the third through fifth metatarsals. (*B*) Lateral view demonstrating underossification and irregular sclerosis of the normal navicular bone (*arrow*). The findings should not be misinterpreted for aseptic necrosis. With aseptic necrosis pain is present.

Achilles tendinitis and tenosynovitis. Am. J. Dis. Child. 128: 486–490, 1974.

8. Shopfner, C.E., and Coin, C.G.: Effect of weight-bearing on the appearance and development of the secondary calcaneal epiphysis. Radiology 86: 201–206, 1966.

9. Starshak, R.J., Simons, G.W., and Sty, J.R.: Occult fracture of the calcaneus—another toddler's fracture. Pediatr. Radiol. 14: 37–40, 1984.

10. Towbin, R., Dunbar, J.S., Towbin, J., and Clark, R.: Teardrop sign: plain film recognition of ankle effusion. A.J.R. 134: 985–990, 1980.

11. Waught, W.: The ossification and vascularization of the tarsal-navicular and a relation to Köhler's disease. J. Bone Joint Surg. 40B: 765, 1958.

12. Weston, W.J.: Traumatic effusions of the ankle and posterior subtaloid joints. Br. J. Radiol. 31: 445–447, 1958.

13. Weston, W.J.: Köhler's disease of the tarsal scaphoid. Australas. Radiol. 12: 332–337, 1978.

FOOT

Normal Soft Tissues and Fat Pads. As in the hand, there are no particularly valuable fat pads to evaluate in the foot. Consequently, except for localized edema, there is little else to analyze.

Detecting Fluid in the Small Joints of the Foot. The detection of fluid in the small joints of the foot rests with noting soft tissue swelling around the involved joint. Occasionally, the joint space can be widened due to distension, but this is not a common finding (see Fig. 4.207).

Injuries of the Metatarsals and Phalanges. Dislocation of the various joints of the foot is uncommon except perhaps for dislocation of the great toe. *Cortical, buckle, or torus fractures* on the other hand, are quite common, and as in the hand often require oblique views for adequate visualization (Fig. 4.195). However, some of these fractures still can be quite subtle, and only telltale soft tissue edema (Fig. 4.196) or meticulous inspection of the films will aid one in detecting them (Fig. 4.197).

Another, more recently documented injury, commonly seen in young infants is the

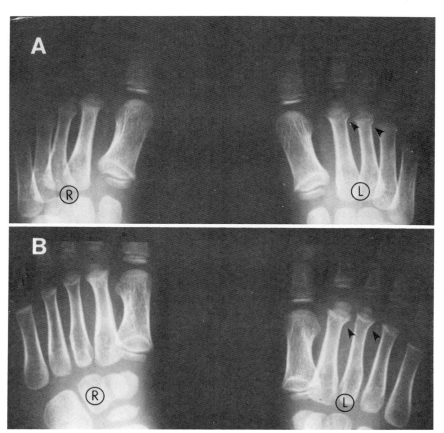

Figure 4.195. *Subtle cortical fractures of metatarsals.* (*A*) On the left, note subtle cortical buckling of the second and third metatarsals (*arrows*). Also note that the soft tissues in the area are a little more opaque due to underlying edema. (*B*) Oblique view more clearly demonstrates the cortical buckles (*arrows*). Compare these findings with the corresponding cortices on the normal right side.

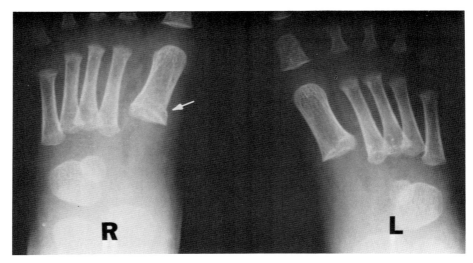

Figure 4.196. *Cortical fracture of first metatarsal.*   First note extensive edema of the soft tissues of the right forefoot. Then note the cortical buckle fracture at the base of the first metatarsal (*arrow*).

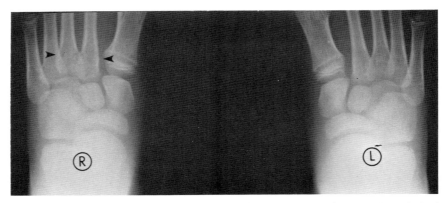

Figure 4.197. *Metatarsal fractures, subtle findings.*   On the right, note subtle fractures through the base of the second and third metatarsals (*arrows*). These fractures easily could be missed unless the findings are compared with those in the normal bones on the left side.

bunkbed or Lisfranc fracture (1, 2). This fracture is believed to be a fracture dislocation of the first metatarsal and cuneiform bone (1, 2) and in subtle cases may be missed. Comparative views are important here except when the avulsed fracture fragment is clearly visible (Fig. 4.198*A*). When these fractures heal they may leave an exostotic-like bony bulge (Fig. 4.198*B*).

Epiphyseal-metaphyseal injuries are much less common in the foot than in the hand, and similarly fractures of the various epiphyses themselves are less common.

A problem, however, can arise in the great toe where the occasional epiphyseal fracture

(Fig. 4.199) is confused with the more common normal bipartite epiphysis (Fig. 4.200).

Salter-Harris type I, and even type II, epiphyseal-metaphyseal injuries also can occur in the small bones of the feet, especially in the great toe. Indeed, these fractures have a propensity to become infected as there often is a break through the nail bed (3). These fractures usually can be suspected when there is excessive widening of the epiphyseal line, and once again, comparative views are indispensable here (Fig. 4.201).

Other fractures of the small bones of the foot include a variety of spiral and transverse fractures, many of which are hairline (Fig.

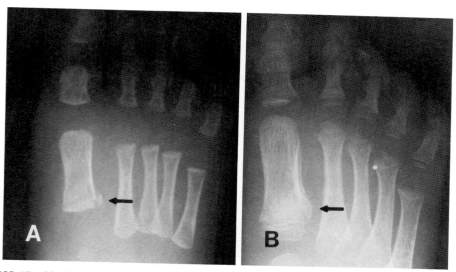

Figure 4.198. *"Bunkbed" fracture of first metatarsal.* (*A*) Note typical location of this dislocation-avulsion fracture (*arrow*). (*B*) Healing phase demonstrates an exostotic-like hump (*arrows*).

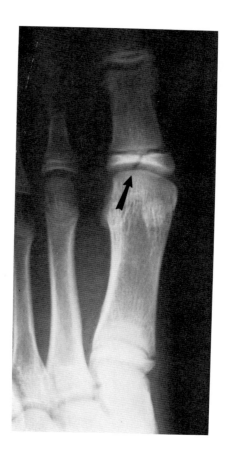

Figure 4.199. *Epiphyseal fracture (Salter-Harris type III injury).* Note the fracture through the epiphysis (*arrow*) of the proximal phalanx of the great toe. Also note that the epiphyseal line is a little wider medially, giving support to the presence of a Salter-Harris type III injury. In addition, there was tenderness over the area clinically, and considerable soft tissue swelling around the area.

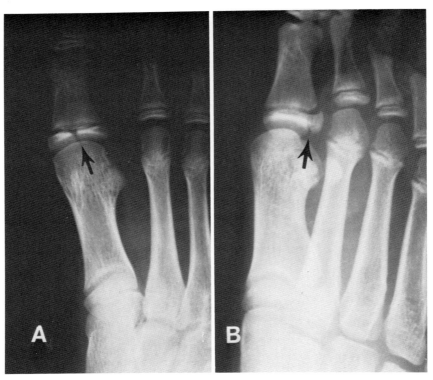

Figure 4.200. *Bipartite epiphysis—pseudofracture of the great toe.*   (*A*) Note the bipartite epiphysis (*arrow*) of the great toe. The findings are virtually indistinguishable from the fracture demonstrated in Figure 4.199. (*B*) Another example of an eccentric bipartite epiphysis mimicking a fracture (*arrow*).

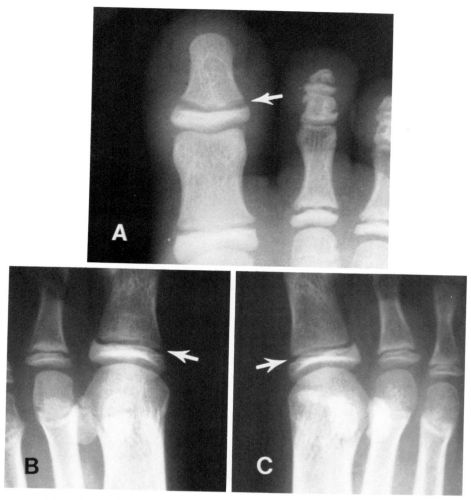

Figure 4.201. *Epiphyseal-metaphyseal fractures of the great toe.* (*A*) Note widening of the epiphyseal line of the distal phalanx (*arrow*). Compare it with the width of the other lines. (*B*) Another patient with somewhat subtle widening of the epiphyseal line, (*arrow*). (*C*) Compare with the same epiphyseal line on the normal side.

4.202), and the **avulsion fracture of the base of the fifth metatarsal.** Actually, this latter injury is common, and usually is sustained with inversion sprains of the ankle. It results from pulling on the base of the fifth metatarsal by the peroneus brevis muscle. However, many times swelling around the ankle diverts attention from this fracture, and it is not until the fracture is detected roentgenographically that the injury comes to light. In this regard, it is most fortunate that, on almost any roentgenogram of the ankle, the base of the fifth metatarsal is included, and thus if one always looks at this area in patients with a sprained ankle, one will be the first to detect a good many of these fractures.

In **differentiating base of the fifth metatarsal fractures from the normal os vesalianum**, it should be noted that the fractures almost always are transverse or near transverse (Fig. 4.203), while the os vesalianum usually is a longitudinal structure (Fig. 4.204). If avulsion of the os vesalianum occurs, a variable degree of separation from the base of the fifth metatarsal will be seen, and clinically, the findings will be accompanied by local tenderness (Fig. 4.205).

Miscellaneous Injuries of the Foot. Stress fractures in the foot are reasonably common in the older child but not in the infant. Of these, the best known is the stress fracture of the second metatarsal or the so-

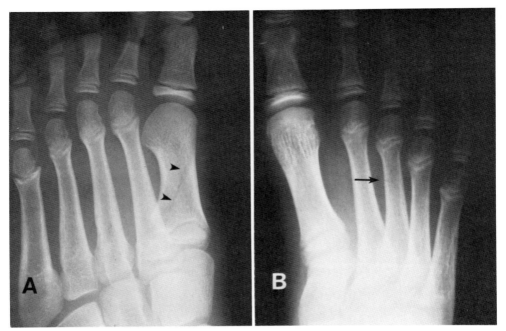

Figure 4.202. *Hairline fractures of the metatarsals.* (*A*) Note the oblique hairline fracture of the first metatarsal (*arrows*). (*B*) Very subtle transverse hairline fracture of the third metatarsal (*arrow*). This is the type of fracture seen with the march (stress) fracture.

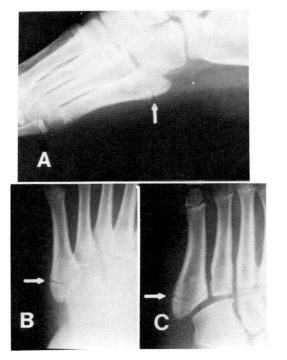

Figure 4.203. *Base of the fifth metatarsal fracture.* (*A*) Typical transverse fracture (*arrow*) through the base of the fifth metatarsal. (*B*) Same fracture (*arrow*) on anteroposterior view. (*C*) Oblique view of the fracture (*arrow*). Typically, this fracture occurs in the transverse plane.

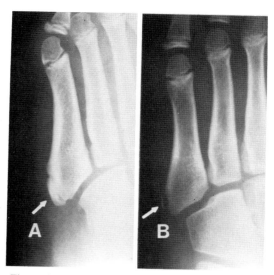

Figure 4.204. *Os vesalianum—base of fifth metatarsal accessory center.* (*A*) Large os vesalianum (*arrow*). (*B*) Thin sliver-like os vesalianum (*arrow*). As opposed to a fracture through the base of the fifth metatarsal, the os vesalianum always lies in the longitudinal plane.

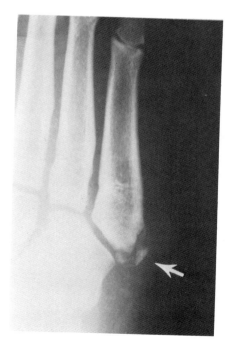

Figure 4.205. *Avulsion of the os vesalianum.* Note the fragmented, partially avulsed os vesalianum (*arrow*). Not visible on this reproduction is localized soft tissue swelling over the avulsed bony fragment. Clinically, point tenderness over the area was present.

called "march" fracture. As with any stress fracture, the fracture line may be difficult to detect in its early stages, but later on it usually is visualized because of its abundant periosteal new bone deposition (Fig. 4.206). Another lesion in the foot causing pain is aseptic necrosis of the second metatarsal head or Freiberg's disease. Roentgenographically, the findings range from increased sclerosis to sclerosis interspersed with focal bony resorption of the second metatarsal head.

Septic Arthritis, Osteomyelitis, and Cellulitis of the Foot. Septic arthritis is manifest by swelling around the joint space, and occasionally, distention of the joint space (Fig. 4.207). Osteomyelitis and cellulitis, on the other hand, usually present with soft tissue swelling only. Indeed, they are difficult to differentiate from one another, but eventually osteomyelitis results in bony destruction (Fig. 4.208). Finally, it should be noted that patients with sickle cell disease can present with extensive soft tissue swelling, bony destruction, and periosteal new bone deposition as part of the hand-foot syndrome. The findings are no different from those seen in the hand (see Fig. 4.99), and are difficult to differentiate from osteomyelitis.

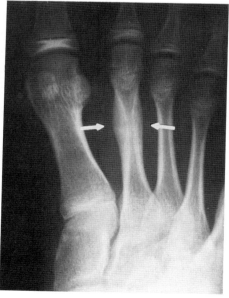

Figure 4.206. *Stress fracture of second metatarsal.* Note extensive periosteal new bone deposition along the second metatarsal (*arrows*). This is a healing stress fracture.

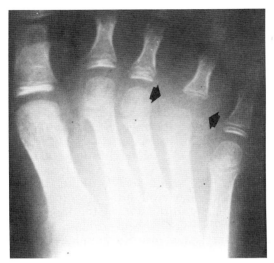

Figure 4.207. *Septic arthritis of the small joints of the foot.* Note the widened joint space between the fourth metatarsal and the adjacent proximal phalanx (*arrows*). Also note that the joint is dislocated and that the epiphysis of the phalanx has been partially destroyed.

Irregular ossifications of the epiphyses or pseudoepiphyses of the metatarsals and phalanges are less commonly misinterpreted for fractures but can be misinterpreted for areas of aseptic necrosis (Fig. 4.209).

The bipartite epiphysis of the great toe, a common normal variation, also has been dealt with earlier (Fig. 4.200) and is a normal finding commonly misinterpreted for a fracture. In addition, bipartite or even tripartite, sesamoid bones over the head of the first metatarsal are common and frequently misinterpreted for fractures of these bones (Fig. 4.210*A*). Finally, it should be noted that the normal proximal epiphysis of the first metatarsal, when seen in oblique projection, can have a very bizarre appearance. In many of these cases, a fracture is suggested (Fig. 4.210*B*), but knowledge of this phenomenon should enable one to avoid such a misinterpretation.

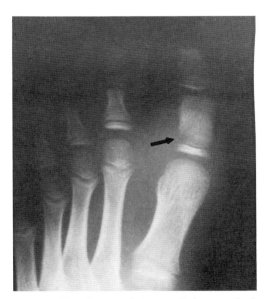

Figure 4.208. *Osteomyelitis—small bones of the foot.* Note swelling around the great toe and early bone destruction (*arrow*).

Normal Findings Causing Problems.
The os vesalianum, or accessory ossification center at the base of the fifth metatarsal, has been dealt with earlier and is a common normal finding misinterpreted for a base of the fifth metatarsal fracture (see Fig. 4.204).

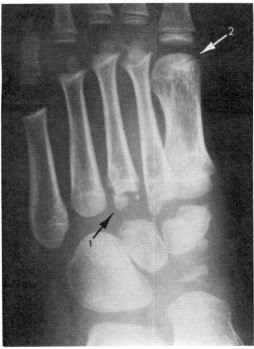

Figure 4.209. *Normal irregular ossification of the metatarsal apophyses.* Note the irregular ossification pattern of the apophysis (pseudoepiphysis) of the third metatarsal (*1*). Also note irregular ossification of some of the tarsal bones. The radiolucent defect through the head of the first metatarsal (*2*) should not be misinterpreted for a fracture. It is a residual defect caused by the apophysis (pseudoepiphysis) of the first metatarsal.

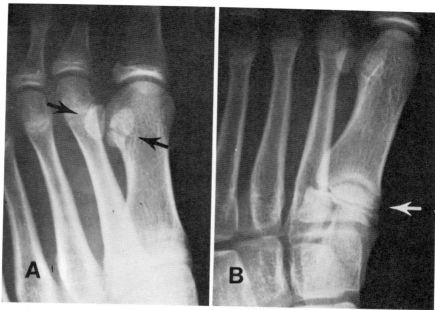

Figure 4.210. *Other normal findings causing problems.* (*A*) Note the *sesamoid bones* of the great toes (*arrows*). One of the bones is bipartite and should not be misinterpreted for a fracture of the sesamoid bone. (*B*) Irregular appearance of the epiphysis of the first metatarsal (*arrow*). The finding should not be misinterpreted for a fracture.

REFERENCES

1. Foster, S.C., and Foster, R.R.: Lisfranc's tarsometatarsal fracture-dislocation. Radiology 120: 79–83, 1976.
2. Johnson, G.F.: Pediatric Lisfranc injury: "bunkbed" fracture. A.J.R. 137: 1041–1044, 1981.
3. Pinckney, L.E., Currarino, G., and Kennedy, L.A.: The stubbed great toe: a cause of occult compound fracture and infection. Radiology 138: 375–377, 1981.

MISCELLANEOUS EXTREMITY PROBLEMS

Battered Child Syndrome. A complete discussion of the battered child syndrome is beyond the scope of this book, but one or two pertinent observations are in order. First, it is not uncommon for a battered infant to first present as an emergency patient, and one should be suspicious if: (a) roentgenographic evidence of trauma is greater than the clinical history would suggest, (b) roentgenographic evidence of trauma is poorly correlated with clinical history, and (c) unsuspected fractures are detected.

In terms of skeletal injury, it first should be noted that many battered children present with calvarial injuries and underlying subdural hematomas. Consequently, any unexplained skull fracture or subdural he-matoma should be treated with a great deal of suspicion. However, the most characteristic lesion in the battered child syndrome is the epiphyseal-metaphyseal fracture (2–4, 8). These fractures usually are Salter-Harris type I and II fractures, and their multiplicity, along with their different stages of healing are characteristic of this syndrome (Fig. 4.211). However, although this type of fracture is the most pathognomonic, it is becoming increasingly apparent that many children, perhaps as many as 50% (1, 5–7), do not present with these injuries. Rather they present with soft tissue injury, unremarkable appearing spiral or transverse fractures of one extremity, or no bony injury at all. Consequently, in the emergency room, any injury which does not seem to fit with the clinical history should be treated with suspicion, and if necessary, a bone survey should be obtained at the time (Fig. 4.212).

It has been suggested that isotope bone scanning should be the initial screening procedure in any patient suspected of child abuse (9). Although there is no doubt that the isotope bone scan can detect areas of fracture, not all subscribe to this philosophy. There are, indeed, two opinions but most

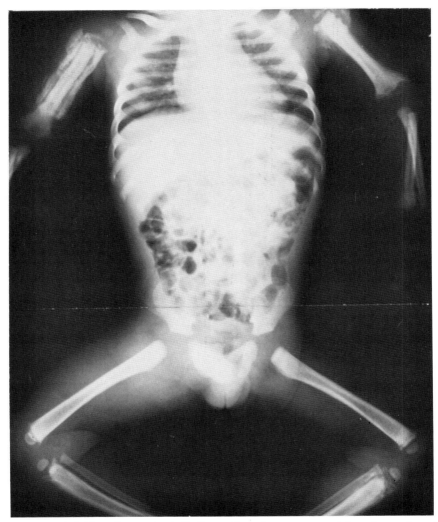

Figure 4.211. *Battered child syndrome, classic findings.*   Note the numerous epiphyseal-metaphyseal fractures in numerous stages of healing in the shoulders, elbows and knees. Periosteal new bone deposition at certain sites is profound. Also note that the right hip joint is distended and that the femur is displaced laterally. This represents an acute hemarthrosis due to an occult hip fracture. On later films, a healing Salter-Harris epiphyseal-metaphyseal injury became evident.

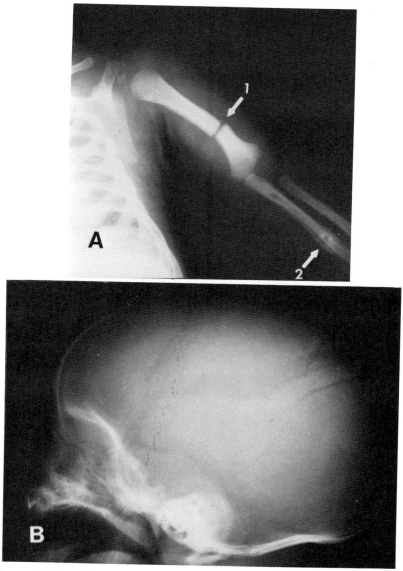

Figure 4.212. *Battered child syndrome—incidental identification.*   (A) This 6-week-old infant was brought to the emergency room by the mother because she thought the arm was broken. A clear-cut fracture through the humerus is visible (*1*), but also note periosteal new bone deposition around an old distal ulnar fracture (*2*). This latter fracture was unexpected and unexplained. Consequently, a bone survey was obtained. (B) Skull film obtained as part of the bone survey demonstrates a number of totally unsuspected calvarial fractures. In addition, this patient demonstrated fractures of the lower extremities and ribs and eventually was determined to be a battered infant.

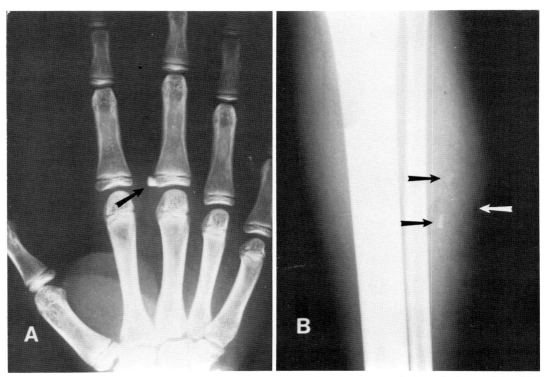

Figure 4.213. *Glass in the soft tissues.* (*A*) Clearly visible glass fragment (*arrow*) in the soft tissues of the third digit. (*B*) Less clearly visualized fragments of glass (*black arrows*) in the soft tissues of the leg. Also note edema in the leg and air in the soft tissues (*white arrow*).

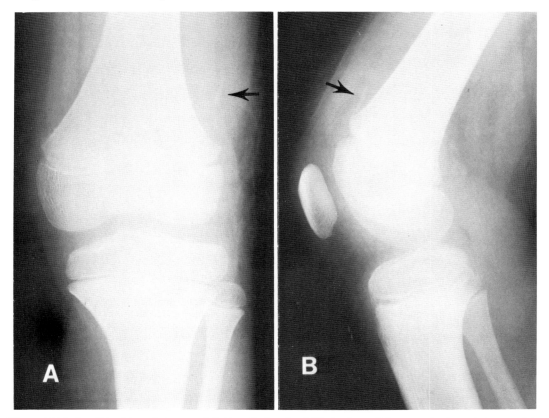

Figure 4.214. *Pencil lead in soft tissues.* (*A*) Note the barely visible lead pencil fragment in the soft tissues of the knee (*arrow*). (*B*) Lateral view demonstrating the same lead pencil fragment (*arrow*).

institutions still obtain the roentgenographic bone survey for the detection of occult trauma. The roentgenogram provides more specific information than does the isotope study, but the isotope study delivers less radiation. On the other hand, when positive areas are identified on the isotope study, roentgenograms of that area are then required.

Visceral injury also is becoming more commonly documented in the battered child syndrome and some of these children can present with acute abdominal problems. Among the more common of these are pancreatic and duodenal injuries, but involvement of the other intra-abdominal organs also is seen.

Foreign Bodies in the Soft Tissues. Soft tissue foreign bodies are a common problem in childhood. Metallic foreign bodies and pebbles or dirt, of course, are readily demonstrable, but less opaque or totally nonopaque foreign bodies present more of a problem. In this regard, pieces of glass may or may not be visible, and visibility depends entirely upon the amount of lead in the glass. In some of these cases, the glass fragment is readily demonstrable while in other cases it is more difficult to see (Fig. 4.213). Lead from a lead pencil is another foreign body commonly embedded in the soft tissues, and in some cases may be demonstrable roentgenographically (Fig. 4.214). In all of these cases, however, xeroradiography may be of considerable aid in the detection of the foreign bodies. In addition, CT scanning can be useful (Fig. 4.215).

Of special interest is the *wooden foreign body* which can become embedded in the soft tissues on a chronic basis (1–6). In such instances, most often one is dealing with a toothpick, although tree twigs, etc. also have been encountered. The toothpick, of course, is not visible roentgenographically, and we have not had great success in demonstrating it with xeroradiography. Consequently, one is left with secondary findings consisting of widening of the soft tissues between the adjacent bones, and eventually, periosteal new bone deposition; i.e., reactive periostitis (Fig. 4.216). In some cases, the resulting periosteal new bone and adjacent demineralization of the bones can lead to a pseudo-osteomyelitis or tumor-like appearance.

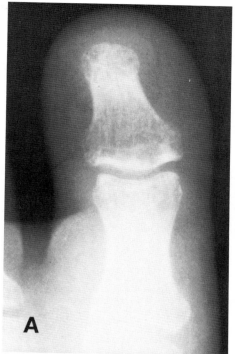

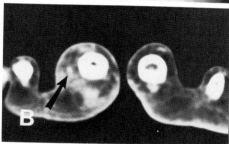

Figure 4.215. *Soft tissue foreign body; CT scan.* (*A*) This big toe was swollen for a prolonged period of time. No clear-cut foreign body is seen but one was suspected medially. (*B*) CT scan clearly demonstrates the foreign body (*arrow*) and the swollen soft tissues around the big toe. (Courtesy C. J. Fagan M.D.)

Soft Tissue Infections, Edema, and Air in the Soft Tissues. Many times children come to the emergency room with extensive soft tissue swelling secondary to trauma or infection. Roentgenographically, the findings in both cases consist of thickening of the soft tissues, obliteration of the fat-muscle interfaces, and a characteristic reticulation of the fatty tissues (Fig. 4.217). Reticulation is caused by the accumulation of fluid within the fibrous septae of the fatty tissues, and as the septae become thicker, they become vis-

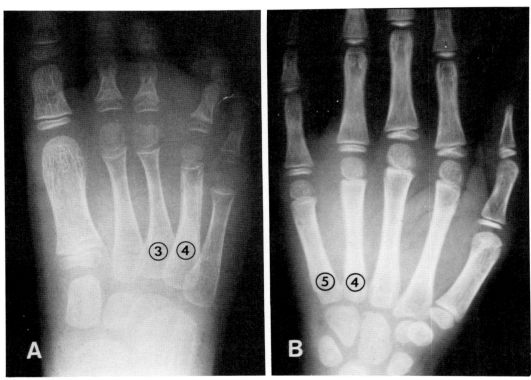

Figure 4.216. *Chronically embedded toothpick.* (*A*) Note widening of the soft tissues between the third (*3*) and fourth (*4*) digits, and periosteal new bone deposition along the fourth metatarsal. This patient presented with a chronically draining lesion between the third and fourth toes. A toothpick was extracted. (*B*) Note increased density of the soft tissues around the fourth (*4*) and fifth (*5*) metacarpals and that the soft tissue space between the fourth and fifth metacarpals is widened. Also note periosteal new bone deposition along the shaft of the fourth metacarpal. This patient had a toothpick embedded between these bones.

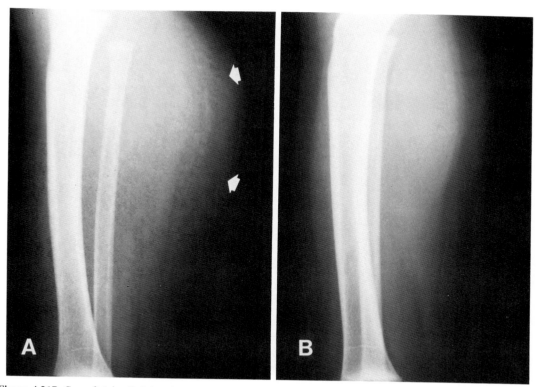

Figure 4.217. *Superficial cellulitis.* (*A*) Note typical reticulated appearance of the edematous soft tissues of the posterior aspect of the calf (*arrows*). (*B*) Compare with normal side.

ible as reticulations. In other instances, deep soft tissue infections are associated with gas-producing organisms and gas will be seen in the soft tissues (Fig. 4.218). Air also can be seen in the soft tissues in association with extensive lacerations, and with blast injuries (see Fig. 4.213).

As noted in the preceding paragraph, superficial edema produces reticulation of the subcutaneous fatty tissue. When edema is deeper, however, a problem arises as to whether it is due to osteomyelitis or soft tissue infection (i.e., pyomyositis, abscess, etc.). In the past, often it was difficult to make this determination, but with ultrasound, it has become increasingly easier. Ultrasound can clearly identify soft tissue abscesses and should be used whenever soft tissue infection is suspected. The findings are not difficult to define or interpret (Figs. 4.219 and 4.220). Such soft tissue abscesses, often involving the muscles, are more common than generally appreciated. The term "pyomyositis" (1–5) often is applied to the

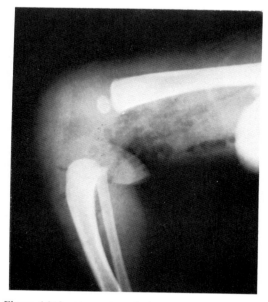

Figure 4.218. *Air on the soft tissues—gas forming organism.* Young infant with cellulitis of the thigh. Note numerous air bubbles and linear collections of air in the soft tissues of the thigh.

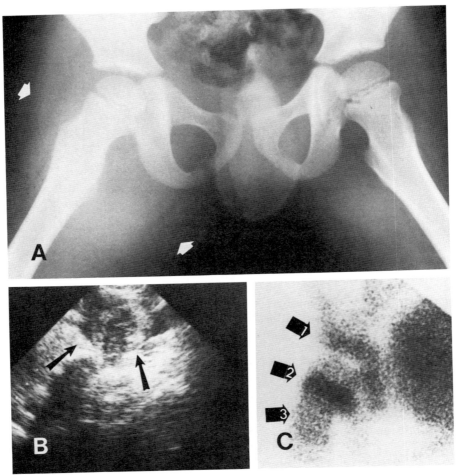

Figure 4.219. *Soft tissue abscess. Value of ultrasound.* (*A*) Note extensive soft tissue swelling around the upper femur (*arrows*). (*B*) Ultrasound study clearly identifies an abscess in the medial soft tissues of the thigh (*arrows*). (*C*) Isotope study performed previously is normal. Normal uptake in acetabular roof (*1*), epiphyseal-metaphyseal junction (*2*), and upper femur (*3*). There is no increased uptake at any of these sites.

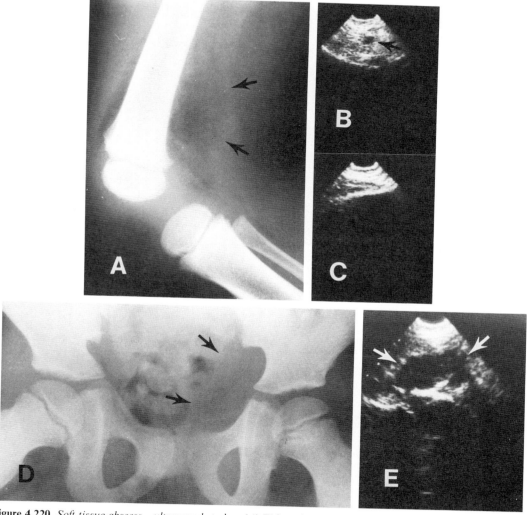

Figure 4.220. *Soft tissue abscess—ultrasound study.* (*A*) This patient demonstrates edematous reticulation of the soft tissues posterior to the knee (*arrows*). (*B*) Ultrasound study demonstrates a sonolucent abscess in the area (*arrow*). (*C*) Normal side for comparison. (*D*) Another patient with deep soft tissue swelling in the pelvis (*arrows*). (*E*) Ultrasonography over the buttocks demonstrates a large abscess (*arrows*).

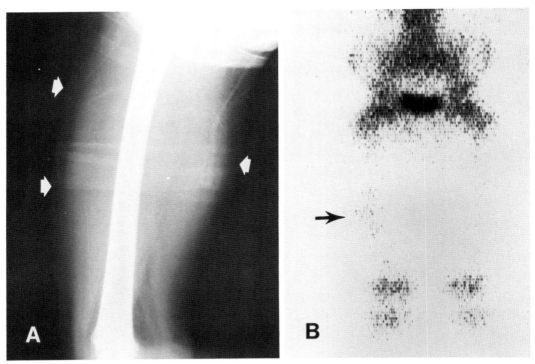

Figure 4.221. *Pyomyositis.* (*A*) Note thickening of the soft tissues of the thigh (*arrows*). (*B*) Isotope scan demonstrates increased, albeit vague, tracer accumulation in the area of muscle inflammation (*arrow*).

condition. Isotope studies frequently are helpful in identifying these sites of infection (Fig. 4.221), but as already noted, ultrasonography is the most valuable study.

REFERENCES

Battered Child Syndrome

1. Akbarnia, B., Torg, J.S., Kirkpatrick, J., and Sussman, S.: Manifestations of the battered child syndrome. J. Bone Joint Surg. 56A: 1159–1166, 1974.
2. Caffey, J.: Multiple fractures in long bones of children suffering from chronic subdural hematoma. A.J.R. 56: 163–173, 1946.
3. Caffey, J.: Parent-infant traumatic stress syndrome (Caffey-Kempe syndrome, battered babe syndrome): First Annual Neuhauser Presidential Address of the Society for Pediatric Radiology. A.J.R. 114: 217–229, 1972.
4. Kempe, C.H., Silverman, F.N., Steel, B.F., Droegenmueller, W., and Silver, H.K.: Battered child syndrome. J.A.M.A. 181: 17–24, 1962.
5. Kogutt, M.S., Swischuk, L.E., and Fagan, C.J.: Patterns of injury and significance of uncommon fractures in the battered child syndrome. A.J.R. 121: 143–149, 1974.
6. Merten, D.F., Radkowski, M.A., and Leonidas, J.C.: The abused child: a radiological reappraisal. Radiology 146: 377–381, 1983.
7. O'Neill, J., Jr., Meacham, W., Griffin, P., and Sawyers, J.: Patterns of injury in the battered child syndrome. J. Trauma 13: 332–339, 1973.
8. Silverman, F.N.: Roentgen manifestations of unrecognized skeletal trauma in infants. A.J.R. 69: 413–427, 1953.
9. Sty, J.R., and Starshak, R.J.: The role of bone scintigraphy in the evaluation of the suspected abused child. Radiology 146: 369–375, 1983.

Foreign Bodies in the Soft Tissues

1. Borgia, C.A.: Unusual bone reaction to organic foreign body in hand. Clin. Orthop. Related Res. 30: 188–192, 1963.
2. Gerle, R.D.: Thorn-induced pseudo-tumours of bone. Br. J. Radiol. 44: 642–645, 1971.
3. Maylahn, D.J.: Thorn-induced "tumors" of bone. J. Bone Joint Surg. 34A: 386–388, 1952.
4. Ritvo, M.: *Bone and Joint X-ray Diagnosis*, pp. 732–735. Lea & Febiger, Philadelphia, 1955.
5. Swischuk, L.E., Jorgenson, F., Jorgenson, A., and Capen, D.: Wooden splinter induced "pseudotumors" and "osteomyelitis-like lesions" of bone and soft tissue. A.J.R. 122: 176–179, 1974.
6. Weston, W.J.: Thorn and twig-induced pseudotumours of bone and soft tissues. Br. J. Radiol. 36: 323–326, 1963.

Soft Tissue Infection

1. Broadfoot, E., and Chaitow, J.: Primary suppurative myositis. Australas. Radiol. 25: 175–176, 1981.
2. Grose, C.: Staphylococcal pyomyositis in South Texas. J. Pediatr. 93: 457–458, 1978.
3. Hirano, T., Srinivasan, G., Jamakiraman, N., Pleviak, D., and Mukhopadhyay, D.: Gallium-67 citrate scintigraphy in pyomyositis. J. Pediatr. 97: 596–598, 1980.
4. Sirinavin, S., and McCraken, G.H., Jr.: Primary suppurative myositis in children. Am. J. Dis. Child. 133: 263–265, 1979.
5. Yousefzadeh, D.K., Schumann, E.M., Mulligan, G.M., Bosworth, E.E., Young, C.S., and Pringle, K.C.: The role of imaging modalities in diagonosis and management of pyomyositis. Skeletal. Radiol. 8: 285–289, 1982.

CHAPTER 5
The Head

HEAD TRAUMA

Trauma to the calvarium and intracranial structures is common in childhood, but roentgenographic examination of the skull in most cases is relatively unrewarding. Indeed, it has been demonstrated that at most only about 25% of patients demonstrate skull fractures (6–8), and even then the presence of a fracture does not necessarily imply the presence of a significant intracranial injury. The contrary also is true, for the absence of a fracture does not rule out a significant intracranial injury. Consequently, *the skull roentgenogram is of limited value unless some selection for its performance is devised.*

A plethora of articles (1–6, 9–12), have appeared in the literature and all attest to the fact that, unless a selection process is instituted, most skull roentgenograms obtained are of no clinical value. A summary of the criteria suggested by these various authors for the selection of patients requiring skull films is presented in Table 5.1. It might be added that these are the same criteria one could use for determining whether a patient should have a computerized tomographic (CT) scan. While it is true that skull films often provide a better overall view of the calvarial fracture configuration, CT scans provide invaluable information regarding intracranial injury (Fig. 5.1). For this reason use of the skull film in the acutely injured patient has decreased significantly.

Table 5.1. *Clinical Findings Predisposing to Skull Roentgenograms (or CT Examination)*

History
- Age less than 1 year*a*
- Unconsciousness or amnesia of greater than 5-min duration
- Gunshot wound or skull penetration
- Focal neurologic symptoms

Physical Examination
- Focal neurologic or ocular signs
- Skull depression; palpable or identified by probe
- CSF discharge from ear or nose
- Blood in middle ear
- Battle's sign
- Blackeye (hematoma)
- Lethargy, coma, or stupor

a With more severe trauma only.

REFERENCES

1. Bell, R.S., and Loop, J.W.: The utility and futility of radiographic skull examination for trauma. N. Engl. J. Med. 284: 236–239, 1971.
2. Boulis, Z.F., Dick, R., and Barnes, N.R.: Head injuries in children—aetiology, symptoms, physical findings and x-ray wastage. Br. J. Radiol. 51: 851–845, 1978.
3. Cummins, R.O.: Clinician's reasons for overuse of skull radiographs. A.J.R. 135: 549–552, 1980.
4. de Lacey, G., Guilding, A., Wignall, B., Reidy, J., and Bradbrook, S.: Mild head injuries: a source of excessive radiography? (analysis of a series and review of the literature). Clin. Radiol. 31: 457–462, 1980.
5. DeSmet, A.A., Fryback, D.G., and Thornbury, J.R.: A second look at the utility of radiographic skull examination for trauma. A.J.R. 132: 95–97, 1979.
6. Harwood-Nash, D.C., Hendrick, E.B., and Hudson, A.R.: The significance of skull fractures in children. A study of 1,187 patients. Radiology 101: 151–155, 1971.
7. Hendrick, E.B., Harwood-Nash, D.C., and Hudson, A.R.: Head injuries in children: a survey of 4,465 consecutive

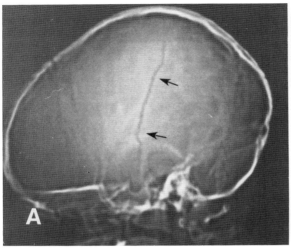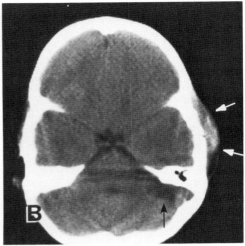

Figure 5.1. *Skull films and CT scanning.* (*A*) Scout film for CT scan demonstrates a clear-cut fracture (*arrows*). (*B*) The fracture is less well visualized on CT scanning, but it is more important to note the hematoma over the fracture (*white arrows*), and the area of contusion (subtle hypodensity), under the fracture. In addition, another area of hypodensity due to contusion is seen in the posterior fossa (*lower arrow*).

cases at the Hospital for Sick Children, Toronto, Canada. Clin. Neurosurg. 11: 46–65, 1974.

8. Jamison, D.L., and Kay, H.H.: Accidental head injury in childhood. Arch. Dis. Child. 49: 376–381, 1974.
9. Jennett, B.: Skull x-rays after recent head injury. Clin. Radiol. 31: 463–469, 1980.
10. Leonidas, J.C., Ting, W., Binkiewiez, A., Vas, R., Scott, R.M., and Pauker, S.G.: Mild head trauma in children: when is a roentgenogram necessary? Pediatrics 69: 139–143, 1982.
11. Masters, S.J.: Evaluation of head trauma: efficacy of skull films. A.J.R. 135: 539–547, 1980.
12. Newman, D.E.: Routine skull radiographs in children with seizures or head trauma. J. Can. Assoc. Radiol. 23: 234–235, 1977.

Which Skull Views Should Be Obtained? Generally speaking, *in the alert patient*, both lateral, a posteroanterior, and Towne's views suffice. If one also is assessing facial injuries, then a Waters' view should be included. In most instances, there is little reason to obtain a base of the skull view, but stereo lateral views can compliment the study if desired. Thereafter, if a fracture is visualized, one may require special projections such as tangential and oblique views to fully visualize the fracture. In the *patient who is not alert* or in the *patient in whom a neck injury also is suspected*, one should confine the initial study to cross-table lateral, anteriorposterior, and Towne's views; all obtained without moving the patient.

    Importance of Site and Type of Fracture. Much more important than the mere detection of a fracture is the determination

of the type and site of the fracture. For example, compound skull fractures and fractures through air-filled structures such as the paranasal sinuses and mastoid air cells are important because they can lead to complications such as meningitis and cerebrospinal fluid leaks. Depressed fractures are obviously important and definitely place the patient into a higher risk category (1, 4, 5). Most of these fractures require elevation and repair of underlying dural tears, and associated brain damage and long lasting complications such as focal seizures are a definite additional problem. Multiple calvarial fractures (eggshell fractures) as might be sustained in automobile accidents or from falls on the head from great heights are of obvious significance, and likewise, linear fractures traversing vascular structures such as the middle meningeal artery and deep venous sinuses are more significant than the same linear fractures not traversing these sites. Base of skull fractures also are generally considered more significant fractures, for they tend to extend into the mastoid air cells, sphenoid sinus, cribriform plate, ethmoid sinuses, nasal cavity, or foramen magnum.

    Can One Predict the Site and Type of Fracture from the Site and Type of Injury? There is usually good correlation of the site of fracture with the site of injury, for the contrecoup phenomenon associated with brain injury is not applicable to calvarial fractures. Restated, this simply says that if trauma occurs over the forehead, then the fracture is most likely to be in this location. This is not to say that the fracture line must lie precisely under the point of impact, but only that the fracture should be in the same general area. Of course, the smaller the object which delivers the blow to the calvarium, the more precisely will one be able to pinpoint the exact fracture site. For example, if the blow is delivered with a small, high velocity object such as a baseball bat, hammer or dashboard knob, the fracture usually lies immediately below the point of impact (Fig. 5.2*A*). On the other hand, if the blow is delivered by a broad surface, low velocity object such as the flat surface of a door, floor, or windshield, the fracture may be somewhat removed from the center of impact (Fig. 5.2*B*). The same general information is useful in predicting the actual type of fracture present. For example, in the first instance, when a small, high velocity object

delivers the blow, the fracture often is focally depressed, while in the other instance, linear, or broad curvilinear fractures result (Fig. 5.2). All of these considerations are important in the assessment of calvarial fractures, and the specific types of fractures produced are dealt with in later sections.

How Important Is the Mode of Injury? The mode of injury is most important for often it leads to information regarding severity of injury. For example, an infant falling backward and striking his occiput on a well cushioned floor represents a problem very different from an infant falling backward on a concrete floor, sidewalk, or the edge of a sink or bathtub. Clearly, one would not expect a fracture in the first instance, but in the latter case, the possibility of calvarial fracturing is much higher. Consequently, it is most important to determine just how the patient was injured for it may well foretell the type and site of fracture.

Types of Fractures Seen. As stated earlier, the type of fracture depends on the

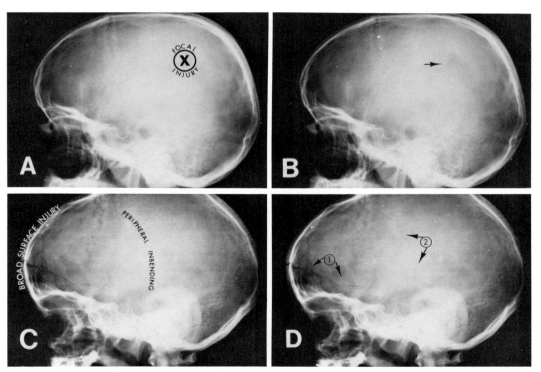

Figure 5.2. *Fracture mechanics.* (*A* and *B*) *Focal injury.* High velocity focal injury results in dissipation of forces over a small area (×). The resulting fracture is a small, stellate depressed fracture (*arrow*). (*C* and *D*) *Broad surface injury.* High velocity broad surface injury results in a central, diastatic, "V"-shaped fracture (*1*), and a more peripheral curvilinear arc-like fracture at the zone of peripheral inbending (*2*).

mode of injury, but generally speaking, one can encounter linear, curvilinear, stellate, eggshell, and depressed fractures, and fractures causing diastasis of the cranial sutures. ***Linear fractures*** are, perhaps, the most common type of fracture encountered (Fig. 5.3*A*), and some may be more difficult to see on one

view than another. When linear fractures result from greater forces, they often spread at the end closest to the point of impact, and the fracture assumes a V-shaped configuration (Fig. 5.3*B*). Another interesting feature of these fractures is that they usually do not cross sutures (Fig. 5.3*B*).

Linear fractures which are not widely dia-

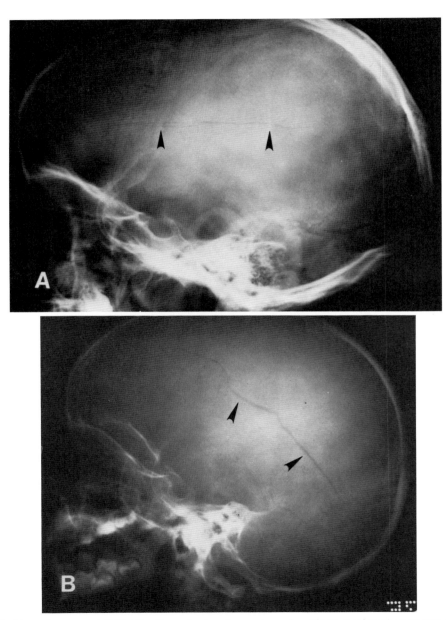

Figure 5.3. *Linear fractures.* (*A*) Hairline linear fracture (*arrows*) crossing middle meningeal artery area anteriorly. (*B*) Slightly diastatic linear fracture (*arrows*). Note that the fracture is wider in the center than at either end, and note that the fracture stops at the coronal and lambdoid sutures.

static are not a cause for alarm unless they: (a) cross a critical area such as the middle meningeal artery groove or the deep venous sinuses, or (b) they extend into the paranasal sinuses or mastoid air cells. When they cross a vascular structure, intracranial bleeding can be a problem, and when they extend into the paranasal sinuses or mastoid air cells, meningitis can be a complication. If linear fractures are widely diastatic, they often are associated with underlying dural or meningeal tears, subdural hematomas, or cerebral injury (Fig. 5.4). In those cases where a dural tear only occurs, the leptomeninges may herniate through the tear and cause the fracture to become progressively wider. This often is termed the **_growing fracture_** and eventually, the bulging, pulsating

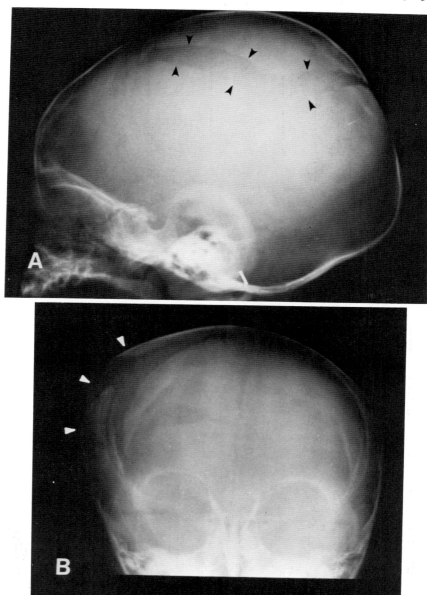

Figure 5.4. *Widely diastatic linear fracture.* (*A*) Note the widely diastatic fracture (*arrows*) on this lateral view. (*B*) Frontal view demonstrating how the bone edges have been displaced outwardly and how the cranial contents bulge outward (*arrows*).

leptomeningial sac causes calvarial erosion, and a round or oval, scalloped calvarial defect around a ***leptomeningeal cyst*** (2) (Figs. 5.5 and 5.6).

Broad, curvilinear fractures, that is fractures with a broad, peripheral arc usually result from high velocity, broad surface injuries and the curvilinear arc-like portion of the fracture outlines the peripheral most points of bony inbending (4). In many cases,

these peripheral curvilinear fractures are associated with linear fractures originating from the point of impact (see Fig. 5.2*B*). ***Stellate fractures*** are classic examples of such a fracture in that the fracture lines radiate from the center of impact, and circumferentially a peripheral arc demarcates the zones of maximal inbending. Because of this, these fractures usually are depressed (Fig. 5.7).

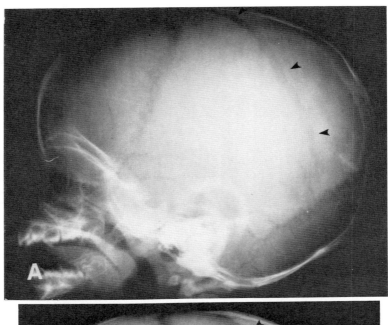

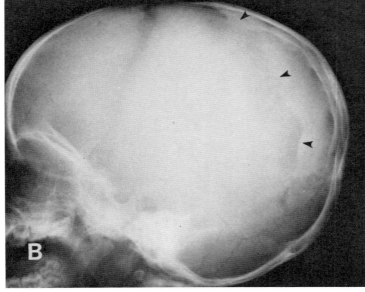

Figure 5.5. *Diastatic fracture with subsequent leptomeningeal cyst.*   (*A*) Note the moderately diastatic linear fracture of the parietal bone (*arrows*). (*B*) Months later note how the fracture has grown, and how its edges have become scalloped (*arrows*). These findings are characteristic of a leptomeningeal cyst.

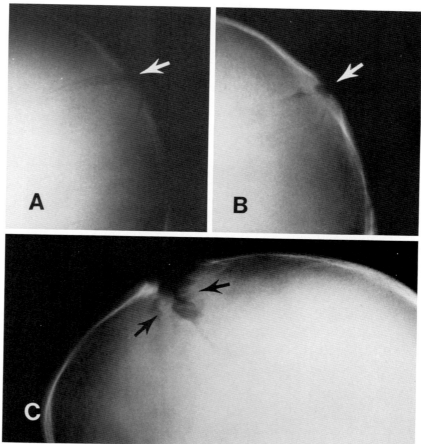

Figure 5.6. *Leptomeningeal cysts, varying configurations.* (*A*) Note initial fracture (*arrow*). (*B*) Months later, note a small leptomeningeal cyst (*arrow*). (*C*) Large leptomeningeal cyst (*arrows*). (Fig. *C* courtesy of Virgil Graves, M.D., Great Falls, Montana.)

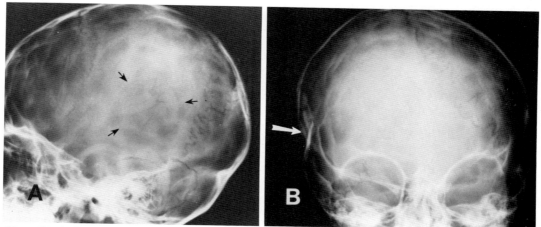

Figure 5.7. *Stellate-depressed skull fracture.* (*A*) Note the round peripheral zone of inbending producing a complete circle (*arrows*). Also note stellate fractures radiating outward from the center of the circle. (*B*) Frontal view. Note degree of depression of the central fragments (*arrow*).

With *depressed fractures*, the injury usually results from: (a) high velocity impacts dissipating their forces over a relatively small area of the skull (i.e., injuries sustained from baseball bats, hammers, dashboard knobs, etc.), and (b) high velocity broad surface blows. In those cases where the impact site is over a small area, a relatively small stellate-peripheral arc type of fracture results (Fig. 5.7). Very often these fractures are visualized better on one view than the other, and tangential views are required for adequate evaluation of the degree of depression (Fig. 5.7). When seen en face, sclerosis along the edge of one of the fracture fragments, undue widening of the space between two fracture fragments, or disproportionate widening of the peripheral arc portion of the fracture can serve to alert one to the presence of the depressed aspect of these fractures

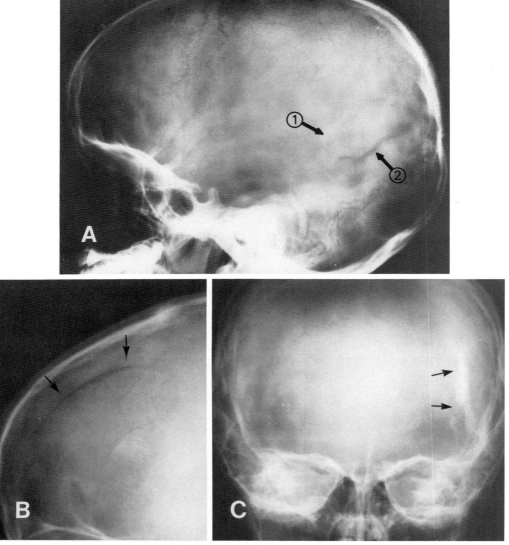

Figure 5.8. *Depressed fractures—other findings.* (*A*) Stellate, depressed fracture similar to the one demonstrated in Figure 5.7. Note the area of increased sclerosis due to overlapping of the bony fragments (*1*), and the radiolucent, diastatic portion (*2*), of this circular, depressed fracture. Also note the diastatic, central stellate limbs of this typically depressed fracture. (*B*) Note the curvilinear frontal bone fracture (*arrows*) and that it is wider in the center than at either end. This denotes depression. (*C*) Frontal view demonstrating the profound degree of depression of the central fragment (*arrows*). The degree of depression is not suspected from the lateral view in (*B*).

(Fig. 5.8). Nonetheless, it cannot be overstated that depressed fractures can be most elusive on the en face view and in such cases, one must learn to suspect the slightest degree of sclerosis, disproportionate radiolucency, etc., and then to pursue these findings with tangential views (Fig. 5.9). In terms of the tangential view, in many cases it is nothing more than the view obtained at right angles to the en face view, but in other instances, the head must be rotated through a number of degrees before the fracture is visualized on tangent.

With depressed fractures resulting from broad area injuries, the stellate peripheral arc appearance is replaced by irregular rectangular- or triangular-shaped bony fragments seen at various angles (Fig. 5.10). Because these fragments are rotated and tilted, one or more may appear unduly sclerotic, or once again one side of a fragment will be sclerotic (overlap) while the other wide and radiolucent (diastasis). The most common normal finding to be misinterpreted for a depressed fracture is a normal inner table convolutional marking. These can occur anywhere over the calvarium (Fig. 5.11).

Depressed fractures also are readily demonstrable with CT, and the study also is obtained before surgical correction is attempted (Fig. 5.12).

Diastatic Sutural Fractures. Diastatic sutural fractures can occur in isolated form or in association with a linear fracture. In these latter cases, the fracture often runs directly into the suture (Fig. 5.13). Diastatic sutural fractures can involve any suture but are especially prone to occur in the posterior fossa, where unilateral sutural spread can serve to alert one to the presence of underlying intracranial injury (Fig. 5.14). ***Generalized sutural diastasis*** in the young infant or young child with a closed head injury is a common problem, and can occur with or without associated fracturing of the calvarium (Fig. 5.15). In explaining this phenomenon, it is most likely that the sutures spread because of an associated acute increase in cerebral mass due to post-traumatic hyperemia. Indeed, this has been shown to be the most common intracranial manifestation of head trauma in childhood (5). Of course, generalized sutural diastasis also can be seen with other intracranial space-occupying problems such as subdural or epidural hematomas, but spread due to post-traumatic hyperemia alone, I believe, is quite common. Such edema is quite readily demonstrable with CT scanning (Fig. 5.16).

Of clinical interest in these infants is that even though the sutures are spread, relatively few symptoms are present. I have never been able to completely explain this phenomenon, but presumably the calvarium's ability to accommodate acute pressure secondary to the increased cerebral mass allows for the general paucity of symptoms. On follow-up

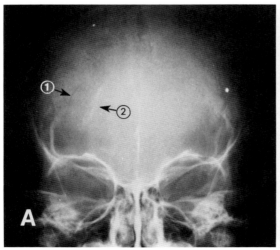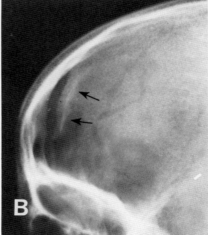

Figure 5.9. *Depressed fracture—subtle findings.* (*A*) Once again, note the combination of a central vertical radiolucent line (*1*), and a vertical area of increased sclerosis just medial to it (*2*). These findings represent a depressed fracture. (*B*) Lateral, tangential view more clearly demonstrates the depressed fracture fragment (*arrows*).

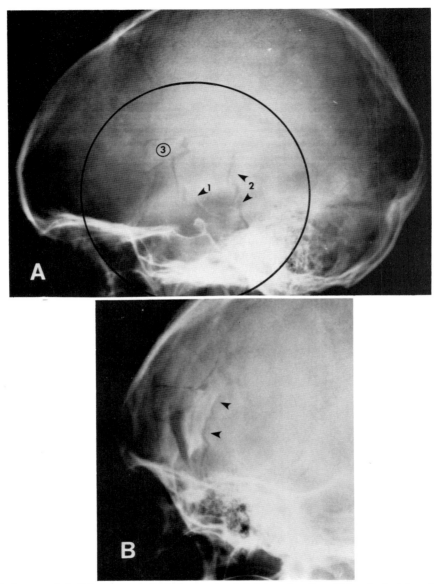

Figure 5.10. *Depressed skull fracture—multiple fragments.* (*A*) A broad surface, high velocity injury has resulted in a mosaic pattern of depressed fracture fragments (*large circle*). Note linear sclerosis due to overlapping (*1*), diastasis due to depression (*2*), and a generalized increase in density of one of the fragments due to depression and tangential positioning (*3*). (*B*) Tangential view demonstrating the degree of depression of one of the fragments (*arrows*). Depression of this fragment causes the fracture to appear wide and radiolucent.

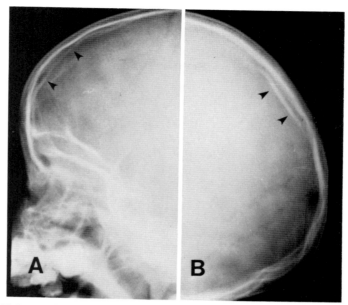

Figure 5.11. *(A and B) Inner table convolutions—"pseudodepressed" fractures.*   Note frontal and posterior parietal inner table sclerosis mimicking fracture fragment depression (*arrows*).

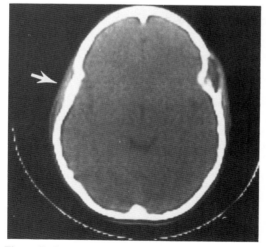

Figure 5.12. *Depressed fracture—CT scan.*   Note depressed fracture (*arrow*).

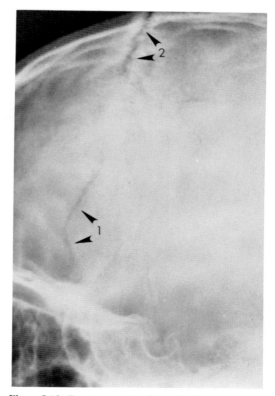

Figure 5.13. *Fracture causing diastasis of suture.*   Note the fracture (*1*) in the lower frontal parietal region. Then note associated spread (diastasis) of the ipsilateral coronal suture (*2*). The radiolucent line above the sella is the normal groove of the middle meningeal artery.

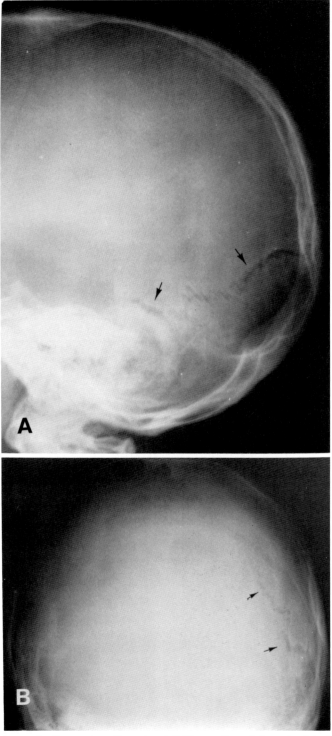

Figure 5.14. *Unilateral posterior fossa suture diastasis.* (*A*) Note unilateral diastasis of the lambdoid and parieto-mastoid sutures (*arrows*). (*B*) Towne's projection confirms unilateral spreading of these sutures (*arrows*). No fracture, however, is present.

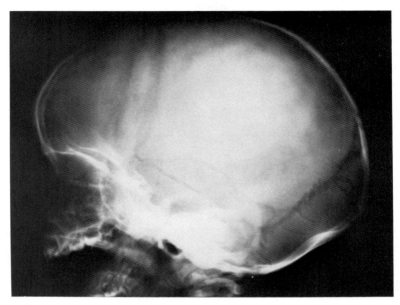

Figure 5.15. *Generalized suture diastasis.* This infant suffered a blow to the head. No fractures were detected but all of the sutures showed moderate spreading. The linear lines extending posteriorly from the lambdoid and occipitomastoid sutures are normal Mendosal and other accessory sutures. They are not fractures.

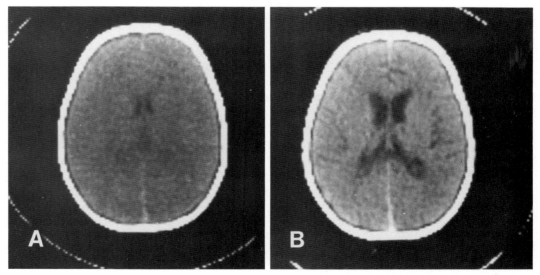

Figure 5.16. *CT scan; brain edema.* (*A*) Note virtual absence of visualization of the sulci and subarachnoid spaces. The ventricles are small. (*B*) Months later the ventricles have dilated and the sulci are prominent, attesting to the development of atrophy.

films a few weeks later, all of these sutures returned to normal, unless, that is, a lesion such as a persistent subdural hematoma is present.

Finally, a few comments on the so-called *eggshell fracture of the calvarium* are in order. This fracture presents a startling roentgenographic picture (Fig. 5.17, *A* and *B*), and obviously, in most of these cases the fracture is not a surprise. However, there is one practical aspect to these fractures, and that is that they should not be confused with similar roentgenographic findings in normal infants with numerous intraparietal accessory sutures (Fig. 5.17, *C* and *D*). With these latter patients, there often is a discrepancy between the clinical history and the apparent extent of calvarial fracturing. However, roentgenographic differentiation often still

is a problem, but it is of some assistance to note that multiple intraparietal accessory sutures usually are very symmetrical (Fig. 5.17*D*).

When Should Follow-up Films Be Obtained? Generally speaking, the mere presence of a linear fracture does not mandate a follow-up roentgenogram. However, widely diastatic fractures, or even mildly diastatic fractures, should be followed up with repeat roentgenograms a few weeks or months later. The reason for this is to check for the development of a post-traumatic leptomeningeal cyst (see Fig. 5.6). Of course, these cysts often are first suspected clinically (i.e., soft, pulsatile, bulge in palpable), but before such a cyst becomes palpable, the radiologist often will be able to detect that the fracture is spreading.

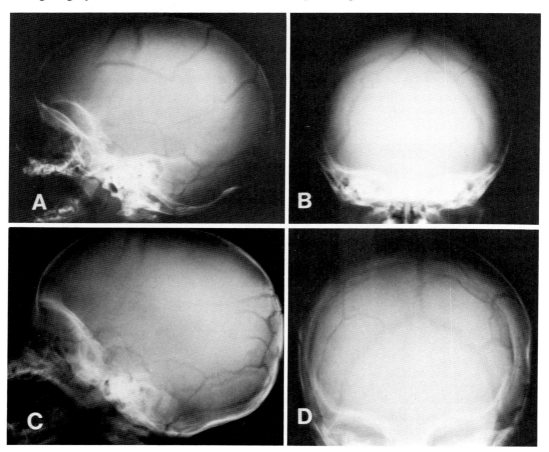

Figure 5.17. *Eggshell fracture versus multiple intraparietal fissures.* (*A* and *B*) *Eggshell fracture.* On the lateral view note the numerous, moderately diastatic fractures and generalized spreading of the sutures. On frontal view note asymmetry of the fractures. (*C* and *D*) *Multiple intraparietal fissures.* Note fracture-like appearance of the numerous intraparietal fissures on lateral view. On frontal view note how symmetric these accessory fissures are.

REFERENCES

1. Genieser, N., and Becker, M.: Head trauma in children. Radiol. Clin. North Am. 12: 333–342, 1974.
2. Gugliantini, P., Caione, P., Fariello, G., and Rivosecchi, M.: Post traumatic leptomeningeal cysts in infancy. Pediatr. Radiol. 9: 11–14, 1980.
3. Gurdjian, E.S., Webster, J.E., and Lissner, H.R.: The mechanism of skull fracture. Radiology 54: 313–339, 1950.
4. Swischuk, L.E.: Childhood head injuries and skull roentgenogram. Pediatr. Ann. 4: 639–649, 1975.
5. Zimmerman, R.A., Bilaniuk, L.T., Bruce, D., Dolinskas, C., Obrist, W., and Kuhl, D.: Computed tomography of pediatric head trauma: acute general cerebral swelling. Radiology 126: 403–408, 1978.

Intracranial Manifestations of Head Injuries. Intracranial manifestations of head injuries are numerous and consist of acute epidural hematomas, acute subdural hematomas, vascular lacerations and aneurysms, cerebral contusions, intracerebral bleeds, focal or generalized cerebral edema, and traumatic pneumocephalus (1, 9, 11). Except for evidence of traumatic pneumocephalus (Fig. 5.18), one usually must resort to studies other than plain films for delineation of these complications, and today, most often the study is CT. Indeed, even intracranial air is more readily demonstrable with CT scanning (Fig. 5.19).

Although eventually, arteriography often is required in certain cases, contrast-enhanced CT scanning usually provides most of the information required (2, 4, 6, 12, 13, 17). This modality has been especially useful in detecting occult, intracranial damage in the battered child syndrome (3, 7, 8, 15, 16).

CT scanning, of course, is excellent in delineating subdural, epidural, and intracerebral hematomas (Fig. 5.21). Contusions and edema also are readily demonstrable (Fig. 5.22), and in addition, evidence of subarachnoid bleeding, in the form of increased density along the falx or tentorium (5), can be seen (Fig. 5.22B).

In terms of subdural hematomas, it should be remembered that, midway through their course, they may appear isodense (see Fig. 5.21C). Under such circumstances they may be missed unless one notices other findings such as ventricular shift. Of course, if the subdurals are bilateral, shift may not be present. Rapid high dose contrast CT scanning has been suggested to circumvent this problem (10). Isodense subdural hematomas also are the problem in anemic patients, where the generally decreased iron content of the blood leads to the problem (14).

As far as the calvarium is concerned, CT scanning, as noted earlier, is very useful in delineating depressed skull fractures (see Fig.

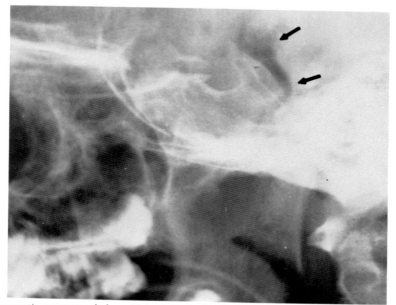

Figure 5.18. *Traumatic pneumocephalus.* Note air in the basal cistern (*arrows*). Also note that the sphenoid sinus has been obliterated by blood. Also note disruption of the base of the skull just anterior to the anterior clinoids and unilateral depression of one of the anterior fossa floors.

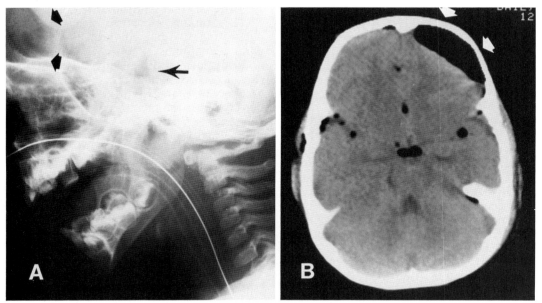

Figure 5.19. *Intracranial air—CT scan.* (*A*) Cross-table lateral view demonstrates large collection of air in the frontal region (*anterior arrows*). Air also is seen in the middle fossa (*single arrow*). (*B*) CT scan study more vividly demonstrates the large collection of air over the frontal region (*arrows*), and scattered throughout the subarachnoid spaces.

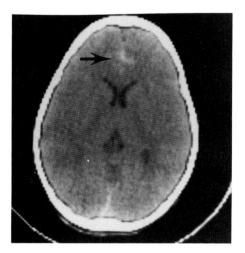

Figure 5.20. *Closed head injury—CT demonstrates contrecoup injury.* This patient had injury to the occiput. Note swelling of the scalp over the occiput. However, also note an area of hemorrhage (*arrow*) anteriorly.

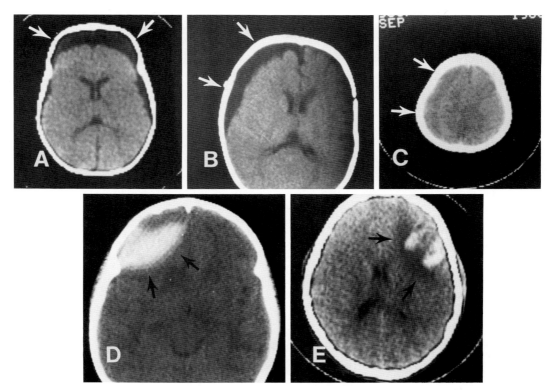

Figure 5.21. *CT scan—intracranial injury.* (*A*) Note extensive bilateral subdural hematomas in a battered child (*arrows*). (*B*) Unilateral subdural hematoma (*arrows*) with contralateral shift of the brain structures. (*C*) Nearly isodense subdural hematoma (*arrows*). (*D*) Typical epidural hematoma (*arrows*). (*E*) Intracerebral hematoma (*arrows*), with surrounding edema (hypodensity) and slight displacement of the ventricles to the other side.

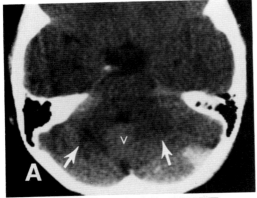

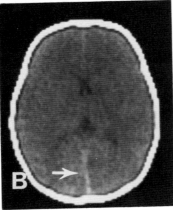

Figure 5.22. *CT findings; intracranial injury.* (*A*) Note contusion (hypodensity), of both lobes of the cerebellum (*arrows*). The normal vermis (*V*) is the dense structure in between. (*B*) Note generalized edema with failure of visualization of the sulci. The ventricles are a little small. In addition note bleeding along the interhemispheric fissure posteriorly (*arrow*).

5.12), but in addition may reveal bony displacement in regular fractures, not recognized on plain films (Fig. 5.23).

REFERENCES

1. Arkins, T.J., McLennan, J.E., Winston, K.R., Strand, R.D., and Suzuki, Y.: Acute posterior fossa epidural hematomas in children. Am. J. Dis. Child. 131: 690–692, 1977.
2. Bruce, D.A., and Schut, L.: The value of CAT scanning following pediatric head injury. Clin. Pediatr. 19: 719–725, 1980.
3. Caffey, J.: The whiplash shaken infant syndrome; manual shaking by the extremities with whiplash-induced intracranial and intraocular bleedings, linked with residual permanent brain damage and mental retardation. Pediatrics 54: 396–403, 1974.
4. Davis, K.R., Taveras, J.M., Roberson, G.H., Acherman, R.H., and Dreisbach, J.N.: Computed tomography in head trauma. Semin. Roentgenol. 12: 53–62, 1977.
5. Dolinskas, C.A., Zimmerman, R.A., and Bilaniuk, L.T.: A sign of subarachnoid bleeding on cranial computed tomograms of pediatric head trauma patients. Radiology, 126: 409–411, 1978.
6. Dublin, A.B., French, B.N., and Rennick, J.M.: Computed tomography in head trauma. Radiology 122: 365–370, 1977.
7. Ellison, P.H., Tsai, F.Y., and Largent, J.A.: Computed tomography in child abuse and cerebral contusion. Pediatrics 62: 151–154, 1978.
8. Guthkelch, A.N.: Infantile subdural hematoma and its relationship to whiplash injuries. Br. Med. J. 2: 430–431, 1971.
9. Harwood-Nash, D.C.: Craniocerebral trauma in children. Curr. Probl. Radiol. 3: 3–24, 1973.
10. Hayman, L.A., Evans, R.A., and Hinck, V.C.: Rapid-high-dose contrast computed tomography of isodense subdural hematoma and cerebral swelling. Radiology 131: 381–383, 1979.
11. Kahn, R.J., and Daywitt, A.L.: Traumatic pneumocephalus. A.J.R. 90: 1171–1175, 1963.
12. Koo, A.H., and LaRoque, R.L.: Evaluation of the head trauma by computed tomography. Radiology 123: 345–350, 1977.
13. Merino-deVillasante, J., and Taveras, J.M.: Computerized tomography (CT) in acute head trauma. A.J.R. 126: 765–778, 1976.

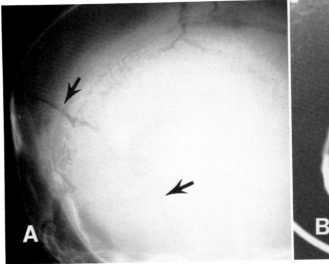

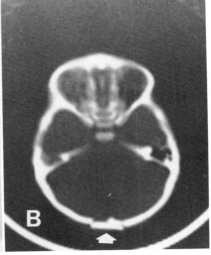

Figure 5.23. *CT scan; fracture information.* (*A*) Note the ordinary appearing parieto-occipital fracture (*arrows*). (*B*) CT scan demonstrates that the fracture fragment is outwardly displaced (*arrow*).

14. Smith, W.P., Jr., Batnitzky, S., and Rengachary, S.S.: Acute isodense subdural hematomas: a problem in anemic patients. A.J.R. 136: 543–546, 1981.
15. Touddry, M., LeFrancois, M.C., LeMarc, B., Gandon, Y., Carsin, M., and Senecal, J.: Computed tomography of the skull on the battered child. Ann. Radiol. 25: 237–243, 1982.
16. Tsai, F.Y., Zee, C.-S., Apthrop, J.S., and Dixon, G.H.: Computed tomography in child abuse head trauma. CT 4: 277–286, 1980.
17. Zimmerman, R.A., Bilaniuk, L.T., Gennarelli, T., Bruce, D., Dolinskas, C., and Uzzell, B.: Cranial computed tomography in diagnosis and management of acute head trauma. A.J.R. 131: 27–34, 1978.

BASAL SKULL FRACTURES

Fractures through the base of the skull often are most difficult to detect roentgenographically. Clinically, they can be suspected when nasal discharge of cerebral spinal fluid is present or when there is bleeding from the ear or blood behind the eardrum. Roentgenographically, when looking for these fractures it is best to divide the skull into three zones: (a) the anterior fossa, (b) the middle fossa, and (c) the posterior fossa. Fractures through the *floor of the anterior fossa* frequently involve the orbital roofs and are best visualized on frontal views. In such cases, discontinuity of the cortex of the roof of the orbit, a clearly visible fracture line, or a depressed orbital fracture fragment usually alert one to the problem (Fig. 5.24). In other instances, air may be present in the orbit (i.e., from the adjacent paranasal sinuses), or decreased aeration, or an air-fluid level, may be noted in the adjacent paranasal si-

nuses. On lateral view, these fractures can be seen to extend through the cribriform plate into the ethmoid sinuses (Fig. 5.25, *A* and *B*), but they are not always easy to detect. Furthermore, they must be differentiated from the normal, unfused planum sphenoidale (7), a commonly occurring "pseudofracture" in this area (Fig. 5.25C).

Fractures through the *floor of the middle fossa* also often are frequently best visualized on frontal projection but, of course, also are visible on lateral view. Many of these fractures also extend into the region of the sella turcica (1, 2), and one may see complete disruption of the sella, fracturing through the various sellar structures, or an air-fluid level in the sphenoid sinus (Fig. 5.26). The air-fluid levels, of course, usually are visualized on cross-table lateral views of the skull, and the fluid represents blood in the sphenoid sinuses. If air from the sphenoid sinuses escapes into the calvarium, one may see air in the basal cisterns (see Fig. 5.18).

Fractures through the *posterior fossa floor* involve the temporal bone and may be associated with hearing and equilibrium problems (3). In some cases one can clearly see the linear fracture extending through the temporal bone (Fig. 5.27), but in other cases one first is alerted to the problem by the presence of unilateral opacification of the mastoid air cells only. Obliteration of the mastoid air cells is due to bleeding, and even if a fracture is not visible, the presence of

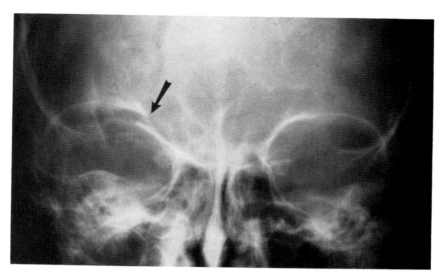

Figure 5.24. *Anterior fossa floor fracture; frontal view.* Note depressed superorbital (anterior fossa floor) fracture (*arrow*).

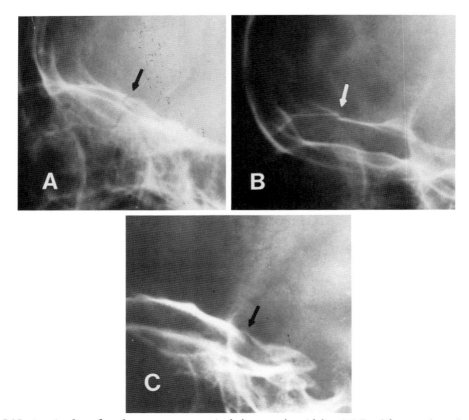

Figure 5.25. *Anterior fossa floor fracture versus ununited planum sphenoidale.* (*A*) Basal fracture through anterior fossa floor. Note the irregular radiolucent fracture (*arrow*) extending into the ethmoid sinus. (*B*) Another basal fracture (*arrow*). (*C*) Normal defect (*arrow*) due to *unfused planum sphenoidale.*

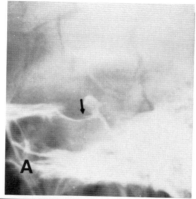

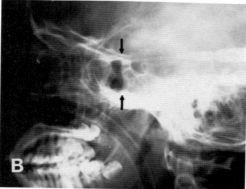

Figure 5.26. *Middle fossa basal fractures.* (*A*) Injured patient demonstrating a barely discernable fracture extending to the base of the skull (*arrow*). (*B*) Indirect evidence of a basal fracture extending into the sphenoid sinus is present in this patient, in the form of an air fluid level in the sphenoid sinus (*arrows*). This was a crosstable lateral view with the face pointing upward.

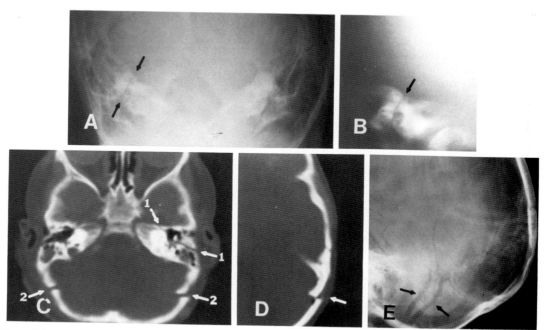

Figure 5.27. *Posterior fossa basal fractures.* (*A*) Note the fracture through the petrous bone on the right. Note also that the mastoid air cells are hazy due to bleeding. (*B*) Tomogram demonstrates the fracture to better advantage (*arrow*). (*C*) CT study in another patient demonstrates a basal fracture (*1*) and bilateral occipitomastoid sutural diastatic fractures (*2*). The one on the right is offset. Also note that both mastoid air cells are hazy due to bleeding. Another fracture was present on the other side, on another cut. (*D*) Slightly higher cut demonstrates pneumocephalus along the right occipitomastoid fracture (*arrow*). (*E*) X-ray demonstrates numerous occipital fractures and the bilateral occipitomastoid suture diastatic fractures (*arrows*).

such obliteration should cause one to assume that an occult fracture is present. Thereafter, clinical correlation will determine whether opacification is in fact due to acute bleeding or to the inflammatory changes of coincidental mastoid and middle ear infection. This, of course, is very important, for middle ear infections with mastoid involvement are common in children. Consequently, if one does not take the time to determine whether opacification of the air cells truly is due to bleeding, one will overdiagnose these injuries. Fractures through the tympanic portion of the temporal bone, or for that matter, any fracture through the temporal bone, usually is best detected with polytomography (3–6, 8). However, these studies usually are accomplished beyond the emergency setting.

The other common fracture of the base of the skull in the posterior fossa is the vertical occipital bone fracture. Most often these fractures are midline, but they may be set off to one side or the other (Fig. 5.28). The midline fracture must be differentiated from the fortuitous superimposition of the normally open metopic suture. In the latter instance, of course, the apparent fracture line will cross the foramen magnum, while with a true occipital bone fracture, the fracture line stops at the posterior lip of the foramen magnum (Fig. 5.29). These fractures also must be differentiated from the infrequently occurring, unusually prominent median occipital bone fissure. Normally these fissures are short and extend upward from the lip of the foramen magnum or downward from the region of the posterior fontanelle. However, in some cases these fissures are unusually long and misinterpreted for occipital bone fractures (see Fig. 5.33). Other occipital bone fractures are dealt with in a later section (see p. 522).

REFERENCES

1. Archer, C.R., and Sundaram, M.: Uncommon sphenoidal fractures and their sequelae. Radiology 122: 157–161, 1977.
2. Dublin, A.B., and Poirier, V.C.: Fracture of the sella turcica. A.J.R. 127: 969–972, 1976.
3. Harwood-Nash, D.C.: Fractures of the petrous and tympanic parts of the temporal bone in children. A.J.R. 110: 598–607, 1970.
4. Kaseff, L.G.: Tomographic evaluation of trauma to the temporal bone. Radiology 93: 321–327, 1969.
5. Potter, G.D.: Trauma of the temporal bone. Semin. Roentgenol. 4: 143–150, 1969.

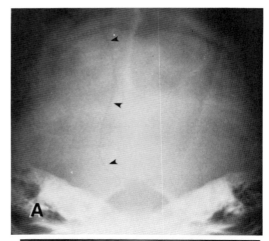

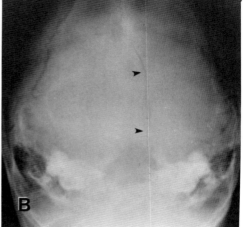

Figure 5.28. *Posterior occipital basal skull fractures.* (*A*) Note the typical appearance of a slightly diastatic occipital fracture (*arrows*). (*B*) Another patient demonstrating a thin linear posterior occipital fracture (*arrows*).

6. Roche, J.: Fractures of the temporal bone involving the ear. Aust. Radiol. 19: 317–325, 1975.
7. Smith, T.R., and Kier, E.L.: The unfused planum sphenoidale: Differentiation from fracture. Radiology 98: 305–309, 1971.
8. Wright, J.W.: Trauma to the ear. Radiol. Clin. North Am. 12: 527–532, 1974.

FRACTURES VERSUS NORMAL SUTURES, FISSURES, AND VASCULAR GROOVES

So common is the problem of a normal suture, fissure or vascular groove mimicking a fracture, that it is just as important to be familiar with these structures as with the fractures themselves. In this regard, it is best to become familiar with the direction in which these normal sutures, fissures, and vascular grooves travel (1, 8–10). The sutures and fissures, more than the vascular

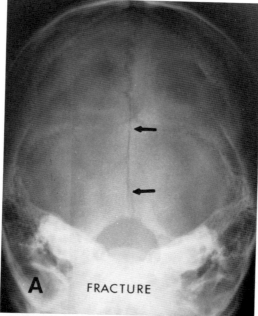

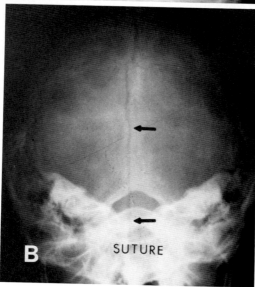

Figure 5.29. *Midline occipital fracture versus metopic suture.* (*A*) Note the typical appearance of a midline occipital fracture (*arrows*). Note that it stops at the posterior lip of the foramen magnum. (*B*) Metopic suture mimicking occipital fracture (*arrows*). Note that the metopic suture crosses the foramen magnum.

grooves, are remarkably consistent from patient to patient and almost always appear in the same place with the same degree of rotation. Consequently, if one sees a radiolucent line which does not conform to the site and location of one of these structures, then one should consider it to represent a fracture. These normal variations are considered in three general areas: (a) the frontal region, (b) the temperoparietal region, and (c) the occipital region.

Frontal Region Fractures and Pseudofractures. One of the most common structures misinterpreted for a fracture in the frontal bone is the vascular groove produced by the supraorbital branch of the ophthalmic artery. The problem is not so great on frontal view (Fig. 5.30), but on lateral view, often it is almost impossible to differentiate the two (Figs. 5.31 and 5.32). However, a few general rules can be applied: (a) most vascular grooves are located in the anterior third of the frontal bone, (b) most vascular grooves run in a vertical fashion with a gentle, posterior curve, (c) vascular grooves tend to have sclerotic edges while fractures have sharp nonsclerotic edges, and (d) vascular grooves seldom run in a horizontal or anteriorly sloping direction.

Another problem arising in the anterior fossa, but this time on frontal view, is the misinterpretation of a persistently open metopic suture (11) for a fracture. This suture commonly is open in children, and to the unwary will suggest a midline frontal bone fracture (Fig. 5.33*A*). This is an even greater problem if the suture is partially closed (Fig. 5.33*B*). The metopic suture also is notorious for mimicking an occipital bone fracture on Towne's projection (see Fig. 5.29*B*). A less common problem in the frontal region, on lateral view, is the misinterpretation of the fissure representing the unfused planum sphenoidale (7) for a basal, anterior fossa floor skull fracture (see Fig. 5.25*C*).

Temporoparietal Region Fractures and Pseudofractures. In terms of vascular grooves in this portion of the skull, it is the outer table groove of one of the branches of the superficial temporal artery which causes most problems (Fig. 5.34). In some of these cases, these vascular grooves virtually defy distinction from fractures except, perhaps, that very often the grooves show sclerosis

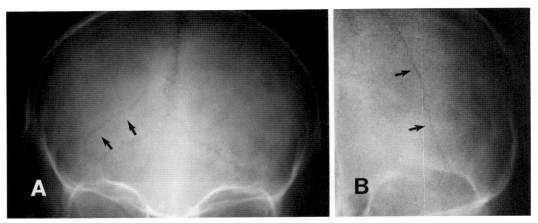

Figure 5.30. *Frontal vascular groove versus fracture.*   (*A*) Note the radiolucent line resulting from a normal frontal vascular groove (*arrows*). (*B*) Thin, long radiolucent line representing a frontal fracture extending into the left orbital roof (*arrows*). Distinction between a vascular groove and fracture on frontal view is not difficult.

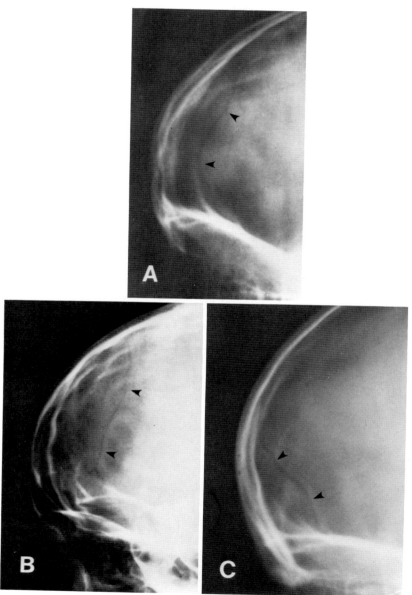

Figure 5.31. *Frontal vascular grooves—lateral view.* (*A*) Note typical appearance of a vascular groove in the frontal region (*arrows*). Characteristically it assumes a gentle posteriorly curving course. (*B*) Another vascular groove, somewhat less typical (*arrows*), and one which might easily be misinterpreted for a frontal bone fracture. (*C*) Unusual direction of another normal vascular groove (*arrows*). However, in this case the slight sclerosis along the edge of the groove identifies it as a vascular groove.

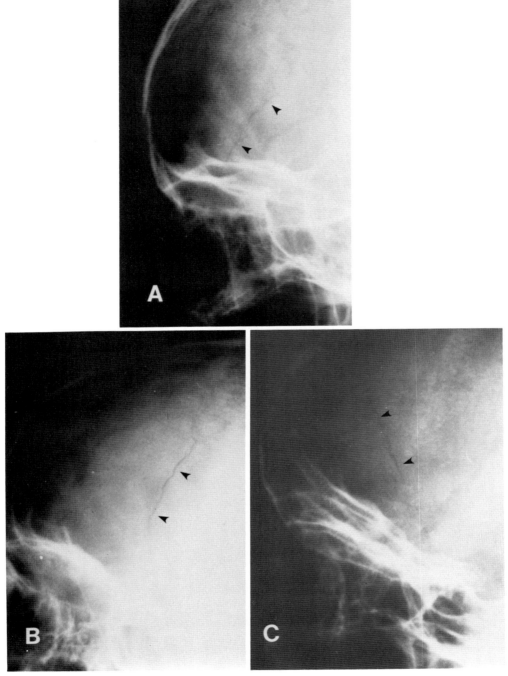

Figure 5.32. *Frontal bone fractures—lateral view.* (*A*) Note the thin radiolucent line representing a frontal bone fracture (*arrows*). Its gentle posterior curving course could cause one to misinterpret it for a vascular groove. A true vascular groove of the middle meningeal artery lies just posterior to the fracture. (*B*) Frontal bone fracture located in the posterior third of the frontal bone (*arrows*). Frontal vascular grooves are quite uncommon in this area and fracture identification is easier. (*C*) Anteriorly sloping frontal fracture (*arrows*). Vascular grooves usually do not head in this direction.

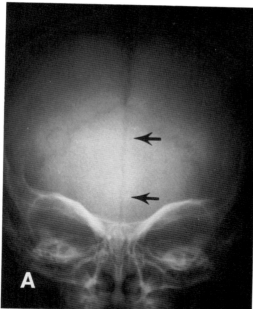

Figure 5.33. *Metopic suture—pseudofracture.* (*A*) Note the typical location of the metopic suture (*arrows*). (*B*) Partially obliterated meopic suture (*arrows*) extending from the anterior aspect of the anterior fontanelle. The fontanelle is not visualized on this reproduction. Note slight sclerosis along the suture edge, identifying it as a normal suture and not a fracture.

along their edges (Fig. 5.34*B*). These grooves can be seen all around the sellar region, and in addition, one also can encounter similar problems with the posterior branch of the middle meningeal artery (Fig. 5.34*A*). Parietal diploic vascular grooves are not easily confused with calvarial fractures nor are the inner table vascular grooves produced by the

main branches of the middle meningeal artery (Fig. 5.35). It is only when either of these vascular grooves is very thin that confusion with calvarial fractures can occur (Fig. 5.35).

As far as sutures in this area are concerned, although a number exist (Fig. 5.36), it is the squamosal suture which causes most difficulty. Indeed, with slight degrees of rotation of the calvarium, either from front to back or top to bottom, these sutures can appear so like a fracture that it is impossible to convince one that they represent a normal suture only (Fig. 5.37). This is less of a problem with the other sutures in the area (Fig. 5.37*C*). On frontal view, the squamosal suture also is a problem and commonly mimics a fracture (Fig. 5.38). Fortunately, however, almost always the sclerotic line along either side of the suture identifies it as such. Either the posterior or anterior limbs of the squamosal suture can present in this fashion.

In the young infant, accessory fissures along the posterior parietal bone can mimic small wedge-like linear fractures. Generally speaking, these fissures occur in the lower two-thirds of the parietal bone and often are multiple. In some cases, they are associated with a posterior parietal bony defect, the so-called third fontanelle (2). In analyzing these fissures, if they occur over the lower two-thirds of the parietal bone, and if no soft tissue swelling overlies them, then they most likely are nothing more than a normal fissure, but if they lie in the upper third of the posterior parietal bone, and soft tissue swelling overlies them, then a fracture is most likely (Fig. 5.39). This rule, of course, is not 100% foolproof, for obviously one can encounter fractures in the lower two-thirds of the parietal bone and normal fissures in the upper third, but still it is useful in a good many cases.

Another problem with accessory sutures in the parietal bone is the one concerned with so-called intraparietal sutures or fissures (5). The fissures have a great propensity to mimic parietal bone fractures, especially if they are unilateral (Fig. 5.40). However, it is of some aid to note that these fissures usually are relatively horizontal in position, and because of this if a vertical, radiolucent line is encountered, it should

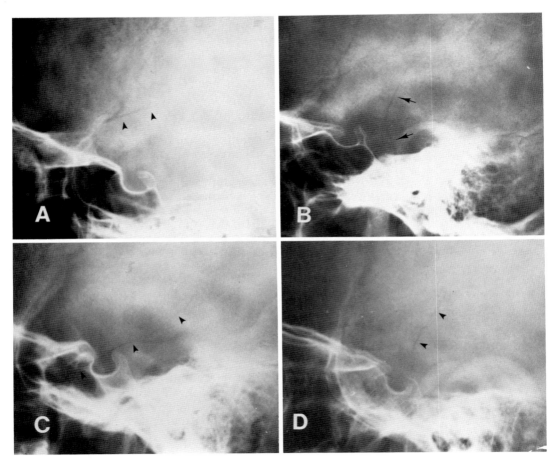

Figure 5.34. *Middle fossa vascular grooves versus fracture.* (*A*) Typical appearance of a vascular groove produced by the posterior branch of the middle meningeal artery (*arrows*). (*B*) Fracture-like appearance of a vascular groove produced by one of the branches of the superificial temporal artery (*arrows*). It would be difficult to differentiate this groove from a fracture. (*C*) True fracture (*arrows*) of the middle fossa. The fracture line is somewhat sharper than the vascular groove in (*B*) but still the two might be confused. (*D*) Small linear fracture in the lower parietal bone (*arrows*). Irregularity of the bone edges suggests a fracture.

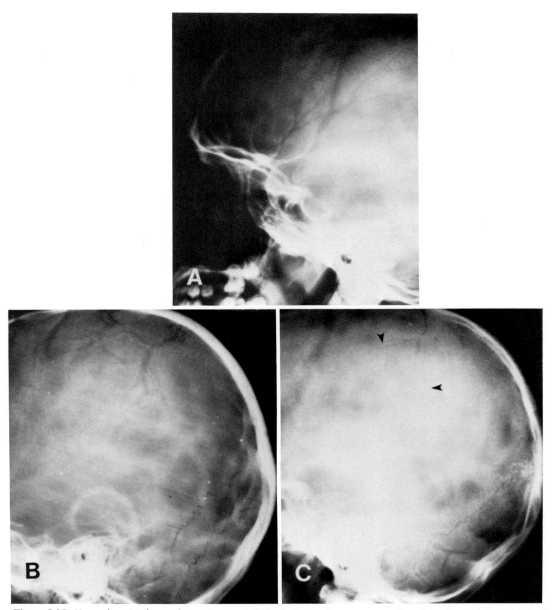

Figure 5.35. *Normal parietal vascular patterns.*   (*A*) Typical vascular grooves produced by the middle meningeal arteries and their branches. (*B*) Typical diploic venous vascularity in the upper parietal bone. (*C*) Small diploic venous channels in the upper parietal bone, some of which (*arrows*) could be misinterpreted for a fracture.

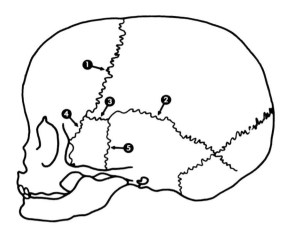

Figure 5.36. *Normal anterior and middle fossa sutures—diagrammatic representation.* Coronal suture (*1*), squamosal suture (*2*), sphenoparietal suture (*3*), sphenofrontal suture (*4*), and sphenosquamosal suture (*5*).

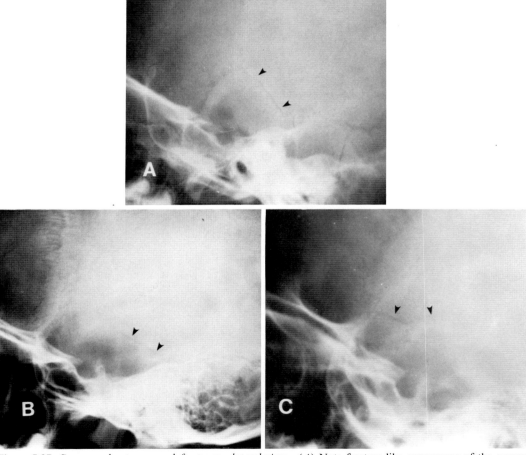

Figure 5.37. *Squamosal suture pseudofractures—lateral view.* (*A*) Note fracture-like appearance of the normal squamosal suture (*arrows*). The near vertical radiolucent line about an inch posteroinferior to it is the occipitomastoid suture which also appears fracture-like because of rotation of the skull. (*B*) Another normal squamosal suture (*arrows*) virtually indistinguishable from a fracture. (*C*) *Normal sphenoparietal suture* (*arrows*), mimicking a fracture. Compare these findings with true fractures in this area demonstrated in Figure 5.34, *C* and *D*.

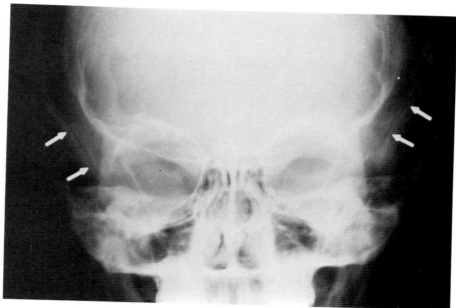

Figure 5.38. *Squamosal suture pseudofractures—frontal view.* In certain patients the anterior or posterior limbs of the squamosal suture can appear slit-like on frontal projection (*arrows*) and suggest a fracture. In this case, note typical sclerosis on either side of the radiolucent lines identifying them as normal squamosal sutures. On the left, both anterior and posterior limbs of the squamosal suture are demonstrated.

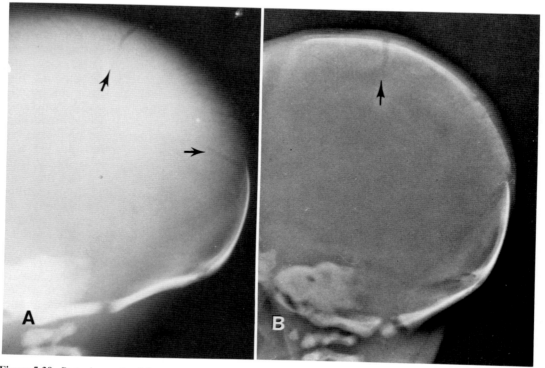

Figure 5.39. *Posterior parietal fissures versus fracture.* (*A*) Typical posterior parietal fissuring. This is a normal. Two of the fissures stand out more prominently (*arrows*), and either one could be misinterpreted for a fracture. (*B*) True parietal bone fracture (*arrow*). Note slight degree of soft tissue swelling over the fracture site. Reproduction enhanced to bring out soft tissues.

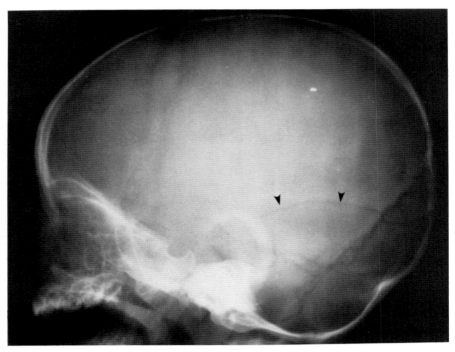

Figure 5.40. *Unilateral intraparietal fissure mimicking fracture.* Note the fracture-like appearance of this normal intraparietal fissure (*arrows*). All of the sutures in the occipital bone also are normal.

represent a fracture. In addition, if the radiolucent line truly represents a fracture, overlying soft tissue edema usually is present (Fig. 5.41). Of course, if the fissures are bilateral, and they commonly are, their remarkable symmetry usually serves to identify them correctly (Fig. 5.42). Nonetheless, when multiple, these sutures can mimic eggshell calvarial fractures (see Fig. 5.17).

Along the base of the skull, in the middle fossa, the only normal structures to be misinterpreted for fractures are the sphenooccipital and intersphenoid synchondroses (Fig. 5.43). The intersphenoid synchondrosis usually disappears by the age of 2 years (6), but the spheno-occipital synchondrosis remains patent until the late teens and early adulthood (4).

Occipital Region Fractures and Pseudofractures. The only vascular groove which can cause confusion in the occipital region of the skull is the groove for the mastoid emissary vein, but usually it is so tortuous that it offers no real problem. Sutures, on the other hand, are a significant problem in this area, for the occipital region of the skull is virtually cluttered with normal and accessory sutures and synchondroses (Fig. 5.44). Familiarity with all of them is mandatory for otherwise one is sure to misinterpret one of them for a fracture. On lateral view, the sutures most commonly visible are the lambdoid, parietomastoid, occipitomastoid, and Mendosal, while the visible synchondrosis is the innominate synchondrosis. The four sutures radiate outward from the region of the posterior-lateral fontanelle, but the Mendosal suture usually is visible in the infant and young child only. The problem with these sutures is not that they are difficult to identify in the average patient, but rather that with slight degrees of rotation any one of them can appear absolutely fracture-like (Fig. 5.45). This is not to say that true fractures do not occur in this area, for indeed they do (Fig. 5.46), and because of this one must be able to differentiate a fracture from a suture. In this regard, when one believes that a radiolucent line represents a normal suture, one should look for its mate on the other side. Whether this contralateral suture appears fracture-like or not, if only two radiolucent lines heading in the same direction are identified, then one can be

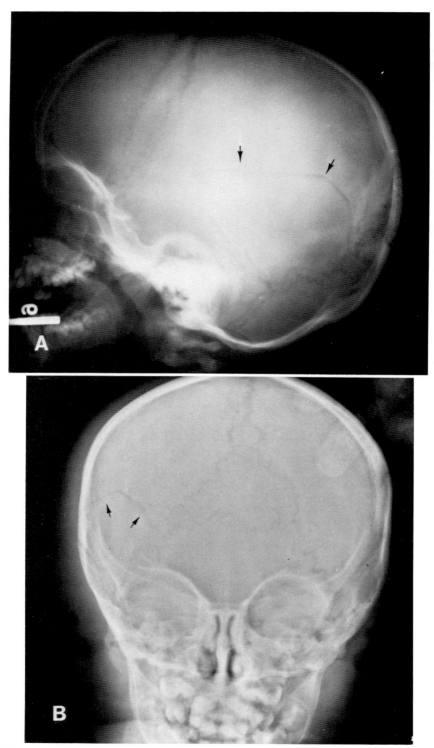

Figure 5.41. *Transverse parietal fracture..* (*A*) Note the transverse parietal bone fracture (*arrows*). Also note that all of the sutures show minimal diastasis. (*B*) Frontal view demonstrating the fracture (*arrows*). Also note extensive soft tissue edema over the right side of the calvarium. Such edema is not present with normal intraparietal accessory fissures. Frontal view altered to bring out soft tissues.

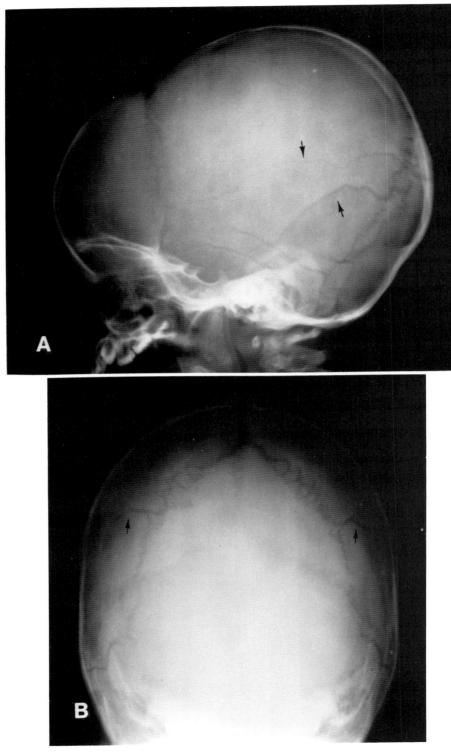

Figure 5.42. *Bilateral intraparietal accessory fissures.*   (*A*) Either one of these normal fissures can be misinterpreted for a fracture (*arrows*). (*B*) Frontal view demonstrating characteristic symmetry of these normal fissures (*arrows*).

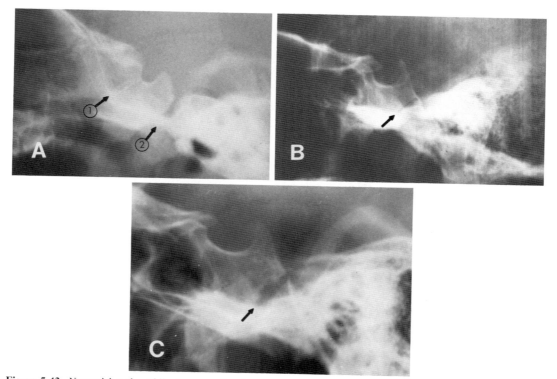

Figure 5.43. *Normal basal middle fossa synchondroses.* (*A*) Young infant. Note the typical appearance of the intersphenoid synchondrosis (*1*), and the wider spheno-occipital synchondrosis (*2*). (*B*) Older child demonstrating residual spheno-occipital synchondrosis (*arrow*) easily misinterpreted for a basal skull fracture. (*C*) Another patient with a very wide but normal spheno-occipital synchondrosis (*arrow*). (Fig. *C* courtesy of M. Kogutt, M.D., New Orleans.)

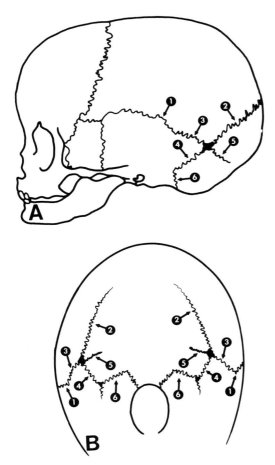

Figure 5.44. *Posterior fossa sutures—diagrammatic representation.* Lateral (*A*) and Towne's (*B*) projections. Squamosal suture (*1*), lambdoid suture (*2*), parietomastoid suture (*3*), occipitomastoid suture (*4*), Mendosal suture (*5*), and innominate synchondrosis complex (*6*).

should be considered a fracture. In addition, of course, if a radiolucent line is located in a totally unexpected place, a fracture should be considered.

In addition to these problems, the occipital bone also is prone to irregular ossification over the posterior lip of the foramen magnum. Furthermore, the median occipital fissure (*3*) visualized just below the posterior fontanelle commonly is misinterpreted for a fracture. This fissure usually is seen in young infants only and usually it is not more than a centimeter or centimeter and a half in length (Fig. 5.49*A*). Very rarely it is longer, and then it is more likely to suggest a midline occipital fracture (Fig. 5.49*B*). A similar problem can occur with an abnormally long, but normal, fissure extending upward from the posterior lip of the foramen magnum (Fig. 5.49*C*).

Finally, one should note that a number of interparietal accessory bones can be seen in the occipital bone, just at the junction of the lambdoid and sagittal sutures. On frontal view, this bone (inca bone) or bones are of characteristic appearance and location, and usually are not misinterpreted for fractures (Fig. 5.50). On lateral view, however, they often appear very sclerotic and frequently are misinterpreted for a depressed fracture (Fig. 5.50).

Base of Skull Pseudofractures. On basal skull views, almost any of the normal sutures mentioned, with certain degrees of obliquity, can be projected so as to mimic a fracture. Most often this occurs with the coronal suture or one of the posterior fossa sutures (Fig. 5.51).

confident that the fracture-like appearing line is simply a normal suture. However, when an extra line exists (i.e., a third radiolucent line) or when one finds these radiolucent lines to be traveling in unusual directions, then one should consider them to be fractures (Figs. 5.46 and 5.47). These sutures also are a problem on frontal and Towne's projections where slight degrees of rotation also can cause them to appear absolutely fracture-like (Fig. 5.48).

In the posterior fossa, if one remembers that most of the sutures are paired, a third radiolucent line, even though heading in a direction suggestive of a normal suture,

REFERENCES

1. Allen, W., Kier, E., and Rothman, S.: Pitfalls in the evaluation of skull trauma: a review. Radiol. Clin. North Am. 11: 479–503, 1973.
2. Chemke, J., and Robinson, A.: Third fontanelle. J. Pediatr. 75: 617–622, 1969.
3. Franken, E.A., Jr.: The midline occipital fissure: Diagnosis of a fracture versus anatomic variants. Radiology 93: 1043–1046, 1969.
4. Irwin, A.L.: Roentgen demonstration of the time of closure of the spheno-occipital synchondrosis. Radiology 75: 451–452, 1960.
5. Shapiro, R.: Anomalous parietal sutures and the bipartite parietal bone. A.J.R. 115: 569–577, 1972.
6. Shopfner, C.E., Wolfe, T.W., and O'Kell, R.T.: The intersphenoid synchondrosis. A.J.R. 104: 184–193, 1968.
7. Smith, T.R., and Kier, E.L.: The unfused planum sphenoidale: Differentiation from fracture. Radiology 98: 305–309, 1971.
8. Swischuk, L.E.: The normal pediatric skull: Variations and

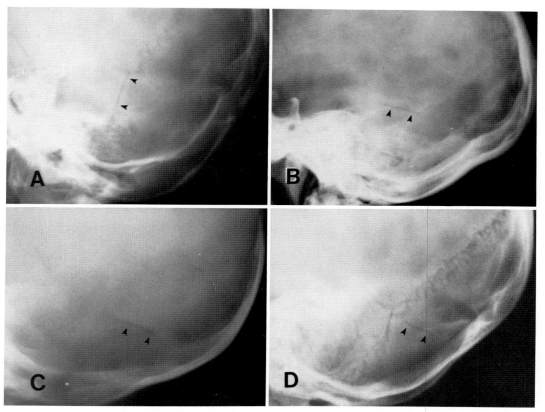

Figure 5.45. *Posterior fossa pseudofractures—lateral view.* (*A*) Note fracture-like appearance of the normal occipitomastoid suture (*arrows*). (*B*) Fracture-like appearance of the normal parietomastoid suture (*arrows*). (*C*) Isolated visualization of one Mendosal suture (*arrows*) in young infant. This, to the uninitiated, is virtually indistinguishable from a fracture. (*D*) Mendosal suture pseudofracture (*arrows*) in an older child.

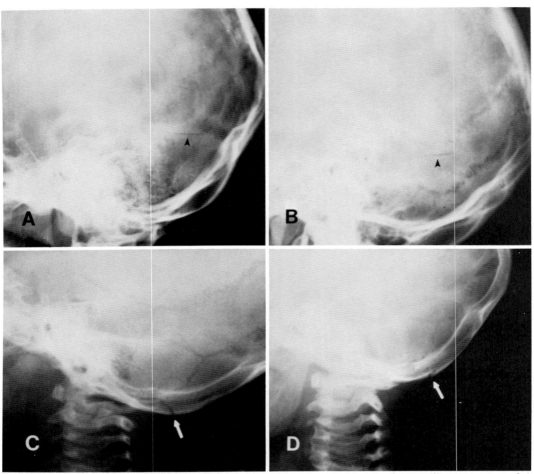

Figure 5.46. *Posterior fossa pseudofractures versus true fracture.* (*A*) Note the fracture-like appearance of the normal parietomastoid suture (*arrow*). (*B*) Fracture of the posterior fossa (*arrow*) mimicking a parietomastoid suture. However, when one lines this radiolucent line up with the two, true parietomastoid sutures one finds that it represents an extra radiolucent line and hence should be a fracture. (*C*) Normal innominate synchondrosis (*arrow*). (*D*) Diastatic, slightly offset fracture of innominate synchondrosis (*arrow*). Normal fissures and synchondroses are not offset, and thus, this should be a fracture.

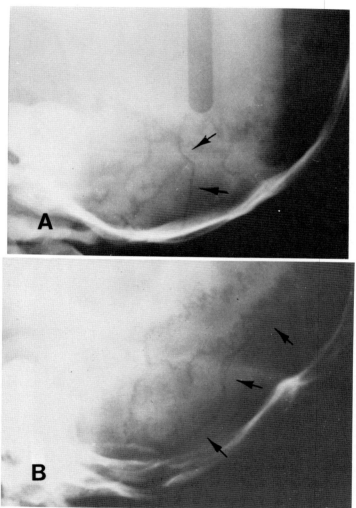

Figure 5.47. *True occipital fractures—lateral view.* (*A*) Note the fracture in the occipital bone (*arrows*). There are no normal sutures in this area. (*B*) Another patient demonstrating a long, linear fracture of the occipital bone (*arrows*). All of the normal sutures are identified and this represents an extra radiolucent line, or in other words, a fracture.

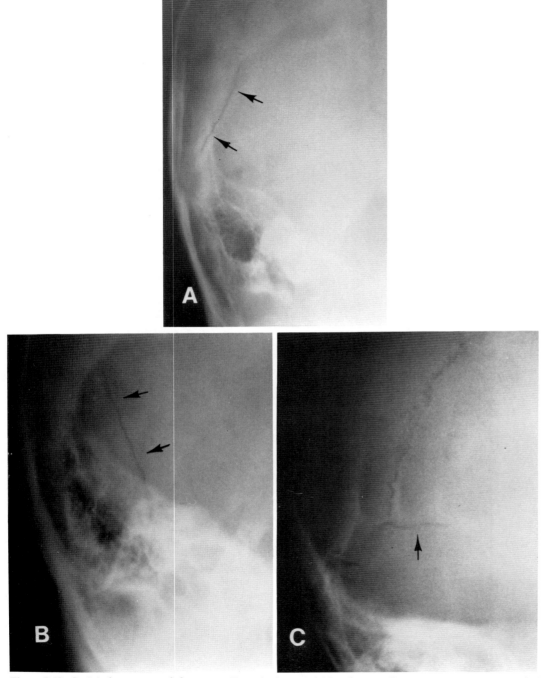

Figure 5.48. *Occipital suture pseudofractures—Towne's view.*   (*A*) Note fracture-like appearance and characteristic slope of the normal parietomastoid suture (*arrows*). (*B*) Pseudofracture appearance and characteristic slope of the occipitomastoid suture (*arrows*). (*C*) Small residual Mendosal suture (*arrow*) mimicking a fracture.

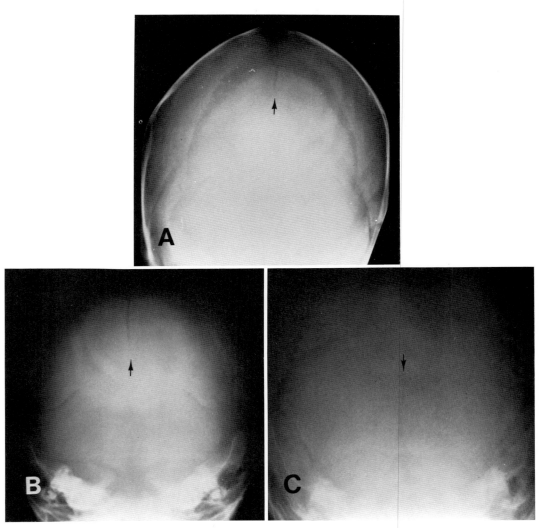

Figure 5.49. *Midline occipital fissures—pseudofractures.*   (*A*) Note typical appearance and length of the median occipital fissure (*arrow*) visualized on Towne's projection in young infants. (*B*) Unusually long but normal median occipital fissure (*arrow*) in another infant. Also note residual Mendosal sutures on both sides. (*C*) Unusually long occipital fissure (*arrow*) arising from the posterior lip of the foramen magnum.

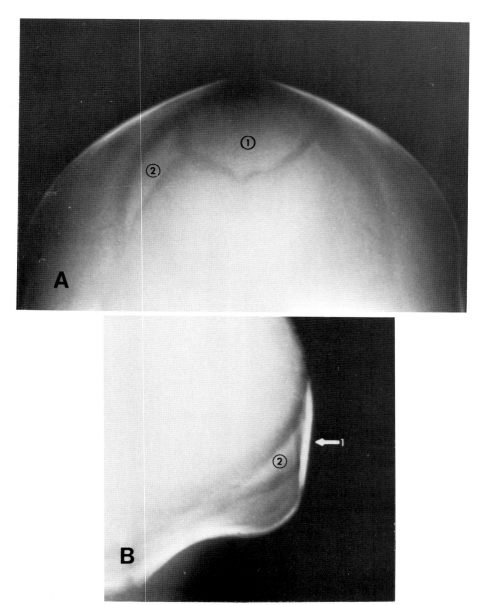

Figure 5.50. *Interparietal bone.* (*A*) Note the large interparietal (inca) bone (*1*) and the other accessory bone (*2*). These usually are not misinterpreted for fractures on this view. (*B*) On lateral view, however, their extremely sclerotic appearance (*arrows*) can strongly suggest a depressed fracture, especially if the skull is slightly obliqued.

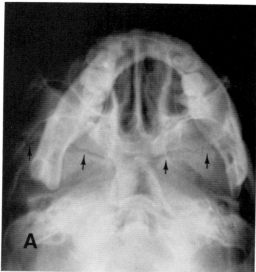

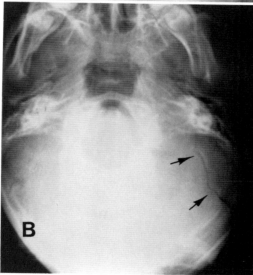

Figure 5.51. *Sutural pseudofractures on basal views.* (*A*) Note the coronal suture crossing the base of the skull (*arrows*). (*B*) Occipitomastoid suture (*arrows*) appearing as though it were a fracture on basal view.

artifacts. Radiol. Clin. North Am. 10: 277–290, 1972.
9. Swischuk, L.E.: The growing skull. Semin. Roentgenol. 9: 115–124, 1974.
10. Swischuk, L.E.: The normal newborn skull. Semin. Roentgenol. 9: 101–113, 1974.
11. Torgerson, J.: A roentgenologic study of the metopic suture. Acta Radiol. 33: 1–11, 1950.

ARTIFACTS MIMICKING CALVARIAL FRACTURES

A number of artifacts can be mistaken for calvarial abnormalities (1). However, one of the most common is the laceration which projects as a radiolucent defect or pseudofracture of the calvarium (Fig. 5.52*A*). Clinical correlation is the rule here, and it is most important that such correlation be accomplished for if the laceration suggests a fracture, it often suggests a depressed one. Other artifacts which can cause problems in the interpretation of skull roentgenograms include dirt and pebbles over the scalp and in the hair (Fig. 5.52*B*), hair soaked with water or blood (Fig. 5.53*C*), hair braids, air trapped in the pinna of the ear so as to suggest pneumocephalus, and abnormal shadows produced by the pinna and earlobe itself (Fig. 5.53).

REFERENCE

1. Swischuk, L.E.: The normal pediatric skull: variations and artifacts. Radiol. Clin. North Am. 10: 277–290, 1972.

FACIAL, ORBITAL, AND MANDIBULAR FRACTURES

Fractures of the face, orbit, and mandible are certainly not as common in the infant and young child as they are in the adult. An exception might be made in regard to nasal fractures, but generally speaking, facial fractures do not become a great problem until the child is older, and at this age, the considerations are not different from those in the adult. In this regard, the presence or absence of symmetry is the key to the assessment of facial bone fractures. Most faces are very symmetrical, and thus, if one encounters any asymmetry of cortical continuity or contour, one should suspect a fracture. In terms of **which views to obtain**, one usually obtains frontal, posteroanterior, lateral, and Waters' views. The Waters' view, however, is the most productive and the single most important view for the assessment of facial injuries. Thereafter, one might require special orbital, zygomatic arch, mandibular, or stereoscopic views for complete assessment. Actually, stereoscopic views are very useful in the evaluation of facial trauma (16), but now generally are supplanted by CT scanning (5, 21). However, in most cases of trauma to the face, plain films still are the starting point and CT scans are obtained in the more severe injuries and in difficult cases where the fracture is occult. Consequently, as opposed to skull fractures, facial fractures still require significant expertise in their assessment on plain films.

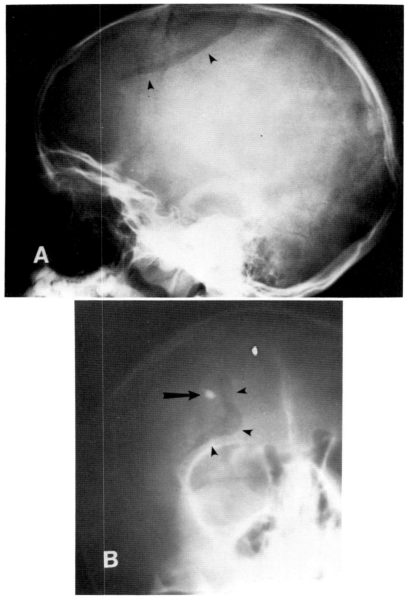

Figure 5.52. *Scalp laceration and pebble artifacts.*   (*A*) Note the radiolucency secondary to a deep laceration over the calvarium (*arrows*). (*B*) Another patient with a laceration over the forehead (*small arrows*), and a pebble embedded in the laceration (*large arrow*). Such a laceration should not be misinterpreted for a depressed skull fracture.

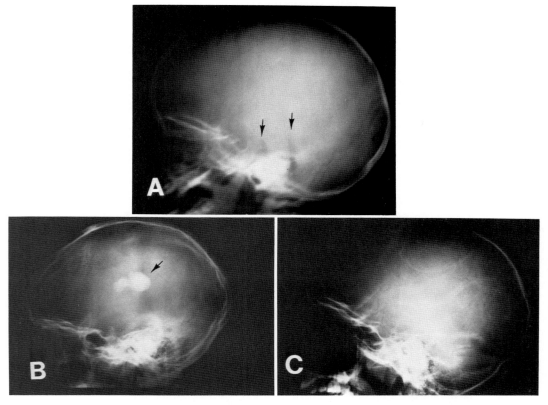

Figure 5.53. *Other artifacts.*   (*A*) Note accumulations of air in the pinnae of both ears (*arrows*). These air collections should not be misinterpreted for pneumocephalus. (*B*) Tightly braided hair mimicking an intracranial calcification (*arrow*). (*C*) Whorl-like configurations of strands of wet hair.

TYPES OF FRACTURES

Facial fractures generally can be divided into: (a) nasal fractures, (b) orbital fractures, (c) zygomatic-maxillary fractures, and (d) mandibular fractures (3–6).

Nasal Bone Fractures. These fractures usually are best demonstrated with moderately penetrated lateral views of the nasal bone and a Waters' view for assessment of nasal septal deviation. Septal deviation also is visible on CT scans (see Fig. 5.63). Fractures of the nasal bone can be simple linear fractures, depressed fractures, or comminuted fractures, and all can be associated with other facial fractures or fractures of the spine of the maxillary bone (Fig. 5.54). Linear fractures must be differentiated from three normal radiolucent lines commonly seen around the nose, i.e., the nasomaxillary suture, the groove for the nasociliary nerve, and the nasofrontal suture (Fig. 5.55). The lines produced by the nasomaxillary suture and groove for the nasociliary nerve are straight, and more or less parallel the anterior aspect of the nasal bone. This is not to say that fractures do not occur in this plane, but only to indicate that if one sees a radiolucent line traveling in the opposite direction, or even better, in the horizontal plane, then one should assume the line to represent a fracture (12).

Orbital Fractures. Fractures of the orbits can be linear or depressed and often occur in conjunction with frontal bone or other facial fractures. However, they also occur alone (9, 17) and it may require Caldwell, Waters', lateral, or olique (optic foramen) views for their complete demonstration (Fig. 5.56). CT scans also are helpful. In any case, the key to proper assessment is the assessment of symmetry. Constant comparison of the normal with the abnormal will allow one to detect the more subtle

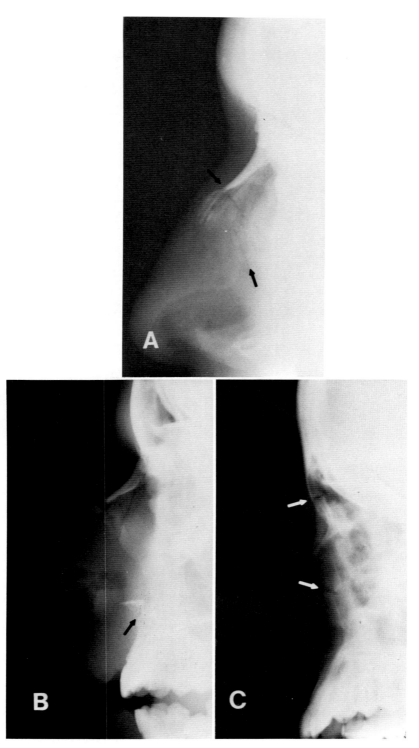

Figure 5.54. *Nasal fractures.* (*A*) Note the comminuted nasal fracture. Two of the fracture lines are identified with arrows. (*B*) Note the comminuted fracture of the nasal bone. the vertical radiolucent line is a fracture. It is too far anterior to be the nasomaxillary suture and too sharp and radiolucent to be the nasociliary groove. Both of these normal structures are demonstrated in Figure 5.55. Also note the fracture through the spinous process of the maxillary bone (*arrow*). (*C*) This patient was hit in the nose and face. Note fractures through the anterior wall of the frontal sinus (*upper arrow*) and the maxillary bone below the nose (*lower arrow*).

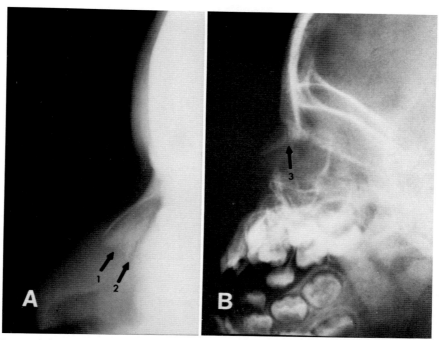

Figure 5.55. *Pseudofractures of nasal bone.* (*A*) Note the barely visible groove for the nasociliary nerve (*1*), and the more prominent vertical radiolucent line representing the nasomaxillary suture (*2*). Both of these structures can be misinterpreted for fractures. (*B*) Normal nasofrontal suture (*3*).

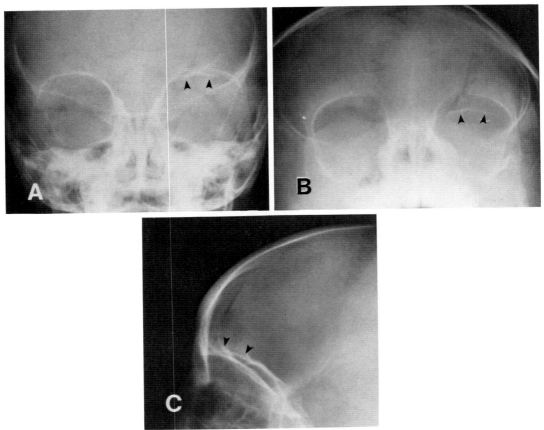

Figure 5.56. *Superior orbital rim fracture.* (*A*) Note generalized increase in soft tissue density over the left orbit and also note discontinuity of the left orbital roof (*arrows*). A depressed fracture fragment and a fracture extending into the frontal bone above the orbit are suggested. (*B*) Waters' view more clearly demonstrates the depressed fragment (*arrows*), and clearly demonstrates the fracture extending into the frontal bone. (*C*) Lateral view demonstrating the fracture of the frontal bone and the malaligned left anterior orbital roof (*arrows*). Compare the configuration of the left orbital roof with the normal right orbital roof beneath it.

fractures involving the orbital rim. This is especially true of medial wall fractures which often are associated with changes in the adjacent ethmoid sinuses (Fig. 5.57). In addition, some of these cases may demonstrate air within the orbit, and in this regard, one should be careful not to misinterpret air trapped between the eyelids for air in the orbit (see Fig. 5.66).

A special type of fracture of the orbit is the **blowout fracture**. This fracture occurs through the floor of the orbit and results from blunt trauma to the eye (2, 4, 5, 15, 19, 22). Usually it occurs in isolated form but can be associated with other facial fractures, especially the tripod fracture of the maxillary bone. In the blowout fracture, the hydrostatic pressure produced within the globe blows out, or displaces, the wall at its weakest point. This point is the inferior aspect or floor of the orbit, and the orbital contents decompress through it. Because of this, the globe becomes partially fixed, and cannot move in all directions. Typically, diplopia secondary to lack of upward gaze is present in these patients.

Roentgenographically, the best view for detecting blowout fractures is the Waters' view. On this view, one should look for asymmetry of the floors of the orbits and in some cases, one may see actual downward displacement of the bony fragments while in others one will note only that a soft tissue mass has prolapsed into the maxillary an-

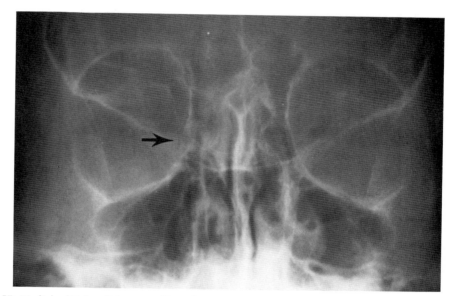

Figure 5.57. *Medial orbital wall fracture.* Note discontinuity of the cortex of the medial orbital wall on the right (*arrow*). Also note that the ethmoid air sinuses are obliterated because of associated bleeding.

trum (Fig. 5.58). The prolapsed soft tissue mass has been referred to as the "teardrop" sign while the depressed bony fragments have been referred to as the "open bomb-bay" door sign. The maxillary sinus may be totally clear or obliterated by blood, and once again the fracture is best demonstrated with conventional laminography or CT scanning. However, plain films (Waters' and Caldwell views), still are quite reliable in detecting this fracture (11). Thereafter, if one requires more delineation, one can use CT scanning (10, 20).

Most often blowout fractures occur

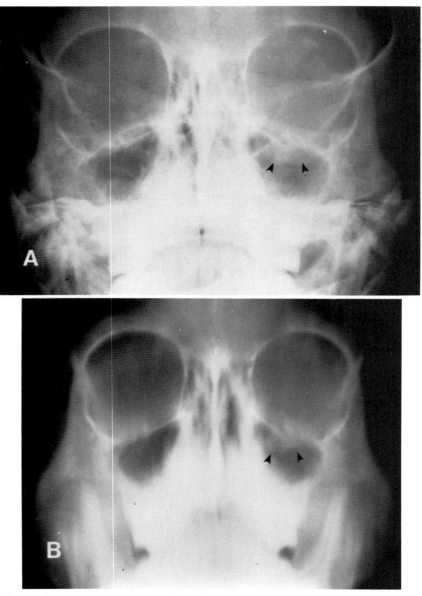

Figure 5.58. *Blowout fracture.*   Note a poorly defined soft tissue mass (*arrows*) bulging into the left maxillary sinus. Also note that the roof of the maxillary sinus is depressed and that a fracture is suggested. Soft tissue swelling above the sinus also is present. Compare these findings with the normal right side. (*B*) Laminogram more clearly demonstrating the "teardrop" configuration of the blowout fracture (*arrows*) and the associated fracture through the orbital floor. For a more subtle blowout fracture, see Figure 5.66*B*.

through the floor of the orbit, but occasionally they can occur medially and extend into the ethmoid sinus cavities. They also have been reported to extend into the frontal sinuses (3), and fractures in all of these latter sites are more difficult to detect. Indeed, this is a very good time to use CT scanning.

Fractures of the Zygomatic and Maxillary Bones. These include solitary zygomatic arch fractures, tripod fractures of the zygomaticomaxillary bone complex, isolated maxillary fractures, and Le Fort fractures of the face. Of course, many times these fractures occur in conjunction with one another, but they also occur in isolated form. Of all the fractures of the maxillary bone, the most common is the *tripod fracture*. This fracture results from a direct blow to the check (7, 8, 18) and characteristically, fracturing occurs at three sites: (a) the zygomatic-frontal suture, (b) the inferior orbital rim and maxillary bone (i.e., junction of the zygoma and maxillary bone), and (c) the zygomatic arch (Fig. 5.59). Depending on the severity of the injury and the extent of the fracture through the inferior orbital rim and maxillary sinus, more or less lateral and downward displacement of the fracture fragment occurs. In actual fact, this fracture fragment is the entire zygoma and roentgenographically its depression results in a variable degree of asymmetry of the lower orbital rims (Fig. 5.60). In children, it is important not to misinter-

pret the normal zygomatic-frontal suture for the superiormost fracture of the tripod fracture complex.

Other fractures of the maxillary bone are less common but also result from direct blows to the cheek. Many of these fractures extend into the alveolar process of the maxilla, and in so doing produce a loose fragment with separation of the teeth.

Fractures isolated to the *zygomatic arch* usually result from direct blows to the side of the face. These fractures can be depressed or nondepressed, and in those cases where depression occurs, the zygomatic arch fractures at three sites. Depression occurs at the middle site (Fig. 5.61). Zygomatic arches can be visualized on Towne's projections (see Fig. 5.64), Waters' projection and posteroanterior projections with the chin tucked tightly against the neck. If these views do not suffice, special tangential views or base of the skull views can be obtained.

One of the more serious facial injuries is the *Le Forte fracture.* This fracture is a transverse maxillary fracture extending across the face (4, 5, 13, 14, 18), and often is associated with a fracture of the pterygoid process (16). Le Fort fractures usually are classified into three types, depending on the level of fracture (Fig. 5.62). The lowermost of these fractures is the Le Fort I or transverse maxillary fracture, and the fracture line is located above the level of the teeth but below the nose. There is separation of the teeth and the hard palate from the upper portions of the maxilla. In the Le Fort II fracture, the fracture line is located at a higher level and generally runs along the upper aspect of the maxillary bones and nose. Laterally, it may extend along the infraorbital ridge. This fracture often is referred to as the pyramidal fracture because of the shape of the main fracture fragment. In Le Fort III injuries, there is craniofacial separation. The fracture is high in position and is located somewhere upward of the bridge of the nose. It usually extends into the orbits, and to a varying degree separates the face from the base of the skull. The main fracture fragment is the entire face. Le Fort fractures usually are complex and serious injuries, and are sustained from head-on blows to the face such as those sustained in automobile accidents.

Very often, with the more complex facial

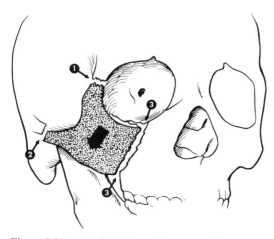

Figure 5.59. *Tripod fracture—diagrammatic representation.* Characteristically fractures occur through the zygomatic-frontal suture (*1*), zygomatic arch (*2*), and the junction of the zygoma and maxillary bone (*3*). In addition, the fracture fragment is displaced downward and outward (*large arrow*).

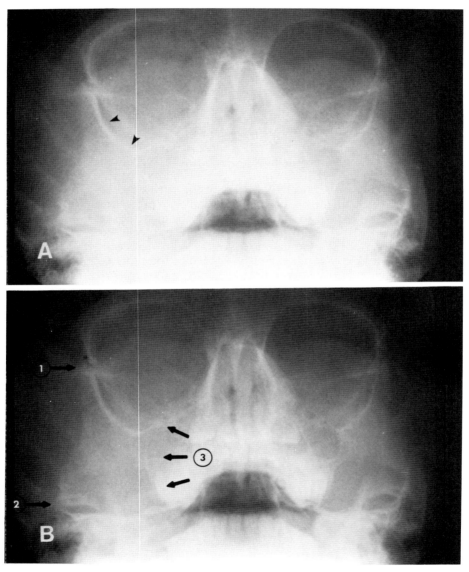

Figure 5.60. *Tripod fracture in infant—subtle findings.* (*A*) First note a generalized increase in soft tissue density over the right orbit and maxillary sinus region. Then note asymmetry of the inferior aspects of the orbits. On the right, there is downward and outward displacement (*arrows*). (*B*) Same patient demonstrating better bony detail. Note the fracture through the zygomaticofrontal suture (*1*), a distorted fractured zygomatic arch (*2*), and a poorly defined, although obligatorily present fracture through the orbital floor and maxillary sinus (*3*). Very often, in young infants, these fractures are difficult to define on plain films, and laminography or CT scanning are required for more accurate definition.

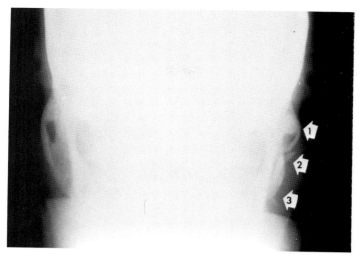

Figure 5.61. *Zygomatic arch fracture.* Note the typical configuration of the fractured zygomatic arch (*arrow*). The fracture occurs at three sites (*1, 2, 3*) and is depressed at the middle site (*2*). Other zygomatic arch fractures are demonstrated in Figures 5.60*B* and 5.64*B*.

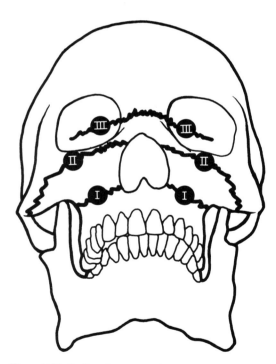

Figure 5.62. *Le Fort fractures—diagrammatic representation.* Note the characteristic position of the Le Fort I, II, and III fractures.

fractures, it was difficult to determine just where all of these fractures occur. However, now that CT scanning is available, one can obtain a much clearer assessment of these

maxillary, and facial fractures in general (Fig. 5.63).

Mandibular Fractures. These fractures usually result from direct blows to the lower jaw, and often, because of the ring-like configuration of the mandible, fractures occur at two sites. However, single fractures also commonly occur and usually are not too difficult to detect (Fig. 5.64*A*). In other cases, fractures can occur through the condylar processes of the mandible. These fractures can be unilateral or bilateral and in young infants often are of the greenstick or bending (1) variety (Fig. 5.64*B*). Usually, these fractures are best demonstrated on Towne's or Caldwell views of the head. On this latter view, if one has the patient tuck the chin tightly against his or her chest, the mandibular condyles become readily visible. With more extensive fractures of the mandible, that is, where fracturing might occur at three sites, the mandible often is noted to be wider than it should be; in other words, the mandible appears magnified on the frontal view and too large for the remainder of the face (17). Mandibular fractures also are readily demonstrable with CT scanning (Fig. 5.65).

Dislocation of the mandible is not particularly common but can occur. Of course, clinically it should be readily apparent, for the patient will be unable to open and close the mouth. On Law's projection and subse-

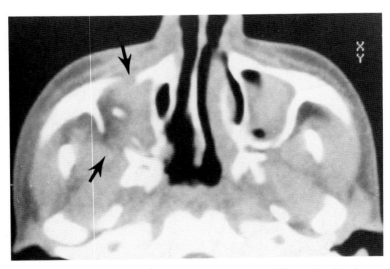

Figure 5.63. *Maxillary fracture; CT scan.*   Note fractures through the maxilla on the right (*arrows*), and a smaller fracture on the left. Also note deviation of the nasal septum to the right, and edema of the soft tissues along the medial left maxillary wall. Both maxillary sinuses are obliterated secondary to bleeding.

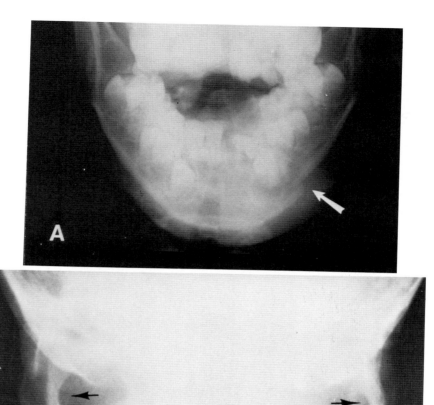

Figure 5.64. *Fractures of the mandible.* (*A*) Note the displaced fracture through the body of the mandible (*arrow*). Alignment of the teeth is disrupted. This patient did not have any other mandibular fractures. (*B*) Bilateral greenstick (bending) fractures of the mandibular condyles (*arrows*) in a young infant. The zygomatic arch, on the right, also is fractured but not depressed. It merely is separated at the zygomatic frontal suture.

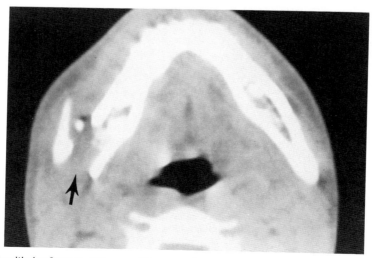

Figure 5.65. *Mandibular fracture; CT scan.* Note gross fracture through the mandible on the right (*arrows*).

quent tomography the condyles are visualized with considerable clarity, and it can be determined that, in the dislocated joint, the condyle lies anterior to the articular fossa.

Soft Tissue Changes with Facial Injury. Very often the soft tissues are swollen and distorted with facial injury. This can occur with or without underlying bony abnormality, and it is important to appreciate these changes. In some instances, considerable edema and swelling is present and can distract one from a more serious underlying problem (Fig. 5.66). In this regard, one of the more distracting soft tissue changes is

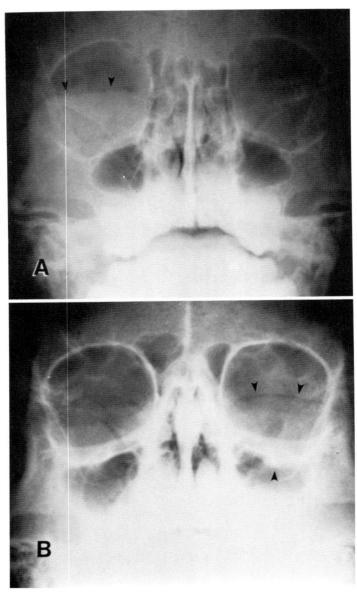

Figure 5.66. *Soft tissue abnormalities in facial trauma.* (*A*) Note extensive swelling of the soft tissues above the right maxillary sinus (*arrows*). This patient suffered a blow to the cheek and swelling was so profound that it was difficult to determine whether any underlying bony injury was present. Roentgenographically, all of the bony structures are normal. (*B*) Another patient sustaining a blow to the left orbit. Note some generalized increase in soft tissue density over the lower left orbit and the slit-like transverse radiolucency caused by air being trapped between the palpebral fissures (*upper arrows*). Swelling of the lower eyelid causes the trapped air to appear slit-like. Note its normal appearance on the right side. In addition, note a minimal blowout fracture on the left (*lower arrow*).

that produced when air is trapped between the palpebral fissures. In such cases, air within the orbit might erroneously be suggested (Fig. 5.66).

Normal Findings Causing Problems. The facial bones are so complexly constructed and united by so many sutures that it is no surprise that many normal structures are misinterpreted for fractures. The most common of these have been dealt with at appropriate places in earlier paragraphs, and perhaps at this point it is best merely to underscore the value of assessing symmetry in the face. If one makes an observation which suggests that a fracture might be present, then one should immediately compare this area with the same one on the other side. If the finding is normal, chances are that it will be seen on the other side. Of course, this is with the understanding that the examination is performed with proper positioning, that is, without rotation, obliquity, etc.

In the mandible, the most commonly misinterpreted normal structure is the synchondrosis of the symphysis menti. This is a radiolucent, vertical line in the middle of the mandible and usually is seen in infants and young children. Knowledge of its midline position should avoid misinterpretation for a fracture. The groove for the mandibular branch of the trigeminal nerve also can be misinterpreted for a fracture of the body of the mandible.

REFERENCES

1. Ahrendt, D., Swischuk, L.E., and Hayden, C.K., Jr.: Incomplete (bending?) fractures of the mandibular condyle in children. Pediatr. Radiol. 14: 140–141, 1984.
2. Brown, O.L., Longacre, J.J., DeStefano, G.A., Wood, R.W., and Kahl, J.B.: Roentgen manifestations of blow-out fracture of the orbit. Radiology 85: 908–913, 1965.
3. Curtin, H.D., Wolfe, P., and Schramm, V.: Orbital roof blow-out fractures. A.J.R. 139: 969–972, 1982.
4. Dolan, K.D., and Jacoby, C.G.: Facial fractures. Semin. Roentgenol. 13: 37–51, 1978.
5. Dolan, K.D., Jacoby, C., Smoker, W.: The radiology of facial fractures. Radiographics 4: 577–663, 1984.
6. Freimanis, A.K.: Fractures of the facial bones. Radiol. Clin. North Am. 4: 341–363, 1966.
7. Fueger, G.F., Milauskas, A.T., and Britton, W.: The roentgenologic evaluation of orbital blow-out injuries. A.J.R. 97: 614–617, 1966.
8. Gerlock, A.J., and Sinn, D.P.: Anatomic clinical, surgical, and radiographic correlation of zygomatic complex fracture. A.J.R. 128: 235–248, 1977.
9. Gould, H.R., and Titus, C.O.: Internal orbital fractures: the value of laminography in diagnosis. A.J.R. 97: 618–623, 1966.
10. Hammerschlag, S.B., Hughes, S., O'Reilly, G.V., Naheedy, M.H., and Rumbaugh, C.L.: Blow-out fractures of the orbit: a comparison of computed tomography and conventional radiography with anatomical correlation. Radiology 143: 487–492, 1982.
11. Hammerschlag, S.B., Hughes, S., O'Reilly, G.V., and Weber, A.L.: Another look at blow-out fractures of the orbit. A.J.R. 139: 133–137, 1982.
12. Lacey, G.F., Wignall, B.K., Hussain, S., and Reidy, J.R.: The radiology of nasal injuries: problems of interpretation and clinical relevance. Br. J. Radiol. 50: 412–414, 1977.
13. Le Fort, R.: Fracture de la machoire superieure. Congr. Internat. de Med. Paris, Sect. Chir. Gen. 1900, pp. 275–278.
14. Le Fort, R.: Etude experimentale sur les fractures de la machoire superieure. Rev. Chir. 23: 208–209, 1901.
15. Lewin, J.R., Rhodes, D.H., Jr., and Pasek, E.J.: Roentgenologic manifestations of fracture of orbital floor (blow-out fracture). A.J.R. 83: 628–632, 1960.
16. Rothman, S.L., Allen, W.E., and Keir, E.L.: Stereo roentgenography in craniofacial injuries: a revival. Radiol. Clin. North Am. 11: 683–696, 1973.
17. Trapnell, D.H.: The "magnification sign" of triple mandibular fracture. Br. J. Radiol. 50: 97–100, 1977.
18. Unger, J.D., and Unger, F.G.: Fracture of the pterygoid processes accompanying severe facial bone injury. Radiology 98: 311–316, 1971.
19. Vinik, M., and Gargano, F.P.: Orbital fractures. A.J.R. 97: 607–613, 1966.
20. Zilkha, A.: Computed tomography of blow-out fracture of medial orbital wall. A.J.R. 137: 963–965, 1981.
21. Zilkha, A.: Computed tomography in facial trauma. Radiology 144: 545–548, 1982.
22. Zismor, J., Smith, B., Fasano, C., and Converse, J.M.: Roentgen diagnosis of blow-out fractures of orbit. A.J.R. 87: 1009–1018, 1962.

DETECTING INCREASED INTRACRANIAL PRESSURE (SPREAD SUTURES)

In infancy and early childhood, increased intracranial pressure is manifest primarily in widening or spreading of the calvarial sutures. The coronal suture usually is the first to spread, and as far as measurements are concerned, in the infant under 3 months of age no valid measurements are available. Consequently, one must rely on one's objective observation that the coronal suture is wider and more V-shaped than normal (4). In addition to this finding, one may well note that the anterior fontanelle is bulging (Fig. 5.67). In the older infant and child, it has been suggested that if the coronal suture measures more than 3 mm at its uppermost aspect, then spread should be present (2). This measurement is the most useful one available at the present time, but yet in some cases borderline measurements still cause uncertainty. It is in such cases that I have found it worthwhile to examine the sagittal suture as well (3). The reason for this is that while the normal coronal suture often appears spread when really it is not, seldom does this occur with the sagittal suture. Consequently, if the sagittal suture is judged to be spread, then increased intracranial pressure is likely (Fig. 5.68). In the older child, that is, the child over 10 years of age, one

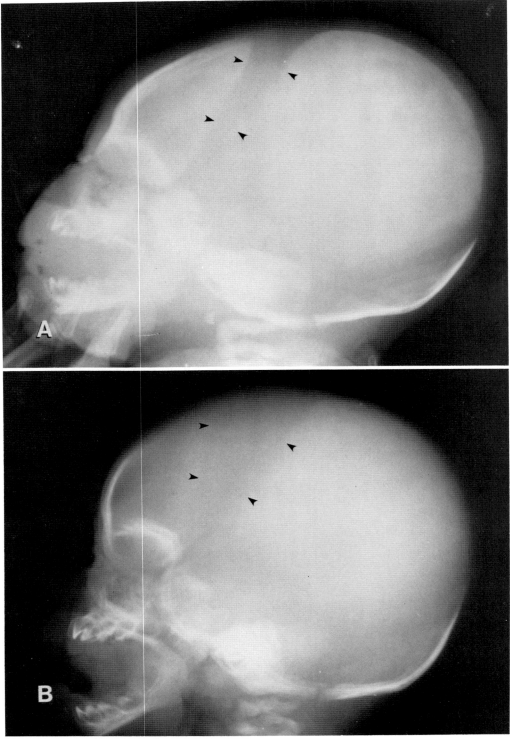

Figure 5.67. *Spread sutures in infancy.*   (*A*) Normal infant demonstrating upper limits of normal of the coronal suture (*arrows*). Note that the coronal suture is slightly V-shaped. (*B*) Exaggerated V-shaped configuration of the coronal suture (*arrows*) due to markedly increased intracranial pressure. Also note that the anterior fontanelle is bulging. In (*A*) the anterior fontanelle is not bulging.

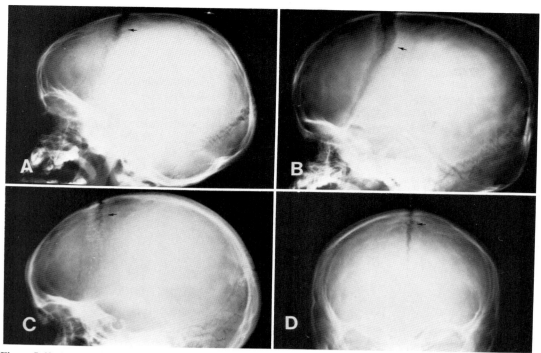

Figure 5.68. *Spread sutures in older infants and children.* (*A*) Note clearly spread coronal suture (*arrow*). (*B*) Gross spreading with an exaggerated V-shaped configuration of the coronal suture (*arrow*) in an infant with meningitis. All of the other sutures also are spread. (*C*) Questionably spread coronal suture (*arrow*). Such a configuration often is difficult to differentiate from normal. (*D*) Frontal view demonstrating definite spread of the sagittal suture (*arrow*). This should suggest that the coronal suture in (*C*) truly is spread. This patient had an intracranial bleed.

does not require the 3-mm width standard for diagnosis of abnormal sutural spread. In this age group, any spread of the coronal suture should be treated with suspicion, for there is little normal leeway. In addition, one should also check the sella for demineralization, for almost surely it also will be present, as in this age group the problem usually is more chronic.

Spread of the cranial sutures is a nonspecific finding and can be seen with increased intracranial pressure secondary to cerebral edema, subdural hematomas, cerebral hematomas, meningitis (1), and brain tumors. In the emergency setting, however, one usually is confronted with sutural spread secondary to calvarial injury with intracranial bleeding or cerebral edema, or meningitis.

REFERENCES

1. Holmes, R.D., Kuhns, L.R., and Oliver, W.J.: Widened sutures in childhood meningitis: Unrecognized sign of an acute illness. A.J.R. 128: 977–979, 1977.
2. Segal, H.D., Mikity, V.G., Rumbaugh, C.L., et al.: Cranial sutures in the first year of life: Limits of normal and the "sprung suture." Presented at the 57th annual meeting of the Radiological Society of North America, Chicago, 1971.
3. Swischuk, L.E.: The growing skull. Semin. Roentgenol. 9: 115–124, 1974.
4. Swischuk, L.E.: The normal newborn skull. Semin. Roentgenol. 9: 101–113, 1974.

MISCELLANEOUS SKULL AND FACE PROBLEMS

Ocular Foreign Body Localization. Ocular foreign bodies are a common problem in the emergency room. Those which are nonopaque pose obvious problems, but most opaque foreign bodies are relatively easily localized. In the past, the most commonly employed method for localizing these foreign bodies was Sweet's localization. Almost every institution was equipped with the appropriate charts for this method of localizing a foreign body. Another method was the so-called lo vac method where a plastic disc was applied to the cornea by the use of a low vacuum apparatus (2). The plastic disc was opaque, and when roentgenograms were obtained, a chart could be superimposed over the roentgenogram and the foreign body localized.

Currently, however, ultrasonography (1) and CT scanning (3) more frequently are utilized for foreign body detection and localization. Opaque foreign bodies, of course, are readily visible with CT scanning (Fig. 5.69).

REFERENCES

1. Coleman, D.J., and Trokel, S.L.: A protocol for B-scan and radiographic foreign body localization. Am. J. Ophthalmol. 71: 84–89, 1971.
2. Erkonen, W., and Dolan, K.D.: Ocular foreign body localization. Radiol. Clin. North Am. 10: 101–114, 1972.
3. Tate, E., and Cupples, H.: Detection of orbital foreign bodies with computed tomography: current limits. A.J.R. 137: 493–495, 1981.

Proptosis and Orbital Cellulitis. Proptosis can result from a number of causes, but in the child, acute unilateral proptosis usually is secondary to trauma or orbital inflammatory disease. Trauma, of course, is self-evident and with orbital inflammatory disease, most often the problem is preorbital cellulitis (1). Thereafter, one should consider orbital inflammation secondary to sinusitis (3, 6–8). In most of these cases, there is no true osteomyelitis of the bones of the orbit, but rather adjacent, sympathetic soft tissue, intraorbital inflammation. Less common causes of proptosis as-

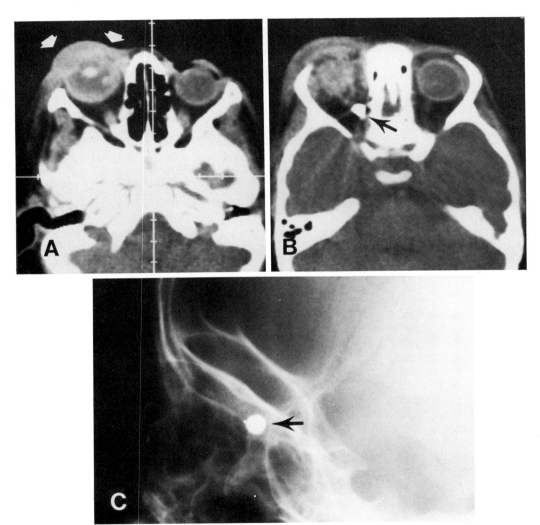

Figure 5.69. *Foreign body; CT scan.* (*A*) Note the proptotic globe, and considerable soft tissue swelling and thickening over its anterior aspect (*arrows*). There also is an area of focally increased density, behind the lens, probably representing blood in the globe. (*B*) A slightly higher cut demonstrates the metallic foreign body (*arrow*), and gross disorganization of the soft tissues within the orbit. (*C*) Plain film provides confirmation as to the general position of the foreign body (*arrow*).

sociated with orbital swelling include orbital bone infarction in sickle cell disease (2, 10), pseudotumor of the orbit (9), and nonspecific orbital cellulitis.

Periorbital and intraorbital inflammatory diseases, in the past, often were difficult to differentiate clinically (4), but currently they are easily differentiated with CT scanning (5). On CT scanning, preorbital cellulitis presents with normal intraorbital contents and swelling over the front of the eye (Fig. 5.70A). Intraorbital inflammatory disease associated with sinusitis usually presents with displacement of the medial rectus muscle and adjacent collections of intraorbital fluid, or an actual abscess. In addition, bone destruction may be seen, but the commonest findings are displacement of the medial rectus muscle and adjacent edema (Fig. 5.70B). Nonspecific intraorbital cellulitis produces mottled increased density behind the globe (Fig. 5.70C), while bleeding into the globe, as may be seen with trauma (11) (battered child syndrome included), presents with opacity in the globe (Fig. 5.70D).

REFERENCES

1. Barkin, R.M., Todd, J.K., and Amer, J.: Periorbital cellulitis in children. Pediatrics 62: 390–392, 1978.
2. Blank, J.P., and Gill, F.M.: Orbital infarction in sickle disease. Pediatric 67: 879–881, 1981.

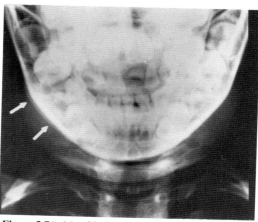

Figure 5.71. *Mandibular periostitis.* Note early deposition of periosteal new bone on the right (*arrows*). This patient presented with soft tissue swelling of the mandible in this area. No osteomyelitis is present. (Courtesy V. Mikity, M.D.)

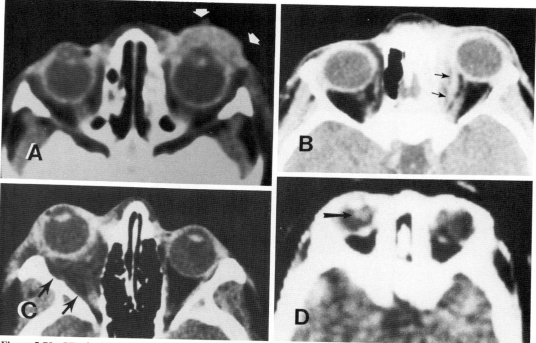

Figure 5.70. *CT of orbital disease.* (*A*) *Preorbital cellulitis.* Note thickening of the soft tissues anteriorly (*arrows*). The retrobulbar structures are normal. (*B*) *Sinusitis with intraorbital inflammation.* Note proptosis and lateral displacement of the medial rectus muscle (*arrows*). There is associated soft tissue edema under the muscle and the adjacent sinus cavities are obliterated. An adjacent abscess can not be ruled out. (*C*) *Retrobulbar inflammation.* Note nonspecific increased density of the retrobulbar soft tissues (*arrows*). (*D*) *Trauma to orbit.* Note intraorbital densities due to bleeding in a battered child (*arrow*).

3. Chandler, J.R., Langenbrunner, D.J., and Stevens, E.R.: The pathogenesis of orbital complications in acute sinusitis. Laryngoscope 80: 1414, 1970.

4. Gellady, A.M., Shulman, S.T., and Ayoub, E.M.: Periorbital and orbital cellulitis in children. Pediatrics 61: 272–277, 1978.

5. Goldberg, F., Berne, A.S., and Oski, F.A.: Differentiation of orbital cellulitis from preseptal cellulitis by computed tomography. Pediatrics 62: 1000–1005, 1978.

6. Hawkins, D.B., and Clark, R.W.: Orbital involvement in acute sinusitits: lessons from 24 childhood patients. Clin. Pediatr. 16: 464–471, 1977.

7. Haynes, R.E., and Crambleth, H.G.: Acute ethmoiditis, its relationship to orbital cellulitis. Am. J. Dis. Child. 114: 261, 1967.

8. Jarret, W.H., II, and Gutman, F.A.: Ocular complication of infection in the paranasal sinuses. Arch. Ophthalmol. 81: 683, 1969.

9. Nugent, R.A., Rootman, J., Robertson, W.D., Lapointe, J.S. and Harrison, P.B.: Acute orbital pseudotumors: classification and CT features. A.J.R. 137: 957–962, 1981.

10. Seeler, R.A.: Exophthalmos in hemoglobin SC disease. J. Pediatr. 102: 90–91, 1983.

11. Tomasi, L.G., and Rosman, N.P.: Purtscher's retinopathy in the battered child syndrome. Am. J. Dis. Child. 129: 1335–1337, 1975.

Swollen Jaw. Very often children presenting with a "swollen jaw" have, as their underlying problem, submandibular adenopathy, and in some of these cases periosteal new bone deposition along the body of the mandible can be seen (Fig. 5.71). These findings, however, do not represent osteomyelitis but rather a reactive periostitis secondary to the soft tissue inflammation (1). Other causes of swelling of the mandible

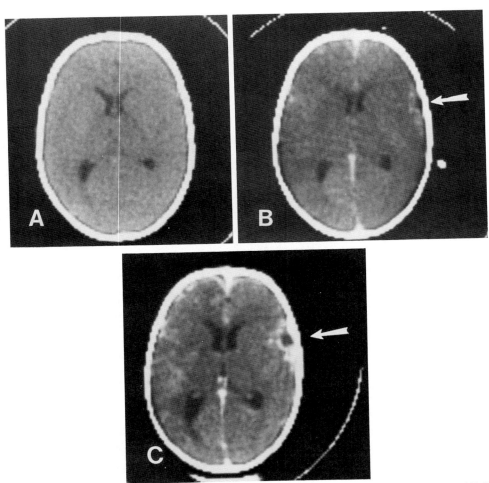

Figure 5.72. *Meningitis—cerebritis.* (*A*) Nonenhanced scan demonstrates generalized cerebral edema. (*B*) Contrast scan shows an area of focal enhancement on the right (*arrow*). (*C*) Later, edema has subsided and the ventricles have enlarged secondary to hydrocephalus. Now there is a focal area of cerebritis or fluid collection on the right (*arrow*). Also note increased enhancement of the meninges.

include Caffey's disease, submandibular salivary gland inflammations, and primary bone tumors and infections. However, the most common cause is submandibular adenopathy.

REFERENCE

1. Suydam, M.J., and Mikity, V.C.: Cellulitis with underlying inflammatory periostitis of the mandible. A.J.R. 56: 133–135, 1969.

Seizures. Seizures are a common problem in pediatrics and while the occasional seizure can herald the presence of an intracranial tumor, most are idiopathic or febrile seizures. In either case, skull roentgenograms are most unproductive (1, 3–6). In addition, although transient postictal edema can be seen on CT scanning (7), CT scans for childhood seizures also are relatively unproductive (2). In the future, magnetic resonance (MR) scanning may be more helpful, but currently, certainly skull films should not be obtained very often, and if one should obtain any study, it should be the CT scan.

REFERENCES

1. Committee on Radiology: Skull roentgenography of infants and children with convulsive disorders. Pediatrics 62: 835–837, 1978.
2. Harwood-Nash, D.C.: Computed tomography and seizures in children. J. Neuroradiol. 10: 130–136, 1983.
3. Hayes, W.G., and Shopfner, C.E.: Plain skull roentgenographic findings in infants and children with convulsions. Am. J. Dis. Child. 126: 785–787, 1973.
4. Nealis, J.G.T., McFadden, S.W., Asnes, R.A., and Ouellette, E.M.: Routine skull roentgenograms in the management of simple febrile seizures or head trauma. J. Can. Assoc. Radiol. 23: 234–235, 1977.
5. Newman, D.E.: Routine skull radiographs in children with seizures or head trauma. J. Can. Assoc. Radiol. 23: 234–235, 1977.
6. Ogunmekan, A.O.: Routine skull roentgenography in the clinical evaluation of children with febrile convulsions. Br. J. Radiol. 53: 815, 1980.
7. Rumack, C.M., Guggenheim, M.A., Fasules, J.W., and Burdick, D.: Transient positive postictal computed tomographic scan. J. Pediatr. 97: 263–264, 1980.

ACUTE INTRACRANIAL VASCULAR AND INFLAMMATORY DISEASES

In the past, the diagnosis of meningitis, for the most part, was nonradiologic. However, with CT scanning, one now can see early brain edema, and later, with contrast enhancement, increased definition (enhancement) of the meninges or areas of associated cerebritis (Fig. 5.72). Enhancement of the meninges is especially profound with tuberculous and fungal meningitis. Brain abscess characteristically produces an area of hypodensity on plain CT scans, and a ring of enhancement on contrast studies (Fig. 5.73).

As far as acute vascular problems are concerned, spontaneous intracranial bleeds are quite uncommon. Nonetheless, they do occur, either with angiomas, aneurysms, or blood dyscrasias (Fig. 5.74). Deep venous thrombosis, now that CT scanning is available, is more readily identified than in the past. When seen, it presents with increased

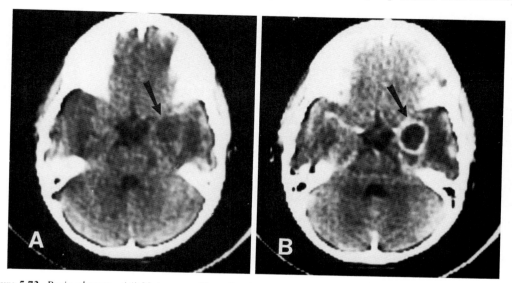

Figure 5.73. *Brain abscess.* (*A*) Note area of hypodensity (*arrow*). (*B*) Contrast-enhanced scan, in same patient, demonstrates typical enhancing ring (*arrow*).

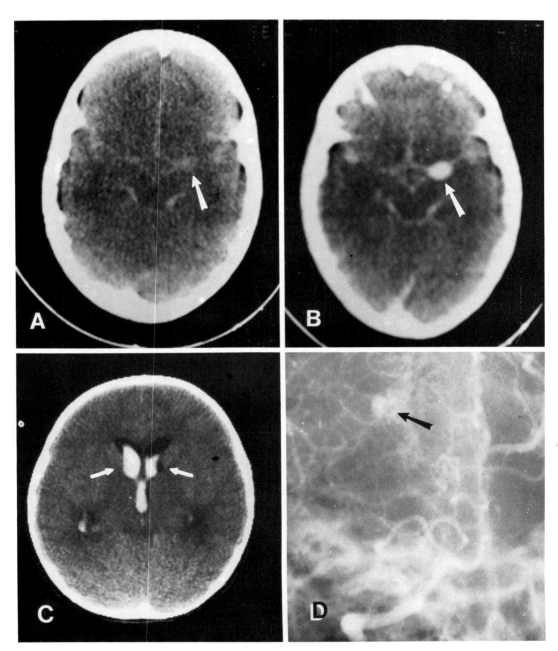

Figure 5.74. *Acute intracranial vascular abnormalities.* (*A*) Intracranial aneurysm with bleeding (*arrow*). Note blood along the falx and in the various sulci. (*B*) Contrast-enhanced CT scan demonstrates the aneurysm to better advantage (*arrow*). (*C*) Extensive intraventricular bleeding from a small arteriovenous malformation, found later on angiography (*arrow* in (*D*)).

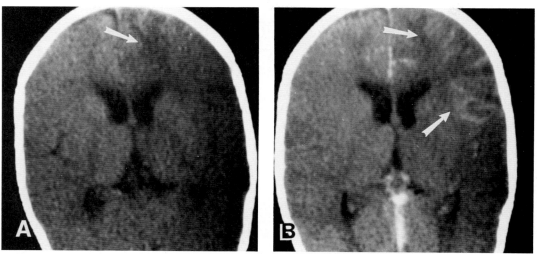

Figure 5.75. *Cerebral infarction.*   (*A*) Note area of hypodensity in the left frontal lobe (*arrow*). The ventricles are enlarged in this patient. (*B*) Contrast enhancement shows luxury perfusion in the area of infarction (*arrows*).

density of the dural sinuses, and on contrast enhancement, a radiolucent, triangular defect is seen at the confluence of the straight and transverse sinuses (1, 2). Stroke, due to vascular occlusive disease, also is uncommon in children, but with CT scanning produces an area of hypodensity (infarction-edema), later followed on the contrast-enhanced scan, by luxury perfusion around the infarcted area (Fig. 5.75). Such infarcts can

occur spontaneously or as a complication of intracranial infection such as meningitis.

REFERENCES

1. Eick, J.J., Miller, K.D., Bell, K.A., and Tutton, R.H.: Computed tomography of deep cerebral venous thrombosis in children. Radiology 140: 399–402, 1981.
2. Rao, K.C.V.G., Knipp, H.C., and Wagner, E.J.: Computed tomographic findings in cerebral sinus and venous thrombosis. Radiology 140: 391–398, 1981.

CHAPTER 6
The Spine and Spinal Cord

CERVICAL SPINE INJURIES

Injuries of the cervical spine are less common in the infant and young child than in the older child, teenager, and adult (3, 4), but one's approach to the analysis of the roentgenograms is the same whatever the age. In this regard, one's most important job is to determine whether the cervical spine is stable or unstable. To do this, one must understand all of the mechanisms of cervical spine injury and the abnormal findings they produce. It is to this end that this chapter is devoted primarily.

What Views Are Necessary? Patients with cervical spine injuries fall into two groups: (a) those who are freely ambulant and can move their neck, and (b) those who are not ambulant and often unconscious. In the latter group, one should confine the examination to cross-table lateral, frontal, and open-mouth odontoid views, and all should be obtained without moving the patient. In the ambulant patient, lateral, frontal, open-mouth odontoid, and oblique views are in order, and in addition, flexion and extension views may be necessary. With these latter views, it is best to have the patients perform the flexion-extension maneuvers themselves, for in this way, it is less likely that they will move their necks beyond safe limits.

Visualize All of the Cervical Spine. This is necessary for it is well known that if the cervical spine is not fully extended, that is,

if the shoulder covers the lower cervical spine, one can miss significant lesions in this area. Consequently, it is most important to count the vertebral bodies and make sure that all of them are included on any given film. Always count seven vertebrae.

It is also important to remember that spinal injuries may occur at multiple levels. This can occur in the cervical spine alone, or throughout the entire vertebral column (2, 5, 8). In addition, it might also be recalled that facial injuries often are associated with hyperextension spinal injuries and that blows to the back of the head can induce concomitant flexion injuries of the cervical spine.

POLYTOMOGRAPHY AND CT SCANNING

Generally speaking, when one can not identify a fracture on plain films, polytomography or more currently, computerized tomography (CT) scanning (1, 6, 7), is in order. However, as opposed to cranial and intracranial injuries, the plain film remains an important study in the assessment of spinal injury. There is no question that both CT scanning and polytomography add another parameter to the assessment of bony injury to the spine, but neither can replace the initial spine roentgenogram. *One still makes one's basic decisions regarding stability or instability of an injury from plain films.*

REFERENCES

1. Brant-Zawadzki, M., Jeffrey, R.B., Jr., Minagi, H., and Pitts, L.H.: High resolution CT of thoracolumbar fractures. A.J.R. 138: 699–704, 1982.
2. Calenoff, L., Chessar, J.W., Rogers, L.F., Toerge, J., and Rosen, J.S.: Multiple level spinal injuries: importance of early recognition. A.J.R. 130: 665–669, 1978.
3. Dunlap, J.P., Morris, M., and Thompson, R.G.: Cervical spine injuries in children. J. Bone Joint Surg. 40A: 681–686, 1958.
4. Gaugin, L.M., and Goodman, S.J.: Cervical spine injuries in infants: problems in management. J. Neurosurg. 42: 179–184, 1975.
5. Gehweiler, J.A., Jr., Clark, W.M., Schaaf, R.E., Powers, B., and Miller, M.D.: Cervical spine trauma: the common combined conditions. Radiology 130: 77–86, 1979.
6. McInerney, D.P., and Sage, M.R.: Computer assisted tomography in the assessment of cervical spine trauma. Clin. Radiol. 30: 203–206, 1979.
7. Radmor, R., Davis, K.R., Roberson, G.H., New, P.F.J., and Taveras, J.M.: Computed tomographic evaluation of traumatic spinal injuries. Radiology 127: 825–827, 1978.
8. Scher, A.T.: Double fractures of the spine—an indication for routine radiographic examination of the entire spine after injury. S. Afr. Med. J. 53: 411–413, 1978.

WHAT TO LOOK FOR IN CERVICAL SPINE INJURIES

One should have some system for analyzing the cervical spine, and in this regard, I have found it best to start with the lateral view. This view is the most informative view, and a number of assessments should be accomplished before turning to the frontal and oblique views. First, one should note the general curvature of the spine, and then one should assess the various structures from front to back. These structures include the prevertebral soft tissues, predental space (C_1 to dens distance), odontoid process, individual vertebral bodies, disc spaces, apophyseal joints, neural arches, and spinous tips.

Loss of Normal Cervical Spine Curvature. On lateral view, the cervical spine in the normal, neutral position assumes a gentle lordotic curve (Fig. 6.1), and on frontal view, it is straight. Deviation from these normal alignments usually reflects the presence of underlying muscle spasm and/or bony/ligament injury. Spasm usually produces a straight spine on lateral view, and in many children may lead to a mild to moderate anterior, kyphotic angulation of C_2 on C_3 (Fig. 6.2). In such cases, there is no anterior displacement of the body of C_2 on the body of C_3, and although the overall configuration may appear worrisome, it is quite reversible and not representative of a fracture or dislocation. Localized kyphosis at lower levels, on the other hand, usually is

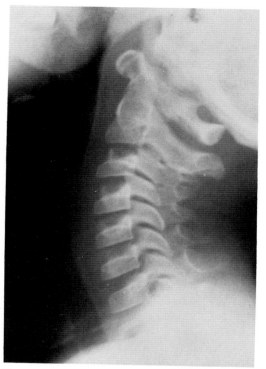

Figure 6.1. *Normal cervical spine curvature.* Note the gentle lordosis of the cervical spine. Also note the normal predental distance, the normal synchondrosis (*horizontal radiolucent line*) between the dens and body of C_2, and the normal prevertebral soft tissues. In addition, note the high position of the anterior arch of C_1. This occurs during extension and is normal. It should not be misinterpreted for posterior dislocation of C_1.

significant and indicates the presence of ligamentous laxity secondary to a hyperflexion injury.

Prevertebral Soft Tissue Thickening. Prevertebral soft tissue thickening due to edema or hematoma formation is a very important ancillary finding in cervical spine injuries. However, it should be noted from the outset that it is not present in all cases (2). There is good reason for this, for in those cases where no anterior spinal ligament or vertebral body injury occurs, there is no reason for the prevertebral soft tissues to become widened. Consequently, in a good many significant cervical spine injuries, the prevertebral soft tissues are normal. This lack of prevertebral soft tissue thickening frequently occurs with minimal anterior compression fractures and undisplaced fractures of the dens (2).

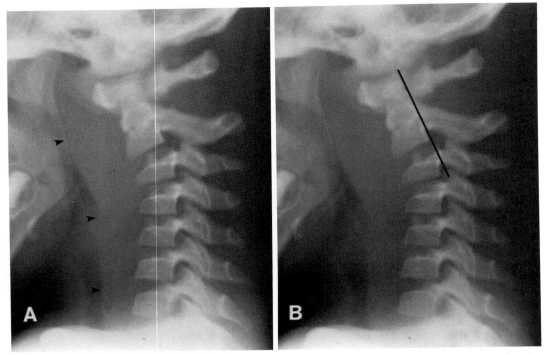

Figure 6.2. *C₂–C₃ angulation pseudoabnormality and pseudoprevertebral soft tissue thickening.*   (*A*) Note that the prevertebral soft tissues appear thickened (*arrows*). Such thickening is due to poor roentgenographic technique (i.e., inadequate distension of the airway and hyperflexion of the spine). Also note that C₂ is angled forward on C₃. However, in (*B*) note that a *line* drawn along the posterior aspect of the dens and body of C₂ demonstrates that there is no associated anterior displacement of C₂ on C₃. In the absence of such displacement, angulation of C₂ on C₃ is of no particular consequence and can be seen with both voluntary and involuntary muscle spasm. Finally, note that the predental distance is wide (4–5 mm in this patient), and that the distance between the spinous tips of C₁ and C₂ also is unusually wide. Both of these findings are normal.

Another problem with the assessment of the prevertebral soft tissues in the infant and young child is that if the airway is not fully distended, or the spine not fully extended, pseudothickening can be suggested (Fig. 6.2). True soft tissue swelling should be reproducible from film to film, and also should cause anterior displacement and indentation of the airway (Fig. 6.3). In the upper soft tissues, however, even these considerations may not solve the problem, for normal adenoidal lymphoid tissue can significantly interfere with interpretation (Fig. 6.4). Over the lower cervical spine, in those cases where soft tissue thickening is borderline, it may be helpful to note whether the prevertebral fat stripe is displaced anteriorly (3). Displacement of this fat stripe can be taken to indicate the presence of an underlying vertebral injury, but it is of limited

value in the pediatric age group, for it is not readily visible in the infant and young child.

In terms of normal measurement guidelines for prevertebral soft tissue thickening in children far too much variability exists for such measurements to be extremely useful. Nonetheless, it has been suggested that above the glottis soft tissue thickness of 7 mm or more be considered abnormal, and that below the glottis over 14 mm of soft tissue space be considered abnormal (1). These measurements are reasonably dependable in the older child, but must be adjusted upward in younger children and infants where vertebral body ossification is incomplete and even greater width variation occurs. In general, however, the measurements do reflect an overall *rule that below the level of the glottis the normal soft tissues double in thickness.* This occurs because be-

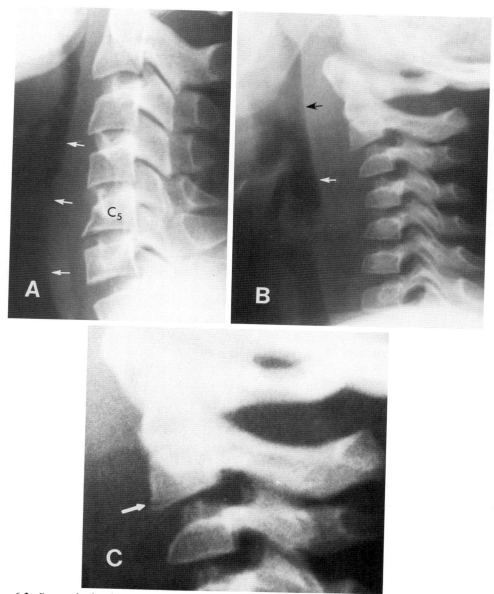

Figure 6.3. *Prevertebral soft tissue swelling.* (*A*) Note prevertebral soft tissue swelling (*arrows*) anterior to a compression fracture of C$_5$. Not only are the tissues thickened, but they also are producing anterior displacement of the airway. Compare these prevertebral soft tissues with the normal ones illustrated in Figure 6.1. (*B*) Another patient with marked prevertebral soft tissue swelling (*arrows*). No bony injury is detected, but there is a subtle, nondisplaced corner, or teardrop avulsion fracture at the bottom of C$_2$. (*C*) Close-up view demonstrates this fracture (*arrow*) to better advantage. Visualization of this fracture infers significant ligament injury, which is manifest, in this case, by marked soft tissue swelling.

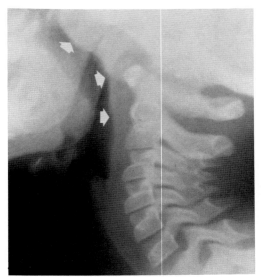

Figure 6.4. *Normal adenoidal prevertebral soft tissues.* Note prominent adenoidal prevertebral soft tissues over the upper cervical spine (*arrows*). This type of soft tissue thickening should not be misinterpreted for pathologic thickening.

low this level the esophagus separates from the airway and becomes part of the airless prevertebral soft tissue mass.

REFERENCES

1. Clark, W.M., Gehweiler, J.A., Jr., and Laib, R.: Twelve significant signs of cervical spine trauma. Skeletal Radiol. 3: 201–205, 1979.
2. Penning, L.: Prevertebral hematoma in cervical spine injury: incidence and etiologic significance. A.J.R. 136: 553–561, 1981.
3. Whalen, J.P., and Woodruff, C.L.: The cervical prevertebral fat stripe. A.J.R. 109: 445–451, 1970.

Increase in the Predental Space (C_1 to Dens Distance). Before beginning any discussion of the predental distance, one must realize that normal variations are much more pronounced in children than in adults. In the adult, a distance of over 2.5 mm usually is considered abnormal, but in children distances of 3–4 mm are commonplace and normal (Fig. 6.5). Indeed, a few children can demonstrate a predental distance of 5 mm and still be normal. This was demonstrated by Locke et al. (2) a number of years ago, and duplicated in our own survey of 100 consecutive cervical spine roentgenograms in normal children (Table 6.1). In addition to these differences, it should be noted that the predental distance can widen significantly between flexion and extension

(Fig. 6.6), often with variations of up to 2 mm (1). Consequently, one must be cautious not to overinterpret an *apparently* abnormally wide predental space in children.

Abnormal widening of the predental space occurs when there is disruption of the transverse ligament between C_1 and the dens, but in actual fact, this is not such a common injury, even with dens fractures. The reason for this is that the dens and C_1 move as a unit, and thus the predental distance is not altered. Actually, widening of the predental space occurs more often with atlantoaxial instability due to underlying abnormalities such as rheumatoid arthritis or congenital hypoplasia of the dens. In either case, these patients are prone to abnormal atlantoaxial movement, and dislocation without fracture is more likely to occur.

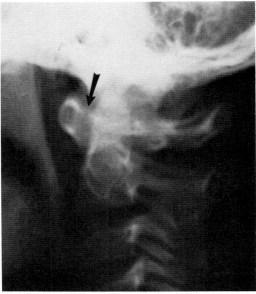

Figure 6.5. *Normal wide predental space.* Note the wide (4–5 mm) predental space (*arrow*) in this normal 8-year-old child.

Table 6.1. *Normal Predental (C_1 to DENS) Distances*

Predental Distance (mm)	Number of Patients
1–1½	7
2–2½	54
3–3½	27
4–4½	9
5	3
Total	100

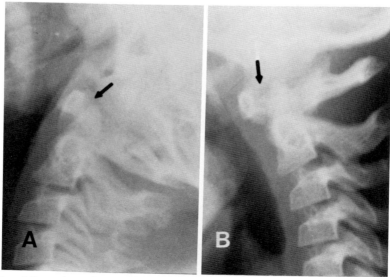

Figure 6.6. *Predental distance—variation with extension and flexion.* (*A*) On extension note the normal appearance of the predental space (*arrow*). (*B*) With flexion note how much widening has occurred (*arrow*). This patient was normal.

Other injuries which can be associated with an increase in the predental distance include rotatory subluxation of C_1 on C_2 and some Jefferson, bursting fractures of C_1.

Finally, a word regarding high positioning of the anterior arch of C_1 during extension in normal children is in order. In these cases, with extension, the anterior arch of C_1 can rise high above the dens and still be normal (see Fig. 6.1). The finding should not be misinterpreted for a posterior dislocation of C_1.

REFERENCES

1. Cattell, H.S., and Filtzer, D.L.: Pseudosubluxation and other normal variations in the cervical spine in children. J. Bone Joint Surg. 47A: 1295–1309, 1965.
2. Locke, G.R., Gardner, J.I., and Van Epps, E.F.: Atlas-dens interval (ADI) in children: a survey based on 200 normal cervical spines. A.J.R. 97: 135–140, 1966.

Displacement of the Vertebral Bodies.

In most instances, displacement of one vertebral body on another is a significant abnormal finding and reflects underlying instability of the spine. Anterior displacement is much more common than posterior displacement and usually occurs with flexion injuries, but it also can occur with rotatory, and some extension injuries.

Anterior displacement of the vertebral bodies in the upper cervical spine of children must be interpreted with a certain degree of caution, for it is well known that such dis-

placement commonly occurs on a physiologic basis (1–3, 5–9). It may involve all of the upper four vertebral bodies or C_2–C_3 only. In those cases where multiple vertebral bodies are involved, the findings are not difficult to interpret (Fig. 6.7), but when isolated anterior displacement of C_2 on C_3

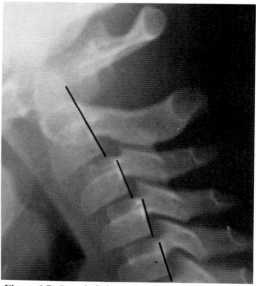

Figure 6.7. *Pseudodislocation of upper cervical spine—multiple levels.* Note that each of the vertebral bodies from C_2 through C_5 demonstrates anterior displacement. Such displacement is normal and physiologic.

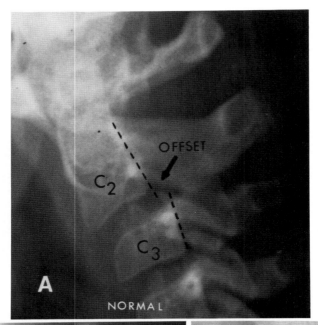

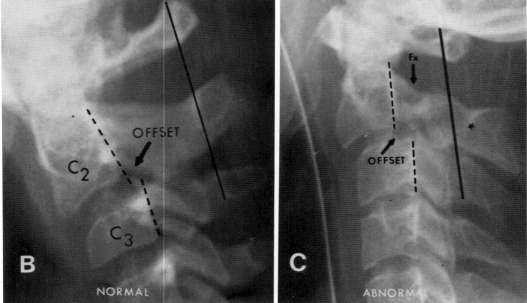

Figure 6.8. *Physiologic dislocation of C_2 on C_3—use of posterior cervical spine.* (*A*) Note that C_2 is anteriorly displaced on C_3 (*dotted lines*). (*B*) The *posterior cervical line* is drawn from the anterior cortex of the spinous process of C_1 to the anterior cortex of the spinous process of C_3. In this case, it passes directly through the middle of the anterior cortex of C_2. This is normal, and thus the findings represent physiologic displacement of C_2 on C_3 only. (*C*) *Pathologic dislocation of C_2 on C_3 secondary to hangman's fracture—use of posterior cervical line.* Note that the body of C_2 is displaced forward on the body of C_3 and that offsetting is present. Also note that the *posterior cervical line* is abnormal in that it misses the cortex of C_2 (*star*) by more than 2 mm. The actual measurement was 4 mm. (Reprinted with permission from L.E. Swischuk: Anterior displacement of C_2 in children—physiologic and pathologic. (A helpful differentiating line), Radiology 122: 759–763, 1977.)

occurs, interpretation can be a problem. Indeed, in some children, the degree of displacement is so pronounced that it is almost impossible to accept that it is physiologic (Fig. 6.8). Nonetheless, it is physiologic in most cases and results from the fact that the fulcrum for flexion of the upper cervical spine is at the C_2–C_3, level and that the cervical spine generally is a lax structure in children. Consequently, a great deal of normal motion can occur at this site, and in most cases it is further enhanced by a more horizontal attitude of the C_2–C_3, and other upper apophyseal joints in children.

As an aid to this problem, I devised the ***posterior cervical line*** (7), and this line has proven to be most helpful to me in differentiating physiologic, from pathologic displacement of C_2 on C_3 (Fig. 6.8). The line is drawn from the anterior aspect of the cortex of the spinous process of C_1 to the same point on C_3 and its relationship to the anterior cortex of C_2 is noted. If it misses the anterior cortex of C_2 by 2.0 mm or more, a true dislocation should be present, and this usually is associated with an underlying hangman's fracture. A measurement of 1.5 mm is borderline, but under 1.5 mm the findings should represent physiologic displacement only (Fig. 6.8). A diagrammatic representation of the normal limits for the posterior cervical line is presented in Figure 6.9, but before one examines these limits, it must be underscored that the ***posterior cervical line should be applied only in those cases where anterior displacement of C_2 on C_3 is present*** (7). This is most important for with the spine in neutral or extended position, the posterior cervical line commonly will miss the posterior arch of C_2 by 2 mm in normal individuals (4, 7). This occurs because in these positions the posterior arch of C_2 lies far back of C_3 and C_1 (Fig. 6.10). It is only when C_2 is displaced forward on C_3 that a distance of 2 mm or more becomes significant (7).

The phenomenon of physiologic anterior displacement of C_2 on C_3 is common in childhood but tends to disappear around the age of 16 years. It has been documented in young adults (3), but generally it is a phenomenon of the early and mid-pediatric age group. In addition, it might be noted that, in a few instances, the posterior cervical line may measure normal and yet ligamentous injury leading to instability of C_2 on C_3 can arise (see Fig. 6.18). ***A normal posterior cervical line excludes a hangman's fracture, but not necessarily pure ligament injury.***

Pathologic posterior displacement of one vertebral body on another is not particularly common but probably occurs during the acute phase of certain extension injuries. Such displacement, however, does not seem to persist for long, and the reason may be that with subsequent return to a more neutral position or with hyperflexion secondary to whiplashing, normal alignment tends to reestablish itself. Normal physiologic posterior displacement also is not particularly

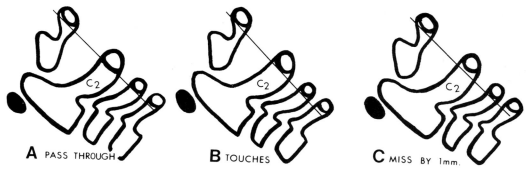

Figure 6.9. *Posterior cervical line—normal limits.* The posterior cervical ine is normal when it: (*A*) passes through or just behind the cortex of C_2, (*B*) touches the anterior cortex of C_2, or (*C*) passes within 1 mm of the anterior aspect of the cortex of C_2. If it passes 1.5 mm in front of the cortex, it is borderline in significance, but if it misses the cortex by 2.0 mm or more, an underlying pathologic dislocation should be present. (Reprinted with permission from L.E. Swischuk: Anterior displacement of C_2 in children—physiologic or pathologic. (A helpful differentiating line). Radiology 122: 759–763, 1977.)

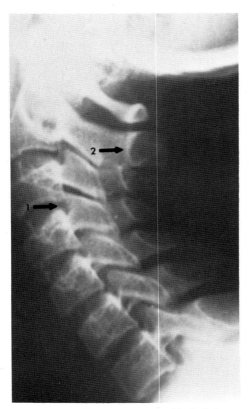

Figure 6.10. *Normal posterior vertebral body dislocation and posterior position of the spinous process of C_2.* Note normal posterior displacement of C_3 on C_4 (*1*) and the normal posterior position of the spinous process of C_2 (*2*). In the neutral or extended position, this is the normal location of the spinous process of C_2. With flexion, it moves forward and lines up with the spinous processes of C_1 and C_3. In so doing, it constitutes the basis for the application of the posterior cervical line as delineated in Figures 6.8 and 6.9.

common (1), but it does occur (Fig. 6.10). In such cases, I have not seen the displacement to result in more than 1–2 mm of offsetting. Displacement of the vertebral bodies in a lateral direction also can occur and usually is associated with severe fracture-dislocations with significant changes also visible on lateral view.

Alterations in the Width of the Disc Space. In most normal patients the width of the intervertebral disc spaces is the same from one level to another. This is most important for if there is a gross discrepancy, underlying longitudinal ligament injury with cervical spine instability should be present. Narrowing of the disc space occurs with

flexion and rotation injuries, but widening of the disc space almost always signifies the presence of an underlying extension injury. Disc space narrowing or widening is best assessed on lateral views, but obviously can also be assessed on frontal views.

REFERENCES

1. Cattell, H.S., and Filtzer, D.L.: Pseudosubluxation and other normal variations in the cervical spine in children. J. Bone Joint Surg. 47A: 1295–1309, 1965.
2. Harrison, R.B., Keats, T.E., Winn, H.R., Riddervold, H.O., and Pope, T.L., Jr.: Pseudosubluxation in the axis in young adults. J. Can. Assoc. Radiol. 31: 176–177, 1980.
3. Jacobson, G., and Bleecker, H.H.: Pseudosubluxation of the axis in children. A.J.R. 82: 472–481, 1959.
4. Kattan, K.R.: Backward "displacement" of the spinolaminal line at C_2: a normal variation. A.J.R. 129: 289–290, 1977.
5. Pennecot, G.F., Gouraud, D., Hardy, J.R., and Pouliquen, J.C.: Roentgenographical study of the stability of the cervical spine in children. J. Pediatr. Orthop. 4: 346–352, 1984.
6. Sullivan, C.R., Bruwer, A.J., and Harris, L.E.: Hypermobility of the cervical spine in children: a pitfall in the diagnosis of cervical dislocation. Am. J. Surg. 95: 636–640, 1958.
7. Swischuk, L.E.: Anterior displacement of C_2 in children: physiologic or pathologic? A helpful differentiation. Radiology 122: 759–763, 1977.
8. Teng, P., and Paptheodorou, C.: Traumatic subluxation of C_2 in young children. Bull. Los Angeles Neurol. Soc. 32: 197–202, 1967.
9. Townsend, E.H., Jr., and Rowe, M.L.: Mobility of the upper cervical spine in health and disease. Pediatrics 10: 567–572, 1952.

Abnormal Apophyseal Joint Configurations. On a true lateral view of the cervical spine, all of the apophyseal joints are visualized (Fig. 6.11*A*), but with rotation the apophyseal joints are thrown one off the other. However, if all are rotated to the same general degree, rotation due to positioning only should be the cause (Fig. 6.11*B*). If, however, there is an abrupt discrepancy at one level, that is if the apophyseal joints are visualized in true lateral position to a certain point and then above this they are visualized in oblique position, one should suspect rotatory subluxation with a locked facet (see Fig. 6.37).

In other cases, the apophyseal joints can be frankly dislocated or subluxated, and almost always this occurs with flexion injuries. In such cases, the joints, in addition to being anteriorly dislocated, also may appear unduly wide or narrow. Either configuration is abnormal and should infer ligamentous injury with instability.

Widening of the Joints of Luschka. On normal frontal projection, with lateral bend-

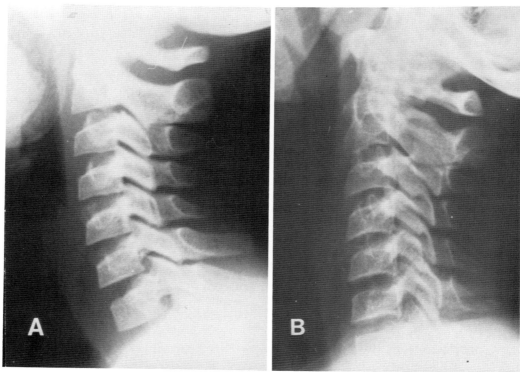

Figure 6.11. *Normal apophyseal joints.* (*A*) Lateral view demonstrating superimposed apophyseal joints at all levels. (*B*) Obliquity due to faulty positioning causes all of the apophyseal joints to be rotated one off the other. However, all are obliqued to about the same degree. This still is normal. If there were an abrupt change in the alignment of the apophyseal joints at one level, a unilateral locked facet would be present (see Figs. 6.36 and 6.37).

ing, the contralateral joints of Luschka uniformly increase in width. This phenomenon is quite common and renders evaluation of the joints of Luschka somewhat difficult. However, if one sees undue widening at one or two levels, then one should suspect underlying ligamentous injury.

Interspinous Distance Widening. Widening of the interspinous distance is seen with hyperflexion injuries which result in tearing of the posterior spinal ligaments. It is most important to determine whether such an increase in distance is present, for if it is, the injury is unstable. In the upper cervical spine, however, it should be noted that very commonly the distance between the spinous tip of C_1 and C_2 appears unusually wide and is entirely normal (see Figs. 6.2 and 6.7). In such cases, I believe that tight ligamentous attachments between the base of the skull and C_1 cause the pseudoabnormal configuration. It is a very common finding in chil-

dren (1) and should not be misinterpreted for pathologic separation of the spinous processes of C_1 and C_2. Widening of the interspinous distance also can be appreciated on frontal view (2).

REFERENCES

1. Cattell, H.S., and Filtzer, D.L.: Pseudosubluxation and other normal variations in the cervical spine in children. J. Bone Joint Surg. 47A: 1295–1309, 1965.
2. Naidich, J.B., Naidich, T.P., Garfein, C., Liebeskind, A.L., and Hyman, R.A.: The widened interspinous distance: a useful sign of anterior cervical dislocation in the supine frontal projection. Radiology 123: 113–116, 1977.

Lateral Deviation of the Spinous Processes. On frontal view, in most normal patients the spinous tips are lined up in a straight line. As long as no anomalies such as bifid or unfused spinous tips are present, the tips are easy to visualize. If rotation secondary to positioning occurs, the spinous tips are deviated to the opposite side, but the degree of deviation is progressive and more pronounced in the upper spine. If deviation of the spinous tips is abrupt at one level, one should suspect underlying rotatory subluxation with a locked facet (see Fig. 6.38).

Interpedicular Space Widening. Widening of the interpedicular space occurs with bursting fractures of the vertebral bodies. In such cases, on frontal view, the pedicles are displaced laterally and the distance between them increased. In addition the apophyseal joints also may widen.

Lateral Mass of C_1 to Dens Relationships. A number of offsetting abnormalities of the lateral masses of C_1 have been described (1–6) and to say the least the subject is confusing. For example, some authorities have stated that unilateral medial insetting of one lateral mass is indicative of rotatory subluxation, while others have indicated that it can be seen normally. Numerous other examples of differences of opinion can be cited, and after reviewing the entire subject, I have come to the conclusion that almost any type of offsetting can be produced by varying degrees of rotation and tilting of the upper cervical spine in normal and abnormal individuals. Because of this, I feel that the only significant abnormal configuration is that of bilateral or unilateral outward offsetting of the lateral masses as seen with Jefferson bursting fractures of C_1 (see Fig. 6.42). Of course, this is not to say that offsetting abnormalities do not occur with the various rotatory problems encountered in this area, but only that they are so inconsistent and intertwined with normal variations that their evaluation becomes difficult and tenuous. For this reason, rather than spending a great deal of time trying to decide whether offsetting is normal or abnormal in these cases, I find it more productive to examine the upper cervical spine from its other aspects.

REFERENCES

1. Fielding, J.W., and Hawkins, R.J.: Atlanto-axial rotatory fixation (fixed rotatory subluxation of the atlanto-axial joint). J. Bone Joint Surg. 59: 37–44, 1977.
2. Jacobson, G., and Adler, D.C.: Examination of the atlanto-axial joint following injury with particular emphasis on rotational subluxation. A.J.R. 76: 1081–1094, 1956.
3. Jacobson, G., and Adler, D.C.: An evaluation of lateral atlanto-axial displacement in injuries of the cervical spine. Radiology 61: 355–362, 1961.
4. Shapiro, R., Youngberg, A.S., and Rothman, S.L.G.: The differential diagnosis of traumatic lesions of the occipito-atlanto-axial segment. Radiol. Clin. North Am. 11: 505–526, 1973.
5. von Torklus, D., and Gehle, W.: *The Upper Cervical Spine.* Grune & Stratton, New York, 1972.
6. Wortzman, G., and DeWar, F.P.: Rotary fixation of the atlanto-axial joint: rotational atlanto-axial subluxation. Radiology 90: 479–487, 1968.

Actual Fracture Visualization. I have left assessment of the cervical spine for the visualization of fractures to the end, not because I feel it is unimportant, but because I think it is more important to first assess the spine in other ways. If one looks for fractures first, then one is more likely to miss the other, perhaps more important, findings. However, when one does get to looking for fractures in the cervical spine, it is most important to appreciate those which are associated with instability. Many of these fractures are clearly visible on regular views but others may remain occult until a variety of oblique views, laminograms or CT scans are obtained.

DETERMINING INSTABILITY OF A CERVICAL SPINE INJURY

In the final analysis, one's most important mission in cervical spine injuries is to determine whether the injury is stable or unstable. In this regard, there are certain abnormal findings which when appreciated should transmit such information. Basically, these

Table 6.2. *Signs of Instability of Cervical Spine Injuries*[a]

Anterior, posterior or lateral dislocation of a vertebral body
Widened or narrowed intervertebral disc spaces
Widened, narrowed or dislocated apophyseal joint
Focally widened (dislocated) joints of Luschka
Bilateral or unilateral locked facets[b]
Separation of the spinous processes with or without associated avulsion fractures
Flexion or extension teardrop fractures
Anterior wedge compression fracture with posterior displacement of involved vertebral body[c]
Widened predental (C_1-dens) space
Bilateral or unilateral outward displacement of the lateral masses of C_1 (Jefferson fracture)
Unilateral anterior displacement of one of the lateral masses of C_1 (rotatory dislocation)
Fracture of the dens, with or without displacement
Bursting fracture of vertebral body

[a] More than one may be present in any case.

[b] May be stable when locked, but after reduction is unstable.

[c] May require flexion views for demonstrable instability.

findings indicate that severe ligamentous injury has occurred, and that because of this, instability is present. These findings are summarized in Table 6.2, and only a few pitfalls exist. These include: (a) the flexion injury which appears normal on extension (see Fig. 6.16), (b) the patient with a central cord syndrome and a normal appearing cervical spine (see Fig. 6.45), and (c) the patient with a non-displaced or minimally displaced fracture through the base of the dens (see Fig. 6.22). In all of these cases, although a significant, unstable injury is present, the cervical spine may appear remarkably normal on initial inspection. Other than under these circumstances, one should be able to correlate the abnormal findings listed in Table 6.2 with the presence of cervical spine instability.

TYPES AND MECHANISMS OF CERVICAL SPINE INJURIES

Injuries to the cervical spine range from minimal soft tissue and ligamentous injury to complete fracture-dislocation with spinal cord injury. Basically, however, the spine is subject to five forces: (a) flexion, (b) extension, (c) lateral flexion, (d) rotation, and (e) axial compression (2, 4, 5, 10, 15, 16, 18, 26, 37). The types of injuries resulting when these forces become excessive are discussed in detail in the following paragraphs.

Flexion Injuries of the Lower Cervical Spine. These injuries usually produce abnormality in three areas: (a) the vertebral body and its ligaments, (b) the apophyseal joints and their ligaments, and (c) the spinous processes and their ligaments (Fig. 6.12). Overall, compressive forces are in effect anteriorly and distraction forces posteriorly. Anteriorly this results in vertebral body compression (Fig. 6.13), and in many cases a triangular, corner, avulsion or "teardrop" fracture (Fig. 6.14). This fracture results from buckling of the anterior longitudinal ligament during hyperflexion and most often it is the lower, anterior corner of the vertebral body which is avulsed (23, 30). When this fracture is noted, an unstable hyperflexion injury can be assumed. In children, the equivalent of the teardrop fracture often consists of displacement of a fragment of the normal vertebral epiphyseal ring (12, 22). An example of such an injury is seen in Figure 6.14C. In other cases, the corner frac-

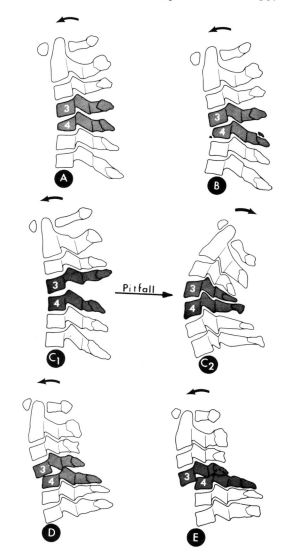

Figure 6.12. *Flexion injuries of the lower cervical space—diagrammatic representation.* (*A*) Minimal flexion causes anterior compression of C_4. (*B*) More pronounced flexion causes anterior dislocation of the apophyseal joints between C_3 and C_4, narrowing of the disc space between the two vertebral bodies, and widening of the interspinous distance between the two vertebrae. Also note an anterior inferior teardrop fracture of C_4, and an avulsion fracture of the spinous process of C_4. (*C*) Flexion injury pitfall. On flexion (Fig. C_1) note that there is separation of the apophyseal joints between C_3 and C_4. Also note that the spinous processes have been separated. On extension (Fig. C_2), however, note that the vertebrae align normally, and that no injury is apparent. This is an important pitfall to avoid in the interpretation of flexion injuries and is illustrated again in Figure 6.16. (*D*) More pronounced flexion causes marked dislocation of C_3 and C_4 and locking of the facets. (*E*) Severe anterior dislocation of C_3 and C_4, with locking of the vertebral bodies.

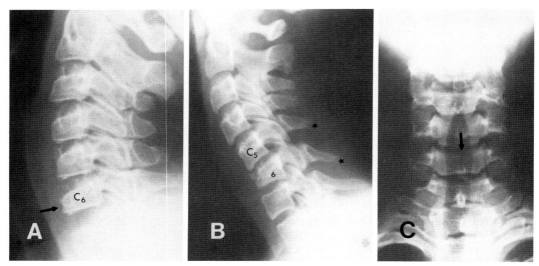

Figure 6.13. *Flexion injuries with compressed vertebrae.* (*A*) Note subtle anterior wedging of C_6 (*arrow*). There is no corresponding soft tissue swelling and no other findings of injury. (*B*) More severe injury demonstrates localized kyphosis at the level of C_5–C_6. The corresponding spinous processes are separated (*), leading to an increase in the interspinous distance. There is anterior apophyseal joint dislocation, narrowing of the intervening disc space, anterior compression and fragmentation of C_6, anterior dislocation of C_5 on C_6, and clear-cut anterior soft tissue swelling. In addition, note that the posterior aspect of C_6 has been displaced into the spinal canal. (*C*) Frontal view demonstrating associated vertical fracture (*arrow*) through the body of C_6.

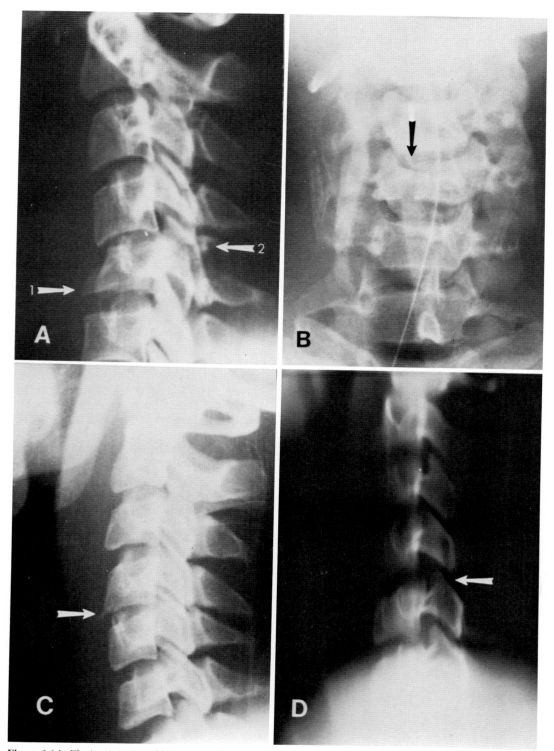

Figure 6.14. *Flexion injuries of lower cervical spine—teardrop and spinous process avulsion fractures.* (*A*) Note the large teardrop fracture (*1*) of C_5. Also note that C_5 is compressed anteriorly and that the disc space between C_4 and C_5 is narrowed. The interspinous distance between C_4 and C_5 also is increased and there is an associated avulsion fracture (*2*) of the posterior elements of C_5. (*B*) Frontal view demonstrating associated vertical fracture (*arrow*) of the compressed and expanded body of C_5. Note again that the disc space between C_4 and C_5 is narrowed. (*C*) Small teardrop fracture along the inferoanterior aspect of C_4 (*arrow*). Actually, this fragment probably represents an avulsed ring epiphysis fragment. Also note marked prevertebral soft tissue swelling and narrowing of the disc space between C_4 and C_5. All of these findings should indicate the presence of an unstable flexion injury. (*D*) Subsequent laminography demonstrates associated anterior dislocation of the apophyseal joint (*arrow*) at the involved level.

ture may be very subtle (see Fig. 6.3*C*). In addition to the findings just noted, accompanying ligamentous injury in and around the disc space can lead to disc disruption and narrowing of the disc space (Figs. 6.13 and 6.14).

Prevertebral soft tissue swelling also is a common finding with flexion injuries, but does not occur in all cases. Indeed, often it is not present with mere anterior compression fractures (Fig. 6.13*A*). However, with more severe injuries, especially when teardrop fractures are seen, the soft tissues appear thickened (Fig. 6.14*C*).

In those cases where significant vertebral body compression occurs, a vertical fracture (27), through the involved vertebra frequently is present (Fig. 6.14*B*). Actually this fracture attests to the presence of associated vertebral compression force. The presence of such compression causes the involved vertebra to become squashed or burst and the vertical fracture is one manifestation of this phenomenon. On lateral view, similar evidence is present in that often there is posterior displacement of the compressed vertebral body into the spinal canal (Fig. 6.13). This finding also is vividly demonstrable with CT scanning (see Fig. 6.54*C*).

The posterior distracting forces associated with hyperflexion injuries lead to ligamentous injury through the apophyseal joints and between the neural arches and spinous processes. At the apophyseal joint level, this can lead either to widening or narrowing of the involved joints and variable degrees of anterior subluxation (Fig. 6.15). Displacement can be minimal and in terms of measurement, 3 mm or more usually is considered abnormal (5). Correspondingly anterior angulation of more than 12–15° also is considered abnormal (5).

At the neural arch and spinous process level, ligamentous injury results in separation of the involved spinous processes, widening of the interspinous distance (25), and in some cases, avulsion fractures of the posterior elements (Fig. 6.14). Once all of these features of flexion injuries of the cervical spine are appreciated, it is easy to understand why the spine becomes unstable. Clearly, when there is damage to the anterior and posterior longitudinal ligaments, the ligaments of the apophyseal joints, neural arches, and spinous processes, instability must result.

At the opposite end of the spectrum of flexion injuries, one can encounter marked

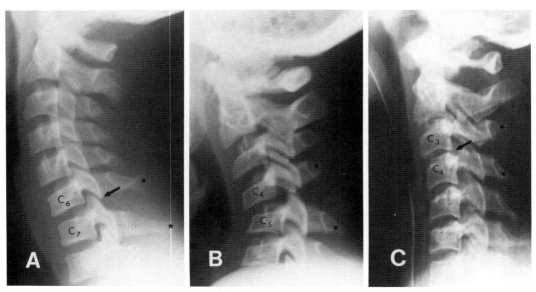

Figure 6.15. *Flexion injury; apophyseal joint dislocation.*   (*A*) Note localized kyphosis at the C_6–C_7 level with slight anterior dislocation through the apophyseal joint (*arrow*). Also note that the posterior aspect of the disc space has widened, and that the distance between the corresponding intraspinous processes has widened (∗). (*B*) Another infant with a marked degree of anterior dislocation of C_4 on C_5. The intraspinous distance also is increased (∗) and the positioning of the facets approaches the perched or locked position. (*C*) Another patient demonstrating anterior dislocation of C_3 on C_4 (*arrow*). This is the only obvious finding of injury. The apophyseal joints are not particularly remarkable, but there is widening of the intraspinous tip distance (∗).

degrees of apophyseal joint and vertebral body dislocation resulting either in bilateral apophyseal joint locking or frank vertebral body locking (see Fig. 6.12, *D* and *E*). These latter two injuries obviously are not difficult to detect clinically or radiographically.

A significant pitfall in the interpretation of flexion injuries of the lower cervical spine deals with the patient whose cervical spine shows little or no abnormality in the neutral or extended position (Fig. 6.16*A*). In these patients, until the spine is flexed, the lesion can escape detection completely (Fig. 6.16*B*). It is important to appreciate this pitfall for the lesion is quite unstable (31).

In addition to this pitfall, it should be recalled that physiologic displacement of the body of C_2 on the body of C_3 is a common phenomenon in childhood (see Fig. 6.8) and should not be misinterpreted for pathologic dislocation. These patients also often demonstrate flattening of the anterosuperior aspect of the body of C3 (Fig. 6.17) and this finding results from chronic compression secondary to the physiologic sliding of C_2 on C_3 during normal flexion. It is a very common finding and should not be misinter-

preted for an acute anterior compression fracture of C_3. Seldom does it go beyond the proportions noted in Figure 6.17. Indeed, when one notes an extremely wedged,

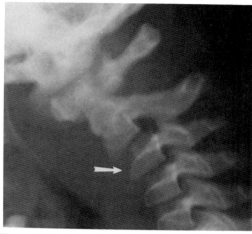

Figure 6.17. *Normal anterior wedging of C_3.* Note anterior wedging of C_3 (*arrow*) due to chronic anterior slipping of C_2 and C_3. Such slipping is physiologic in children and the anterior wedging of C_3 is an extremely common finding which should not be misinterpreted for a compression fracture.

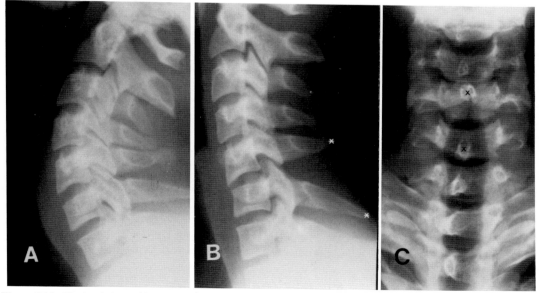

Figure 6.16. *Flexion injury of lower cervical spine—pitfall.* (*A*) On this neutral or extended view, there is little to see in the way of abnormality. Some soft tissue swelling over the anterior lower cervical spine might be suggested, but no fractures or dislocations are visualized. (*B*) With flexion, however, note that the interspinous distance between C_5 and C_6 has increased markedly (*asterisks*). In addition, the apophyseal joints at the same level show anterior dislocation and the disc space at the same level shows a little narrowing. Prevertebral soft tissue swelling again is suggested, but the finding still is equivocal. (*C*) On frontal view, note the increased distance between the involved spinous processes (*x's*). This patient was asymptomatic except for some neck pain, but if the flexion view had not been obtained the injury might have gone undetected. (Courtesy C. Mott, M.D.)

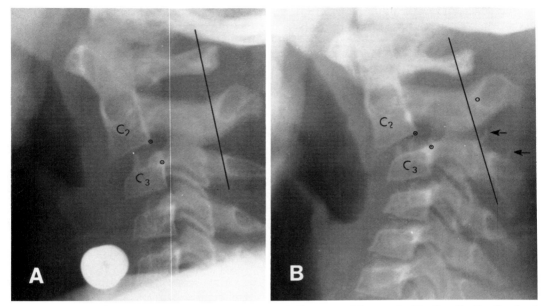

Figure 6.18. *Occult flexion injury C_2–C_3.* (*A*) Note normal alignment of the vertebral bodies. C_2–C_3 offsetting is minimal (*dots*) and appears physiologic. The posterior cervical line lies within normal range. There may be a little prevertebral soft tissue swelling. (*B*) After 2 months in a collar and then 1 month out of a collar, the patient returned with chronic neck pain. Note acute kyphosis at the C_2–C_3 level, anterior displacement of C_2 on C_3 (*dots*) and widening of the C_2–C_3 intraspinous distance. The posterior cervical line is abnormal now and misses the cortex of C_2 by at least 2 mm. Also note calcifications in the ligaments (*arrows*). Such ligamentous injuries are not common, but with persistent neck pain, reexamination of the cervical spine should be obtained. For application of the posterior cervical line, see Figure 6.9.

beaked vertebra in this region, chronic hyperflexion should be considered, and most often this results from a previously unrecognized, unstable, ligamentous injury (26). In these patients initial films usually are normal but later, as symptoms persist, a chronic hyperflexion deformity results (Fig. 6.18). In addition, other findings suggesting injury, such as calcification along the posterior, interspinous ligaments, due to previous avulsions, may be seen (21, 26).

Flexion Injuries of the Atlas and Axis. These injuries most commonly result in fractures through the base of the dens with anterior displacement of the dens (Fig. 6.19). Widening of the predental distance may be present if there is associated anterior dislocation of the atlas on the axis (see Fig. 6.24). In infants and young children, fractures through the base of the dens usually occur through the dens-body synchondrosis (13, 32) (Fig. 6.20). This synchondrosis remains open until late childhood and should not be misinterpreted for a fracture (Fig.

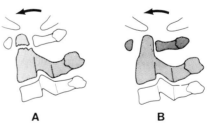

Figure 6.19. *Flexion injuries of the upper cervical spine—diagrammatic representation.* (*A*) Fracture through the base of the dens with slight anterior displacement. (*B*) Isolated atlantoaxial dislocation with no fracture of the dens. Note that the predental distance has increased.

6.21). Lesser degrees of flexion injury may result in an undisplaced fracture of the dens which usually is more difficult to detect (Fig. 6.22). In young infants, such fractures may go unrecognized (32), until pain and loss of normal motion bring the patient back for examination. At that time, some 1–2 weeks later, resorption of bone at the dens-body synchondrosis is seen (Fig. 6.23). These dens

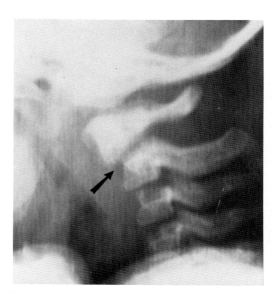

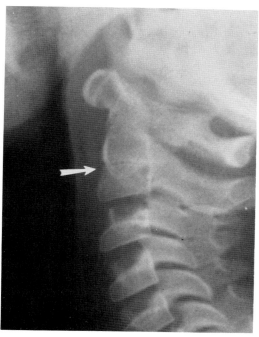

Figure 6.20. *Fracture of dens in infant.* Note that the dens has been displaced anteriorly in this infant who sustained a fracture through the dens-body synchondrosis (*arrow*). Also note that C₁ has been displaced anteriorly and that there is some prevertebral soft tissue swelling.

Figure 6.21. *Normal dens-body synchondrosis of* C₂. Note the normal residual dens-body synchondrosis (*arrow*) of C₂ in this older child. It appears thin and fracture-like except for its smooth, sclerotic edges.

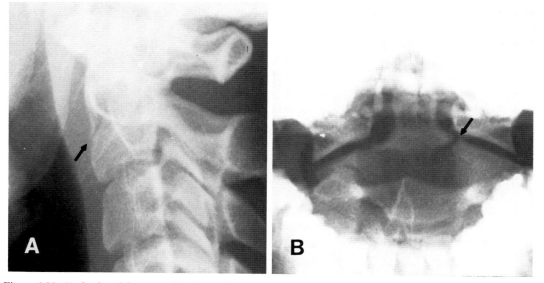

Figure 6.22. *Undisplaced fracture of the base of the dens; subtle findings.* (*A*) Note a subtle fracture through the base of the dens (*arrow*). There is no displacement of the dens, but the prevertebral soft tissues might be slightly widened. (*B*) Frontal view demonstrating the fracture more clearly (*arrow*) and subsequent laminography demonstrated the fracture to extend across the entire base of the dens. (Courtesy T. Brown, M.D.)

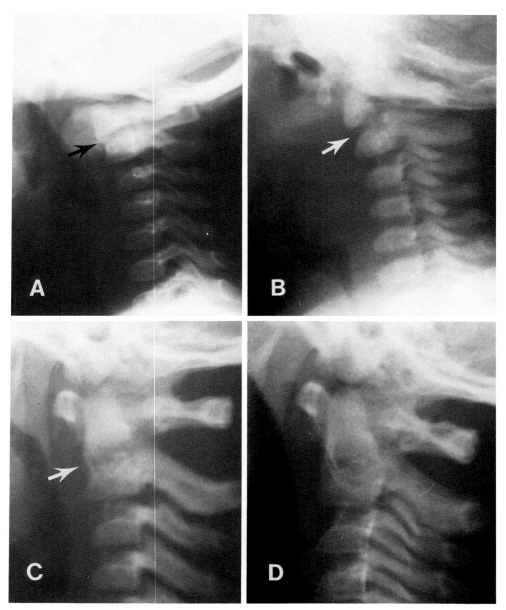

Figure 6.23. *Fracture of dens with widened synchondrosis.* (*A*) Note the widened synchondrosis (*arrow*), and anteriorly cocked dens. (*B*) Another infant demonstrating similar findings. Note especially, the widened synchondrosis (*arrow*), and even some bone resorption along the posterior aspect of the dens. (*C*) Still another patient with neck pain 3 weeks after an automobile accident. Note bone resorption at the junction of the dens and body leading to widening of the synchondrosis (*arrow*). The dens also is cocked forward. (*D*) One year later, note that the dens and body have fused, but that the dens still is cocked forward.

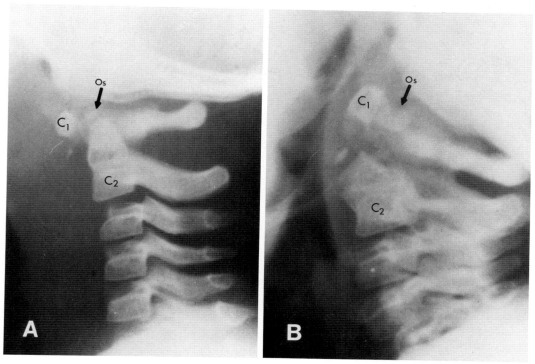

Figure 6.24. C_1 *dislocation, and dens injury with resorption.* (*A*) Note marked soft tissue swelling, anterior displacement of C_1 with an increased C_1-dens distance, and an avulsed bony fragment from C_1. Not clearly seen, but also present is a dislocated os terminale (*Os*). (*B*) Years later, the dens has completely resorbed and the os terminale has overgrown to produce an acquired os odontoideum (*Os*). (From J. E. Ricciardi, H. Kaufer, and D. S. Louis: Acquired os odontoideum following acute ligament injury, J. Bone Joint Surg. 58A: 410–412, 1976.)

fractures probably are more common than generally realized, and indeed, frequently are missed entirely. However, increased width and radiolucency of the synchondrosis (32) should signal their presence and one should be doubly suspicious when the dens is cocked anteriorly (Fig. 6.23). While posterior tilting of the dens is a common, normal phenomenon (see Fig. 6.32*A*), anterior tilting is not, and should suggest injury. In other instances, blood supply to the entire dens may be disrupted and the dens slowly may be resorbed and disappear (Fig. 6.24). In such cases, the normal os terminale overgrows, in a compensatory fashion, and results in the so-called acquired os odontoideum (9, 11, 17).

Anterior atlantoaxial dislocations generally are uncommon but do occur. They may be isolated injuries, or associated with other upper cervical spine injuries (Fig. 6.24). In the pediatric age group, however, isolated atlantoaxial dislocations are more likely to be seen in patients with ligament laxity due to underlying conditions such as rheumatoid arthritis or hypoplasia of the dens with an associated os odontoideum.

Roentgenographically, when anterior atlantoaxial dislocation is present, no matter what the cause, the predental distance is widened. However, it should be remembered that the predental distance in children normally is wider than in adults, and that it is not unusual for it to measure up to 4 or 5 mm and still be normal (see Fig. 6.5). In addition to this finding, it should be recalled that the interspinous distance between C_1 and C_2 also frequently is unusually prominent in some normal children (see Fig. 6.2) and should not be misinterpreted as being indicative of posterior ligamentous injury at this level.

Extension Injuries of the Lower Cervical Spine. These injuries, as opposed to flexion injuries, result in compressive forces posteriorly and distracting forces anteriorly (Fig. 6.25). Consequently, often there is little in the way of vertebral body fracturing, but

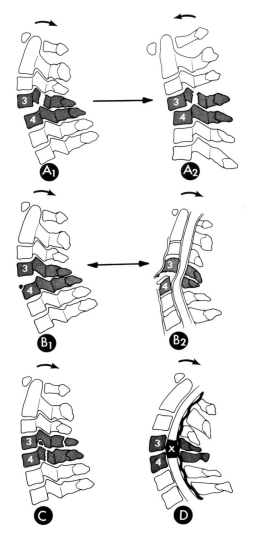

considerable evidence of fracturing of the articular facets, pillars, and posterior elements (Fig. 6.26). However, this is not to say that anterior vertebral body fractures never occur with hyperextension injuries, for actually, one of the most significant hyperextension fractures is the extension type "teardrop" fracture (Fig. 6.27). This fracture occurs anteriorly, and just as the flexion "teardrop" fracture, indicates the presence of significant ligamentous injury and an unstable spine. However, as opposed to the flexion "teardrop" fracture, the extension "teardrop" fracture most commonly involves the upper anterior corner of the ver-

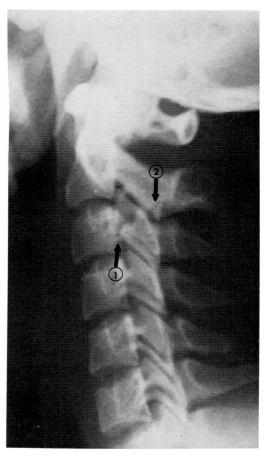

Figure 6.26. *Extension injury—multiple posterior element fractures.* Note fractures through the base of the articular facet of C_3 (*1*) and the posterior articulating facet of C_2 (*2*). The involved facet of C_3 is dislocated posteriorly to a slight degree, and probably rotated. Actually, the injury is most likely the result of a combination of extension and rotation forces.

Figure 6.25. *Extension injuries of the lower cervical spine—diagrammatic representation.* In A_1 extension produces bilateral fractures through the neural arches or pedicles of C_3. Subsequent return to a more neutral position in A_2 leads to anterior displacement of C_3, and narrowing of the intervening disc space. This is the same type of fracture as seen at the C_2 level with the hangman's fracture. In B_1, hyperextension causes widening of the disc space between C_3 and C_4, a characteristic upper anterior teardrop (corner) fracture of C_4, and alteration of the associated apophyseal joint. B_2 demonstrates how stretching and tearing of the anterior longitudinal ligament leads to the avulsion-teardrop fracture and how cord damage occurs with this type of injury. (*C*) Note that hyperextension can produce a variety of posterior element fractures of the involved vertebrae. No anterior injury is present. (*D*) Central cord syndrome. In this type of injury, no fracture occurs, but buckling of the ligamentum flavum during hyperextension causes compression and injury to the cord (×).

tebral body (Fig. 6.27). It results from undue stretching or tearing of the anterior longitudinal ligament during hyperextension (see Fig. 6.25*B*), and because of this, rather than being associated with a narrowed disc space, it usually is associated with a widened disc space (3) (Fig. 6.27).

When an extension "teardrop" fracture is present, prevertebral soft tissue swelling also is present, but if there is no anterior ligamentous injury in patients with hyperextension injuries, the prevertebral soft tissues remain normal. Posteriorly, with hyperextension injuries, a variety of fractures through the neural arches, pedicles, articular facets, pillars, spinous process, etc., can occur. When these latter fractures are unilat-

eral and not associated with any other injuries, the spine is not particularly unstable, but when they are bilateral, and occur through the neural arch or pedicles, they result in an unstable injury. This injury, of course is the same type of injury as occurs with the classic hangman's fracture of C_2, and very often it is not until laminography (Fig. 6.28) or CT scanning are obtained that the posterior element fractures come to one's attention. In addition, many of these injuries are combination flexion-extension injuries (i.e., whiplash injuries), and signs of both flexion and extension damage to the spinal column are seen (Figs. 6.27 and 6.28).

An important pitfall in the evaluation of hyperextenion injuries of the lower cervical spine occurs with the so-called central cord syndrome. This syndrome is discussed at a later point (see Fig. 6.45), but at the present time it should be noted that the cervical spine in these patients usually appears normal. What occurs is that rather than fracture-dislocation, there is buckling of the ligamentum flavum during hyperextension, and this causes focal compression of the spinal cord (Fig. 6.25*D*). Consequently, while clinically there is definite evidence of cord injury, cervical spine films appear remarkably negative.

Extension Injuries of the Atlas and Axis. These are quite common (Fig. 6.29), and among the most common are fractures through the posterior arch of C_1, fractures of the dens, and the classic hangman's fracture of C_2 (7, 24, 33). Fractures through the posterior arch of C_1 can be bilateral or unilateral and can be seen alone or in association with other fractures of C_1 or C_2 (Fig. 6.30). These fractures usually produce narrow defects through the posterior arch of C_1, and in this way can be differentiated from commonly occurring congenital defects of the arch. The latter usually are quite wide and associated with triangular, tapered, or otherwise peculiarly shaped residual, ossified fragments of the posterior arch of C_1 (Fig. 6.31). Less commonly, extension injuries produce transverse fractures of the anterior arch of C_1 (Fig. 6.29*A*). These fractures usually remain occult until laminagraphy is performed and currently all C_1 fractures are best visualized with CT scanning (see Fig. 6.42).

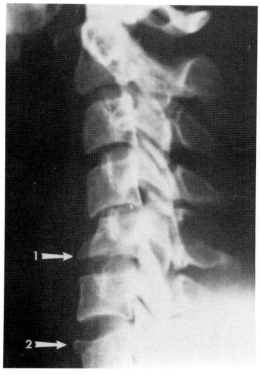

Figure 6.27. *Extension and flexion teardrop fractures.* This patient sustained a whiplash injury, and on this lateral view shows evidence of both flexion and extension injuries. A typical flexion teardrop fracture of C_5 is demonstrated at level *1*. Note that the vertebra above it is anteriorly displaced and that the intervening disc space is narrowed. An extension teardrop fracture is demonstrated at level *2*. Note that it is located at the upper anterior corner of the involved vertebra, and that the disc space is widened. Such widening is characteristic of extension injuries.

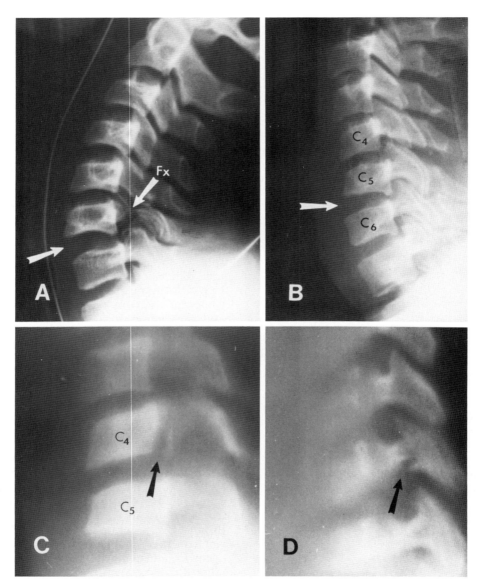

Figure 6.28. *Hyperextension injuries; lower cervical spine.* (*A*) Note the fracture through the posterior elements (*Fx*) and the widened disc space (*anterior arrow*). There is slight anterior displacement of the vertebra above the widened disc space. (*B*) Another patient with anterior displacement of C_4 and widening of the disc space between C_5 and C_6 (*arrow*). Fractures of the posterior elements are not visualized. (*C* and *D*) Tomography, however, demonstrates a number of fractures through the posterior elements (*arrows*), consistent with a hyperextension injury. Most likely in both these patients, both hyperextension and hyperflexion (whiplash) forces were in effect, for anterior dislocation is best explained by the latter.

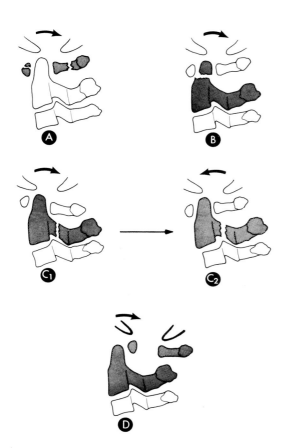

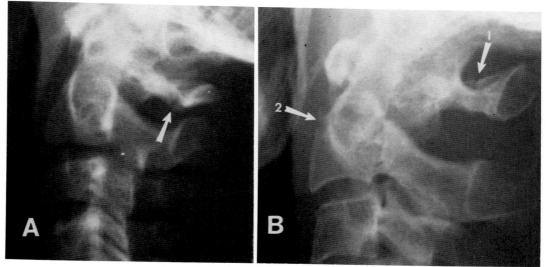

Figure 6.29. *Extension injuries of the upper cervical spine.* (*A*) Typical transverse fracture through the interior arch of C_1 and vertical fracture through the posterior arch of C_1. (*B*) Fracture of the base of the dens with posterior displacement. (*C*) Hangman's fracture of C_2. With initial extension in Fig. C_1, bilateral fractures through the arch or pedicles of C_2 occur. There may or may not be anterior displacement of the body and dens of C_2 at this time. In Fig. C_2 with a subsequent return to a more neutral position, or with hyperflexion secondary to whiplashing, abnormal motion through the fracture site occurs, and the body and dens of C_2, along with all of C_1, move forward. The posterior arch and spinous process of C_2, along with all of C_3, remain posterior. (*D*) Posterior atlantoaxial dislocation without fracture of the dens. This is a very uncommon injury.

Figure 6.30. *Hyperextension, posterior arch of C_1 fractures.* (*A*) Note the typical thin radiolucent line of a fracture (*arrow*) through the posterior arch of C_1. Such fractures can be unilateral or bilateral. (*B*) Another patient demonstrating a vertical fracture through the posterior arch of C_1 (*1*), but in addition there is a fracture through the base of the dens (*2*). Note associated posterior tilting and angulation of the dens. Both of these injuries result from hyperextension.

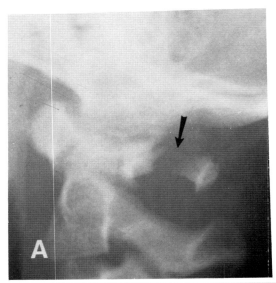

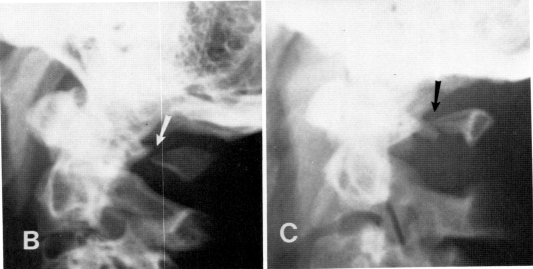

Figure 6.31. *Congenital defects of the posterior arch of* C_1. (*A*) Wide defect (*arrow*) in a young girl who was in an automobile accident. Note the bizarre appearance of the remaining ossicles of the posterior arch of C_1. (*B*) Typical triangular posterior ossicle and tapered ossicle ends seen with congenital defects (*arrow*) of C_1. (*C*) Another patient demonstrating a generally thin and hypoplastic posterior arch of C_1 and typical tapering of the bone ends on either side of the congenital defect (*arrow*). These defects should not be misinterpreted for posterior arch fractures (Fig. C courtesy P. S. Kline, Jr., M.D.).

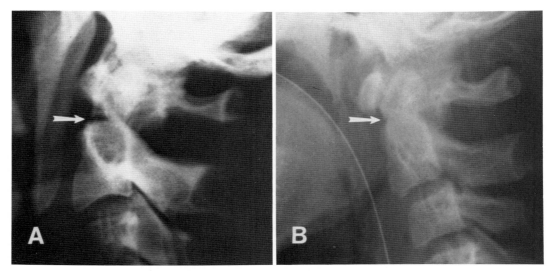

Figure 6.32. *Hyperextension fracture of the dens with posterior tilting.* (*A*) Note a fracture through the base of the dens (*arrow*), and readily visible posterior tilting of the dens. A similar fracture is demonstrated in Figure 6.30*B*. (*B*) *Normal posteriorly tilted dens.* This patient was in an automobile accident and the normal posteriorly tilted dens was misinterpreted for a fractured dens. This type of misinterpretation often is enhanced by the presence of a slight notchlike defect at the base of the dens (*arrow*). Subsequent laminography failed to reveal any type of fracture in this patient.

Fractures of the dens secondary to extension injuries often are associated with a variable degree of posterior tilting or displacement (Fig. 6.32*A*). Minimal such displacements or tilts must be differentiated from the normally tilted or lordotic dens (Fig. 6.32*B*) occurring with surprising frequency in many normal individuals (36). With the hangman's fracture of C_2, initial hyperextension causes bilateral fractures through the neural arch and/or pedicles (Fig. 5.29*B*), and with subsequent return to a more neutral position, or indeed, with hyperflexion due to whiplashing, abnormal motion through the fracture site and associated disc space is induced. This results in anterior displacement of the body of C_2, the dens, and all of C_1. In some of these cases, the fracture is clearly visible while in others it remains obscure. In these latter cases, if any degree of anterior displacement of C_2 on C_3 is suspected, one should apply the posterior cervical line (see Figs. 6.8 and 6.9) and almost always it will be abnormal (i.e., it will miss the posterior arch of C_2 by 2 mm or more, Fig. 6.33). Unilateral neural arch fractures may be more difficult to detect, but usually are not associated with cervical spine instability (Fig. 6.34).

Another injury of the cervical spine sustained during hyperextension is the pure posterior atlantoaxial dislocation (Fig. 6.29*D*). This injury, however, is rare, for the strong transverse ligament usually causes a dens fracture to occur instead.

Lateral Flexion Injuries of the Cervical Spine. These injuries can result in simple ipsilateral vertebral body compression, contralateral fractures of the transverse or uncinate processes (28), and contralateral brachial plexus avulsions (Fig. 6.35). This latter injury is discussed later (see Fig. 6.44), and the other injuries are self-evident and require little in the way of illustration. However, a comment regarding disruption of the joints of Luschka is in order. With some lateral flexion injuries, contralateral widening of the joints of Luschka can occur. If such widening occurs at every level, it most likely is normal, but if there is a marked disparity at one or two levels, significant underlying ligamentous tear with potential instability of the cervical spine should be suspected (see Fig. 6.37*B*). Indeed, very often when this finding is present, considerable injury to the cervical spine has occurred and significant findings also will be present on the lateral view. In the upper cervical spine,

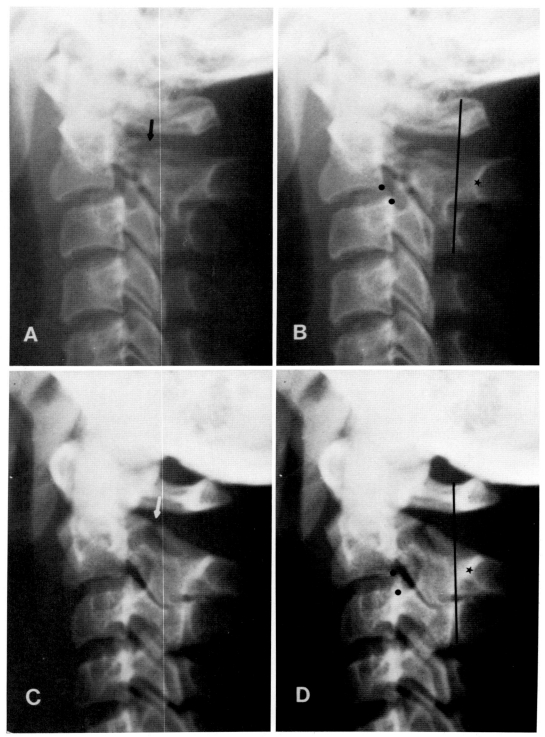

Figure 6.33. *Hangman's fracture of C₂.* (*A*) Typical location of the bilateral fractures through the neural arch-pedicle junctions of C₂ (*arrow*). (*B*) Same patient. Note that C₂ is displaced on C₃ (*dots*), and that the posterior cervical line lies more than 2 mm anterior to the cortex of the spinous process of C₂ (*star*). (*C*) Another patient with more subtle findings. However, note the characteristic location of the fracture (*arrow*). (*D*) Same patient as in C. Very little anterior displacement of C₂ on C₃ is present (*dots*) but the fact that such displacement is present becomes significant. Under these circumstances, the posterior cervical line should be applied, and in this case it misses the anterior cortex of the spinous process of C₂ by more than 2 mm. Consequently, it is abnormal and should reflect the presence of pathologic dislocation secondary to a hangman's fracture. For more discussion of the posterior cervical line in normal and abnormal cases, see Fig. 6.9.

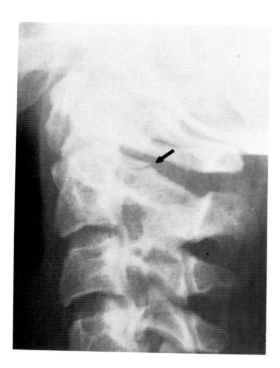

Figure 6.34. *Extension injury of C₂—unilateral arch fracture.* Note the fracture (*arrow*) through the neural arch-pedicle junction of C₂. This was a unilateral fracture and no instability was present.

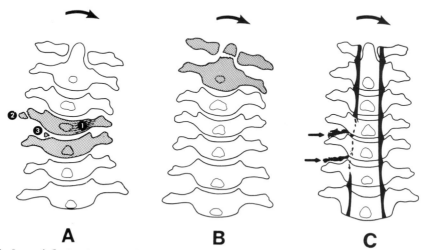

A   **B**   **C**

Figure 6.35. *Lateral flexion injuries of the cervical spine—diagrammatic representation.* (*A*) With flexion, a fracture (compression) can occur through the ipsilateral side of a vertebral body (*1*), on the contralateral side through the transverse process (*2*), or through the uncinate process (*3*). With more pronounced lateral flexion injuries, these latter two fractures also can occur on the ipsilateral side. (*B*) Fracture of the base of the dens with some lateral displacement to the side of flexion. (*C*) Brachial plexus avulsion. These avulsions occur on the side opposite the side of bending. Myelography is required to demonstrate the avulsions and characteristically shows extravasation of contrast material along the avulsed nerve roots (*lower arrows*).

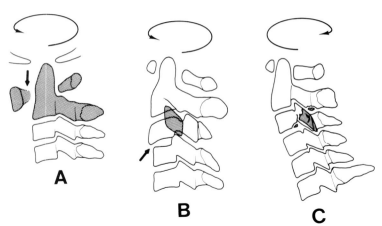

Figure 6.36. *Rotation injuries of the cervical spine—diagrammatic representation.*   (*A*) Rotatory subluxation of C_1 on C_2. One of the anterior masses will be displaced forward and the predental distance (*arrow*) will be increased. (*B*) Unilateral locked facet. In these cases, the involved facet (*shaded*) comes to lie anterior to its mate. In addition, the involved vertebral body becomes anteriorly displaced on the one below it (*arrow*), and the disc space often is narrowed. Both the locked facet and the rotatory subluxation of C_1 result from flexion rotation forces. (*C*) Flexion extension forces usually result in a variety of fractures through the articular pillars, articular facets, and posterior elements.

lateral flexion can produce fractures of the dens with associated lateral displacement of this structure (Fig. 6.35*B*).

Rotation Injuries of the Cervical Spine. These frequently are missed and can occur both in the upper and lower cervical spine (Fig. 6.36). Usually they are associated either with a flexion or extension injury, but most often it is the former. In the lower cervical spine, flexion-rotation injuries result in the so-called unilateral "locked" or "jumped" facet (29). This injury can be suspected on lateral views of the cervical spine either by noting that the rotated vertebral body is anteriorly displaced on the one below it, or that there is an abrupt change in alignment of the apophyseal joints at the level of injury (Fig. 6.37). Anterior

displacement of the vertebral body usually is not difficult to detect and most often is associated with narrowing of the disc space and swelling of the soft tissues anterior to the site of injury. Abnormal alignment of the apophyseal joints, on the other hand, may be more difficult to detect and frequently is missed. However, if one recalls that for the apophyseal joints to be normal, they either should all be in true lateral projection or all rotated to the same degree (see Fig. 6.11), then if one notes an abrupt change in the alignment of the apophyseal joints at one level, one should suspect injury (Fig. 6.37). In many of these cases, associated fractures through the articular facets, pillars, and posterior elements occur, and often there is associated lateral displace-

Figure 6.37. *Unilateral locked facet; rotation-flexion injury.*   (*A*) First note prevertebral soft tissue swelling and then note that C_6 is anteriorly displaced on C_7 (*arrow*). The intervening disc space is narrowed and only one apophyseal joint (the posterior one) is visualized. Above this level, the spine is rotated, and the normal apophyseal joints are visualized in pairs. The fact that only one apophyseal joint is visualized at the site of injury, should suggest that a locked facet is present. (*B*) Frontal view demonstrating deviation of the body, and to some degree the spinous process, of C_6 to the left. Marked widening of the joint of Luschka on the right also is present (*arrow*). (*C*) Another patient demonstrating typical findings of unilateral locked facet at the C_3–C_4 level. Note that the inferior articular facets of C_3 are thrown one off the other; one lies anterior while the other lies posterior (*arrows*). In addition, note that only the upper anterior articular facet is visualized (i.e., the joint is incomplete). Below the level of the injury, both apophyseal joints are superimposed, one on the other, in true lateral position. This abrupt change in alignment of the articular facets and apophyseal joints is characteristic of unilateral locked facet. In addition, note that the body of C_3 is slightly anteriorly displaced on C_4, and that the intervening disc space is a little narrowed. (*D*) Same patient 2 years earlier when the cervical spine was normal. Compare the apophyseal joints and articulating facets with those in the abnormal cervical spine in (*C*).

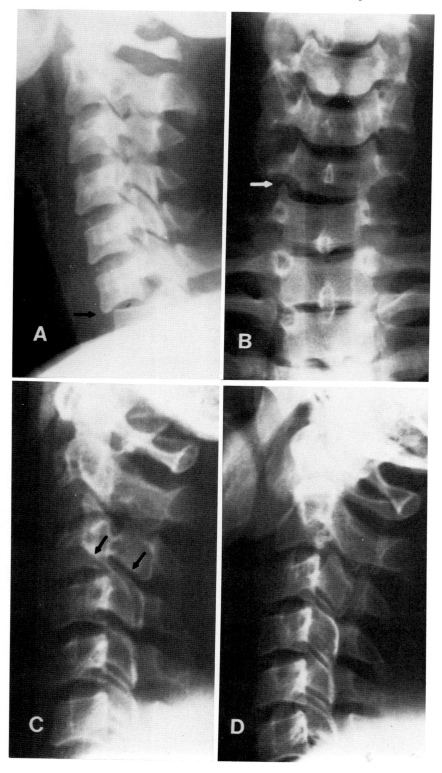

Fig. 6.37.

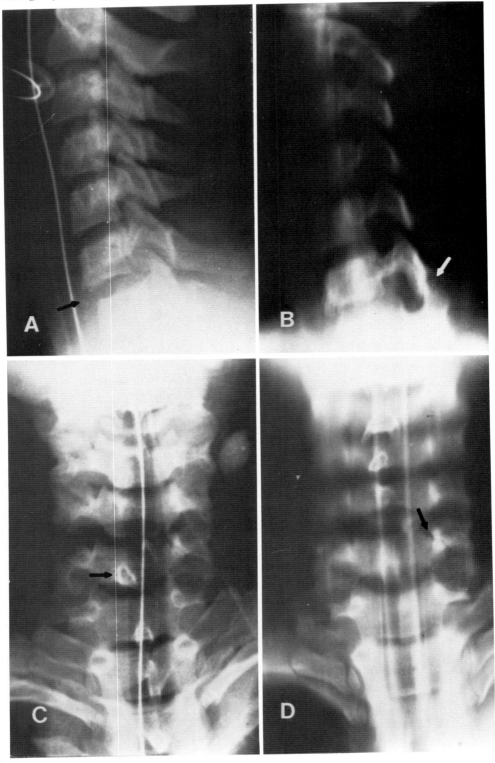

Fig. 6.38.

ment of the upper vertebral body and local-ized widening and dislocation of the joints of Luschka (Figs. 6.37*B* and 6.38). Actual demonstration of the associated fractures and the "locked" or "jumped" facet often is best accomplished with oblique views and/or laminography (Fig. 6.38). On frontal view, a locked facet can be suspected when it is noted that the spinous processes of the rotated vertebra and the vertebrae above it are shifted off midline (Fig. 6.38).

Extension-rotation injuries of the cervical spine usually result in fractures of the artic-ular facets, pillars, and posterior elements (Fig. 6.36*C*). In this regard, the resulting injury is not particularly different from that seen with pure hyperextension injuries.

Rotation Abnormalities of the Atlas and Axis. These consist of rotatory dislocation, rotatory subluxation, and rotatory fixation (8, 19, 20, 34, 38). Rotatory dislocation and subluxation probably represent different de-grees of the same problem, but whereas ro-tatory subluxation usually is reversible with conservative measures, rotatory dislocation requires proper surgical treatment for cor-rection. Actually, rotatory subluxation of C_1 on C_2 is the classic problem in the typical wryneck or torticollis abnormality of child-hood (4, 6, 34). Clinically, these patients present with acute onset of a stiff neck, and often with a history of "catching a draft," or previous "minor trauma." Roentgenograph-ically, lateral views of the cervical spine may be relatively normal or may demonstrate a peculiar cocking or dislocated appearance of C_1 on C_2 (Fig. 6.39). However, in spite of this disturbing appearance of C_1, there will be no evidence of true atlantoaxial disloca-tion in that the predental distance will be normal. On frontal view, however, a char-acteristic alignment of the spinous process of C_2 and the tip of the mandible occurs. Normally when the head is turned to one side, the spinous tips of the vertebral bodies rotate to the opposite side (i.e., opposite to the side to which the mandible has rotated or points). With torticollis, on the other hand, the rotated anterior facet of C_1 be-comes "locked" on the underlying facet of C_2, and because of this C_2 cannot rotate properly. The end result is that the spinous tip of C_2, rather than rotating to the side opposite to which the mandible has rotated, stays on the same side. This is demonstrable on frontal roentgenograms when a line is dropped from the tip of the dens through the midsagittal plane of the dens (Fig. 6.39).

With rotatory dislocation of C_1 on C_2, the same general abnormalities are visualized on frontal view, but on lateral view cocking of C_1 on C_2 is more pronounced and fixed. In addition, there is visible anterior displace-ment of the rotated articular mass of C_1 and widening of the predental space (Fig. 6.40, *A* and *B*). In this way, the findings are quite different from simple torticollis. However, always make sure these assessments are made on a true lateral view of the spine. I mention this because some of these patients have so much torticollis that while the head is in lateral position the spine is obliqued and one's assessments then can become er-roneous. On frontal view, in addition to deviation of the spinous process of C_2 off the midline, it has been noted that inward offsetting of the rotated lateral mass of C_1 also occurs (19, 20). However, while there is no question that such a malalignment occurs in many cases, similar malalignment can be seen under normal circumstances (34). Fur-thermore, it is not uncommon for similar or other offsetting abnormalities of the lateral masses of C_1 to occur with simple torticollis. Consequently, as I have stated previously, I have come to the conclusion that it is best to ignore what the lateral masses are doing in these cases, for there are other, more important, findings to assess.

Rotatory fixation is a peculiar problem

Figure 6.38. *Unilateral locked facet with associated fractures.* (*A*) Note that C_6 is anteriorly displaced on C_7 (*arrow*) and that while above this level the apophyseal joints are seen in pairs, at the level of dislocation only one joint is visualized (the posterior one). Once again, this should signify the presence of a unilateral locked facet. (*B*) Subsequent laminagram demonstrates the locked or jumped facet (*arrow*) at the C_6–C_7 level. (*C*) Frontal view demonstrating the spinous process of C_6 to be displaced to the right (*arrow*). The spinous processes above this level all line up with C_6, while those below the level line up with C_7. This is characteristic of unilateral locked facet. (*D*) Subsequent laminagraphy demonstrates extensive fractures through the lateral aspect of C_6 (*arrow*). The bony ossicles just adjacent to the inner aspect of the ribs are normal secondary ossification centers.

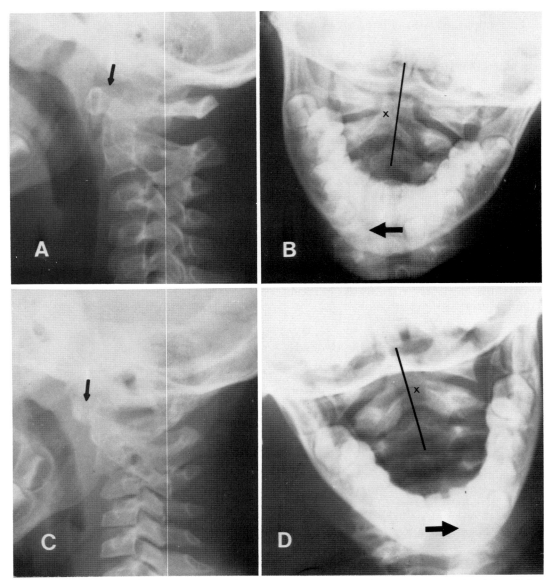

Figure 6.39. *Torticollis or wryneck.* (*A*) Note that in this patient the spine is somewhat rotated and that C_2 is a little cocked forward on C_3. However, the predental distance is normal (*arrow*). (*B*) Frontal view demonstrating that the spinous process of C_2 (×) lies to the same side of the midline as the mandible points (*arrow*). (*C*) Another patient with torticollis showing completely scrambled upper cervical spine. However, the predental distance (*arrow*) is normal. (*D*) Frontal view demonstrating characteristic findings in that the spinous process of C_2 (×) lies to the same side of the midline as the mandible points (*arrow*).

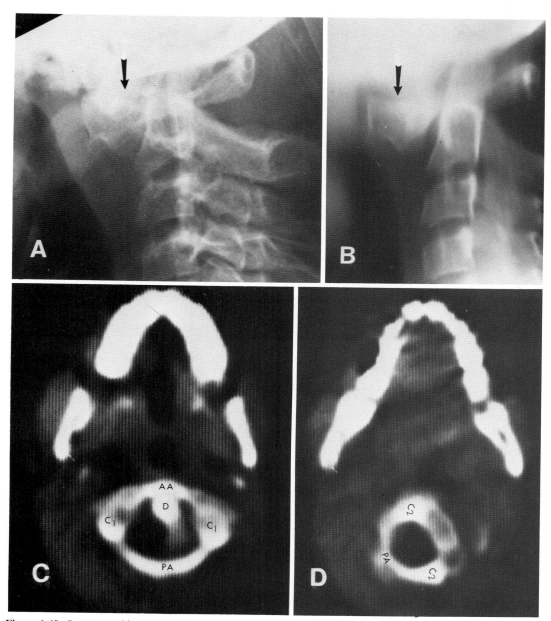

Figure 6.40. *Rotatory subluxation of C₁ on C₂.* (*A*) Note the peculiarly cocked appearance of C₁. Also note that the predental distance, although not clearly visualized, appears abnormally wide (*arrow*). A little prevertebral soft tissue swelling also is present. (*B*) Subsequent laminograms demonstrate the anterior position of the rotated lateral mass (*arrow*). (*C*) CT scan in another patient. Note the position of the lateral masses (*C₁*), the anterior arch (*AA*) and the posterior arch (*PA*) of C₁. The dens (*D*) is off the midline. (*D*) Lower cut. Note the position of the articular facets of C₂ (*C₂*), and the position of the posterior arch (*PA*). Almost 90° dislocation is present. (Courtesy, F. L. G. Rothman, M.D.)

wherein there is persistent offsetting of the involved lateral mass of C_1 (34, 38). In these cases, it is said, no matter which way the patient turns his head, offsetting remains the same (34, 38). The injury is believed to result from invagination of the ligaments into the involved joint, and on lateral view, as opposed to rotatory dislocation, there is no widening of the predental distance. Overall, however, this abnormality is quite uncommon.

Finally, it should be noted that CT is ideal, and aids considerably, in the detection of some of these lesions. This modality can clearly delineate C_1–C_2 positions, and rotatory subluxation should become more readily demonstrable. This is most important, for very often it is virtually impossible to obtain good roentgenograms in these patients (Fig. 6.40).

Axial Compression Injuries of the Cervical Spine.   These injuries generally result in bursting of the involved vertebra (Fig. 6.41). In the upper cervical spine, the classic bursting fracture is the Jefferson fracture of C_1 (6, 14, 34). In the other vertebral bodies, including the body of C_2, axial compression injuries result in bursting and expansion of the vertebral body in all directions (Fig. 6.41).

The Jefferson bursting fracture is unstable and is characterized by bilateral outward displacement of the lateral masses of C_1. The

fractures through the anterior and posterior arches of C_1 usually are not visible until laminography or CT scanning is performed. Consequently, it is most important to detect lateral mass of C_1 displacements on frontal views. Most often both lateral masses are displaced (Fig. 6.42*A*), but with surprising frequency, only one is displaced (Fig. 6.42 *B*). In such cases, a unilateral, or partial, Jefferson fracture is present. In other words, fractures may occur at two sites only, but as long as the "ring" is broken instability with lateral displacement, to one side or the other, can occur. Less commonly, with compression injuries, one may note an isolated fracture of the medial portion of the lateral mass of C_1 (1). These bursting fractures, in general, and those specifically involving C_1 are dramatically depicted with CT scanning (Fig. 6.42*D*).

A recently identified normal variation in infants has been noted to mimic a Jefferson fracture (35). In these patients, on frontal view, the lateral masses appear widely displaced, and as such, suggest a Jefferson fracture (Fig. 6.42*E*).

Axial compression injuries of the body and dens of C_2 cause vertical or oblique fractures and expansion of the vertebral body in all directions (Fig. 6.43, *A* and *B*). The same is true of axial compression fractures of the lower cervical vertebrae (Fig. 6.43*C*).

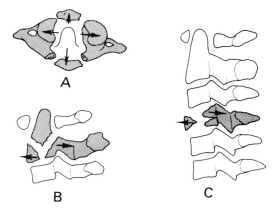

Figure 6.41. *Axial compression injuries of the cervical spine.* (*A*) Typical Jefferson bursting fracture of C_1. Fractures occur posteriorly and anteriorly and the fracture fragments are displaced in all directions. (*B*) Bursting fracture of C_2. The findings are self-evident. (*C*) Similar findings in a bursting fracture of one of the lower cervical vertebrae.

REFERENCES

1. Barker, E.G., Krumpelman, J., and Long, J.M.: Isolated fracture of the medial portion of the lateral mass of the atlas: a previously undescribed entity. A.J.R. 126: 1053–1058, 1976.
2. Beatson, T.R.: Fractures and dislocations of the cervical spine. J. Bone Joint Surg. 45B: 21–35, 1963.
3. Cintron, E., Gilula, L.A., Murphy, W.A., and Gehweiler, J.A.: The widened disk space: a sign of cervical hyperextension injury. Radiology 141: 639–644, 1981.
4. Clark, R.N.: Diagnosis and management of torticollis. Pediatr. Ann. 5: 43–57, 1976.
5. Dolan, K.D.: Cervical spine injuries below the axis. Radiol. Clin. North Am. 15: 247–259, 1977.
6. Donaldson, J.S.: Acquired torticollis in children and young adults. J.A.M.A. 160: 458–461, 1956.
7. Elliott, J.M., Jr., Rogers, L.F., Wissinger, J.P., and Lee, J.F.: The hangman's fracture. Fractures of the neural arch of the axis. Radiology 104: 303–307, 1972.
8. Fielding, J.W., and Hawkins, R.J.: Atlanto-axial rotatory fixation (fixed rotatory subluxation of the atlanto-axial joint). J. Bone Joint Surg. 59: 37–44, 1977.
9. Fielding, J.W., and Griffin, P.O.: Os odontoideum: an acquired lesion. J. Bone Joint Surg. 56A: 187–190, 1974.
10. Forysth, H.F.: Extension injuries of the cervical spine. J. Bone Joint Surg. 46A: 1792–1797, 1964.
11. Freiberger, R.H., Wilson, P.D., Jr., and Nicholas, J.A.: An

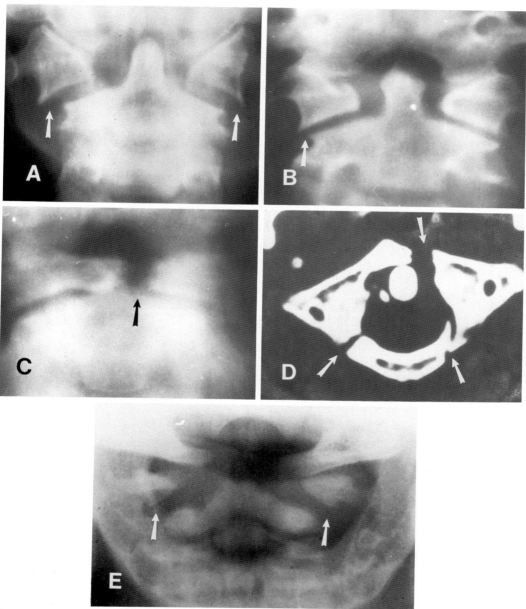

Figure 6.42. *Jefferson fracture of C₁.* (*A*) Typical outward displacement (*arrows*) of both lateral masses of C₁. The one on the right is more displaced than the one on the left. Because of this, the distance between the dens and lateral mass on the right is greater than on the left. (*B*) *Unilateral Jefferson fracture of C₁.* Note unilateral outward displacement of the right lateral mass of C₁ (*arrow*). There is an associated increase in distance between the right lateral mass and the dens. (*C*) Laminograms demonstrate the associated fracture through the anterior arch of C₁ (*arrow*). (*D*) CT findings. Note how clearly the bursting phenomenon is depicted at the three fracture sites (*arrows*). (*E*) *Pseudo-Jefferson fracture—infant.* Note how the lateral masses of C₁ (*arrows*), appear laterally displaced, in this normal infant.

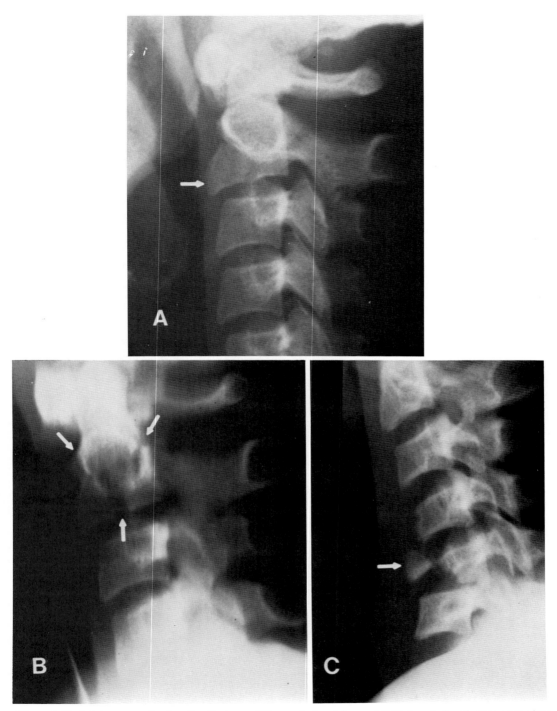

Figure 6.43. *Axial compression bursting fractures of the cervical vertebrae.*   (*A*) Note anterior displacement of the expanded body of C$_2$ (*arrow*). There is some associated disc space narrowing but clear-cut fractures are difficult to define. (*B*) Laminagraphy demonstrates a Y-shaped bursting fracture (*arrows*) involving the body and lower aspect of the dens of C$_2$. (*C*) Bursting fracture of C$_5$ (*arrow*). The findings represent a combination of an axial compression fracture of C$_5$ and a hyperflexion injury at this level. In this regard, note that there is kyphosis at the level of injury, and marked narrowing of the disc space between C$_5$ and C$_6$. Prevertebral soft tissue swelling is extensive. Very often axial compression injuries of the lower cervical spine are accompanied by a flexion component.

acquired absence of the odontoid process. A case report. J. Bone Joint Surg. 47A: 1231–1236, 1965.

12. Gooding, C.A., and Hurwitz, M.E.: Avulsed vertebral rim apophysis in a child. Pediatr. Radiol. 2: 265–268, 1974.

13. Griffiths, S.C.: Fracture of odontoid process in children. J. Pediatr. Surg. 7: 680–683, 1972.

14. Han, S.Y., Witten, D.M., and Musselman, J.P.: Jefferson fracture of the atlas: report of six cases. J. Neurosurg. 44: 368–371, 1976.

15. Hanafee, W., and Crandall, P.: Trauma of the spine and its contents. Radiol. Clin. North Am. 4: 365–382, 1966.

16. Harris, J.H., Jr., and Harris, W.H.: *The Radiology of Emergency Medicine*, pp. 60–111. Williams & Wilkins Baltimore, 1975.

17. Hawkins, R.J., Fielding, J.W., and Thompson, W.J.: Os odontoideum—congenital or acquired: a case report. J. Bone Joint Surg. 58A: 413–414, 1976.

18. Holdsworth, F.W.: Fractures, dislocations, and fracture-dislocations of the spine. J. Bone Joint Surg. 52A: 1534–1551, 1970.

19. Jacobson, G., and Adler, D.C.: Examination of the atlanto-axial joint following injury with particular emphasis on rotational subluxation. A.J.R. 76: 1081–1094, 1956.

20. Jacobson, G., and Adler, D.C.: An evaluation of lateral atlanto-axial displacement in injuries of the cervical spine. Radiology 61: 355–362, 1961.

21. Jones, E.T., and Hensinger, R.N.: C_2-C_3 dislocation in a child. J. Pediatr. Orthop. 1: 419–422, 1981.

22. Keller, R.H.: Traumatic displacement of the cartilaginous vertebral rim: a sign of intervertebral disc prolapse. Radiology 110: 21–24, 1974.

23. Lee, C., Kim, K.S., and Rogers, L.F.: Triangular cervical vertebral body fractures; diagnostic significance. A.J.R. 138: 1123–1132, 1982.

24. McGrory, B.E., and Fenichel, G.M.: Hangman's fracture subsequent to shaking an infant. Ann. Neurol. 2: 82, 1977.

25. Naidich, J.B., Naidich, T.P., Garfein, C., Liebeskind, A.L., and Hyman, R.A.: The widened interspinous distance: a useful sign of anterior cervical dislocation in the supine frontal projection. Radiology 123: 113–116, 1977.

26. Pennecot, G.F., Leonard, P., Des Gachons, S.P., Hardy, J.R., and Pouliquen, J.C.: Traumatic ligamentous instability of the cervical spine in children. J. Pediatr. Orthop. 4: 339–344, 1984.

27. Richman, S., and Friedman, R.L.: Vertical fracture of cervical vertebral bodies. Radiology 62: 536, 1954.

28. Schaaf, R.E., Gehweiler, J.A., Jr., Miller, M.D., and Powers, B.: Lateral hyperflexion injuries of the cervical spine. Skeletal Radiol. 3: 73–78, 1978.

29. Scher, A.T.: Unilateral locked facet in cervical spine injuries. A.J.R. 129: 45–48, 1977.

30. Scher, A.T.: "Tear-drop" fractures of the cervical spine—radiological features. S. Afr. Med. J. 61: 355–356, 1982.

31. Scher, A.T.: Anterior cervical subluxation: an unstable position. A.J.R. 133: 275–280, 1979.

32. Seimon, L.P.: Fracture of the odontoid process in young children. J. Bone Joint Surg. 59A: 943–948, 1977.

33. Seljeskog, E.L., and Chou, S.N.: Spectrum of the hangman's fracture. J. Neurosurg. 45: 3–8, 1976.

34. Shapiro, R., Youngberg, A.S., and Rothman, S.L.G.: The differential diagnosis of traumatic lesions of the occipito-atlanto-axial segment. Radiol. Clin. North Am. 11: 505–526, 1973.

35. Suss, R.A., Zimmerman, R.D., and Leeds, N.E.: Pseudo-spread of the atlas: false sign of Jefferson fracture in young children. A.J.R. 140: 1079, 1983.

36. Swischuk, L.E., Hayden, C.K., Jr., and Sarwar, M.: The posteriorly tilted dens (a normal variation mimicking a fracture of the dens). Pediatr. Radiol. 8: 27–28, 1979.

37. Whitley, J.E., and Forsyth, H.F.: The classification of cervical spine injuries. A.J.R. 83: 633–644, 1960.

38. Wortzman, G., and DeWar, F.P.: Rotary fixation of the atlanto-axial joint: rotational atlanto-axial subluxation. Radiology 90: 479–487, 1968.

CERVICAL CORD AND NERVE ROOT INJURIES

Brachial Plexus Injuries (1–4). These injuries are avulsion injuries of the brachial plexus resulting from excessive lateral flexion-rotation of the spine. They also can result from excessive posterior stretching of the arm. In either case, there is paralysis of the affected limb and with C_5–C_7 root injuries, a Duchenne-Erb's paralysis of shoulder and upper arm results, while a Klumpke's paralysis of the hand results from C_8–T_1 injuries. With C_8–T_1 injuries, Horner's syndrome also may be present. The diagnosis usually is made clinically, for until myelography is performed there is little in the way of roentgenographic abnormality. Typical myelographic findings consist of extravasation of contrast material along the nerve roots in so-called "traumatic meningoceles" or "cysts" (Fig. 6.44).

Central Cord Syndrome. The central cord syndrome usually results from hyper-

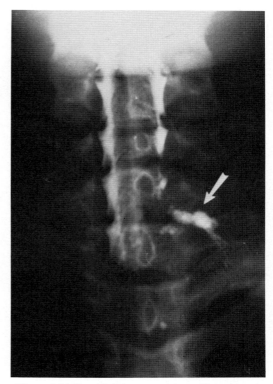

Figure 6.44. *Brachial plexus avulsion.* Note characteristic extravasation of the contrast material along a nerve root (*arrow*).

extension injuries of the cervical spine. Clinically, there is a definite cord level with neurologic deficit clearly apparent (5–8). However, the roentgenograms usually show no fracture or dislocation (Fig. 6.45), but in spite of these rather negative findings, the lesion should be considered unstable and the neck properly immobilized. Cord injury results from pinching or squeezing of the cord between the anterior and posterior walls of the spinal canal secondary to buckling of the ligamentum flavum during hyperextension (see Fig. 6.25D).

REFERENCES

1. Davies, E.R., Sutton, D., and Blight, A.S.: Myelography in brachial plexus injury. Br. J. Radiol. 39: 362–371, 1966.
2. Lester, J.: Pantopaque myelography in avulsion of the brachial plexus. Acta Radiol. 55: 186–192, 1961.
3. Murphey, F., Hartung, W., and Kirklin, J.W.: Myelographic demonstration of avulsing injury of the brachial plexus. A.J.R. 58: 102–105, 1947.
4. Murphey, F., and Kirklin, J.: Myelographic demonstration of avulsing injuries of the nerve roots of the brachial plexus—a method of determining the point of injury and the possibility of repair. Clin. Neurosurg. 20: 18–28, 1972.
5. Rand, R.W., and Crandall, P.H.: Central spinal cord syndrome in hyperextension injuries of the cervical spine. J. Bone Joint Surg. 44A: 1415–1422, 1962.
6. Schneider, R.C., Cherry, G., and Pantek, H.: The syndrome of acute central cervical spinal cord injury. J. Neurosurg. 11: 546–577, 1954.
7. Taylor, A.R., and Blackwood, W.: Paraplegia in hyperextension cervical injuries with normal radiographic appearances. J. Bone Joint Surg. 30B: 245–248, 1948.
8. Taylor, A.R.: The mechanism of injury to the spinal cord in the neck without mage to the vertebral column. J. Bone Joint Surg. 33B: 543–547, 1951.

C₁-OCCIPITAL INJURIES

These injuries, by and large, are not particularly common. Atlanto-occipital dislocations can result from both flexion or extension forces and both often are associated with sudden death. With anterior atlanto-

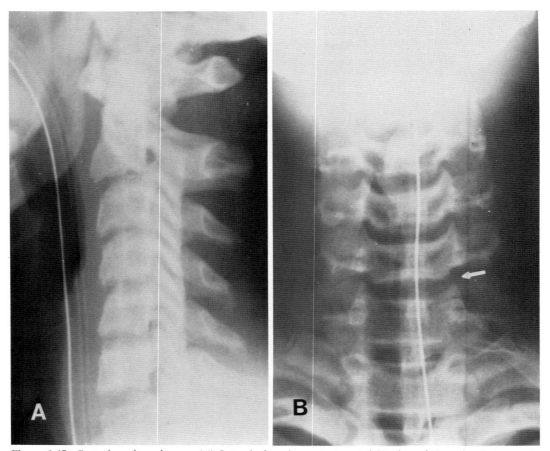

Figure 6.45. *Central cord syndrome.* (*A*) Lateral view demonstrates straightening of the spine but no other abnormalities. Offsetting of C₂ on C₃ is physiologic. This patient had a C₆–C₇ cord level. (*B*) Frontal view demonstrating questionable widening of the joint of Luschka at the C₆–C₇ level on the left (*arrow*). This was the only roentgenographic evidence of injury in this patient.

occipital dislocations, the dens lies anterior to the anterior lip of the foramen magnum while with posterior dislocations, the dens lies posterior to the anterior lip of the foramen magnum. Normally, of course, it lies

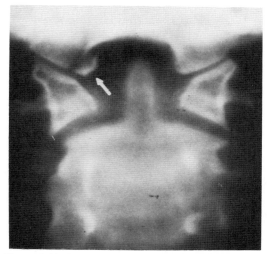

Figure 6.46. *Occipital condyle fracture.* Note the fracture (*arrow*) of the occipital condyle on the right. Also note that the right lateral mass of C_1 is displaced outwardly, suggesting the associated presence of a unilateral Jefferson fracture of C_1.

just below the anterior lip of the foramen magnum.

Other injuries of the cervical occipital junction consist of fractures through the occipital condyles, but often these fractures are not detected until subsequent laminography, or CT scanning is performed (Fig. 6.46). The basic mechanisms through which these fractures occur are poorly understood, but since they can be associated with fractures of C_1, it might be that they result from axial compression and hyperextension forces.

NORMAL FINDINGS AND ANOMALIES OF THE CERVICAL SPINE CAUSING PROBLEMS

Most of the significant normal findings in the cervical spine have been covered at appropriate points in previous sections, but a few others should be discussed for completeness. In this regard, one of the most common normal findings to be misinterpreted for a fracture is the ***dens-arch synchondrosis of*** C_2 (3, 5). Actually, this synchondrosis is part of a triad of synchondroses between the dens, body, and arch of C_2 (Fig. 6.47). All of these synchondroses lie anterior and are seen only on oblique views of the cervical spine. In the

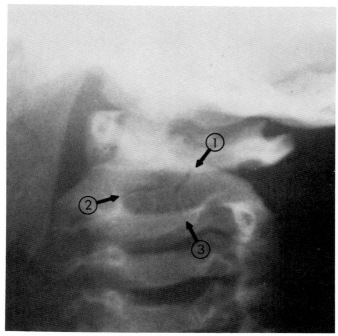

Figure 6.47. *Normal synchondroses of* C_2. Synchondrosis between the dens and arch (*1*), synchondrosis between the dens and body (*2*), and synchondrosis between the body and arch (*3*). The synchondrosis between the dens and arch is the one most commonly misinterpreted for a fracture of C_2.

injured child, this most commonly occurs fortuitously, on skull roentgenograms. In such cases while the head is in lateral position, the cervical spine is in the rotated, oblique position (Fig. 6.48).

In assessing these synchondroses, it is important to recall that they are anterior structures, and thus visible only when the spine is obliqued. Once this is appreciated, they can be differentiated from fractures through the neural arch of C_2 with ease, for these fractures are visible on both oblique and lateral views (Fig. 6.49). Indeed, if one notes a defect in the neural arch of C_2 on lateral view, it should be considered a fracture until proven otherwise. Congenital defects in this region are extremely rare (1). The synchondroses between the bodies and arches of the lower cervical vertebrae are less of a problem (Fig. 6.50).

Other normal findings causing problems include the ***transverse processes*** being projected through the intervertebral disc spaces and the normal ***ring epiphysis*** of the growing vertebral body. These ring epiphyses can be misinterpreted for corner (teardrop) frac-

tures of the vertebral bodies while the transverse processes can be misinterpreted for intervertebral disc calcifications (Fig. 6.51). In the upper cervical spine, especially at the C_2 and C_3 levels, the ring epiphyses normally may appear tilted and suggest avulsion (Fig. 6.51).

In terms of anomalies causing problems, although a number exist, the most important is the ***hypoplastic dens associated with an os odontoideum*** (2, 4, 6). In these cases, the os odontoideum can appear as though it were a fractured dens (Fig. 6.52). Actually, the os odontoideum probably is an overgrown os terminale, and it overgrows when the dens is hypoplastic (6). The os terminale is a small ossicle occurring in all children, just at the tip of the dens (Fig. 6.52*A*), and by adolescence, it becomes fused with the dens. The presence of dens hypoplasia and an os odontoideum is of more than passing interest, for very often they are associated with hypermobility at the C_1-C_2 area and associated cord injury. Indeed, the lesion is unstable and frequently requires surgical stabilization. Occasionally an os odontoideum can

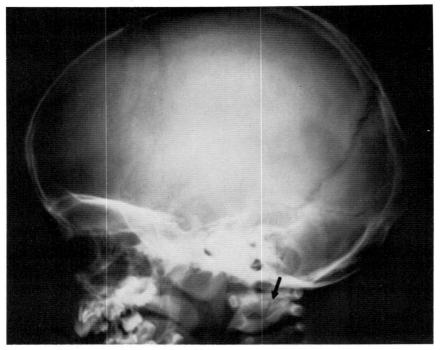

Figure 6.48. *Fortuitous visualization of the dens-arch synchondrosis of C_2 on a skull film.* Note the fracture-like appearance of the synchondrosis between the dens and arch of C_2 (*arrow*). This synchondrosis is visible on oblique views of the cervical spine in all infants and young children. In older children, it fuses and disappears.

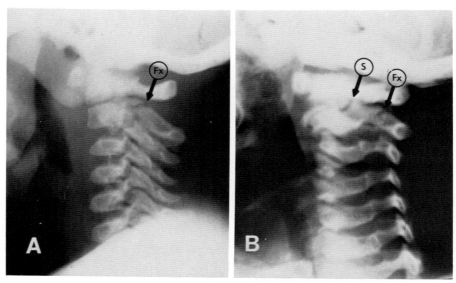

Figure 6.49. *Dens-arch synchrondrosis of C_2 versus hangman's fracture.* (*A*) Lateral view demonstrating a defect (*Fx*) through the arch of C_2. This should be a hangman's fracture. (*B*) Oblique view demonstrates the posterior position of the fracture (*Fx*) and the anterior position of the normal dens-arch synchrondrosis (*S*) of C_2.

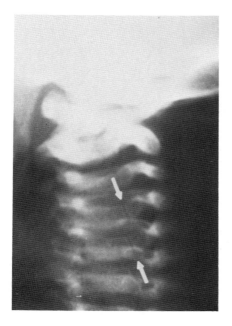

Figure 6.50. *Synchrondroses of lower cervical vertebrae.* Note the typical appearance of the synchrondroses between the bodies and arches of the lower cervical vertebrae (*arrows*).

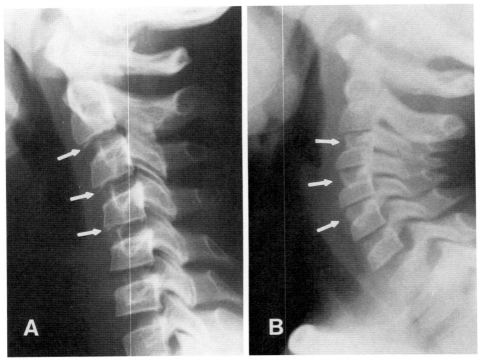

Figure 6.51. *(A) Ring epiphyses.*   Note normal ring epiphyses (*arrows*). The one off C₃ appears tilted and avulsed. This, however, is a normal appearance. For a truly avulsed ring epiphysis, see Figure 6.14C. (*B*) *Transverse processes projected through intervertebral discs.* Note the transverse processes of the cervical vertebrae (*arrows*) projected through the intravertebral discs. They should not be confused with intravertebral disc calcifications (compare with Fig. 6.60).

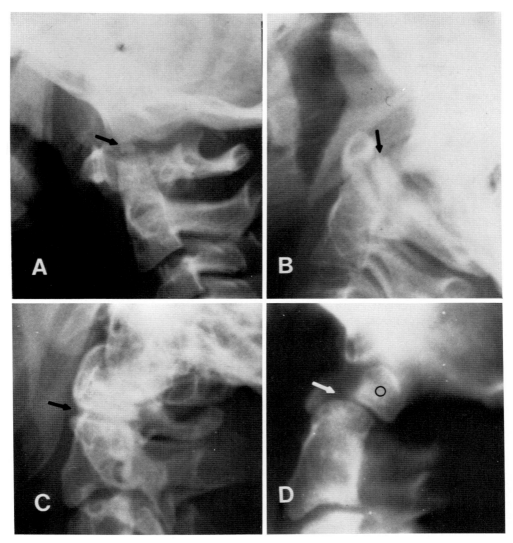

Figure 6.52. *Os terminale-os odontoideum anomalies.* (*A*) Normal os terminale (*arrow*) at the tip of the dens. (*B*) Large os odontoideum (*arrow*); actually an overgrown os terminale. Note that the dens is hypoplastic. (Courtesy D. Binstadt, M.D. Minnesota.) (*C*) This 15-year-old boy was in an automobile accident and at first the defect through the base of the dens (*arrow*) was thought to represent a dens fracture. However, note how smooth it appears and that considerable anomalous development of the upper cervical spine is present. More specifically, C_1 is markedly hypoplastic and deformed. (*D*) Subsequent laminography demonstrates that the defect is not a fracture, but rather a persistent congenital defect between the hypoplastic dens and overgrown os terminale or os odontoidium (*O*). The os odontoidium shows marked displacement and attests to the instability of this lesion.

be acquired, resulting from pronounced dens resorption (interrupted blood supply?) after dens injuries in infancy (see Fig. 6.24).

REFERENCES

1. Harwood-Nash, D.C., and Fitz, C.R.: *Neuroradiology in Infants and Children.* p. 1094. C. V. Mosby, St. Louis, 1976.
2. Kattan, K.R.: *"Trauma" and "No Trauma" of the Cervical Spine.* Charles C Thomas, Springfield, Ill., 1975.
3. Keats, T.: *Normal Roentgen Variants That May Simulate Disease.* Year Book, Chicago, 1973.
4. Shapiro, R., Youngberg, A.S., and Rothman, S.L.G.: The differential diagnosis of traumatic lesions of the occipito-atlanto-axial segments. Radiol. Clin. North Am. 11: 505–526, 1973.
5. Swischuk, L.E., Hayden, C.K., Jr., and Sarwar, M.: The dens-arch synchondrosis versus the Hangman's fracture. Pediatr. Radiol. 8: 100–102, 1979.
6. von Torklus, D., and Gehle, W.: *The Upper Cervical Spine: Regional Morphology, Pathology and Traumatology: An X-ray Atlas.* Grune & Stratton, New York, 1972.

THORACOLUMBAR SPINE TRAUMA

In the thoracolumbar spine, much as in the cervical spine, injuries can result from flexion, extension, lateral flexion, rotation, and axial compression forces.

Flexion Injuries. Most often flexion injuries of the thoracolumbar spine result in anterior compression of the vertebral bodies (Fig. 6.53 and 6.54). However, the more severe the injury the greater is the likelihood there will be posterior ligament tear, widening of the interspinous distance, and associated spinous tip or neural arch avulsion fractures. Actually, the mechanics of injury are exactly the same as those encountered in flexion injuries of the cervical spine, and in addition to the preceding fractures, teardrop fractures also can be seen (Fig. 6.54). In the lumbar spine, teardrop fractures often are referred to as limbus fractures. If the injury is severe enough, patients with these fractures will also demonstrate anterior subluxation through the apophyseal joints, and once this finding, or separation of the spi-

nous processes is present, the fracture is considered unstable.

Extension Injuries. Extension injuries of the thoracolumbar spine are not as common as flexion injuries. In some cases, nothing more than non-displaced neural arch and spinous process fractures result, but in other cases a hangman's type fracture mechanism is at play and anterior dislocation of the superior vertebral body can occur. Actually, this is what happens in so-called "traumatic spondylolisthesis." Most cases of spondylolisthesis, of the lumbosacral spine, however, are more insidious in onset.

Another fracture which might be sustained when excessive extension forces are applied to the thoracolumbar spine is the so-called "limbus" or corner fracture of the vertebral body. Actually, this is the same fracture as the teardrop fracture seen in the cervical spine, and should indicate underlying ligamentous injury with instability. In addition, there may be associated disc space widening, and actual posterior displacement of the involved vertebral body.

Lateral Flexion Injuries. As in the cervical spine, lateral flexion injuries can result in ipsilateral compression fractures of the vertebral bodies or contralateral transverse process fractures. Most often these injuries are not particularly serious if lateral flexion only is the force involved. If other forces are involved, more serious injuries can occur. Transverse process fractures must be differentiated from rudimentary lumbar ribs or bipartite transverse processes (see Fig. 6.64).

Rotation Injuries. These are either rotation-flexion or rotation-extension injuries. The upper thoracic spine is especially prone to severe wrenching injuries and considerabvle spinal damage can result (Fig. 6.55).

Axial Compression Injuries. Axial compression results in a "burst" vertebra, and actually many times this type of injury is associated with some degree of hyperflexion injury (see Fig. 6.54). When axial compression is a prominent component of these injuries, the vertebral body bursts and spreads outwards in all directions. Once again the mechanics are the same as those seen in the cervical spine. On frontal view, in these cases one may note widening of the interpedicular distance and/or widening of the apophyseal joints. On lateral view, the

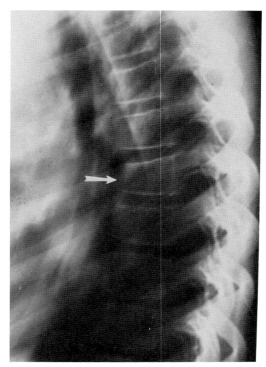

Figure 6.53. *Compression fracture—thoracic vertebra.* Note the typical appearance of the anteriorly compressed vertebra (*arrow*).

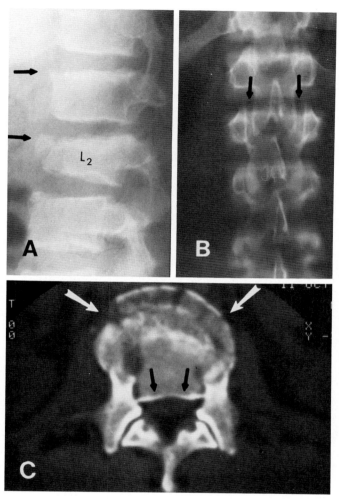

Figure 6.54. *Combined hyperflexion-axial compression injury of lumbar spine.* (*A*) Lateral view demonstrating marked anterior compression of L_2, anterior teardrop fractures of L_2 and L_3 (*arrows*), and minimal anterior compression of T_{12} and L_1. Also note that the posterior part of L_2 is displaced posteriorly into the spinal canal to a minor degree. (*B*) Frontal view demonstrating widening of the apophyseal joints of L_2 (*arrows*) and some widening of the corresponding interpedicular distance. These findings result from the compression-induced bursting of the vertebra. This patient fell directly on his buttocks and sustained an axial compression-hyperflexion injury of the thoracolumbar spine. (*C*) CT scan demonstrating compression fracture of a lumbar vertebra (*white arrows*), with protrusion of the posterior fragment (*black arrows*) into the spinal canal.

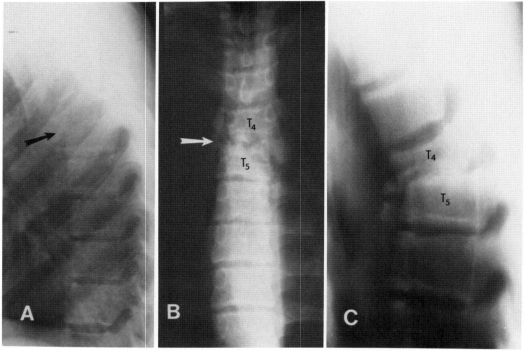

Figure 6.55. *Wrenching injury of thoracic spine.*   (*A*) Note acute kyphosis at the T_4–T_5 level (*arrow*). The vertebral bodies and intervening disc space are difficult to identify. (*B*) Frontal view demonstrating obliteration of the disc space between T_4 and T_5 (*arrow*), and lateral displacement of T_4 on T_5. (*C*) Subsequent laminography demonstrates the extensive nature of the rotation-flexion injury of T_4 and T_5.

compressed vertebra will be squashed, and the posterior part of it will protrude into the spinal canal. When significant associated interspinous ligament laxity or tearing occurs, the lesion becomes unstable.

Other Injuries of the Thoracolumbar Spine. Transverse fractures of the vertebral body with anterior or lateral dislocation of the upper half of the fractured vertebra are a well known injury occurring in patients wearing lap seatbelts (1–5). They are termed Chance fractures (2) and can readily be detected on frontal views (Fig. 6.56). However, it is not uncommon for the fracture to remain undetected for some time, for often these patients obtain supine roentgenograms for abdominal pain and not enough attention is paid to the lumbar spine. Chance fractures of the lumbar vertebra usually are seen in older children.

Spinal injuries in the battered child syndrome also can be encountered, and although they are not particularly common, one can see simple compression fractures, compression fractures with notched vertebrae, and actual fracture dislocations (6).

SACROCOCCYGEAL SPINE TRAUMA

Injuries of the coccyx are quite uncommon except in older children who might fall on their buttocks, and if the injury is severe enough, the lateral view will demonstrate tilting of the fractured coccyx. Sacral fractures have been dealt with in the section on pelvic injuries.

REFERENCES

1. Carroll, T.B., and Gruber, F.H.: Seat belt fractures. Radiology 91: 517–518, 1968.
2. Chance, G.Q.: Note on type of flexion fracture of spine. Br. J. Radiol. 21: 452–453, 1948.
3. Rogers, L.F.: The roentgenographic appearance of transverse or chance fractures of the spine: the seat belt fracture. A.J.R. 111: 844–849, 1971.
4. Smith, W.E., and Kaufer, H.: Patterns and mechanisms of lumbar injuries associated with lap-seat belts. J. Bone Joint Surg. 51A: 239, 1969.
5. Steckler, R.M., Epstein, J.A., and Epstein, B.S.: Seat belt trauma to lumbar spine: unusual manifestation of seat belt syndrome. J. Trauma 9: 508–513, 1969.
6. Swischuk, L.E.: Spine and spinal cord trauma in battered child syndrome. Radiology 92: 733–738, 1969.

MISCELLANEOUS PROBLEMS OF THE SPINE

Infections of the Spine. Generally speaking, infections of the spine consist of osteomyelitis and the so-called spondyloarthritis or discitis of childhood (1–7, 9). In all of these conditions, the hallmark of radiographic diagnosis is disc space narrowing with destruction of the two adjacent vertebral body surfaces (Fig. 6.57). Most often these patients present with back pain, hip pain, or a limp. The degree of systemic reaction is variable, and the underlying organism usually is staphylococcus aureus. In some of these cases, however, an infectious agent is not demonstrable, and this has prompted some to consider such cases as traumatic, rather than infectious, in origin. Bone scanning is very worthwhile in the detection of these infections (5, 8), especially since the roentgenographic changes are somewhat late in onset (Fig. 6.57). CT scans eventually also can demonstrate vertebral body destruction (Fig. 6.58).

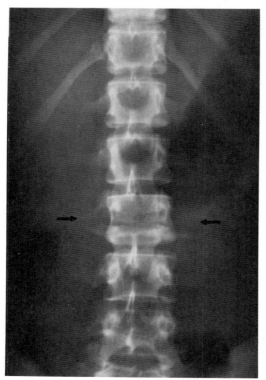

Figure 6.56. *Chance fracture of lumbar vertebra body.* Note the transverse fracture through the third lumbar vertebra (*arrows*) in this teenager who was in a car accident. Actually the film was obtained because of abdominal pain. However, note that the vertebra and its transverse processes are completely fractured. Also note that the pedicles of the involved vertebra are distorted because of the fracture.

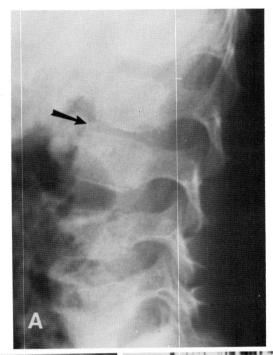

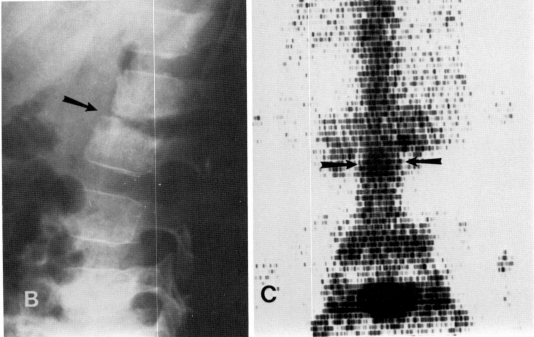

Figure 6.57. *Discitis or spondyloarthritis.* (*A*) Typical early changes consisting of disc space narrowing only (*arrow*). (*B*) Two weeks later, note how much destruction has occurred at the site of infection (*arrow*). In addition, there has been some posterior displacement of the upper vertebral body. (*C*) Bone scan obtained after the first roentgenogram demonstrates increased activity over the lesion (*arrows*).

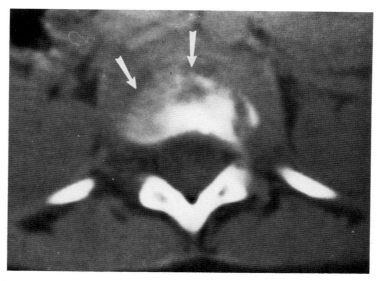

Figure 6.58. *Discitis; CT scan findings.*   CT scan demonstrating vertebral body destruction (*arrows*).

REFERENCES

1. Alexander, C.J.: The aetiology of juvenile spondyloarthritis (discitis). Clin. Radiol. 21: 178–187, 1970.
2. Brass, A., and Bowdler, J.D.: Non-specific spondylitis of childhood. Ann. Radiol. 12: 343–354, 1969.
3. Bolivar, R., Kohl, S., and Pickering, L.K.: Vertebral osteomyelitis in children: report of four cases. Pediatrics 62: 549–553, 1978.
4. Childe, A.E., and Tucker, F.R.: Spondyloarthritis in infants and children. J. Can. Assoc. Radiol. 12: 47–51, 1961.
5. Fischer, G.W., Popich, G.A., Sullivan, D.E., Mayfield, G., Mazat, B.A., and Patterson, P.H.: Diskitis: a prospective diagnosis analysis. Pediatrics 62: 543–548, 1978.
6. Gates, G.F.: Scintigraphy of discitis. Clin. Nucl. Med. 2: 20–25, 1977.
7. Moes, C.A.F.: Spondyloarthritis in childhood. A.J.R. 91: 578–587, 1964.
8. Norris, S., Ehrlich, M.G., Keim, D.E., Guitermann, H., and McKusick, K.A.: Early diagnosis of disc-space infection using gallium-67. J. Nucl. Med. 19: 384–386, 1978.
9. Wenger, D.R., Bobechko, W.P., and Gilday, D.L.: The spectrum of intervertebral disc-space infection in children. J. Bone Joint Surg. 60A: 100–108, 1978.

Pathologic Fractures. Pathologic fractures of the spine are an occasional cause of acute back pain. In this regard, the most commonly encountered condition is eosinophilic granuloma or histiocytosis X. However, metastatic neuroblastoma, other metastatic disease, or underlying solitary primary bone lesions such as aneurysmal bone cysts, interosseous hemangiomas, etc., also can lead to pathologic compression. Histiocytosis X and eosinophilic granuloma, differ a little from these latter conditions in that they produce a very flat vertebra, the so-called vertebra plana (Fig. 6.59). Patients with leukemia or lymphoma also can present with compression fractures of the vertebrae, but most often these patients also are on steroid therapy. Compression fracture secondary to poorly mineralized bone such as might be seen with hyperparathyroidism, rickets, and osteogenesis imperfecta also can be encountered, especially if the children

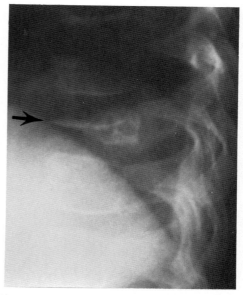

Figure 6.59. *Pathologic fracture of vertebral body.* Note typical flat vertebra associated with pathologic compression secondary to histiocytosis X (*arrow*).

with these conditions are active and ambulant.

The roentgenographic hallmark of all these fractures is loss of vertebral body height due to compression. The adjacent intervertebral discs, however, remain normal. This is a most important point, for the configuration is completely opposite to that which is seen with osteomyelitis of discitis. The only exception to this rule is coccidioidomycosis or other fungal disease, which can be associated with retention of the disc space.

Calcified Intervertebral Discs. Commonly this condition occurs in the cervical spine (Fig. 6.60), but it also can be seen in the thoracic spine. Usually, it is associated with neck pain and stiffness, but the etiology is unknown (1, 2, 4–6). There is debate as to whether the calcification results from trauma or inflammation, but no conclusive data to support either etiology are currently available. Systemic response in these patients is variable, and while some show signs of marked inflammation and muscle spasm, others are less symptomatic. If followed, these calcifications eventually disappear, but some have been noted to herniate and protrude either anteriorly or posteriorly (3, 7). Of course, those protruding posteriorly will do so into the spinal canal, but they do not seem to cause cord injury (3, 7).

REFERENCES

1. Blomquist, H.K., Lindqvist, M., and Mattsson, S.: Calcification of intervertebral disc in childhood. Pediatr. Radiol. 8: 23–26, 1979.
2. Henry, M.J., Grimes, H.A., and Lane, J.W.: Intervertebral disk calcification in childhood. Radiology 89: 81–84, 1967.
3. Mainzer, F.: Herniation of the nucleus pulposus. A rare complication of intervertebral disk calcification in children. Radiology 107: 167–170, 1973.
4. Melnick, J.C., and Silverman, F.N.: Intervertebral disk calcifications in childhood. Radiology 80: 399–408, 1963.
5. Mikity, V.G., and Isenbarger, J.: Intervertebral disk calcification in children. A.J.R. 95: 200–202, 1965.
6. Sonnabend, D.H., Taylor, T.K.F., and Chapman, G.K.: Intervertebral disc calcification syndromes in children. J. Bone Joint Surg. 64B: 25–31, 1982.
7. Sutton, T.J., and Turcotte, B.: Posterior herniation of calcified intervertebral discs in children. J. Can. Assoc. Radiol. 24: 131–136, 1973.

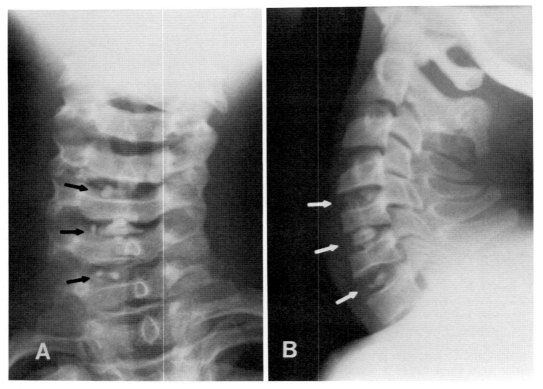

Figure 6.60. *Disc space calcifications.* (*A*) Frontal view demonstrating acute scoliosis and multiple disc space calcifications (*arrows*). This boy presented with acute neck pain and torticollis. (*B*) Lateral view demonstrating characteristic appearance of the calcified intervertebral discs (*arrows*). Note that the spine is normal in other respects.

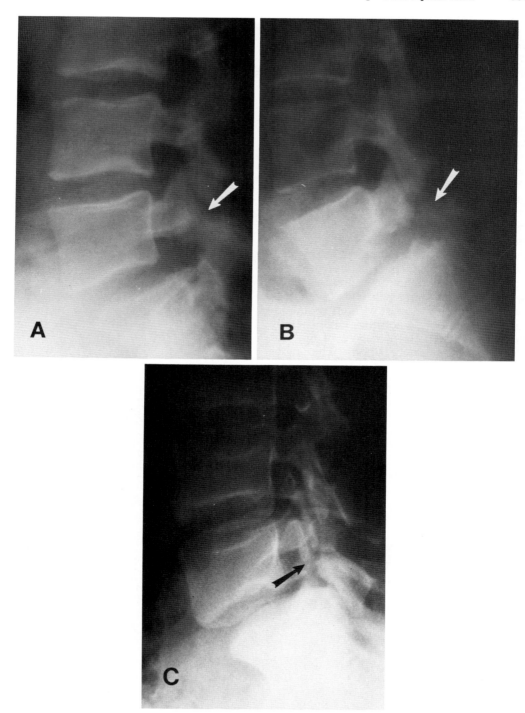

Figure 6.61. *Spondylolisthesis.* (*A*) Note typical spondylolysis (*arrow*) with minimal spondylolisthesis. (*B*) More extensive lytic changes producing a dysplastic appearance through the pedicle (*arrow*). Also note bone resorption along the posterior aspect of the vertebral bodies, some disc space narrowing, and at least a grade II spondylolysthesis. (*C*) Acute spondylolysis. Patient in car accident with acute back pain. Note defect in the pedicle (*arrow*). On this oblique view, spondylolisthesis is suggested, but on true lateral view, none was present.

Spondylolysis and Spondylolisthesis
Generally not a cause of acute pain, spondylolysis occasionally can result from acute trauma. Nonetheless, most cases are chronic in nature and generally accepted opinion is that most are acquired (1–4). In this regard there is considerable feeling that the initial problem may be a fatigue fracture (4). Some familial tendency toward the problem has been documented (1), but most cases are sporadic.

In early cases the defect is rather straight and subtle (Fig. 6.61*A*), but later on, bony resorption occurs and a more dysplastic appearance results (Fig. 6.61*B*). This has prompted dividing the condition into those cases with a small defect and those with a dysplastic appearing pedicle, but probably both are the same, merely representing different stages of abnormality (1). Spondylolysis, of course, can exist without spondylolisthesis, and spondylolisthesis is generally graded on the basis of degree of anterior slippage of the vertebral body. The grades usually consist of grade I through grade IV.

REFERENCES

1. Albanese, M., and Pizzutillo, P.D.: Family study of spondylolysis and spondylolisthesis. J. Pediatr. Orthop. 2: 496–499, 1982.
2. McKee, B.W., Alexander, W.J., and Dunbar, J.S.: Spondylosis and spondylolisthesis in children. J. Can. Assoc. Radiol. 22: 100–109, 1971.
3. Wertzberger, J., and Peterson, H.: Acquired spondylolysis and spondylolisthesis in the young child. Spine 5: 437, 1980.
4. White, L.L., Widell, E.H., and Jackson, D.W.: Fatigue fracture: the basic lesion in isthmic spondylolisthesis. J. Bone Joint Surg. 57A: 17–22, 1975.

Intervertebral Disc Herniation. Disc herniations are extremely uncommon in infants and young children, but are not so uncommon in the active adolescent (1–3). Roentgenographically, there is little to see except for muscle spasm causing straightening or curvature of the spine. Occasionally, one may note an acutely narrowed disc space secondary to extrusion of nuclear material, but for the most part these patients require myelography for definitive diagnosis. CT scanning may demonstrate an apparent destructive lesion in the vertebral body, if the disc material herniates into the vertebral body (Fig. 6.62).

REFERENCES

1. Clarke, N.M.P., and Cleak, D.K.: Intervertebral lumbar disc prolapse in children and adolescents. J. Pediatr. Orthop. 3: 202–206, 1983.
2. Kurihara, A., and Kataoka, O.: Lumbar disk herniation in children and adolescents. Spine 5: 443, 1980.
3. Zamani, M.H., and MacEwen, G.D.: Herniation of the lumbar disc in children and adolescents. J. Pediatr. Orthop. 2: 528–533, 1982.

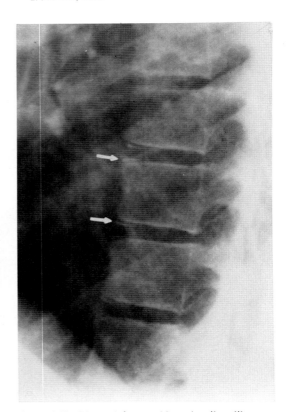

Figure 6.63. *Ring epiphyses.* Note the silver-like appearance of the normal ring epiphyses of the vertebral bodies (*arrows*). These should not be misinterpreted for teardrop fractures.

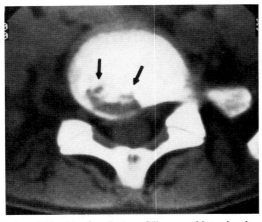

Figure 6.62. *Disc herniation; CT scan.* Note the defect, produced in the vertebral body (*arrows*), by the herniated disc. Surgically proven.

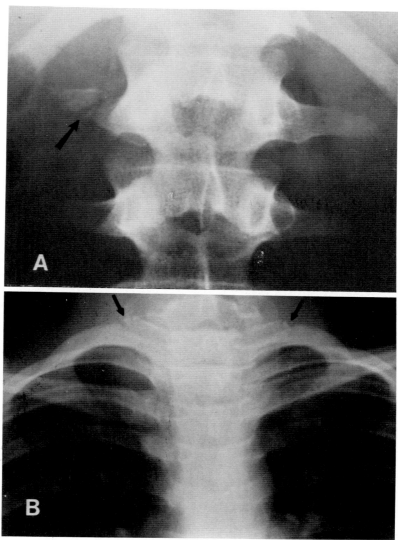

Figure 6.64. *(A) Rudimentary lumbar rib or bipartite transverse process (arrow).* This finding should not be misinterpreted for a fracture. *(B)* Normal secondary ossification centers of the upper thoracic transverse processes *(arrows).*

NORMAL VARIATIONS CAUSING PROBLEMS IN THE THORACOLUMBAR SPINE

One of the most common normal variations causing problems is the normal ***ring epiphysis*** of the vertebral body (Fig. 6.63). These ring-like growth plates of the vertebral bodies occur throughout the entire spine in childhood, and to the uninitiated can suggest a corner, avulsion, teardrop, or limbus fracture. This, however, is not to say that the ring epiphysis never is involved in this type of fracture, for in children, a portion of the ring epiphysis can be avulsed with certain flexion or extension injuries. In these cases, the ring epiphysis fragment constitutes a true teardrop fracture (Fig. 6.14).

The ***bipartite transverse process or rudimentary rib*** of a lumbar vertebra can be misinterpreted for a fracture (Fig. 6.64A), and a similar problem can arise in the upper thoracic spine where ***accessory ossicles of the transverse processes*** also are prone to misinterpretation (Fig. 6.64B).

Index